who have never studied economics or who took the subject long ago will find everything they need in Chapter 2. Read the chapter and then attempt the review questions at the end of the chapter. But you need not commit the structure of Chapter 2 to memory: later in the book when we use a concept developed in Chapter 2, we refer you back to the relevant part of that review so that you can get a quick refresher. At several points later in the book we develop some microeconomic tools that are not covered in Chapter 2. Your ability to assimilate those new tools will be greatly enhanced the more familiar you are with the material in the review chapter. Although we have kept the amount of mathematics to a minimum, we have also explained briefly in Chapter 2 some of the mathematical tools and terminology that will come in handy later in the book. For example, we explain what a function is, what the difference is between a dependent and an independent variable, and how to read graphs.

Economists will need to read Chapter 3 to learn something about the common law system and how it differs from the civil law tradition and to become familiar with the structure of the court systems. If your training in microeconomics is rusty or you are not certain whether you need to read Chapter 2, you should look at the questions at the end of that chapter. If you can comfortably answer them, you probably do not need to read the chapter.

Even those economists who are familiar with microeconomic theory will want to read the Appendix to Chapter 2. That appendix introduces the economics of risk and insurance, specifically, the expected utility model of decisionmaking under uncertainty. It is not at all unusual for undergraduates or graduate students with an otherwise first-rate formal training in microeconomics not to have studied the economics of uncertainty. But because one of the recurring themes of this book is the ability of legal rules to induce efficient risk allocation, the material in the Appendix to Chapter 2 is extremely important.

After the introductory and review chapters, the book turns to the economics of the principal areas of the common and criminal law. These substantive chapters are organized in pairs. The first chapter of the pair begins with examples of the sorts of issues that arise in that area of the law. Next there is a summary of the conventional legal or jurisprudential theory of the law. Then we develop an economic theory of that area of the law and show how it compares with the received legal theory. The second chapter in each pair applies the economic theory of the previous chapter to various legal topics. Thus, Chapter 4 describes "An Economic Theory of Property," and Chapter 5 applies that theory to "Topics in the Economics of Property," such as defining property rights to intellectual creations and the economics of allowing the government to compel private citizens to sell their property. Chapter 6 develops "An Economic Theory of Contracts," and that theory is elaborated and applied in Chapter 7 to such issues as the enforcement of promises to give a gift and how and when the law should discourage breach of contract. Chapter 8 proposes "An Economic Theory of Torts," a theory that is applied to a wide-ranging set of problems in Chapter 9. In particular, Chapter 9 discusses the crisis in products liability law and evaluates the various proposals for remedying the ills of that part of the tort liability system. Chapter 10 ("The Economic Efficiency of the Common Law Process") deals with some of the issues found in what lawyers know as civil procedure. That chapter somewhat breaks the mold in that the theory and applications are found in the same chapter. The book concludes with two chapters on the economics of the criminal law. Chapter 11 proposes a theory to explain why there is a criminal law distinct from the law governing civil disputes and why some people commit crimes. Chapter 12 turns to the policy issues of crime: Is there a crime wave? Should criminals be fined or sent to prison? Does the death penalty deter murders? What is the connection between drug use and crime?

Some law students and others familiar with the law may find that they can skip the first half of each of the theory chapters, the part in which a summary of an area of the law is given. However, our experience in teaching this material to law students is that they find the summaries of property, contract, and tort law to be extremely helpful reviews, just as economics students have found Chapter 2 to be a useful review.

There are several other notable pedagogical features of *Law and Economics*. Each chapter contains numerous boxed examples of the material that is being discussed. For example, in the chapter that introduces various topics in the economics of property, we have included a boxed example that explains whether and how property rights are defined in the oceans and in satellite tracking orbits. And in the second chapter on crime, we use a boxed example to discuss the development of state prisons operated by private profit-maximizing corporations.

In addition to the boxed examples, there are discussion questions sprinkled throughout the text. We have found these and similar questions to be very helpful in teaching law and economics. In this course, more than in any other course either of us has ever taught, students benefit from discussing the course material through questions. We have included extensive suggested answers to all of the questions at the end of the book.

We have taken pains to see that both the theory and applications of that theory are given a full and balanced treatment. Students frequently find the economic theory of the law to be intrinsically interesting, but they also demand—and rightly so—that they be shown how this theory can help them understand a practical problem or lead to a policy prescription that could not be reached save for the theory they have taken pains to learn. We are in complete sympathy with this demand and have tried to show in each chapter why the theory is not merely dry academic stuff but, rather, vital to some terribly important policy issues.

Finally, because we think that it is important for students to know what additional professional literature is available in the event that they wish to pursue some topic introduced in the text, we have included extensive references in footnotes and in selected bibliographies at the end of each chapter.

ACKNOWLEDGMENTS

Several colleagues have been kind enough to read the manuscript of this book with care and to offer us helpful criticisms and suggestions. For their thoughtful efforts, we would like to thank the following people:

Merritt Fox
Indiana University, Bloomington

Henry Hansmann
Yale University

James R. Kearl
Brigham Young University

Neil N. Komesar
University of Wisconsin, Madison

Lewis Kornhauser
New York University

Richard N. Langlois
New York University

Henry G. Manne
Emory University

Julianne Nelson
New York University

George Priest
Yale University

Susan Rose-Ackerman
Columbia University

Daniel Rubinfeld
University of California, Berkeley

Steven Shavell
Harvard University

Matthew L. Spitzer
University of Southern California

Robert Wolf
Tufts University

Many colleagues at Illinois, Berkeley, and elsewhere have spared many hours to discuss law and economics with us. Of those colleagues, two deserve special thanks: John Lopatka of the University of Illinois College of Law and Mel Eisenberg of Boalt Hall.

We must also thank the many economics and law students at the University of Illinois and the University of California at Berkeley who have suffered through earlier versions of this manuscript. Their suggestions, questions, and criticisms have forced us to refine our thoughts and to clarify our methods of conveying them. We have learned a great deal from our students and are reminded each semester that the opportunity to work with first-rate students is one of the great rewards of the academic life.

We also want to thank several people at Scott, Foresman and Company. George Lobell is everything that authors could ask for in an editor. From the time we first proposed doing this book through the later ups and downs, he was unfailingly encouraging. His commitment to excellence in scholarship is without equal. We were also fortunate in having Bruce Kaplan as an editor. Bruce's skill as a writer and his familiarity with both the law and with economics immeasurably improved the book. Finally, Deb DeBord saw the manuscript through the final stages of correction and production with thoroughness and patience.

Our final and greatest debt is to our families—to Julia, Ted, and Tim Ulen, and to Blair, John, Bo, and Joe Cooter. The list of sacrifices they have made in order for us to complete this book is long. Their support and love have been wonderful.

Robert D. Cooter
Thomas S. Ulen

CONTENTS

CHAPTER 5   Topics in the Economics of
            Property   123

CHAPTER 6   An Economic Theory of Contract   212

CHAPTER 7   Topics in the Economics of
            Contract Law   248

CHAPTER 1

An Introduction to Law and Economics

Let's begin our study of law and economics with a very broad definition of the subject matter of economics: economics studies rational behavior, defined as the pursuit of consistent ends by efficient means. By this expansive definition, economics is a suitable tool for studying the behavior of anyone who knows of the law or administers it: legal officials—e.g., lawyers and judges—are expected to act rationally and are criticized for acting irrationally; common citizens usually respond in a rational way to legal rules and institutions by, for example, not driving too fast for the prevailing conditions and not stealing their neighbor's lawnmower. It follows from our very broad definition of the subject matter of economics that economic concepts and models are useful for explaining laws and legal institutions. In this chapter we will give you some concrete examples of how economics explains legal institutions by using models of rational behavior. The subsequent chapters will teach you to construct these explanations in some of the principal areas of the law: property, contracts, torts, and crime.

I. WHAT IS LAW AND ECONOMICS ABOUT?

The best way to discover the subject matter of law and economics is to plunge right in. The following three examples give a flavor of the topics we will discuss and reveal how economics may be used to explain legal rules and institutions.

> **Example 1:** An oil company signs a contract to deliver oil by a certain date from the Middle East to a European manufacturer. Before the oil is delivered, war breaks out in the exporting country, so that the oil company cannot perform the contract as promised. The lack of oil causes the European manufacturer to forego profitable business investments. The manufacturer brings an action

1

against the oil company for breach of contract and asks the court to award damages equal to the amount of profits the manufacturer would have realized if the oil had been delivered as promised. Unfortunately, the contract is silent about the risk of nonperformance in the event of war so that the court cannot simply read the contract and resolve the dispute on the contract's own terms. In resolving the suit, the court must decide whether to excuse the oil company from performance on the grounds that the war made the performance "impossible" or to find the oil company in breach of contract and to require the oil company to compensate the manufacturer for lost profits.[1]

For an economist analyzing this case, the crucial point is that the parties failed to allocate between themselves the risk of a certain contingency—in this instance, war—that has arisen to frustrate performance of the contract. War is a risk of doing business in the Middle East, a risk that must be borne by one of the parties to the contract. Because the contract is silent about the allocation of this risk, the court must allocate it, and, depending on how the court decides the case, one party or the other will have to bear the costs of that risk. What are the *consequences* of different court rulings on how to allocate the loss?

If the court excuses the oil company from responsibility for performing the contract, then the manufacturer is going to bear the losses that arise from the non-delivery of oil. On the other hand, suppose that the court holds the oil company responsible for compensating the European manufacturer for the profits lost because of the failure to deliver the oil. In that case, the oil company bears the losses that arise from non-delivery of the oil. Therefore, the way the court decides the case accomplishes an apportionment of losses between the two parties.

Can economics provide a method for the court to decide which apportionment is better? From the standpoint of economic efficiency, the court should assign the loss from non-delivery so as to make future contractual behavior more efficient.[2] And a rule for doing this is *to assign the losses to the*

---

[1]This example is taken from Posner & Rosenfield, *Impossibility and Related Doctrines in Contract Law,* 6 J. LEGAL STUD. 88 (1977). This is an example of the citation style detailed in A UNIFORM SYSTEM OF CITATION, published periodically by the Harvard Law Review Association and used throughout the American legal profession. It is such a clear method of directing the reader to the author's sources that we will employ it in all our footnotes and end-of-chapter bibliographies in this book. Here is what the citation means: the authors of the work are Posner and Rosenfield; the title of the work is "Impossibility and Related Doctrines in Contract Law"; and the article may be found, beginning on page 88, in volume 6 of the *Journal of Legal Studies,* which was published in 1977.

[2]We are ignoring for the moment the possibility that the court should apportion the loss between the two parties on the basis of some distributional goal, e.g., that, whenever possible, manufacturers should be made wealthy and exporters should be made less wealthy. We return to these issues in the chapters on the economics of contract law.

party who can bear the risk of such a loss at least cost.[3] In this case it seems that a company doing business in the Middle East is in a better position than a European manufacturer to assess the risk of war in that region and to take steps to mitigate its effects. For example, the oil company might be able to purchase insurance against non-performance because of war much more cheaply than could the European manufacturer. The oil company could more cheaply arrange for alternative shipping routes that might not be blocked by a Middle Eastern war. That company could make arrangements with other oil companies in other, less sensitive parts of the world to make emergency purchases of oil in the event of war in the Middle East.

In so far as it is true that the oil company is better able to bear the risk of non-performance because of war, a court whose objective was to promote economic efficiency would hold the oil company liable for breach of contract. This conclusion is consistent with the outcome of some actual cases that arose as a consequence of the 1967 war in the Middle East.

How does the economic justification for deciding this case promote economic efficiency? To see the connection, we need first to extract the general rule from the case and then examine the economic consequences of that rule for future contracting parties. The rule that our economically-minded court proposes would seem to be this: *if in your contract you fail to allocate the risk of loss from non-performance of the contract due to a particular contingency and that contingency arises to frustrate performance of the contract, the court will determine which party could have borne the risk of such a loss at lower cost and will then allocate the loss to that party.* That rule is economically efficient if it induces future contracting parties to write more or better contracts than they would under any alternative rule. We will consider this matter in much greater detail in Chapters 6 and 7; here, let us merely suggest the efficiency consequences of the above general rule. One way in which the rule promotes efficient contracting is that it mimics the allocation of risk that the contracting parties would have probably agreed upon if only they had thought of the contingency that has arisen to frustrate performance. Thus, the rule corresponds to what the parties would have wanted to have happened. (Of course, *after* the frustrating contingency has occurred, the losing party—the

---

[3]We will assume in this example that the entire loss from non-performance must be allocated by the court to one of the parties. Although considerations of economic efficiency argue for this method of allocating losses, this is not necessarily the way courts would behave. Courts might divide the loss between the parties, perhaps because they feel that that was fair or more just. For example, if the manufacturer has lost $10,000 in profit as a result of the non-delivery of oil, a court might have divided the losses by awarding the manufacturer only $5,000.

In our much more complete discussion of these issues in Chapters 6 and 7, we will show that economic efficiency is served by allocating the loss entirely to one party or the other. This is your first glimpse at the potential conflict between economic efficiency and justice, a conflict that we will confront again in this book.

cheaper bearer of the risk of loss—may well deny that he would have willingly assumed the risk. Nonetheless, he might have willingly accepted the risk at the time the contract was formed.) Another way in which the general rule promotes efficiency is that, by alerting future contracting parties that this is the rule that courts will apply in allocating loss from non-performance, it encourages future contracting parties to devise *explicit* allocations of the risk of loss if for whatever reason they would be made better off by that alternative allocation. That might be the case if one contracting party was risk-neutral while the other party, although the cheaper risk-bearer, was highly risk-averse. The risk-averse party would prefer that the risk-neutral party bear the risk. This allocation may increase the cost of concluding the contract, but if both parties feel themselves better off with that allocation of risk than they would if the risk-averse party bore the risk (as would be the case under the general rule above), their contract is efficient.

Notice that these beneficial effects of the court's general rule extend well beyond the market for the delivery of Middle Eastern oil. After all, the general rule is not tailored just to that market but spreads much more broadly to include all contracts where there is a risk of non-performance.

Here is a second example of the subject matter and style of analysis of law and economics:

> **Example 2:** A factory emits smoke that dirties the clothes being cleaned at a nearby commercial laundry. Suppose that the laundry initiates court proceedings to have the damage stopped; depending on the evidence presented to the court, the case might be resolved in one of two ways. If, as seems most likely, the court decides that the factory is infringing upon the laundry's right to be free from smoke damage, the court may take steps to stop the factory from polluting. If, however, the court decides that there has been no infringement by the factory—because, perhaps, the factory was in the neighborhood first; the laundry, that is, "came to the nuisance"—then the court may dismiss the laundry's complaint without any remedy. Will the efficiency of production by the factory and the laundry be affected by which option the court selects?[4]

The traditional legal approach in nuisance law attempts to assess the rights of the two parties and to balance those rights in such a way as to do justice. An economic analysis of nuisance has this focus: the determination of which of the two options faced by the court is more likely to promote the efficient use of scarce resources. These may strike you as completely different approaches, and, indeed, they are. But we will see repeatedly in this book that, as different as the legal and economic approaches are, they frequently

---

[4]An additional question we will want to answer when we deal with this situation in Chapters 4 and 5 is what form of relief the court should award to the laundry if it finds that the laundry is entitled to be free from the factory's pollution. Court-imposed relief may take two forms: an injunction against the factory's continuing to pollute and the payment of money damages by the factory to the laundry.

lead to the same conclusions. The same legal rule that legal scholars defend as just, economists defend as efficient. This is not always true, as we will make plain when those instances arise. But in a surprisingly large number of circumstances, the economic and legal approaches reach the same destination by different routes.

Now, to return to the example of the factory emitting smoke that damages a nearby laundry, will the efficiency of production by the factory and the laundry be affected by which option the court selects—relief for the laundry or dismissal of the action? An early economic analysis of this problem suggested that the answer is "None." It may not matter to the efficient use of resources by the factory or the laundry, nor to the amount of pollution emitted, whether the court protected the laundry's right to be free from pollution or allowed the factory to pollute at will by dismissing the complaint. Where the cost to the laundry and to the factory of concluding a private agreement limiting pollution is very low, the pollution level and the amount of production by both parties will be the same level under either rule of law.

This remarkable conclusion, commonly called the "Coase Theorem" after its author, Professor Ronald Coase, asserts that where the costs of concluding a transaction are very low, the rule of law—that is, whether the laundry is entitled to be free from pollution by the factory or the factory is entitled to pollute as much as it likes—will not affect the level of pollution or the amount of laundry cleaned; the amounts will be the same regardless of how the law resolves the dispute.[5]

To see why, let us imagine an unlikely but dramatic solution to this pollution problem: suppose that the owner of the laundry marries the owner of the factory. As a result, the cost of coordinating the activities of the factory and the laundry become very low. We would confidently expect the couple to set pollution at the level that maximizes the total profits of the two enterprises, in order to maximize their combined income, regardless of whether the law would protect the laundry from pollution.

Rational bargainers facing low bargaining costs will do just as well as a married couple, because they will bargain until they exhaust the possibilities for mutual gain, which occurs when total profits of the two enterprises are maximized. For example, suppose the pollution damage suffered by the laundry is $5,000 and the cost to the factory of installing equipment or cutting back on production to eliminate the pollution is $10,000. Assume, furthermore, that the two parties can bargain between themselves at low cost.

How will different rules of law affect this situation? If the rule of law entitles the factory to pollute as much as it likes, then the factory can pollute

---

[5]Strictly speaking, the level of pollution and the amount of laundry cleaned will be *efficient* under the conditions specified by the Coase Theorem, regardless of how the rights are allocated. This usually implies that the quantities of pollution and of laundry will also be invariant to the assignment of rights.

with impunity, so it will go on polluting. The laundry will simply have to suffer $5,000 in losses.

But what if the law gives a right to the laundry to be free from the factory's pollution? One might think that the result of this different assignment of rights would force the factory to spend $10,000 to eliminate pollution entirely. But under our assumption of low bargaining costs, that result is unlikely. A mutually beneficial transaction is possible that allows the factory to continue its production and pollution and also allows the laundry to be compensated for the loss of $5,000 that the pollution inflicts. If the factory stops pollution entirely, then it loses $10,000 and the laundry benefits $5,000. Both will benefit if some alternative can be found that pays the laundry more than its $5,000 in losses but costs the factory less than $10,000. Suppose, for example, that the polluter pays the laundry $7,500 in exchange for the laundry's waiving its right to be free from pollution and allowing the factory to continue to pollute. Under this alternative, the laundry is paid $7,500 for putting up with $5,000 in pollution damages, thus enjoying a net profit of $2,500. Similarly, the factory is better off paying $7,500 to the laundry instead of incurring the expense of $10,000 to install the pollution abatement equipment. Both parties are better off. So, under the assumption of low bargaining costs, the factory will continue polluting whether the law gives the pollutee the right to be free from pollution or gives the polluter the right to pollute.

There is a useful, general way to describe these facts: if someone values an asset—whether it be automobiles, wheat, labor, or pollution rights—more than its owner, then there is scope for mutual gain by exchange. We may think of the agreement between the laundry and the factory as an exchange of pollution rights. The potential gains from exchange are not exhausted unless the total profits from the two enterprises are maximized.

In our chapters on property, we will return to the important issues raised in this example. Among other things, we will want to determine the circumstances in which it *does* matter to the efficient use of resources how the law assigns rights.

And here is the final example of what law and economics is about:

Example 3. A commission has been appointed to consider some reforms of the criminal law. The commission has identified certain white-collar crimes that are committed for money after rational computation of the risk of getting caught and punished and the potential gain. Currently, those convicted of committing these crimes are sentenced to a term in prison. After taking extensive testimony, much of it from economists, the commission decides that a monetary fine, rather than incarceration, is the appropriate punishment for these offenses. The commission ranks each offense by seriousness and determines that the fine should increase with the seriousness of the offense, but by how much?

One important consideration in answering this question is the effectiveness of the schedule of fines in discouraging potential offenders. Any desired level of deterrence for these white-collar crimes can be achieved by setting the risk at the appropriate level. The risk depends upon the *probability* and *magnitude* of the punishment. If apprehending offenders is costly and administering fines is cheap, then the cheapest way to achieve any desired level of deterrence is to invest little in apprehending offenders but to fine severely those who are apprehended. Specifically, it can be shown that the most serious offense should be punished by the maximum fine that the offender can bear. Indeed, it can also be shown that it is never efficient from a social viewpoint to incarcerate *any* criminal offender—not just white-collar criminals—unless the ability to pay fines has been completely exhausted. These are a few of the remarkable findings that result from the economic analysis of crime and punishment.

The reader of this book will learn to analyze legal problems like those in these examples using the tools of microeconomic theory. Let us outline the steps in a complete economic analysis of a legal problem. The first step is to assume that the individuals or institutions who make decisions are maximizing well-known and clearly specified economic objectives, for example, that businesses are maximizing profits and that consumers are maximizing wealth and leisure. The second step is to show that the interaction among all relevant decisionmakers settles down into what economists call an equilibrium, a condition that does not spontaneously change. The third step is to judge the equilibrium on the criterion of economic efficiency.

Scientific method requires an additional step beyond the logically consistent economic analysis suggested above—testing the predictions of that analysis against the facts. For example, before fully accepting the prediction that the assignment of liability for pollution does not influence the amount of pollution when the parties can bargain together cheaply, it is necessary to confront that hypothesis with data from the real world. A convincing test would involve statistics and, possibly, econometrics. Because it is still a new field of study, the economic analysis of law has generated far more logically consistent analyses than tests. An additional reason for the paucity of empirical tests of the hypotheses is that the data available for these tests are of poor quality. The law has only recently become interested in gathering data in such a way that statistical hypothesis-testing is feasible, and there is no doubt that both the quality and quantity of that data will increase. As that happens and as the set of economic hypotheses about the law continues to flower, these tests will become a vital part of the law and economics literature in the future.[6]

---

[6]This suggests that lawyers and economists concerned to equip themselves with a complete tool kit for future scholarship should learn mathematical statistics and econometrics. Indeed, many lawyers have already done so. The legal literature on such issues as employment, sex, and age discrimination has become very statistically sophisticated.

II. THE METHODOLOGIES OF ECONOMICS AND OF THE LAW[7]

The rest of this introductory chapter compares the methodologies of economics and law. We make this comparison with some trepidation because methodological discussions are a good cure for insomnia. A discussion of methodology is required because this book brings together scholarship in two very different disciplines. We will do our best to make the discussion lively.

Since the 17th century, social scientists have tried to accomplish in the study of society what Newton achieved in the study of nature. Everyone who buys groceries or seeks work knows that the power of economics is feeble compared to that of physics, but economists have managed to make Newton's mathematics the structure of their discipline. In the process of absorbing Newton's mathematics, which began in the 1880s and was completed by the time Samuelson published *Foundations of Economic Analysis* in 1942, economics gained technical superiority over the other social sciences. The technical superiority of economics makes its spread into other social sciences irresistible, just as Newtonian mechanics spread into economics. Indeed, the fields of political science, history, demography, biology, and sociology have been revolutionized by scholars who have imported into those disciplines an approach that combines the traditional modes of analysis of each discipline with the quantitative methods and behavioral theories of microeconomics. The law of entropy appears to work backwards for ideas: rigor drives out less structured modes of thought.

This aggression against softer subjects has been called the "imperialism of economics." One recent beneficiary, or victim, is the law. Left to its own devices, the law stood no more chance of developing quantitative methodology than Australia stood of independently developing the rabbit. The traditions of legal scholarship point in a different direction from that of quantitative analysis. Most lawyers conceive of empirical research as analyzing appellate cases in an effort to discover consistencies in the interpretation of the law. And in so far as the law has a theory that informs this empirical work, that mainstream legal theory continues to be the philosophy of law, whose technical foundation is the analysis of language. The lawyer poring over cases contrasts vividly with the economist manipulating equations.

The contrast was not so vivid fifty years ago when mathematical economics was still a narrow specialty within the economics profession. At that time empirical economics consisted partly of descriptive case studies, such as a case study of the shoe industry. The emphasis was on such questions as the number of firms in the shoe industry, how large each of them was, which firms had introduced new methods of production or new styles for consum-

---

[7]Some of the material in this section is adapted from Cooter, *Law and the Imperialism of Economics*, 29 U.C.L.A. L. REV. 1260 (1982).

ers, and whether the firms marketed their own shoes in their own retail outlets or hired other firms to do the retail sales for them. This is important work and is still being done today, but there has been a subtle shift in emphasis between those earlier case studies and today's. The modern economist is more interested in explanation than in description and uses sophisticated theories of economic behavior in these explanations. The most widespread technique of inquiry among economists today is to propose a thorough mathematical theory of some important aspect of behavior and then to confront this theory with data from the real world to see if the model accurately explains and predicts behavior. Thus, the modern economist must be comfortable with advanced mathematical tools from the differential and integral calculus, from linear algebra, and from mathematical statistics and econometrics. Forty years ago, theoretical economics could still be conducted in ordinary language, as opposed to mathematics. But those past forty years have revealed that economic knowledge can be advanced more by analyzing statistics than by scrutinizing descriptive case studies, more by taking derivatives than by parsing phrases.

Many economists today confidently expect the recent history of economics to be repeated in the study of the law. In fact, economic models have already found their way into law journals, and analyses ultimately derived from these models are presented in the basic law school curriculum. There is a competition between alternative styles of research whose potential effects upon legal education and scholarship are profound.

Watching law respond to economic analysis is rather like watching an ecological system rearrange itself after the release of an exotic animal. Like the rabbits in Australia, economists have discovered an unoccupied niche in legal scholarship, specifically, the absence of quantitative reasoning, and are moving quickly to fill it. Their reception into this new area has been a mixed one. Many traditional lawyers have been contemptuous of and unsettled by the work of economists who analyze the law. Their attempts to refute the economic approach have often been undertaken without going through the intermediate step of understanding it. The detractors claim that the economic approach is too abstract, untested, and irrelevant to the courtroom. "It is all very well to theorize," they argue, "but it has little to do with the practice of law." In response to these criticisms, economists have not done much to raise the level of the debate. Often they have belittled the traditional legal method, its concentration on the "fuzzy" idea of justice, and its lack of formal, mathematical sophistication without bothering to study the law.

The strengths and weakness of the economic analysis of law are better revealed by examining its substance, rather than by engaging in ill-informed methodological disputes. What are the novel substantive claims of the economic analysis of law? The central claim is that the fundamental economic concepts, such as maximization, equilibrium, and efficiency, are also fundamental to understanding and explaining the law. This claim comes in several versions that can be arranged by their strength.

The strongest claim is that the law can be reduced to economics by substituting economic concepts for such traditional legal concepts as justice, right, duty, negligence, and so forth. According to this claim, after the substitution is made, the legal language can be jettisoned as excess baggage.[8] For example, some theorists propose to replace the concept of justice with the concept of economic efficiency.[9]

Weaker than reductivism is the claim that economic concepts can be used to explain much of the law but not to eliminate and replace legal concepts. Explaining the law involves discovering unity and structure in its diverse elements, revealing its purposes and consequences, and accounting for the origins of rules and practices. For example, it has been suggested that the negligence rule of liability for certain kinds of accidents can be explained as the means by which judges implement a social policy of minimizing the social costs of accidents. If successful, such a deduction would reveal that there is an economic aspect to the logic of the law that is hidden from the eye that has not been educated in economics.

A distinct claim from the one we have just made is that economists can explain why courts and legislators make certain changes in the law. For example, and roughly speaking, the history of tort law in the last several centuries shows remarkable changes for which we do not yet have an adequate explanation. Until the late 18th century the general rule was that if you *caused* harm, you were responsible for paying for its consequences, a standard called "strict liability." In the 19th century the common law judges found this rule to be too harsh and amended it to say that only if you *negligently* caused harm were you responsible for paying for the consequences, a standard known as "negligence." More recently, there has been an increased interest in jettisoning the whole tort liability system in favor of so-called administered compensation systems such as no-fault insurance and workers' compensation.

A multitude of theories can be adduced in an attempt to explain these changes in tort law. For example, one scholar has argued that the change from strict liability to negligence in the 19th century was made by common law judges in order to subsidize the new industrial enterprises of the period.[10] Such proffered explanations of broad changes in the law, though

---

[8]The claim that law can be reduced to economics is similar to the claim that used to be made in psychology that mind can be reduced to behavior. This proposition, called "reductivism" in philosophy, is dead in psychology, and it ought to be laid to rest in the economic analysis of law, too.

[9]The theme that concepts of justice are merely expressions of individual preferences, which should be replaced in law by the more substantial concept of efficiency, occurs in the work of Judge Richard Posner. For example, see his pathbreaking THE ECONOMIC ANALYSIS OF LAW (3d ed. 1986) and *The Ethical and Political Basis of the Efficiency Norm in Common Law Adjudication,* 8 HOFSTRA L. REV. 487 (1980). For a reply, *see* Jules Coleman, *Efficiency, Utility, and Wealth Maximization,* 8 HOSTRA L. REV. 509 (1980).

[10]*See* M. Horowitz, THE TRANSFORMATION OF AMERICAN LAW, 1790–1860 (1977).

stimulating, are bound to be received with skepticism and caution, if not with hostility. In contrast, the economic analysis of law is on firmer ground when, instead of trying to explain the history of legal rules, it confines itself to predicting their economic consequences. For example, economics might predict that replacing a negligence rule with one of strict liability for injuries caused by defective products will cause producers to invest additional resources in finding safer designs for products. And, indeed, some studies of this sort have been done; we will discuss their results in the chapters on the economics of tort law.

As another example, there is a general theory that courts, like competitive markets, cannot achieve equilibrium in the common law process until the legal rules are efficient. This theory, when applied to the history of torts, leads to the hypothesis that the law will evolve toward more efficient rules.

This book deals with economic explanations of the law and predictions of the consequences of legal rules. In order to explain these rules and their consequences, we propose to use the tools of microeconomic theory. The reason is this: *the rules created by law establish implicit prices for different kinds of behavior, and the consequences of those rules can be analyzed as the response to those implicit prices.* Furthermore, we contend that economic concepts such as maximization, equilibrium, and efficiency are fundamental categories for explaining society, especially the behavior of rational people responding to rules of law. Thus, the scope for the economic analysis of law is as broad as the scope of rational behavior by legal officials and by people subject to the law.

How broad is this scope? The ideal decisionmaker in legal theory is described as "reasonable," whereas the ideal decisionmaker in economics is described as "rational." Explaining the relationship between the reasonable man and the rational man is one way to assess the scope of the economic analysis of law. The difference between reason and rationality is a celebrated topic in philosophy. According to a conventional view, rational behavior is the pursuit of consistent ends by efficient means. Irrationality arises when ends are contradictory or means are inefficient. By this definition, rationality allows for substantial arbitrariness of ends. Specifically, behavior can be rational even though the ends are anti-social, and the means are immoral.

However, pursuing anti-social ends or adopting immoral means is generally regarded as *unreasonable.* A reasonable person is socialized into the norms and conventions of a community, so his ends are consistent with shared values and his pursuit of them conforms to group norms. For example, a reasonable person obeys the community standards of care in dangerous activities like driving a car, and a reasonable person knows how to respond when placed on a jury and asked to decide whether the preponderance of evidence favors the plaintiff or the defendant.

The ideal decisionmaker in law—whether a judge, juror, plaintiff, defendant, potential plaintiff, or potential defendant—is reasonable and, therefore, conforms to these social norms. It is usually true that these norms include the norms of economic rationality, specifically those of consistency and efficiency. This claim that a person must be rational in order to be reasonable is a very strong one. Yet, it is close to the truth when applied to legal officials. For example, a judge may feel obligated to achieve legal objectives without wasting resources. And most of us feel that to say that the decision of a legal official was irrational is to make a strong condemnation of it. The fact that legal officials are expected to pursue consistent ends by efficient means implies that there is broad scope for legal theory based upon economic analysis. The fundamental hypothesis of the economic analysis is that law is rational, and hence analyzable by economic concepts. This book attempts to present the best existing evidence on the strengths and weaknesses of that hypothesis.

However, legal officials are subject to additional constraints and norms besides consistency and efficiency, constraints and norms inherent in the notion of reasonable decisions, and this implies that economics cannot provide a complete explanation of law. These norms are imbedded in long traditions of thought and analysis, especially in ethical and political philosophy, which are not themselves a part of economics. This fact suggests that the economic approach to law is fundamental, but incomplete. For this reason we say that the aim of our book is to explain the rationality of law, which is a fundamental, but incomplete, part of the explanation of law.

Instead of knock-down proofs, arguments about reasonable behavior appeal to various philosophical and humanistic traditions of thought. These traditions, which are *disciplines* but not *sciences,* are sometimes difficult for economists to appreciate. Infatuated by the model of natural science, economists tend to regard theories of ethics worked out over several thousand years of debate as insubstantial. Like prophets in the desert, this conceit insulates economists from the mainstream of legal theory. Unfortunately, contempt for these other traditions frequently leads to crude language and shallow arguments that make some lawyers hostile to the economic analysis of law. Our approach in this book will be to try to bring economics into contact with the philosophy of law in order to connect the analytical methods for explaining rational behavior with the sensibilities motivating reasonable behavior.

III. WHY SHOULD LAWYERS STUDY ECONOMICS? WHY SHOULD ECONOMISTS STUDY LAW?

The economic analysis of law is an inter-disciplinary subject, bringing together the tools of two great fields of study. As we will see in the course of this book, this melding of the two areas allows us to gain a greater understanding of both. Economics allows us to perceive the legal system in a new way, one that is extremely useful to lawyers and to anyone interested in issues of public policy. You probably are already accustomed to thinking of rules of law as important tools for society to achieve its goals of justice and fairness. Indeed, it is not an exaggeration to suggest that most people, especially lawyers, view the law *only* in its role as a provider of justice. We do not wish to supplant this view so much as to supplement it. This book will teach you also to view the law in its role as allocating legal rights according to standards of economic rationality. Specifically, you will learn to assess the consistency and efficiency of different allocations of legal rights.

There is another area upon which this book will enhance your understanding, and that is your understanding of economics. While our main focus will be on what economics can add to the analysis of legal rules and institutions, we will also find that the law has something to teach economists. Lawyers spend a great deal of their time trying to resolve practical problems. As a result, they are somewhat impatient with abstractions that stray too far from practicalities; the techniques of legal analysis have been shaped by this sensibility. Law students learn sensitivity to verbal distinctions; indeed, the outcome of a case often turns upon the labels that are used to describe the facts. These verbal distinctions sometimes strike non-lawyers as being sophistry or pettifoggery. But often these legal, verbal distinctions are based on subtle but important points about practical problems that economists have ignored. By way of illustration, economists frequently extoll the virtues of voluntary exchange, but economics does not have a detailed account of what it means for exchange to be *voluntary.* As we will see, contract law has a complex, well-articulated theory of volition. If economists will listen to what the law has to teach them, they will find their models being drawn closer to reality.

This mutual enhancement of understanding is the great benefit of interdisciplinary study. But it will come as no surprise to you to learn that this benefit can be had only at a cost: lawyers must learn some economics, and economists must learn something about the law. We ask the reader to incur this cost in the next two chapters. In order to construct proofs or tests, you must be able to use the tools of microeconomics, and in order to apply these techniques to the law, you need to understand the elements of legal analysis, especially the case method. The next chapter reviews the microeconomic tools, and the subsequent chapter, Chapter 3, reviews the elements of legal analysis. The trained economist or lawyer may wish to skip the familiar parts of these two chapters and focus only upon the unfamiliar parts.

SUGGESTED READINGS

Ackerman, Bruce, ed., ECONOMIC FOUNDATIONS OF PROPERTY LAW (1975).

Easterbrook, Frank, *Foreword: The Court and the Economic System,* 98 HARV. L. REV. 4 (1984). [*See also* Laurence Tribe, *Constitutional Calculus: Equal Justice or Economic Efficiency?* 98 HARV. L. REV. 592 (1984) and Easterbrook, *Method, Result, and Authority: A Reply,* 98 HARV. L. REV. 622 (1984).]

Friedman, Lee S., MICROECONOMIC POLICY ANALYSIS (1984).

Goetz, Charles, LAW AND ECONOMICS (1984).

Hirsch, Werner Z., LAW AND ECONOMICS: AN INTRODUCTORY ANALYSIS (1979).

Kronman, Anthony and Richard A. Posner, eds., THE ECONOMICS OF CONTRACT LAW (1979).

Leff, Arthur, *Economic Analysis of Law: Some Realism about Nominalism,* 60 VA. L. REV. 451 (1974) [A book review of the first edition of Posner, ECONOMIC ANALYSIS OF LAW].

Michelman, Frank I., *Norms and Normativity,* 62 MINN. L. REV. 1015 (1978).

Polinsky, A. Mitchell, *Economic Analysis as a Potentially Defective Product: A Buyer's Guide to Posner's Economic Analysis of Law,* 87 HARV. L. REV. 1655 (1974).

Polinsky, A. Mitchell, AN INTRODUCTION TO LAW AND ECONOMICS (1983).

Posner, Richard A., ECONOMIC ANALYSIS OF LAW (3d ed., 1986).

CHAPTER 2

A Review of Microeconomics

"For the rational study of the law the black-letter man may be the man of the present, but the man of the future is the man of statistics and the master of economics."

Oliver Wendell Holmes, Jr., *The Path of the Law*, in COLLECTED LEGAL PAPERS (1921).

The economic analysis of law draws upon the principles of economics, which are reviewed in this chapter. For those of you who have not studied economics, reading this chapter will prove challenging but essential for an understanding of the material in the remainder of the book. For those who have already mastered economic theory, reading this chapter is unnecessary. For those readers who are somewhere in between these extremes, we suggest that you begin reading this chapter, skimming what is familiar and studying carefully what is unfamiliar. A good test of your level of understanding is to try the questions at the end of the chapter.

I. OVERVIEW

The part of economics that will prove most useful in our analysis of the law is called *microeconomics*. Microeconomics is frequently defined as the study of how scarce resources are allocated among competing ends. That is, it is the study of how individuals and the society that they form make choices. Economists have, over the past one hundred years, elaborated an elegant and powerful theory of choice. We cannot hope to reproduce that entire theory here, but we can give you the general conclusions of that theory and a glimpse of how economists use it.

Microeconomics is often divided into four sections. The first is the theory of consumer choice and demand, in which a model is developed of how the typical consumer, constrained by a restricted amount of income, chooses among the many goods and services offered to him in the economy. From this axiomatic study of consumer choice, it is possible to derive one of the most important tools of microeconomic analysis—the demand curve.

The second section of microeconomics deals with the other side of the market, the supply of goods and services. After we develop a model of the basic business unit, the firm, we will see how the firm decides what to produce for sale, how much to produce, and at what price to sell its output. We will combine the material on consumer choice and the theory of the firm in order to derive a theory of market equilibrium.

The third section of microeconomic theory treats the special theory of markets for factors of production, such as labor and capital. We will not deal with that topic in this book.

The final section of our review of microeconomics will deal with the topic known as welfare economics. The "welfare" studied in this section of microeconomics is not the set of governmental programs designed to aid the less advantaged. Rather, it is the aggregate welfare or well-being of all consumers. We review the economists' debate about the goals of efficiency and equity and then explore various theoretical tools that economists have proposed to allow them to talk about issues of income and wealth distribution.

Finally, the appendix to this chapter introduces the economic theory of decisions under uncertainty. We will be using that theory repeatedly in the course of this book.

There are additional tools of microeconomic analysis beyond those we shall review here. Later in the book we will introduce those special tools of analysis where they are more immediately necessary.

II. MAXIMIZATION, EQUILIBRIUM, AND EFFICIENCY

From a mathematical viewpoint, there are two fundamental concepts in economics, both of which were borrowed from calculus and are now being applied to social phenomena as different as warfare and marriage. The first concept is *maximization*. Maximization of something is taken to be the goal of every economic actor: consumers are said to maximize utility; firms, to maximize profits; politicians, to maximize votes; bureaucracies, to maximize revenues; charities, to maximize social welfare; and so forth. The second important mathematical concept is that of an *equilibrium*, a pattern of interaction that tends to persist because everyone is maximizing simultaneously. There is no apparent limit to the situations in which this notion can be and has been applied: equilibria have been studied in markets for goods and services, elections, club memberships, competitive games, team effort, budgetary allocation on Capitol Hill, and more. No habit of thought is so deeply ingrained among economists as the urge to characterize each social phenomenon as an equilibrium in the interaction of maximizing individuals or institutions.

The assumption that decisionmakers maximize is a simple way to quantify social behavior. Suppose that an individual or institution can rank alternative states of the world from bad to good. Because real numbers can be ranked from small to large, the qualitative ranking of alternatives can be associated with a quantitative ranking by real numbers. In this way the values of the individual or institution can be quantified.

Once these values are quantified—that is, once the various states of the world are ranked and numbers are assigned to the ranking—and once we ask the individual or institution to choose which state is most preferred, then it is natural to assume that the state with the highest numerical value or rank will be chosen. Thus, economists assume that individuals and some institutions act as if they rank alternative states of the world and maximize by choosing the best available alternative. In principle, it does not matter what it is that individuals or institutions maximize. They could be attempting to maximize money income, votes, subjective feelings of well-being, the average welfare of society, or something else. All that is required is the minimum level of purposefulness necessary for quantification. Nor is an economist's definition of purposefulness demanding: the maximization may be the product of thoughtful, careful deliberation, as when a firm computes profits, or a rote response, as when a laboratory rat presses a bar to obtain food.

From an analytic standpoint the simplest pattern of interaction among maximizing individuals is one that does not change. It is much simpler to analyze a change by comparing the initial and final end-states (equilibria) of the process than by attempting to trace out the entire path of development. Advanced microeconomic theories of growth, cycles, and disequilibria exist, but we will not need them here. The comparison of equilibria (what is called among economists "comparative statics") will be the basic approach in this text.

The concept of *efficiency* is less fundamental in the mathematical sense, but just as prominent in microeconomics as maximization and equilibrium. Economists use the word "efficiency" to describe an equilibrium among consumers or producers. A production process is said to be *productively efficient* if it yields a given level of output with the least cost combination of inputs.[1] That is, the firm cannot produce the given level of output at lower cost. Equivalently, a process is *productively efficient* if it maximizes the level of output attainable from a given combination of inputs. For the purposes of illustration, consider a firm that uses labor and special tools (called, because of their durability, "capital" or "capital goods") to produce a consumer good called a "widget." Suppose that currently the firm produces 100 widgets per week using 10 workers who are using 15 special tools. Is the firm productively efficient? It is if (1) it is not possible to produce 100 widgets per

---

[1]Equivalently, a process is efficient if it used the minimum number of inputs to yield a given level of output. Or, productive efficiency can be defined as a condition in which a given output is produced at least cost.

week using a less expensive combination of workers and tools or (2) it is not possible to produce more widgets per week from the combination of 10 workers and 15 special tools.

A related kind of efficiency, *allocative efficiency*, describes an equilibrium distribution of goods and services among individual consumers. A particular distribution of goods among consumers is said to be *allocatively efficient* if it is not possible to redistribute the goods so as to make at least one consumer better off (in his own estimation) without making another consumer worse off (again, in his own estimation). For simplicity's sake, assume that there are only two consumers, Smith and Jones, and two goods, umbrellas and food, and that there is some existing distribution of those goods between them. Is the existing distribution of umbrellas and food between Smith and Jones allocatively efficient? It is if it is not possible to rearrange the distribution of food and umbrellas between the two consumers without making one of them worse off. (As we will see, if it is possible to rearrange the distribution of goods so as to make *both* of them better off, they will engage in an exchange or market transaction.) The point of this example is to introduce the notion of allocative efficiency, not to suggest that the distribution is *fair* or *just* or *equitable*. As we have indicated before, fairness and efficiency are distinguishable concepts. Welfare economics tries to reconcile the goals of efficiency and fairness, so we will leave a more detailed discussion of that important topic until later in this chapter.

The basic concepts-maximization, equilibrium, and efficiency-are fundamental to explaining rational behavior, especially in decentralized institutions like markets that involve the coordinated interaction of many different people. Nonetheless, some lawyers who are critical of the economic analysis of law are doubtful that these concepts are really useful in explaining important social phenomena. They ask, "Why stress equilibria instead of change? Isn't it better for the analysis to be dynamic rather than static? Why stress maximization instead of psychological or sociological theories? Isn't it better to base predictions upon the psychology of choice rather than postulate rationality, to recognize social norms rather than assume selfishness or self-interest?" These claims sometimes have merit, as economists have known for a long time. But microeconomists are well aware that these criticisms fit only some actions and situations, whereas the more basic economic concepts (such as maximization, equilibrium, and efficiency) have a very broad application.

III. MATHEMATICAL TOOLS

Some readers must reach far back into their memories to recall simple mathematical notation; for others the math may be fresh in their minds, but they have never learned economics. This section reviews mathematical notation and applies it to the fundamental economic concepts of maximization, equilibrium, and efficiency.

Economics is rife with functions: production functions, utility functions, cost functions, social welfare functions, and others. A function is a *relationship between two sets of numbers such that for each number in one set there corresponds exactly one number in the other set.* To illustrate, the columns below correspond to a functional relationship between the numbers in the left- and those in the right-hand column. Thus, the number 4 in the *x*-column below corresponds to the number 10 in the *y*-column.

y-column	*x*-column
2	-3
3	0
10	4
10	6
12	9
7	12
7	15

In fact, for each number in the *x*-column there corresponds exactly one number in the *y*-column. Thus, we can say that the variable *y* is a function of the variable *x*, or in the most common form of notation

$$y = f(x).$$

This is read as "*y* is a function of *x*" or "*y* equals some *f* of *x*."

Note that the number 4 is not the only number in the *x*-column that corresponds to the number 10 in the *y*-column; the number 6 also corresponds to the number 10. In this table, for a given value of *x*, there corresponds one value of *y*, but for some values of *y*, there corresponds more than one value of *x*. A value of *x* determines an exact value of *y*, whereas a value of *y* does not determine an exact value of *x*. Thus, in $y = f(x)$, *y* is called the "dependent variable," since it depends on the value of *x*, and *x* is called the "independent variable." Since *y* depends upon *x* in this table, *y* is a function of *x*, but since *x* does not (to our knowledge) depend for its values on *y*, *x* is not a function of *y*.

Now suppose that there is another dependent variable, named *z*, that also depends upon *x*. The function relating *z* to *x* might be named *g*:

$$z = g(x).$$

When there are two functions, $g(x)$ and $f(x)$, with different dependent variables, *z* and *y*, remembering which function goes with which variable can be hard. To avoid this difficulty, the same name is often given to a function and the variable determined by it. Following this strategy, the preceding functions would be renamed as follows:

$$y = f(x) <=> y = y(x)$$
$$z = g(x) <=> z = z(x).$$

This is a useful way to keep track of functions when there are several dependent variables.

Sometimes an abstract function will be discussed without ever specifying the exact numbers that belong to it. For example, the reader might be told that y is a function of x, and never be told exactly which values of y correspond to which values of x. If exact numbers are given, they may be listed in a table, as we have seen. Another way is to give an exact equation. For example, a function $z = z(x)$ might be given the exact form.

$$z = z(x)$$
$$= 5 + x/2,$$

which states that the function z matches values of x with values of z equal to five plus one-half of x. The table below gives the values of z associated with several different values of x:

z	x
6.5	3
12.5	15
8.0	6
6.0	2
9.5	9

A function can relate a dependent variable (there is always just one of them to a function) to more than one independent variable. If we write $y = h(x,z)$, we are saying that the function h matches one value of the dependent variable y to every pair of values of the independent variables x and z. This function might have the specific form

$$y = h(x,z)$$
$$= -3x + z,$$

according to which y decreases by 3 units when x increases by 1 unit, and y increases by 1 unit when z increases by 1 unit.

Economic models typically consist of several interrelated functions. Intuition into the properties of the models can be improved by graphing the functions so that they can be visualized. In a graph, values of the independent variable are usually read off the horizontal axis, and values of the dependent variable are usually read off the vertical axis. Each point in the grid of lines corresponds to a pair of values for the variables. For example, point a on the graph in Figure 2.1 represents the pair of values $y = 10$ and $x = 5$. The heavy line on the graph represents all of the pairs of values that satisfy the function $y = 5 + x/2$. Notice that point a is off the graph of the function, whereas point b represents a pair of values on the graph of the function, specifically $y = 12.5$ and $x = 15$.

The graph in Figure 2.1 is two-dimensional and, usually, graphing a function with two variables is straightforward. How can we graph a function

Figure 2.1 Graphing a Function

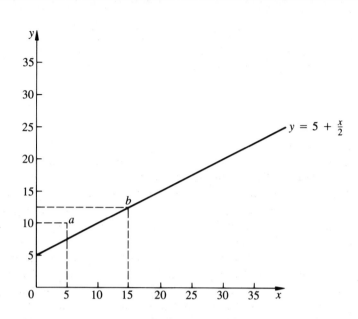

The figure gives a two-dimensional, graphical representation of the equation $y = 5 + x/2$. Values of the independent variable, x, are measured along the horizontal axis, and the corresponding values of the dependent variable, y, are measured along the vertical axis. The heavy line represents all the pairs of values of x and y that satisfy the function $y = 5 + x/2$. Point a, which represents the combination $x = 5$ and $y = 10$, is off the line because that pair does not satisfy the function. Point b, which represents the combination $x = 15$ and $y = 12.5$, is on the line because that pair of values does satisfy the equation.

with three variables, such as $y = y(x,z)$? This may be done by drawing a three-dimensional graph, but that is often a very difficult thing to do. A simpler alternative is to graph the relationship between any *two* of the variables in a function of several variables while holding the values of the other variables constant. Consider the function $y = y(x,z) = -3x + z$. Let's hold z constant at some value, say $z = 6$, so that the function can be simplified by eliminating z:

$$y = -3x + z$$
$$= -3x + 6 \text{ when } z = 6.$$

The reduced function contains only two variables, so it can be graphed just like the preceding example. This process can be repeated for $z = 15$, in which case the equation to be graphed is $y = -3x + 15$, and so forth for many different values of z. The result is shown in Figure 2.2.

Figure 2.2 Graphing Three Variables in Two Dimensions

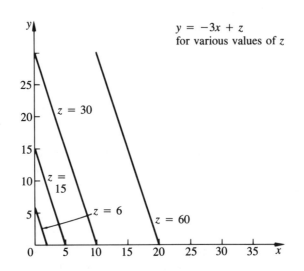

In the equation $y = -3x + z$, there is one dependent variable, y, but two independent variables, x and z. To represent three variables in two dimensions, one of the independent variables is held constant at various values while y is then measured along the vertical axis as a function of x, measured along the horizontal axis. z is held constant at 6, 15, 30, and 60, and the heavy lines represent all the pairs of values of x and y that satisfy the resulting equations $(y = -3x + 6; y = -3x + 15;$ and so on).

IV. THE THEORY OF CONSUMER CHOICE AND DEMAND

We have now described the fundamental economic concepts (maximization, equilibrium, and efficiency) and have reviewed the mathematical tools necessary for using them. Now we bring together the economics and math to review microeconomic theory.

The construction of the economic model of consumer choice begins with an account of the preferences of consumers. Consumers are assumed to know the things they like and dislike and to be able to rank the available alternative combinations of goods and services according to their ability to satisfy the consumer's preferences. This involves no more than ranking the alternatives as being better than, worse than, or equally as good as one another. For example, the consumer might be a shopper deciding how much beef and chicken to buy. If x denotes beef and y denotes chicken, then a function $u = u(x,y)$ can be used to describe the consumer's ranking of alternative combinations of beef and chicken.

This function is called the "utility function," with u standing for the utility that the consumer derives from consuming various amounts of x and y.

"Utility" is a slippery concept that means different things in different contexts. Usually it just means "preference ranking," but sometimes it means satisfaction, welfare, happiness, or even pleasure. For now we stick to the simplest meaning–preference ranking or ordering–and in subsequent chapters we will alert the reader when we introduce more complicated and controversial meanings. A higher ranking is indicated by a higher value of the utility function. To illustrate, if two units of beef and one unit of chicken rank higher than one unit of beef and 3 units of chicken, then the value of $u(2,1)$ will be larger than the value of $u(1,3)$. The specific numbers might be, say, $5 = u(2,1)$ and $3 = u(1,3)$.

It is important to remember that the preferences of the consumer are purely *subjective*. That is, they are his or her preferences, to be discovered by finding out what he or she likes, not by telling him or her what to like. Economists leave to other disciplines, such as psychology and sociology, the study of whence these preferences came. We take them as given.

A useful device for visualizing the preferences of the consumer is a graph that shows the alternative combinations with the same ranking, that is, those combinations that give the consumer the same utility. The alternatives with the same ranking are the alternatives to which the utility function assigns the same number. For example, all the values of x and y whose utility value is 10 might be joined by a line, which is the graph of $10 = u(x,y)$. By repeating this construction for utility values 15, 20, 30, and so forth, the decisionmaker's preferences are mapped as in Figure 2.3. The lines on the map are called utility curves (lines of constant utility) or indifference curves (alternatives that tie in the preference ordering). Each indifference curve connects those combinations of x and y that give the individual the same utility. It follows that a "higher" indifference curve represents combinations of x and y that are preferred by the individual to combinations that lie on "lower" indifference curves.

The problem of consumer choice arises from the collision of the consumer's preferences with obstacles to their satisfaction. The obstacles are the constraints that force decisionmakers to choose among alternatives. Foremost among these constraints is the fact that income is limited. Naturally, the consumer would prefer to reach the highest indifference curve. For example, the consumer might prefer an indefinitely large quantity of beef and chicken. However, he must pay for those commodities, and the amount he can pay is constrained by his income. The rational consumer will choose the highest ranking alternative that is feasible. He will, that is, choose the bundle that is on the highest attainable indifference curve, given his income. In Figure 2.4, the budget line shows which alternatives are affordable given the consumer's income of I, and the indifference curves show the ranking of alternatives. To find the best feasible alternative, start the search at the top of the budget line where it touches the vertical axis. Move along the budget line in the direction of the arrows and notice that at first the utility numbers increase on the indifference curves that you pass, indicating that you are moving toward higher-ranked alternatives. Eventually you will reach a point where you begin crossing indifference curves with lower utility numbers,

Figure 2.3   *Consumer Indifference Curves*

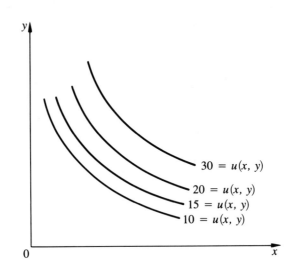

Indifference curves (or utility curves) are used to visualize the preferences of the consumer. All the combinations of the commodities x (measured along the horizontal axis) and y (measured along the vertical axis) that give the consumer the same utility and have, therefore, the same preference ranking are joined along a line called an "indifference curve" or a "utility curve." For example, all the combinations of x and y whose utility value is 10 are joined by a line, which is labeled $10 = u(x,y)$. Those combinations of x and y that give utility values 15, 20, and 30 are also joined along separate indifference curves. Any combination on a "higher" indifference curve is preferred to a combination on a "lower" indifference curve. For instance, any combination of x and y along $20 = u(x,y)$ is preferrable to any combination of x and y along $15 = u(x,y)$.

indicating that you are moving towards lower-ranked alternatives. The tipping point, where you stop passing to higher alternatives and start passing to lower alternatives, is the best feasible alternative, denoted (x_m, y_m) in the figure. This point is called the *constrained maximum* because the decisionmaker's utility is maximized subject to the feasibility constraint. (A more sophisticated description of a constrained maximum is possible by using more sophisticated techniques, including calculus.[2])

---

[2]Maximizing $u(x,y)$ subject to the constraint $I = p_x x + p_y y$ (the income constraint) can be written

$$\max [u(x,y) + \lambda (I - p_x x - p_y y)],$$

where λ is a Lagrangean multiplier. The first order conditions for an interior maximum are

$u_x = \lambda p_x$
$u_y = \lambda p_y$, and
$I = p_x x + p_y y.$

The Lagrangean multiplier, λ, is the shadow price, or marginal utility of income, I.

Figure 2.4 The Consumer's Optimum

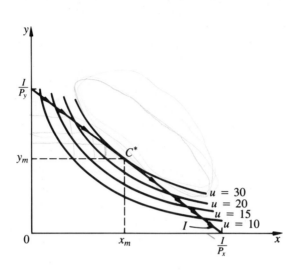

Given his income, the consumer chooses the combination of x and y that lies on the highest feasible indifference curve. The "budget line," drawn between the points I_1/P_y and I_1/P_x, represents the combinations of x and y that are affordable by a consumer whose income is I_1 when the prices of the commodities are P_x and P_y. Any combination along the budget line costs the same amount, I_1. The combination y_m and x_m is optimal for this consumer because it lies on a higher indifference curve ($u = 30$) than does any other affordable combination of x and y. This combination is denoted by the point C^*, called the constrained maximum. At this point, marginal costs equal marginal benefits—small movements in either direction on the budget line will only lead to a lowering of consumer utility.

Because of the central importance of constrained maximization in microeconomic theory, let us take a moment to examine a more general way of characterizing such a maximum. A constrained maximum can be described as a point where marginal cost equals marginal benefit. The word "marginal" in this context refers to very small changes. The decisionmaker is assumed to have altered his decisions by these marginal amounts in accord with the rule that a small change is recommended so long as the cost of doing so is less than the benefit. He continues to make these small, or marginal, adjustments until the marginal cost of the last change made equals the marginal benefit. That point is the maximum.

We can characterize the consumer's income-constrained maximum, C^* in Figure 2.4, in terms of the equality of marginal cost and benefit. Small changes in either direction along the budget line, I, represents a situation where the consumer spends a dollar less on one good and a dollar more on the other. To measure the cost and benefit of these marginal changes along the budget line, we use the notion of small or marginal changes in utility.

For example, a dollar less for y means fewer units of y can be purchased, so that this shift causes a loss in utility that we may call the marginal cost of the budget re-allocation. But the dollar previously spent on y can now be spent on x. More units of x mean greater utility, so that we may call this increase the marginal benefit of the budget re-allocation. Suppose that the consumer is initially somewhere along I between the vertical axis and C^* and is contemplating spending a dollar less on good y and a dollar more on x. Should he do so? Yes, if the marginal cost (the decrease in utility from one dollar less of y) is less than the marginal benefit (the increase in utility from having one dollar more of x). The consumer will continue to re-allocate dollars away from the purchase of y and toward the purchase of x so long as the marginal benefit of this re-allocation is greater than the marginal cost. The process will stop and the consumer's income-constrained maximum will be attained when the marginal benefit of the last change made is equal to the marginal cost. This occurs at the point C^* in Figure 2.4.

As we will see, marginal cost equal to marginal benefit has a similar meaning for a firm making decisions about how much and what to produce and to an individual deciding how much time to spend working for pay and how much to spend in other ways. Indeed, if you will firmly understand and realize that for economists the optimum for nearly all decisions occurs at the point at which marginal benefit equals marginal cost, then you will have gone a long way towards mastering the microeconomic tools necessary to answer most questions where a choice must be made. Having discovered that "marginal cost equals marginal benefit" is a good answer to the question "What is best?", economists are always on the lookout for some specific questions to which the answer fits, and this approach is responsible for many of the insights that economists have brought to the study of the law.

There is another method of describing a constrained maximum that we will use again in this book. A maximum is said to be an *interior solution* or *interior maximum* if, like C^* in Figure 2.4, it contains some of each good and lies, therefore, away from the x- and y-axes and along the interior of the budget line, I. Most maxima are interior solutions. A *corner solution* is a constrained maximum that lies along one of the axes, at a corner of the triangle formed by the axes and the budget line, and indicates that the maximum contains only one good. For corner solutions it is not true that at the maximum the marginal cost and marginal benefit are equal. Corner solutions are unusual in microeconomic theory and are typically an indication that something is not right in the market.

We have described how a rational consumer, facing definite prices for goods and having a definite amount of money to spend, would choose which goods to buy. Repeating this process for all the consumers active in a market is known as *aggregating demand*. In almost every case the aggregate demand for a good rises when its price falls. This is the famous Law of Demand. This relation between price and quantity demanded is plotted in Figure 2.5, where we have put units of the good x on the horizontal axis and the price of x on the vertical axis.

Figure 2.5 The Aggregate Demand Curve

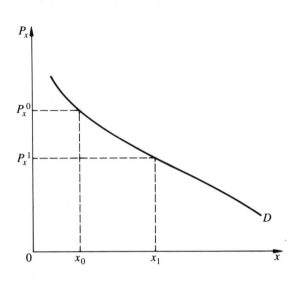

When the demands of all consumers active in a market are summed, the result is the "aggregate demand curve" for that commodity. The graph shows the inverse relationship between price and quantity demanded that is called the Law of Demand: when the price of a commodity falls, as from P_x^0 to P_x^1, the quantity demanded increases, as from x_0 to x_1.

Aggregate demand for a good is a function of several variables but, in a graph like Figure 2.5, the only determinant of the quantity demanded of the good x that is explicitly shown in the figure is the price of x. As the price of x varies in the graph, other variables are implicitly held constant. Prominent among the background variables that are being held constant is the income of consumers and the prices of other goods. If either of those things (income or other prices) changes, the demand curve for x also changes.

Suppose, for example, that x is chicken. In drawing the demand curve for chicken, we are assuming that the prices of all other commodities are being held constant. Thus, when the price of chicken falls, the price of chicken *relative* to everything else falls, and we may safely conclude that the quantity of chicken demanded increases. But if the price of beef falls at the same time that the price of chicken falls and if consumers perceive beef and chicken to be substitutes, we cannot be certain what will happen to the quantity of chicken demanded. To take an extreme case, if the fall in the price of beef is much greater than the fall in the price of chicken, then the *relative* price of chicken increases and the quantity of chicken demanded may well *decline*. Thus, the law of demand (that price and quantity demanded move inversely) holds only when all other prices are constant.

Similarly, consumer income must be held constant for the law of demand to hold. Suppose again that x is chicken but now let us assume that at the same time that the price of chicken falls, the consumer's income increases. This simultaneous change introduces several complications. To take the easier case first, suppose that the consumer considers chicken to be what economists call a "normal good," i.e., as the consumer's income increases, all other things equal, he consumes more of the good. The shift in the demand curve to the northeast, from D to D', in Figure 2.6 indicates this situation: an increase in the demand for a normal good when the consumer's income increases. When there is this sort of shift in the demand curve at the same time that the price of the good is falling, it is certain that the quantity of the good demanded will increase. However, because of the simultaneous

Figure 2.6 Shifting Demand Curves

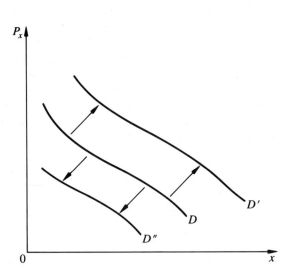

The demand for a good is a function of several variables such as the price of the good, consumer income, the price of substitute goods, and so on, but the demand curve focuses on the relationship between the quantity demanded of a good and the price of the good. As the price of x varies in the graph, the values of other variables are held constant. If the other variables change, the demand curve shifts. The graph shows what might happen to the demand for x from Figure 2.5 if consumer income increases, everything else held constant: the demand curve shifts to the northeast from D to D'. Such a shift indicates that at any given price, the total quantity demanded is larger. This shift takes place when the good demanded is a *normal good*. For *inferior goods*, increases in consumer income, everything else held constant, lead to a shift in the demand curve to the southwest from D to D''. An inferior good is some good such as peanut butter: people who can afford to eat only peanut butter switch to meat when their incomes rise, rather than purchase even more peanut butter.

change in price and income, it is difficult to say by how much. To take a more troubling complication, suppose that the consumer considers chicken to be what economists call an "inferior good," i.e., as the consumer's income increases, all other things equal, he consumes less of the good. The shift in the demand curve to the southwest, from D to D'', in Figure 2.6 indicates this situation: a decrease in the demand for an inferior good when the consumer's income increases. (Notice, however, that even though this is an inferior good, the demand curve is still downward sloping. Inferiority is a condition relating to changes in income, all other things equal.) When there is this sort of shift in the demand curve at the same time that the price of the good is falling, there is no clear relationship between quantity demanded and the price of the good: the quantity of the good demanded may decrease, increase, or remain constant. Thus, the law of demand (that price and quantity demanded move inversely) holds only when consumer income is constant.

There is one last, important point to be made about consumer demand. The demand curve we have drawn could have had a different slope than that shown: it might have been either flatter or steeper. This matter of slope, of the steepness of the demand curve, is related to an important concept called the *price elasticity of demand*, or simply, *elasticity of demand*. Elasticity of demand is a numerical measure of how responsive demand is to changes in price. It is calculated as the percentage change in quantity demanded divided by the percentage change in price. The measure is frequently denoted by the letter "e," and the ranges of elasticity are called "inelastic" ($e < 1$), "elastic" ($e > 1$), and "unitary elastic" ($e = 1$).[3] For an inelastically demanded good, the percentage change in price exceeds the percentage change in quantity demanded. Thus, a good that has $e = 0.5$ is one for which a 50% decline in price will cause a 25% increase in the quantity demanded or for which a 15% increase in price will cause a 7.5% decrease in quantity demanded. For an elastically demanded good, the percentage change in price is less than the percentage change in quantity demanded. As a result, a good that has $e = 1.5$ is one for which a 50% decline in price will cause a 75% increase in quantity demanded or for which a 20% increase in price will cause a 30% decline in quantity demanded. The most important determinant of the price elasticity of demand is the presence of substitutes for the good. The more substitutes for the good, the greater the elasticity of

---

[3]Economists are agreed that e, the price elasticity of demand, should be measured as a positive (or absolute) number, even though the calculation we suggested will lead to a negative number. Because price and quantity demanded move inversely, the percentage change in price and the percentage change in quantity demanded will be of opposite sign. For example, a 50% *increase* (a positive number) in price might lead to a 25% *decrease* (a negative number), so that e, without the agreement, would be equal to -0.5. Everyone has problems trying to remember if -1 is greater or less than -1.5. To avoid those problems, we assume that e is always a positive (or absolute) number.

demand; the fewer the substitutes, the lower the elasticity. Thus, one would expect a relatively large price elasticity of demand for individual kinds of food such as beef, pork, chicken, or white bread, and a relatively small price elasticity for a more encompassing category of goods like food.

Economists have measured price elasticities of demand for numerous goods and services. Table 2.1 shows these measurements for some goods. We have included both short-run (up to one year) and long-run (more than one year) elasticities. The reason for this distinction is that the longer the period of time during which consumers can make an adjustment to a price change, the more elastic one would expect their demand to be. Consider the case of gasoline. Suppose that there is a sudden increase in the price of gasoline. In the very short-run, say, the next several months, there will be few substitutes for gasoline, and consumers will be able to make only limited adjustments in their gasoline consumption habits. As a result, one would expect a relatively highly inelastic demand for gasoline in the short-run. In fact, the reported figure in Table 2.1 is 0.14, which indicates that if the price of gas doubles, there will only be a 14% decline in the quantity of gasoline demanded. But over a longer period of time, consumers can make more extensive adjustments to the increase in the price of gas by, for example, walking more, car

Table 2.1   Price Elasticity of Demand in the Short-Run and in the Long-Run

Good	Elasticity	
	Short-Run	Long-Run
Alcohol	0.92	3.63
Sports equipment, boats	0.88	2.39
Movies	0.87	3.67
Bus travel (local)	0.77	3.54
Air travel (foreign)	0.70	4.00
Rail travel (commuter)	0.54	1.70
Medical insurance	0.31	0.92
Bus travel (intercity)	0.20	2.17
Theater, opera	0.18	0.31
Natural gas (residential)	0.15	10.74
Gasoline, oil	0.14	0.48
Electricity (residential)	0.13	1.90
Newspapers, magazines	0.10	0.52

Source: Heinz Kohler, INTERMEDIATE MICROECONOMICS: THEORY AND APPLICATIONS 103 (2d ed. 1986).

pooling, and bicycling. Thus, one would expect the long-run elasticity of demand to be higher than the short-run figure, as in fact it is. In the long-run a doubling of the price of gasoline causes a 48% decrease in the quantity of gasoline demanded.

There is a well-known and important relationship between the price elasticity of demand and total consumer expenditures on a good. Total consumer expenditures on a good are equal to the price of the good times the quantity of goods sold. When price and quantity demanded change, their product may change. Suppose that the price elasticity of demand for commodity x is 1, and consider the effect of a 10% increase in price. Because $e = 1$, there will be a 10% decrease in the quantity of x demanded. What will happen to total consumer expenditures on x? Because price has increased by exactly the same amount that quantity demanded has decreased, total consumer expenditures, which equal p times q, remain unchanged.

What happens to total consumer expenditures when demand is elastic or inelastic? Suppose that the demand for good y is elastic ($e > 1$) and that price has increased by 10%. We know by the definition of price elasticity that the quantity of y demanded has decreased by more than 10%. Because the quantity demanded has decreased by more than the price has increased, the product of price and quantity will decline as a result of the price increase for an elastically demanded good. If price has *decreased*, the exact opposite would be true: total consumer expenditures would increase because the quantity demanded would increase by more than the price had decreased. Finally, suppose that the demand for good z is inelastic ($e < 1$) and that price has increased by 10%. By the definition of price inelasticity we know that the quantity of z demanded has decreased by less than 10%. Because price has increased by more than quantity demanded has decreased, total consumer expenditures (the product of price and quantity) will *increase*. If the price of an inelastically-demanded good decreases, the reverse is true: total consumer expenditures would decrease because the quantity demanded would increase by less than the price had decreased. These relationships may be summarized in Table 2.2.

Table 2.2   Price Elasticity of Demand and Consumer Expenditures

Elasticity	When Price Increases, Consumer Expenditures	When Price Decreases, Consumer Expenditures
Inelastic ($e < 1$)	Increase	Decrease
Unitary elasticity ($e = 1$)	Are unchanged	Are unchanged
Elastic ($e > 1$)	Decrease	Increase

Information about price elasticity of demand is extremely valuable to private businesses and to public officials. A business that is contemplating a price change would very much like to know how consumer demand will respond to that change so that it might project the impact on its revenues. If the business's good is elastically demanded, then a decrease in prices will cause consumers to spend more on the good, thus increasing the firm's revenues. Government officials who are thinking of altering the price of a commodity through, say, the imposition of an excise tax must be aware of the price elasticity of demand for that commodity if they wish to predict the consequences of the imposition of that tax for governmental tax revenues and the private businesses that supply the good.

V. THE THEORY OF SUPPLY

We now turn to a review of the other side of the market. Here we will meet the business firm, review how it makes its decisions, derive the supply curve, and then merge supply with demand to see how the independent maximizing activities of consumers and of firms achieve a market equilibrium.

The firm is the institution in which output (products and services) is fabricated from various factors of production (or inputs) for sale to consumers. Just as we assume that consumers are rationally maximizing their utility subject to the constraint imposed by their income, we assume that firms are attempting to maximize their profits subject to the constraints imposed on them by consumer demand and the technology of production.

In microeconomics, profits are defined as the difference between total revenue and the total costs of production. Total revenue for the firm is simply the product of the number of units of output sold and the price of each unit. Total costs are the costs of each of the inputs times the number of units of input used, summed over all inputs. The profit-maximizing firm produces that amount of output that leads to the greatest positive difference between the firm's revenue and its costs. Microeconomic theory demonstrates that the firm will maximize its profits if it produces that amount of output whose marginal cost equals its marginal revenue. There are some new terms here, and we must define and explain them.

Marginal cost is defined as the increase in total costs that results from producing the last (marginal) unit of output. Similarly, *marginal revenue* is defined as the increase in total revenue that results from the sale of one more unit of output. Suppose that a firm is attempting to maximize its profits and is producing some level of output, q_1. Further suppose that in producing q_1 the firm's accountants report that the addition to total revenues from the sale of the q_1th unit was greater than the addition to total costs from producing that unit. What may be concluded? Clearly, the production of the q_1th unit of output increased the firm's profits since total revenues increased more than total costs. Now suppose that the firm continues to expand output and is now contemplating the production of the q_2th unit of output. The accountants report that for that unit of output the marginal cost will exceed the marginal revenue; that is, the production of q_2 will add more to total costs than it will add to total revenue. Clearly then, production of q_2 will decrease profits.

These considerations suggest that when marginal revenue exceeds marginal cost, the firm should expand production, and that when marginal cost exceeds marginal revenue, it should reduce the amount of output produced. It follows that profits will be maximized for that output for which marginal cost and marginal revenue are equal. Note the economy of this rule: the firm need not concern itself with its total cost or total revenues (even though there are other reasons that it certainly will); instead, it can simply experiment unit-by-unit of production in order to discover the output level that maximizes its profits.

In Figure 2.7 the profit-maximizing output of the firm is shown at the point at which the marginal cost curve and marginal revenue curve of the firm are equal.[4] There are several things you should note about the curves in the graph. For the sake of convenience we have drawn the marginal revenue curve as horizontal. This implies that the firm can sell as much as it likes at that prevailing price. As a result, marginal revenue equals the price. The profit-maximizing level of production, denoted q^* in Figure 2.7, occurs at the point where the marginal revenue curve intersects the marginal cost curve. Total profits at this level of production, denoted by the shaded area in Figure 2.7, equal the difference between the price and the average cost of production,[5] multiplied by the quantity of output, q^*.

In microeconomics the firm is said to operate in two different time frames: the short run and the long run. These time periods do not correspond to calendar time. Instead they are defined in terms of the firm's inputs. In the short run at least one input is fixed, and the usual factor of production that is fixed is capital (the firm's buildings, machines, and other durable inputs). Since captial is fixed in the short run, all the costs associated with capital are called fixed costs. In the short run the firm can, in essence, ignore those costs: they will be incurred regardless of whether the firm produces nothing at all or 10 million units of output. The long run is distinguished by the fact that all factors of production become variable.

---

[4]Note that there are two output levels for which marginal cost and revenue are equal. Can you see why profits are *not* maximized at output level q_m?

[5]If the total cost of producing q units is $C(q)$, then the average cost equals $C(q)/q$. Note the relationship between average cost and marginal cost. When average cost is declining, marginal cost is less than average cost; when average cost is rising, marginal cost is greater than average cost; and when average cost is at its minimum, average and marginal cost are equal.

Figure 2.7 The Firm's Profit-Maximizing Output

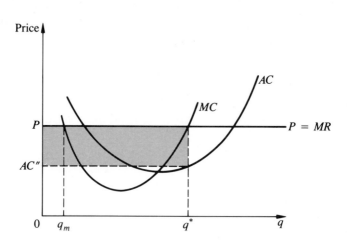

The firm's profit-maximizing output level, q^* in the figure, is the one for which the marginal cost of production (the cost of producing that last unit of output) is equal to the marginal revenue (the revenue generated by the sale of that last unit of output). Note that if the firm produced and sold the $(q^* + 1)$st unit of output, the marginal cost of that unit would exceed its marginal revenue. Thus, that unit would add more to the firm's total costs than it adds to its total revenues. Because profit in microeconomics is the difference between total revenue and total cost, the production and sale of the $(q^* + 1)$st unit of output would reduce profits below those at q^*.

There are no longer any fixed costs. Established firms may expand their productive capacity or leave the industry entirely, and new firms may enter the business.

Another important distinction between the long and the short run has to do with the equilibrium level of profit-maximizing output for each firm. At any point in time there is an average rate of return earned by capital in the economy as a whole. When profits being earned in a particular industry exceed the average profit rate for industry as a whole, firms will enter the industry if they can, i.e. if there are no barriers to entry. As entry occurs, the price of the output in the industry goes down, causing each firm's revenue to decrease. Also, the increased competition for the factors of production causes input prices to rise, pushing up each firm's costs. The combination of these two forces causes each firm's profits to decline. Entry ceases when profits fall to the average rate. Economists have a special way of describing these facts. The average return on capital is treated as part of the costs that are subtracted from revenues to get "economic profits." Thus, when the rate

A Digression: Opportunity Cost and Comparative Advantage

We have been implicitly using one of the most fundamental concepts in microeconomics—*opportunity cost*. This is such an important notion that we want you to be clear about it. Because microeconomics studies the process of allocating scarce resources among competing ends, opportunity cost, or the economic cost of an alternative that has been foregone, is a pivotal concept. When you decided to attend college, graduate school, or law school, you gave up certain other valuable alternatives, e.g., taking a job, training for the Olympics, or traveling around the world on a tramp steamer. In reckoning the cost of going to college or to law school, the true *economic* cost was that of the next best alternative. This point is true of the decisions of *all* economic actors: when maximizing utility, the consumer must consider the opportunities given up by choosing one bundle of consumer goods rather than another; when maximizing profits, the firm must consider the opportunities foregone by committing its resources to the production of widgets rather than of something else.

In general, the economic notion of opportunity cost is more expansive than is the more common notion of *explicit* or *accounting* cost. An example will make this point.[1] Suppose that a rich relative gives you a car whose market value is $15,000. She says that if you sell the car, you may keep the proceeds but that if you use the car yourself, she'll pay for the gas, oil, maintenance, repairs, and insurance. In short, she says, "The use of the car is FREE!" But is it? Suppose that the $15,000 for which the car could be sold would earn 12% interest per year in a savings account, giving $1,800 per year in interest income. If you use the car for one year, its resale value will fall to $11,000—a cost to you of $4,000. Therefore, the opportunity cost to you of *using* the car for one year is $4,000 plus the foregone interest of $1,800—a total of $5,800. This is far from being *free*. The explicit or accounting cost of using the "free" car is zero, but the economic or opportunity cost is the cost of what has been given up by taking one action rather than another.

Related to the notion of opportunity cost is another useful economic concept: *comparative advantage*. The law of comparative advantage asserts that people should engage in those pursuits where their opportunity costs are lower than others. For example, someone who is seven feet tall has a comparative advantage in pursuing a career in professional basketball. But what about someone whose skills are such that he can do many things well? Suppose, for example, that a skilled attorney is also an extremely skilled typist. Should she do her own typing or hire someone else to do it while she specializes in the practice of law? The notion of comparative advantage argues for specialization: the attorney can make so much more money by specializing in the practice of law than by trying to do both jobs that she could easily afford to hire someone else who is less efficient at typing to do her typing for her.

[1]This example is taken from R. Ruffin & P. Gregory, PRINCIPLES OF MICROECONOMICS 156 (2d ed. 1986).

of return on invested capital in this industry equals the average for the economy as a whole, it is said that "economic profits are zero."[6] This leads to the conclusion that economic profits are zero in an industry that is in long-run equilibrium.[7] For more on implicit and explicit costs and how they affect profit, see the box on "Opportunity Cost and Comparative Advantage."

A. Equilibrium

Having described the behavior of utility-maximizing consumers and profit-maximizing producers, our next task is to put them together and explain how they interact. For each price, p, there is a unique quantity that consumers will demand, so aggregate demand d can be written as a function of the price: $d = d(p)$. Graphing this function gives the aggregate demand curve that is depicted in Figure 2.8. Similarly, for each price p there is a quantity that producers will supply, so aggregate supply s can be written as a function of the price: $s = s(p)$. Graphing this function gives the aggregate supply curve that is depicted in Figure 2.8. Our next task is to explain the interaction of demand and supply.

Suppose the price is too high in the sense that the producers supply more than the consumers demand. This situation is represented by the price p_1 in Figure 2.8. At the price p_1, the quantity supplied is q_{s1}, and the quantity demanded is q_{d1}. Since supply exceeds demand at this price, $q_{s1} > q_{d1}$, and the market will adjust. Specifically, the excess supply relative to the demand will cause the price to fall. As the price falls, consumers will demand more and producers will supply less, so the gap between supply and demand will diminish. Eventually the price may reach p_c. In Figure 2.8 it is apparent that the quantity demanded exactly equals the quantity supplied when the price equals p_c: $d(p_c) = s(p_c)$ at q_c.

Once demand equals supply, there is no longer a force causing the price to change. This situation is called an *equilibrium*: a situation that will persist unchanged unless it is disturbed by an outside force, such as the introduction of a new technology or a change in the tastes of consumers. In the analysis of markets, an equilibrium usually corresponds to the intersection of the supply and demand curves, as in Figure 2.8.

---

[6]When profits in a given industry are less than the average in the economy as a whole, economic profits are said to be negative. As a result, firms exit this industry for other industries where the profits are at least equal to the average for the economy. As an exercise, see if you can demonstrate the process by which profits go to zero when negative economic profits in an industry cause exit to take place.

[7]Since this can occur only at the minimum point of the average cost curve, where the costs of production are as low as they can possibly be, inputs will be most efficiently used in long-run equilibrium.

Figure 2.8 Market Equilibrium

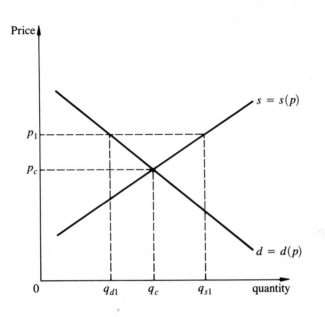

Given the downward-sloping aggregate demand curve, $d = d(p)$, and the upward-sloping aggregate supply curve, $s = s(p)$, there is only one combination of price and quantity, p_c and q_c, for which the decisions of utility-maximizing consumers and profit-maximizing producers are consistent. For any other price, say, p_1, the decisions of consumers and producers are inconsistent: at p_1 consumers demand q_{d1} and producers supply q_{s1}; there is, thus, an excess supply equal to $(q_{s1} - q_{d1})$. This excess supply will cause the price to fall. At lower prices, consumers demand more and producers supply less. Eventually the price will reach p_c, at which point the quantity supplied equals the quantity demanded. The intersection of supply and demand defines an *equilibrium*, a situation that will persist unchanged unless it is disturbed by an outside force, such as the introduction of a new technology of production or a change in the tastes of consumers.

B. Market Structure and the Theory of Supply

An economic analysis is not complete until one has described the market environment in which the firm operates. The polar extremes in the microeconomic theory of market structure are perfect competition and monopoly. In perfect competition there are a large number of buyers and sellers; in monopoly there is only one seller.[8] The number of buyers and

---

[8]The situation in which there is only one *buyer* is called *monopsony*. If a monopoly faces a monopsony, that is said to be a situation of *bilateral monopoly*. The distinguishing feature of bilateral monopoly is that market price depends on the bargaining abilities of the two parties and is, in general, indeterminate.

sellers in perfect competition is left vague for a good reason. The operating feature is not the number of traders but rather how they behave.[9] If they behave in such a way that no individual buyer or seller can influence the market price of the good in question, then the market is said to be *perfectly competitive*. An individual is unable to influence the market price where there are so many other participants in the market that alternative buyers or sellers are readily available. All firms are said to be price-takers under these conditions because they take the output price as given and invariant to their actions. This leads to the firm's perceiving a horizontal demand curve for its output and an identical horizontal marginal revenue curve, like that shown in Figure 2.7.

Although each firm in a perfectly competitive industry believes that it faces a horizontal demand curve, the aggregate demand curve facing the industry is the usual downward-sloping one. Thus, for a perfectly competitive industry the output price and total quantity produced are the equilibrium price and quantity, p_c and q_c, shown in Figure 2.8.

At the other extreme of market structure is monopoly. In a monopoly there is only one supplier, so that firm and industry are identical.[10] A monopoly can arise and persist only where there are barriers to entry that make it impossible for competing firms to appear. In general, such barriers can arise from two sources: first, from statutory and other legal restrictions on entry, and second, from technological conditions of production known as economies of scale. An example of a statutory restriction on entry was the Civil Aeronautics Board's refusal from the 1930s until the mid-1970s to permit entry into the market for passenger traffic on such major routes as Los Angeles-New York and Chicago-Miami. Another legal restriction on entry is the policy of awarding a 17-year monopoly, called a "patent," to inventors. The second barrier to entry is technological; economies of scale are a condition of production in which the greater the level of output, the lower the average cost of production. Where such conditions exist, there is a technological advantage to having only one firm in that the total cost of producing total industry output will be less than if multiple firms produce the same total output at higher average cost. A monopolist that owes its existence to economies of scale is sometimes called a "natural monopoly." Public utilities, such as local water, telecommunications, cable, and power companies, are often natural monopolies. The technological advantages of a natural

---

[9]There are formal, technical definitions of perfect competition in terms of product characteristics, information availability, the mobility of resources into and out of the industry, and so on. Where it is appropriate in the text, we will refer to these technical definitions. Here we want to stress the behavioral aspects of perfect competition.

[10]A cartel is a collusion among several firms that are acting to maximize profits jointly. The cartel, like a single-firm monopolist, can exist only behind effective barriers to entry. However, unlike a single-firm monopolist, a cartel has coordination and cheating problems that make the collusion difficult to maintain.

monopoly would be partially lost if the single firm is allowed to restrict its output and to charge a monopoly price. For that reason, natural monopolies are typically regulated by the government in order to preserve the technological advantages of economies of scale while preventing monopoly pricing and production by the natural monopoly.

The monopolist, like the competitive firm, maximizes profit by producing that output for which marginal cost equals marginal revenue. Marginal cost for the monopolist, as for the competitive firm, is the cost of producing one more unit of output. This cost curve is the monopolist's supply curve and is represented in Figure 2.9 by the curve labeled $S = MC$. But marginal revenue for the monopolist is different from what it was for the competitive firm. Recall that marginal revenue describes the change in a firm's total revenues for a small, or marginal, change in the number of units of output sold.

Figure 2.9 Price and Quantity in a Monopolized Market

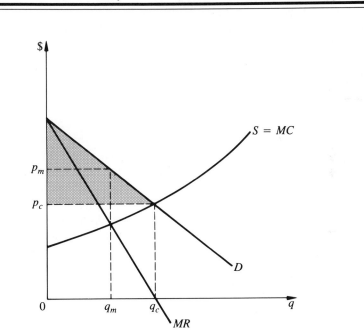

For the monopolist the firm is the industry supplier, and so, the relevant demand curve is the aggregate demand curve, which is downward-sloping. This also means that the monopolist's marginal revenue curve is downward-sloping. Just as was the case for the competitive firm, the monopolist's profit-maximizing output, q_m is that for which the marginal cost of production is equal to the marginal revenue. Note that this quantity is less than the quantity, q_c, that would be produced if this industry were competitive. The price, p_m, that consumers are willing to pay for this output is found by going up to the demand curve, D. Note that this price is greater than the price, p_c, that would prevail if this industry were competitive.

For the competitive firm marginal revenue was equal to the price of output: because the competitive firm can sell as much as it likes at the prevailing price, each additional unit of output sold added exactly the sale price to the firm's total revenues. But for the monopolist marginal revenue declines as the number of units sold increases. This is indicated in Figure 2.9 by the downward-sloping curve labeled MR. Notice that the MR curve lies below the demand curve. This indicates that the marginal revenue from any unit sold by a monopolist is always less than the price. MR is positive but declining for units of output between 0 and q_c; thus, each of those units increases the firm's total revenues but at a decreasing rate. The unit q_c actually adds nothing to the firm's total revenues ($MR = 0$), and for each unit of output beyond q_c, MR is less than zero, which means that each of those units actually reduces the monopolist's total revenues. The reason for this complex relationship between marginal revenue and units sold by the monopolist is that the demand curve is downward sloping. The downward-sloping demand curve means that to sell an additional unit of output the monopolist must lower the price; but (assuming he cannot price discriminate) he must lower the price not just on the last or marginal unit but on *all* the units he sells. From this fact it can be shown, using calculus, that the addition to total revenues from an additional unit of output sold will always be less than the price charged for that unit. Thus, because MR is always less than price for all units of output and because price declines along the demand curve, the MR curve must also be downward sloping and lie below the demand curve.

The monopolist maximizes his profit by choosing that output level for which marginal revenue and marginal cost are equal.[11] This output level, q_m, is shown in Figure 2.9. The demand curve indicates that consumers are willing to pay p_m for that amount of output. Notice that if this industry were competitive instead of monopolized, the profit-maximizing actions of the firms would have resulted in an equilibrium price and quantity at the intersection of the aggregate supply curve, S, and the industry demand curve, D. The competitive price, p_c, is lower than the monopolistic price, p_m, and the quantity of output produced and consumed under competition, q_c, is greater than under monopoly, q_m.

Economists distinguish additional market structures that are intermediate between the extremes of perfect competition and monopoly. Among these the most important are oligopoly and imperfect competition. An oligopolistic market is one containing a few firms who recognize that their individual profit-maximizing decisions are interdependent. That means that what is optimal for firm A depends not only on its marginal costs and the demand for its output but also on what firms B, C, and D have decided to produce and the prices they are charging. The economic analysis of this interdependence requires a knowledge of game theory and may lead to dif-

---

[11]This is yet another example of our point that maxima in microeconomics are points at which marginal benefit and marginal cost are equal. For a firm, marginal benefit is equal to marginal revenue.

ferent conclusions from those that obtain in perfectly competitive and monopolistic markets. We will introduce some elements of game theory in this chapter. An imperfectly competitive market is one that shares most of the characteristics of a perfectly competitive market—for example, free entry and exit of firms and the presence of many firms—but that has one important monopolistic element: firms produce differentiable output rather than the homogeneous (or fungible, as lawyers call it) output produced by perfectly competitive firms. Thus, imperfectly competitive firms distinguish their output by brand names, colors, sizes, quality, durability, and so on. Economists have reached significant conclusions regarding output levels, price, and consumer welfare in imperfectly competitive markets, but they are beyond the scope of this survey. If you would like to explore those conclusions, you should consult one of the intermediate microeconomic textbooks mentioned at the end of this chapter.

C. An Example of Equilibrium Analysis

It is useful to have an example in which the theory developed here is applied to a real problem. Let us imagine a market for rental housing like the one shown in Figure 2.10. The demand for rental housing is given by the curve D, and the supply of rental housing is given by the upward-sloping supply curve S. Assuming that the rental housing market is competitive, then the independent actions of consumers and of profit-maximizing housing owners will lead to a rental rate of r_1 being charged and of h_1 units of rental housing being supplied and demanded. Note that this is an equilibrium in the sense we discussed above: the decisions of those demanding the product and of those supplying it are consistent—that is, stable—at the price r_1. Unless something causes the demand curve or the supply curve to shift, this price and output combination will remain in force.

But now suppose that the city government determines that, for whatever reason, r_1 is too high. It passes an ordinance that specifies a maximum rental rate for housing of r_m, considerably below the equilibrium market rate. The hope of the government is that at least the same amount of housing will be consumed by renters but at a lower rental rate. A look at Figure 2.10, however, leads one to doubt that that will be the outcome. At r_m, consumers demand h_d units of rental housing, an increase over the quantity demanded at the higher rate, r_1. But at this lower rate suppliers are only prepared to supply h_s. Apparently it does not pay them to devote as much of their housing units to renters at that lower rate; perhaps if r_m is all one can get from renting housing units, suppliers prefer to switch their units to condominiums, which they sell, not rent, to occupants. The result of the rate ceiling imposed by the government is a shortage of rental units equal to $(h_d - h_s)$.

If the regulation of maximum rental rates is very strict, then this shortage will simply persist until something causes either the demand curve to shift inward or the supply curve to shift outward. It is also possible that landlords will let their property deteriorate by withholding routine mainte-

Figure 2.10   The Economics of Rent Control

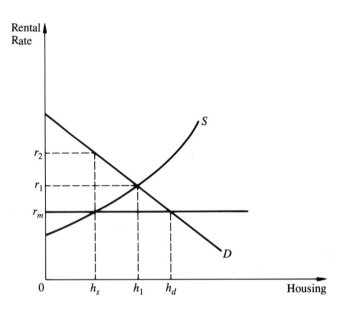

The demand for rental housing is given by the curve D, and the supply of rental housing is given by the curve S. If the rental housing market is competitive, then the equilibrium rental rate, r_1, and quantity of rental housing, h_1, are determined at the intersection of D and S. But suppose that the city government imposes a ceiling on rental rates: no unit may rent for more than r_m. At that rate consumers demand h_d units of rental housing, and suppliers are willing to supply h_s units; there is an excess demand or shortage of ($h_d - h_s$) units of rental housing. If the rate ceiling is strictly enforced, the shortage will persist. Some non-price methods—e.g., queuing—of determining who gets the h_s units of rental housing must be found. However, if the ceiling is not strictly enforced, then renters will find a way to make secret payments to landlords equal to ($r_2 - r_m$) so that the price really does adjust to erase the shortage.

nance and repairs, so that the value of their property falls to such an extent that r_m provides a competitive rate of return to them.

If, however, the rate ceiling is not strictly enforced, then consumers and suppliers will find a way to erase the shortage. For example, renters could offer free services or secret payments (sometimes called "side payments") to landlords in order to get the effective rental rate above r_m and induce the landlord to rent to them rather than to those willing to pay only r_m. Those services and side payments could amount to ($r_2 - r_m$) per housing unit.

D. The Theory of Games and the Nash Equilibrium

The previous sections introduced the concepts of demand, supply, equilibrium, and market structure. In our discussion we noted that for the market structure known as oligopoly, where there are so few firms that their maximizing decisions are interdependent, a different analytical tool called the theory of games was needed. The law sometimes confronts situations that are analogous to those in oligopoly: there are few decisionmakers and what is optimal for one actor to do depends on what another actor chooses. So our understanding of the economics of some legal rules will be enhanced if we are familiar with the elements of game theory. The economic theory of games is highly developed and very mathematical. We cannot begin to develop it fully, but we can introduce one important feature of games: the most fundamental equilibrium concept.[12]

Assume that you own one of the six gasoline stations that form "gasoline alley" on an otherwise empty and isolated stretch of highway. You wish to set the price you charge for gas to maximize your own profits, but the best price for you depends upon the prices that the other stations charge. Specifically, it is best for you to undercut the others so that you get a lot of business, but not by so large an amount that you sell at a loss. Assume that a combination of legal obstacles and personal animosities has made explicit or implicit cooperation in setting prices impossible among the six owners. The result is a price war. A rational way for you to behave is to keep a wary eye on the other five station owners and set your price at a level that maximizes your profits, given the prices set by the other five stations. But this rule of rational behavior applies to everyone, not just to you.

Given that everyone uses this rule for setting prices, it is easy to characterize the equilibrium price: an equilibrium is a situation in which each player is at a maximum given the behavior of the other players. Consequently, in equilibrium, no individual player can do any better by changing his behavior so long as the other players do not change theirs. This is called a *Nash equilibrium*. (Notice that the competitive equilibrium that we discussed in the previous section is an example of a Nash equilibrium when there are many players in the game.) We will use this idea in subsequent chapters, sometimes explicitly but more often implicitly.

VI. WELFARE ECONOMICS

The microeconomic theory we have been reviewing to this point has focused on the fundamental concepts of maximization, equilibrium, and efficiency in describing the decisions of consumers and firms. The part of microeconomic theory called welfare economics explores how the decisions of many individuals and firms interact to affect the well-being of individuals. Welfare economics is, as a result, much more abstract and philosophical than the other topics in microeconomic theory. It is in this section that the great policy

---

[12]An accessible introduction to the subject is Morton D. Davis, GAME THEORY: A NON-TECHNICAL INTRODUCTION (rev. ed. 1983). A more formal treatment of the subject with special reference to economics is Martin Shubik, GAME THEORY IN THE SOCIAL SCIENCES: CONCEPTS AND SOLUTIONS (1982).

issues are raised. For example, is there an inherent conflict between efficiency and fairness? To what extent can unregulated markets maximize individual well-being? When and how should the government intervene in the market place? Can economists identify a just distribution of goods and services? In this brief introduction, we can only hint at how microeconomic theory approaches these questions. Nonetheless, this material is fundamental to the economic analysis of legal rules. The central concepts developed in this section will be used repeatedly in the remainder of the book.

A. Efficiency Theorems

One of the great accomplishments of modern microeconomics is the specification of the conditions under which the independent decisions of utility-maximizing consumers and profit-maximizing firms will lead to the inevitable, spontaneous establishment of equilibrium in all markets simultaneously. Such an equilibrium is known as *general equilibrium*. General equilibrium will be achieved only where competitive forces have led to the equality of marginal benefit and marginal cost in the market for every single commodity. As you can well imagine, this is a stringent condition, unlikely to be realized in the real world. However, there are two good, practical reasons for knowing what the conditions of general equilibrium are. First, while it may be unlikely that *all* real-world markets obey those conditions, it is not unlikely that many of them will. Second, the specification of the conditions that lead to general equilibrium provides a benchmark for evaluating various markets and making recommendations for public policy.

Modern microeconomics has gone even further than this and has shown that the general equilibrium established under the condition known as "perfect competition" is socially optimal. This remarkable conclusion is sometimes called the Theorem of the Invisible Hand.[13] The term "social optimum" has a special meaning in welfare economics. The equilibrium achieved is socially optimal because it is efficient both with respect to the production of goods and to their allocation to consumers. Recall that production is efficient when it is impossible to produce more goods using the available resources, or, equivalently, when output is maximized for given inputs. Goods are distributed efficiently among consumers when it is impossible to transfer or reallocate goods and services among consumers so as to make any consumer better off (i.e., causing him or her to move to a higher indifference curve) without making some other consumer worse off (i.e., causing him or her to fall to a lower indifference curve). When an economy

---

[13]The unusual name comes from a famous passage in Adam Smith, THE WEALTH OF NATIONS (1776), in which Smith says that the unfettered market, through the signals transmitted by prices, will guide self-interested individuals, "as if by an invisible hand," to do what is best not only for themselves but also for society as a whole.

is efficient in production and the allocation of goods to consumers, there is no way to make a change that benefits someone without harming someone else. This condition bears the technical name "Pareto efficiency," which is fundamental to the economic analysis of law. An economy that is efficient in production and allocation is "socially optimal" in the sense of being Pareto efficient.[14]

B. Market Failure

Let us now turn to a discussion of the sorts of things that can go wrong in a market that prevents it from being Pareto efficient. There are four kinds of things that can go wrong to cause what economists call "market failure": monopoly, external effects, public goods, and informational asymmetry.

The first source of market failure is monopoly in its various forms: monopoly in the output market, collusion among otherwise competitive firms or suppliers of inputs, and monopsony (only one buyer) in the input market. If the industry were competitive, marginal benefit and marginal cost would be equal. But as illustrated in Figure 2.9, the monopolist's profit-maximizing output and price combination occurs at a point where the price per unit exceeds the marginal cost of production. The price is too high from the viewpoint of efficiency. For this reason, the general public policy is to replace monopoly with competition where possible. That, for example, is the rationale for antitrust laws. But sometimes it is not possible or even desirable to replace a monopoly. Natural monopolies—such as public utilities—are an example; those monopolies are allowed to continue in existence but are closely regulated by the government in order to minimize their monopolistic inefficiencies while at the same time maximizing their technological efficiencies. Another example of a monopoly that is encouraged but regulated is the patent system; inventors are allowed a 17-year monopoly as an inducement to invest in the inventive process, but the monopoly right can only extend for the fixed period. (We will investigate the efficiency of the patent system in Chapter 5.)

The second source of market failure is the presence of what economists call "externalities." Exchange inside a market is voluntary and mutually beneficial; in contrast, an economic effect *external* to a market exchange may be involuntary and harmful. So, a harmful externality is defined as a cost or benefit that the voluntary actions of one or more people imposes or confers on a third party or parties without their consent. An example of an external cost is pollution. (We will not discuss external benefits here, principally because they do not figure prominently in law and economics. Any of the textbooks recommended at the end of this chapter will introduce you to

---

[14]Vilfredo Pareto was an Italian political scientist who wrote at the turn of the 20th century.

the economics of external benefits.) Suppose that a factory located upstream from a populous city dumps toxic materials into the river as a by-product of its production process. This action by the factory imposes an unbargained-for cost on the townspeople downstream since they are forced to incur some additional costs to clean up the water or to bring in safe water from else-where. The reason the market fails in the presence of external costs is that the generator of the externality does not have to pay for harming others, and so exercises too little self-restraint. In a technical sense, the externality-generator produces too much output and the associated harm because there is a difference between private marginal cost and social marginal cost.

Private marginal cost, in our example, is the cost of production for the factory, the generator of the externality. *Social* marginal cost is the sum of private marginal cost and the additional costs imposed on third parties. The difference is shown in Figure 2.11, where the private cost curve and the social cost curves are both drawn. Since the former lies below the latter, social marginal cost is greater than private marginal cost at every level of output. Because the profit-maximizing firm operates along its private marginal cost curve, the firm will produce more than it should from a socially optimal point of view, where, as here, there is a difference between social and private marginal cost. We would like the firm to take into account *all* the costs of production, including the costs imposed on others, in choosing its profit-maximizing output. It is clear from Figure 2.11 that where there are external costs, the firm will produce q_p rather than q_s. The key to achieving the social optimum where there are externalities is to induce private profit-maximizers to restrict their output to the socially optimal, not privately optimal, point. This is done by policies that cause the firm to operate along the social marginal cost curve rather than along the private marginal cost curve. When this is accomplished, the externality is said to have been "internalized" in the sense that the private firm now takes it into consideration.

The third thing that can lead to market failure is the presence of a commodity called a "public good." A public good is a commodity with two very closely related characteristics: first, consumption of the good by one person does not leave less for any other consumer, a situation sometimes referred to as "non-rivalrous consumption"; and second, the costs of excluding non-paying beneficiaries who consume the good are so high that no private profit-maximizing firm is willing to supply the good. Consider the conventional example of a public good: national defense. The fact that one citizen is secure from the threat of invasion by a foreign army does not leave any less security for other citizens. Furthermore, it is difficult to exclude any citizen from enjoying the security provided to others. Because of these two characteristics, public goods are not likely to be provided at all by the market, or if they are privately provided, provided in less than socially optimal amounts.

Suppose, for the purposes of illustration, that national defense is provided by a private company. For a fee the company sells protection to its

Figure 2.11 Private and Social Marginal Cost

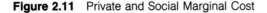

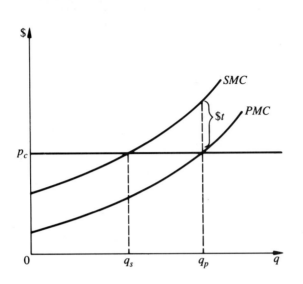

The costs that utility- or profit-maximizing behavior involuntarily imposes on others are called "external costs" or "social costs." Examples are tobacco smoking and air pollution. The consumer or firm that imposes these costs does not take them into account when deciding how much to consume or produce. This causes "market failure." In the figure, a firm's production is assumed to impose external costs of $t per unit of output. The private profit-maximizing output level for the firm is q_p because the firm does not take the external costs it imposes into account. The socially optimal amount of output for this firm is q_s. The task for public policy, including the law, is to devise efficient methods of getting the generator of the external costs to "internalize" those costs: to take them into its private utility- or profit-maximizing calculations.

customers against loss from foreign invasion by air, land, or sea. Only those customers who purchase the company's services will be protected against foreign invasion. Perhaps these customers could be identified by special garments, and their property denoted by a large white X painted on the roof of their homes. The company will protect only those and their property who have the proper identification; all others, unless protected by a rival defense company, will be at the mercy of invaders. Who will purchase the services of the private national defense company? Some will but many will not. Many of the non-purchasers will reason that if their neighbor will purchase a protection policy from a private national defense company, then they, too, will be protected: it will prove virtually impossible for the private company to protect the property and person of the neighbor without also providing security to the nearby non-purchaser. That is, the consumption of national defense is non-rivalrous: consumption by one person does not leave less for any other consumer. For that reason, there is a strong inducement for consumers of the privately-provided public good to try to be "free riders": they hope to benefit at no cost to themselves from the payment of others. The related problem for the private supplier of a public good like national defense is that it is very costly to exclude non-paying beneficiaries of the service. The attempt to distinguish those who have from those who have not subscribed to the private defense company is almost certain to fail: for example, the identifying clothes and property markings can easily be counterfeited. As a result of the presence of free riders and the high cost of distinguishing non-paying beneficiaries, it is not likely that the private company will be able to induce many people to purchase defense services. If private profit-maximizing firms are the only providers of national defense, too little of that good will be provided.

How can public policy correct the market failure in the provision of public goods? There are two general correctives. First, the government (local, state, or federal) may undertake to subsidize the private provision of the public good, either directly or indirectly through the tax system. An example is vaccination against epidemic disease. Vaccination shots are usually provided by private doctors with the government paying for the serum or compensating the doctors for the number of vaccinations they administer. The government pays for this subsidization out of general tax revenues, not from a user fee. Second, the government may undertake to provide the public good itself and to pay the costs of providing the service through the revenues raised by compulsory taxation. This is, in fact, how national defense is supplied.

The fourth source of market failure is a lack of information, for example, about who is selling the desired good or about the quality of goods offered for sale.[15] It is often the case that sellers know more about the quality of goods than do buyers. For example, a person who offers his car for sale knows far more about its quirks than does a potential buyer. Similarly, when a bank presents a depository agreement for the signature of a person opening a checking account, the bank knows far more than the customer about the legal consequences of the agreement. When sellers know more about a product than do buyers, or *vice versa*, information is said to be distributed asymmetrically in the market. Under some circumstances, these asymmetries can be corrected by the mechanism of voluntary exchange, for example, by the seller's willingness to provide a warranty to guarantee the quality of a product. But severe asymmetries can disrupt markets so much that a social optimum cannot be achieved by voluntary exchange. When that happens, government intervention in the market can correct for the informational asymmetries and induce more nearly optimal exchange. For example,

---

[15]Information is a special type of public good, but it is sufficiently different from other kinds of public goods to warrant being treated as a separate cause of market failure. We will introduce you to some of these special differences in Chapter 4, where we discuss the economic theory of information and how it might guide us in fashioning property rights in information.

the purchasers of a home are often at a disadvantage *vis-a-vis* the current owners in learning of latent defects—such as the presence of termites or of a cracked foundation—in the home. As a result, the market for the sale of homes may not be functioning in a socially optimal manner; purchasers may be paying too much for homes or may inefficiently refrain from purchases because of a fear of latent defects. Many states have corrected for this informational asymmetry by requiring sellers to disclose knowledge of any latent defects to prospective purchasers. If the sellers do not make this disclosure, then they may be responsible for correcting those defects. For similar reasons, the Federal Trade Commission requires the sellers of used cars to be truthful in disclosing information about the cars to prospective purchasers. We will discuss how the law can correct informational asymmetries in greater detail in our treatment of contract law.

C. Efficiency and Optimality

An economy that is both productively and allocatively efficient satisfies the Pareto criterion, viz., that no one can be made better off without making someone else worse off. The importance of this criterion can be clarified by imagining a society consisting of only two people, A and B. A two-person society can deploy its productive resources in various ways that benefit A and B differentially. To represent the different outcomes, individual A's utility is shown in Figure 2.12 on the vertical axis and individual B's utility on the horizontal axis. The downward-sloping curve, called the "utility possibility frontier," represents the outer boundary of the points that society can achieve. Any point on this frontier, or inside, can be achieved by an appropriate deployment of resources. This frontier represents all the Pareto efficient points achievable by this society. To see why, notice that starting from initial point a, any move into the quadrant bounded by P_a makes both A and B better off, which is a Pareto improvement. Or from initial point b, any move into the quadrant bounded by P_b is a Pareto improvement. In general, for any point inside the frontier, there is at least one Pareto superior point on the frontier.

There is a connection between the Pareto frontier in Figure 2.12 and the model of perfect competition. If all the sources of market failure in the economy have been corrected so that the economy is perfectly competitive, the actions of utility-maximizing consumers and profit-maximizing firms will result in the attainment of a social optimum. In terms of Figure 2.12, this means that starting from *any* point within the utility possibility frontier, A and B—each of whom acts as both a consumer and a producer—can, through mutually beneficial voluntary exchange, reach the utility possibility frontier. Second, note that the particular Pareto optimum that the two-person society reaches depends on its starting point. Each starting point represents a different initial allocation of goods and services (and its resulting utility to A and B), and each of them can lead to a different social optimum. Third, once the

Figure 2.12 The Utility Possibility Frontier

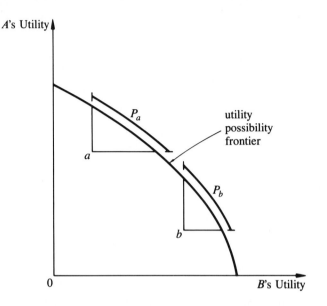

Assume that there are only two people, A and B, in society and that utility can be measured cardinally. The "utility possibility frontier" represents the combinations of A's and B's utility that can be realized if this society's resources are used Pareto efficiently. That means that it is impossible from any point on the frontier to make A and B better off simultaneously; on the frontier, A can be made better off only by making B worse off and *vice versa*. But from a point like *a* that is not on the frontier, both persons can be made better off by a northeasterly move toward the segment of the frontier labeled P_a. Notice that the final distribution of utility between A and B along the utility possibility frontier depends on the initial point from which this hypothetical two-person society begins: if from *a*, then the distribution will be along the P_a-segment; if from *b*, then the distribution will be along the P_b-segment.

two-person society has reached the utility possibility frontier, any move along that frontier is *not* a Pareto improvement: one person can be made better off only by making the other worse off. The great conclusion of all this is that, given some initial allocation of resources, mutually beneficial voluntary exchange and profit-maximizing production will achieve a social optimum *but* that the resulting optimum depends on the initial allocation.

We have, as yet, no standard for choosing among all the Pareto optima on the utility possibility frontier. Let us now turn to microeconomists' various attempts to posit a way for society to choose which optimum is the best. First, there is the notion of a *potential* Pareto improvement. This is an attempt to surmount the restriction of the Pareto criterion that only those changes are recommended in which at least one person is made better off and no one is made worse off. A *potential* Pareto improvement allows changes in which there are both gainers *and* losers, but requires that the gainers gain more than the losers lose. If this condition is satisfied, the gainers can, in principle, compensate the losers and still have a surplus left for themselves. Compensation does not actually have to be made, but it must be possible in principle for the change to be a potential Pareto improvement. In essence, this is the technique of cost-benefit analysis. There are both theoretical and empirical problems with this standard,[16] but it is indispensable to applied welfare economics.

Second, there is the notion of a social welfare function, a mathematical function that indicates how the utility of individuals in society are to be aggregated in order to compute social welfare. In our two-person society, we could suppose such a function to have the general form

$$\text{Social Welfare} = f(U_A, U_B).$$

Let us further assume that this function has properties such that it appears as the set of social indifference curves labeled SWF_1, SWF_2, and so on in Figure 2.13. Higher curves represent higher levels of social well-being. Any combination of A's utility and B's utility along a given social welfare curve represents the same level of *societal* well-being. Thus, all points on SWF_2 indicate combinations of the two individuals' utilities that give the same *social* utility. But every point along SWF_2 represents a combination that has less social utility than any combination along SWF_3. Just as the budget line represented the feasible combinations of goods available to the consumer, the points along the utility possibility frontier represent the feasible Pareto optima in this two-person society. Given the social welfare function above, the best of the available optima is the combination at point R. Thus, we conclude that if there is a social welfare function like the one we have been describing, then we can determine which among all the Pareto optima is the best for society.

Economists generally agree that specifying an exact social welfare function requires drawing upon theories from ethics and political philosophy, such as utilitarianism, which lie outside the scope of economics. We will have occasion to refer to some of these theories in subsequent chapters.[17]

In this survey of welfare economics, efficiency is a prominent concept, but equity or fairness has not figured in the discussion. This is not because those areas are unimportant but rather because they are beyond the typical economist's professional competence. Nevertheless, an interdisciplinary subject like law and economics forces economists to acquire new competencies, and on that note we turn from a review of economic methods to a review of legal methods.

---

[16]On the theoretical problems, *see* Jules Coleman, *Efficiency, Utility, and Wealth Maximization*, 8 HOFSTRA L. REV. 487 (1980). On the empirical problems, *see* E.J. Mishan, COST-BENEFIT ANALYSIS (1972).

[17]A discussion of the theoretical problems connected with social welfare functions may be found in Kenneth J. Arrow, COLLECTED PAPERS, VOL. 1: SOCIAL CHOICE AND JUSTICE (1983).

Figure 2.13 The Social Welfare Function

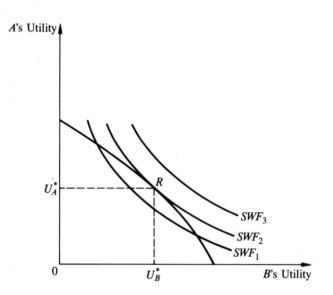

One theoretical method of determining which of the points on the utility possibility frontier is the best is to imagine a social utility (or welfare) function analogous to the individual's utility function. The social welfare function aggregates the utility or well-being of the individuals in society in order to determine society's utility or well-being. (Specifying the exact form of a social welfare function requires going outside the boundaries of economics to ethics and political philosophy.) If the social welfare function has the same characteristics as the individual utility functions, then social indifference curves (SWF_1, SWF_2, and SWF_3) may be drawn. The socially optimal distribution of well-being is then the highest attainable distribution, given by the tangency between the utility possibility frontier and the highest social indifference curve. In the graph, the highest attainable social welfare is SWF_2, which is distributed between A and B as u_A^* and u_B^*.

QUESTIONS

2.1. Define the role of the mathematical concepts of maximization and equilibrium in microeconomic theory. (Suggested answers are at the end of this book.)

2.2. Define and distinguish between *productive efficiency* and *allocative efficiency*.

2.3. What are consumers assumed to maximize? Describe the individual consumer's constrained maximum. Can you characterize this constrained maximum as a point where marginal cost and marginal benefit are equal?

2.4. A married couple with children is considering divorce. They are negotiating about two elements of the divorce: the level of child support that will be paid to the partner who keeps the children and the amount of time that the children will spend with each partner. Whoever has the children would prefer more child support from the other partner and more time with the children. Furthermore, the partner who keeps the children believes that as the amount of child support increases, the value of more time with the children declines relative to the value of child support.

    a. Draw a typical indifference curve for the partner who keeps the children with the level of child support on the horizontal axis and the amount of time that the children spend with this partner on the vertical axis.

    b. Suppose that the partner who keeps the children has this utility function: $u = cv$, where c = the weekly level of child support and v = the number of days per week that the children spend with this partner. Suppose that initially the support level is $100 and the number of days per week spent with this partner is c. What is the utility to this partner from that arrangement? If the other partner wishes to reduce the weekly support to $80, how many more days with the children must the child-keeping partner have in order to maintain utility at the previous level?

2.5. Define price elasticity of demand and explain what ranges of value it may take. What is the relationship between the value of price elasticity of demand, changes in price, and changes in total consumer expenditures?

2.6. Street crimes committed by heroin addicts grow so numerous in New York City that a reform administration is voted into office with a mandate to "get tough" on those responsible for the crimes. The new police commissioner undertakes a vigorous program of suppressing the drug traffic, which results in a leftward shift (i.e., a reduction) in the supply curve of heroin. No other steps are taken to stop the connection between street crime and heroin addiction. Using a graph showing the supply of and demand for heroin and other economic concepts developed in this chapter, explain the connection between the elasticity of demand and the statistics on street crime. For example, what will happen to the amount of street crime if the demand for heroin by addicts is inelastic? If it is elastic?

    Suppose that, after the sad consequences of the supply-oriented policy are revealed, the commissioner comes to you for advice on how to break the connection between heroin addiction and street crime. Suppose that you determine that the demand for heroin is inelastic. Would a policy of *reducing* the price to addicts achieve the goal of lessening street crime?

    [Be sure you re-evaluate these conclusions after the discussion of heroin and crime in Chapter 12.]

2.7. Use the notion of opportunity cost to explain why "There's no such thing as a free lunch."

2.8. What are firms assumed to maximize? Describe how the individual firm determines the output level that achieves that maximum. Can you characterize the firm's constrained maximum as one for which marginal cost equals marginal benefit?

2.9. Characterize these different market structures in which a firm may operate: perfect competition, monopoly, oligopoly, and imperfect competition. Compare the industry output and price in a perfectly competitive industry with the output and price of a monopolist.

2.10. What conditions must hold for a monopoly to exist?

2.11. Suppose that a governmental policy regulates a competitive industry by placing a ceiling on the market price below the equilibrium price. Explain the consequences of this ceiling.

2.12. What is general equilibrium and under what conditions will it be achieved? What are the welfare consequences of general equilibrium?

2.13. What are the four sources of market failure? Explain how each of them causes the Invisible Hand to lead to sub-optimal results. What general policies might correct each of the instances of market failure?

2.14. Which of the following are private goods and might, therefore, be provided in socially optimal amounts by private profit-maximizers? Which are public goods and should, therefore, be provided by the public sector or by the private sector with public subsidies?

    a. A swimming pool large enough to accommodate hundreds of people.
    b. A fireworks display.
    c. A heart transplant.
    d. Vaccination against a highly contagious disease.
    e. A wilderness area.
    f. Vocational education.
    g. On-the-job training.
    h. Secondary education.

2.15. What is meant by *Pareto efficiency* or *Pareto optimality*? What is the importance of the initial distribution of resources in determining what the distribution of resources will be after all Pareto improvements have been made?

SUGGESTED READINGS

A. Microeconomic Theory Generally

Baxter, William A., PEOPLE OR PENGUINS: THE CASE FOR OPTIMAL POLLUTION (1974).

Hirschleifer, Jack, PRICE THEORY AND APPLICATIONS (3d ed. 1984).

Levi, Maurice, THINKING ECONOMICALLY (1985).

Miller, Roger, and Douglass C. North, THE ECONOMICS OF PUBLIC POLICY ISSUES (4th ed. 1984).

Mishan, E. J., INTRODUCTION TO NORMATIVE ECONOMICS (1981).

Ruffin, Roy J., and Paul R. Gregory, PRINCIPLES OF MICROECONOMICS, (2d ed. 1986).

B. Microeconomic Theory in the Law

Calabresi, Guido, THE COSTS OF ACCIDENTS: A LEGAL AND ECONOMIC ANALYSIS (New Haven, Conn.: Yale University Press, 1971).

Cooter, Robert D., *Law and the Imperialism of Economics: An Introduction to the Economic Analysis of Law and Review of the Major Books,* 29 UCLA L. REV. 1258 (1982).

Posner, Richard A., ECONOMIC ANALYSIS OF LAW, ch. 1 (3d ed. 1986).

See also the suggested readings at the end of Chapter 1.

The Economics of Risk and Insurance[18]

In nearly all of the economic models we have examined so far we have implicitly assumed that there was little or no uncertainty that clouded the perceptions and thus the behavior of the actors. This is clearly a simplifying assumption, one that has served us well thus far. But it is time to expand our basic economic model by explicitly allowing for the presence of uncertainty.

A. Uncertainty and Consumer Behavior

Economists distinguish between two different kinds of uncertainty. The first, sometimes called "primary" or "event" uncertainty, exists because certain future events that are crucial to economic decisions taken today are unknown or unknowable. For example, a farmer's decisions about what to plant and how much of it to plant this spring depends in large part on the future prices of various farm outputs, on the weather during the growing season, on whether there will be an embargo on the export of various commodities, and so on, all of which events lie in the future and are unknown. Clearly, a decisionmaker like the farmer has some information on the various possibilities for these future events—e.g., the history of weather patterns in the area—but this information is not complete and perfect, as we have been implicitly assuming in our simpler models.

A second form of uncertainty, sometimes called "secondary" or "market" uncertainty, arises because information about certain future or present events is known to some but not to all economic actors. (We have already mentioned this condition as an informational asymmetry and have noted that may be a source of market failure.) This asymmetry may arise because there is uncertainty about what prices are being charged by different retail-

---

[18]The material in this section draws on the chapter on decisions under uncertainty in Heinz Kohler, INTERMEDIATE MICROECONOMICS: THEORY AND APPLICATIONS (2d ed. 1986).

ers, about the quality of various products (e.g., their durability and service record), and about what may and may not be legally done in the future to correct a problem. We will postpone a discussion of the economics of this important aspect of uncertainty until the chapters on the economics of contract law. In what follows here, we concentrate on primary uncertainty.

Let us begin by analyzing a simple business decision about the future. Suppose that a certain entrepreneur is considering two possible uses of investment capital. The first, D_1, involves the production of an output for which the market is well known and stable. For all intents and purposes there is no uncertainty about the output under D_1; regardless of the future course of events, the entrepreneur can be confident of earning a profit of $200 if he takes D_1.

The second course of action, D_2, is less certain. It involves a new and untried output whose reception by the consuming public is highly uncertain. If consumers like the new product, the entrepreneur can earn profits of $400. However, if they do not take to it, he stands to lose $50.

How is the entrepreneur supposed to compare these two courses of action, D_1 and D_2? One possibility is to compare their *expected monetary values*. An "expected value" is defined as the sum of the probabilities of each possible outcome times the value of each of those outcomes. For example, suppose that there are four possible numerical outcomes, labeled O_1 through O_4, to a decision. And suppose, also, that there are four separate probability estimates, labeled p_1 through p_4, associated with each of the four outcomes. These probabilities must sum to 1, which indicates that these four outcomes are the only ones possible. We then define the expected value (EV) of this decision as being equal to the expression

$$EV = p_1 O_1 + p_2 O_2 + p_3 O_3 + p_4 O_4.$$

An expected value can be converted into an expected *monetary* value if the outcomes are monetary outcomes. To return to our entrepreneur, he may compute the expected monetary value (EMV) of D_1 as the product of the probability of that event (here, since we have assumed the outcome is certain, the probability is 1) and the monetary value of the outcome (here, profits of $200):

$$EMV(D_1) = 1 (200) = 200.$$

The computation of the expected monetary value of the decision D_2 is more problematic. Here there are two possible outcomes, and in order to perform the calculation the entrepreneur needs to know the probabilities of the two outcomes. Since we do not have that information, let us explore the calculation in more general terms. Let p be the probability of the new output's being a success. Thus, $(1 - p)$ is the probability that it is a failure. Then, the expected monetary value of D_2 is given by the expression

$$EMV(D_2) = 400p + (-50)(1 - p),$$
$$= 400_p - 50 + 50p,$$
$$= 450p - 50, \text{ for any } p.$$

Thus, if the probability of success for the new product is 0.3, the expected monetary value of the decision to introduce that new product is $85.

The question obviously arises as to where the decisionmaker is to get the information about the probabilities of the various outcomes. It could be that the seasoned entrepreneur has some intuition about p or that, having done extensive marketing surveys, he may have a more scientific basis for assessing p. Still another possibility might be that he calculates the level of p that will make the expected monetary value of D_2 equal to that of the certain event, D_1. A strong reason for doing that would be that, although he might not know for sure what p is, it would be valuable to know how high p must be in order for it to give greater expected profits to the entrepreneur than the safe course of action D_1. For example, even if there was no way to know p for sure, suppose that one could calculate that in order for the uncertain course of action to have a higher expected value than the safe course of action the probability of success of the new product would have to be 0.95. That would be valuable information.

It is a simple matter to calculate the level of p that equates the expected monetary value of D_1 and D_2. That is the p that solves the following equation:

$$450p - 50 = 200, \text{ or}$$
$$p = 5/9 = 0.556.$$

The implication, of course, is that if the probability of the new product's success is 0.556 or greater, then D_2 has a higher expected monetary value than does D_1, and the entrepreneur will choose D_2. The economic analysis typically assumes that decisionmakers can form probabilities one way or another so that expectations can be computed.

Let us now go beyond this simple model of decisionmaking under uncertainty to ask if it is really true that when facing decisions in which there is some uncertainty, people tend to take the action that has the higher expected monetary value. First, suppose that the two decisions, D_1 and D_2, have the *same* expected monetary value. (This equality occurs when the probability p equals 0.556.) Ask yourself if you were in the entrepreneur's shoes whether you would automatically choose D_2. Many of us upon reflection would hesitate to take D_2 unless the expected monetary value of D_2 was substantially greater than that of D_1. The reason for this hesitation may lie in the fact that many of us are reluctant to gamble, and D_2 certainly is a gamble. We are generally much more comfortable with a sure thing like D_1.

The formal explanation for this phenomenon of avoiding gambles was first offered in the 18th century by the Swiss mathematician and cleric Daniel Bernoulli. Bernoulli's insight was to notice that people making decisions under uncertainty do not attempt to maximize expected monetary values. Rather they seek to maximize expected *utility*. This is a subtle but crucial difference. The introduction of utility allows us to introduce the notion of risk and of decisionmakers' attitudes toward risk.

Assume that utility, as defined in the main text of this chapter, is, among many other things, a function of money income; that is,

$$U = U(I).$$

Bernoulli suggested that a common relationship between money income and utility was that as income increased, utility increased, but at a decreasing rate.[19] A utility function in money income with that property is said to exhibit diminishing marginal utility of income. The sense of such a function is that if one's income level is $10,000, an additional $100 in income will add more to one's total utility than will $100 added to that same person's income of $40,000. A utility function like that shown in Figure A2.1 has this property. When this person's income is increased by $1,000 from $10,000 to $11,000, her utility increases from 100 to 125 units, an increase of 25 units. But when her income is increased by $1,000 from $40,000 to $41,000, her utility increases from 250 to 255 units, an increase of only 5 units. Thus, for a risk-averse person the marginal utility of income decreases. The slope of the curve in Figure A2.1 is flatter at higher income levels to indicate this relationship.

One example of a utility function with this property is

$$U = \text{square root}(I).$$

A money income level of $10,000 thus has a utility level of 100; one of $40,000 has a utility level of 200. Thus, a four-fold increase in money income increases this person's utility level only two-fold.

A person whose utility function in money income exhibits diminishing marginal utility is said to be "risk averse." A more formal definition of risk aversion is this: a person is said to be a risk averse if she considers the utility of a certain prospect of money income to be higher than the expected utility of an uncertain prospect of equal expected monetary value. We can illustrate this definition with the help of Figure A2.1. Suppose that the person whose utility function is shown faces two courses of action. The first, A_1, will result in income I_0 with certainty. The second, A_2, has two possible outcomes, $10,000 and $40,000. Let the probability of the outcome's being $10,000 equal p; the probability of an outcome of $40,000 is then $(1 - p)$. Depending on the value of p, the expected monetary value of A_2 lies along the line segment TS in Figure A2.1. The greater the probability of $10,000$'s being the outcome, the closer the point will be to T. Suppose that p is such that the expected monetary value of A_2 is at point B on line segment TS; thus, the expected monetary value of this second course of action is I_0,

$$EMV(A_2) = I_0 = 10{,}000p + 40{,}000(1 - p).$$

And by assumption

$$EMV(A_1) = I_0.$$

---

[19]In terms of the differential calculus, $U' > 0$ and $U'' < 0$.

Figure A2.1   The Utility Function of a Risk-Averse Person

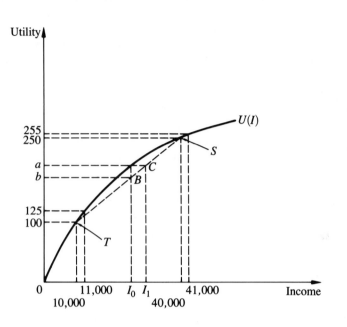

Units of utility are measured on the vertical axis, and income is measured along the horizontal axis. The heavy line, $U(I)$, shows a utility function that exhibits a diminishing marginal utility of income: utility increases as income increases but at a diminishing rate. Thus, when income increases from \$10,000 to \$11,000, utility increases by more than when income increases by the same increment from \$40,000 to \$41,000. A person for whom the marginal utility of income is diminishing is said to be "risk-averse."

More formally, a risk-averse person considers the utility of a certain prospect of income to be higher than the expected utility of an uncertain prospect of income of equal expected monetary value. Consider an action that has two possible outcomes: if it is a success, it will earn \$40,000; if it is a failure, it will earn \$10,000. Depending on the probability of success, the expected monetary value of this uncertain prospect can be read off the line segment TS. Suppose that the probability of success is at point B on the line TS so that the expected monetary value of the uncertain course of action is I_0. The expected utility of this uncertain prospect of I_0 income is the distance Ob on the vertical axis. However, a certain prospect of I_0 income will give utility equal to the vertical distance Oa. This shows that a risk-averse person prefers a certain prospect of income to an uncertain prospect of equal expected monetary value.

The expected monetary values of the two courses of action are equal.

We now know that risk-averse people are not indifferent between actions that have equal expected monetary value. Can we show graphically that they prefer the more certain outcome? In the figure the expected utility of A_2 can be seen by measuring the vertical distance from the income axis at income I_0 to the point B on the line segment TS. Thus, the expected utility of A_2 is the distance Ob. The utility of the certain course of action, A_1, is the vertical distance from the income axis at income I_0 to the point on the utility function $U(I)$. This is the distance Oa. Because $Oa > Ob$, the utility of a certain prospect of income I_0 is greater than the expected utility of an uncertain prospect of income I_0.

Notice that the risk-averse person will prefer the certain outcome unless the probability of an uncertain outcome of $40,000 increases substantially. To be specific, only if the probability of an uncertain outcome places the expected monetary value of A_2 above point C on line segment TS will this risk-averse person get greater utility from the uncertain prospect of income I_1 than from the certain prospect of income I_0.

Economists presume that the attitude of most people toward risk is one of aversion, but they also recognize that there may be those who are either neutral toward risk or, like gamblers, rock climbers, and race car drivers,

Figure A2.2   (a)   The Utility Function of a Risk-Neutral Person

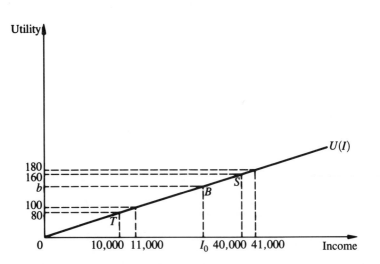

The heavy line, $U(I)$, shows a utility function that is a straight line passing through the origin, which indicates a constant marginal utility of income: utility increases as income increases and at a constant rate. Thus, whether income increases from $10,000 to $11,000 or from $40,000 to $41,000, the increase in utility is 20 units. A person for whom the marginal utility of income is constant is said to be "risk-neutral."

More formally, a risk-neutral person is one who is indifferent between a certain prospect of income and an uncertain prospect of income of equal expected monetary value. Suppose that this person faces a course of action with two possible outcomes: if it is a success, it will earn $40,000; if it is a failure, it will earn $10,000. Depending on the probability of success, the expected monetary value of this uncertain prospect can be read off the line segment TS. Suppose that the probability of success is at point B on the line TS so that the expected monetary value of the uncertain course of action is I_0. The expected utility of this uncertain prospect of I_0 income is the distance Ob on the vertical axis. But because of the constant marginal utility of income, the utility of a certain prospect of I_0 income is exactly the same, Ob. This shows that a risk-neutral person is indifferent between a certain prospect of income and an uncertain prospect of equal expected monetary value.

actually seek risk. Like aversion, these alternative attitudes toward risk may also be defined in terms of the individual's utility function in money income and the marginal utility of income. Someone who is risk neutral has a constant utility of income and is, therefore, indifferent between a certain prospect of income and an uncertain prospect of equal expected monetary value. Figure A2.2, panel (a), gives the utility function for a risk-neutral person. It is a straight line because the marginal utility of income to a risk-neutral person is constant.

In Figure A2.2(a) we compare the change in utility when the risk-neutral person's income is increased by $1,000 at two different levels of income. When this person's income is increased by $1,000 from $10,000 to $11,000, his utility increases from 80 to 100 units, an increase of 20 units. And when

(b) The Utility Function of a Risk-Preferring Person

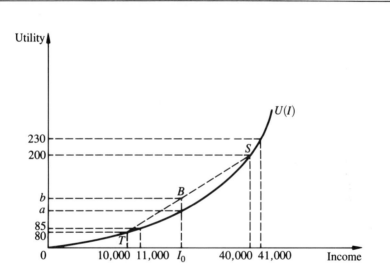

The heavy line, $U(I)$, shows a utility function that indicates an increasing marginal utility of income: utility increases as income increases but at an increasing rate. Thus, when income increases from $10,000 to $11,000, utility increases by less than when income increases by the same increment from $40,000 to $41,000. A person for whom the marginal utility of income is increasing is said to be "risk-preferring" or "risk-seeking."

More formally, a risk-preferring person prefers an uncertain prospect of income to a certain prospect of income of equal expected monetary value. Suppose that this person faces a course of action with two possible outcomes: if it is a success, it will earn $40,000; if it is a failure, it will earn $10,000. Depending on the probability of success, the expected monetary value of this uncertain prospect can be read off the line segment TS. Suppose that the probability of success is at point B on the line TS so that the expected monetary value of the uncertain course of action is I_0. The expected utility of this uncertain prospect of I_0 income is the distance Ob on the vertical axis. However, the utility of a certain income of I_0 has utility of Oa, which is less that Ob. Thus, a risk-preferring or risk-seeking person prefers an uncertain prospect of income to a certain prospect of income of equal expected monetary value.

his income is increased by $1,000 from $40,000 to $41,000, his utility increases by exactly the same amount, 20 units, from 160 to 180 units. Thus, for the risk-neutral person the marginal utility of income is constant.

A more formal definition of risk neutrality is this: a person is said to be risk neutral if he is indifferent between a certain prospect of money income and an uncertain prospect of money income of equal expected monetary value. We can illustrate this definition with the help of Figure A2.2(a). Suppose that the person whose utility function is shown faces two courses of action. The first, A_1, will result in income of I_0 with certainty. The second, A_2, has two possible incomes, $10,000 and $40,000. Depending on the probability of these outcomes, the expected monetary value of A_2 lies along the line segment TS in Figure A2.2(a). The greater the probability of $10,000 being the outcome, the closer the point will be to T. Suppose that p is such that the expected monetary value of A_2 is at point B on line segment TS. The expected monetary values of the two courses of action are equal to I_0.

Because the utility function in income for a risk-neutral person is a straight line through the origin, the expected utility of A_2 (the vertical distance from the income axis at income I_0 to the point B on the line segment TS) and the utility of A_1 (the vertical distance from the income axis at income I_0 to the point on the utility function $U(I)$) are both equal to Ob. Because both courses of action give the risk-neutral person the same utility, he is indifferent between them. Notice that an implication of this more formal definition of risk neutrality is that the course of action with the higher expected monetary value will always be chosen by a risk-neutral decisionmaker.

Someone who is risk-seeking or risk-preferring has an increasing marginal utility of income and, therefore, prefers an uncertain prospect of income to a certain prospect of equal expected monetary value. Figure A2.2, panel (b), gives the utility function of a risk-preferring individual. The figure allows us to compare the change in utility when the risk-preferring person's income is increased by $1,000 at two different levels of income. When this person's income is increased by $1,000 from $10,000 to $11,000, her utility increases from 80 to 85 units, an increase of 5 units. However, when her income is increased by $1,000 from $40,000 to $41,000, her utility increases from 200 to 230 units, an increase of 30 units. Thus, for the risk-preferring person the marginal utility of income increases.

A more formal definition of risk-seeking or risk-preferring is this: a person is said to be risk-seeking or risk-preferring if she considers the expected utility of an uncertain prospect of money income to be higher than the utility of a certain prospect of equal expected monetary value. We can illustrate this defintion with the help of Figure A2.2(b). Suppose that the person whose utility function is shown faces two courses of action, A_1 (a certain income of I_0) and A_2 (uncertain outcomes of $10,000 or $40,000), that have the same expected monetary value I_0. The probabilities of the outcomes from A_2 are such that the expected monetary value of A_2 is at point B on line segment TS.

The expected monetary values of the two courses of action are equal. But the risk-preferring person prefers the uncertain course of action to the certain course of action of equal expected monetary value. In Figure A2.2(b) the expected utility of A_2 can be seen by measuring the vertical distance from the income axis at income I_0 to the point B on the line segment TS. Thus, the expected utility of A_2 is the distance Ob. The utility of the certain course of action, A_1, is the vertical distance from the income axis at I_0 to the point on the utility function $U(I)$. This is the distance Oa. Because $Ob > Oa$, the expected utility of an uncertain prospect of income I_0 is greater than the utility of a certain prospect of income I_0.

From the figure we may also conclude that the risk-preferring person will prefer the uncertain outcome unless the expected monetary value of the certainty increases substantially. Specifically, only if the expected monetary value of the certain course of action exceeds I_1 will this risk-preferring person get greater utility from the certain prospect of income I_1 than from the uncertain prospect of income I_0.[20]

The general presumption in economics is that people are risk-averse over gambles affecting a significant proportion of their wealth. One of the most important behavioral implications of risk aversion is that people will pay to avoid having to face uncertain outcomes. There are three ways in which a risk-averse person may convert an uncertain into a certain outcome. First, he may purchase insurance from someone else. Second, he may self-insure. This may involve incurring expenses to minimize the probability of an uncertain event's occurring or to minimize the monetary loss in the event of a particular contingency. An example is the installation of smoke detectors in a home. Another form of self-insurance is the setting-aside of a sum of money to cover possible losses.[21] Third, a risk-averse person who is considering the purchase of some risky asset may reduce the price he is willing to pay for that asset. At some price, as we shall see, he prefers surrendering this certain amount of income to holding the uncertain asset.

For the purposes of illustrating the market insurance option, consider Figure A2.3. The utility function is for a risk-averse person. Suppose that this person is facing an uncertain prospect, say, the loss of earnings due to catastrophic illness in the coming year. He is self-employed and is currently not covered by a medical insurance plan. His annual salary is $25,000, which, if he does not get ill, he is certain to earn over the course of the year. A money income of $25,000 gives him a utility of $0g$, corresponding to the vertical distance from $25,000 on the income axis to the point G on the utility function. If he falls catastrophically ill, this person will be unable to

---

[20]Still another possibility is that people are averse to large risks and preferrers of small risks. These preferences combine elements of the curve in Figure A2.1 and Figure A2.2.

[21]Large business organizations frequently practice self-insurance in this form for their employees' health expenses.

Figure A2.3 The Decision to Insure

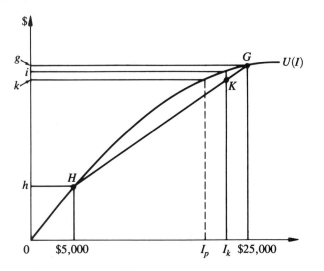

The utility function $U(I)$ is for a risk-averse person. In the absence of catastrophic illness, this person will have an annual income of $25,000. The utility of this certain income is $0g$. But if he falls severely ill, his income will be only $5,000. Suppose that the probability of becoming catastrophically ill is given by the point K on the line segment GH. The expected monetary value of such an illness is I_k, and the expected utility is $0k$. This person is willing to pay a sum up to $(25,000 - I_p)$ as an insurance premium. The insurance policy converts the uncertain outcome from illness into a certain loss (the insurance premium). This person gets greater utility from a lower certain income of, say $(I_p + 5)$ than from an uncertain income of I_k. (Notice that the expected monetary value of I_k is greater than that of I_p.)

work, and his income will decrease to $5,000. An income of $5,000 will give him a utility of $0h$.

To see if he should purchase insurance against catastrophic illness, the individual needs to estimate the probability that he will get ill, compute the expected monetary value of that outcome, and compare that expectation with the cost of an insurance policy (the premium). The probability of catastrophic illness determines a point along the line segment GH from which the expected monetary value of the uncertain event can be computed. Assume that the probability of illness is given by point K on GH. The expected monetary value of that uncertain outcome is I_k, and the expected utility is $0k$. Notice that a certain income of I_p would give this person a utility of $0k$, exactly equal to that of the uncertain income I_k. It follows that this risk-averse person would be willing to surrender up to $(25,000 - I_p)$ of his certain income in exchange for not having to bear the risk of catastrophic illness and that he would consider himself better off with a lower but certain income of slightly more than I_p than with an uncertain income I_k.

This is precisely what an insurance contract will provide the risk-averse person: in exchange for giving up a certain amount of income (the insurance premium), the insurance company will bear the risk of the uncertain event. The risk-averse person considers himself better off with the lower certain income than facing the uncertain higher income.

The example we have just discussed concerned the purchase of market insurance. Recall that there are other options available by which the risk-averse person can avoid risk: self-insurance by setting aside a contingency fund or, in the case of illness, incurring the extra costs of being very, very careful about diet, exposure to illness, and so on. In general, the risk-averse person will choose whichever of these options is the cheapest method of avoiding a given risk.

B. The Supply of Insurance

The material we have just finished concerns the demand for insurance by risk-averse individuals. Let us now turn to a brief consideration of the suppliers of insurance, the insurance companies. There is a common belief among non-specialists that insurers must be risk-seeking, as though they must stand in a mirror-like relationship to their risk-averse insurees. This view is incorrect. Insurance companies are presumed to be profit-maximizing firms. They offer insurance contracts not because they prefer gambles to certainties but because of a mathematical theorem known as the law of large numbers. This law holds that what may seem random, unpredictable, and undependable to the individual becomes deterministic and predictable among large groups of individuals. For example, each of us is hard pressed to imagine on our own what the probability of a fire in our home is likely to be, or what the most likely extent of loss is likely to be in the event of a fire; we do not have enough experience with that phenomenon to make anything more than an educated guess. But for all the individuals in a city or a state or the nation the occurrence of fire is regular enough so that someone who looks to that larger set of information can easily determine the probabilities. For an insurance company, one of the ways to be more certain about the probability of insurable events is to attempt to insure a broad sample of the relevant population on the principle that the larger the sample the more dependable are the probabilities.[22]

Any insurer faces several well-known problems to which we will return throughout this book whenever we discuss insurance. These problems are referred to as "moral hazard" and "adverse selection." Moral hazard is the

---

[22]This connection between large sample size and dependability highlights the extraordinary risks that the legendary Lloyd's of London routinely insures. Lloyd's has become famous for insuring events—such as the injury to a pianist's fingers or the launch of a telecommunications satellite—for which the sample size is very small and for which, therefore, the risk exposure of the *insurer* is high.

name for the problem that arises when the behavior of the insuree changes *after* the purchase of insurance so that the probability of loss or the size of the loss increases. An extreme example is the insured's incentive to burn his home when he has been allowed to insure it for more than its market value. A more realistic example comes from loss due to theft. Suppose that you have just purchased a new stereo tape deck for your car but that you do not have insurance to cover your loss in the event that the deck is stolen. Under these circumstances you are likely to lock your car whenever you leave it, to park it in well-lighted places at night, to patronize only well-patrolled parking garages, and so on. The extra expenses that this involves constitute your self-insurance.

Now suppose that you discover that it is possible to purchase an insurance policy under which, for the payment of a premium, the insurer agrees to replace your tape deck if it is stolen or destroyed and that the premium is less than the extra expenses you were incurring to achieve self-insurance. Naturally, with the policy in force you now may be less assiduous about locking your car or parking in well-lighted places. In short, the very fact that your loss is insured may cause you to act so as to increase the probability of a loss.

Since insurance companies attempt to set their premiums so that, roughly, the premium equals the expected monetary value of the loss, the presence of moral hazard implies that a premium that has been set without regard for the increased probability of loss due to moral hazard will be too low and thus threaten the continued profitability of the firm.

Every insurer is aware of this problem and has developed methods to minimize it. Among the most common are coinsurance and deductibles. Under coinsurance the insuree shoulders a fixed percentage of his loss; under a deductible plan, the insuree shoulders a fixed dollar amount of the loss, with the insurance company paying for all losses above that amount. Both methods are intended to minimize the moral hazard problem by having the insured participate in coverage of his potential losses and thus to induce him not to change his behavior after the purchase of insurance. Additional methods of minimizing moral hazard problems are cancellation provisions: e.g., life insurance benefits are not payable in the event of suicide, nor are fire insurance losses payable in the event that the insured committed arson. Lastly, some insurance companies attempt to induce safer behavior by offering premium reductions for certain easily established acts by the insured: e.g., life insurance premiums are less for non-smokers and for those engaged in regular physical exercise; auto insurance premiums are less for non-drinkers; and fire insurance rates are lower for those who install smoke detectors and fire extinguishers.

The other major problem faced by insurance companies is called adverse selection. This arises because of the high cost to insurers of accurately distinguishing between high- and low-risk insurees. Although the law of large numbers helps the company in assessing probabilities, what it calculates from the large sample are *average* probabilities. And the insurance premium must be set using this average probability of a particular loss. But there are groups within the sample who are better risks than average, and those who are worse risks than average. Let us assume, as seems reasonable, that in many cases the individuals know better than the insurance company what their true risks are. For example, the insured alone may know that he drinks heavily and smokes in bed or that he is intending to murder his spouse, in whose insurance policy he has just been named principal beneficiary. If so, then this asymmetrical information may induce only high-risk people to purchase insurance and low-risk people to purchase none. This is because the premium, set on the basis of the *average* probability of loss, may be perceived as being too high by low-risk people and as being very low by high-risk people. The implication is that adverse selection could lead to only those most likely to have a loss seeking insurance. Indeed, if the problem is great enough it could be that there are markets in which no insurance is available because the costs to an insurance company of distinguishing between good and bad risks are too high.

The same devices that insurance companies employ to minimize risks of moral hazard also may serve to minimize the adverse selection problem. Coinsurance and deductible provisions are much less attractive to high-risk than to low-risk insurees so that an insuree's willingness to accept those provisions may indicate to the insurance company to which risk class the applicant belongs. Exclusion of benefits for losses arising from pre-existing conditions is another method of trying to distinguish high- and low-risk people. The insurer can also attempt, over a longer time horizon, to reduce the adverse selection bias by developing better methods of discriminating among insured—e.g., medical and psychological testing—so as to place insurees in more accurate risk classes.

> **Question A2.1:** Assume that there is unimpeachable evidence that some characteristic is strongly correlated with the occurrence of an insurable event. For example, women live longer than men. What would be the *efficiency effects* if insurance companies were forbidden from using that characteristic to establish different premiums for the higher- and lower-risk classes of insureds?

C. Discounting for Uncertainty

Let us now consider the behavior of a risk-averse person when neither market nor self-insurance is available. In that case the only method of accommodating the risk is by paying so little for the uncertain asset as to prefer the risky asset to the certainty of the income given up for it. This possibility will become plainer through the use of an example.

Consider Figure A2.4. The utility function reflects risk-aversion. The person here is thinking of purchasing a parcel of land. But the value of the parcel to the potential purchaser is not certain. He is concerned, with good reason, that the local government may impose some restrictions on the uses to which the parcel may be put. If the parcel's uses are not restricted, then the land is worth $25,000. But if restrictions are imposed, then it is only worth $5,000. The expected monetary value of the parcel to this purchaser

Figure A2.4   Discounting for Uncertainty

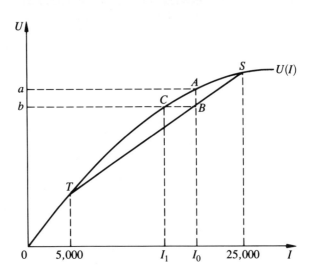

The figure shows the utility function of a risk-averse person who is thinking of purchasing a parcel of land. If the local government does not restrict the uses of the parcel, it is worth $25,000. But if it does impose restrictions, then the parcel is worth only $5,000. The expected monetary value of the parcel to the purchaser lies along the line *TS*, with the exact expected monetary value on that line being determined by the probability that the restrictions will be imposed. Suppose that the probability is such that the relevant point on *TS* is *B* so that the expected monetary value of the parcel is I_0 with expected utility *Ob*. Because the utility of a certain income of I_0, *Oa*, is greater than the expected utility of an uncertain income of I_0, *Ob*, this risk-averse person gets the greater utility from having a certain income of I_0 than from having an uncertainly-valued parcel for which he paid I_0. However, if the price of the parcel were to fall below I_1, then he would prefer the uncertainly-valued parcel of land to the certain income of less than I_1. Thus, risk-averse people will buy risky assets if they are priced low enough.

varies along the line *TS* depending on the probability that the purchaser places on the restrictions being imposed.

Let us assume that the probability estimate is at point *B* on *TS*. The expected monetary value of the land is thus I_0. The expected utility of the parcel of land is then $0b$. Note that that utility is less than the utility, $0a$, of a certain income of I_0. That means that this individual will get greater utility from having a certain income of I_0 than from having an uncertain prospect— here, the parcel of land—of equal expected monetary value. In short, I_0 is more than this individual will pay for the land.

Is there some certain amount of income that this individual is willing to give up in exchange for the land, whose expected value is I_0 and whose expected utility is $0b$, and consider himself better off? Note that the utility,

$0b$, of a certain income of I_1 equals the expected utility of the uncertain outcome from the parcel of land. That implies that this risk averse individual is indifferent between giving up I_1 and having the land. And of course, that suggests that he would *prefer* to give up anything less than I_1 and get the land in return.

> **Question A2.2:** What will happen to the maximum amount this individual is willing to pay for this parcel of land if he revises his probability estimate so that the restrictions on land use are *less* likely?

> **Question A2.3:** Suppose that an insurer announces that he is willing to insure against reductions in property values because of future governmental restrictions. The premium is slightly less than ($25,000 − I_0). Will the risk-averse person purchase this insurance? What will happen to the maximum amount the risk-averse individual is willing to pay for the parcel? If he purchases the parcel plus the insurance policy, is the total amount he pays for the parcel greater or less than when he offered less than I_1? Is he better or worse off as a result?

Consider one last aspect of this matter. Suppose that there are several risk-averse people interested in purchasing the parcel of land we have been discussing. And suppose that these purchasers have different degrees of risk aversion.[23] In Figure A2.5 these different utility functions are shown. The function *TRPS* indicates a greater degree of risk aversion than does *TUVS*. The relevant endpoints representing the two possible outcomes of a given decision are the same for the two different utility functions: $5,000 and $25,000. Let us assume that the two potential buyers are agreed that the probability of regulation affecting the value of the parcel is at point H on the segment TS such that the expected monetary value of the parcel is I_0. For both of them, then, the expected utility of the uncertain event is the distance $0b$. But they place different utilities on the certainty of income I_0. The less risk-averse individual derives $0a$ utility from that certainty; the more risk-averse individual, $0c$. For the less risk-averse person, the certain income I_1 gives just as much utility as does the uncertain outcome I_0. Therefore, the maximum that he is willing to pay for this parcel is I_1. The more risk-averse person gets equal utility from a certain income of I_2 as from an uncertain income of I_0. Thus. I_2 is the most that he is willing to give up in exchange for the parcel. If the seller is indifferent between the two buyers, then the less

---

[23]Economists formally distinguish between degrees of risk aversion in two different ways. *Absolute risk aversion* measures one's willingness to pay to avoid an uncertain event of a fixed monetary value as one's income or wealth changes. (This method of measuring the degree of risk aversion is formally written as $(-U''/U')$.) It is generally agreed that risk-averse people have declining absolute risk aversion. Thus, as their income increases, they are more willing to take a $25 gamble. *Relative risk aversion* measures the willingness to pay to avoid an uncertain event that is a fixed percentage of one's wealth or income. (The formal measure is $-I(U''/U')$.) What happens to relative risk aversion as income increases is uncertain, but most are agreed that it is constant and may decline. Thus, as income increases, relative risk aversion may predict an increasing willingness to wager 10% of one's income.

Figure A2.5 Different Degrees of Risk-Aversion

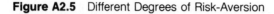

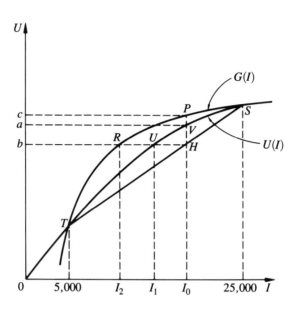

The utility functions of two different risk-averse people are shown. The function *TRPS* indicates a greater degree of risk-aversion than does *TUVS*. They both are considering purchasing the parcel of land whose value will be $25,000 if the local government does not impose use restrictions and $5,000 if it does. They are agreed that the probability of the restrictions being imposed is given by point *H* on the segment *TS*. Thus, for both persons the expected monetary value of the parcel is I_0. And the expected utility of this uncertain income is also the same for both, *Ob*. But because they have different degrees of risk aversion, they have different utilities from a certain income of I_0. The less risk-averse individual derives *Oa* utility from a certain income of I_0; the more risk-averse person, *Oc*. This affects the amount they are willing to pay for the parcel. The more risk-averse person will not be willing to purchase until the price falls below I_2; the less risk-averse person will not be willing to purchase until the price falls below I_1. If the seller is indifferent between these two buyers, he will prefer to sell to the less risk-averse person because he is willing to pay more for the parcel.

risk-averse person, being able to offer a higher price, will end up as the owner of the parcel.

The expected utility model of decisionmaking under uncertainty is the most widely-used in economic discussions. And yet that model has been subjected to an increasing amount of scholarly criticism. One implication of this criticism is that the expected utility model must be applied to a certain restricted class of decisions taken under uncertainty. Alternative models are suggested as more appropriate to other decisions under uncertainty. Until we return to a consideration of these alternative models, we will confine our application of the expected utility model to those circumstances in which it is most likely to be a helpful explanatory tool.

CHAPTER 3

An Introduction to Law and Legal Institutions

"You are old," said the youth, "and your jaws are too
  weak for anything tougher than suet.
Yet you finished the goose, with the bones and the beak
  —Pray, how do you manage to do it?"
"In my youth," said his father, "I took to the law,
  and argued each case with my wife;
And the muscular strength, which it gave to my jaw,
  has lasted the rest of my life."
From "Father William" in Lewis Carroll, ALICE'S ADVENTURES IN
WONDERLAND

An economist who picks up a law journal will understand much more of what is being said than a lawyer who picks up an economics journal. For this reason, it is not hard to convince a lawyer that he does not know economics. (Convincing him that he *should* learn economics is harder!) On the other hand, economists sometimes wonder what lawyers know; their suspicion is that lawyers know very little except a list of facts about legal rules. Perhaps economists imagine that knowledge must have a mathematical form, rather than being a verbal facility, and that is why they are unappreciative of the law and lawyers. In any case, in order for an economist to contribute to an understanding of the law, he must understand the rudiments of legal analysis. This chapter provides an introduction to the law for non-lawyers.

The first year of a Ph.D. program in economics is largely devoted to teaching the student micro- and macroeconomic theory and econometrics, the general tools for specialized research. By contrast, the first year of law school is not concerned with teaching a general theory of law. Classes in the theory of law are not offered until the second or third year of law school, and enrollments are often low. While there may not be a widely accepted theory of the law, there is, nonetheless, a general method and a generally accepted core in the practice of law and in legal scholarship. The purpose of this chapter is to introduce this general method by developing a shared core of knowledge about what the law is, how it develops, how it changes, and how it is administered.

I. THE COMMON LAW SYSTEM

There are two legal traditions that have shaped the legal systems of the modern world: the common law tradition and the civil law tradition. The common law tradition originated in England (the traditional beginning date is the Norman invasion of 1066) and is the prevailing tradition in Great Britain, Ireland, the United States, Canada, Australia, New Zealand, and the parts of Africa and Asia that were once part of the British Empire (for example, India). The civil law tradition is older and far more widely accepted than is the common law tradition. Its origins are the Roman codifications, especially that of the Emperor Justinian published in AD 533, and, more importantly, the revolutionary and nationalistic ferment of the late 18th and early 19th centuries. The civil law tradition is the predominant tradition in most of Western Europe, Central and South America, the socialist countries (including the Soviet Union), most of Africa and Asia, and even here and there in the common law world (for example, Louisiana, Quebec, and Puerto Rico).

What distinguishes these two legal traditions? The most striking distinction is each tradition's answer to the question, "What is the source of law?" In the common law systems there are multiple sources that stand in a loose hierarchy: the constitution (although England, the source of the common law tradition, has no written constitution), the legislature, the executive branch, and the judiciary. Of these sources it is, perhaps, the presence of the judiciary as a source of law that is the most distinctive to the common law tradition. As we will see in the first part of this chapter, judicial decisions are one of the most important sources of law in the common law countries. By contrast, in the civil law systems the sources of law stand in a strict hierarchy with the legislature being pre-eminent. The judiciary is precluded from making law; instead, judges merely apply the law created by the legislature. Judicial opinions do not have the effect of creating law, as they do in the common law systems. In large part, the different roles of the judiciary in the common law and civil law traditions reflect the particular histories and associated political philosophies of the modern countries (England and France) from which these traditions emerged.[1]

---

[1] It is sometimes said that an important distinction between the common law and civil law traditions is the presence of a comprehensive code of the law drawn up by the legislature. The model code for the civil law countries was, historically, the *Corpus Juris Civilis* of Justinian and,

In the remainder of this chapter and the other chapters of this book, we will focus on the rules and institutions of the common law tradition. However, this does not mean that the analysis we develop here might not be applied to the rules and institutions of the civil law countries. Indeed, some comparative law scholars have recently argued that there is a discernible convergence between the common law and civil law traditions; that although the procedures for determining the law and other aspects of the traditions are markedly different, the substantive rules of the two traditions exhibit an increasing similarity. To the extent that this is true, the economic analysis of this book has a direct application to the rules of the civil law systems.

A. Introduction

When the legislature enacts a bill and certain subsequent procedures are followed, the bill becomes law. The legislature is not, however, the only source of laws. Rules and orders have the force of law; laws also emanate from the executive branch of government and from regulatory agencies such as the Food and Drug Administration and the Federal Reserve Board.

In addition, the countries with legal systems that originated in England, including the United States, have laws that are made by *judges*. These laws consist of decisions by appeals courts that lower courts are required to follow.[2] Most of us are far more familiar with statute than with judge-made or "common" law; for example, most of us are far more likely to know the names of our legislators than those of our state or federal judges. And yet the body of judge-made law regulates many of our actions. Many of the rules of contractual relationships, of property law, and of tort liability originated with judges.

---

in modern times, the Code Napoleon of 1804. But many of the common law countries also have codes. For example, in the United States every state has adopted the Uniform Commercial Code (a codification of the rules of commercial transactions), and it is said that California has more codes than any civil law nation. Moreover, several of the civil law countries (for example, South Africa) do not have a code. These brief examples indicate that the distinction between common law and civil law traditions lies more in the matter of the source of the law than in the presence or absence of a statutory code.

On these and other matters concerning the operation of the civil law and its differences from the common law, *see* John H. Merryman, THE CIVIL LAW TRADITION: AN INTRODUCTION TO THE LEGAL SYSTEMS OF WESTERN EUROPE AND LATIN AMERICA (2d ed. 1985).

[2]We will explain the difference between an appeals court and a lower court in just a moment.

Besides *making* law, judges also serve other important functions. They interpret and decide the constitutionality of statutes, orders, regulations, and other rules made by the other branches of government. In practice there is a fine line between *interpreting* law and *making* it. Moreover, convincing a judge to decide a case in favor of one's client, which is the task of lawyers, is essentially the same whether the issue is interpreting a statute or making law.

This common law system of judge-made law surprises many observers. After all, judges are frequently appointed, not elected, officials; not only are *all* federal judges appointed but they also serve for life and are removable only by death, resignation, or impeachment. Allowing appointed officials to make laws may seem undemocratic. Shouldn't our laws be made only by those elected by a majority of the voters? For just that reason many countries outside the English common law tradition have severely circumscribed the power of judges and prevented them from creating a body of rules similar to the common law. But England and her former colonies have taken another course by allowing judges to make law. In the first part of this chapter we will show how such a system of judge-made law works and how it achieves the ends that are asked of any legal system—uniformity, stability, and flexibility. In a subsequent chapter we will consider how a common law system can be defended and justified, but for now we concentrate upon what it is, rather than what is good about it.

Any system of law must strike a balance between stability, uniformity, and flexibility. The reasons for desiring uniformity and stability in the law over time and space are obvious. A widely-held principle of justice is that the law should be the same for everyone. To a large extent, that means that the law should reach the same conclusion in similar cases, regardless of the particular persons who are involved. If the law were otherwise, there would not be what most of us would call justice; law would instead be capricious, with cases being decided differently not because the facts were different but because the people were different. Furthermore, if the law is not uniform and if it is subject to sharp changes, then people cannot easily make rational plans for the future. They would spend inordinate amounts of time and money planning for the contingencies that different legal rules would create. The cost savings from having a uniform, dependable law are also substantial. But at the same time that it is uniform and stable, a legal system must be flexible. This flexibility must be available in two dimensions. First, at any given point of time, different jurisdictions within the same legal system may wish to preserve different legal rules that take account of distinctive characteristics in that jurisdiction. For example, there is no uniform law in the United States for dealing with harms arising from product-related accidents. Some states rely on a rule of negligence with contributory negligence; others, on comparative negligence; still others, on strict liability. Additionally, as we will see in Chapter 5, the rules for assigning rights to water are different in the Eastern and Western United States, probably due to the vastly different endowments of water in those areas. Second, a legal system must also be flexible enough over time to accommodate new circumstances and changing societal tastes. For example, legal rules that are appropriate for a rural, largely agricultural society may be inappropriate for an urban, highly industrialized society.

How does the common law system of judge-made law achieve uniformity and stability? The principal method by which uniformity and stability are achieved in the common law is through the use of *precedent* or, as it is sometimes called, *stare decisis* (Latin meaning "to stand by things decided"). Precedent is the principle that, in deciding a new case, the judge should reach the same conclusion, called a "holding," as he or other judges reached in previous cases if the facts in the new case are not sufficiently different from the facts of the previously-decided cases. This means that in most litigation the attorneys for the plaintiff and defendant do their best either to demonstrate that the facts of their dispute are just like those in a previous case whose result they applaud; alternatively, if the result of the previous cases is not what they want, the attorneys strive to distinguish the present case from past cases in order to show that they are different. Another implication of the definition of precedent is that in order for judge-made law to change, new facts that distinguish a case must be presented.

To achieve uniformity and stability in judge-made law through following precedent, the courts in the common-law countries are organized hierarchically. Those who seek the assistance of the common law courts in resolving their dispute enter the system through the trial courts of general jurisdiction. Either disputant may appeal the decision of these courts to the next tier of courts, the intermediate appellate courts. And if they are still not satisfied, they may appeal to the court of last resort. Each tier of courts in this hierarchy evaluates the adjudication of the courts below to make certain that they have conformed with precedent. We will describe the institutional details of this hierarchy below.

> **Question 3.1:** There are many different forms of law: statutes, constitutions, administrative agency regulations, and the holdings of the courts are a few. Answer the following questions about these examples of the different forms of the law:
> a. What governmental body issues each of these forms of law?
> b. By what processes are these forms of law legitimately changed?
> c. What processes and governmental bodies guarantee uniformity and stability for each of these forms of law?
> d. What processes and governmental bodies guarantee uniformity *among* the forms of law? For example, what happens if a statute and the constitution are in conflict? If a statute and a holding are in conflict?

B. How the Common Law Establishes and Changes Rules: A Case Study

Let us turn now to several actual cases to see how the common law works and how it evolves to take account of new circumstances.

The first case we will examine is *Butterfield v. Forrester*, which is cited as "11 East 60 (K. B., 1809)." Because we will be using this system of legal citation throughout this book, let's take a moment to understand it. The first number, 11, refers to the volume number in which the court's opinion is to be found. The second entry is "East," which is the title of the series of books, called "court reporters," in which the opinion is collected. The number "60" tells the reader on which page the opinion begins in volume 11 of East's reports. The parenthetical entry tells you the court in which the case was heard (in this case it is one of the English courts called the King's Bench) and the year in which the opinion was handed down, 1809. You will discover that United States cases are cited in exactly the same fashion, and that law review and other scholarly articles have a similar citation system.

The opinion in *Butterfield v. Forrester* (reproduced below) provided the basis for the doctrine of contributory negligence. After the text of the opinion we discuss the major points of the case and the structure of the opinion.

Butterfield v. Forrester, 11 East 60 (K.B., 1809)[3]

> This was an action on the case for obstructing a highway, by means of which obstruction the plaintiff [Butterfield], who was riding along the road, was thrown down with his horse, and injured, etc. At the trial before BAY-LEY, J.[4] at Derby, it appeared that the defendant [Forrester], for the purpose of making some repairs to his house, which was close by the roadside at one end of the town, had put up a pole across part of the road, a free passage being left by another branch or street in the same direction. That the plaintiff left a public house [a tavern] not far distant from the place in question at 8 o'clock in the evening in August, when they were just beginning to light candles, but while there was light enough left to discern the obstruction at one hundred yards distance; and the witness who proved this, said that if the plaintiff had not been riding very hard he might have observed and avoided it; the plaintiff, however, who was riding violently, did not observe it, but rode against it, and fell with his horse and was much hurt in consequence of the accident; and there was no evidence of his being intoxicated at the time. On this evidence, BAY-LEY, J., directed the jury, that if a person riding with reasonable and ordinary care could have seen and avoided the obstruction; and if they were satisfied that the plaintiff was riding along the street extremely hard, and without ordinary care, they should find a verdict for the defendant, which they accordingly did.
>
> [The plaintiff, having lost his case, then moved for a new trial. The opinion of the judge in this appeal follows.]
>
> LORD ELLENBOROUGH, C.J. A party is not to cast himself upon an obstruction which had been made by the fault of another, and avail himself of it, if he does not himself use common and ordinary caution to be in the right. In case of persons riding upon what is considered to be the wrong side of the road, that would not authorize another purposely to ride

---

[3]The cases we have selected and our discussion of them owe a great debt to the stimulating lectures given by Professor Bob Summers to the Fifth Legal Institute for Economists.

[4]"J." means judge and by tradition opinions are headed by the last name of the justice who wrote the majority opinion, followed by "J." or, as below, "C.J." for chief judge or chief justice.

up against them. One person being in fault will not dispense with another's using ordinary care for himself. Two things must concur to support this action: an obstruction in the road by the fault of the defendant, and no want of ordinary care to avoid it on the part of the plaintiff.

[A new trial was denied. Lord Ellenborough and his colleagues felt that the lower court's decision not to allow Butterfield to recover from Forrester for his injuries was correct.] ▬

The heading states that the parties to the dispute are named Butterfield and Forrester. Because both of these people are private citizens, this is a private, or civil, dispute. If one party had been accused of a crime, then it would have been a public dispute, in which the government, as a representative of all of society, would have been the plaintiff.

One party to the dispute, the plaintiff (Butterfield) alleges that he was wrongfully harmed by the other party, the defendant (Forrester). Thus, the plaintiff has come to a court of law to seek judicial relief, specifically, the payment of money to compensate him for the harm he has suffered. In *Butterfield* the plaintiff says that it was wrong for the defendant to leave the obstruction in the road where someone might stumble across it and be harmed, as Butterfield in fact did. The defendant typically denies having done wrong and says that he should not be held responsible for the plaintiff's harm. Forrester does not deny that he left the obstruction sticking slightly into the roadway, but he says that this act should not entitle the plaintiff to recover from him because Butterfield's injury was not so much due to Forrester's obstruction as it was to Butterfield's having been intoxicated and riding dangerously.

Most private disputes have this form—one party seeks money damages from the other. However, the vast majority of such disputes never go to trial: only 5–10% of all disputes go to trial in contemporary America, the remaining 90–95% being settled out of court before a trial even begins. One reason such disputes do not go to trial is that litigation is costly, so much so that both parties frequently prefer a less expensive out-of-court settlement. Another reason is that the law is clear enough in most disputes that the dispute can be settled against this background.

There is another point about *Butterfield v. Forrester* that merits notice. Not only was there a trial, but the loser in the trial (Who was he: the defendant Forrester, or the plaintiff Butterfield?) appealed the case to a higher court, where a second tribunal considered the matter. The text of the case that you read is the appellate opinion. The organization of this opinion is so typical that it is worth drawing your attention to it.

The opinion begins with a description of the original trial, which occurred before Judge Bayley in the court held in the town of Derby. The text first states the facts as they were determined at that trial. In general, the first trial of a dispute determines the facts and these facts are then taken as given at each stage of the appeals process. In principle, an appeals court never inquires further into the facts that were established by the trial court but instead confines itself to an interpretation of the law pertaining to those facts.[5]

A case must be decided by combining the facts with the law. In cases tried to a jury (that is, tried before a jury), there is a simple division of labor: the judge decides the law and the jury decides the facts on the basis of evidence developed in the trial.[6] There is usually no appealing the jury's finding of facts; appeals must be based upon the judge's interpretation of the law. There are two aspects to deciding the law that often result in appeals. First, the judge decides what evidence the law allows the jury to hear and to take into account, and it is frequently contended by the losing party that the judge improperly or prejudicially excluded (or included) some evidence from (for) the jury's consideration. Second, after the presentation of the case by both parties, the judge explains to the jury the law that they must use in deciding the case. This explanation takes the form of an instruction by the judge to the jury. In *Butterfield v. Forrester*, the trial judge

> *... directed the jury, that if a person riding with reasonable and ordinary care could have seen and avoided the obstruction; and if they were satisfied that the plaintiff was riding along the street extremely hard, and without ordinary care, they should find a verdict for the defendant, which they accordingly did.*

If the judge had explained the law differently, the verdict might have gone the other way. Knowing this, the plaintiff in *Butterfield v. Forrester*, who lost at the trial level, appealed the case. The plaintiff wanted the appeals court to rule that the jury instruction was improper in the sense that the judge incorrectly specified the law to the jury. As we will see, the plaintiff here was, to a degree, correct in claiming that the judge's instruction was not in keeping with precedent.

If the appeals court had ruled that the jury instruction was improper, several things could have happened: the appellate court could have ordered a new trial in which the trial judge used the jury instruction provided by the appeals court; or the court could have reversed the verdict and simply declared the plaintiff the winner, on the grounds that there is no other deci-

---

[5]This is true only generally. An appeals court may occasionally hear fresh evidence in both criminal and civil cases in order to determine whether a new trial should be ordered. However, if the appellate court does determine on the basis of this new evidence that a new trial is warranted, that new trial will be conducted by a lower court, not by an appeals court. The possibility of the appellate court's ordering a new trial does not violate the restriction in criminal law against double jeopardy or the civil law doctrine of *res judicata* (Latin for "the thing has been adjudicated" to indicate that a particular dispute, once adjudicated, cannot be re-litigated).

[6]If both parties agree, a civil dispute may be tried as a "bench trial" in which there is no jury. Instead, in a bench trial the judge serves as both the determiner of the facts and the law. In England and many other countries *all* civil disputes are tried as bench trials. (A defendant has a right to be tried by a jury of his peers only in some criminal cases; that right can be waived by the defendant, in some circumstances, in favor of a bench trial.)

sion the jury could have reached, if they had been instructed properly. However, the appeals court decided not to overturn the decision of the trial court nor to remand the case back to the lower court for a new trial. Instead, the appeals court affirmed the lower court ruling and stated the law more precisely in what is called the "holding" of the case. (The holding is frequently easy to find because it is what follows the words "We hold that . . . .")

A holding is important because lower courts are bound to follow it. In principle, a trial court can never decide matters of law, so a trial court cannot go against the holding of a higher court. Eventually, appeals courts may modify the holding; indeed, at some point in the distant future it may be discarded and replaced with an entirely different holding, but courts generally make such changes very gradually, if at all.[7]

Deciding exactly what Lord Ellenborough held in *Butterfield v. Forrester* is essential to predicting how courts will decide similar cases, but it is not exactly clear what he held. The holding of a judge can always be construed broadly or narrowly, so there is always scope for the law to evolve and change by judicial decisionmaking.

Under a narrow interpretation, the judge held that riders of horses cannot recover money damages for their injuries from a negligent defendant if they do not ride with ordinary care and this lack of care contributes to the accident. This narrow interpretation says that the rule applies only to accidents like this one. Indeed, Lord Ellenborough's example of a horseman riding on the wrong side of the road not being allowed to collect for injuries sustained when he runs into another horseman riding on the correct side would seem to support this narrow interpretation.

But a much broader interpretation of the court's holding is possible, and did, in fact, come to be the common interpretation. Under a broad interpretation of the holding, Lord Ellenborough held that *no* plaintiff can recover when his own negligence contributes to his injury (even if the defendant was negligent). This was new law. Although the issue had arisen before 1809, it had never been decided in the way that Lord Ellenborough and his colleagues here held. This is apparently the substance of the plaintiff's appeal: the judge in the trial court did not apply the prevailing rule of law. The defendant presumably has no objection to the trial court's view of prevailing law. And even if the plaintiff's interpretation is correct, the defendant presumably favors revising the law in the way that the trial court has changed it. For various reasons, some of them reproduced by Lord Ellenborough in his opinion, the defendant argues that there are circumstances in which, even if the defendant was negligent, the plaintiff's negligence was such that he, not the defendant, should bear the burden of paying for his injuries. After all,

---

[7]The technical name for judicial conservatism is, as we have seen, *stare decisis*. For an economic interpretation *see* Martin Shapiro, *Toward a Theory of Stare Decisis*, 1 J. LEGAL STUD. 125 (1972).

the facts give us reason to believe that Butterfield was tipsy, if not drunk. He had just left a pub, and a witness said that the horseman was riding "violently," which presumably means very fast and perhaps recklessly. If we add the further fact that it was dusk (". . . candles were just being lit . . ."), then it does not seem unreasonable to excuse Forrester from having to pay for Butterfield's injuries. This new law came to be summarized in the expression: "contributory negligence is a complete bar to recovery."

Notice that Lord Ellenborough did not refer to any Act of Parliament in deciding this case. In Britain and America, judges have fairly broad scope to shape law, which is why the study of holdings by appeals courts is the core of legal education.

Our discussion of *Butterfield v. Forrester* has demonstrated the manner in which the common law creates new law. But let us pursue this topic further by seeing what happened to the rule that contributory negligence is a complete bar to recovery in the years after 1809. The next step in this development is the seminal case of *Davies v. Mann*.

Davies v. Mann, 10 M. & W. 545 (Ex., 1842)

At the trial, before ERSKINE, J., it appeared that the plaintiff, having fettered the fore-feet of an ass belonging to him, turned it into a public highway, and at the same time in question the ass was grazing on the off side of a road about eight yards wide, when the defendant's wagon, with a team of three horses, coming down a slight descent, at what the witness termed a smartish pace, ran against the ass, knocked it down, and the wheels passing over it, it died soon after . . . The learned judge told the jury, that . . . if they thought that the accident might have been avoided by the exercise of ordinary care on the part of the driver, to find for the plaintiff. The jury found their verdict for the plaintiff . . .

Godson now moved for a new trial, on the ground of misdirection.[8] The act of the plaintiff in turning the donkey into the public highway was an illegal one, and, as the injury arose principally from that act, the plaintiff was not entitled to compensation for that injury which, but for his own unlawful act would never have occurred. . . . The principle of law, as deducible from the cases is, that where an accident is the result of faults on both sides, neither party can maintain an action. Thus, in *Butterfield v. Forrester*, 11 East 60, it was held that one who is injured by an obstruction on a highway, against which he fell, cannot maintain an action, if it appear that he was riding with great violence and want of ordinary care, without which he might have seen and avoided the obstruction. . . .

---

[8]That is, the defendant's lawyer appealed the judgment on the grounds that the judge in the trial court had incorrectly instructed the jury on the law to be applied to the facts in this case.

LORD ABINGER, C.B.[9] . . . [A]s the defendant might, by proper care, have avoided injuring the animal, and did not, he is liable for the consequences of his negligence, though the animal may have been improperly there.

PARKE, B . . . [T]he negligence which is to preclude a plaintiff from recovering in an action of this nature, must be such as that he could, by ordinary care, have avoided the consequences of the defendant's negligence. . . . [A]lthough the ass may have been wrongfully there, still the defendant was bound to go along the road at such a pace as would be likely to prevent mischief. Were this not so, a man might justify the driving over goods left on a public highway, or even over a man lying asleep there, or the purposely running against a carriage going on the wrong side of the road. . . .

[New trial denied.]

The facts of this case, as well as the commentary in the appellate court's opinion, make it clear that the situation here was similar to that in the case of *Butterfield v. Forrester*. A plaintiff has suffered a loss—his donkey was killed—allegedly because of the wrongful act of the defendant, who was here driving a wagon too quickly for the conditions on the road. However, the plaintiff himself was at fault for having left his donkey unattended, although fettered, beside a public road. Strictly following the rule in *Butterfield v. Forrester* would seem to preclude the plaintiff's recovering. The plaintiff's fault or negligence contributed to his losses and thus should bar his recovery. That is precisely what Mann's lawyer argued in appealing the judgment for the plaintiff in the lower court.

---

[9]The traditional English court system that took shape in the late 12th century and prevailed until the late 19th century consisted of three common law courts and a court of equity. The first of the common law courts was the Court of Common Pleas. The members of that court were called "justices" and were presided over by the Chief Justice. The court originally concentrated on civil disputes concerning land but came to consider a wide range of civil disputes. The Court of King's Bench, the second common law court, was originally a criminal court but in time became a court of review over the civil issues from the Court of Common Pleas. The third common law court was the Court of Exchequer of Pleas or, simply, the Court of Exchequer. The Exchequer was the king's treasury, and this court originally heard disputes arising from tax liability and other matters concerning the king's revenue. By the late 16th century the Court of Exchequer had extended its jurisdiction to cover nearly all civil disputes. Members of this court, in which the appeal in *Davies v. Mann* was heard, were called "Baron," abbreviated "B." and were presided over by the Chief Baron, abbreviated "C.B." The equity court was the Court of Chancery, so called because it was presided over by the Chancellor, the most important member of the king's Council. By the late 15th century Chancery was established as a separate court that dispensed a more flexible justice, especially in regard to remedies, than did the common law courts. (We will distinguish between equitable and legal (or common law) remedies throughout this book.) In the Judicature Act of 1873 and the Supreme Court of Judicature (Consolidation) Act of 1925 the British Parliament replaced all of these courts with a greatly simplified structure that drew no distinction between common law and equity. Today Britain has a Court of Appeals with separate civil and criminal divisions.

But at the trial the jury believed that the facts in *Davies v. Mann* were distinguishable from those in earlier cases in which a contributorily negligent plaintiff was not allowed to recover from a negligent defendant. Discerning precisely what the distinguishing characteristic is in this case is difficult, but it is crucial to your understanding of the manner in which the common law changes. There appear to be two reasons for excusing the plaintiff's negligence in Lord Abinger's and Baron Parke's opinions. First, there is the element of time. Although the plaintiff was negligent in leaving his donkey unattended on the public highway, the defendant's negligence came afterward. And, very importantly, if the defendant had not been driving recklessly, he would have had time to avoid the donkey by stopping or swerving. The fact that the defendant's negligence came afterward and was controlling is crucial. This doctrine has come to be known as "the last clear chance" rule: if both parties to an accident are negligent, the party that had the last clear chance to avoid the accident and did not take that chance will be held responsible for the losses arising from the accident.

The second argument that the justices give for excusing the plaintiff's negligence is that to allow the defendant to escape the consequences of his negligence in cases like this will cause future behavior to be altered in an inefficient manner. Again, Baron Parke puts the point nicely, "[A]lthough the ass may have been wrongfully there, still the defendant was bound to go along the road at such a pace as would be likely to prevent mischief. Were this not so, a man might justify the driving over goods left on a public highway, or even over a man lying asleep there, or the purposely running against a carriage going on the wrong side of the road." This interpretation of the law is quite congenial to an economist; it suggests that people know what the rules of law are and behave in accord with them. It follows then that if the rules create incentives for inefficient behavior, people will behave inefficiently.

The notable thing for our purposes about *Davies v. Mann* is that the law handed down in *Butterfield v. Forrester* has been changed and that we have seen the process by which that judge-made law was altered. The blanket rule from the earlier case that contributory negligence is a complete bar to recovery has been amended through the process of introducing a new situation unthought of in the earlier case. We may say that after *Davies v. Mann* the legal rule has become this: contributory negligence is a complete bar to recovery unless the defendant had the last clear chance to avoid the accident and did not take that chance.[10] This case was not the end of the process of

---

[10]In order for you to be sure that you understand the difference between *Butterfield v. Forrester* and *Davies v. Mann*, imagine that Davies was the case first decided and that the rule of law developed there was the one we have laid out in the text. Then suppose that *Butterfield* came up for decision with the relevant law being that developed in *Davies*. Would *Butterfield* still be decided in favor of the defendant?

the development of this legal rule of contributory negligence; the law has been revised several times subsequently.[11]

Notice how flexible the principles of common law are. An argument that arose originally in the context of an accident involving a horse and rider was applied to nearly all accidents, not just those involving transportation modes. Those principles apply to most accidents in which there is a negligent plaintiff seeking relief from a negligent defendant.

II. THE FEDERAL AND THE STATE COURT SYSTEMS

Now that we have explained how the common law system works, we will describe the basic institutional structure of the court systems in this country that apply the common law. The items upon which we will focus are the following: the hierarchical structure of the courts, the subject matter jurisdiction of the different courts, and how judges in the various systems are selected and the length of time for which they serve.

In the United States, whether at the state or the federal level, the court systems are organized in three tiers. At the lowest level are the trial courts of general jurisdiction. These are the "entry level" courts where a wide array of both civil and criminal disputes are first heard. The trial courts of general jurisdiction are "courts of record"; that is, the proceedings there are written down and officially saved by the government. In the state systems these courts are usually organized along county lines. For example, in the State of Illinois there are 103 counties, and each has a Circuit Court, which serves as the trial court of general jurisdiction within the county. These trial courts have different names in different states: in California they are called Superior Courts; in New York State, Supreme Courts. The nearly universal practice is for each civil and criminal case to be tried to a single judge and possibly to a jury.

---

[11]For example in *British Columbia Electric Railway Company v. Loach*, 1 Appeal Cases 719 (Privy Council, 1915 [1916]), the facts in a new situation caused the rule of last clear chance from *Davies v. Mann* to be amended. Two men were seriously hurt when their wagon was struck by a train at a crossing. The train's engineer had seen the men on the crossing and had applied his brakes. If the brakes had been in working order, the train would have stopped short of the wagon, causing no harm. However, the brakes had not been properly maintained. The railway company, as the original defendant, contended that they did not have the last clear chance because of the defective brakes. The court held for the plaintiffs. How do you think the court amended the last clear chance rule to take account of this new situation?

More recently, dissatisfaction with contributory negligence's complete bar has been one of the important reasons that most states and most European countries have adopted *comparative* negligence. Under that standard a plaintiff's negligence is a partial but not a complete bar to recovery. We will discuss the economics of contributory and comparative negligence in Chapters 8 and 9.

In the federal system the entire country is divided into 93 judicial districts, each of which contains a federal district court, which is the trial court of general jurisdiction for the federal judiciary. Every state in the Union has at least one federal district court, and about half have only one. The District of Columbia has its own district court. The larger states, where larger numbers of disputes involving federal questions arise, have up to four district courts, usually organized along geographical divisions of the state. New York has four districts: the Southern, the Northern, the Eastern, and the Western. Illinois has three federal districts: the Northern, the Eastern, and the Southern. The number of federal judicial districts has remained fixed at 93 for a long time. As the volume of federal litigation has grown, Congress has responded not by creating more districts but by appointing more judges within each district. One of the busiest districts is the Southern District of New York, which contains most of New York City, and there are twenty-five judges on that district's bench. Another busy district, the Northern District of Illinois, has twelve. Wisconsin's Eastern District (Milwaukee) has three, while the Western District (Madison) has only one. The usual procedure in the federal districts is for a single judge to hear each case, but there are instances where a three-judge panel hears a case.

Above the trial courts in the state and federal systems are appellate courts or courts of appeal. In most state court systems, there is only one appellate court, beyond which there is no further appeal. But about one-third of the states and all of the federal districts have intermediate appellate courts that stand between the trial courts of general jurisdiction and the highest court or court of last resort. For example, in Illinois there are twenty intermediate appellate courts. Where these courts exist, parties from the trial court may appeal that lower decision "as of right." That means that, so long as they are willing to pay the costs involved, parties may *always* seek appellate review. Appeal is also a right in the federal judiciary.[12] However, in both the state and the federal judiciary the highest appellate court has a discretionary right to review. That is, the Supreme Court of Illinois, the Supreme Court of the United States, and all other courts of last resort may generally select which cases they will review.[13]

The intermediate courts of appeal in the federal judiciary are called "Courts of Appeal for the _____ Circuit." There are now twelve of these circuits, as Figure 3.1 indicates. Eleven of these Courts of Appeal are numbered; for example, the First Circuit is in New England; the Seventh Circuit covers Indiana, Illinois, and Wisconsin; and the Ninth Circuit covers the

---

[12]The Federal Courts of Appeal may also take appeals from administrative adjudications. The Court of Appeals for the District of Columbia Circuit receives much of its docket from this source because the federal administrative agencies are located in the District.

[13]This statement is only generally true. The United States Supreme Court and the highest courts in the states control most but not all of their docket. For example, some cases—e.g., disputes between two states—come to the United States Supreme Court directly and without the discretion of the justices. And in many states the highest court is obligated to review death sentences.

West Coast, some of the Mountain states, and Alaska and Hawaii. The District of Columbia constitutes its own circuit as well as being its own district court. All the other circuits include several states. An unsuccessful litigant from the federal district court can take an appeal, as a matter of right, to the Court of Appeals. Those courts usually sit in a panel of three judges, sometimes including in that panel a district court judge or a circuit judge from another circuit. Sometimes, for a particularly significant case, all of the circuit judges will sit together to decide the case. In that case the court is said to be sitting *en banc* or "in bank." Where more than one judge hears a case, the matter is decided by majority vote.

In the federal judiciary the highest court is the Supreme Court of the United States. That court has nine members, consisting of the Chief Justice of the United States and eight Associate Justices. All of the justices, rather than a panel, take part in the deliberations on each case. The Court begins its work on the first Monday in October and concludes its term some time in June. The workload of the Supreme Court has increased significantly over the last quarter of a century. Typically, the justices decide less than 10% of the cases submitted to them for review. There is lively dispute about whether this figure is too large or too small. Some of the justices have urged Congress to establish a National Court of Appeals that would handle a certain set of appeals arising from the twelve circuits and thereby free up the Supreme Court to pursue a larger caseload than it can currently manage.

Finally, there are rules that specify what disputes the state and federal court systems may hear. In the state courts jurisdiction is limited to litigation involving state statutes or civil actions between residents of that state or to cases arising under federal law when Congress has not given exclusive

Figure 3.1   United States Courts of Appeal and United States District Courts

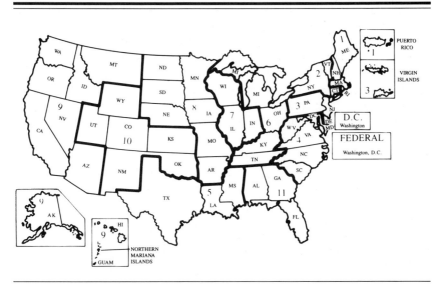

jurisdiction to the federal courts. For the federal courts Congress, through the powers assigned it in the Constitution, defines the jurisdiction. For the federal district courts that jurisdiction is limited to three areas:

1. Federal questions, that is, those matters involving monetary amounts in excess of $10,000 and arising under the United States' Constitution or federal laws or treaties.
2. Cases to which the United States is a party. Typically, these are criminal cases under federal statute law.
3. Diversity cases—any civil dispute, involving more than $10,000, between citizens of different states. In the late 18th century, Congress allowed these disputes to be removed from state to federal courts because it felt that state loyalties were so strong that the citizen of another state might lose in a state court, regardless of the merits of his case, simply because he was a "foreigner."

The Federal District Courts generally apply the law of the state in which they sit. There is a good reason to doubt that diversity of citizenship is any longer a compelling reason for the federal courts to assume jurisdiction. Indeed, former Chief Justice Burger has recently urged Congress to ease the caseload of the federal judiciary by removing the diversity jurisdiction.

As to the selection and tenure of judges, there are two broad groupings. For the federal bench the rule is appointment by the President with the advice and consent of the Senate for life tenure. For state judges in a majority of states the rule is election to the bench and limited tenure. For the remainder of the states, the state judiciary is appointed for varying periods of tenure.

The American Bar Association and the American Judicature Society have proposed and supported a compromise system for selecting state judges. This compromise has characteristics of the federal system of appointment for life and of the state system of election. The plan, called the "Missouri Plan," works as follows: initially judges are appointed for a fixed term by the governor from a list of names submitted to him by a commission with representatives from the bar, the judiciary, and the public; later, the incumbent judge must run for election after the expiration of his term but on his own record, that is, not against a rival; if he is not retained, then a new appointment is made from a new list of names, and the process begins anew.

CONCLUSION

This chapter has provided a brief introduction to the mechanisms and institutions of the common law system of judge-made law. As you can no doubt imagine, this survey has scratched the surface of a remarkably rich and interesting body of learning. Despite our simplifications, the chapter has introduced most of the concepts that you will need to understand the legal aspects of the issues raised in the remainder of this book.

Having reviewed microeconomic theory in Chapter 2 and having reviewed the common law system and its institutions in this chapter, we are now equipped to apply economic analysis to the law. In the following chapter we begin that study by discussing the economics of property.

SUGGESTED READINGS

Abraham, Henry J., THE JUDICIAL PROCESS (5th ed. 1986).

American Bar Association, *Law and the Courts in the News,* ABA Publications (1960).

Berman, Harold H., and William R. Greiner, THE NATURE AND FUNCTIONS OF LAW (4th ed. 1980).

Franklin, Marc A., THE BIOGRAPHY OF A LEGAL DISPUTE: AN INTRODUCTION TO AMERICAN CIVIL PROCEDURE (1968).

Fuller, Lon L., *The Forms and Limits of Adjudication,* 92 HARV. L. REV. 353 (1978).

Levi, Edward H., AN INTRODUCTION TO LEGAL REASONING (1949).

Mermin, Samuel, LAW AND THE LEGAL SYSTEM (1973).

Mishkin and Morris, ON LAW IN COURTS: AN INTRODUCTION TO JUDICIAL DEVELOPMENT OF CASE AND STATUTE LAW (1965).

Murphy, Walter F., ELEMENTS OF JUDICIAL STRATEGY (1964).

Rombauer, Marjorie D., LEGAL PROBLEM SOLVING: ANALYSIS, RESEARCH, AND WRITING (1978).

Ulmer, Sidney, ed., COURTS, LAW, AND JUDICIAL PROCESS (1981).

CHAPTER 4

An Economic Theory of Property

This morning in a remote meadow in Wyoming, a deer was born. To whom does that fawn belong?
—Professor John Cribbet[1]

There is no concept more central to the study of law than that of property. And yet, for an economist first approaching the great body of legal scholarship on that subject, there is little that is readily familiar. Here are some hypothetical examples of the sorts of questions with which property law deals:

Example 1: Orbitcom Inc. spent $125 million designing, launching, and maintaining a satellite for the transmission of business data between Europe and the United States. The satellite is positioned in a geosynchronous orbit 25 miles above the Atlantic Ocean. Recently a natural resource-monitoring satellite belonging to the Windsong Corporation has strayed so close to Orbitcom's satellite that the company's transmissions between Europe and the United States have become unreliable. As a result, Orbitcom has lost customers and has sued Windsong for trespassing upon Orbitcom's right to its geosynchronous satellite orbit.

Example 2: Foster inspects a house under construction in a new subdivision on the north side of town and decides to buy it. The day after she moves in, the wind shifts and begins to blow from the north. She smells a powerful stench. Upon inquiring, she learns that a large cattle feedlot is located north of the subdivision, just over the ridge, and, to make matters worse, the owner of this old business plans to expand it. Foster joins other property owners in a suit to shut down the feedlot.

---

[1]This remarkable question is how Professor Cribbet, one of the leading scholars of property law, has frequently opened his first lecture on property to first-year law students at the University of Illinois College of Law.

Example 3: Bloggs inherits the remnant of a farm from his father, most of which has already been sold for a housing development. The remaining acreage, which his father called "the swamp," is currently used for fishing and duck hunting, but Bloggs decides to drain and develop it as a residential area. However, scientists at the local community college have determined that Bloggs' property is part of the wetlands that nourish local streams, including the fish in the town's river. The town council, hearing of Bloggs' plans, passes an ordinance forbidding the draining of wetlands. Bloggs sues for the right to develop his property, or, failing that, he asks the court to compel the town to buy the property from him at the price that would prevail if development were allowed.

Example 4: A county ordinance requires houses to be set back five feet from the property line. Joe Potatoes buys some heavily wooded land in an undeveloped area and builds a house on it. Ten years later Fred Parsley, who owns the adjoining lot, has his land surveyed and discovers that Potatoes' house extends two feet over the property line onto Parsley's property. Potatoes offers to compensate Parsley for the trespass, but Parsley rejects the offer and sues to have Potatoes relocate the house in conformity with the ordinance.

The first example concerns the question, "Can a satellite orbit be privately owned?" Orbitcom apparently asserts such a claim of ownership, and Windsong denies it. Perhaps Windsong will defend by denying that orbits can be privately owned and arguing instead that space, like the high seas, is an unowned resource that is open to all on the same terms. This dispute raises the general question, "What things can be privately owned?" Must they be tangible like land, or may they also be intangible like a satellite orbit, a musical tune, or the design for a new line of clothes? Economics has a lot to say about the consequences of resources' being privately owned, publicly owned, or unowned.

Orbitcom apparently bases its ownership claim on having placed a satellite in the orbit in dispute before anyone else. This claim appeals to a legal principle called the "Rule of First Possession," according to which the first party to use an unowned resource acquires a claim to it. The general issue raised here is, "How does a person acquire ownership of something?" The Rule of First Possession provides one possible answer to this question, at least for previously unowned resources. As we will see, a different answer must be given for goods that are abandoned, mislaid, newly created, stolen, or inherited.

The second example concerns whether the law allows one property owner to create a stench that offends other property owners. The law tries to prevent property owners from interfering with each other, but in this example, as in many other cases, there is a tradeoff between competing activities. Is the cattle feedlot interfering with the homeowner by creating the stench, or is the homeowner interfering with the feedlot by seeking to shut it down? The legal outcome turns in part upon whether the stench constitutes a "nuisance" as defined by law. Economics has a lot to say about this determination.

The third example is a dispute about whether a property owner can develop his land according to his own wishes or whether he must conform to severe restrictions upon development imposed by a local government. The underlying question concerns the extent to which local government can regulate the exercise of property rights. We will show that economics has a lot to say about appropriate and inappropriate regulation.

Notice that Examples 2 and 3 both raise the question, "What may owners legitimately do with their property?" The difference is that Example 2 concerns a dispute between private owners and Example 3 concerns a dispute between a private owner and a government.

In Example 4, one property owner has encroached upon the land of another. The question raised by this example concerns the remedy for trespass. Should the owner be denied a remedy because the trespass has persisted for so long? Alternatively, should the court award compensatory damages to the owner? Or should the court enjoin the trespasser and force him to move his house? As we will see, economics provides a powerful tool for fashioning remedies because it provides means for predicting the effects of the various alternatives.

There are, then, four fundamental questions of property law raised by these examples:

1. What can be privately owned?
2. How are ownership rights established?
3. What may owners legitimately do with their property?
4. How are property rights protected? What are the remedies for their infringement?

In the next two chapters we will be using economics to answer these questions. Traditional legal scholarship on property law is notoriously weak in its use of theory, at least in comparison to contracts and torts.[2] This fact contributes to the feeling of many students that the common law of property is diffuse and unorganized. Through economics it is possible to give the subject more coherence and order. In this chapter we concentrate upon developing fundamental tools for the economic analysis of property: bargaining theory, public goods theory, and the theory of externalities. In the next

---

[2]In contracts and torts there was a classical theory that dominated American law at the beginning of the twentieth century. The introductory chapters on contracts and torts describe these classical theories. There was, however, no classical theory of property of comparable coherence, detail, or stature. Instead there is a long philosophical tradition of analyzing the institution of property at a very abstract level. Some of these philosophical theories of property are described at the end of this chapter.

chapter we apply these tools to a large number of property laws and institutions.

I. THE LEGAL CONCEPT OF PROPERTY

Property is a complicated institution. In order to come to terms with its complexity, we must try to capture its essential aspects. From a legal viewpoint, property is a *bundle of rights*. These rights describe what a person may and may not do with the resources he owns: the extent to which he may possess, use, transform, bequeath, transfer, or exclude others from his property. These rights are not immutable; they may, for example, change from one generation to another. But, at any point in time, they constitute the detailed answer of the law to the four fundamental questions of property law listed above.

The bundle of legal rights constituting ownership has two dimensions that are so important to our later understanding that they are worth expounding briefly. First, the owner is free to exercise his rights over his property, by which we mean that no law forbids or requires him to exercise those rights. In our example at the beginning of the chapter, Parsley can farm his land or leave it fallow, and the law is indifferent as to which he chooses to do. Second, others are forbidden to interfere with the owner's exercise of his rights. Thus, if Parsley decides to farm his land, Potatoes cannot put stones in the way of the plough. This protection is needed against two types of interlopers, private persons and the government. As we will see, one of the strengths of the economic theory of property is the precision of its analysis of when and how others, including the government, should be allowed to interfere with the owner's property rights and of the remedies that should be available for illegal interference.

The legal conception of property is, then, that of a bundle of rights over resources that the owner is free to exercise and whose exercise is protected from interference by others. A right to choose that is protected from interference is often called a "liberty." We may thus define property as the legal institution that, by allocating a bundle of rights over resources to people, gives people liberty over resources. Property creates a zone of privacy in which owners can exercise their will over things without being answerable to others. This general definition of property is compatible with many different theories of what particular rights are to be included in the protected bundle and of how to protect those rights.

The law has tended to look beyond itself to philosophy for these theories of what rights to include in the bundle of property rights. In the appendix to this chapter we discuss some of these philosophical approaches, but our immediate concern is with the economic approach. In order to develop the economic approach to property, we will have to call upon a fundamental tool of economic analysis. Many of you may be familiar with the economic analysis of markets, but probably less of you are familiar with the economic analysis of games. Yet, for studying law, game theory is at least as important as market theory. To develop an economic theory of property, we must first develop the economic theory of bargaining games, which is the subject of the next section.

> **Question 4.1:** We have defined property as a type of liberty. Another type of liberty is religious liberty. In what ways are these two types of liberty similar and in what ways are they different? For example, why is religious liberty distributed more equally than property?

II. BARGAINING THEORY

In this section we develop a simple bargaining model in detail. At first you may not see its relevance to property law, but later you will recognize that it is the very foundation of the economic theory of property.

The elements of bargaining theory can be developed through an example of a familiar exchange: selling a used car.

> **Facts:** Adam, who lives in a small town, has a 1957 Chevy convertible in good repair. The pleasure of owning and driving the car is worth $3,000 to Adam. Blair, who has been coveting the car for years, inherits $5,000 and decides to try to buy the car from Adam. After inspecting the car, Blair decides that the pleasure of owning and driving it is worth $4,000 to her.

According to these facts, an agreement to sell will enable the car to pass from Adam, who values it at $3,000, to Blair, who values it at $4,000. The potential seller values the car less than the potential buyer, so there is scope for a bargain. Assuming that sales are voluntary, Adam will not accept less than $3,000 for the car, and Blair will not pay more than $4,000, so the sale price will have to be somewhere in between. A reasonable sale price would be $3,500, which splits the difference.

The logic of the situation can be clarified by restating the facts in the language of game theory. The kind of game represented by this example is called a "cooperative game" because the parties can both benefit from cooperating with each other. To be specific, they can move a resource (the car) from someone who values it less (Adam) to someone who values it more (Blair). Moving the resource in this case from Adam, who values it at $3,000, to Blair, who values it at $4,000, will create $1,000 in value. The value created by moving the resource to a more valuable use will be available for the parties to share. The share that each receives depends on the price at which the car is sold. If the price is set at $3,500, each will enjoy an equal share of the value created by the exchange, or $500. If the price is set at $3,800, the value will be divided unequally, with Adam enjoying $\frac{4}{5}$ or $800, and Blair enjoying $\frac{1}{5}$ or $200. Or if the price is set at $3,200, Adam will enjoy $200 or $\frac{1}{5}$ of the value created, whereas Blair will enjoy $800 or $\frac{4}{5}$.

An agreement over price, if reached, will be the product of negotiation. In the course of negotiating the parties may assert facts ("The motor is mechanically perfect . . ."), appeal to norms ("$3,700 is an unfair price . . ."), threaten ("I won't take less than $3,500 . . . "), cajole and wheedle ("I would be so grateful if . . ."), and so forth. These are the tools used in the art of bargaining in an attempt to find terms on which the parties can cooperate. The fact that the parties can negotiate is an advantage of bargaining games relative to other games, such as the famous Prisoner's Dilemma,[3] in which the inability of the parties to communicate makes achieving a cooperative surplus difficult or impossible. Even when negotiation is possible, however, there is no guarantee that it will succeed. If the negotiations break down and the parties fail to cooperate, their attempt to shift resources to a more valuable use will fail and they will not create value. The obstacle to creating value is that the parties must agree on how to divide it. Value will be divided between them at a rate determined by the price at which the car is sold. Agreement about the car's price marks successful negotiations, whereas disagreement marks a failure in the bargaining process.

To apply game theory to this example, let us characterize the possible outcomes as a *cooperative* solution and a *noncooperative* solution. The cooperative solution is the one in which Adam and Blair reach agreement over a price and succeed in exchanging the car for money. The noncooperative solution is the one in which they fail to agree upon a price and they fail to exchange the car for money. To analyze the logic of bargaining, we must first consider the consequences of noncooperation. If the parties fail to cooperate, they will each achieve some level of well-being on their own. Adam will keep the car and use it, which is worth $3,000 to him. Blair will keep her money—$5,000—or spend it on something other than the car. For simplicity, assume that the value she places on this use of her money is its face value, specifically, $5,000. Thus, the payoffs to the parties in the non-

---

[3]In this two-person, non-cooperative game two suspects in a crime are taken into custody, put in separate cells, and not allowed to communicate. The authorities offer each prisoner the opportunity to confess to the crime. Suppose that if either prisoner confesses and his partner does not, the confessor will receive half a year in prison and the non-confessor will receive 10 years. If they both confess, they will each receive 5 years in prison. And if neither confesses, they will each receive 1 year in prison. The prisoners will be best off if neither of them confesses. But if either prisoner adopts the strategy of not confessing, he might be left open to a long prison sentence if his partner confesses. In these circumstances, the best strategy is for each prisoner to confess. Thus, each will spend 5 years in prison. Note how different the solution to this game would have been if the participants could have communicated. Presumably, they would have coordinated their strategies so that each would have refused to confess, with the result that each would have spent only 1 year in prison.

cooperative solution, called their *threat values*, are $3,000 for Adam (the value to him of keeping the car) and $5,000 to Blair (the amount of her cash). The total value of the noncooperative solution is $3,000 + $5,000 = $8,000.

In contrast, the *cooperative solution* is for Adam to sell the car to Blair. Through cooperation, Blair will own the car, which is worth $4,000 to her, and in addition the two parties will each end up with a share of Blair's $5,000. (For example, Adam might accept $3,500 in exchange for the convertible. Blair then has the car, worth $4,000 to her, and $1,500 of her $5,000.) Thus, the value of the cooperative solution is $4,000 + $5,000 = $9,000. The *surplus* from cooperation is the difference in value between cooperation and noncooperation: $9,000 − $8,000 = $1,000.

In any agreement, each player must receive at least the threat value or there is no advantage to cooperating. A reasonable solution to the bargaining problem is for each player to receive the *threat value plus an equal share of the cooperative surplus*, specifically $3,500 for Adam and $5,500 for Blair.[4] To accomplish this division, Blair should pay Adam $3,500 for the car. This leaves Adam with $3,500 in cash and no car, and leaves Blair with a car worth $4,000 to her and $1,500 in cash.

> **Question 4.2:** Suppose Adam receives a bid of $3,200 from a third party named Clair. How does the fact of Clair's bid change the threat values, the surplus from cooperation, and the reasonable solution?

We have explained that the process of bargaining can be divided into three steps: establishing the threat values, determining the cooperative surplus, and agreeing upon terms for distributing the surplus from cooperation. These steps will be used in the next section to understand the origins of the institution of property.

III. THE ORIGINS OF THE INSTITUTION OF PROPERTY: A THOUGHT EXPERIMENT

The bargaining model shows how cooperation can create a surplus that benefits everyone. This type of reasoning can be used to perform a thought experiment that is helpful in understanding the origins of property.

Let us imagine a simplified world in which there are people, land, and agricultural and military technology but in which there are no courts and no

---

[4]Economists have long struggled with the fact that self-interested rationality alone does not seem sufficient to determine the distribution of the cooperative surplus. That is why we use the term "reasonable solution," which invokes social norms, rather than "rational solution."

Bargaining in a Civil Dispute

Since trials are costly, both parties can usually gain by settling out of court. That is why so few disputes ever come to trial. Here is a problem in which you must apply bargaining theory to a civil dispute.

Facts: Arthur alleges that Betty borrowed a valuable kettle and broke it, so he sues to recover its value, which is $300. The facts are very confusing. Betty contends that she did not borrow a kettle from Arthur; even if it is proved that she borrowed a kettle from Arthur, she contends it is not broken; even if it is proved that she borrowed a kettle from Arthur and that it is broken, she contends that she did not break it.

Since the facts in the case are so unclear, Arthur and Betty believe that the chances of either side winning in court are an even 50%. Litigation in small claims court will cost each party $50, whereas the transaction costs of settling are nil. So, cooperation in this case is a matter of settling out of court and saving the transaction cost of a trial. Noncooperation in this case means trying the dispute.

QUESTION 4.3:

a. Arthur's threat value is _____.

b. Betty's threat value is _____.

c. If Arthur and Betty cooperate together in settling their disagreement, the net cost of resolving the dispute will be

_____.

d. The surplus from cooperating is _____.

e. A reasonable settlement would be for Betty to pay Arthur

_____.

f. Suppose that instead of both sides' believing that there is an even chance of winning, both sides are optimistic; specifically, Arthur thinks that he will win with probability 2/3, and Betty thinks that she will win with probability 2/3.

    1. Arthur's putative threat value (what he believes he can secure on his own without Betty's cooperation) equals

    _____.

    2. Betty's putative threat value (what she believes she can secure on her own without Arthur's cooperation) equals

    _____.

    3. The putative cooperative surplus equals _____.

    4. Describe the obstacle to settlement in a few words.

government. In this imaginary world people live on land to which they may have a moral claim, but there is no government to vindicate and protect those claims. These ownership claims are self-enforced by individuals, families, or alliances of families to the extent that they are willing and able to defend their property. Why do people in this imaginary world take the time and trouble to defend various pieces of land? The answer is straightforward for economically rational people: the land must have some value to its occupiers that exceeds the cost of defending it. That value can arise from a number of characteristics of the land. Perhaps a family learns by continuous occupation how to use that land and its resources more effectively. Or perhaps continuous occupancy gives the land a special non-pecuniary significance, for example, a religious value, to the families living on it. Or the land might be astride a crucial trade route so that its occupier can exact tribute from those who wish to pass. In any case, we assume that excluding others from the property is worthwhile.

In our imaginary world, the right of exclusion is enforced by the military strength of the occupants, not by appeal to legal institutions. In these circumstances, are resources used efficiently? If people are rational, they allocate their limited resources so that, as we saw in Chapter 2, the marginal cost of defending land is just equal to the marginal benefit. This means that at the margin, the value of the resources used for military ends (the marginal benefit) equals their value when used for productive ends, such as raising crops and livestock (the marginal (opportunity) cost). For example, if the occupants are rational, allocating a little more time to patrolling the perimeter of the property preserves as much additional wealth for the defenders as they would enjoy by allocating a little more time to raising crops. The same statement could be made about allocating land between crops and fortifications, or about beating metal into swords or plowshares.

These facts describe a world in which it makes good sense to be both a warrior and a farmer. Although it is individually rational, is it socially efficient? In Chapter 2 we offered the following definition of inefficient production: the same (or fewer) inputs could be used to produce a greater total output. Our imaginary society is socially inefficient if it could be reorganized so that the same inputs could be used to produce a greater total output. Can some mechanism be found that is less expensive than military strength in securing the ownership claims to land? Such a mechanism would allow some or all of the military resources previously devoted to protecting the land to be given over to expanded or more intensive crop cultivation.

One possible mechanism is the establishment of a system of legally enforceable property rights. Suppose that the costs of operating this system of property rights are less than the sum of all individual costs of private defense. It might be, for example, that a tax payment submitted by each occupier to a government to operate the property rights system would be less than each occupier had been spending on the provision of each individual army. In economic terms it could well be that there are economies of scale to be realized in having one large army in the society to defend against invasion of land rather than many small, privately-owned armies.[5] In other words, there may be natural monopoly on force.

We could imagine the parties bargaining together over the terms for establishing a government to recognize and enforce their property rights. They are motivated by the realization that there are economies of scale in protecting property. By reaching an agreement to have one government backed by one army, everyone can enjoy greater wealth and security. The bargain eventually reached by such negotiations is called the "social contract" by philosophers because it establishes the basic terms for social life.[6] It would be rational for the parties negotiating the social contract to take account of other rights of owners besides the right to exclude. Many of the rights that are currently in the bundle called property could be considered, such as the right to use, sell, bequeath, and transform. Indeed, many rights other than property rights could be a part of the social contract, such as freedom of speech and freedom of religion, but they do not concern us in this chapter.

The same bargaining model used to explain the sale of a second-hand car can be applied to this thought experiment in which a primitive society develops a system of property rights. First, a description is given of what people would do in the absence of civil government, when military strength alone established ownership claims. That situation—called the "state of nature"—corresponds to the threat values of the *noncooperative solution*, which prevails if the parties cannot agree. Second, a description is given of the advantages of creating a government to recognize and enforce property rights. Civil society, in which such a government exists, corresponds to the game's *cooperative solution*, which prevails if the parties can agree. The social surplus, defined as the difference between the total amount spent defending land in the state of nature and the total cost of operating a property rights system in civil society, corresponds to the *cooperative surplus* in the game. Third, an agreement is described for distributing the advantages from cooperation. In the car example, this agreement is merely the price that the buyer offers and the seller accepts. In the thought experiment, this agreement is the social contract that includes the fundamental laws of property.

---

[5]Recall that economies of scale occur when the cost per unit (or average cost) of production declines as the total amount of output increases. A production technology for which the unit costs are falling at every level of production, even very large levels, is called a natural monopoly because a larger producer can sell at a lower price than any smaller producer.

[6]The social contract has usually been thought of as a logical construct, but some theorists have used it to explain history. For example, it has been argued that feudalism in the Middle Ages corresponds roughly to the conditions of our imaginary world. The economic factors that caused this system to be replaced in some parts of Western Europe by a system of private property rights enforced by a central government are discussed in Douglass C. North and Robert Paul Thomas, THE RISE OF THE WESTERN WORLD (1973).

Table 4.1   The State of Nature

	Corn Grown	Corn Gained by Theft	Corn Lost by Theft	Net Corn Consumption
A	50	40	− 10	80
B	150	10	− 40	120
Totals	200	50	− 50	200

To see the parallel more clearly, imagine that our world consists of only two people, A and B. In a state of nature, each one grows some corn, steals corn from the other party, and defends against theft. Each of the parties has different levels of skill at farming, stealing, and defending. Their payoffs in a state of nature are summarized in Table 4.1. Taken together, A and B produce 200 units of corn, but it gets reallocated by theft. Notice that A ultimately enjoys 80 units of corn, and B enjoys 120 units, after taking into account the gains and losses from theft.

Instead of persisting in a state of nature, A and B may decide to enter into a cooperative agreement, recognize each other's property rights, and adopt an enforcement mechanism that puts an end to theft. Let us assume that cooperation will enable them to devote more resources to farming and fewer resources to fighting, so that total production will rise from 200 units to 300 units. 100 units thus constitutes the social or cooperative surplus. In civil society there will be a mechanism for distributing the surplus from cooperation, such as government taxes and subsidies. The parties must decide through bargaining how this is to be done. A reasonable division of that surplus gives each party an equal share. So, in civil society, each party receives half the cooperative surplus plus the individual net consumption in the state of nature, which is each party's threat value. These facts are summarized in Table 4.2.

Question 4.4:

a. Is the cooperative solution fair? Can the resulting inequality in civil society be justified?

b. Suppose that the bargaining process did not allow destructive threats, such as the threat to steal. How might this restriction affect the distribution of the surplus?

Table 4.2   Civil Society

	Threat Value	Share of Surplus	Net Corn Consumption
A	80	50	130
B	120	50	170
Totals	200	100	300

c. What is the difference between the principle, "To each according to his threat value," and this principle, "To each according to his productivity"?

IV. A (NORMATIVE) ECONOMIC THEORY OF PROPERTY

The fact that the same theory of bargaining can be applied to selling a used car or creating a civil society is proof of that theory's generality and power. There are, however, significant differences between bargaining to form a civil society and bargaining to form a business contract. The negotiations between Adam and Blair occur within an established legal framework, whereas negotiations to form a civil society are directed at *creating* a legal framework. To illustrate, if Blair offers $3,500 and Adam balks, Blair can threaten to withdraw from the negotiations, but harsher threats, such as threatening to steal the car, are unlawful. In contrast, if *A*, in our example above, proposes terms for cooperating and *B* rejects them, *A* can threaten to return to the state of nature and resume stealing *B's* corn. So, one of the differences is that the threats in a state of nature, being unconstrained by law, are far worse than in civil society.

Threats are often a symptom of disagreement or that cooperation is on the verge of failing. Disagreements and failure to cooperate are costly and should be minimized. The importance of minimizing the losses from disagreements was especially appreciated by the 17th-century philosopher Thomas Hobbes. Hobbes thought that people would seldom be rational enough to agree upon a division of the cooperative surplus even when there were no serious impediments to bargaining.[7] Their natural cupidity would lead them to quarrel unless a third, stronger party forced them to agree. These considerations suggest our first principle of property law, which can be called the *Normative Hobbes Theorem: Structure the law to minimize the harm caused by failures in private agreements.*[8] According to this principle, the law should be designed to prevent coercive threats and to eliminate the destructiveness of disagreement. (Can you give an example of this principle's application to collective bargaining? Negotiating a bank loan? Losing an election?)

Besides coercive threats, there are many obstacles to cooperative bargaining, whether it is done in a state of nature or in a modern legal framework. And this points up a central purpose of law, especially of property and contract law: *to remove the obstacles to private bargaining.* Why should this

---

[7]Since Hobbes wrote in the 17th century, he did not express himself in quite these terms, but this kind of argument is pervasive in his classic work, LEVIATHAN.

[8]This idea is developed at length in Cooter, *The Cost of Coase*, 11 J. LEGAL STUD. 1 (1982).

be a central purpose of law? One important reason comes from the modern theory of welfare economics that we reviewed in Chapter 2 and from the discussion of game theory in the previous section: successful bargaining generates a cooperative surplus, or, as a fundamental theorem of welfare economics puts it, voluntary exchange is mutually beneficial. Thus, one of the most important things we can do in developing an economic theory of property is to identify the obstacles to private bargaining and to demonstrate how legal rules can contribute to overcoming those obstacles.

The obstacles to successful bargaining can be identified by our model. According to our model, bargaining proceeds by identifying the threat points of the parties, determining the cooperative solution, and finding a reasonable way to divide the surplus from cooperation. Conversely, there are obstacles to cooperation when there is uncertainty about the threat points, when there are high costs of identifying and enforcing the cooperative solution, and when one or both parties act unreasonably about dividing the surplus. Let us discuss these obstacles in turn.

One well-confirmed result in the literature on bargaining is that bargainers are more likely to cooperate when their rights are clear, and less likely to agree when their rights are ambiguous.[9] Put in more formal terms, bargaining games are easier to solve when the threat points are public knowledge. The rights of the parties define their positions or threat points in legal disputes. This consideration helps explain why property law favors criteria for determining ownership that are clear and simple. For example, a system for the public registering of ownership claims to land avoids many disputes and makes settlement easier for those that arise. Similarly, the fact that someone possesses or uses an item of property is easy to confirm. In view of this fact, the law gives weight to possession and use when determining ownership.

Turning to the second obstacle, discovering the cooperative solution may require extensive negotiation and enforcing it may require monitoring and policing. These aspects of bargaining can be costly. Negotiation involves communication, and the costs of communicating depend in large part upon the number of parties to the dispute and their geographical dispersion. When there are a small number of disputants all of whom are near each other, communication costs do not pose a significant obstacle to bargaining. After an agreement is reached, there are costs of enforcing the agreement among the parties. In Example 3 at the beginning of the chapter, if Bloggs promises the town that he will not drain or fill wetlands, officials must watch him to be sure that he keeps his promise. Monitoring costs are low when, among other things, violations of the agreement are easy to observe.

Unreasonableness in dividing the surplus from cooperation can occur because the parties to the dispute have emotional concerns that interfere

---

[9]*See* Elizabeth Hoffman & Matthew Spitzer, *The Coase Theorem: Some Experimental Tests,* 25 J. LAW & ECON. 73 (1982), and Hoffman & Spitzer, *Experimental Tests of the Coase Theorem with Large Bargaining Groups,* 15 J. LEGAL STUD. 149 (1986).

with rational agreement, as when a divorce is bitterly contested. However, unreasonableness can also result when the parties form rational strategies that press their own advantage "too hard." An essential aspect of bargaining is forming a strategy and trying to decipher an opponent's moves.[10] For example, Bloggs may have to hire a lawyer to negotiate on his behalf and to inform him of the likely moves by the town. In forming a bargaining strategy, each party tries to anticipate how much the opponent will concede. If the parties make a mistake in assessing the other party's resolve or threat point and each takes a hard line, each will be surprised to find that the other does not concede, and as a result, the parties may end by failing to cooperate. Familiarity and continuity eliminate many of the surprises that disrupt bargaining. Costly mistakes in strategy are likely when the parties are unfamiliar with each other and when their relationship is temporary, whereas mistakes of strategy are unlikely when the parties know each other well and when they expect to have a long, continuing relationship.

On the basis of this discussion, the obstacles to cooperation can be grouped into three kinds of costs:

1. communication costs,
2. monitoring costs, and
3. strategic costs.

Property law facilitates private agreements by reducing these costs. The idea that property law *ought* to facilitate private agreements by reducing these costs was argued powerfully by Professor Ronald Coase in a famous paper.[11] In recognition of this fact, we name our second principle of property law the *Normative Coase Theorem: Structure the law to remove the impediments to private agreements.*

The two normative principles of property law—minimize the harm caused by private disagreements over resource allocation (the Normative Hobbes Theorem) and minimize the obstacles to private agreements over resource allocation (the Normative Coase Theorem)—have wide application

---

[10]Strategic behavior raises some very complex problems in bargaining theory. Economics usually assumes that people behave rationally and looks for the equilibrium in their interaction. Economists have not, however, successfully found a solution to the bargaining problem based upon rationality alone. Rationality alone does not decide how the cooperative surplus will be distributed. Recall that in our discussion of the division of the cooperative surplus in the examples of the sale of the used car or the establishment of civil society we called an equal division a "reasonable solution," not a "rational solution." As we noted there, the term "reasonable solution" takes account of social norms, whereas "rational solution," as currently used in economics, only takes account of self-interest.

[11]The theorem is suggested, but not explicitly stated, in the classic article by Professor Coase, *The Problem of Social Cost,* 3 J.L. & ECON. 1 (1960). There are many different versions of the Coase Theorem. Here is another: "If there are no obstacles to exchanging legal entitlements, they will be allocated efficiently by private agreement, so the initial allocation by the courts does not influence the efficiency of the final allocation." Yet another is this: "The assignment of property rights does not matter when transaction costs are zero." The alternative formulations are systematically described by Cooter in *The Coase Theorem,* in THE NEW PALGRAVE (1985).

in law.[12] In fact, these normative principles will form the heart of our economic analysis of property law in the remainder of this and in the following chapter. A strategy of analysis that we will employ repeatedly is to ask *whether, and how, a property rule or institution lubricates the transfer of resources by facilitating private bargaining.* Indeed, since the law does in fact take as one of its purposes the facilitation of private bargaining, and hence the efficient allocation of resources, the two normative principles also turn out to be useful descriptive principles, as we will demonstrate.

V. HOW ARE PROPERTY RIGHTS PROTECTED?

We developed bargaining theory and used it in a thought experiment to explain the origins of property. Now we will apply bargaining theory to a fundamental question in the theory of property law: "What remedies should be awarded to a property owner when someone else, either a private citizen or the government, illegitimately interferes with the owner's property rights?" Our discussion of this question will focus principally on situations in which the illegitimate interference comes from another private citizen. In the next chapter we will analyze the circumstances in which the government may take a private citizen's property rights and what remedies the private citizen may invoke when this property is taken.

The remedies available to a common law court are either *legal* or *equitable.* The principal legal remedy is the payment of compensatory damages by the defendant to the plaintiff. If the defendant is held liable for damages, then he is obligated to compensate the plaintiff, in the form of money, for the harm he has caused. If he fails to make that compensatory payment, his property may be seized and sold at public auction to raise the amount due the plaintiff. The general rule in common law courts is that legal relief will be awarded to a successful plaintiff unless he can clearly demonstrate that the award of money damages would under-compensate him for the harm the defendant has caused him.[13]

Equitable relief consists of an order by the court directing the defendant to perform an act or to refrain from acting in a particular manner. This order is frequently in the form of an "injunction," which is said to "enjoin" the defendant from doing the act. The consequences to a defendant of violating an equitable decree are far more serious than the consequences of failing to pay a monetary judgment. Failure to abide by an injunction not only leaves the plaintiff at a loss but, from the court's point of view, it also consti-

---

[12]The mathematician will recognize immediately that two objectives affected by the same variables cannot be minimized simultaneously. In view of this fact, these two principles could be combined and restated as one complicated principle.

[13]Note that this is a different thing from "punitive damages," which are money damages over and above compensatory damages assessed against the defendant. The purpose of punitive damages is to punish the defendant, not to compensate the plaintiff. We return to a discussion of punitive damages in the chapters on the economics of tort law.

tutes an insult to the authority of the court. Such an insult cannot be tolerated. A defendant who ignores an injunction may be held in contempt of court and imprisoned until he agrees to abide by the injunction.

One important distinction between the two forms of relief is that legal relief is backward-looking, in the sense that it compensates a plaintiff for a harm already suffered, while equitable relief is often prospective or forward-looking, in the sense that it frequently seeks to prevent a defendant from inflicting a harm on the plaintiff in the future.

Courts today are reluctant to issue equitable decrees for at least two reasons. First is the widely-held belief that compensatory money damages are almost always adequate for plaintiffs. Second is the court's reluctance to place itself in a confrontational position in which the defendant might be found in contempt of court; imprisonment without a definite term is a harsh punishment, and courts are understandably loathe to use it except in extreme circumstances.

Which remedy is better from an economic viewpoint: the legal remedy of damages or the equitable remedy of injunction? To decide whether an injunction or damages is more efficient, it is necessary to consider the impediments to private bargaining again. To carry out that analysis, we turn to another example.[14]

> **Facts:** The *E* Electric Company emits smoke, which dirties the wash at the *L* Laundry. No one else is affected because *E* and *L* are near to each other and far from anyone else. *E* can abate this external cost by installing scrubbers on its stacks, and *L* can reduce the damage by installing filters on its ventilation system. The installation of scrubbers by *E* or filters by *L* completely eliminates pollution. Table 4.3 shows the profits of each company, depending upon what action is taken to reduce the pollution. (The profits that are shown in the matrix exclude any compensation that might be paid or received as a consequence of a legal dispute.)

The numbers in Table 4.3 can be explained as follows. When *E* does not install scrubbers, *E's* profits are 1,000. When *L* does not install filters and when *L* does not suffer pollution damage, *L's* profits are 300. Pollution destroys 200 of *L's* profits. *L* can avoid this by installing filters at a cost of 100, or *E* can avoid it by installing scrubbers at a cost of 500. Check to see that you can use these facts to explain the numbers in Table 4.3.

The most efficient outcome is, by definition, a situation in which the total profits for the two parties, called the "joint profits," are greatest. The joint profits are found by adding the two numbers in each cell of the table. Following this procedure, it is easy to see that joint profits are maximized in the northeast cell, where 1,200 is attained when *E* does not install scrubbers and *L* installs filters.

The harm caused by pollution represents a source of contention between *E* and *L*. They may be able to settle their disagreement and cooperate with each other, or they may fail to cooperate and litigate their dispute. What we

---

[14]This is a quantitative version of the qualitative example used in Chapter 1.

Table 4.3 Profits Before Legal Action*

| | | Laundry | |
		No filter	Filter
Electric Company	No Scrubbers	100	200
		1,000	1,000
	Scrubbers	300	200
		500	500

*L's profits in top of each cell; E's profits in bottom of each cell.

are interested in determining here is how rules of property law may be used to induce the parties to achieve the efficient solution and thus to minimize the harm of pollution.

Suppose that E and L litigate their disagreement. Three alternative rules of law could be applied in the event of a trial:

   i. E is free to pollute.
  ii. L is entitled to *compensatory damages* from E. (Compensatory damages are a sum of money that E pays to L to make up for L's reduced profits due to E's pollution.)
 iii. L is entitled to an *injunction* forbidding E to pollute. (An injunction is a court order requiring E to stop polluting.)

Let us determine the value of the noncooperative solution under each of these rules.

Beginning with rule (i), if E is free to pollute, the most profitable action for E is not to install scrubbers and to enjoy profits of 1,000, whereas the most profitable response for L is to install filters and enjoy profits of 200. Thus, the noncooperative value of the rule of free pollution is 1,200. This is the efficient solution, which is in the northeast cell of the table.

Turning to rule (ii), if E must pay damages to L for polluting, then L will not bother to install filters. E will have to pay damages to L equal to the difference between the profits L enjoys when there is no pollution, 300, and the profits L enjoys with pollution, 100. E has a choice between installing the scrubbers and eliminating pollution damage, or not installing the scrubbers and paying damages of 200 to L ($200 = 300 - 100$). The most profitable alternative is for E not to install the scrubbers, thus initially enjoying 1,000 in profits, from which 200 must be subtracted to pay damages, leaving E with net profits of 800. Thus, E enjoys net profits of 800, L enjoys net profits of 300, and the noncooperative value under the rule of liability for compensatory damages is $1,100 = 300 + 800$. This is the value in the northwest cell in the table.

Turning to rule (iii), if E is enjoined from polluting and responds by installing scrubbers, E's profits equal 500. When E installs scrubbers, L will not bother to install filters, so L's profits will be 300. Thus, the noncooperative value under the rule of enjoining pollution is $800 = 500 + 300$, which corresponds to the southwest cell of the table.

Under the pessimistic assumption that E and L cannot cooperate, only one of the legal rules produces an efficient outcome, specifically rule (i). Instead of making the pessimistic assumption that the parties will be unable to cooperate, suppose we make the optimistic assumption that the parties will settle their disagreements and cooperate. When E and L cooperate, their best strategy is to maximize the joint profits of the two enterprises. The joint profits are maximized when they take the efficient course of action, which, in this case, is for L to install filters and E not to install scrubbers, yielding joint profits of 1,200.

There are, thus, two ways to achieve the efficient solution. One way is for the law to *adopt the rule for which the noncooperative solution is efficient.* In our example (but not necessarily in other pollution examples), the non-cooperative solution is efficient under rule (i), which gives E the freedom to pollute. The other way to achieve efficiency is for *the parties to cooperate.* Notice that the cooperative solution is efficient under all three of the possible laws.

This leads to the following general rule: *when parties can bargain together and settle their disagreements by cooperation, their behavior will be efficient regardless of the underlying rule of law.* This proposition, called the *Positive Coase Theorem*, is one of the most celebrated insights in the economic analysis of law. According to the Positive Coase Theorem, inefficient allocations of legal rights by laws such as rules (ii) and (iii) will be cured by private agreements, provided that bargaining in successful.[15]

If successful bargaining can cure inefficient laws, what difference does the law make? One answer is that the law affects the distribution of the cooperative product, which makes a great deal of difference to the parties to the negotiations. To illustrate this point about distribution, recall how the structure of the law, such as rules (i), (ii), and (iii), affects the threat values of the parties. A reasonable bargaining solution is for each party to receive his threat value plus an equal share of the cooperative surplus. Each party to a bargain would prefer the rule of law that provides him with the largest threat value. Specifically, the threat value of the plaintiff in a property dispute is at

---

[15]In Chapter 1 when we were introducing the subject matter of law and economics, we gave a simplified account of the laundry-polluting factory example, including an oversimplification of the Coase Theorem, saying that "the quantities of pollution and laundry will also be invariant to the assignment of rights." The more detailed development of that example in this chapter has also led to a more general statement of the Coase Theorem that must be carefully distinguished from the over-simplified statement of Chapter 1. Here we stress the Positive Coase Theorem's conclusion that, whatever the assignment of rights, the resulting mix of output will be *efficient*. We do not say that the output of the laundry and the electric factory will be invariant to the assignment of rights. As we noted in Chapter 2, the competitive equilibrium in a pure exchange economy depends upon the initial endowments of the traders, including the allocation of rights. However, as we also saw, under competitive behavior, *all* equilibrium allocations will be Pareto optimal, regardless of initial endowments. Thus, there is no unique competitive equilibrium, as the oversimplified Coase Theorem of Chapter 1 implied.

least as great when the remedy is injunctive relief as when the remedy is damages. The plaintiff, consequently, prefers the remedy of injunctive relief, whereas the defendant prefers the damage remedy or, better yet, no remedy.

The effect of the rule of law on the distribution of the cooperative product can be computed precisely for E and L. Imagine that E and L enter into negotiations, and, to keep the arithmetic simple, assume that negotiating a settlement or going to trial is costless for the parties (swallow hard!). The noncooperative payoffs—that is, the profits each can get on his own if negotiations fail—are shown in Table 4.4 under each of the three rules. The surplus, which equals the difference between the joint profits from cooperation and the threat values, is also shown. A reasonable bargaining solution is for each party to receive his threat value plus half the surplus from cooperation. The payoffs to the two parties from cooperation are given in the two columns on the right side of the table. Notice that in each case the cooperative payoffs sum to 1,200, but L receives the largest share under the injunctive rule, an intermediate share under damages, and the smallest share when E is free to pollute.

We have explained that the assignment of legal entitlements makes no difference to efficiency so long as the parties can cooperate together and bargain to an agreement, although the distribution of the cooperative surplus is affected. There are, however, other important effects of the law: it affects the *probability* that bargaining will succeed and the *consequences* of a failure. The two normative principles (Hobbes and Coase) that we developed earlier direct us to take these two considerations into account when choosing between the alternative remedies of injunction or damages.

That type of analysis was carried out in a famous article by Calabresi and Melamed on the choice of remedy for resolving disputes about incompatible property uses, that is, in circumstances where somone was illegitimately interfering with another's property.[16] They assume that society has already allocated property rights, which they call "entitlements," to resources. They then suggest that where an externality has arisen, the court

Table 4.4 Profits from Bargaining Under Three Legal Rules

	Non-cooperation		Surplus	Cooperation	
	E	L		E	L
E free to pollute rule (i)	1,000	200	0	1,000	200
Damage rule (rule ii)	800	300	100	850	350
Injunction (rule iii)	500	300	400	700	500

[16]Calabresi & Melamed, *Property Rules, Liability Rules, and Inalienability: One View of the Cathedral*, 85 HARV. L. REV. 1089 (1972).

should choose between compensatory damages and an injunction on the basis of the parties' ability to cooperate in resolving the dispute. Where there are obstacles to cooperation, the preferred remedy is the award of compensatory money damages. Where there are few obstacles to cooperation, the preferred remedy is the award of an injunction against the defendant's interference with the plaintiff's property.

When this standard is applied in practice, the preferred legal remedy depends in large part upon how many parties must participate in a settlement. The obstacles to cooperation are usually few in disputes involving a small number of geographically concentrated people who know each other well. Property disputes frequently involve small numbers of contiguous property owners. In those circumstances, communication costs are obviously low; the parties can monitor the agreement at low cost since each person can observe what happens on his own land; and, finally, the strategic costs are low if land ownership is stable and contiguous owners know each other well. Thus, bargaining is likely to be successful in these circumstances and, therefore, the most efficient remedy for resolving these property disputes is injunctive relief. In contrast, private bargaining is unlikely to succeed in disputes involving a large number of geographically dispersed strangers because communications costs are high, monitoring is costly, and strategic behavior is likely to occur.

To illustrate, the laundry and the electrical company are next to each other, and (by assumption) no one else is affected by the smoke, so private bargaining is likely to succeed. In contrast, in Example 3, the case of Bloggs' wetlands, the affected parties include everyone in the watershed, and in Example 2, the case of the cattle feedlot, the affected parties include all residents downwind of the feedlot. The costs of communication, monitoring, and strategy are high in these examples because the bargaining process must bring together many strangers. As a result of these high bargaining costs, cooperation is unlikely. In Calabresi and Melamed's terms, the court can contribute to the efficient use of resources in these property disputes by performing a "hypothetical market analysis." That is, the court should determine the price at which a bargain would have taken place had there been few obstacles to cooperation and assess that price against the defendant as compensatory money damages. In the following chapter we will see how courts might actually do this.

We will use the term *private bad* to describe a harm that affects few people, and the term *public bad* to describe a harm that affects many people. Thus, our prescription for remedies in property disputes is to *use the injunctive remedy for private bads and damages for public bads.*

Externalities of the public bad variety should be priced by requiring the party who causes them to compensate the victims fully. But when the harm is a private bad, the equitable remedy of injunction is preferred because the private character of the harm will enable the solution of the problem by private negotiations. With private bads, the threat of an injunction will seldom be exercised because the conditions are right for private solutions as described by the Positive Coase Theorem. In the next sections we will develop a more thorough account of the public-private distinction by introducing the theory of public goods.

VI. WHAT CAN BE PRIVATELY OWNED?

In the previous section we showed how economic theory can help answer one of the fundamental questions of property law: how should property rights be protected? In this section we turn to another of those fundamental questions: over what resources should property rights be defined? First, we use the economic distinction between public and private goods (developed in Chapter 2) to delineate those resources that will be most efficiently used if privately owned from those that will be most efficiently used if publicly owned. Second, we investigate how the economic theory of information suggests that property rights might be defined for some important intangible resources, such as ideas.

A. Public and Private Goods[17]

Most examples of property that we have discussed thus far in this book are what economists call "private goods." Goods that economists describe as purely private have the characteristic that one person's use precludes another's: for example, when one person eats an apple, others cannot eat it; a pair of pants can only be worn by one person at a time; a car cannot go two different directions simultaneously; and so forth. These facts are sometimes summarized by saying that there is *rivalry* in the consumption of private goods.

The polar opposite is a purely public good, for which there is no rivalry in consumption and for which the costs to a private supplier of excluding non-paying beneficiaries are high. A conventional example of a public good is military security in the nuclear age. Supplying one citizen with protection from nuclear attack does not diminish the amount of protection supplied to other citizens. In fact, it is virtually impossible to supply different amounts of protection against nuclear attack to different citizens. (Citizens do, however, disagree about how much protection is afforded by military expenditures.)

This distinction between public and private goods has a great deal to do with determining how property law can facilitate private exchange. The role

---

[17]Before reading this section, you may find it helpful to review the material on public goods in Chapter 2.

of government is very different in the supply of public and private goods. In the case of purely public goods like security, the obstacles to private supply are so overwhelming that government must be the primary supplier. To illustrate, suppose that a particular city block is plagued by crime, so some residents propose hiring a private guard. Many residents will voluntarily contribute to the guard's salary, but suppose that some refuse. The paying residents may instruct the guard not to aid non-payers in the event of a mugging. The presence of the guard on the street, however, will make it safer for *everyone*, whether they paid or not, because muggers are unlikely to know who has and who has not paid for the guard's services. Given these facts, there is not much that the payers can do to compel non-payers to contribute.

Those who do not pay for their consumption of a public good are called "free-riders." To appreciate this concept, imagine that a street car has an electric meter in it and, in order to make the street car move, the riders must put money into the meter. The riders will realize that anyone who pays provides a free ride for everyone else. Many riders will, nonetheless, put their full fare into the meter (perhaps they do not wish to risk being branded as "cheap"); some will put some money in but not their full fare; and some will not put anything in at all. Because there are partial or full "free riders" and because it is difficult for the street car company to distinguish them from those who pay their full fare, it may not be possible for the street car company to make a profit. To the extent that that is the case, there may be fewer street cars than are desirable.

The fact that excluding free riders is difficult or impossible for purely public goods disrupts the workings of markets for these goods. When public goods are supplied by private means, the level of supply is usually deficient. In Chapter 2 we showed that to correct for this deficiency two public policies should be considered: (1) governmental provision of the public good with the costs of production being paid from general tax revenues or (2) private provision of the public good with governmental subsidization indirectly through the tax system or directly out of general governmental revenues. The choice between these policies should be made by comparing their net benefits.[18]

In the case of private goods, the proper role of the law in assuring their supply is very different. For private goods, the obstacles to markets are not so severe as for public goods. When markets work tolerably well, private supply has great advantages over public supply. The essential role of the law with regard to private goods is, then, to insure that markets work tolerably well in accord with the Hobbes and Coase Theorems discussed above.

---

[18]We are not, of course, suggesting that the current division of responsibility between public and private providers of goods and services necessarily follows the rules we have just set down. That is, there are current instances of the government provision or subsidization of *private* goods and of the private (under) provision of *public* goods. The extent to which these anomalies exist and why they persist is one of the central concerns of the branch of microeconomic theory called "public choice theory."

Graphing the Distinction
Between Private and Public Goods

One of the first clear accounts of the difference between private and public goods was offered by Paul Samuelson.[1] Panel a of Figure 4.1 shows the demand for a *private* good, say, apples, by person A and person B. Reading from the graph, if the price is p_1, person A demands x_{a1} and person B demands x_{b1}. Thus, at the price p_1, the total amount demanded by A and B, denoted x_1, equals the sum of their individual demands. That is,

$$x_1 = x_{a1} + x_{b1}.$$

x_1 is one point on the total demand curve for this private good, which is called the aggregate demand curve because it is found by aggregating the individual demands. To find other points, we repeat the same process: choose another price on the vertical axis; read the corresponding individual demands on the horizontal axis; and then add the resulting quantities. The aggregate demand curve for a private good is thus found by summing the individual quantities, or by summing the individual demand curves *horizontally*.

Panel b depicts the equivalent calculation for a *public* good, such as clean air. The horizontal axis depicts reductions in the level of pollution from 0% to 100%; thus, a movement to the right on the horizontal axis represents a cleaner level of air. Choose any level of reduction in pollution, say x_2. Reading from the graph, the amount that individual A would be willing to pay for this level of pollution reduction is p_{a2}, and the amount that individual B would be willing to pay for this level of pollution reduction is p_{b2}. Thus the total amount that A and B would be willing to pay for pollution reduction x_2, denoted p_2, is the sum

$$p_2 = p_{a2} + p_{b2}.$$

p_2 is one point on the aggregate demand curve for the *public* good, pollution reduction. To find other points, we simply repeat the same process: choose another level of pollution reduction; find the corresponding amounts the individuals are willing to pay on the vertical axis; and then add the prices. The aggregate demand curve for a public good is thus found by summing the individual prices, or summing the individual demand curves *vertically*.

Why is the aggregate demand for a private good derived by summing individual demand curves *horizontally* but the aggregate demand curve for a public good is derived by summing individual demand curves *vertically*?

The aggregate demand for public goods is found by summing vertically because everyone enjoys the same quantity of the good but values it differently, whereas the aggregate demand for private goods is found by

---

[1] Paul Samuelson, *Diagrammatic Exposition of a Theory of Public Expenditure*, 37 REV. ECON. & STAT. 350 (1955).

summing horizontally because everyone pays the same price for those goods but consumes different quantities. We could say that with public goods the quantity is public (no rivalry and no exclusion) and the willing-ness-to-pay is individual, whereas with private goods the price is public and the quantities are individual (rivalry and exclusion).

Figure 4.1

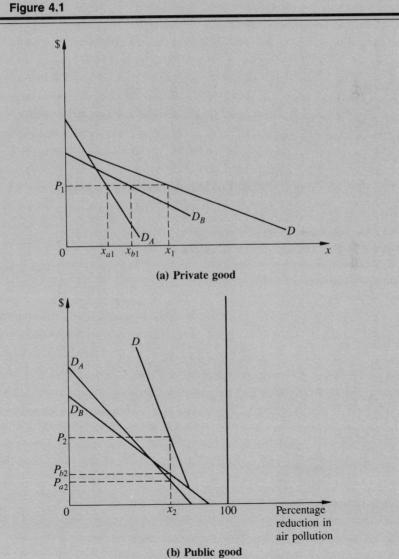

(a) **Private good**

(b) **Public good**

The microeconomic distinction between private and public goods should guide the development of property rules to answer the question, "What can be privately owned?" It is private goods, which exhibit rivalry and exclusion, that ought to be privately owned, and it is public goods, which exhibit nonrivalry and nonexclusion, that ought to be publicly owned. To be more precise, the economic theory of property suggests that ownership claims should be granted to any resource if the bundle of rights called property will lead to a more efficient use of that resource and thus an increase in social wealth, and if the costs of establishing and enforcing those ownership claims is less than the benefits. The costs of establishing and enforcing ownership claims is low for private goods and high for public goods. The characteristics of private goods enable the establishment of markets for their allocation, whereas the characteristics of public goods prevent markets from forming. Because of these practical considerations, there is a convergence between reality and the economic ideal: private goods like land, wheat, and labor tend to be privately owned, and public goods like the air and the high seas tend not to be privately owned.

> **Question 4.5:** If everyone has free access to a public beach, who, if anyone, has discretion over use of this resource?

B. Intangible Resources: Property Rights in Information

In the next chapter we will continue developing these themes by discussing two important questions: For what specific resources is private ownership more efficient than public or communal ownership and *vice versa*? And under what circumstances should government be allowed to take private property from citizens? For now we illustrate how to use this theory by applying it to an example.

What special problems exist for defining property rights in intangible but valuable resources? The example upon which we will here focus is information. For economists there is something extraordinary about the commodity *information*. On the demand side, consumers are uncertain about the utility of information because it is difficult to determine the value of information until one has it. But they cannot have information until they have paid for it. But they cannot know how much to pay for information until they have determined its utility by having it. There is no easy way into this circle. The problems on the supply side are just as formidable. Information is costly to produce, and yet it costs relatively little to transmit. Thus, it is extremely hard for anyone who has devoted resources to the production of information to appropriate its value through the sale of that information. This is because the instant the producer sells the information to one consumer, that consumer becomes a potential competitor of the original producer, owing to the low cost of transmitting information. Consumers desire to become "free riders" for information, paying no more than the cost of transmission for the commodity. (Have you ever copied for free a computer program or taped a friend's record or a televised concert?)

In short, information has one of the attributes of a public good, namely, that it is costly to prevent non-paying beneficiaries from consuming the commodity. And, as we have seen, where this is the case, the private market may provide sub-optimal amounts of the public good. In the literature on the economics of information this problem is frequently referred to as the problem of *non-appropriability*.

These theoretical considerations suggest that the unregulated market will produce sub-optimal amounts of information in inventive ideas and in creative works such as books, paintings, and music. And this, in turn, suggests the need for govenmental intervention in the market for information in order to increase the amount of information generated. As with other public goods, this governmental intervention in the market for information can take one of two general forms: (1) governmental supply of information or (2) governmental subsidization of the private provision of information (either directly from general governmental revenues or indirectly through the tax system). In fact, the government does both of these things. An example of the governmental production and dissemination of information is the weather forecasting services offered by federal and state governments. Examples of the governmental subsidization of the private provision of information are the governmental funding of basic research in the sciences, humanities, and the arts and the awarding of monopoly rights to the creators of information through the patent, copyright, and trademark systems.

The conventional theory that we have explained leads to the conclusion that an unregulated market will produce sub-optimal amounts of information. Economics is, however, a profound and subtle instrument of thought. For every theoretical argument pointing to one conclusion, another argument can usually be constructed pointing to the opposite conclusion. Recently, economists have identified conditions under which the conventional conclusion that unregulated markets produce too little information is wrong; instead, under certain conditions, no regulation results in either just the right amount of information[19] or, under alternative conditions, too much information.[20] Let's briefly explore these alternative explanations.

Consider an inventor who has developed a means of forecasting the weather with great accuracy. Clearly this is an important and valuable invention. But the standard interpretation of the economics of information suggests that this invention is unlikely because the costliness of the inven-

---

[19] *See* J. Hirschleifer, *The Private and Social Value of Information and the Reward to Innovative Activity*, 61 AM. ECON. REV. 561 (1971).

[20] *See* R. Posner, *The Social Costs of Monopoly and Regulation*, 83 J. POL. ECON. 807 (1975). *But see* E. Rice & T. Ulen, *Rent-Seeking and Welfare Loss*, 3 RES. IN LAW & ECON. 53 (1981).

tor's appropriating the value of his information from his customers will dissuade anyone from investing resources in developing it. If the inventor were to sell his information to, say, farmers, most would be reluctant to buy, not because they doubt the value of the information about the weather, but because if they can wait for some other farmer to buy the information, the rest of them can get that information from him, directly or indirectly by observing his actions, at no cost. The standard theory argues that the costlessness of transmission of information makes it unlikely that the inventor will reap the reward of his innovative activity through the sale of his information.

But the standard theory may be misleading in this case. Although it correctly points out that the inventor will not be able to appropriate the value of his invention through the direct sale of that information, the standard theory ignores the possibility that there may be alternative, less direct means for inventors to appropriate this value. The inventor of the weather forecast, for example, may use the information he generates to make money by buying and selling futures contracts in farm output on his own account or by buying and selling futures contracts in factors of production specialized to farming.[21]

To see how this might work, let's suppose that the inventor uses his invention to determine that the upcoming weather will be terrible. He knows, therefore, that the harvest will be low and that the resulting low supply of farm output will cause the price of that output to be high. He can keep this information secret and buy farm output futures, committing him to buy output in the future at a price, specified today, that he alone knows to be too low. When the harvest comes in, farmers will fulfill their contracts with the inventor by selling their output to him at the previously specified low price. The inventor will then be free to resell that output at the higher price, which his investment in the invention allowed him to predict. The profit thus earned may well be enough to justify his costs in having developed the information.

> **Question 4.6:** Suppose that the inventor of a weather-forecasting technique uses his invention to determine that the weather during the growing season will be perfect. Therefore, he knows that there will be a very large crop. Using the analysis of this section, show how he might keep this knowledge secret and use futures contracts to realize enough profit to justify incurring the investment in his invention.

The point of this example is that there may be circumstances in which it is possible to appropriate the benefits of information in ways alternative to that of selling it directly to consumers. When this is true, the economic argument in favor of government intervention in the market for information is weakened. In fact, where indirect appropriation of this sort can occur,

---

[21]A "futures contract" is a commitment to buy or sell something at some specified date in the future at a fixed price determined today.

the unregulated market may produce precisely the optimal amount of information.

Some have argued that competitive markets may produce *too much* information, for which the recommended policy cure is a restriction on competition in information. For instance, consider the fact that there are many investigators looking for a cure for cancer. The suggestion of some scholars has been that much of this research is duplicative and, thus, wasteful. To minimize this competitive waste, some have suggested restricting competition by, for example, requiring a license of those engaged in cancer research and licensing only a limited number of researchers. Before this sort of restriction becomes public policy, a careful taxonomy of informaton must be produced; it must become possible to differentiate those kinds of information for which competitive duplication is a problem from those for which competitive *under*-provision is the problem and from those for which competition provides just the right amount of information. Currently, we do not have such a taxonomy and until one is produced, a policy of restricting competition among the producers of information is premature.

When one stands back and tries to come to grips with the economic theory of information in order to determine the appropriate role of property law in leading to an efficient amount of information, one finds three competing hypotheses with very different public policy prescriptions:

1. The standard theory, which holds that the market will *under*-produce information because of the problem of non-appropriability. To correct the problem of the sub-optimal provision of information, the government should either produce and disseminate information itself, subsidize the private production of information, or grant special monopoly rights to creators of information.
2. The theory that the market will, unaided, produce the optimal amount of information because of the possibility of the original producer's indirectly appropriating enough revenue to justify incurring the costs of producing information. The recommended public policy is not to intervene, other than to guarantee competitive conditions in the market for information.
3. The theory that competitive markets for information generate *over*-production of information in the form of duplicative investment. The recommended public policy in this case is to restrict competition, for example, by assigning a monopoly right to a single producer of a particular type of information at a very early stage of production.

Clearly, not all three theories can be simultaneously true. Just as certainly, there are circumstances or different kinds of information for which only *one* theory is appropriate. To the extent that this is so, a policymaker who mistakenly assumes that there is only *one* kind of information and that there is, therefore, only *one* rule of property law for all markets in information will create inefficiencies, leading to the wrong amount and kinds of information being generated. What is required—and what the economics profession has not yet provided—is a taxonomy of information so that we may decide which theory of information is appropriate to different kinds of information. If categories of information can be distinguished, then the appropriate public policy may be invoked to produce the socially optimal amounts of information.

Bear these considerations about the economics of information in mind when, in the next chapter, we explore the current legal system in the United States for securing property rights in intellectual property.

VII. WHAT MAY OWNERS DO WITH THEIR PROPERTY?

We used the theory of public goods and the economic theory of information to begin answering the question, "What can be privately owned?" Closely related to the theory of public goods is the theory of externalities. Now we turn to that theory in order to develop an answer to the question, "What may owners do with their property?"

In Chapter 2 we discussed external costs, which are involuntary costs imposed upon one person by another. Since market transactions are voluntary, externalities are *outside* the market system of exchange—hence their name. In the next chapter, and again in the chapters on torts, we will deal extensively with externalities, including developing a mathematical framework. For now, we restrict ourselves to a few remarks about their connection to property law.

The law can impose restrictions upon what persons may do with their property. But at common law there are few restrictions, with the general rule being that any use was allowed that did not interfere with other people's property. This general restriction from the common law of property corresponds to the economic concept of external cost. For example, a factory that emits thick, cloying smoke into a residential neighborhood is generating an externality. In Example 2, the stench from the cattle feedlot is an externality that interferes with Foster's enjoyment of her house. In Example 3, the development of Bloggs' wetlands will interfere with the town's enjoyment of its rivers and streams. Notice that these types of interference are like a public good in that they affect many property owners. There is, at it were, no rivalry or exclusion from smelling the feedlot's stench among Foster and her neighbors. These forms of interference are thus like a public good, except they are bad rather than good.

We have already explained why markets cannot arise to supply public goods efficiently. The same set of considerations explain why private bargaining solutions cannot solve the problem of externalities, or, as we called them in a previous section, public bads. To illustrate, suppose that Foster had enough money to pay the feedlot to stop emitting its stench. If she made this private deal with the feedlot, all of her neighbors would benefit as much as she does since all of them would be free from the stench. As with a public good, the obstacle to the private solution is that there will be some free riders so that not all the beneficiaries of the restriction of the public bad will contribute. Thus, the private solution will not lead to an optimal restriction of a public bad.

In view of these facts, public bads are not self-correcting. Some form of public policy remedy is called for. We have already noted how bargaining theory can help to design the form—the payment of money damages—that that remedy should take. An alternative remedy that we will consider in the following chapter is regulation of the public bad or external-cost-generating activity by an administrative agency.

On the other hand, recall that private bads are self-correcting through private agreements, so there is no need for an intrusive, governmental solution. Instead, the courts can stand prepared to issue an injunction in the confident expectation that they will seldom be required to issue it.

CONCLUSION

We defined property as the institution that, by allocating things to people, gives people liberty over things. The bundle of protected rights that constitutes property can be analyzed using economic theory in two steps. The first step is to consider how property might be established. This involves analyzing the obstacles to bargaining that exist when the rights of the parties are not defined by law. This stage of analysis leads to the normative conclusion that property law should be constructed to facilitate private bargaining and to minimize the harm that results from failures to reach private agreements. We, thus, viewed property law as a device for removing the obstacles to allocating resources by bargaining and voluntary exchange.

The second stage analyzed a system of property rules in economic terms. We developed the distinction between private goods and public goods to answer the question, "What can be privately owned?" We concluded that private ownership is appropriate when there is rivalry and exclusion in the use of goods. We also introduced the economic theory of information to investigate how and whether private ownership claims could be defined for intangible resources such as ideas. We then asked, "What can owners do with their property?" We developed an account of unwarranted interference based upon the economic concept of an externality and showed that this economic analysis fits the common law rule of property that allows owners to do anything with their property that does not interfere with others. Finally, we asked how property rights are protected. We concluded that owners should be protected against externalities of the private-bads type by the injunctive remedy and that they should be protected against externalities of the public-bads type by receiving compensatory damages.

There is a common theme in this economic analysis that concerns the use of property rules and institutions to remove the obstacles to voluntary private exchange. We began the chapter by considering the state of nature in social contract theory, where the absence of a legal framework creates serious obstacles to private exchange. We explained how to remove some of these obstacles by creating a framework of property law. Then we discussed how property law could be refined to identify and cope with other obstacles to exchange that exist even when the elements of the institution of property are in place.

Property law thus establishes in our legal system a market structure for allocating resources. Creating, protecting, and enhancing this transactional structure is one of its central functions.[22]

SUGGESTED READINGS

Ackerman, Bruce, ed., THE ECONOMIC FOUNDATIONS OF PROPERTY LAW (1976).

Becker, Lawrence, PROPERTY RIGHTS: PHILOSOPHICAL FOUNDATIONS (1977).

Cribbet, John, PRINCIPLES OF THE LAW OF PROPERTY (2d. ed. 1975).

Dukeminier, Jesse, and James Krier, PROPERTY (1981).

Epstein, Richard, *Possession as the Root of Title,* 13 GA. L. REV. 1221 (1979).

Furubotn, E., and S. Pejovich, eds., THE ECONOMICS OF PROPERTY RIGHTS (1974).

Manne, Henry, ed., THE ECONOMICS OF LEGAL RELATIONS: READINGS IN THE THEORY OF PROPERTY RIGHTS (1975).

Polinsky, A. Mitchell, *Controlling Externalities and Protecting Entitlements: Property Rights, Liability Rules, and Tax-Subsidy Approaches,* 8 J. LEGAL STUD. 1 (1979).

Polinsky, A. Mitchell, *Resolving Nuisance Disputes: The Simple Economics of Injunctive and Damage Remedies,* 32 STAN. L. REV. 1075 (1980).

Regan, Donald, *The Problem of Social Cost Revisited,* 15 J. LAW & ECON. 427 (1972).

Rose, Carol M., *Possession as the Origin of Property,* 52 U. CHI. L. REV. 73 (1985).

Umbeck, John, *Might Makes Rights,* 19 ECON. INQUIRY 38 (1981).

---

[22]In the discussion of the economic theory of contract, we will complete this analysis by discussing the model of perfectly competitive markets, in which all obstacles to voluntary exchange are removed.

Appendix

The Philosophical Concept of Property

Philosophers generally perceive property to be an instrument for achieving fundamental values. Some philosophers of property have concentrated on its ability to advance values such as utility, justice, self-expression, and social evolution. These traditions of thought have influenced the law. This Appendix introduces the reader to four of these traditions and relates them to the economic analysis of property.

1. Utilitarianism

Utilitarians measure the value of a good or an act by the net pleasure or satisfaction that it creates. For utilitarians, the purpose of the institution of property is to maximize the total pleasure or satisfaction obtained from material and other resources. Bentham thus defines property as an expectation of utility: "Property is nothing but a basis of expectation; the expectation of deriving advantages from a thing, which we are said to possess, in consequence of the relation in which we stand towards it."[23] The objective of maximizing total utility constitutes a standard against which property rules can be evaluated. In our examples at the beginning of the chapter, each of the disputes could be resolved on utilitarian grounds by establishing a legal rule that seeks to maximize the sum of utilities or pleasure of society as a whole.

The utilitarian approach makes a person's claim to his property tentative. It can be taken from him in principle if the beneficiaries of the expropriation gain more in utility than the owner loses. Suppose, for example, that a young son is living with his aged parents in their home. On utilitarian

---

[23]Jeremy Bentham, THEORY OF LEGISLATION: PRINCIPLES OF THE CIVIL CODE 111–113 (Hildreth ed. 1931).

grounds, the young son may be excused for throwing the parents out of the home if their loss in utility from being dispossessed is less than his gain in utility from having them out of the house. Critics of utilitarianism have often wondered whether the theory makes ownership rather *too* tentative. Isn't ownership more than an expectation? Do we really think that a person could be rightfully deprived of his property just because his loss is more than offset by the gain to others?

This objection to the utilitarian theory of property applies with equal force to the conventional economic theory that holds that the purpose of property is to maximize wealth. Isn't ownership more than a right to a stream of income? Do we really think that a person could be rightfully deprived of his property just because his loss of wealth is more than offset by the gain in wealth to others?

2. Distributive Justice

Another philosophical approach to property law emphasizes property law's ability to achieve *distributive justice*, rather than pleasure or satisfaction. Aristotle, for example, held that a conception of distributive justice is implicit in various forms of social organization. For Aristotle, the principle of justice is different for different societies, but it is appropriate for each type of society to promote its own conception of distributive justice through its constitution and laws, including its notion of property rights. He argued that a democracy will favor an equal distribution of wealth, whereas an aristocracy (the form preferred by Aristotle) will favor the distribution of wealth according to the *virtues* of various classes. In Aristotle's conception, it is just that aristocrats receive an unequal share of wealth because they use it for more worthy ends than do others.

From the Aristotelian conception of democratic equality we might infer a policy of redistributive justice whereby the valuable assets of society are periodically redistributed so as to achieve a roughly equal distribution of that property. In general, this sort of redistribution would favor the poor and penalize the wealthy. On the other hand, from the Aristotelian justification of aristocratic inequality we might infer the polar opposite policy of redistributive justice whereby the assets of society would be periodically redistributed to the aristocrats. To the extent that the aristocracy and the wealthy are the same group, this redistribution of property would favor the rich and penalize the poor. In either case, these notions of distributive justice make property claims as tentative as they were under utilitarianism and, therefore, open to the same criticisms.

There is another school of philosophical thought relating distributive justice and property that emphasizes a just *process* for defining and enforcing property rights rather than a just *outcome* or *end-result* in the distribution of wealth from property.[24] According to one version of this theory, any distribution of wealth is just provided that it starts from a just initial distribution of resources and achieves the final distribution by voluntary exchange. In practice this means that the process of market exchange is just and that ownership claims are most justly established and enforced in an unfettered market in which there is free and perfect competition. In Nozick's memorable rephrasing of Marx, "From each as he chooses; to each as he is chosen." Whatever distribution of wealth results from this just process is also just. Thus, according to this theory, redistributing property to dilute the effects of competition is unjust.

Several criticisms have been made of this notion of distributive justice. The most telling criticism is that the competitive process can lead to a multitude of distributive outcomes, from one in which each individual has an equal share to one in which one individual has 99% of the property and everyone else divides up the remaining 1%. All of these outcomes are *efficient*. But clearly not all of them are equitable or just. The notion of the competitive process as distributive justice is not a sufficient guide to designing rules of property law. At a minimum, there must be an additional, independent standard by which to appraise various initial endowments of property.

3. Liberty and Self-Expression

Besides utility and distributive justice, another value that may underlie property law is liberty. Private property is a precondition for markets, and markets are a decentralized mechanism for allocating resources. Most markets can, and do, operate without extensive government interference or supervision. The practical alternative to markets in the modern economy is some form of government planning. Government planning involves centralizing power over economic matters in the hands of state officials. Control over economic life provides officials with leverage that can be used to control other aspects of life, whereas private property creates a zone of discretion within which individuals are not accountable to government officials. Private property has thus been viewed by some philosophers as a bulwark against the dictatorial authority of governments.[25] It has been argued, for

---

[24]The most forceful modern statement of this view is in R. Nozick, ANARCHY, STATE, AND UTOPIA (1974).

[25]This is a theme in the FEDERALIST PAPERS and is the work of Friedrich Hayek, for example, THE CONSTITUTION OF LIBERTY (1972).

example, that capitalism was deliberately invented to thwart absolutism by depriving the king of economic power. The United States Constitution was probably drafted with this idea in mind.

Another connection between property and liberty focuses on individual self-expression. Hegel stressed the idea that people, through their works, transform nature into an expression of personality, and, by doing so, perfect the natural world. A painter takes materials in no particular order—the paints on the palette—and rearranges them into a work of art. By investing personality in work, the artist transforms natural objects and makes them the artist's own. It is difficult to imagine a system of property law that did not recognize this fact. Thus, to encourage self-expression, the state needs to recognize the creator's rights of ownership over his creation. Notice that this proposition extends beyond art to most of the works of man.

4. Conservatism and the Origins of Property

The philosophical theories discussed so far tend to regard the institution of property as serving ultimate values, such as utility, distributive justice, or liberty. Another philosophical tradition focuses, not upon the purposes of property, but upon its origins. To illustrate, in medieval times there were many encumbrances and restrictions on the use and sale of real estate. The common law of private property emerged from feudalism and acquired its modern character by chipping away at these encumbrances upon the marketability of real property. Political conservatives like Burke and Hayek idealize forms of social order that, like the common law of property, evolve spontaneously from the decentralized decisions of many individuals. This view considers society to be an evolving organism not unlike other species of life, and thus, subject to the same sorts of ecological rules. These conservative philosophers condemn institutions imposed upon us by planners, engineers, politicians, and other social decision makers for much the same reasons that environmentalists condemn actions that interfere with an area's ecology. The conservative ideal arose from the common law of property, which followed the ecological model, not the planning model.

CHAPTER 5

Topics in the Economics of Property

In the preceding chapter, we developed an economic theory of property rights and remedies and related that theory to the dominant legal and philosophical conceptions of property. We saw that property law creates a bundle of rights that the owners of property are free to exercise as they see fit and protects them from interference by the state or by private persons. Bargaining and voluntary exchange is the system of allocation that is consistent with this freedom. Property law fosters voluntary exchange by removing the obstacles to bargaining. The economic theory of property rights and remedies holds that, if the rules of property law are centered on this purpose, resources will be used efficiently.

In the preceding chapter we posed four questions that must be answered by a theory of property law. Recall that those questions are:

1. What can be privately owned?
2. How are ownership rights established?
3. What may owners do with their property?
4. How are property rights protected? What are the remedies for their infringement?

We used economics to begin sketching answers to these questions. To answer the first question, we distinguished between private and public goods, and we claimed that the former should be privately owned. As for the second question, we merely remarked in passing that the rules of acquisition must be shaped according to their incentive effects. We answered the third question by developing the theory of externalities, especially the connection between public bads in economics and nuisance in law. In answering the fourth questions, we used bargaining theory to conclude that the injunctive remedy is preferred for private bads and the damage remedy is preferred for public bads.

These answers are very general. Now we will re-examine some aspects of each of these questions in greater detail. This chapter consists of a series of topics, rather than a continuous argument, so the reader may wish to pick and choose among them. The topics are organized roughly according to the four fundamental questions of property law. There will be some overlap and a few round pegs in square holes because property law does not neatly separate into distinct questions. First, we examine problems that arise in deciding what resources should be property and how the rights of ownership should be delineated; next, we consider different forms of ownership, such as private and public ownership; then, we investigate some economic considerations for deciding what rights should be included in the bundle called property; and finally, we consider the use of various remedies to protect property owners from expropriation and interference by other private citizens and the government.

I. WHAT RESOURCES SHOULD BE PROTECTED BY PROPERTY RIGHTS?

In the preceding chapter we explained that the clear delineation of property rights facilitates bargaining and voluntary exchange. The practical problem is that the delineation and enforcement of property rights is costly, especially for intangible resources such as ideas. It is necessary, consequently, to balance the benefit from delineating property rights against the costs. In this section we consider how the law strikes such a balance.

A. Fugitive Property

The problem of defining property rights seems straightforward for objects like land and houses, which have definite boundaries and stay put, but what about objects that are difficult to pin down, like natural gas or wild animals? Fugitive property—as things such as natural gas and wild animals are called—creates a legal problem that can be illustrated by the case of *Hammonds v. Central Kentucky Natural Gas Co.*, 255 Ky. 685, 75 S.W.2d 204 (Ct. of Appeal of Kentucky, 1934).

The Central Kentucky Natural Gas Company leased tracts of land under which there were large deposits of natural gas. Some of the land leased by the company was contiguous, but some parcels were separated by land that the company did not own or lease. The geological dome of natural gas from which the company drew its supply lay partially under the leased land and partially under nearby unleased land. Hammonds owned 54 acres of land that lay above the geological dome tapped by the Central Kentucky Natural Gas Company, but she had not leased the sub-surface rights of her land to the company. When the Central Kentucky Natural Gas Company extracted gas and oil from the dome, she sued the company on the theory that some of the natural gas that was under her land had been wrongfully appropriated by the defendant.

It is extremely difficult, if not impossible, to identify which of the natural gas came from under unleased land and which came from under leased land. This means that there is a problem here, and we might see that problem lessened by the adoption of either of two legal rules:

1. "that oil and gas are not the property of anyone until reduced to actual possession by extraction" or
2. "that the owner of the surface has the exclusive right to sub-surface deposits."

Under the first rule, the Central Kentucky Natural Gas Company was entitled to extract all the oil and gas from the dome, regardless of whether it held the surface rights. But under the second rule the Central Kentucky Natural Gas Company was only entitled to extract the oil and gas under the ground that it owned or leased. The consequences of these two rules for the efficient exploration and extraction of such natural resources as natural gas and oil are very different. What are those efficiency consequences?

According to the first rule, fugitive oil is not owned by anyone until someone *possesses* it, and the first person to possess it thereby becomes the owner. This rule can, consequently, be called the *rule of first possession*, which is an application of the important legal maxim "first in time, first in right." In recent history people have often attempted to claim unpossessed resources under the rule of first possession. For example, in the U.S. in the 19th century, there were a series of homesteading laws whereby pioneers could obtain title to lands on the frontier. (The laws did not confer title based upon aboriginal practices such as hunting, so Indians could not claim their ancestral lands under these laws.[1] We will see in a moment what requirements the homestead acts imposed on those who claimed title to public lands.) In the arid American Southwest, a person could obtain a right to water in a stream by being the first to tap it for use in mining or irrigation. (See the box entitled "Owning Water".) By now, there are few opportunities to claim unpossessed land or water, but even today nations make claims to

---

[1]The rule of first possession favors particular uses of the land and disfavors others; specifically, it favored the activities that the pioneers wished to engage in, such as agriculture, and disfavored the activities of Indians, such as hunting and worshipping natural objects. To illustrate, the Cherokee homeland in Georgia, South Carolina, and Tennessee, where the topsoil contains the blood and bones of generations of Cherokees, was not regarded as belonging to the Cherokees and, when they were dispossessed of it by act of Congress, the courts did not protect them or require compensation.

Property Rights in Wild Animals

A famous case that raises issues similar to those in *Hammonds* concerns ownership claims to a wild animal. A hunter flushed a wild fox from hiding, and, while he was chasing it, the fox ran across the path of a bystander who shot and kept it. The question is, who owns the fox, the original hunter or the person who shot it? As was the case with fugitive natural gas, there are apparently two possible legal rules:

1. A wild animal is not the property of anyone until reduced to actual possession by catching or killing it, or
2. A person who locates and pursues a wild animal with the intention of catching or killing it thereby acquires a right to it so long as there is a reasonable chance that his pursuit will succeed.

See how the New York Court decided which rule was preferable.

Pierson v. Post, 3 Cal. R. 175, 2 Am. Dec. 264 (Supreme Court of New York, 1805)

". . . Post, being in possession of certain dogs and hounds under his command, did, 'upon a certain wild and uninhabited, unpossessed and waste land, called the beach, find and start one of those noxious beasts called a fox,' and whilst there hunting, chasing and pursuing the same with his dogs and hounds, and when in view thereof, Pierson, well knowing the fox was so hunted and pursued, did, in the sight of Post, to prevent his catching the same, kill and carry it off. A verdict having been rendered for the plaintiff below [Post], [Pierson appealed] . . .

TOMPKINS, J. . . . The question submitted by the counsel in this cause for our determination is, whether Lodowick Post, by the pursuit with his hounds in the manner alleged in his declaration, acquired such a right to, or property in, the fox, as will sustain an action against Pierson for killing and taking him away? . . . It is admitted that a fox is a *ferae naturae*, and that property in such animals is acquired by occupancy only. These admissions narrow the discussion to the simple question of what acts amount to occupancy, applied to acquiring rights to wild animals? . . .

If the first seeing, starting, or pursuing such animals, without having so wounded, circumvented or ensnared them, so as to deprive them of their natural liberty, and subject them to the control of their pursuer, should

parts of the Antarctic or the ocean by appeal to rules similar to first possession.

A great advantage of the rule of first possession is that it proposes a relatively easy and inexpensive method of determining ownership claims. To illustrate, it is very easy to observe who first possessed the wild fox and less easy, though feasible, to determine who first possessed

afford the basis of actions against others for intercepting and killing them, it would prove a fertile course of quarrels and litigation.

However uncourteous or unkind the conduct of Pierson towards Post, in this instance, may have been, yet his act was productive of no injury or damage for which a legal remedy can be applied. We are of opinion the judgment below was erroneous, and ought to be reversed.

[Justice Livingston now gives his dissenting opinion.]

LIVINGSTON, J. My opinion differs from that of the court. . . . By the pleading it is admitted that a fox is a 'wild and noxious beast'. . . . His depradations on farmers and on barn yards have not been forgotten; and to put him to death wherever found, is allowed to be meritorious, and of public benefit. Hence it follows, that our decision should have in view the greatest possible encouragement to the destruction of an animal, so cunning and ruthless in his career. But who would keep a pack of hounds; or what gentleman, at the sound of the horn, and at peep of day, would mount his steed, and for hours together, '*sub jove frigido*,' or a vertical sun, pursue the windings of his wily quadruped, if, just as night came on, and his stratagems and strength were nearly exhausted, a saucy intruder, who had not shared in the honours or labours of the chase, were permitted to come in at the death, and bear away in triumph the object of pursuit? . . .

[W]e are at liberty to adopt one of the provisions just cited . . . that property in animals *ferae naturae* may be acquired without bodily touch or manucaption, provided the pursuer be within reach, or have a *reasonable* prospect (which certainly existed here) of taking, what he has *thus* discovered an intention of converting to his own use. . . .

Question 5.1: What was the lower court's judgment? Why does the majority here reverse that judgment? What benefits does the majority believe will flow from adopting the rule that the ownership of wild animals is established by catching or killing it, not by chasing it with the intent to catch or kill it? Do you agree with the majority's analysis? Why or why not?

Question 5.2: What reason does the minority opinion give for preferring the alternative rule that ownership of wild animals is established by chasing the animal with the intent to catch or kill it? Do you agree? Why or why not?

the fugitive oil. This ease of observability makes adjudication cheap and simple.[2]

---

[2]It does not, however, remove all problems. For example, there can be troublesome uncertainties about who was *really* the first possessor. But at least the rule of first possession focuses the issue on a few central and relatively easily-answered questions.

Owning Water

Water has always been one of the most valuable natural resources, but because it tends to run away, there have always been problems in defining and assigning property rights in water. Centuries ago in England the low density of population and the relative plenitude of water meant that disputes about use and ownership rights to water were infrequent. The leading uses of water were for the home and as the source of reservoirs to create controlled streams, called "mill races," to turn water wheels. Such cases as arose usually were between a landowner and the owner of a mill regarding their respective rights of access to a stream or river. The general rule that the law established in resolving competing claims to water was that rights would be assigned based on priority in time (the rule of first possession) and that these rights would vest in the riparian owner, that is, in the person who owned the land on the bank of the river. The riparian owner's principal right was to a *flow* of water past his land. This rule for initial assignment was supplemented by the restriction placed on the initial right-holder to use his water rights so as to cause no harm to others. Since the principal attribute of the water rights was a right to a *flow*, the implication was that it would be a violation of someone else's rights for an upstream user to use the water that passed by his property in such a way as to harm downstream users with similar rights. The upstream user could not, therefore, divert so much of the water to his own use that the flow was significantly diminished for those downstream.

The English common law property rules governing water, which are known as the "natural flow theory," were accepted unchanged into the law of the early United States. However, in the nineteenth century this legal arrangement had to be altered. There were two reasons spurring the change: the first was the great increase in the demand for water as a source of power for industry and the second was the expansion of settlement in the United States into the relatively dry and sparsely populated West.

The increase in the use of water as a source of power meant that the demands on the natural flow of a river frequently exceeded the supply. Indeed, it became necessary in some circumstances to alter the natural course or dimensions of the river in order to accommodate the demands of the industrial users. The law handled this change by, first, refining and applying to the new circumstances the principles of priority and of no-harm-to-others and, second, by focusing not on the flow of the stream but rather on the *use* of that flow. Since it was the case that the demand for the use of the flow exceeded the supply, the courts had to discover some means of allocating this increasingly scarce resource. In England and the eastern United States, these issues were resolved by elaborating the *natural flow theory* of water rights. Under that theory, each riparian owner was entitled to the limited use of the natural flow of a stream of water by his property, the use being limited by the necessity of not impairing the flow available to downstream users. One of the important aspects of the natural flow theory was that the right of the riparian owner to use the water was limited to use on the riparian owner's land. Thus, the riparian owner who had no intention of using the flow on his own land could not divert water in order to re-sell it to someone who was removed from the bank but desired to purchase access to the flow. The reason for this restriction was to prevent just the sort of unproductive, speculative ownership of riparian land that is likely to take place under a pure rule of first possession.

An alternative theory of water rights appeared in the western United States and is now the predominant theory in this country. Under the *reasonable use theory*, the riparian owner is entitled to use the water flow in any way that does not unreasonably interfere with the reasonable use of others. The differences between this theory and the natural flow theory are subtle but important. They are as follows:

1. Under the reasonable use theory a riparian owner does not have a fundamental right to have the natural integrity of a body of water maintained.
2. A riparian owner whose rights are established under the reasonable use theory may use those rights for either riparian or non-riparian uses so long as his use does not interfere with the reasonable use of others. There are no other proscriptions on the use of the water.
3. One owner may use *all* of the water in a stream or lake when others are making no use of it.
4. A riparian owner may transfer his rights to use to non-riparians, so long as their use does not interfere with the reasonable use of others.

Is there an underlying economic explanation that caused the reasonable use theory to be attractive in the western United States but not in the eastern or southern United States or in England? In the West the land is arid, meaning that access to water for farming as well as for livestock was one of the most important attributes of land. In order for settlement to proceed, the law had to accommodate uses, such as irrigation, that were almost unknown in the much wetter sections of the country and that sometimes completely dried up the stream. The reasonable-use theory allowed the appropriation of water in ways that facilitated agricultural and industrial development of that region. The value of a body of water for other uses—for example, scenery—was virtually nil. Thus, the law had to change in order to reflect the different relative prices of the underlying factors of production. In the East and the South, as well as in England, a stream is an amenity that can add value to land even though it is not being used. Thus, in those regions there was an emphasis on preserving the natural flow and other amenities of a stream.

See Coffin v. The Left Hand Ditch Co., 6 Colo. 443 (1882) and Gaffney, *Economic Aspects of Water Resource Policy*, 28 AM. J. ECON. & SOC. 131 (1969).

But the rule of first possession does leave a gap in the system of property rights: specifically, the fugitive objects that are not possessed by anyone are, as yet, no one's property. This fact may create an incentive for some people to pre-empt others by making uneconomic investments to obtain ownership of the property. And that consequence of the rule of first possession causes inefficiencies because pre-emptive investment is not necessarily efficiency-enhancing.

There is a simple explanation of why the rule of first possession creates an incentive to invest too much too early. Under the rule of first possession, an investment yields two types of benefits to the investor: (i) a productive return (more is produced from existing resources) and, (ii) a speculative return (the ownership of some resources is transferred to the investors so that future increases in value are transferred to the current owner). For example, fencing unowned land increases the productivity from grazing cattle on it and, under the appropriate circumstances, title is transferred to the person who built the fence. Profit-maximizing investors will, consequently, fence land until the marginal cost equals the marginal value of the sum of the increased productive value *plus* the value of transferred ownership. Economic efficiency, however, concerns the *production* of wealth, not the *transfer* of it. For the sake of efficiency, investors ought to fence land until the marginal cost equals the marginal increase in productive value. Investors ought to ignore the transfer of ownership for the sake of social efficiency but, under the rule of first possession, it is not in their self-interest to do so. The transfer-effect under the rule of first possession thus causes over-investment in the activities that the law defines as necessary to obtain legal possession.

Sometimes the over-investment effect of the rule of first possession may be used by public policymakers to achieve beneficial consequences; at other times the effect is overlooked with undesirable and unintended consequences. As an example of the first possibility, consider the homesteading acts. The Homestead Act of 1862 established rules for private citizens to acquire ownership of up to 160 acres of the public domain. The Act required claimants to fulfill certain requirements before they acquired title; for example, the claimant had to file an affidavit swearing that he or she was the head of a family or 21 years old and that the claim was "for the purpose of actual settlement and cultivation, and not, either directly or indirectly, for the use or benefit of any other person or persons whomsoever"; moreover, before full title was acquired for $1.25 per acre, the claimant had to reside on the claim for six months and make "suitable" improvements on the land. Clearly these requirements were meant to minimize the transfer effect of speculative possession and to encourage the productive use of the public domain. But in practice the requirements were either fleetingly enforced (as was usually the case with the residence requirement) or easily evaded (as was the case when the suitable improvement requirement was satisfied by placing miniature homes, really large doll houses, on the claim). The result was that there was a great deal of speculative demand for acreage under the Homestead Act. As a result, economic occupation and development of the frontier occurred at a faster pace than competitive markets or a strictly-enforced Homestead Act would have produced. It is possible, although unproved, that the framers of the Homestead Act intended this over-investment.

But more usually the over-investment stimulated by the rule of first possession has undesirable and unintended consequences. Consider briefly the fate of sea creatures. They are unowned until someone possesses them. The consequence of this instance of the rule of first possession has been over-investment in fishing for such sea mammals as whales, seals, and sea otters to the point that some species are in danger of extinction.

In contrast to the rule of first possession, there is no gap in ownership under the second rule for fugitive gas, according to which all the gas under the ground already belongs to the people who own the surface. By extension, this second rule suggests that, wherever possible, ownership claims in fugitive property should be tied to ownership in other, easily observed forms of property. Thus, the ownership of natural gas should be tied to that of land; that of wild animals should also be tied to land; that of fish and other marine resources should perhaps be tied to the ownership of the ocean floor (but this presents special problems to which we turn in a moment). The advantage of tying ownership of fugitive property to ownership of settled property is that this rule does not induce inefficient investment in speculative pre-emption *so long as the ownership claims in the resource to which the fugitive property is tied are already established.* Under the second rule all the gas is already owned because all the surface rights are already owned, and so the rule does not provide an incentive to acquire ownership to gas by extracting too much gas too soon.

However, the problem with the second rule, as illustrated by the facts in *Hammonds*, is that this method of establishing and verifying ownership rights is sometimes difficult to administer and enforce. Because of the geographic dispersity of underground caverns and because of the homogeneity of natural gas, it is costly and difficult to establish in court the original underground location of natural gas that has been pumped to the surface.

Our analysis of fugitive resources reveals a tradeoff that is very common in property law: *Rules that tie ownership to possession have the advantage of being easy to administer and the disadvantage of providing incentives for uneconomic investment in possessory acts, whereas rules that allow ownership without possession have the advantage of avoiding pre-emptive investment and the disadvantage of being costly to administer.* From an economic perspective, choosing between the two rules in a case such as *Hammonds* or *Pierson* is a matter of balancing the incentive to over-invest under the rule of first possession against the cost of administering and enforcing ownership without possession.

This line of thought suggests that some intangible but valuable resources, such as the ocean floor (see the box entitled "Owning the Ocean") or the electromagnetic spectrum, will remain unowned until the cost of administering a system of property rights is not prohibitive. Insofar as law tends to evolve towards economic efficiency, a society will incur the costs of

Owning the Ocean

Water covers 70% of the Earth's surface, yet almost all of that vast amount of water is devoid of well-defined property rights. In the late 16th and early 17th centuries the great voyages of discovery and the resulting sea-borne empires necessitated internationally-accepted rules on rights to use the ocean. These rights were first catalogued in the famous MARE LIBERUM of Hugo Grotius of Holland. He noted that the "sea, since it is as incapable of being seized as the air, cannot have been attached to the possessions of any particular nation." In the system that Grotius suggested and that prevailed in international law for nearly 300 years, each nation was to have exclusive rights to the use of the ocean within 3 miles of its shoreline, with that area to be called the "territorial seas." (The 3-mile distance was not picked at random; it was the distance that an early 17th century cannonball could carry.) Beyond the 3-mile limit, Grotius urged that the "high seas" should be a common resource from which none, save pirates, could legitimately be excluded. Increasing use of the high seas in the early and mid-19th century led to the replacement of the doctrine of "free use" with that of "reasonable use."

This allocation of property rights in the ocean began to crumble after World War II. In 1945 President Truman unilaterally announced that the United States' exclusive rights to subaqueous organic resources—e.g., oil and natural gas—extended to the continental margin, an area that stretched 200 miles from the Atlantic coast. Other nations quickly made similar claims.

The increasing importance of offshore oil and gas discoveries and the pressure that these discoveries made on the pre-World War II system of ocean rights led to the First United Nations Conference on the Law of the Sea in 1958. The work of that convention was never generally accepted (only one-third of UN member states ratified the treaty), yet the following four conventions regarding private property rights in the oceans emerged:

1. Without adopting a common distance, the conference specified a 12-mile maximum limit on territorial sea;
2. the conference recognized freedom of navigation, fishing, overflight, and the laying of submarine cables and pipelines on the high seas;
3. coastal states were allowed to regulate fisheries around their shores, even beyond the 12-mile territorial sea limit; and
4. the conference recognized exclusive national rights of exploration and exploitation of continental-shelf resources.

In the late 1960s and early 1970s there were several important developments that made it important that property rights in the ocean be more clearly defined. First, the volume of sea-borne commerce increased at a rapid rate. Between 1950 and 1975 that volume quadruped, with a consequent increase in the number of territorial and other disputes. Second, during the same period the world fish catch, largely in non-territorial waters, rose by 16 million tons to a total of 69 million tons. And lastly, there was the discovery of staggeringly large amounts of organic resources on the ocean bed. By 1970 the fraction of the world's oil and gas reserves that were known to be in the oceans reached 40%. Most important of these discoveries of organic material were the so-called "manganese nodules." These are coal-sized lumps lying on the floor of the deep oceans and containing commercially- and strategically-important quantities of copper, cobalt, nickel, and manganese. The total amount of resources held in these deposits is not known, but it is widely believed to be far greater than known reserves of those resources on land. Nearly all of the manganese nodules lie beyond the 200-mile continental margin.

In response to these developments, the late 1960s and early 1970s saw a rapid increase in the unilateral assertion of new jurisdictional claims; for example, Iceland announced a 50-mile exclusive fishing zone, sparking the first of its "Cod Wars" with Great Britain.

When the 3rd United Nations' Conference on the Law of the Sea (UNCLOS) convened in 1974, there was widespread agreement that the territorial sea would be established at the 12-mile limit and that there should be an "economic zone," largely but not completely controlled by the coastal state, stretching to 200 miles, the extent of the continental shelf, beyond the shoreline. There was not general agreement on what to do with property rights to the areas beyond this 200-mile limit, and it was the disposition of these areas that raised the really hard issues in the late stages of the Third Law of the Sea Conference. (It is worth noting that the 200-mile economic zone took care of the allocation of 35% of all ocean spaces and that that 35% contains almost all the known offshore oil and gas reserves, 95% of harvestable living resources, and, perhaps, a significant percentage of the manganese nodules. Just as important is the fact that one-third of the 35% allocated on the 200-mile economic zone principle will lie within 10 states, 7 of which are among the wealthiest in the world—Australia, Canada, Japan, New Zealand, Norway, the Soviet Union, and the United States.)

There were two principal positions on how to allocate rights to the manganese nodules that lie beyond 200 miles. The developed countries, following a suggestion made to the UN Seabed Committee in 1970, urged a private property rights-based system of development. Under this system the nodules would be owned and exploited by private individuals, who, because of the superior mining technology and financial resources of the developed countries, were most likely to come from those nations. The UN's role would be limited to the creation of an International Seabed Authority to register title claims to nodules and to collect royalties from the owners for distribution to UN members. The feeling of the developed countries was that this system would take advantage of the superior mining technology of the richer countries, thus allowing more rapid development of the nodules, but at the same time, through the payment of royalties, would allow the poorer nations to participate in the profits of the venture.

The developing countries offered a common property rights system in which the resources of the deep ocean floor would be the "common heritage" of all mankind. A UN-supervised company would be the only entity authorized to develop the mining rights and to distribute the profits.

In the end a compromise, called the "parallel" system, was agreed upon. There would be both private development and a UN-funded and UN-operated company, called "The Enterprise." In order to give the Enterprise the ability to compete with the more advanced countries of the developed world, an International Seabed Authority would be created to allocate rights to mine the oceans. The conference specified an ingenious variant of the "I cut; you choose" method of cake-cutting in order to allocate mining rights. Before it could begin operation, a private or state organization had to submit to the ISA two prospective sites of operations. The Authority would then choose one of those sites for later development by the Enterprise and allow the applicant to proceed with the mining of the other.

The United States refused to sign the final treaty, although 117 countries eventually signed in December, 1982.

See Northcutt Ely, *One OPEC is Enough!*, REGULATION (Nov./Dec. 1981); John Temple Swing, *Who Will Own the Oceans?*, 54 FOREIGN AFFAIRS 527 (1976); and J. Sebenius, NEGOTIATING THE LAW OF THE SEA (1984). Note that the considerations raised here apply to the determination of property rights to Antarctica. The problems associated with defining property rights arise in this part of the world, too, because of the recent discovery there of oil and because of the very valuable fishing in krill off its shores. Currently, 13 nations are signatories to a 1961 treaty that suspends all territorial claims to Antarctica for 30 years and sets aside the entire continent for peaceful, scientific purposes. A supplemental treaty about mining rights is currently under negotiation. The same arguments also apply to such important public policy issues as property rights to satellite orbital tracks (*see* Macauley & Portney, *Property Rights in Orbit*, REGULATION (July/August, 1984), to the moon, to outer space, to the other planets, and so on.

defining property rights over a resource only when the benefits of that definition exceed the costs.

This thesis about the evolution of property law can be applied wholesale to history.[3] For example, it has been argued that it was not until the benefits

---

[3]Far-reaching claims for this proposition are made by Professor Demsetz, *Toward a Theory of Property Rights,* 57 AM. ECON. REV. 347 (1967). He argues, for example, that Indians did not establish property rights in land where the costs of administering the rules exceeded the benefits from private ownership. Proceeding along these lines, he tries to explain why certain North American Indian tribes, such as those in the Northeast, whose principal economic activity was trapping animals for their fur, developed a notion of property rights and others, such as the Plains Indians, whose principal resource was the migratory buffalo, did not. The extent to which his arguments can be squared with history or anthropology is still open to question.

of settled agriculture exceeded those of nomadic agriculture or hunting that human society first incurred the costs of defining property rights in land. Whether these wholesale claims prove useful in understanding history, underlying them is a real tradeoff between ease of administration and incentives for productive investment that is one of the fundamental tensions in property law.

B. Intellectual Property: Patents, Copyrights, and Trademarks

One of the most valuable intangible resources is information. In the previous chapter we argued that the creation and enforcement of property rights in information can encourage efficient investment in and use of information. Now we will examine how the laws granting property rights to ideas actually work. Here, as with fugitive property, the law must balance the incentive to over-invest under the rule of first possession against the higher costs of administering and enforcing ownership claims under an alternative system.

Society provides three distinct systems for granting property rights in ideas. The *patent system* establishes ownership rights to inventions and other technical improvements. The *copyright system* grants ownership rights to authors, artists, and composers. The *trademark system* establishes property in distinctive commercial marks or symbols.

The distinguishing economic characteristic of each of these methods for establishing property rights in information is that they are *monopoly* rights. This seems paradoxical in that, in general, a monopoly is less efficient than a competitive industry, but information is an unusual commodity. Recall that the producer of new information may have difficulty appropriating its value in an unregulated market. By giving monopoly power to the creator of an idea, that person is presented with a powerful incentive to discover new ideas. However, a monopolist tends to discourage use of a good by over-pricing it. Put succinctly, the dilemma is that without a legal monopoly not enough information will be produced but with the legal monopoly too little of the information will be used.

1. Patents   The system of granting patents for inventions began in the Republic of Venice in 1474 and was formalized in England in the Statute of Monopolies in 1623. Article I, Sec. 8, of the United States Constitution gives Congress the power "to promote the progress of science and useful arts, by securing for limited times to authors and inventors the exclusive right to their respective writings and discoveries." To put this power into action, Congress passed the first patent law in 1790. There have been revisions of that basic act in 1793, 1836, and 1952.

To secure an exclusive right to an invention an application must be submitted to the United States Patent Office for "any new and useful process, machine, manufacture, or composition of matter, or any new and useful improvement thereof." (35 U.S. Code 101.) The invention must be non-obvious, must have practical utility (a characteristic that is more or less presumed for all applicants), and must not have been commercialized or known to the public for more than a year before the date of application. The applicant who successfully passes these tests is given a 17-year monopoly on the use of the patent. Others who wish to use the invention or improvement must purchase the right to do so from the patent holder. He may, at his discretion, "license" the use of his patent in exchange for the licensee's payment of a fee known as a "royalty."

About three-fourths of all applications are granted by the Patent Office. Throughout the 1970s between 70,000 and 80,000 patents were granted per year. Of those issued between 1971 and 1975, 51% were assigned to domestic corporations, 23% to foreign corporations and governments, 2% to the United States federal government, and 23% to individual inventors.[4] This distribution represents a secular trend in the century toward corporate ownership and away from individual ownership of most new patents.

Economists have long been concerned with several important efficiency aspects of the patent system: for example, the optimal patent life. If the monopoly right is granted for too long a time period, then the usual monopoly distortions may exceed the social benefits realized from granting an inventor an exclusive right to his creation. In that case the social costs of the patent might well be greater than the social benefits. There are several components of these social costs. First are the extraordinary costs that potential users of the invention or competitors of the inventor may incur in trying to "invent around" the patent. Second are the costs to consumers of underutilization of the monopolized product. These social costs could have been reduced on balance if the invention's patent monopoly had been adjusted so that it expired before the social costs exceeded the social benefits.

The balancing of these considerations is depicted in Figure 5.1. The horizontal axis indicates the life of patents in years. The vertical axis indicates the dollar costs and benefits of inventions. The marginal social cost of the monopoly given to an inventor is indicated by the *MSCM* curve that slopes up to indicate that the annual social cost of the monopoly right increases with the length of time of the patent. The marginal social benefit of inventive activity is indicated by the *MSBI* curve that slopes down to indicate that extending the life of patents increases the amount of investment activity, but at a diminishing rate. The intersection of the two curves indicates the optimal patent life, denoted t^* in the figure.

One can understand the problem with the current law by recognizing that a major invention is given the same 17-year monopoly right as is a minor improvement in an existing production process. The long period may be justifiable in the case of the major invention in order to allow the inventor time to realize enough profit to have made his investment worthwhile and to encourage other inventors to press on with their projects. But for the minor improvement, the investment in skill, time, and resources by the pat-

---

[4]Frederick Scherer, INDUSTRIAL MARKET STRUCTURE AND ECONOMIC PERFORMANCE, (2d ed. 1980).

Figure 5.1 The Optimal Life of Patents

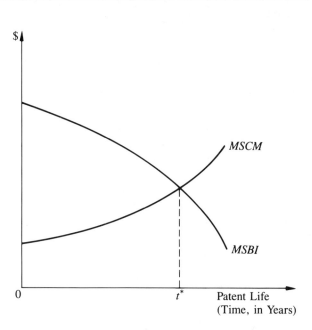

The *MSCM* curve represents the marginal social cost of granting a monopoly to the patent-holder; it slopes upward because all monopolies impose efficiency losses, and the social costs of a patent monopoly increase with the length of time of the patent. The *MSBI* curve indicates the marginal social benefit of the inventive activity that the patent rewards; it slopes downward to indicate that although extending the life of patents increases the total amount of inventive activity, the rate of increase diminishes. The length of patents should be extended if the extension generates more social benefits than costs. The optimal patent life is t^*, where the marginal social costs and marginal social benefits are equal.

entee was probably minor, too, so that the optimal period of time necessary for the monopoly right to run is probably much shorter than 17 years. (Can you use Figure 5.1 to explain why this should be so?)[5]

Determining *a priori* the optimal patent life of any given invention is costly and in some cases may simply be impossible. Nonetheless, some improvement in the efficiency of the current system may be feasible. The Federal Republic of Germany, for example, has established a two-tiered patent system in which major inventions receive full-term patents, while minor

---

[5]Assume that the curves shown in Figure 5.1 are those for a major invention. How would those curves be different for a minor invention? The *MSBI* curve would probably be lower because the social benefits of the minor invention at any given level of patent life are less than for the major invention shown in the figure. If the social costs of the monopoly are invariant to whether the invention is major or minor, then the lower *MSBI* curve for a minor invention means that the optimal patent life for a minor invention (at the point of equality of the social costs and benefits of the invention) occurs at a lower t than that shown in Figure 5.1.

inventions and improvements receive "petty patents" for a term of three years. There are disputes about whether an invention is major or minor, but this two-tier system has worked well in Germany to reduce the social costs of patents.

A second issue arising in the optimal patent life literature has been the search for some way in which to forestall the use of the patent system to achieve anticompetitive ends. Examples of such ends are the suppression of inventions or the fencing-off of some vital area of technology, known respectively as "patent shelving" and "patent blitzing." There is one tool already available to prevent these inefficient uses of patent law: the antitrust laws.[6] But in most circumstances, antitrust law is unnecessary because the use of a patent to suppress an invention is exceedingly unlikely. The far more common case is that the licensing of a patent for a fee is much more valuable to the patentee than is the act of not revealing an invention. And it can be argued that being able to "fence off" an area—for example, by patenting the microchip, an invention that is crucial to all subsequent developments in microcomputer technology—presents precisely the sort of reward for inventive activity that is most likely to encourage substantial improvement.

In the recent past there have been two additional policies proposed to minimize the predatory or anti-competitive use of the patent system. The first is a proposal to subject all patents in force to an annual tax or renewal fee. If the fee is not paid, the patent is cancelled. In West Germany, where this policy is in force, the annual fee is relatively modest for the first several years of a patent's life but thereafter escalates at regular intervals until the patent period is exhausted. The result of the West German renewal fee system is that fewer than 5% of German patents remain in force for their entire term, the average patent life being a little less than 8 years. Thus, the renewal fee system reduces the social costs of patent monopolies. In addition, it has apparently had no adverse effect on inventive activity in Germany.

We can explain how to set the annual renewal fee by reference to Figure 5.1. The fee should be set equal to the marginal social costs imposed by the patent-holder's monopoly right. Thus, in the figure the fee should be equal to the height of the curve labelled *MSCM* in each year. The *MSCM* curve slopes upward to indicate that the cost to society of extending the patent monopoly for an additional year increases as the patent becomes older. Thus, the renewal fee also increases in each year of the patent's life. Presumably, the patent-holder will pay the fee in the early years of his patent because the benefits from maintaining his monopoly exceed the renewal fee (or social cost). But as the renewal fee increases and the private benefits of the monopoly decrease, there comes a point beyond which it is better for the patent-holder to discontinue paying the fee because the benefit to him of the monopoly right has fallen below the annual renewal fee. If the fee is calcu-

---

[6]The antitrust literature on patents is extensive. *See, e.g.,* R. Posner & F. Easterbrook, ANTITRUST LAW (1982).

lated correctly, then this discontinuance will occur at t^*, the socially optimal patent life.

A far more intrusive proposal is that of compulsory licensing. This policy, which forms part of the patent system of most West European countries, allows a frustrated licensee to ask a court to compel the patentee to license to him if he can show that the patent holder has failed to use his patent in the domestic market within a specified time period, has failed to license when that is essential to bringing a complementary invention into use, or when the patent owner abuses his position by, for example, excessively restricting the supply of his invention. If the court is persuaded by the licensee to compel licensing, then it also determines a "reasonable" royalty. In countries that have compulsory licensing, its use is extremely rare, but that may reflect the fact that the mere possibility of compulsion is enough to encourage transactions between reluctant patentees and licensees. It may also reflect the possibility that it would be so difficult to enforce that no one wants to venture on such a gray area.

2. Copyright   The copyright laws attempt to convey the same monopoly rewards to writers, composers, and other artists as incentives to creative activity as the patent laws do for inventors. Article I, Section 8, of the Constitution empowers Congress to establish protection for authors' works. Since 1787 the Copyright Act has been re-written four times, most recently in 1976. Each revision may be explained as an attempt to include new forms of original composition: the 1802 act added artistic prints to the list of protected works; the 1831 act added musical composition; and the 1870 law added paintings, statues, and other examples of fine arts. Unlike the patent system, the copyright system does not require anything more than registration of the work by the creator, and in many instances the creator is protected even without having registered. Until the Copyright Act of 1976 the United States granted copyright in multiples of 14 years. For example, the 1909 act allowed for an initial term of 28 years with renewal for another 28 years. The 1976 act granted copyright protection for the creator's lifetime plus 50 years.[7]

The twin pillars of the current copyright act are that only *expressions* of an *original* idea are granted monopoly rights. Seven categories of original

---

[7]Before 1976 there was a distinction between *common law copyright* and *statutory copyright*. The first was perpetual and belonged to an author and all his heirs, successors, and assigns. However, this form of copyright was good only so long as the material remained unpublished. Once the material was published, the monopoly rights to its use were limited in time by statute, beginning in 1710. The feeling was apparently that once an author decided to commercialize his creation he forfeited his perpetual rights in exchange for the state's protection of his exclusivity for a limited duration.

This division between pre- and post-publication rights was abolished in the 1976 act in favor of a longer time period of *statutory* protection from the time that the creation was put in some concrete form.

▌Computer Chips and Computer Software

Computer programs, called "software," are protected by copyright. As with all copyrighted material, the author does not have to register his work in order to receive copyright protection. Nonetheless, because the registration confers substantial advantages at a very low cost—for example, it erases any doubt about the primacy of creation in the event of a later dispute—software authors have been encouraged to register. To register, the author of any copyrightable work must submit at least the first and last several pages of the work to the Copyright Office and allow these pages to become part of the public record. This divulgence of even a small part of the program has made many computer programmers reluctant to register for fear that their thoughts will be stolen. Recently the Copyright Office has indicated its willingness to accept the first and last pages of a program in a highly arcane form called "machine language," a move that would render the registered documents intelligible to only a very few.

For those who produce the semiconductor chips upon which much of the computer's logic and memory reside, the property rights situation has been less satisfactory. Only recently have some courts granted copyright protection for the design of wires and switches that constitutes a chip. But the extent of that protection is less than complete, making it profitable for some firms to invest millions of dollars in pirating the design of chips, producing them at a fraction of the cost of the major developers and manufacturers, and thus removing much of the incentive to develop new, more efficient computer chip designs.

Nor may the pattern on a chip be protected by a patent. As we have seen, a patentable invention must be non-obvious, a hurdle that the pat-

expressions are enumerated for protection—literary works, musical works, dramatic works, choreographic works, graphic works, audiovisual works, and sound recordings—but the Act notes that this list is not exclusive.

The economic efficiency argument in favor of a system of copyright comes from the standard economic theory of information that we reviewed in the previous chapter: in the absence of monopoly protection for original artistic creations, there will be "too little" creative activity. This is because, once a creation is disseminated, it becomes very difficult to exclude nonpaying beneficiaries, who will enjoy the creation without having to pay the creator for the pleasure. As a result, creators cannot easily recoup enough revenue through market transactions to justify the expense of producing their work or foregoing other profitable uses of their time and talent. (See the box on the California Resale Royalties Act to see how one state has attempted to correct for this apparent public goods problem.) The copyright monopoly gives the creator the right to bring an action against nonpaying beneficiaries of his creation and so reduces the public goods problem associ-

terns of wires and switches on a silicon chip has not been able to clear. The prevailing view is that computer chip patterns are—like fashion designs—variations on a single underlying idea and, for that reason, unpatentable. Moreover, the chip patterns, technically known as "masks," are changing so rapidly that a pattern is likely to become obsolete by the time the two- or three-year patent-approval process is completed.

To resolve this problem, in the fall of 1984 Congress passed and the President signed the Semiconductor Chip Protection Act. The Act creates a special system that combines some of the aspects of patent and some of those of copyright. For example, as with a patent, the Act grants a limited, 10-year period of exclusive protection to a chip pattern that has been registered with the federal government. But unlike the patent system, the registrant need not demonstrate uniqueness, only that the pattern is, like a copyrighted work, an original expression.

This resolution of the domestic status of semiconductor chip patterns now shifts the focus of attention to the international arena. Currently, the international conventions on patent and copyright do not recognize an exclusive right like that embodied in the Semiconductor Chip Protection Act. That has meant that a great deal of the piracy has been international. Prospects for the United States' solution being widely adopted are not great, although the Act does create incentives (in the form of reciprocal rights and trade concessions) for other countries to comply with the protection granted to chips.

ated with original artistic creation. As Lord Macaulay put it, copyright is "a tax on readers for the purpose of giving a bounty to writers."[8]

Recall that our survey of the economic theory of information in the previous chapter revealed that there are alternatives to the standard theory's perception that most information is a public good. One of those alternatives holds that some information is such that competition will lead to "too much" information, not too little as the standard theory holds. We discussed that alternative theory in the context of possibly duplicative research into a cure for cancer. Another alternative to the standard theory holds that some information is sufficiently private so that the unregulated market will produce an efficient amount of it. We discussed this theory in the context of an invention of a weather forecasting technique. Recently, Judge Stephen Breyer has argued that this latter alternative theory comes close to describ-

---

[8]T. Macaulay, SPEECHES ON COPYRIGHT 25 (C. Gaston ed. 1914).

Droit de Suite: The California Resale Royalties Act

Many European countries supplement an artist's copyright protection with a "droit de suite." This right entitles the artist to a fixed percentage of the sale price of his or her work whenever it changes hands.

California, the home of many artists, is the only state in the United States that has a *droit de suite:* the California Resale Royalties Act [CAL. CIV. CODE Sec. 986 (1976); amended in 1982.] The Act entitles an artist to a 5% royalty on the sale price of his or her work each time it is sold. The initial sale by the artist is excluded. No royalty is given if the gross sale price is less than $1000. If he is not paid, the artist may bring an action for damages. However, the action must be brought within three years of the date of sale or one year after the artist's discovery of the sale, whichever is later. In the original Act no royalty was due for any resale after the artist's death. But in the Amendment of 1982, the rights of the artist were to continue and inure to the benefit of his heirs, legatees, and assigns until the 20th anniversary of his death. In general, this right to royalties is not transferable to others.

The reasons for assigning this right to royalties upon resale are several. First, the right would seem to put artists on an equal footing with authors. Copyright affords the right to control *reproductions* of one's work, and this allows an author or graphic artist or composer to participate in the proceeds from every new sale or re-issue of his work. But an artist's work is rarely reproduced; indeed, much of its value comes from its being unique. In the absence of a *droit de suite*, the artist's only opportunity to participate in the value of his work is at its initial sale. By granting her the right to participate in resale, the artist is put in the same position as authors and composers.

ing the market for many original artistic creations currently protected by copyright. He concludes that, because the unregulated market for creative output is not as inefficient as the standard theory indicates, the case for granting a copyright monopoly and for extending it to new types of creative activity is weak.[9]

Judge Breyer's intriguing analysis is worth looking at more closely. He focuses on book publishers (not authors) and asks if it is true, as the standard economic theory argues, that in the absence of copyright there will be an inefficiently small number of books published. Recall from the standard theory that one of the difficulties in a market for information is that a consumer of the information becomes a rival to the original disseminator.

---

[9]S. Breyer, *The Uneasy Case for Copyright: A Study of Copyright in Books, Photocopies, and Computer Programs,* 84 HARV. L. REV. 281 (1970).

It was also argued that the *droit de suite* would encourage artistic activity. Many artists sell their first works at relatively low prices because they are unknown talents. If the value of those works appreciates later, then the benefit inures to the current owners rather than to the artist. The classic example of this phenomenon is Vincent Van Gogh (1853–1890), who is today considered a great painter but is said to have sold only one painting during his life. If artists were allowed to participate in this increase in the value of their work, then they would stick to their creative activity rather than try some more lucrative and non-artistic employment.

The economic issues raised by the *droit de suite* are fascinating but complex. To take but one such issue, it may be doubted whether the Act really encourages creative activity. This is because of the fact that without the Act an artist can already participate in the appreciation of the value of his work. Typically, an artist keeps an inventory of his work on hand so that if his work catches on and its value rises, he may participate in this increase by selling other works out of his inventory. Alternatively, the artist can simply produce more original work after his talent becomes known. In fact, it is possible that these actions accomplish the same end as that intended by the *droit de suite*. If so, then a persuasive case has not been made for that legislation. Indeed, to the extent that artists indirectly participate in the increase in the value of their previous work by keeping inventories and by increasing their later output, legislation like the California Resale Royalties Act introduces inefficiencies into the market for artistic activity. (Can you see how?)

Because the rival's costs of transmitting the information are so low, he can almost always undercut the original disseminator. As applied to book publishing, this analysis predicts that the original publisher of a book could always be undercut by another publisher. The copying publisher does not incur the fixed costs of discovering and editing the author's work, cutting plates, making corrections, and so on; instead, he can produce the book for the relatively low cost of photographing the pages of the original and of distributing it. Because his costs are lower, the copying publisher can sell the book at a lower price than the original publisher. In fact, actual estimates suggest that a copying publisher's costs will be about one-third lower than the original publisher's. This much seems to confirm the standard theory.

However, Judge Breyer points out that the original publisher has countervailing advantages that may more than offset the cost advantages of the copier. One of these countervailing advantages is "lead time": the original publisher's product reaches the market first. This advantage is meaningful only for certain types of books. For books that must make a profit in their first few months on the market or not at all (Judge Breyer suggests this is the case for novels and general nonfiction books), the original publisher's lead time advantage may swamp a copier's cost advantage. Moreover, the more rapidly a copier attempts to cut this lead-time advantage by rushing his copies to market, the more likely he is to incur higher production costs and thus to reduce his cost advantage. For those books for which there is not much of a lead-time advantage (Judge Breyer indicates that college textbooks are an example), the copier's cost advantage cannot be so easily overcome.

A second countervailing advantage that the original publisher may have is that of retaliation. At a minimum, the original publisher can match the copier's lower retail price, and this action reduces the incentive to copy. But additionally the original publisher may have better quality reproduction, a better distribution network, and the ability to claim his as the "authorized" edition. Taken together, these retaliatory actions may offset a copier's cost advantages.

There is much more to Judge Breyer's economic analysis of the case for copyright. For example, he discusses whether private contractual arrangements between book consumers organized in buying clubs and book publishers might further reduce the copying publisher's profits. He asks if a policy of subsidizing book publishers out of general tax revenues is a more efficient method of correcting for the small inefficiencies of the market for books than is the system of granting copyright monopolies. His analysis is invariably stimulating and instructive. Judge Breyer concludes that there is a case to be made for copyright protection of books (and other original creations) but that the case is not as strong as the standard theory makes out and that, as a result, the protections granted by copyright law need not be as extensive as they currently are.

3. Trademarks and Servicemarks   Many modern businesses and service organizations invest vast sums of money to establish an easily recognizable symbol that the consuming public will use to identify particular sellers. For example, every American with small children is aware of how distinctive the golden arches are in signaling the location of a McDonald's franchise. Those arches and numerous other examples demonstrate one of the most important aspects of a trademark or servicemark: its ability to minimize consumers' search costs. Almost inseparably coupled with that function is a trademark's value as a reliable indicator of the quality of output. Moreover, it is probably the case that an anonymously produced item is of lower quality than one with a brand name. As an example of this point, consider that when the Soviet Union abolished marks identifying the producing plant of various consumer goods, the average quality of those goods fell.[10]

---

[10]See Goldman, *Product Differentiation and Advertising: Some Lessons from Soviet Experience*, 68 J. POL. ECON. 346 (1960) and Scherer, INDUSTRIAL MARKET STRUCTURE AND ECONOMIC PERFORMANCE 379, n. 14 (2d ed. 1980).

The relationship between product quality and brand name is much disputed within the economics profession. Some claim that product differentiation, of which trademarks are an aspect, is not a good thing. The principal argument is that this differentiation serves to obscure otherwise physically identical products, such as sugar and aspirins and, therefore, to cause producers to waste money artificially distinguishing their products. The resources that go into this differentiation are, it is argued, a social waste. Other economists assert that product differentiation is maintained only where consumers find some reason to believe that there is really a distinction. For example, those who spend lots of money for vodka (which, let us assume, is an identical product, regardless of who produced it) apparently wish to be known as people who are able to spend lots of money on vodka. If that desire gives them utility, then the efforts of producers to distinguish their output increases consumer well-being and, therefore, produces a net social benefit.

Trademarks have their origin in the markings that ancient craftsmen in the Middle and Far East placed on their work. The clear intention was to establish in the consumer's mind a connection between a particular craftman's work and its high quality. It must have been obvious at an early date that unscrupulous traders could imitate the marks of established craftsmen in an effort to capture some of their market without having incurred the costs of establishing themselves as the makers of high quality merchandise. This practice was known as "palming off." In an effort to minimize its adverse effects, both the common law and statutes from as early as the 13th century in England provided protection for trademarks.

In 1870, Congress for the first time provided guidelines for federal trademark registration. That act was held to be unconstitutional in 1879 because it did not limit the federal registration to goods in interstate or foreign commerce, the only areas of commerce that the Constitution allowed Congress to oversee.[11] Those cases also noted that, unlike patent and copyright, there is no Constitutional provision for federal protection of trademarks.

Modern trademark law stems from the Federal Trademark Act of 1946, commonly called the Lanham Act. That Act defines "trademark," "servicemark," and several other important categories of commercial symbols and provides a method for obtaining federal registration for those marks. As in the case of patents, the applicant must establish that the mark passes certain criteria, the most important of which is distinctiveness, before gaining registration. That registration entitles the holder to certain protections and rights, among which is the privilege of placing beside one's trademark a sign, ® or ™, to indicate that that is a registered trademark.

The law of trademarks (and of the closely-related field of unfair competition) is large and complex. One of the most fascinating and instructive aspects of that law for our purposes of learning about the economic effi-

---

[11]*United States v. Steffens*, 100 U.S. 82 (1879) (The Trademark Cases).

"Coke" Is It!

One of the best-known trademarks in the world is the word "Coke" to describe the Coca-Cola Company's cola soft drink. Precisely because it is so well known, there is the danger to the Coca-Cola Company that consumers might use the designation "Coke" to refer to *any* cola soft drink and not just the one the Coca-Cola Company produces. If that should happen, then "Coke" will have become a generic product name that any producer may use. Thereafter, a patron of a restaurant who asked for a Coke would be happy to receive any cola drink, not necessarily the one produced by the Coca-Cola Company.

Precisely this sort of thing happened to the Sterling Drug Company in 1921. In that year a federal district court determined that Sterling's trademarked name for acetyl salicylic acid, Aspirin, had become the common word for *any* brand of that drug, not just Sterling's. Thus, all producers of acetyl salicylic acid have used the term "aspirin" to describe their product. (Sterling has managed to prevent this erosion of its trade name Aspirin in Mexico and Canada, where no one but Sterling may describe his acetyl salicylic acid as "aspirin.") Similarly, the Otis Elevator Company, once the proprietary owner of the trademark "Escalator," lost the exclusive use of that mark in 1950 when, among other things, its own ads described its moving stairway as an "escalator," with a small "e".

The Coca-Cola Company incurs some elaborate expenses in order to prevent its famous trademark from becoming a generic name. The Coca-Cola Trade Research Department, which has an annual budget of about $2 million, employs a team of about 25 investigators whose job is to roam the United States asking at restaurants and soda fountains for "Coke" and "Coca-Cola." The investigators then send samples of what they are served back to the corporate headquarters in Atlanta for chemical analysis. If the company determines that a restaurateur has served them something other than Coca-Cola, then that business is advised of its wrongdoing and instructed to serve only Coke if customers ask for that or to point out to the customer that the restaurant serves a different brand of cola drink. If the abuse continues or is flagrant, then Coca-Cola may sue

ciency of property rights has to do with generic terms. Nothing is more settled in the law of trademark than the proposition that product or service names cannot be trademarks. For example, no producer of cameras may register as a trademark the word "camera." To allow a producer to do so would be to give it the ability to proceed against every other camera manufacturer that advertised its product by use of the word "camera," a situation that would make for chaos. Generic names are free for all to use; that is, they are communal property.

But what about the possibility that a product, with a registered trademark, may become so successful that the trademark becomes a generic

the party for trademark infringement. Since 1945, Coca-Cola has sued over 800 retailers on these grounds, at a rate of approximately 40–60 per year. The company asserts that it has won all of these suits. The largest action was one launched in 1974 against the 900 restaurants in the Howard Johnson's Company chain. In preparation for that suit, the Trade Research Department's investigators placed orders for "Coke" or "Coca-Cola" at different Howard Johnson restaurants on 2,480 separate occasions. Howard Johnson claimed that it instructed its employees to inform patrons who made that request that they would receive Howard Johnson cola, the chain's own brand. Coca-Cola's investigators said that they were not so informed 2,115 times. The federal district court in Atlanta in 1976 granted Coca-Cola an injunction against Howard Johnson's use of the terms "Coke" or "Coca-Cola" to describe anything other than the Coca-Cola Company's cola drink.

Retailers claim that what lies behind the company's vigorous campaign is not a fear of trademark infringement but an insidious and anti-competitive attempt to browbeat retailers into dealing only with the Coca-Cola Company. They note that it is frequently too costly for them—as on a busy night—to tell each customer who asks for a rum and Coke that they are really going to get a rum and Pepsi. Rather than face a lawsuit for trademark infringement, many of the retailers claim that it is less costly for them simply to sign up with Coca-Cola as their exclusive supplier. The Coca-Cola Company's competitors assert that their bigger rival is terrorizing mom-and-pop stores, to the detriment of competition. They point to the fact that Coke has an 80% market share in the fountain soda market but a much smaller share of the supermarket sales as evidence of the fact that the Trade Research Department's work is part of an anti-competitive marketing operation. Pepsi, with less than one-quarter the fountain soda market share of Coke, does not have a trade research department.

[See "Mixing with Coke Over Trademarks Is Always a Fizzle: Coca-Cola Adds a Little Life in Court to Those Failing to Serve the Real Thing," WALL STREET JOURNAL, March 9, 1978, p. 1, col. 4.]

name? When this happens, the trademark loses its protected status and becomes a generic name. From that point on, anyone may use the former trademark to advertise the product. This makes the issue of generic names one of the most frequently litigated issues in trademark law. Furthermore, as the box on the word "Coke" indicates, this creates a powerful incentive for firms to spend resources to protect their trademark from becoming a generic name. The dilemma for entrepreneurs is this: they desire their product to become so successful as to become a household name but not so successful that people begin to use the product's name to mean any similar product.

To show you how widespread this phenomenon is, consider the following list of names that were once trademarks but have since become generic product names. The former trademark is given in capital letters, and the former generic product name is given in parentheses:[12]

ASPIRIN (acetyl salicylic acid)

BRASSIERE (women's bust support)

CELLOPHANE (transparent cellulose sheets and film)

COLA (type of soft drink)

EASTER BASKET (Easter floral bouquet)

ESCALATOR (moving stairway)

HOAGIE (type of sandwich)

LIGHT BEER (beer light in body and taste)

MONOPOLY (real estate trading game)

MONTESSORI (educational method and toys used for such method)

POCKET BOOK (paperback books)

SHREDDED WHEAT (baked wheat biscuit)

SOFTSOAP (liquid hand soap)

SUPER GLUE (rapid setting cyanoacrylate adhesives)

THE PILL (birth control oral contraceptive)

THERMOS (vacuum-insulated bottles)

TRAMPOLINE (rebound tumbling equipment)

YO-YO (return top)

The other side of this coin is the following list, which gives trademarks that have been challenged as being generic but were held to be valid trademarks:

COKE (cola beverages)

DICTAPHONE (dictating machines)

LEVI'S (denim pants)

POLAROID (light polarizing materials)

TEFLON (non-stick resin coating)

THE UNCOLA (non-cola soft drinks)

TINKERTOY (construction toy sets)

TIPARILLO (small cigar)

WING-NUT (wire connectors)

---

[12]This list comes from J. Thomas McCarthy, TRADEMARKS AND UNFAIR COMPETITION 533–37 (2d ed. 1984). This source also identifies the reported cases in which the determination was made that the trademark had become a product name.

Question 5.3: This is a question concerning remedies for infringing property rights in intellectual activity.

In a recent Supreme Court case, several plaintiffs, who were the owners of the copyrights to certain audiovisual material, sued the manufacturers of videocassette recorders (VCRs) for infringement of their property rights. The VCRs produced by the defendants could be used by their owners to record the plaintiffs' copyrighted material when it was telecast. The plaintiffs argued that home recording of their property was an invasion of their property rights, and they asked the court to prevent future infringements by enjoining the production and retail sale of VCRs and to award them money damages as compensation for past infringements of their property rights.

Assuming that the defendants have infringed the plaintiffs' property rights, what is the most efficient remedy, money damages or an injunction? Is it possible that some other form of relief is even more efficient than either legal or equitable relief, for example, a federal tax on the sales of videocassette tapes, with the proceeds divided among the copyright holders of televised material? (*Sony Corporation of America v. Universal City Studios, Inc.,* 104 S.Ct. 774 (1984) (*Betamax*).) [On the economics of the Betamax case, *see* M.B.W. Sinclair, *Fair Use Old and New: The Betamax Case and its Forebears,* 33 BUFF. L. REV. 269 (1984) and W. Gordon, *Fair Use as Market Failure: A Structural and Economic Analysis of the Betamax Case and its Predecessors,* 82 COLUM. L. REV. 1600 (1982).]

II. HOW ARE PROPERTY RIGHTS ESTABLISHED AND VERIFIED?

The difficulty with assigning property rights to fugitive objects is that, until they are possessed, their identity remains uncertain. It is difficult to put one's mark on natural gas that remains in the ground or fish that remain in the sea. Once the natural gas or fish are firmly in someone's possession, identity is no longer a problem and ownership rights are relatively easy to establish and enforce. But even after objects are identified, it may be desirable to provide some means of verifying ownership other than the mere fact of possesson of the object. These remarks hold not only for intangible property; they also hold for tangible items such as land and television sets. This section concerns the economics of registering and verifying ownership claims.

A. Recording and Transferring Title

Let's examine this important issue through an example. Suppose that you have decided to purchase some land in order to fulfill a lifelong dream of becoming a farmer. You locate a parcel in the country that you like and approach the man who is living there and appears to be the owner in order to gather more information. After discussing its boundaries, fertility, and drainage, he proposes a price that strikes you as reasonable; you decide to buy and shake hands to seal the agreement. The next week you return with a check, hand it over to the man, and shortly thereafter move onto the property. One week after you take up residence, another man knocks on the door, announces that he is the owner of the property and explains that he has come to evict the nefarious tenant who rented the house in which you are living. At this point you recall the joke that begins: "Hey buddy, how would you like to buy the Brooklyn Bridge?"

The point of this example is that when you buy real estate, you must ascertain the name of the rightful owner of the property. What is needed to prevent scams, such as tenants representing themselves as owners, is a reliable and relatively inexpensive method of determining rightful ownership. In modern land transactions there is such a system: every time real property changes hands the transaction is recorded by the filing of a deed in the County Recorder's Office. The process of recording is a formal one with the records open for scrutiny by the public. For each piece of property in the county the Recorder's Office contains a file that tells the legal boundaries of the property, any restrictions that apply to its use, who has owned the property at each point in time, and other important aspects of the ownership.

There is no common and uniform method of land registration in this country,[13] but every state has some system for the public recording of title to land. The presence of the system of recording important property transactions and of making them available to the public means that disputes like the one in which you purchased land from someone who had no right to sell the property should not arise. For minimal expense—the cost of going to the County Recorder's Office and examining the files or, more likely, the cost of hiring an attorney to search the title for you—any purchaser can ascertain who rightfully owns the property.

Registering property is not the only way to certify ownership of valuable property. Consider, for example, the ownership determination problems that arose in the Old West where ranching involved turning cattle onto the range to forage for themselves, untended, for months at a time. Inevitably, cattle from different ranches would intermingle. When the time came to round up the cattle for the drive to market, some method had to be found of determin-

---

[13]Most of the rest of the world has adopted a method known as the Torrens system, after Sir Richard Torrens, who introduced this simplified mechanism into South Australia in 1858. Several states have introduced the system, but in only three—Illinois, Massachusetts, and Minnesota—is most land registered under the Torrens system. Despite the fact that the American Bar Association and the Commissioners on Uniform State Laws have urged adoption of the Torrens system, certain vested interests, such as land title insurance companies and certain attorneys, have successfully opposed its introduction. A recent study found that if the Torrens system of land registration were in place in Cook County (Chicago), Illinois, the savings in the costs of transferring title would amount to $76 million. *See* Jancyzk, *Land Title Systems, Scale of Operations, and Operating and Conversion Costs,* 8 J. LEGAL STUD. 569 (1979).

ing whose cattle were whose. The problem was partially solved by the practice of branding each ranch's cattle with a distinctive mark.

Consider, also, the story—perhaps apocryphal but nonetheless instructive—of how the transfer of title was "recorded" in England in the Middle Ages. Most people, including landowners, could not read, so that written documentation of the conveyance of land from one person to another would not have been helpful. But land was scarce and, therefore, valuable, and its ownership was essential to survival, so some method of recording transfers had to be found. It is said that when one owner sold land to someone else, the conveyance of the land was marked by a public ceremony on the land being transferred. The former owner, in front of witnesses, handed the new owner a clod of turf and a twig from the property in a ceremony known as "livery of seisin." Then, the adults present at the ceremony would beat up a child who had witnessed the passing of turf and twig. The thrashing would be severe enough so that the child would never forget that day as long as he lived. And so, by the child's pain and fear, a living record of the transfer was created.

A system of recording title is maintained for land and a few other valuable items, like automobiles, but for most goods there is no such system. In most exchanges the buyer does not devote resources to determining whether the seller truly owns what he or she is selling. You rarely question whether the books you purchase at the bookstore were rightly the bookstore's to sell. Nor do you routinely wonder if the person sitting across the aisle from you rightfully owns the pen with which she is taking notes. A system of recording the ownership of books and fountain pens would burden commerce and impede the efficient movement of goods and services. In both cases, our presumption is that whoever possesses something rightfully owns it. Further proof of ownership is in the memory of witnesses to the sale, like the child in the medieval example, or perhaps in a written contract of sale.

We have, thus, encountered another example of a tradeoff in property law. On the one hand, verifying title by formal means, such as recording the transfer of a deed, reduces uncertainties and eliminates disputes arising from sales. On the other hand, the verification of title through formal means is costly. Property law thus has to develop rules that *balance the impediments to bargaining created by uncertain ownership against the cost of maintaining a system of verification.*

Question 5.4: Every state has laws, called "mechanics' lien laws," that grant a lien against the property to those—such as contractors, subcontractors, laborers, and the retailers of building materials—who provide services and goods in the process of constructing or making improvements to property. The lien allows the contractor to take the property as security or collateral for the credit extended by doing the work. If the owner fails to pay, the party holding the lien can foreclose on the property and sell it to settle the debt. Are such lien laws efficient? Do they minimize the costs of making improvements to property? What additional costs would be incurred by the contractor and the property owner in the absence of such laws?

B. Can a Thief Give Good Title?

Balancing these considerations is essentially a problem of designing incentives for the efficient verification of ownership. To examine this incentive problem, let's consider a variation on the example with which we began the previous section. Imagine that you have made what you consider to be a shrewd deal for the purchase of a color television set. The seller was not a retail merchant but rather a person whom you met in the parking lot outside a local bar. The seller handed over the set from the trunk of his car. He allayed your suspicions with a story that was plausible enough to convince you that the set was his to sell. One evening while you are enjoying your recent acquisition in your apartment, the police arrive and inform you that the set you are watching was stolen and that they have come to reclaim it for the rightful owner.

What should be done? Would it be best to return the set to the original owner, or should you be allowed to keep it? The current legal rule in America is that a transferor can convey only those property rights that he legitimately has; thus, a person with void title, such as a thief or a tenant, cannot convey clear title to a good faith purchaser.[14] In other words, the thief did not have good title to the television set he sold you, so he could not and did not give you good title—enforceable against everyone else—to that set. Thus, the entire risk of loss arising from the purchase of stolen goods is placed on the *buyer*. (After returning the television set to its owner, you are entitled to recover your money from the thief—technically, the thief breached his warranty of title—but this legal nicety does you no good unless he is caught and has money.)

But note that there is an alternative legal rule. Instead of putting the risk of loss on the buyer, the law might put that risk on the *original owner*. Indeed, in some parts of Europe, this alternative is the law; the buyer is presumed to have good title; if he has innocently purchased stolen goods, the loss lies on the original owner. Of course, there are some restrictions on the buyer's behavior, such as the requirement that he bought the good "in good faith." The good faith requirement, which means that the buyer genuinely believed that the seller owned the good, prevents a professional "fence" of stolen goods from hiding behind the law. The law may also require the buyer to make reasonable efforts to verify ownership, such as checking to be sure that the serial number was not filed off the television set.

Our general point is that *law must allocate the risk that stolen goods will be bought in good faith and this risk must fall either upon the original owner or the buyer.* For costly items like houses and cars, the risk can be reduced by refusing to recognize unrecorded transactions, so all sales are forced through

---

[14]This is true as a generalization, but there are important exceptions. For example, if a thief steals money and uses it to buy goods from a merchant, the original owner of the money cannot recover the money from the merchant. A thief can convey good title to money.

Credit Cards

Verification is an important problem where credit cards are used extensively. Consider two situations:

Situation A: The Visa card issued to you by your bank is stolen and, before you notify the bank, $500 worth of goods are purchased using it. Are you liable for the $500? For a fraction of it? Or are you not liable?

Situation B: You lend your Visa card to a friend to pay for a $25 dinner. He mails it back to you a week later. At the end of the month your Visa bill shows $500 in purchases that he made. Are you liable for the $500? For just $25? For nothing?

In Situation A, the use of the card was unauthorized, and by statute you have no liability beyond $50. Even the $50 liability would have been avoided if you had notified your bank of the theft before the illegal purchases were made. Notice that this limit on liability gives financial institutions a strong incentive to devise better ways of verifying that the user of the card is its owner.

In Situation B, you authorized your friend to use the card (although not to the extent to which he actually used it). You are liable for the full amount of the loss from your friend's use of your card, which in this case is $500. Notice that this rule creates a strong incentive for the owners of cards to be careful about whom they permit to use them. This incentive effect is especially important where a business owns credit cards and authorizes employees to use them.

Question 5.5: Do you think that the rule of unlimited liability of the cardowner for authorized misuse, as illustrated in situation B, benefits the banks that issue credit cards? Or do you think that most of the benefit is passed on to consumers in the form of lower costs for credit cards? Suppose the market for credit cards is perfectly competitive. Does this assumption affect your answer?

the process of recordation. Recordation, however, is an excessive burden on small transactions, including the sale of color televisions. For these items the law must either give title to the buyer, thereby assigning the risk to the original owner, or *vice versa*. The rule prevailing in parts of Europe, which assigns the risk to the original owners, gives them an extra incentive to protect their property against theft and to mark it for certain identification. The American rule, which assigns the risk to the buyers, gives them an extra incentive to verify that the seller is truly the owner.

One of these rules is more efficient in the sense that it imposes a lower burden upon commerce and promotes the voluntary exchange of property. But it is unclear from casual inspection which of these rules that is. Here is a way to conceptualize the problem. Let C_1 indicate the cost to the original owner of protecting himself against theft, say, by engraving his Social Security number on the object. Let C_2 indicate the cost to the purchaser of verifying that the seller is the owner, say, by confirming with the party from whom the seller originally obtained the good. For the sake of efficient incentives, liability should fall on the party who can verify ownership at least cost. Thus, the efficiency of the competing rules may be determined according to which one of these hypotheses is correct:

1. If it is generally true that $C_1 < C_2$, then it is more efficient for the good faith purchaser to acquire good title against the original owner; but
2. If it is generally true that $C_1 > C_2$, then it is more efficient for the original owner to retain title against the good faith purchaser.

As we said, this is the way to conceptualize this problem of determining which of the competing legal rules for allocating the risk of loss from theft is more efficient. Unfortunately, we cannot definitively answer the question we have posed because there is very little empirical evidence about the values of C_1 and C_2. (See the box "Credit Cards" for an example of how to apply this model.)

III. HOW LONG DO PROPERTY RIGHTS LAST?

Machines deteriorate with the passage of time, especially if they are heavily used; muscles, however, strengthen when regularly exercised and deteriorate from idleness. What about property rights? Are they like machines or like muscles? Do they strengthen with time and exercise, or do they depreciate? This question, to which we now turn, is directed at the third fundamental question the theory of property must answer: what rights are included in the bundle of property? Specifically, we will investigate the relationship between the passage of time, the exercise of property rights, and their strength.

A. Adverse Possession

In the preceding chapter we discussed an example in which Joe Potatoes built his house so that two feet of it extended over the property line onto Fred Parsley's lot. Recall that Parsley did not discover the trespass and sue to stop it until ten years had passed.

Most states have *statutes of limitations* on trespass and many other legal claims. These statutes specify a period of time by the end of which a claimant must exercise his rights or they expire. The conventional argument used to justify statutes of limitation is that the quality of evidence available to the court deteriorates as the events in dispute become more distant.[15] With the passage of time, memory fades and the testimony of witnesses becomes unreliable. Even the interpretation of written documents, which often depends upon the intentions of the drafters and the context in which they are drafted, becomes more difficult.

With regard to property disputes, if the statute of limitation for trespass expires before the owner complains, the right to the property may be lost by the owner and acquired by the trespasser. When someone acquires ownership to another's property by using it without timely objection by the original owner, the new owner is said to have acquired title through *adverse possession*. Thus, in our example from the beginning of Chapter 4, Potatoes might acquire a two-foot strip of Parsley's property through adverse possession. In essence, the doctrine of adverse possession asserts that one's property rights are held under a statute of limitations. If one "sleeps on one's rights," allowing those rights to age without being exercised, the law may allow someone else to assume rightful possession of your property.

There are two efficiency reasons for the rule of adverse possession. First, it lowers the administration costs of establishing rightful ownership claims in the event of a delayed dispute about rightful ownership. Like other statutes of limitations, adverse possession frees the party who has openly possessed land for the requisite period from the fear that someone else can assert ownership rights. *Adverse possession clears title of the clouds (as they are called) upon it from past wrongs, so buyers need not fear the assertion of third party claims based upon events of the distant past.* This makes the cost of land transactions less because they are not burdened by the risk that ownership will be disputed on the basis of the distant past.[16] In fact this attempt to remove clouds on title was the origin of adverse possession statutes.

Adverse possession originated in the ancient common law, but at an early date it became part of statutory law. In 1275 an English statute named

---

[15]This is the major argument for statutes of limitations, but there are others. Another is the fact that, as time passes, the person who violated another's property right by trespassing, perhaps inadvertently or unknowingly, acquires a reasonable expectation that he will not be held to account. A case can be made that law should protect such expectations.

[16]There are, however, some problems with this justification, which is not entirely convincing. Usually a statute of limitations applies to the passage of time between the performance of a *discrete* act and a complaint or charge filed against the actor. However, the trespass in adverse possession cases is *continuous*. To illustrate, suppose the statute of limitations for torts and adverse possession is, in both cases, 10 years. If *A* caused a tortious accident in 1960 that harms *B*, *B* cannot sue in 1971 because the tort occurred 11 years ago. Similarly, if *A* built a house on *B*'s property in 1960, *B* cannot bring suit in 1971 because *A* has acquired the property by adverse possession. Unlike the tort, however, the trespass that is the subject of the complaint did not occur 11 years ago; rather, it has occurred continuously for the past 11 years.

1189, the date of the death of Henry II, as the date beyond which no one could go in adducing evidence of his title to land. The effect was to enable ownership claims based on recent events, including the seizure of land by the Norman invaders from the indigenous Saxons after 1066, to prevail against claims whose origin was lost in the mists of time. Furthermore, and more germane to adverse possession, ancient claims by owners who never occupied or improved the land would lose against the claims of current users of the land. Periodically this benchmark was changed until, in 1540, instead of referring to a calendar year in the past, the statute stipulated the maximum number of years that could elapse between a legal action and the event cited as evidence of ownership in court. This new method of creating by statute a limiting period during which ownership claims must be exercised has become the modern norm. Every state now has a statute that establishes the procedures by which someone may acquire rights to another's property through adverse possession.

As in England, adverse possession statutes were initially important in America in securing the title of land essentially acquired through conquest, in this case from the Indians. To illustrate, when the Cherokee Nation in Oklahoma was dissolved by Act of Congress, the land belonging to the tribe was divided as follows: each Cherokee household was given 60 acres around the homestead and 60 acres some distance from the homestead. However, white settlers who occupied Cherokee land could acquire title simply by paying taxes on it for five years. This was one of the devices by which the Cherokee ownership of most of eastern Oklahoma in 1880 was reduced to a small part of two counties by 1950.

Thus, the first efficiency justification for the rule of adverse possession is made on the basis of minimizing the costs of administering property claims: stale evidence is bad evidence.

The second efficiency justification for the rule of adverse possession is that it tends to prevent valuable resources from being left idle for long periods of time by specifying procedures for a productive user to take title from an unproductive user. Under the rule of adverse possession, a person who does not put his land in production and monitor its boundaries runs the risk of losing it to someone who makes use of it. In this respect the rule tends to move property to higher-valued uses, as required for efficiency, by redistributing it to aggressive owners.

However, there is a potential inefficiency of the rule: if the original owner values *not using* his property more than the adverse possessor values its use, then title should remain with the original owner. These considerations must be balanced when deciding the rules for determining title through adverse possession. As the box on legal requirements for adverse possession points out, the statutory requirements for transferring title to an adverse possessor seem to minimize the possibility of inefficiently transferring title from a higher-valuing original owner to a lower-valuing adverse possessor.

Before leaving this subject, it is worth bringing together the material in the previous section on acquiring title from a thief and the material in this section on adverse possession to note the parallel treatment of real property (real estate) and personal property (chattels) in the case of disputed ownership. For real property, a trespasser who represents himself as the owner and "sells" it to a good-faith buyer cannot give the buyer a good title to the property. The buyer, not the owner, bears the risk of purchasing from a trespasser. There is, however, a statute of limitations on trespass. After a trespasser adversely possesses property for the stipulated period (and satisfies other statutory requirements), he acquires title to it. This law for real property is very similar to the law for chattels. A thief who represents himself as the owner of a television cannot give a good-faith buyer title to it. There is, however, a statute of limitation on theft; after it expires, the thief has title and can sell the good. For real property and personal property, the law strikes a balance between protecting the rights of ownership and unburdening commerce of claims based upon ancient wrongs. These facts illustrate our thesis that property law, whether for real property or personal property, facilitates the efficient use of resources.

B. Estray Statutes

Suppose that while strolling down an alley in Manhattan you stumble over a brown paper bag. Opening the bag, you find that it contains a diamond brooch. Naturally, you would like to claim it for your own. But clearly someone has lost it. Are you entitled to keep it if the owner does not demand it back after a reasonable period of time? Or are you obligated to make positive efforts to locate the owner, such as advertising in the paper? Every state has an "estray statute" to answer these questions and most of the statutes are similar. (The workings of these statutes in a fascinating, real case are illustrated in the box concerning lost cash.)

Consider the economic reasons for the law's concerning itself with property that has been abandoned, lost, or mislaid. First, some orderly procedure is necessary for determining the ownership of every valuable resource, including something that is apparently lost. Without such a procedure, there might be an incentive for finders simply to take the property they have found rather than making an attempt to discover the true owner. Even worse, there might be an incentive for some people to steal other people's property and then claim, if confronted, that they found it. ("Where did you get it?" Sherlock asked the suspect. "It fell off the back of a truck," he replied.) This possibility suggests that the statute should specify procedures for a finder to follow in order to locate the true owner and impose penalties on finders who do not take these steps. That is just what most state laws do. Here is the Illinois statute that was applied in the *Paset* case reproduced in the box on lost cash:

"If the owner is unknown and if such prope.. ty found is of value of $15 or upwards, the finder or finders shall, within 5 days after such finding as aforesaid, appear before some circuit judge residing in the county, and make affidavit of the description thereof, the time and place when and where the same was found, that no alteration has been made in the appearance thereof since the finding of the same, that the owner thereof is unknown to him and that he has not secreted, withheld or disposed of any part thereof. . . .

[T]he county clerk, within 20 days after receiving the certified copy of the judge's order shall cause an advertisement to be set up on the court house door, and in three other of the most public places in the county, and also a notice thereof to be pub-

Legal Requirements for Adverse Possession

There are four requirements in the typical adverse possession statute. (Ask yourself if these requirements minimize the problem noted in the text of inefficiently transferring title by adverse possession from an owner who values not using his property more than the adverse possessor values its use.)

1. The adverse possessor must have actually entered the contested property and have assumed exclusive possession. In the preceding chapter we gave an example in which Joe Potatoes built a house that extended onto Fred Parsley's land. That action by Potatoes satisfies this first requirement.
2. That possession must be "open and notorious." This phase means that the trespass must not be done in secret; an alert owner should be able to detect it.
3. The possession must be adverse or hostile and under a "claim of right." This condition requires the trespass to be inconsistent with the owner's use-rights and against the owner's interests.
4. Finally, the trespass must be continuous for the statutorily-specified period.[1]

These conditions are indifferent with respect to whether the trespasser knew the land belonged to someone else or whether he sincerely thought that it was his own. There is evidence, however, that courts are not really indifferent to this issue and the outcome in court may in fact turn upon the trespasser's intentions.[2] In our example from the previous chapter, the court is more likely to be sympathetic to Potatoes' claims to adversely possess two feet of Parsley's property if Potatoes made an honest mistake about the location of the property line when he built the house, rather than setting out in the beginning to acquire some of Parsley's land. (From an efficiency standpoint, are the trespasser's intentions relevant or irrelevant?)

Economics does suggest a method of improving the efficiency of at least one of the requirements in the typical adverse possession statute. Suppose the statute of limitations mentioned in condition 4 above is 10

lished for three weeks successively in some public newspaper printed in this state and if the owner of such goods, money, bank notes, or other [things] does not appear and claim the same ... within one year after the advertisement thereof as aforesaid, the ownership of such property shall vest in the finder. ...

If any person taking up any estray or other property, or finding any property, fails to comply with the provisions of this Act, he shall, for every such offense, forfeit and pay to the informer the sum of $10, with costs, recoverable before any circuit judge residing in the county where such offense shall be committed; one-half to the use of the county, and the other half to the use of the person suing for the same."

years. After 9.9 years of trespass the owner retains his full rights, but after 10.0 years of trespass the owner loses all of his rights. A legal rule that creates a discontinuity like this one may also create inefficient incentives for decisionmakers. Wherever possible, discontinuities should be replaced by continuities to create more efficient incentives for behavior. Economists have long decried the adverse incentive effects that discontinuities in tax rates can cause. For example, if the marginal income tax rate jumps from 15% to 27% at an income level of $20,000, there is a strong incentive for those close to that level to underreport their income or, in the extreme, to forego work opportunities that would push their income into the higher bracket. A more finely calibrated tax schedule would not have these sharp discontinuities and would thus reduce these disincentive effects. The argument is precisely the same for the statutes of limitations in adverse possession. Instead of the owner's losing his rights abruptly at the end of 10 years, the statute could be written so that his rights depreciate gradually over time, like a machine and like the proposed revision to patent law discussed above. For example, the trespasser could be granted a 10% interest in the property for each year of adverse possession that meets the other three requirements, so that after one year the trespasser would own 10% of it and after 10 years he would own all of it. Do you think that incremental transfer at a gradual rate would be better than total, abrupt transfer?

[1]Some states, notably those in the West, require the adverse possessor to pay property taxes for the statutorily-specified period. We have already seen this requirement at work in eastern Oklahoma as a device for transferring title from the original Cherokee owners to adversely possessing white settlers. An additional proponent of the property-tax payment requirement were the 19th century railroads. They were the owners of vast tracts of land that were costly to police against squatters. Requiring an adverse possessor to make known his claim by paying property taxes was thus an inexpensive way for the railroads to discover adverse possessors. *See* Lawrence Friedman, A HISTORY OF AMERICAN LAW 360–361 (2d ed. 1985).

[2]Richard Helmholtz, *Adverse Possession and Subjective Intent*, 61 WASH. U. Q. 331 (1983).

Lost Cash

Paset v. Old Orchard Bank & Trust Co., 62 Ill. App. 3d 534, 378 N.E.2d 1264 (1978)

SIMON, J. "On May 8, 1974, the plaintiff, Bernice Paset, a safety deposit box subscriber at the defendant Old Orchard Bank (the bank), found $6,325 in currency on the seat of a chair in an examination booth in the safety deposit vault. The chair was partially under a table. The plaintiff notified officers of the bank and turned the money over to them. She then was told by bank officials that the bank would try to locate the owner, and that she could have the money if the owner was not located within 1 year.

The bank wrote to everyone who had been in the safety deposit vault either on the day of, or on the day preceding, the discovery, stating that some property had been found and inviting the customers to describe any property they might have lost. No one reported the loss of currency, and the money remained unclaimed a year after it had been found. However, when the plaintiff requested the money, the bank refused to deliver it to her, explaining that it was obligated to hold the currency for the owner. . . .

The plaintiff sought a declaratory judgment that the Illinois estray statute was applicable to her discovery and granted her ownership of the $6,325. The circuit court judge, however, found that the money was "deemed mislaid" . . . and that the bank should continue to hold the money as bailee or trustee for the true owner. . . . Mislaid property is that which is intentionally put in a certain place and later forgotten; at common law a finder acquires no rights to mislaid property. The element of intentional deposit present in the case of mislaid property is absent in the case of lost property, for property is deemed lost when it is unintentionally separated from the dominion of its owner. The general rule is that the finder is entitled to possession of lost property against everyone except the true owner. We are not concerned in this case with abandoned property where the owner, intending to relinquish all rights to his property, leaves it free to be appropriated by any other person. . . . [A]t common law the finder is entitled to keep abandoned property. . . . Our conclusion is that the estray statute should be applied, and ownership of the money vested in the plaintiff finder. . . .

It is complete speculation to infer, as the bank urges, that the money was deliberately placed by its owner on the chair located partially under a table in the examining booth, and then forgotten. . . . The failure of an owner to appear to claim the money in the interval since its discovery is affirmative evidence that the property was not mislaid. . . .

Because the evidence, though ambiguous, tends to indicate that the money probably was not mislaid, and because neither party contends that the money was abandoned, we conclude that the ambiguity should, as a matter of public policy, be resolved in favor of the presumption that the money was lost. . . .

Accordingly, the judgment of the circuit court is reversed and the case is remanded with directions to enter judgment in favor of the plaintiff finder. Judgment reversed and remanded with directions.''

An intriguing aspect of the *Paset* decision is the court's attempt to distinguish between *mislaid* property and *lost* property. Recall that the court says that the important difference is the true owner's intent: if the true owner intended to put the property where it was found but forgot to come back to get it, then the court says the property is mislaid, and the finder cannot acquire title under the estray statute; if the true owner unintentionally put the property where it was found, then the court says the property is lost, and the finder may acquire title under the estray statute. If you find this distinction mysterious and even silly, you are in good company. Many states have dropped the distinction between mislaid, abandoned, and lost property in their estray statutes. For example, New York defines lost property to include lost, mislaid, and abandoned property.[1]

There is an efficiency reason for not preserving the distinction between mislaid and lost property. First, recall that the economic purpose of the estray statute is to facilitate the efficient use of property by providing a procedure for filling gaps in the ownership of property. It is difficult to perceive a connection between this purpose and the intent of the owner of lost property. More importantly for an economic interpretation, it is unlikely that the behavior of true owners or of finders would be made more efficient by preserving a distinction between mislaid and lost property.

---

[1]The New York statute also includes yet another form of property in the list—treasure trove. (The expression comes from the old French *tresor trové*, ''found treasure.'') This was something that was hidden, usually but not necessarily below ground, by an owner but was discovered by someone else. In English law all treasure trove originally belonged to the king. Subsequently, the common law drew a distinction between treasure that was abandoned by the true owner, which went to the finder, and that which had been hidden with the intention of later recovery, which went to the king.

The New York estray statute has some interesting and important exceptions to the rule that the finder takes title unless the true owner shows up. For example, ''the state takes title to any negotiable instrument or to any property found by a public employee in the course of his official duty; an employer takes title if the property is found by an employee under a duty to deliver the lost property to his employer; a bank takes title if the lost property is discovered upon the enclosed safe deposit premises of the bank.'' Are the exceptions efficient? That is, do they encourage the use or discovery of different forms of property at minimum cost?

Note that the finder who is honest has a positive inducement to follow the process specified in the statute for finding the owner. That arises from the finder's desiring to acquire a clear and unsullied title to the found property. Compliance with the terms of the statute vests ownership of the resource in the finder after one year. Thereafter, not even the original owner can assert a stronger claim to the property than can the finder/new owner.

The important economic point about estray statutes is that they address the problem of removing a cloud upon title while at the same time trying to protect the owner's rights. The effect of the law is to permit the finder of lost or mislaid property to establish good title, so that a buyer can purchase it free from the risk of third-party claims. At the same time, the requirement on the finder to take affirmative steps to discover the true owner protects against the possibility that a thief will obtain title over stolen goods under the guise that they were merely lost. The structure of the economic problem addressed by estray statutes should be familiar to you by now since it is essentially the same as for adverse possession.

Question 5.6: In admiralty law, there have to be rules for allocating ownership rights to property lost at sea in a shipwreck. In the United States, the finder of an abandoned ship is generally awarded ownership, but in some cases the State takes possession of abandoned ships in its waters. Where that latter condition holds, a salvor [one who salvages an abandoned ship] is usually entitled to a salvage award determined by the court.

Does this practice of making awards to salvors encourage dishonesty or attract an efficient number of resources into the business of searching for lost ships? Is the system of awarding complete ownership rights to the finder more or less efficient?

C. Bequests and Inheritances

In the first chapter we defined property as the institution that, by allocating things to people, gives people liberty over things. We stressed that liberty consists in having a bundle of rights that gives owners a zone of personal discretion over their property. One such right is the right to name who will inherit the property upon the owner's death. This freedom is consistent with the general purposes of decentralizing power over property and permitting individuals to determine the best use to which resources should be put. The owner's freedom to structure his own will is, however, a relatively new development in the history of property law. In most of England from 1066 (the date of the Norman Conquest) until 1925 the general rule, called *primogeniture*, was that the eldest son inherited *all* the decedent's land. This old system of inheritance was based upon the status of the parties, specifically their blood relationship, not the preferences of owners.

These two considerations, owner's preferences and kin status, are both at work in modern property law. Some people make some formal provisions for the disposition of their property after their death by means of a will. The

What To Do When There Is No Will? Rules of Intestacy

Common law and state statutes usually define different rules for the disposition of an intestate's real and personal property. Those who succeed to the decedent's real property are called "heirs," and those succeed to the decedent's personal property are called "next of kin."

The rights of heirs are usually ranked in the following order. First, issue or descendants, which includes children and further descendants and, by statute, adopted children, usually share equally. (This is a change from the old common law rule of primogeniture—the eldest son inherits all the land.) At common law the spouse was not an heir, but in most modern statutes of descent the spouse is guaranteed some share, with the rules differing greatly from state to state. Second, parents (also known as "ancestors") succeed as heirs if the decedent had no issue. At common law land could not ascend in this manner, but every state allows parents to succeed if there are no direct descendants. Third, in the absence of issue or parents, collaterals—those who are neither issue nor ancestors but are related by blood, e.g., brothers, sisters, aunts, and cousins—succeed to shares. The rules for determining these shares are complicated. Lastly, if the decedent left no heirs, his property is said to "escheat" to the state in which the property is located. This rule is a modern reflection of the feudal rule by which a tenant's real property escheated to his lord at the tenant's death. (Under modern rules if no next-of-kin can be found, the intestate decedent's personal property also escheats to the state.)

If you followed all this on first reading, your future as a specialist in wills and trusts is assured. For the rest of us, these rules of intestacy give a glimpse of how arcane this area of the law can be. Note, however, that this complexity is inherent in the very nature of the problem of filling this particular gap in the chain of title to property. It is not a complexity unnecessarily imposed on non-lawyers by lawyers.

rules and formalities of writing a will are many, but generally modern property law permits owners to structure a will and dispose of their property as they see fit. However, there are circumstances in which the old system based upon kin-status asserts itself. It frequently happens that someone will fail to leave *any* instructions on what is to be done with property at death or that the instructions are incomplete or garbled. In the former case the person is said to have died "intestate," that is, without a testament (the original word for the document that gave instructions for disposing of one's land; the *will* originally gave instructions for the decedent's personal property). The intestate owner represents a problem similar to that created by lost or fugitive property: the possibility of a gap in property rights. To deal with this contingency, originally the common law and now state legislatures through statutes of descent provided rules for allocating property at the death of someone who died without a will. (The typical form of the rules is explained in the box on rules of intestacy.)

These rules of intestacy follow a principle of consanguinity: the closer the kin tie, the stronger the claim over the intestate's property. The consanguinity principle mimics the typical dispositions made in written wills—children before nephews and nieces, first cousins before second cousins, and so forth. The principle of consanguinity thus disposes of property according to common practices. These practices will often correspond to what intestate persons would have wanted done with their property if they had written a will. The rules of intestacy can be regarded, consequently, as both an expression of general values and practices in society, and an imputation to the deceased of presumptive intentions in the absence of a definitive statement of them.

As explained, the laws governing inheritance generally respect the principle that owners should be able to dispose of their property as they see fit. But other principles are imaginable and, indeed, some have been used in the past. For example, the decedent's property could be automatically re-allocated to the youngest child, called *ultimogeniture*, or to the oldest child, called, as we saw, *primogeniture*.[17] Another principle—one that has never been tried—is governmental re-allocation of title to the decedent's property by lottery or by auction. Society has an interest in the efficient use of resources, and that includes a desire that the costs of transferring ownership rights and of settling questions of rightful title should be minimized. Why are the current laws—generally allowing the decedent to dispose of his property as he sees fit—preferable to the alternatives on efficiency grounds?

One advantage of allowing the owner to choose his heirs is that any rule abridging that choice creates an incentive for him to circumvent it. Imagine an owner with a strong desire to see that a particular friend will have his property after his death, and imagine, counterfactually, that the law will award the property to someone else. The owner can satisfy his desire only by transferring his ownership rights to the friend *before he dies*. It is possible that this would involve some inefficiency, as would be the case if the owner transferred his property long before his death and lost control of it prematurely. (See Shakespeare's *King Lear* for an example of the agony this can cause.) Or perhaps he could transfer title to the friend or relative today and then lease it back from the owner for $1 per year till his death. The only way the government can make this circumvention more difficult is to impose more stringent restrictions on the owner's ability to transfer ownership before his death. For instance, the government might void transfers that occur within 5 years of the transferor's death. But the property owner's response to these more stringent regulations is to develop more elaborate methods of circumventing the regulations. The point is that legal obstacles

---

[17]An intriguing historical puzzle is why, in medieval England, the rule of inheritance of land for the rich was primogeniture but for the poor was ultimogeniture.

to the owner's choosing his heirs can usually be surmounted and that the costs of doing so are a social waste.

A second possibility is that the current owner will be stymied in his attempt to choose an heir. If so, then he may decide to use his property up entirely before he dies. Or the owner might forego some improvement to his property because it will not accrue to the person of his choice. Efficiency considerations argue for rules of inheritability that interfere minimally with the timing and amount of investment in property.

The principle that the current owner may designate the person to whom his property rights should pass at his death runs up against a difficulty, however, when the owner, instead of merely willing his property to others, wishes to constrain their use by stipulating various restrictions and conditions on how they use it. To illustrate, suppose that land is willed with the restriction that it should forever be used as a church, or the trees should never be cleared, or perhaps a fast-food magnate wills his property to his daughter with the restriction that it should be used forever as a Wimpy's Hamburger Shoppe. Frequently a bequest attempts to keep property in the family: an owner leaves instructions that, at his death, his land is to be given to his oldest son, at whose death the land is to be given to *his* oldest son, and so on. At other times a bequest attempts to protect someone from the consequences of his own irresponsibility or bad judgment: a trust is created in which the beneficiary receives the interest but cannot touch the capital until he is middle-aged. In all these cases we have conflicting freedoms: the older generation's freedom to draft restrictive wills conflicts with the younger generation's freedom to use property as they see fit.

If restrictions in wills were unenforceable, the freedom of the testator to structure the will as she sees fit would be greatly impaired. On the other hand, if all restrictions in wills were enforceable according to their terms, a time might eventually come when the property of the living would be controlled by the dead. The law must balance the freedom of the testator and her heir. There is a rule of law, known as the Rule Against Perpetuities, that attempts to strike this balance by prescribing a definite time limit after which restrictions in wills or trusts expire. A famous summary of the rule is this:

> *"No interest is good unless it must vest, if at all, not later than twenty-one years after some life in being at the creation of the interest."*[18]

This rule is like a statute of limitations on property restrictions. To see how it works, consider our owner who wished his property to remain as a

---

[18]John Chipman Gray, THE RULE AGAINST PERPETUITIES sec. 201 (4th ed. 1942). This famous rule was first enunciated in the *Duke of Norfolk's Case*, 3 Ch. Cas. 1, 22 Eng. Rep. 931 (1681). The student who would like to experience the Rule Against Perpetuities in all its complex glory is urged to see W. Leach, *Perpetuities in a Nutshell*, 51 HARV. L. REV. 638 (1938) and Leach, *Perpetuities: The Nutshell Revisited*, 78 HARV. L. REV. 973 (1965).

hamburger stand. If at the time he placed this restriction on his property the youngest beneficiary of the will was his great-grandson, who was then 1 year-old, the restriction would be maintainable for that great-grandson's lifetime and an additional 21 years. If the great-grandson lived to be 80, then the property could be used to make hamburgers exclusively for 101 years. Thereafter, no restrictions could apply.

Is there an efficiency argument in favor of the sort of restriction embodied in the Rule Against Perpetuities? The answer is yes. The efficiency problem that can arise from a testator's restriction on the future use of his property is that prices change with time so that the most valuable use of the property in the future will be different from the one prescribed by the testator. And yet the terms of the bequest prevent the resource from being transferred to that higher-valued use. This imposes a cost on society, as well as on the future owners.

We summarize these costs of the restriction in Figure 5.2. On the vertical axis are dollar costs. Time is measured along the horizontal axis, with the origin representing the time of death of the current owner. The line labeled *MSC* measures the marginal social costs of imposing a restriction today on the use of a resource at some point in the future, *t*. These costs are both private and social. The private component consists of the costs to the decedent's estate and to the future owners of complying with the testator's proscription on use. These costs can be considerable. There must be provision for the many contingencies that can arise after the testator's death to frustrate his desires. For example, one of his heirs might die childless, or it could be that selling hamburgers becomes illegal because they are found at some future date to be seriously carcinogenic. As the time from the testator's death increases, the private component of *MSC* increases. The second component of *MSC* is the *social* cost of the proscription on future use. These are the efficient opportunities for the use of the property that must be foregone because of the decedent's restriction, such as the surplus a buyer would enjoy if the will had not prevented its sale. Like the private cost component of *MSC*, the social costs increase the longer the restriction is in place. Thus, *MSC* slopes upward over time, as the graph indicates.

These costs in *MSC* are not, however, *net* social costs because there are some offsetting *benefits* of the property owner's being able to restrict the use of his property in the future. These benefits, shown in the *MSB* (marginal social benefit) curve, have a private and a social component. The purely private component of the benefits of being able to restrict the use of one's property is the property owner's satisfaction enjoyed during his lifetime from contemplating the restriction on his property's use after his death. Perhaps the current owner's satisfaction increases with each year that the restriction on use is in place, but eventually the *marginal* benefit from each additional year of restriction declines. In that case, the private component of *MSB* declines over time, as depicted in the graph. The social benefit of a restriction on the future use of a decedent's property is the satisfaction that *other* property owners enjoy from observing that the restrictions that others have

Figure 5.2 Optimal Restrictions on Property Use after Death

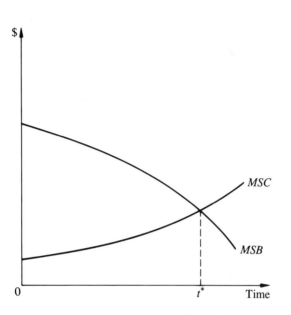

A property-owner derives benefits from imposing restrictions on the use of his property by others after his death. These purely private benefits to the owner probably decline as the number of years of restriction increases. Other property owners also benefit from seeing another property-owner's restrictions enforced; this social benefit probably also declines as the number of years of restriction increases. The *MSB* curve sums these private and social benefits; its downward slope indicates that although lengthening the number of years during which a restriction on property will be enforced after the owner's death increases the total private and social benefit of those restrictions, it does so at a declining rate.

These posthumous restrictions on property use also impose private and social costs. The private costs of providing for all the uncertain contingencies that may arise to frustrate the restriction increases as each additional year of restriction is added. The social cost of restricting property use also increases as the opportunity cost of alternative uses grows. Together, these marginal social costs, as indicated by the *MSC* curve, rise as the length of the restriction increases.

Restrictions on future use should be allowed so long as the marginal social benefit of one more year of restriction exceeds the marginal social cost. The optimal length of time to allow owners to restrict the use of their property after death is given by t^*, where the marginal social costs and benefits of the restriction are equal.

imposed on their property before their death are being honored. Like the private component, the marginal value of this social component presumably declines for each additional year of restriction. Thus, because both the private and social marginal benefits from increasing the length of time of a property restriction decline, *MSB* slopes down over time, as the figure indicates.

When the curves have the shape indicated in the graph, there is a time period, denoted t^*, that indicates the optimal duration for restrictions. The graph indicates that up to time t^*, $MSB \geq MSC$, so there is a net social *benefit* to allowing the restriction on future uses. After t^*, $MSB < MSC$, so that there is a net social *cost* to the restriction. The implication for property law is that there is an efficiency argument in favor of *some* rule terminating the ability of current owners to control the use of their property after their deaths. It is, of course, a different matter to demonstrate that t^* is equal to lives-in-being plus 21 or that t^* is the same for different types of property. The relationship between the current rule and the optimal rule is a matter of speculation and empirical research.

It is important to note that there are also non-efficiency arguments for not allowing a property owner to control the use of his property interminably after his death. It is possible that the restriction on use imposed by a dead property owner may come to violate changing conceptions of social justice. For example, suppose that a landowner in 1850 left land to the city in which he lived on the condition that the land be used only as a city park from which blacks and other minorities were to be excluded. That restriction on who might use the park came to be a poignant and anger-provoking violation of community standards long after the testator's death. In such circumstances, there is an overwhelming *equity* or *fairness* argument for terminating the testator's restriction, regardless of any efficiency arguments that might be made. (For a discussion of how courts solve problems like these, see the box on the doctrine of *Cy Pres*.)

A challenging exercise of a legal education is to figure out ways to circumvent the Rule Against Perpetuities. It is sometimes said that any good lawyer specializing in estates and trusts can find a way to circumvent the rule and accomplish the desire of any testator or donor. If it is true that the main effect of the rule is to trap the unwary and impose legal costs upon the prudent, then it should be abolished.[19] However, the general principle that it represents—that the dead should not be permitted to abolish completely the discretion of the living over property—should be upheld.

IV. CONFLICTING PROPERTY RIGHTS: THE PROBLEM OF SEPARABILITY

The institution of property allocates resources to people in order to give them liberty over things. The essential idea is to create a zone of discretion within which owners are free to exercise their will over their property. The very idea of creating a zone of privacy assumes that one owner's use can be disentangled from another's. It follows that when it is difficult to separate the property interests of different individuals, the essential role of property

---

[19]This is the position taken by Richard Epstein in *Past and Future: The Temporal Dimension in the Law of Property,* 64, WASH. U.L. QUART. 667 (1986).

Cy Pres

Suppose that a benefactor endowed a scholarship fund in 1950 that specified that the interest should be used to pay tuition at a particular private school for "high school seniors who are Caucasian boys of outstanding achievement and limited means." The interest on the fund is used as prescribed in the will for 10 years, but in 1960 this private school decides to eliminate its high school program in order to concentrate its educational efforts on the elementary grade students. Shortly thereafter the racial restriction in the will ("Caucasian boys") is judged to be illegal. (If the proposed Equal Rights Amendment to the Constitution were enacted, the restriction of the scholarship to males might also be regarded as illegal.)

These changes render the strict performance of some terms of the will impossible, and the performance of others is rendered illegal, so the will must be reinterpreted.

Under these circumstances, the law will apply the doctrine of *cy pres* (pronounced "see-pray" and meaning, in law-French, "so nearly"). The doctrine requires the trustees to administer the trust in a way that conforms to the intentions of the donor as nearly as possible, given the fact that exact conformity is impossible or illegal. To illustrate, the trustees might decide to award the scholarship to able boys of limited means in the last year of elementary school, regardless of race. Or the trustees might decide to transfer the scholarship to another private school that still maintains a high school.

cannot be easily fulfilled. For example, your desire to use your property as a refuge of peace and quiet from school and work may not easily be separated from your neighbor's desire to use his property as a place to listen to loud music. In terms of microeconomic theory, non-separability of individual property rights occurs when there are externalities and when one of the resources is a public bad.

In the first part of this section we will briefly review the economic theory of externalities and public bads. In the second part, we will apply the economic analysis of remedies for externalities and public bads to two cases, *Boomer v. Atlantic Cement* and *Del Webb v. Spur Industries*.

A. Introduction: Externalities and Public Bads

We have defined an externality as "a cost or benefit that the voluntary actions of one or more people impose or confer on a third party or parties without their consent." The problem created by the existence of externalities is that each owner's use of his goods directly affects other owners. Technically, this means that individuals' or firms' functions are interdependent. If person A smokes tobacco and person B is allergic to tobacco smoke, then B's utility depends not just upon his own consumption decisions but also upon the extent of A's smoking. This sort of externality is called a "consumer-on-consumer" externality. One can also construct examples of externalities between producers and consumers (e.g., consumer-on-producer and producer-on-producer).

The essence of the problem created by externalities is that they make the utility-maximizing actions of consumers and the profit-maximizing actions of firms inefficient. Rationally self-interested decisionmakers usually do not take account of how their decisions affect the utility or production of third parties. As a result, where there are externalities, there are effects on third parties that are imposed without those parties' consent. Efficiency can be restored by getting the externality-generator to *internalize* these external effects. Thus, one of the important economic aspects of property law is to try to induce this cost internalization when property rights are not separable.

Our examples of externalities above illustrated two-person externalities. There are, however, situations in which an externality affects a large number of persons. For example, the smoke from a factory affects many households; in formal terms, the factory's output of smoke is a harmful input in the utility functions of many consumers. Similarly, when one additional car enters a congested freeway, all the other drivers are slowed down just a little bit. Externalities that affect many people are similar to public goods, except that they are bad rather than good, hence their name, "public bads."

If the externality appears in the utility function of only one consumer or in the production function of only one firm, we say that its character is private. But if the externality is widespread enough so that it affects many consumers or many producers, we say that its character is public. This suggests picturing the public-private distinction as a continuum with externalities arrayed along it, some of which are more nearly private, and some of which are more nearly public. This way of looking at externalities will have an important application in our discussion of efficient remedies for infringements on property rights.

B. Remedies for Externalities and Public Bads

In property law, a harmful externality is called a nuisance. In the first chapter on property we presented an example of a nuisance: the stench from a cattle feedlot blanketed Foster's house. Our discussion of this externality distinguished between two different remedies: injunction and damages. Recall that an injunction would require the feedlot to eliminate the obnoxious odors, which in practice means closing the feedlot down, whereas the alternative would be to permit the feedlot to continue operating and pay damages to property owners like Foster.

It turns out that the choice between remedies has a lot to do with the public-private distinction we have just explained. If the nuisance is private, few parties are affected by it. Since few parties are affected, the costs of bargaining together are low. When bargaining costs are low, the parties will ordinarily be able to reach a cooperative agreement, and it is always in their interests to do what is efficient. Consequently, the choice of remedies makes little difference to the efficiency of the bargaining outcome. The traditional property law remedy—injunctive relief—is attractive under these circumstances because it preserves the property owner's freedom and, in addition, the threat that it represents is unlikely to be exercised.

In contrast, trying to correct a harmful externality of the public-bad type by private bargaining would involve the cooperation of all the affected parties. Bargaining is unlikely to succeed in these circumstances because the cooperation of so many people is required, so the choice of a remedy makes a difference to the efficiency of the outcome. The law refers to a harmful externality of the public type as a "public nuisance." Our analysis suggests that damages will be a better remedy of a public nuisance than injunction. The law has not traditionally conformed to this suggestion. When the public is harmed by a nuisance, the affected parties are traditionally allowed by law to enjoin it. But, as we are about to see, the law may be changing in this respect and becoming more receptive to damage remedies for public nuisances.

Because we believe that one of the most important things that the study of law and economics can teach you is how to use the theoretical tools to resolve important public policy questions, we now turn to the application of the theories we have just been developing to the analysis of a famous case of conflicting property rights, *Boomer v. Atlantic Cement*, in which an externality of the public type resulted in a nuisance suit with a novel remedy. Because this is our first attempt to apply our analysis of bargaining to a real case, we have followed the case with an extensive discussion of the economic issues raised.

Boomer v. Atlantic Cement Co., Inc., 26 N.Y.2d 219, 309 N.Y.S.2d 312, 257 N.E.2d 870 (Court of Appeals of New York, 1970)

BERGAN, J. Defendant operates a large cement plant near Albany. These are actions for injunction and damages by neighboring land owners alleging injury to property from dirt, smoke and vibration emanating from the plant. A nuisance has been found after trial, temporary damages have been allowed;[20] but an injunction has been denied . . .

A court performs its essential function when it decides the rights of parties before it. Its decision of private controversies may sometimes

---

[20]*Temporary* damages are a compensatory payment for past harms inflicted. They are to be distinguished from *permanent* damages, which attempt to compensate the plaintiff for all past and all reasonably anticipated future harms. In our discussion of the case we will see which form of damages is more efficient.

greatly affect public issues. Large questions of law are often resolved by the manner in which private litigation is decided. But this is normally an incident to the court's main function to settle controversy. It is a rare exercise of judicial power to use a decision in private litigation as a purposeful mechanism to achieve direct public objectives greatly beyond the rights and interests before the court.

Effective control of air pollution is a problem presently far from solution even with the full public and financial powers of government. In large measure adequate technical procedures are yet to be developed and some that appear possible may be economically impracticable.

It seems apparent that the amelioration of air pollution will depend on technical research in great depth; on a carefully balanced consideration of the economic impact of close regulation; and of the actual effect on public health. It is likely to require massive public expenditure and to demand more than any local community can accomplish and to depend on regional and interstate controls.

A court should not try to do this on its own as a by-product of private litigation and it seems manifest that the judicial establishment is neither equipped in the limited nature of any judgment it can pronounce nor prepared to lay down and implement an effective policy for the elimination of air pollution. This is an area beyond the circumference of one private lawsuit. It is a direct responsibility for government and should not thus be undertaken as an incident to solving a dispute between property owners and a single cement plant—one of many—in the Hudson River valley.

[At the trial court and on appeal, the defendant's cement-making operations were found to be a nuisance to the plaintiff neighbors. Temporary damages were awarded, but an injunction against future dirt, smoke, and vibration from the plant causing the same or greater harms was denied.] The total damage to plaintiffs' properties is, however, relatively small in comparison with the value of defendant's operation and with the consequences of the injunction that plaintiffs seek.

The ground for denial of injunction . . . is the large disparity in economic consequences of the nuisance and of the injunction. This theory cannot, however, be sustained without overruling a doctrine which has been consistently reaffirmed in several leading cases in this court and which has never been disavowed here, namely that where a nuisance has been found and where there has been any substantial damage shown by the party complaining an injunction will be granted.

The rule in New York has been that such a nuisance will be enjoined although marked disparity be shown in economic consequences between the effect of the injunction and the effect of the nuisance . . .

Although the court at Special Term [the trial court] and the Appellate Division held that injunction should be denied, it was found that plaintiffs had been damaged in various specific amounts up to the time of the trial and damages to the respective plaintiffs were awarded for those amounts. The effect of this was, injunction having been denied, plaintiffs could maintain successive actions at law for damages thereafter as further damage was incurred.

The court at Special Term also found the amount of permanent damage attributable to each plaintiff, for the guidance of the parties in the event both sides stipulated to the payment and acceptance of such permanent damage as a settlement of all the controversies among the parties. The total of permanent damages to all plaintiffs thus found was $185,000 . . .

This result . . . is a departure from a rule that has become settled; but to follow the rule literally in these cases would be to close down the plant at once. This court is fully agreed to avoid that immediately drastic remedy; the difference in view is how best to avoid it. [Footnote by Court: Atlantic Cement Co.'s investment in the plant is in excess of $45,000,000. There are over 300 people employed there.]

One alternative is to grant the injunction but postpone its effect to a specified future date to give opportunity for technical advances to permit defendant to eliminate the nuisance; another is to grant the injunction conditioned on the payment of permanent damages to plaintiffs which would compensate them for the total economic loss to their property present and future caused by defendant's operations. For reasons which will be developed the court chooses the latter alternative.

If the injunction were to be granted unless within a short period— e.g., 18 months—the nuisance be abated by improved methods, there would be no assurance that any significant technical improvement would occur.

The parties could settle this private litigation at any time if defendant paid enough money and the imminent threat of closing the plant would build up the pressure on defendant. If there were no improved techniques found, there would inevitably be applications to the court at Special Term for extensions of time to perform on showing of good faith efforts to find such techniques.

Moreover, techniques to eliminate dust and other annoying by-products of cement making are unlikely to be developed by any research the defendant can undertake within any short period, but will depend on the total resources of the cement industry nationwide and throughout the world. The problem is universal wherever cement is made.

For obvious reasons the rate of the research is beyond control of defendant. If at the end of 18 months the whole industry has not found a technical solution a court would be hard put to close down this one cement plant if due regard be given to equitable principles.

On the other hand, to grant the injunction unless defendant pays plaintiffs such permanent damages as may be fixed by the court seems to do justice between the contending parties. All of the attributions of economic loss to the properties on which plaintiffs' complaints are based will have been redressed . . .

It seems reasonable to think that the risk of being required to pay permanent damages to injured property owners by cement plant owners would itself be a reasonable effective spur to research for improved techniques to minimize nuisance . . . Thus it seems fair to both sides to grant permanent damages to plaintiffs which will terminate this private litigation. The theory of damage is the "servitude on land" of plaintiffs imposed by defendant's nuisance . . . The judgment, by allowance of permanent damages imposing a servitude on land, which is the basis of the actions, would preclude future recovery by plaintiffs or their grantees.

This should be placed beyond debate by a provision of the judgment that the payment by defendant and the acceptance by plaintiffs of permanent damages found by the court shall be in compensation for a servitude on the land.[21]

. . . The orders should be reversed, without costs, and the cases remitted to Supreme Court, Albany County, to grant an injunction which shall be vacated upon payment by defendant of such amounts of permanent damage to the respective plaintiffs as shall for this purpose be determined by the court.

JASEN, J. dissenting. I agree with the majority that a reversal is required here, but I do not subscribe to the newly enunciated doctrine of assessment of permanent damages, in lieu of an injunction, where substantial property rights have been impaired by the creation of a nuisance . . .

I see grave dangers in overruling our long-established rule of granting an injunction where a nuisance results in substantial continuing damage. In permitting the injunction to become inoperative upon the payment of permanent damages, the majority is, in effect, licensing a continuing wrong. It is the same as saying to the cement company, you may continue to do harm to your neighbors so long as you pay a fee for it. Furthermore, once such permanent damages are assessed and paid, the incentive to alleviate the wrong would be eliminated, thereby continuing air pollution of an area without abatement.

It is true that some courts have sanctioned the remedy here proposed by the majority in a number of cases, but none of the authorities relied upon by the majority are analogous to the situation before us. In those cases, the courts, in denying an injunction and awarding money damages, grounded their decision on a showing that the use to which the property was intended to be put was primarily for the public benefit. Here, on the other hand, it is clearly established that the cement company is creating a continuing air pollution nuisance primarily for its own private interest with no public benefit . . . The promotion of the interests of the polluting cement company, has, in my opinion, no public use or benefit.

Nor is it constitutionally permissible to impose servitude on land, without consent of the owner, by payment of permanent damages where the continuing impairment of the land is for a private use . . . This is made clear by the State Constitution (art. I, sec. 7, subd. [a]) which provides that "[p]rivate property shall not be taken for *public* use without just compensation" (emphasis added). It is, of course, significant that the section makes no mention of taking for a *private* use.

In sum, then, by constitutional mandate as well as by judicial pronouncement, the permanent impairment of private property for private

---

[21]A *servitude on the land* is a restriction imposed on a piece of real property. The servitude "runs with the land," which means that it becomes permanently attached to the particular piece of land and is not, therefore, dependent on the identity of the owner. Whoever is the owner must obey the servitude. In our discussion of the case, we will see why the court wishes to make the payment of damages for the nuisance attach a servitude to the land rather than being a mere payment to particular individuals.

purposes is not authorized in the absence of clearly demonstrated public benefit and use.

I would enjoin the defendant cement company from continuing the discharge of dust particles upon its neighbors' properties unless, within 18 months, the cement company abated this nuisance. . . .   ▬

How would an economist analyze this case? Assume that the neighbors were in their homes before the cement company began its operations. The smoke, noise, dirt, and vibration of the defendant's operations constitute an involuntary cost imposed on the neighbors; Atlantic Cement's production function and Boomer's utility functions are interdependent. Assume that the plaintiffs-neighbors have a legal right to a remedy from invasion by the defendant-cement company's pollution. Given this assumption, the next question facing the court is to choose between injunctive relief and damages. Our theory of bargaining provides the following recommendation: if bargaining costs facing the parties are low, the most efficient remedy is compensatory money damages for past harms and an injunction against future harms; if, however, bargaining costs are high, the court should award compensatory damages for past harms and, if possible, also for future harms.

In *Boomer*, it seems likely that the bargaining costs are high, since Boomer is just one of many actual (the case is *Boomer et al. v. Atlantic Cement*) and potential plaintiffs. Because of the large number of neighbors involved, each has an incentive to hold out in an injunction settlement with the defendant. The last neighbor to settle with the cement company can extract an excessive amount for his consent not to enforce the injunction. And for that reason, many of the neighbors would like to be the last to settle, which implies that few would be willing to be the first to settle. So, there is little possibility for a voluntary exchange to resolve the dispute.

Thus, the award of an injunction in favor of the neighbors against future harms by the cement company could work an inefficiency if the defendant company values the right to pollute more than the neighbors collectively value the right to be free from pollution. Because of the high level of bargaining or transaction costs, it would be impossible for the defendants to purchase the rights to enforce the injunction away from all the neighbors in whose favor the injunction runs. And so the right might be inefficiently frozen in the hands of the neighbors by the award of an injunction. We conclude that because the level of transaction costs between the parties here is high, the most efficient remedy is some form of compensatory money damages. Thus, the economic analysis of the dispute reaches the same general conclusion as did the New York Court of Appeals—viz., that money damages are the superior remedy. But note that the court's reasons for preferring legal relief (money damages) to equitable relief (an injunction) are different from ours. Our inquiry focused on the level of transaction costs between the parties in resolving the dispute. The court, in essence, performed a cost-benefit analysis, a species of "balancing test," as it is known to lawyers. The court does not seem to have any doubt about assigning the entitlement to the neighbors, but the majority was deeply troubled by the fact that, as they saw it, enjoining the defendant's operations would impose greater costs than benefits. Specifically, the majority believe that $45 million in capital and 300 jobs would be lost if the court followed precedent in the State of New York and issued an injunction against the defendant's nuisance. But their reason for believing that these consequences follow from the issuance of an injunction is probably not correct. The majority apparently believes that an injunction *necessarily* causes the cessation of the enjoined activity. But the *economic* view of an injunction is different: an injunction will forbid the pollution *only if the bargaining costs between the two parties are too high for a voluntary exchange of rights to take place.*

The distinction is subtle but important. If one thinks like the *Boomer* court, one believes that the court must perform a cost-benefit analysis to choose between injunctions and damages. But courts are not very good at cost-benefit analysis. Instead, the court should focus upon transaction costs and decide the case according to whether the externality is private or public, without attempting a cost-benefit analysis. Furthermore, if one views an injunction as always and forever prohibiting the offensive activity, then one is likely to be reluctant to impose that inflexibility, save in the most drastic circumstances. However, if one views an injunction as, in essence, an instruction to the parties to resolve their dispute through voluntary exchange, then the circumstances in which one is willing to award an injunction are much broader.

> **Question 5.7:** The dissenting judge would issue an injunction against the defendant corporation unless the company abated the nuisance within 18 months. His criticism is that "[i]n permitting the injunction to become inoperative upon the payment of permanent damages, the majority is, in effect, licensing a continuing wrong. It is the same as saying to the cement company, you may continue to do harm to your neighbors so long as you pay a fee for it." That is, of course, precisely what the majority has said. Suppose you could convince the dissenting judge that the payment of damages accomplishes this internalization and that whatever results thereafter is socially optimal and socially efficient. Could you also convince him that the result is *fair*?

An economic analysis agrees with the majority (but for different reasons) that the payment of compensatory money damages is the appropriate remedy for internalizing the cement company's external cost and for compensating the neighbors for suffering these costs. The next step in resolving this dispute and thereby creating an efficient rule to guide future parties is to decide whether the damages should be "temporary" or "permanent." The majority instructed the lower court to reformulate its measure of permanent damages. But is that the most efficient form for the damages to take?

Recall the difference between these two forms of damages. Under temporary damages the plaintiff is awarded an amount to compensate him for the harms the defendant has inflicted upon him in the past. If in the future the defendant again inflicts this harm on the plaintiff, then the plaintiff must come back to court in order to receive another payment of temporary damages to compensate him for the harms he has suffered since he was last in court. The greatest benefit of temporary damages is that the limited time period over which the damages are computed means that they are probably more accurately measured and that the court may respond more flexibly to changes that may make the external cost more or less serious. For example, the sensitivity of the plaintiff to the harm may have lessened because the original plaintiff has sold his home. Or the polluter may have responded to the original judgment by reducing his output or in some other way lessening his pollution. In either case, the court can take account of these changes by decreasing the award of temporary damages in subsequent time periods. The greatest cost of temporary damages is that they require repeated litigation of the dispute, although it may be the case that the costs of periodically resolving the dispute fall.

Damages may alternatively be permanent, in which case they are made up of payments for past harms plus the present discounted value of all reasonably anticipated future harms.[22] The plaintiff receives a lump-sum payment. The greatest benefit of permanent damages is that it resolves the dispute between the parties once and for all, with the proviso that the defendant has paid for all past and future harms only at the level specified in the judgment. That is, the payment of permanent damages does not entitle the defendant to double the amount of pollution he inflicts. The costs of permanent damages are two-fold. First, the estimation of present discounted harms is an exercise fraught with a large amount of uncertainty and, therefore, is subject to error. Second, this form of damages does not allow either the parties or the court much flexibility to take account of future changes in the technology of the externality-generator's production or changes in the sensitivity and identity of those harmed.

What this means is that, in general, the choice between the two forms of damages must be made depending on the particular circumstances of the dispute. Where the damages are easily measured and not subject to much variance, then permanent damages may be superior to temporary damages. But where there is difficulty in measuring damages or where they are subject to large variance, then efficiency in the internalization of external costs may best be served by an award of temporary damages.

Another important factor is whether one form of damages creates a greater incentive for injurers to adopt improvements in the technology of production that lessen the external costs of their activity. Temporary dam-

---

[22]Discounting future values to the present is a method of converting a stream of future values into a single current value. The practice is particularly widespread among businesses who need some method of determing the current value of the future net income from a productive investment.

Suppose that a harm is anticipated to impose costs for the next ten years. Let the damages that will occur in those years be represented by the series D_1, D_2, D_3, through D_{10}. Let the rate of interest be r. Then, the present discounted value, M, of this stream of future damages is equal to

$$M = D_1/(1 + r) + D_2/(1 + r)^2 + D_3/(1 + r)^3 + \ldots + D_{10}/(1 + r)^{10}.$$

ages, by allowing for a reduction in future damage awards in response to a reduction in harm, creates a superior incentive to adopt a less-polluting technology than does an award of permanent damages. Under permanent damages the polluter has "purchased" from the plaintiffs the right to pollute up to the amount of pollution that he is currently engaged in and, therefore, would seem to have little incentive to reduce his pollution. In his dissent in *Boomer*, Justice Jasen was worried about this consequence of the majority's award of permanent damages:

> *"Furthermore, once such permanent damages are assessed and paid, the incentive to alleviate the wrong would be eliminated, thereby continuing air pollution of an area without abatement."*

This is a complex issue, and for us to appreciate the efficiency analysis of the relationship between the form of damages and investment in new technology, we must return to one of the most fundamental points in the economic analysis of law. Remember our contention in the introductory chapter that the economic analysis of law begins from the observation that legal rules imposed by courts create implicit prices for different kinds of behavior and that the responses of decisionmakers to those implicit prices can be studied in the same way that economists have analyzed consumers' or producers' responses to *explicit* prices.

The problem we have addressed here arising out of the *Boomer* decisions is an ideal example. Although we are interested in how the Atlantic Cement Company responds to the type of damages assessed, we are also interested in how *other* nuisance creators respond to the economic incentives created by the rule in *Boomer*. After all, the point of this method of dealing with external costs is to make it plain to those nuisance creators that they will be held liable in a court for the costs they involuntarily impose on others. It follows that polluters should alter their behavior under this threat of liability so as to avoid this liability. Thus, in analyzing the efficiency aspects of the form of damages, we are interested in knowing how the decisions of other polluters to adopt a new, cleaner technology will be affected by the form of damages they might expect a court to impose upon them.

Let us make the usual economist's simplifying assumptions. First, let us assume that we are looking for the impact of the form of damages on a firm that is currently inflicting external costs; the firm learns that, because of *Boomer*, it will be liable for those harms. The situation facing the firm is shown in Figure 5.3. There we have drawn the company's private marginal cost curve, *PMC*, and two social marginal cost curves representing two different technologies. Under the old technology, the addition of external costs of pollution to the private costs of production yields the social cost curve *SMC*. This curve depicts the true cost to society of each level of production under the old technology. There is, however, a new technology that is less polluting. Let the superiority of the new technology lie in the fact that, compared to the older technology, the new one causes half as much pollution at any given level of output. This is indicated by the fact that *SMC'* has half the slope of *SMC*.

Figure 5.3 Legal Remedies and Technological Change

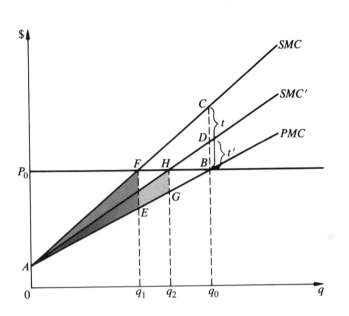

Suppose that a firm that is currently polluting learns from *Boomer* that it will be liable for the harms it inflicts. Will the form of damages in *Boomer* affect this firm's decision to adopt a less-polluting production technology? The company's private marginal cost curve is *PMC*. There are two marginal social cost curves: *SMC* represents the social and private marginal costs under the old technology, and *SMC'* represents the social and private marginal costs under a new, less-polluting technology; at every level of output, q, this new technology inflicts half as much social cost as the old technology.

Under either technology and without any legal constraint, the profit-maximizing output rate is q_0 where private marginal cost equals price, P_0. Under the old technology and with the firm held legally responsible for its external costs, the profit-maximizing output is q_1, where $SMC = P_0$. The total external cost inflicted is the area *AEF*. Under the new technology and with the firm held legally responsible for its external costs, the profit-maximizing output is q_2, where $SMC = P_0$. The total external cost inflicted is the area *AGH*. By assumption, $AEF = AGH$, but because $q_2 > q_1$, society prefers the firm to adopt the new technology and to operate along *SMC'* rather than *SMC*. The firm will probably be quicker to adopt the less-polluting technology under temporary rather than permanent damages.

Under either technology and in the absence of any court or regulatory action, the cement company's profit-maximizing rate of output, q_0, is determined at the intersection of the private marginal cost curve and the prevailing output price, P_0. Under the old technology the total amount of external cost inflicted by the output rate q_0 is the area ABC. Under the new technology the total amount of external cost inflicted by the output rate q_0 is the area ABD. The social cost inflicted by the last unit of output is t under the old technology and t' under the new technology.

If the firm is *not* required to internalize these external costs, it has no incentive to adopt the less-polluting technology. However, if the firm can be made to internalize the social cost of its production of cement, it will prefer the less-polluting technology. From society's point of view the superior technology is preferable to the older one. Under the old technology and with the firm held responsible for its external costs, the profit-maximizing rate of output is determined by the intersection of P_0 and SMC at q_1; under the new technology, it is determined at the intersection of P_0 and SMC' at q_2. The total social cost inflicted by those two rates of output is, under our assumptions, the same; that is, the area AEF is equal to the area AGH. But because $q_2 > q_1$, society prefers the firm to adopt the new technology and to operate along SMC'.

How do these considerations relate to the question we asked above about the incentives for adopting superior technologies of production under the alternative damage measures? The intuitively plausible answer is that the cement company will adopt the cleaner technology more quickly under temporary damages than under permanent damages, and that intuition is borne out by our formal analysis.[23] However, these economic advantages to temporary damages over permanent damages must be balanced against the potentially higher administrative costs of temporary awards.

In our initial comparison of the two types of damages above, we referred to the fact that they differ in their ability to deal with changing sensitivities and identities of those affected by the cement company's pollution. To illustrate, suppose that shortly after the nuisance is resolved by an award of *permanent* damages, Mr. Boomer and some of the neighbors independently decide to take their share of the judgment and move to Florida. They put their houses up for sale, and new people buy them and move in. If the new homeowners awake to discover the smoke, noise, dirt, and vibration from the cement company, can they maintain a nuisance action? The answer is no, for sound economic reasons. As part of its bargaining with Boomer and his neighbors, the cement company is likely to insist that the beneficiaries of the bargain agree to insert a release or other covenant into their deeds of title acknowledging the fact that they have been compensated for pollution at the specified level that the cement company's operations might cause. This agreement will become a "servitude on the land" (as the court has instructed), which means that it applies not just to the current beneficiaries of the settlement but to whoever occupies that land. The economic purpose of this servitude is to internalize the external costs once and for all. Thus, the new homeowners are on notice from the covenant in the title deed that there is a pollution problem, and they will make their decisions about home-buying with that in mind. For example, they will discount the amount they are willing to pay for homes close to the Atlantic Cement Company to reflect the disutility they expect from the cement plant's operation. One way of put-

---

[23] Assuming the firm pays pollution costs, its maximum profits under the old technology are AP_0F, whereas maximum profits under the new technology are AP_0H. It is obvious that $AP_0H > AP_0F$.

ting this is to say that the new homeowners have already been compensated for the externality because of the lower prices they pay for the homes near the cement plant. And because they had already received this compensation, it would be inefficient to allow them to seek compensation from the cement company again. In following this economic argument, the law would dismiss the new homeowner's nuisance action on the grounds that they had "come to the nuisance." The new homeowners knew *or should have known* what they were getting into.

> **Question 5.8:** Suppose that at some time in the future the cement company doubles its rate of output, thus increasing the noise, smoke, dust, and vibration inflicted on the neighborhood. Even if the old homeowners received permanent damages, does efficiency argue for allowing the new homeowners to seek compensation for the additional harms?

Finally, let us address an issue raised in the majority opinion that will return again in our investigation of the economic analysis of law. That is, might there be a social policy, other than exposure to liability in a common law nuisance suit, that might more efficiently induce polluters to internalize the costs they impose on others? The most important policy alternative to *ex post* exposure to liability is *ex ante* administrative agency regulatory control. We have discussed the efficiency aspects of only the first policy: holding nuisance creators liable for the harm they do others involuntarily *but only after the nuisance has been created. Ex ante* regulatory controls attempt to minimize external costs *by stopping them from ever occurring.* In the *Boomer* case, an example of an *ex ante* regulatory control would have been prior requirements on the cement company or administrative agency restrictions on the amount of pollution that all stationary polluters generate. While the economic and legal arguments for and against such administrative agency solutions to the presence of externalities are interesting, the consideration of these arguments would take us far beyond the common law of property.

> **Question 5.9:** Could it be said on efficiency grounds that, in general, *ex post* liability is the more efficient remedy in the case of a *private* nuisance but that *ex ante* regulation is the more efficient remedy in the case of a *public* nuisance?

With this analysis of the *Boomer* case in mind, read the following famous case (on which our example in the previous chapter of the unfortunate Foster is based) and answer the questions afterwards.

Spur Industries, Inc. v. Del E. Webb Development Co., 494 P.2d 701 (Ariz. 1972)

> CAMERON, Vice Chief Justice. From a judgment permanently enjoining the defendant, Spur Industries, Inc., from operating a cattle feedlot near the plaintiff Del E. Webb Development Company's Sun City, Spur

appeals. . . [W]e feel that it is necessary to answer only two questions. They are:

1. Where the operation of a business, such as a cattle feedlot, is lawful in the first instance, but becomes a nuisance by reason of a nearby residential area, may the feedlot operation be enjoined in an action brought by the developer of the residential area?

2. Assuming that the nuisance may be enjoined, may the developer of a completely new town or urban area in a previously agricultural area be required to indemnify the operator of the feedlot who must move or cease operation because of the presence of the residential area created by the developer? . . .

The area in question is located in Maricopa County, Arizona, some 14 to 15 miles west of the urban area of Phoenix. . . In 1956, Spur's predecessors in interest, H. Marion Welborn and the Northside Hay Mill and Trading Company, developed feedlots, about 1/2 mile south of Olive Avenue. . . The area is well suited for cattle feeding and in 1959, there were 25 cattle feeding pens or dairy operations within a 7-mile radius of the location developed by Spur's predecessors. . .

In May of 1959, Del Webb began to plan the development of an urban area to be known as Sun City. For this purpose, the Marinette and the Santa Fe Ranches, some 20,000 acres of farmland, were purchased for $15,000,000 or $750.00 per acre. This price was considerably less than the price of land located near the urban area of Phoenix. . .

By September 1959, Del Webb had started construction of a golf course south of Grand Avenue, and Spur's predecessors had started to level ground for more feedlot area. In 1960, Spur purchased the property in question and began a rebuilding and expansion program extending both to the north and south of the original facilities. . .

Accompanied by an extensive advertising campaign, homes were first offered by Del Webb in January, 1960, and the first unit to be completed was south of Grand Avenue and approximately 2 1/2 miles north of Spur. By 2 May 1960, there were 450 to 500 houses completed or under construction. At this time, Del Webb did not consider odors from the Spur pens a problem, and Del Webb continued to develop in a southerly direction, until sales resistance became so great that the parcels were difficult if not impossible to sell. . .

By December 1967, Del Webb's property had extended south to Olive Avenue, and Spur was within 500 feet of Olive Avenue to the north. . . Del Webb filed its original complaint alleging that in excess of 1,300 lots in the southwest portion were unfit for development for sale as residential lots because of the operation of the Spur feedlot.

Del Webb's suit complained that the Spur feeding operation was a public nuisance because of the flies and the odor which were drifting or being blown by the prevailing south to north wind over the southern portion of Sun City. At the time of the suit, Spur was feeding between 20,000 and 30,000 head of cattle, and the facts amply support the finding of the trial court that the feed pens had become a nuisance to the people who resided in the southern part of Del Webb's development. The testimony indicated that cattle in a commerical feedlot will produce 35 to 40 pounds of wet manure per day, per head, or over a million pounds of wet manure per day for 30,000 head of cattle, and that despite the admittedly good feedlot management and good housekeeping practices by Spur, the resulting odor and flies produced an annoying if not unhealthy situation as far as the senior citizens of southern Sun City were concerned. There is no doubt that some of the citizens of Sun City were unable to enjoy the outdoor living that Del Webb had advertised and that Del Webb was faced with sales resistance from prospective purchasers as well as strong and persistent complaints from the people who had purchased homes in that area. . .

It is noted, however, that neither the citizens of Sun City nor Youngstown are represented in this lawsuit and the suit is solely between Del E. Webb Development Company and Spur Industries, Inc. . .

[The court next discusses the difference between a public and a private nuisance. The former threatens to harm the *general* public rather than any specific individual while the latter is a harm only to easily identifiable individuals. The court assets that, in general, a private nuisance, for which the injury is slight, can be adequately dealt with through the payment of money damages but that a public nuisance, for which the harm is much greater, is subject to an injunction. The trial court held that Spur's feedlot was a *public* nuisance, and the Arizona Supreme Court agrees.]

The judgment of the trial court permanently enjoining the operation of the feedlot is affirmed. . .

In the so-called "coming to the nuisance" cases, the courts have held that the residential landowner may not have relief if he knowingly came into a neighborhood reserved for industrial or agricultural endeavors and has been damaged thereby. [In a Kansas case that dealt with similar issues the court said]: "Plaintiffs chose to live in an area uncontrolled by zoning laws or restrictive covenants and remote from urban development. In such an area plaintiffs cannot complain that legitimate agricultural pursuits are being carried on in the vicinity, nor can plaintiffs, having chosen to build in an agricultural area, complain that the agricultural pursuits carried on in the area depreciate the value of their homes. The area being *primarily agricultural*, any opinion reflecting the value of such property must take this factor into account. The standards affecting the value of residence property in an urban setting, subject to zoning controls and controlled planning techniques, cannot be the standard by which agricultural properties are judged.

People employed in a city who build their homes in suburban areas of the county beyond the limits of a city and zoning regulations do so for a reason. Some do so to avoid the high taxation rate imposed by cities, or to avoid special assessments for street, sewer and water projects. They usually build on improved or hard surface highways, which have been built either at state or county expense and thereby avoid special assessments for these improvements. It may be that they desire to get away from the congestion of traffic, smoke, noise, foul air and the many other annoyances of city life. But with all these advantages in going beyond the area which is zoned and restricted to protect them in their homes, they must be prepared to take disadvantages." Dill v. Excel Packing Company, 183 Kan. 513, 525, 526, 331 P.2d 539, 548, 549 (1958).

Were Webb the only party injured, we would feel justified in holding that the doctrine of "coming to the nuisance" would have been a bar to the relief asked by Webb, and, on the other hand, had Spur located the feedlot near the outskirts of a city and had the city grown toward the feedlot, Spur would have to suffer the cost of abating the nuisance as to those people locating within the growth pattern of the expanding city. . .

There was no indication in the instant case at the time Spur and its predecessors located in western Maricopa County that a new city would spring up, full-blown, alongside the feeding operation and that the developer of that city would ask the court to order Spur to move because of the new city. Spur is required to move not because of any wrongdoing on the part of Spur, but because of a proper and legitimate regard of the courts for the rights and interests of the public.

Del Webb, on the other hand, is entitled to the relief prayed for (a permanent injunction), not because Webb is blameless, but because of the damage to the people who have been encouraged to purchase houses in Sun City. It does not equitably or logically follow, however, that Webb, being entitled to the injunction, is then free of any liability to Spur if Webb has in fact been the cause of the damage Spur has sustained. It does not seem harsh to require a developer, who has taken advantage of the lower land values in a rural area as well as the availability of large tracts of land on which to build and develop a new town or city in the area, to indemnify those who are forced to leave as a result.

Having brought people to the nuisance to the foreseeable detriment of Spur, Webb must indemnify Spur for a reasonable amount of the cost of moving or shutting down. It should be noted that this relief to Spur is limited to a case wherein a developer has, with foreseeability, brought into a previously agricultural or industrial area the population which makes necessary the granting of an injunction against a lawful business and for which the business has no adequate relief.

It is therefore the decision of this court that the matter be remanded to the trial court for a hearing upon the damages sustained by the defendant Spur as a reasonable and direct result of the granting of the permanent injunction. Since the result of the appeal may appear novel and both sides have obtained a measure of relief, it is ordered that each side will bear its own costs.

Affirmed in part, reversed in part, and remanded for further proceeding consistent with this opinion.

Question 5.10:

a. What is the economic interpretation of the defense of "coming to the nuisance"? Could it be said that Webb, by paying less for the property, was already compensated for the nuisance because the land values reflected the stench? Should Spur's contention that they were there first—"first in time, first in right" is the old legal saw—dispose of the issue?

b. Suppose that the price Webb paid for the land was *not* lower than the price of comparable land that was free from the stench. Could you argue that Webb knew or *should have known* about the nuisance so that whether the price of land was lower is irrelevant?

c. Would the result have been less efficient if the court had dismissed Webb's suit on the grounds that he came to the nuisance?

d. How might the behavior of other nuisance-creators be affected by this decision? Would those nuisance-creators behave differently if the court had dismissed Webb's suit?

e. Was a cooperative solution to the nuisance possible between Spur and Webb? Between Spur and the affected residents?

f. Suppose that the case is dismissed on the grounds that if the residents have a cause of action, it lies against Del Webb for fraudulent advertising, not against Spur feedlot for causing a nuisance. Spur remains where they are and so do the residents. But five years later, the Surgeon General of the United States announces that persistent exposure to odor and flies like that emanating from the feedlot causes cancer. Do the residents now have a cause of action against the feedlot? Against Del Webb? How should that dispute be resolved?

V. WHY SHOULD PROPERTY RIGHTS BE PRIVATE?

The first part of this chapter concerned delineating the rights of property owners, and we discussed the content of these rights at length. But we did not discuss who the owners should be. Should ownership of valuable resources be assigned only to individuals? Or to families, communities, organizations, or to all of society? In this section, we turn from discussing the content of the bundle of rights called "property" to a discussion of the types of owners—individual, organizational, the community.

A. Private Versus Public Ownership

An issue we have so far avoided is whether the type of owner matters for the efficient use of resources. Economists have frequently asserted that private property rights are more efficient than other arrangements. "Private" in this context refers to ownership by individuals and non-governmental organizations, such as families, corporations, and cooperatives, whereas the alternative, "public," usually refers to some form of state or governmental ownership.

The question of private versus public ownership goes to some of the deepest ideological disputes and divisions in modern life. However, we will try to provide a discussion of the private-public debate that emphasizes analysis and insight rather than ideology.

The case for private ownership rather than public or communal ownership is easy to make within a narrow context in which economic efficiency is taken as the goal. (In a broader context the choice between private and public ownership would take consideration of additional values such as equity, freedom, human dignity, and shared community norms.) Imagine that a town owns a meadow that is suitable for pasture or crops but not both. No individual owns the meadow in the sense that he may legally exclude others from it or sell it. Will these communal or public property rights lead to the efficient use of the meadowland? Not if these rights are interpreted to mean that every member of the community should have free and unlimited access to the meadow.

Under this assumption about the meaning of communal ownership, many members of the community will perceive that their cost of pasturing livestock in the meadowland is zero. That is, they must make no payment nor incur any other expense to use the pasture. Since demand curves reveal an inverse relationship between price and quantity demanded, it follows that at a zero price the demand for the use of the pasture will be as large as it can possibly be. The crush of livestock on the meadow will result in overgrazing and the destruction of the soil. This outcome has been called "the tragedy of the commons."[24] The tragedy is that communal ownership, understood as open access to a natural resource, results in over-use and destruction, and this result, like a Greek tragedy, follows a remorseless logic to a terrible ending.

Recall, as we saw in Chapter 2, that resources will be efficiently used when, among other things, the price for using that resource reflects its value in the next best alternative use, what economists call its "opportunity cost." Suppose that cropland is the best alternative use of the meadow. Thus, the price for grazing should be greater than zero to reflect this opportunity cost. The zero price implied by communal rights for pasturing is sub-optimal. Specifically, too many of the community's other resources are devoted to raising livestock since the price of pasturage is set inefficiently low.

If the meadowland were held as private property rather than as communal property, it would be much more likely that the land, as well as society's other resources, would be efficiently used. This is because private owners do not let others use their property at no charge. They would charge them a positive price to use their property as a pasture, and the price they would charge would be such that the profit to be made from leasing the land as pasture would be greater than the profit to be made from any alternative use of the land. This pricing scheme will lead to the efficient use of property (where by "private" we mean an individual, a family, a corporation, or cooperative—any non-communal organization).[25]

---

[24] This is the famous problem of over-grazing of the commons or of over-fishing a communal stream or lake. The seminal article in this area is H. S. Gordon, *The Economic Theory of a Common Property Resource: The Fishery*, 62 J. POL. ECON. 124 (1954).

[25] Throughout much of history and across a wide spectrum of societies, grazing land has typically been held in common even though cropland has been individually owned. (A particularly famous example of this is the beautiful Boston Commons, whose name indicates that it was originally a common grazing plot.) In nearly every instance of communal grazing rights, the society imposed restrictions on the use of the common resource in order to minimize the inefficiencies of that form of property ownership. A frequent restriction was to limit the number of cattle one could graze to one's proportion of the community's total landholding, a practice called "stinting."

An interesting empirical verification of the superior efficiency of private over common property rights has come from a study of oyster beds along the Atlantic and Gulf Coasts of the United States.[26] At an early stage in their lives oysters attach themselves permanently to some subaqueous material such as rock. This attachment to something relatively easily defined makes it possible to imagine defining private property rights in oysters for commercial fishermen. However, the states along the Atlantic and Gulf Coasts that have commercial oyster industries have not settled on a single system of property rights for oysters. Some states have determined that the subaqueous areas where oysters tend to congregate are to be *common* property for oyster fishermen; any fisherman may take oysters from those areas and none may exclude another.[27] Other states have held that these areas are to be available for private leasing from the State, and that the lessee will have the usual rights to exclude and transfer (with some limitations). This difference allowed Professors Agnello and Donnelly to compare the relative efficiency of the private and communal property rights systems. The measure of efficiency they used was labor productivity (output per person-hour in oyster-fishing). Their finding was that labor was much more productively employed in the privately-leased oyster beds than in the communal oyster beds. Put dramatically, the authors of this study conclude that if all oyster beds had been privately leased in 1969, the average oyster fisherman's income would have been 50% higher than it was. That implies a sizable welfare loss due to reliance on communal property rights.

In discussing the superiority of private ownership over public ownership, we assumed that the public would be given free access to public property. The free access assumption is what leads to the tragedy of the commons. But this condemnation of public ownership is far too broad, since free access is not in fact given to most public property. To illustrate, the National Parks in the United States are publicly owned, but a fee is charged to enter; many activities, like camping in the more popular parks, require reservations in advance (a form of rationing by time); furthermore, visitors to the national parks are not permitted to graze animals or cut wood. The tragedy of the commons does not occur in the national parks because, while the land is publicly owned, use is restricted.

The tragedy of the commons, in its fully disastrous form, requires a political paralysis that prevents government from stopping the destruction of a resource. This paralysis seems to have reached an advanced stage for some resources, such as fisheries. For other resources, there are symptoms of paralysis, but not the full disaster. For example, the federal government owns vast lands in the American west and sells permits for grazing, forestry,

---

[26] *See* R. J. Agnello and L. P. Donnelly, *Property Rights and Efficiency in the Oyster Industry*, 18 J. L. & ECON. 521 (1975). *See also*, G. Power, *More About Oysters Than You Wanted to Know*, 30 MD. L. REV. 199 (1970).

[27] Sometimes the state government excludes fishermen by allowing only *licensed* oyster fishermen to use the communal property. Using licenses to ration access to a resource has its own inefficiencies, which we will ignore in this brief discussion.

and mining on these lands. There is evidence that much of this federal domain is inefficiently managed. As a result, the ecology is deteriorating, in no small part because the communal interest provides much less incentive for efficient use of a resource than would private ownership.[28]

One solution that has been proposed is to put an end to public ownership by selling or leasing some of the federally-owned land. There seems little doubt that the market value of the products yielded by lands in the American west would be higher if the land currently under public control were under private control. This argument, however, is unlikely to persuade those who love the wilderness and *want* to see it under-utilized. They believe that public land should *not* be managed with the aim of maximizing the market value that it yields. Everyone tends to think that some things are more valuable than wealth (at least at the margin), such as liberty or truth; for some people, wilderness is such a value. Just as people who love liberty would never decide whether someone has the right to speak by asking whether people would pay more to hear him or to shut him up, so those who love the wilderness would never decide whether to build condominiums on the nesting site of the California condors by asking whether developers would pay more for the land than would the conservationists.[29] Ecologists usually oppose the sale of public lands to private interests because their aim is to limit development, rather than to increase yield.

Economists cannot hope to settle such a profound dispute. Their task is to clarify the costs and benefits at stake: just how much waste is involved in the federal government's management of western lands, and how much protection is being afforded to wildlife?

Another example of a valuable resource—this time not land—over which private property rights might be defined but as yet are not is the electromagnetic spectrum. That spectrum consists of radio and light waves over which various kinds of communication, such as radio and television signals, can be transmitted.[30] When it first became technologically feasible to use that spec-

---

[28] The literature on this topic is vast. For an introduction that is favorable to federal ownership and is yet cognizant of the inefficiencies that result, *see* Marion Clawson, THE FEDERAL LANDS REVISITED (1983).

[29] Correction. There are no more nesting sites of California condors. In December of 1985, the few remaining California condors were removed to captive breeding programs. There are none in the wild.

[30] Currently the spectrum, defined over the frequencies between 50 and 1,000 MHz or megaherz (one million cycles per second), is divided up in the following way:

  54- 72 MHz Television channels 2 to 4
  76- 88 Television channels 5 and 6
  88-108 FM radio broadcasting
  108-136 Aircraft navigation
  174-216 Television channels 7 to 13
  225-420 Primarily federal government uses
  420-470 Amateur, citizens', domestic public, and industrial uses
  470-890 UHF television channels 14 to 83

These rules have become somewhat antiquated because of the advent of the new technology of cable television, sometimes called community antenna television (CATV).

trum commercially, in the early 1920s, there was no system for allocating rights to use the spectrum. The result of this was some chaos as private broadcasters interferred, usually inadvertently, with each other's signals by transmitting at frequencies that were too close together. This confusion threatened to make the new technology unusable. Congress sought to end the confusion in the Federal Radio Act of 1927, later amended by the Federal Communications Act of 1934. The statutes explicitly rejected a private property rights approach to the spectrum in favor of the allocation of frequencies through licenses issued by a regulatory agency, the Federal Communications Commission.[31] The most-frequently cited rationale for this method of determining ownership rights is that that spectrum is a limited resource and that, therefore, the government and not market forces should allocate rights to it. This rationale is not to be taken seriously: *all* resources are scarce. There must be more to the argument justifying the licensing method of allocating this particular scarce resource.

When the broadcast media first developed, there was some feeling among the public that the media should serve cultural values. Government regulation of the media seemed to provide a possibility of diverting the media from purely commercial purposes. In addition to this communitarian argument for regulation of the electromagnetic spectrum, there was an efficiency argument for not allowing common law property rights in the spectrum. This was that the technology of broadcasting was not sufficiently developed to prevent stations from inadvertently interfering with each other across wide bands of the spectrum. That is, the property rights of private owners of the spectrum were not sufficiently separable for private, common law property rights to lead to efficient use of this resource. Because it could minimize this problem of non-separability, allocation of rights to the spectrum by a public agency was thought to be superior to a rule of first possession. Even if it once was persuasive, this justification for public allocation of the electromagnetic spectrum is no longer defensible. The technology of broadcasting has changed so that cross-frequency interference is rare, and this suggests that the property rights may now be sufficiently separable that private, common law property rights may be the most efficient rights-allocation mechanism for the spectrum.

There is strong evidence that the current non-market system of allocation imposes inefficiencies on the broadcasting industry. The two major inefficiencies are that the ownership rights granted by the FCC are not as flexible as common law private property rights, with the result that the broadcasting industry inefficiently uses the radio spectrum, as well as the other, complementary resources, such as transmitters, receivers, and labor. For example, it is possible that both the mixture of music, news, and other offerings on existing stations and the total number of stations are less than they would be under a system of private property rights in the electromagnetic spectrum. Secondly, the procedures for allocating ownership rights

---

[31]*See* R. Coase, *The Federal Communications Commission*, 2 J. L. & ECON. 1 (1959).

established by the FCC until very recently forestalled the development and introduction of new technologies in broadcasting. There have been proposals for privatizing that spectrum, and the recent trend toward deregulation in all areas of federal regulation has moved the Federal Comunications Commission toward a more market-like approach to spectrum allocation.

The consideration of federal lands and the electromagnetic spectrum suggests several conclusions about the efficient forms of ownership. In general, property is most efficiently used when it is privately owned. However, when non-separability and public goods problems make the definition of private rights too costly, some alternative form of ownership may be more efficient. Additionally, alternatives to private ownership may be appropriate when efficiency is not the predominant value at stake.

> **Question 5.11:** In general, should property rights in the valuable resources of personal talent, including brain power, be assigned to individuals on a private basis or to society on a communal basis? Consider this case: suppose that a talented pianist, capable of giving great pleasure to millions of listeners, decides to become an auto mechanic. If his talent belongs to the community and not to himself, he may be compelled to continue his training as a pianist. If his talent belongs to him alone, he will become an auto mechanic, and society will lose immense utility. Which should it be—private or communal? Is an alternative public policy available to encourage socially-pleasing uses of private property? [*See* Kronman, *Talent Pooling*, NOMOS (1981).]

B. Individuals and Groups

Private ownership can take many forms: individuals, families, partnerships, corporations, cooperatives, charities, churches, universities, etc. Each of these types of institutions is governed by separate laws. The body of law dealing with organizations is so large and complicated that separate courses are usually offered in law school on each. To illustrate, family law deals in part with the property arrangements created by marriage and children; corporation law deals with the law of corporations; sometimes there is a separate course on non-profit organizations. We mention these different forms of ownership to suggest their variety, but we will not consider these organizations in this chapter. We will, however, briefly comment on the direction of economic analysis in this area.

Economists try to explain organizations just as they explain markets, as an equilibrium in the interaction of rationally self-interested individuals. For example, economists analyze the political process as a competition in which candidates and parties try to adopt platforms and positions that will secure office for them. Similarly, economists analyze the modern corporation as a long-run contract between owners, managers, and workers, whose basis is no different than, say, a long-run contract from a mine to deliver coal to a factory. By this approach, economists have tried to discover laws and regularities that can explain and predict the behavior of organizations. An economic theory of different forms of ownership must be built upon these laws and regularities.

Notice that the economic approach is atomistic in the sense that it traces the behavior of an organization back to the choices of individuals who occupy positions in it. In this respect, economics is thoroughly individualistic. The law, however, tends to regard legal persons, such as corporations, as if they were natural persons. It can be argued that legal persons are not like natural persons with respect to their rights. Specifically, persons have fundamental rights that ought not to be violated, whereas the rights of organizations are only derivative from the rights of individuals. This is essentially the approach in most economic models of law. To illustrate, in economics it is only consumers, not producers, who are final consumers. All demand by firms is "derived demand"—that is, derived from demand by consumers. In cost-benefit analysis, individuals are the final source of utility or welfare.

VI. THE PUBLIC USE OF PRIVATE PROPERTY: THE ECONOMICS OF GOVERNMENTAL TAKING

One of the restrictions on property with which all owners must deal is that they may at some time be required to sell their property to the government. The private property owner cannot, in general, decline to sell to the government as he might to a private purchaser. Nor can he insist that he be paid his reservation price for his property, that is, the price that compensates him for his subjective, as well as the market or objective, valuation of his property. Both the federal and state governments have this power to *take*, as it is called, private property. The taking power is also called the government's right of *eminent domain* and, sometimes, the government's right of *condemnation* or to *condemn* private property. Because this power is such a strong one, it is granted to government in federal and state constitutions as part of government's fundamental prerogatives. That is important to note: the state's right to take private property is not the product of the common law process—although in England, where there is no written constitution of fundamental rights, the common law *did* deal with the sovereign's right to condemn private property and compel its sale to the Crown—nor of mere statutory action by the legislature, but is rather a *constitutional* privilege.

But as can well be imagined, the taking power of government is so far-reaching that at the same time that it is authorized in the Constitution, that power is also restricted. The Fifth Amendment of the United States Constitution allows the federal government to take private property subject to two constraints: the taking must be for a *public* purpose and the owner must be *justly compensated*. State constitutions that create the power to take private property generally impose similar constraints.

The economic analysis of takings is poorly understood by many experts on property, so we will develop it in detail. Let's proceed in four stages.

First, we will see how the potential inefficiencies of the taking power are off-set by potential *efficiencies*. Second, assuming that there are potential net benefits from allowing such a power, we wish to see if the two restrictions—that the taking be for a public purpose and that the private owner be paid just compensation—are likely to confine the government's use of the taking power to those circumstances in which the benefits of the taking exceed the costs. Third, we will consider in detail the incentive effects of takings upon private investment. Finally, we will discuss one of the thorniest of the efficiency issues that arises under the taking power, that of "regulatory takings." A regulatory taking arises not when the government condemns private property but rather when a regulatory action of the government so lowers the value of private property that the owners consider it to have been *taken* by the government and demand compensation. For example, a regulation forbidding nuclear power plants from building on an earthquake fault line does not directly take anyone's private property for public use. However, the regulation may deprive the power company of some or all of the value of a piece of property that it had acquired in anticipation of building a nuclear reactor. The power company contends that the lowering of value is so large that the effect of the regulation is to take its property. In reply, the government contends that the change in value is not large and that the regulation is justified as a reasonable attempt to affect the public safety, morals, or welfare. The government also implies that the loss in the value of the private owner's property is more than offset by the increase in the value of public safety, morals, or welfare. We will discuss the economics of these competing claims shortly. The government, however, typically considers the lowering in value to be insubstantial and refuses to compensate the owners.

A. The Costs and Benefits of Governmental Taking

One of the largest potential inefficiencies of allowing the government to compel a sale of private property is that the forced sale may move the property from a higher-valued use to a lower-valued use. This almost never happens in a voluntary sale of property. A property owner who willingly sells his property to another is presumed to do so only if he is made better off. It follows that if a property owner is *compelled* to sell his property, he may well not be better off.

Let's consider an example. Suppose that Samson owns a plot of land. His ancestors have occupied that land for time out of mind so that the property has a special sentimental value to Samson, although it is not likely that anyone else would share that sentimental attachment. Let us assume that Samson's valuation on his property is $10,000. Further suppose that the government has the right to compel Samson to sell his property to the state so long as the state pays him just compensation. Assume for the moment that "just compensation" means "fair market value." An assessor tells the government that Samson's lot is worth $3,000 on the open market. The government wishes to take the land and put it to use for a public purpose (say, a public highway) whose value is $4,000. The government decides to take the land because its public use is worth $4,000, and its market value is $3,000. However, if the state exercises its right to compel the sale of Samson's property to the state for $3,000, the plot will have moved from the hands of one who valued the plot at $10,000 into the hands of the state, which values it at more than $3,000. That is clearly not a mutually beneficial transaction.

The possibility that the taking of private property will be inefficient can be minimized if we interpret "just compensation" to mean the owner's *reservation price*, the minimum price the owner is willing to accept for his property. If the government is willing to pay the owner his reservation price, then the transaction is mutually beneficial: the government would be willing to pay this reservation price only if the value of the use it envisions for the property exceeds the owner's valuation. Under these circumstances, the government would be indistinguishable from a private purchaser. The prescription to cure the potential inefficiency of taking is, therefore, straightforward: *require the government to pay not merely just compensation but whatever the private owner requests.*

But this prescription is deceptively simple and, indeed, simplistic. Determining a private owner's reservation price in a non-market transaction is fraught with difficulties, not the least of which is that the owner has a powerful incentive to exaggerate that price. However, there is an additional and more subtle reason why the proposed solution of re-defining just compensation to include the owner's reservation price is too simple. That reason arises from the fact that the public purpose for which the government takes the private property is frequently a large project involving many transactions with private property owners. The bargaining costs of these multiple transactions are often high because each owner has an incentive to hold out to be the last person to settle. This means that the costs of putting the project together would be prohibitively high if the government has to pay the reservation price of each owner. This problem will become clearer once we explain what sorts of projects might satisfy the public purpose requirement of the taking clause.

Recall that there is a constitutional requirement that the government may take private property only for a *public purpose*. Thus, the government may not compel a sale of Samson's property in order to transfer it to Delilah, who covets the property but has not been able to convince Samson to sell to her. (Why would that be inefficient and unfair?) The public purpose issue is at the heart of determining the benefits of the taking power. We may invoke the theories we have developed regarding bargaining and the distinction between public and private goods to formalize the benefits of taking. Recall that the government is the most efficient supplier of some public goods. This suggests that the taking power should be invoked to facilitate the governmental provision of *public goods* but not private goods. Thus, taking private property is justified when it is needed to supply goods characterized by non-exclusion and non-rivalry.

But this is only half the matter because, in principle, the government could provide those public goods by purchasing the necessary inputs, including land, from private owners at whatever price the owners asked. Why should the government be allowed to purchase its inputs without regard for subjective values of property owners? The answer is that providing some public goods often requires the government's purchasing property from large numbers of owners. If the government had to strike a bargain with each individual whose property lay in the proposed path of an interstate highway through an urban area, the bargaining costs could be astronomical. Many individuals would have an incentive to hold out to capture as much of the cooperative surplus of the bargain as they could. This way of looking at the public purpose requirement that limits the taking power is consistent with the fact that most taking is done to facilitate large, complex projects for the provision of public goods like highways, public hospitals, public schools, airports, and the like.

Notice an important implication of this economic justification of the public purpose requirement and just compensation. If the government is contemplating the provision of a public good that requires the private property of a small number of persons, the government should not necessarily be allowed to compel those owners to sell at fair market value. This is because the bargaining costs for the government's purchase of the few resources involved may be small. In those circumstances, the government should behave much as would a private developer, purchasing at whatever price the private owner demands. The government should only resort to compulsory sale when there are many sellers, each of whom controls resources that are necessary to the project. Thus, the economic justification for takings is essentially the same as the economic justification given above for using the damage remedy in public nuisance suits.

> **Question 5.12:** What if the government needs to purchase a single, large piece of property in order to provide a public good, say, a satellite tracking station? There is only one private owner with whom to deal. And his property is the *only* one that is suitable for the station. Should the government, a monopsonist for satellite tracking stations, be allowed to compel this individual, a monopolist for the contemplated public use, to sell at fair market value?

Read the following case and answer the questions to see how one might apply the principles we have discussed and how far the public purpose doctrine may be pushed.

Poletown Neighborhood Council v. City of Detroit, 304 N.W.2d 455, 410 Mich. 616 (1981).

PER CURIAM. This case arises out of a plan by the Detroit Economic Development Corporation to acquire, by condemnation if necessary, a large tract of land to be conveyed to General Motors Corporation as a site for construction of an assembly plant. The plaintiffs, a neighborhood association and several individual residents of the affected area, brought suit in Wayne Circuit Court to challenge the project on a number of grounds [,principally that] the city abused its discretion in determining that condemnation of plaintiffs' property was necessary to complete the project.

The trial lasted 10 days and resulted in a judgment for defendants. . .

This case raises a question of paramount importance to the future welfare of this state and its residents: Can a municipality use the power of eminent domain granted to it by the Economic Development Corporations Act . . . to condemn property for transfer to a private corporation to build a plant to promote industry and commerce, thereby adding jobs and taxes to the economic base of the municipality and state? . . .

The Economic Development Corporations Act is a part of the comprehensive legislation dealing with planning, housing and zoning whereby the State of Michigan is attempting to provide for the general health, safety, and welfare through alleviating unemployment, providing economic assistance to industry, assisting the rehabilitation of blighted areas, and fostering urban redevelopment. . . . To further the objectives of this act, the legislature has authorized municipalities to acquire property by condemnation in order to provide industrial and commercial sites and the means of transfer from the municipality to private users.

What plaintiffs-appellants do challenge is the constitutionality of using the power of eminent domain to condemn one person's property to convey it to another private person in order to bolster the economy. They argue that whatever incidental benefit may accrue to the public, assembling land to General Motors' specifications for conveyance to General Motors for its uncontrolled use in profit making is really a taking for private use and not a public use because General Motors is the primary beneficiary of the condemnation.

The defendants-appellees contend, on the other hand, that the controlling public purpose in taking this land is to create an industrial site which will be used to alleviate and prevent conditions of unemployment and fiscal distress. The fact that it will be conveyed to and ultimately used by a private manufacturer does not defeat this predominant public purpose. . .

The power of eminent domain is to be used in this instance primarily to accomplish the essential public purposes of alleviating unemployment and revitalizing the economic base of the community. The benefit to a private interest is merely incidental. . . If the public benefit was not so clear and significant, we would hesitate to sanction approval of such a project. The power of eminent domain is restricted to furthering public uses and purposes and is not to be exercised without substantial proof that the public is primarily to be benefited. Where, as here, the condemnation power is exercised in a way that benefits specific and identifiable private interests, a court inspects with heightened scrutiny the claim that the public interest is the predominant interest being advanced. Such public benefit cannot be speculative or marginal but must be clear and significant if it is to be within the legitimate purpose as stated by the Legislature. We hold this project is warranted on the basis that its significance for the people of Detroit and the state has been demonstrated. . .

RYAN, Justice (dissenting) . . . This is more than an example of a hard case making bad law—it is, in the last analysis, good faith but unwarranted judicial imprimatur upon government action taken under the policy of the end justifying the means. . .

It was, of course, evident to all interested observers that the removal by General Motors of its Cadillac manufacturing operations to a more favorable economic climate would mean the loss to Detroit of at least 6,000 jobs as well as the concomitant loss of literally thousands of allied and supporting automotive design, manufacture and sales functions. There would necessarily follow, as a result, the loss of millions of dollars in real estate and income tax revenues. . . [General Motors insisted that the city make extensive improvements to the freeways, streets, sewers, and other aspects of the site. The cost of the acquisition of the property and of making these improvements was over $200 million. The City intended to sell the site to General Motors for $8 million.] . . . Faced with the unacceptable prospect of losing two automotive plants and the jobs that go with them, the city chose to march in fast lock-step with General Motors to carve a "green field" out of an urban setting which ultimately required sweeping away a tightly-knit residential enclave of first- and second-generation Americans, for many of whom their home was their most valuable and cherished asset and their stable ethnic neighborhood the unchanging symbol of the security and quality of their lives. . .

[T]he central jurisprudential issue is the right of government to expropriate property from those who do not wish to sell for the use and benefit of a strictly private corporation. It is not disputed that this action was authorized by statute. The question is whether such authorization is constitutional. . .

It is plain, of course, that condemnation of property for transfer to private corporations is not wholly proscribed. For many years, and probably since the date of Michigan's statehood, an exception to the general rule has been recognized. The exception, which for ease of reference might be denominated the instrumentality of commerce exception, has permitted condemnation for the establishment or improvement of the avenues of commerce—highways, railroads, and canals, for example . . . It cannot for an instant be maintained, however, nor has anyone suggested, that the case before us falls within the instrumentality of commerce exception. . . It may be argued, however, that the fact that the case before us lies outside the exception does not end the inquiry if the reasons justifying the existing exception are present here. I turn now to determine whether such reasons exist.

Examination of the cases involving the instrumentality of commerce exception reveal[s] that three common elements appear in those decisions that go far toward explicating and justifying the use of eminent domain for private corporations: 1) *public* necessity of the extreme sort, 2) continuing accountability to the *public,* and 3) selection of land according to facts of independent *public* significance. . .

With regard to highways, railroads, canals, and other instrumentalities of commerce, it takes little imagination to recognize that without eminent

domain these essential improvements, all of which require particular con-
figurations of property—narrow and generally straight ribbons of land—
would be "otherwise impracticable"; they would not exist at all. . . [I]t
could hardly be contended that the existence of the automotive industry
or the construction of a new General Motors assembly plant requires the
use of eminent domain. . .

One of the reasons advanced by the defendants as justification of the
taking in this case, and adopted by the majority, is the claim of alleviation
of unemployment. Even assuming, *arguendo*, that employment per se is a
"necessity of the extreme sort," there are no guarantees from General
Motors about employment levels at the new assembly plant. . . But the
fact of the matter is that once [the Central Industrial Park or CIP] is sold to
General Motors, there will be no public control whatsoever over the management, or operation, or conduct of the plant to be built there. . . The
level of employment at the new GM plant will be determined by private
corporate managers primarily with reference, not to the rate of regional
unemployment, but to profit. . .

The third element common to our cases has to do with the recognition
that when property is condemned for a private corporation, determination
of the specific land to be condemned is made without reference to the private interests of the corporation. The determination is based instead upon
criteria related to the public interest. . .

Eminent domain is an attribute of sovereignty. When individual citizens
are forced to suffer great social dislocation to permit private corporations
to construct plants where they deem it most profitable, one is left to wonder who the sovereign is. . .

With this case the Court has subordinated a constitutional right to private corporate interests. As demolition of existing structures on the future
plant site goes forward, the best that can be hoped for, jurisprudentially, is
that the precedential value of this case will be lost in the accumulating
rubble.   ▬

Question 5.13

a. Recall our argument that the taking power is part of the government's tools
for providing public goods. Would you characterize what the City of Detroit
intends to do with this land as being the provision of a public good?

b. Justice Ryan describes the area where the taking is to occur as a "tightly-
knit residential enclave of first- and second-generation Americans, for many
of whom their home was their most valuable and cherished asset and their stable ethnic neighborhood the unchanging symbol of the security and quality of
their lives." If this description is accurate, does it raise any special efficiency
concerns about the government's taking this property at fair market value?
Specifically, is there a particular problem here in under-compensating the residents of Poletown for their large subjective valuation on their homes and
community?

c. What other policies were available to the City of Detroit? How else, other
than taking this property, might the City have assisted General Motors to
remain in Detroit?

B. The Incentive Effects of Takings on Investment and on Government Regulators: The Paradox of Compensation[32]

The incentive effects of takings on private investment and on governmental regulators are often misunderstood. We will develop a detailed explanation of those effects by considering the following situation:

> **Facts:** Xavier is a government official whose wall is covered by a large map with a thick blue line across it. Currently, the area to the south of the blue line may be used for any commercial, industrial, or residential purpose. The government proposes that the area be downzoned to forbid industrial uses, although commercial uses would still be allowed.
>
> Yvonne owns a building that is located on the blue line. The building is currently being used as a retail outlet, but she is contemplating expanding and improving the building so that it can be used as a factory. If the government leaves the zoning as it is, she will be able to use the building as a factory, but if the government downzones the area, she will be prohibited from using the building as a factory.
>
> Yvonne must decide how much to invest in improving her building. If she abandons the idea of using her building as a factory, she will make a small investment and the government's zoning decision will not affect her. But if she proceeds with the idea of using her building as a factory, she will make a large investment and the government's zoning decision will affect her. Should the government carry out its downzoning plan, she will lose money on the large investment, and a court will then have to decide whether she is entitled to compensation for the loss. The decision will turn upon whether the court declares the government restriction to be a regulation, in which case no compensation is due, or a taking, in which case compensation is due.

The incentive effects of the court's decision on whether a taking has occurred has profound effects on people like Yvonne. If downzoning is almost certain to be deemed a taking so that the government will have to compensate Yvonne, she bears no risk from making a large investment, so she will invest as if there were no risk of downzoning. On the other hand, if downzoning is almost certain to be deemed a regulation so the government will not compensate Yvonne, she bears the risk that the value of her investment will be destroyed by downzoning, and she will restrain her investment.

Is it efficient for Yvonne to invest as if downzoning would not occur, or is it efficient for her to take account of the risk of downzoning? Just as a private person is uncertain about her future needs, so a government is uncertain about its future needs. There is a real risk that government will need to downzone the area, although whether this possible need will mature remains to be seen. Social efficiency requires Yvonne to take account of real risks, including the risk that the value of her investment will be destroyed by the need to downzone the area. It is thus inefficient for government to guarantee Yvonne the full value of any investment that she makes.

---

[32]The discussion in this section relies on Cooter, *Unity in Tort, Contract, and Property: The Model of Precaution,* 73 CAL. L. REV. 1 (1985).

Figure 5.4 The Incentive Effects of Governmental Taking on Private Investment

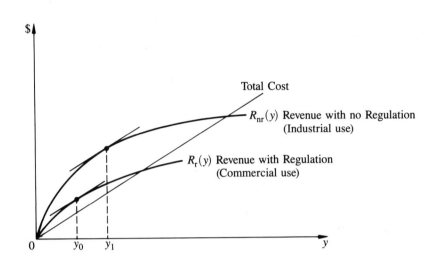

Whether a particular government action is likely to be deemed a compensable taking or a non-compensable regulation has effects on the investment decisions of private property owners. If the action is almost certain to be deemed a compensable taking, then the private investor bears no risk of loss from making a large investment. But if the action is almost certain to be deemed a non-compensable regulation, then the private investor bears all the risk that the value of the investment will be lost. The higher curve, labeled R_{nr}, indicates the revenues Yvonne will realize if her investment can be used in its highest-valued use because government action will almost certainly be deemed a compensable taking. Under those circumstances, y_1 is the optimal investment level: it represents the point at which the marginal revenue of the investment (the slope of R_{nr}) is equal to the marginal cost of the investment (the slope of the Total Cost curve). The lower curve, labeled R_r, gives the revenues obtainable when the investment cannot be used in its highest-valued use because government action will almost certainly be deemed a non-compensable regulation. Under those circumstances, y_0 is the optimal investment level: it represents the point at which the marginal revenue of the investment (the slope of R_r) is equal to the marginal cost of the investment (the slope of the Total Cost curve). Note that $y_1 > y_0$.

The argument can be seen graphicallly. In Figure 5.4, the vertical axis indicates dollars and the horizontal axis measures the size of Yvonne's renovated building. The total cost of Yvonne's investment in the building is shown by the line labeled "Total Cost." There are two curves, labeled R_{nr} and R_r, indicating possible revenues yielded by the building as a function of its size. The higher revenue curve is labelled R_{nr} to indicate the revenues obtainable when there is no regulation, so the building can be used as a factory. The lower revenue curve is labelled R_r to indicate the revenues obtainable when there is regulation, so the building cannot be used as a factory.

y_0 is the point at which the slope of the lower revenue curve (which equals the marginal revenue of Yvonne's investment) equals the slope of the total cost curve (which represents the marginal cost of Yvonne's investment). Because y_0 is the investment level for which the marginal costs and marginal revenues are equal, it is the profit-maximizing investment level when industrial use is forbidden.

y_1 is the point at which the slope of the higher revenue curve (which equals the marginal revenue of Yvonne's investment) equals the slope of the total cost curve (which represents the marginal cost of Yvonne's investment). Thus, y_1 is the profit-maximizing investment level when industrial use is allowed.

If it were certain that government would *not* downzone, then efficiency requires Yvonne to invest at the high level y_1. On the other hand, if it were certain that government would downzone, then efficiency requires Yvonne to invest at the low level y_0. In reality, it is uncertain whether government will downzone, so efficiency requires Yvonne to invest at a level in between y_1 and y_0.[33] Efficiency requires Yvonne to restrain her investment in light of the possibility that its value will be destroyed by government action.

If Yvonne were certain that downzoning would be deemed a taking by the courts so that she would be entitled to full compensation, then her net profits (including compensation) would be the same as if there were no downzoning. Consequently, it will be in her interests to invest at the high level y_1. But this level of investment is too high relative to the efficient level. We conclude that *full compensation for the loss of value in investments caused by government provides incentives for excessive private investment when there is uncertainty about the government's needs.*

On the other hand, if downzoning would be deemed a regulation by the courts so that Yvonne's losses would be uncompensated, then she has an incentive to take full account of the probability of downzoning. Thus, regulations cause private persons to internalize the risk that government action will destroy the value of their investments. We conclude that *no compensation for the loss of value in investments caused by government provides incentives for efficient private investment when there is uncertainty about the government's needs.*

So far it appears that the compensability of takings provides inefficient incentives for private investment, whereas the noncompensability of regulations provides efficient incentives for private investment. But this argument takes account of incentive effects only on private persons, not incentive effects on government officials. The effect of the two legal institutions—regulations and takings—is quite different when we turn from private persons to government officials. If the court decides that downzoning is a mere regulation so that compensation need not be paid, downzoning is costless to the government. On the other hand, if the court decides that downzoning is a taking so that compensation must be paid, downzoning is very costly to the

---

[33]To be precise, efficiency requires her to make additional improvements until the resulting increase in her profits when there is no government action, multiplied by the probability of no government action, equals the loss in profits when there is government action, multiplied by the probability of government action.

c. Would this problem of distinguishing between compensable takings and noncompensable regulations be lessened if the purchase option suggestion of the previous section were adopted as part of government takings?

D. Zoning and the Regulation of Development

There are some goods, called "complements," that are better consumed together, such as hot dogs and sauerkraut, and there are other goods, called "substitutes," that are better consumed separately, such as ice cream and sauerkraut. A similar categorization may be made regarding the spatial separation of economic activities—it is best to locate restaurants near offices, and it is best to separate smoke-stack industries from residences. There is, however, an important difference between culinary and spatial separation: no law prohibits eating ice cream with sauerkraut, but zoning ordinances in most localities prohibit locating industry in residential neighborhoods.

It is the element of compulsion in the segregation of economic activities by zoning laws that we seek to explain. It is possible to make a case for zoning as a response to an important kind of market failure. When demand for a good increases, the price rises and producers respond by supplying more of it. The rise in price is a signal for producers to devote more resources to producing the good. This signal is usually appropriate in the sense that society is better off by shifting resources to producing goods whose price is rising. There are, however, special circumstances in which the signals get crossed. In these special circumstances, it would be better for society if producers responded to a price rise by supplying *less* of the good but, in a free market, they will respond by supplying *more* of it.

To illustrate by an historical example, suppose that in 1900 industry locates on the shore of an undeveloped bay in California. The original purpose for locating industry on the shore was to have easy access to boats, but by 1960 the manufacturers were supplied by truck rather than by boat. While the reason for locating industry on the harbor has disappeared, the harbor now has great esthetic and recreational appeal. Given the change in circumstances, efficiency requires gradually relocating industry in the interior and constructing residences or recreational parks on the harbor.

What ought to happen to cause factories to move out and residences to move in is that the residential developers should bid up the price of harbor land relative to land in the interior, so that factories move out and make way for residences. There is, however, an obstacle to the unregulated market's accomplishing this end. The problem is that no one wants to live next door to a factory, so residential developers are unwilling to pay much for harbor land as long as industry is present. Instead of factories moving away from the harbor, the opposite may happen: as industry expands, residences may be driven farther away from the water. If the relative price of land near the water is falling as residents flee to the interior to escape industry, the unregulated market in this situation is giving the wrong signals.

The technical explanation for the false signal given by the market, and the resulting justification for compulsory zoning, is the existence of a *nonconvexity* in the production technology. This idea can be explained by our example from the end of Chapter 4 concerning the laundry and the electrical company. Recall that the electrical company burns coal and the soot soils the laundry. There is, then, a tradeoff between the amount of electricity that can be generated and the amount of laundry that can be produced using a given amount of resources. This tradeoff is depicted by the production frontier in Figure 5.5, panels a and b. In panel a, the production frontier has the standard shape assumed in microeconomic theory—the frontier bows out in a direction that carries it away from the origin of the graph. Along the vertical axis we measure the amount of laundry that can be produced in a given time period; if all resources are devoted to laundry production, then the maximum amount of laundry output that can be produced is L^*. Along the horizontal axis we measure the amount of electricity that can be generated in a given time period; if all resources are devoted to the production of electricity and none to the cleaning of laundry, then E^* electricity can be produced. The production frontier thus represents the combinations of laundry and electricity that are feasible when a given amount of productive resources is allocated between the two uses (and each enterprise uses its resources efficiently). We will indicate in a moment how the market signals to the producers how those resources are to be allocated.

Suppose that panel a depicts the production frontier when the laundry is 10 miles away from the electrical company. The curves in panel b depict the consequences of moving the laundry closer to the electrical company. The main effect of moving the industries closer together is that the interference with the laundry from soot is greater. To illustrate, when the distance is, say, 6 miles, for any given level of electrical production, the amount of laundry that can be produced is lower than at 10 miles, so the interior points on the production frontier shift towards the origin. The end points, however, do not shift, since they represent a situation in which one of the plants shuts down, so there is no problem of soot interfering with laundry. Moving from 6 miles to 3 miles, another shift occurs. At a distance of 3 miles the production frontier has shifted so that it bows in towards the origin of the graph rather than out. At 10 miles, where the production frontier bows out, the production possibilities form a convex set, but at 3 miles, where the production frontier bows in, the production possibilities form a nonconvex set.[34] The point of this example is that spatial externalities can produce nonconvex production sets.

---

[34]A set is convex if, for any pair of points in it, a straight line connecting the two points is entirely contained in the set. Circles and rectangles form convex sets; a quarter-moon forms a nonconvex set.

Figure 5.5   Production Possibilities and Convexities

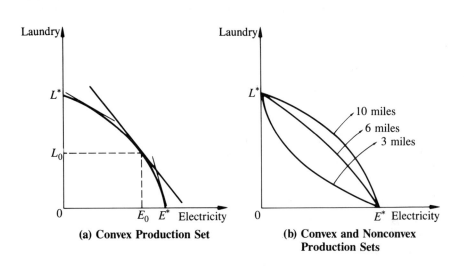

(a) Convex Production Set

(b) Convex and Nonconvex Production Sets

In Panel a, the curve labled L^*E^* represents a convex production frontier for a laundry and an electricity-generating plant located far enough apart so that the smoke from the plant does not impose an externality on the laundry. If all the local resources are devoted to the production of laundry, L^* can be produced. If all the local resources are devoted to generating electricity, E^* can be produced. Any division of resources between the two possibilities gives a combination of laundry and electricity on the convex production possibility frontier. The optimal combination, L_0 and E_0, is given by the point of tangency between the straight line, whose slope indicates the relative prices of laundry and electricity, and the convex production possibility frontier.

In Panel b, the three production possibility frontiers represent the effect of moving the laundry and the electricity-generating plant closer together. (Note that the end points of the frontiers are unchanged because the total amount of laundry and electricity that can be produced if all local resources are devoted only to the production of one commodity is not affected by the closeness of the enterprises.) The effect of moving closer is to make the plant's smoke ever more of a nuisance for the laundry. The closer the two firms are, the less total output can be produced if both firms operate. When they are three miles apart, the production possibility frontier becomes nonconvex. Nonconvexities mean that the price system will send the wrong signal about the relative valuation of the two production possibilities.

But what is so bad about a nonconvex production set? The difficulty is that when a production set is nonconvex, the unregulated market sends the wrong price signals to producers regarding the efficient allocation of resources between competing productive ends. To see the problem, start at the top of the production frontier (at L^*) in panel a and begin drawing lines tangent to the production frontier as you move down it. The slope of these lines represents the relative price of laundry and electricity at different levels of production in a free market. Notice that as you move down the production set, the tangent lines become steeper, which indicates that the production of clean laundry becomes more valuable as it becomes more scarce.

For the nonconvex production set in panel b—the production frontier when the laundry and the electrical plant are 3 miles apart—the opposite is true: as you move down the production set from L^* toward E^*, the tangent line becomes *flatter*, indicating that the laundry's output becomes less valuable relative to electricity as it becomes more scarce. The result of the nonconvex production set is that, in formal economic terms, the optimal solution is a "corner solution," in which all resources are used by one or the other enterprise—that is, either L^* or E^* is going to be produced, but not both. In contrast, where the production set is convex, there is an "interior solution" in which both clean laundry and electricity are produced. (In panel a, L_o and E_o represent the optimal combination of laundry and electricity for a convex production set for an arbitrary relative price of the two outputs.)

Now this analysis can be applied to the example of industrial and residential use of a harbor. This is done in Figure 5.6, panels a and b. The vertical axis in the figures indicates the level of industrial production in the harbor area, and the horizontal axis indicates the level of residential use in the harbor area. The curved line is the production frontier, which shows the feasible combinations of industry and housing. The production frontier in panel a forms a convex set, whereas the production frontier in panel b a nonconvex set. Our example assumes that the production set is nonconvex, like that in panel b. Where that is the case, the unregulated market will generate a harbor area given over entirely to industrial use or to residential use (a corner solution) but not some of both (an interior solution). Because there is a strong suspicion that the more valuable use of the harbor area is now as a residential area, some corrective action is required to prevent the wrong price signals from generating the inefficient outcome of all industrial use.

Although zoning can be justified in this way as a device to correct a market failure and produce an efficient spatial allocation of resources, in reality zoning is a highly political institution that bears little resemblance to the cool, technocratic balancing of benefits and costs implied by our model. A change in zoning or the granting of an exemption, called a "variance," to a particular property owner can often result in doubling or tripling the value of the land. With these multiples at stake, zoning boards are bound to be politically charged, and there is the strong possibility that they will be corrupt.

Several investigators have attempted to discover the objectives that zoning boards actually follow. One plausible idea is that zoning boards tend to impose restrictions upon new developments that maximize the value of the property of the people who elect the board. To illustrate, a wealthy suburb might require a residential developer to donate land for a new park for the town and a new school as the price of granting the variances required to construct new homes. The zoning board may figure that the new park and school will cause the property values of existing voters to rise. Another plausible idea is that zoning makes little difference to the spatial allocation of economic activities because much the same ends can be accomplished by inserting restrictive covenants in deeds. To illustrate, in Houston, where

Figure 5.6   Spatial Nonconvexities and Competing Land Uses

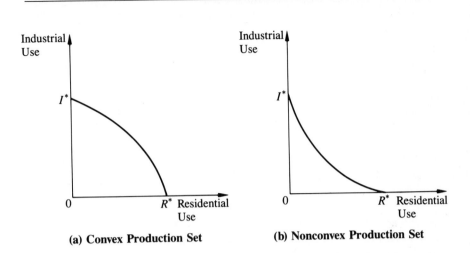

(a) Convex Production Set   **(b) Nonconvex Production Set**

In Panel a, if there are no externalities between the two competing uses of the land, then the convex curve labeled *I*R** shows the feasible combinations of industry and housing. In this case, industry and housing may exist simultaneously in the harbor area.

In Panel b, if there are external effects between the use of land for industry and housing in the harbor area, then the production possibility frontier is the nonconvex curve labeled *I*R**. The likely result of the nonconvexity will be a corner solution: the harbor area will be given over entirely to industrial use or to residential use but not to some of both (which would be an interior solution).

until recently there has been virtually no zoning, the developer of a housing estate often inserts restrictions against industrial or commercial uses of the property into the deeds.[35]

CONCLUSION

In this and the preceding chapter we have developed an economic theory of property and applied that theory to a wide-ranging set of property law problems. Our theory views property as the institution that gives people freedom over resources; property law can contribute to this freedom and encourage the efficient use of resources by creating rules that facilitate bargaining and exchange and that minimize the losses from failing to bargain and exchange. We organized our theoretical discussion of property rules in

---

[35]There is no better place to begin an investigation of the law and economics of zoning than Ellickson, *Alternatives to Zoning: Covenants, Nuisance Rules, and Fines as Land Use Controls*, 40 U. CHI. L. REV. 681 (1973).

the previous chapter and our applications in this chapter around four questions that a system of property must answer:

1. What can be privately owned?
2. How are ownership rights established?
3. What may owners do with their property?
4. How are property rights protected? What are the remedies for infringement?

The analysis of these questions in this chapter has revealed that there is an underlying economic logic to many of the rules of property law. For example, the constraints of the taking power—that the taking must be for a public purpose and the owner must be paid just compensation—help to limit taking to circumstances in which the government is the most efficient supplier of such large, complex public goods as highways and wilderness areas. And the rules for determining ownership claims to lost property limit potentially troubling gaps in the chain of ownership and at the same time encourage the efficient protection of property and efficient attempts to locate rightful owners. This is not to say that *all* the rules of property law may be justified as economically efficient. Our investigation has been somewhat selective because of a desire to apply the economic theory of property. As we have taken pains to point out, there are other values besides efficiency, and rules of property law may sometimes aim to serve these other values at the expense of efficiency. That possibility arose in our discussion of regulatory takings, where the uncompensated lowering of the value of private property as the result of a governmental regulation may be excused if the regulation is reasonably designed to promote a nonefficiency goal like societal morality. Nonetheless, we have established in this and the preceding chapter that the great diversity and richness of property law may be organized according to a purposive and rational economic theory and that that theory helps to explain many of the important issues with which property law deals.

We now turn to the second great area of the common law in order to develop an economic theory of contracts.

SUGGESTED READINGS

Baxter, William, and Lillian R. Altree, *Legal Aspects of Airport Noise*, 15 J. LAW & ECON. 1 (1972).

DeVany, A., R. Eckert, C. Meyers, D. O'Hara, and R. Scott, *A Property System Approach to the Electromagnetic Spectrum*, 21 STAN. L. REV. 1499 (1969).

The Economics of Patents and Copyrights, 8 RES. IN LAW & ECON. 1 (R. Zerbe & J. Palmer, eds., 1986).

Ellickson, Robert, *Alternatives to Zoning: Covenants, Nuisance Rules, and Fines as Land Use Controls*, 40 U. CHI. L. REV. 681 (1973).

Ellickson, Robert, *The Irony of Inclusionary Zoning*, 54 SO. CAL. L. REV. 1167 (1981).

Ellickson, Robert, *Suburban Growth Controls: An Economic and Legal Analysis*, 86 YALE L. J. 385 (1977).

Epstein, Richard, TAKINGS: PRIVATE PROPERTY AND THE POWER OF EMINENT DOMAIN (1985).

Epstein, Richard, *Why Restrain Alienation?*, 85 COL. L. REV. 970 (1985).

Fischel, William, THE ECONOMICS OF ZONING LAWS: A PROPERTY RIGHTS APPROACH TO AMERICAN LAND USE CONTROLS (1985).

Kessel, Reuben, *Transfused Blood, Serum Hepatitis, and the Coase Theorem*, 17 J. LAW & ECON. 265 (1974).

Knetsch, Jack, PROPERTY RIGHTS AND COMPENSATION: COMPULSORY ACQUISITION AND OTHER LOSSES (1983).

Libecap, Gary, *Property Rights in Economic History: Implications for Research*, 23 EXPLORATIONS IN ECONOMIC HISTORY 227 (1986). [An excellent survey of the empirical work done by economic historians on the impact on economic efficiency of different property rights systems.]

Michelman, Frank, *Property, Utility, and Fairness: Comments on the Ethical Foundations of 'Just Compensation' Law*, 80 HARV. L. REV. 1165 (1967).

Rose, Carol M., *Mahon Reconstructed: Why the Takings Issue is Still a Muddle*, 57 SO. CAL. L. REV. 561 (1984).

Rose-Ackerman, Susan, *Inalienability and the Theory of Property Rights*, 85 COL. L. REV. 931 (1985).

Rubinfeld, Daniel, and Lawrence Blume, *Compensation for Takings: An Economic Analysis*, 72 CAL. L. REV. 569 (1984).

Sax, Joseph, *Takings and the Police Power*, 74 YALE L. J. 36 (1964).

White, Michelle, and Donald Wittman, *A Comparison of Taxes, Regulation, and Liability Rules Under Imperfect Information*, 12 J. LEGAL STUD 413 (1983).

CHAPTER 6

An Economic Theory of Contract

People continually make promises—sales people promise happiness, lovers promise marriage, generals promise victory, children promise to behave better, and so forth. The law becomes involved when someone seeks to have a promise enforced. Here are some examples:

Example 1: The Rich Uncle. The rich uncle of a struggling college junior promises to give him a trip around the world if he graduates with honors. The student stops partying and starts studying, graduates with honors, but his uncle reneges on his promise. The student sues his uncle, asking the court to compel the uncle to pay for a trip around the world.

Example 2: The Rusty Chevy. One neighbor offers to sell a used car to another for $1,000. The buyer gives the money to the seller, and the seller gives the car keys to the buyer. To her great surprise, the buyer discovers that the keys fit the rusting Chevrolet in the backyard, not the shiny Cadillac in the driveway. The seller is equally surprised to learn that the buyer expected the Cadillac. The buyer asks the court to order the seller to turn over the Cadillac.

Example 3: The Grasshopper Killer. A farmer, in response to an advertisement for a sure method to kill grasshoppers, sends in $25. He is mailed two wooden blocks with the instructions, "Place grasshopper on Block A and smash with Block B." The buyer asks the court to require the seller to return the $25 and to pay $500 in punitive damages.

The first question faced by the courts in these examples is whether the promise is enforceable. A promise is enforceable if the courts offer a remedy to the victim of the broken promise. Traditionally, courts have been cautious about enforcing promises that are not given in exchange for something. In Example 1, the trip around the world is promised as a prize for the nephew's accomplishments. According to the traditional analysis, the rich uncle does not receive anything in exchange, so the courts would be reluctant to enforce the uncle's promise.

In Example 2, money is exchanged for a promise, but there is confusion about what was promised. The promise that the seller thought he was giving is different from the promise that the buyer thought she was receiving. The courts have also been cautious about enforcing exchanges of confused promises.

In Example 3, there is deception rather than confusion because a reasonable farmer would have understood the promise of "a sure method to kill grasshoppers" to mean something more than what was delivered. The courts ordinarily offer a remedy to the victims of deceptive promises.

Once the court has determined that an enforceable promise was broken, the next problem is to fashion a remedy. One remedy is to force the promise-breaker to keep his promise. For example, if the court decides that the seller in Example 2 broke his promise, then the court might order the seller to turn the Cadillac over to the buyer. This kind of remedy is unavailable in Example 3 because the seller cannot exterminate grasshoppers as promised. Instead, the remedy in Example 3 must involve the payment of money damages as compensation for deceiving the farmer and thereby breaking the promise.

As our examples illustrate, there are two fundamental questions in contract law: "What promises should be enforced?" and "What should be the remedy for breaking enforceable promises?" These questions must be faced by courts when they decide contract disputes and by legislatures when they debate bills to regulate contracts. And these two questions must also be answered by a theory of contract law.

In the late 19th and early 20th centuries, Americans developed the "bargain theory of contracts" to answer the fundamental questions of contract law. The approach taken in that theory is to isolate and abstract the minimal elements of a typical bargain. Having isolated the minimal elements in the typical case, the theory then took the position that those elements are necessary for a binding contract in *every* case. Thus, the basic approach was to describe the essentials of a bargain and raise them up to the level of a legal principle. This approach was so successful among American lawyers that the bargain theory achieved the status of a classic. It no longer enjoys the popularity of former times, but the distinction among the elements of a bargain made by the bargain theory remains fundamental to the way lawyers think about contracts.

Our principal interest will be the economic theory of contracts that has been developed in the last fifteen years or so. Nevertheless, the bargain theory is a useful starting point for our exposition because it will enable us to isolate the essential elements of a bargain. We will use these elements as building-blocks in the economic theory of contracts.

I. THE CLASSICAL OR BARGAIN THEORY OF CONTRACT

In this section we will see how the classical theory answered the two fundamental questions of contracts. Section A will show that the classical theory believed that only promises that were given as part of a bargain or exchange should be legally enforceable. That meant that a gift, like that of the rich uncle to the college student in Example 1 at the beginning of this chapter, would not be enforceable at law because there was no exchange or bargain, merely a one-sided promise. We will also see what evidence the classical theory required in order to infer that promises had been exchanged as part of a bargain. In Section B, we will see how the classical theory answered the second fundamental question of contracts. The classical theory argued that if a promisor breached a legally enforceable promise, he should have to pay compensatory money damages to the victim of the breach. Moreover, the theory specified that these damages should be enough so that the victim was just as well off with the money damages as he or she would have been had the promise been performed.

A. What Promises Should Be Legally Enforceable?

The first question that any theory of contracts must address is "What promises should be enforceable at law?" The classical or bargain theory had a clear answer: a promise is legally enforceable if it is given as part of a bargain and is unenforceable otherwise.

Let's consider some familiar promises to see whether they are enforceable under this principle, which we may call the "bargain principle." The principle excludes any promise that is given gratuitously, rather than being given as part of a bargain: "I promise not to smoke for the rest of the day," or "I promise I won't think less of you in the morning." These promises are usually given freely, not extracted as part of a bargain. So they would be unenforceable under the bargain principle. For the same reason, the bargain principle withholds enforcement from promises to give gifts: "I promise to give Old Siwash University one million dollars when I reach the age of 40," or "If you get an A in this course, I promise to give you a new Corvette." Note that the principle does not deny that the maker of any of these promises may be under a *moral, religious,* or *social* obligation to perform his promise. But it asserts that the person who receives such a promise must look *only* to those non-legal institutions for help should the promise be broken. The law, according to this principle, should not enforce promises that are not part of a bargain. On the other hand, bargains should be enforced according to this principle, even if they are morally tainted: "I pledge my wedding ring as security on this loan," or "I will trade my inheritance for a bowl of soup." Hard bargains are still bargains, according to this theory, and hence enforceable at law.

From these examples it is apparent that the classical theory makes a lot hinge upon classifying promises into "bargains" and "nonbargains." The bargain theory thus required an exact specification of the necessary and sufficient elements for a bargain.[1] The classical or bargain theorists distinguished three such elements: offer, acceptance, and consideration.

"Offer" and "acceptance" have the same meaning in this theory as they do in ordinary speech: one party must make an offer ("I'll take that rusty Chevy over there for $500"), and the other must accept it ("Done"). Contract law and certain statutes specify procedures that must be followed in making and accepting offers. For example, in some states contractual transactions involving sums greater than a certain amount must be concluded "under seal," that is, in writing. In a different context, the Securities and Exchange Commission carefully regulates how business organizations may offer to sell new shares of their stock. However, in most exchanges the signs and symbols of offer and acceptance are prescribed by business practices and social conventions rather than being prescribed by law. For example, a buyer at an auction may signal an offer to buy by raising his hand, and the auctioneer may signal acceptance by shouting "Sold!"

Once an offer is made and accepted, the next step is an exchange. At this stage in a contract, one of the parties (the "promisor") gives the other (the "promisee") a promise. Now enters one of the most important but mysterious elements of the classical theory of contract: the doctrine of consideration. The law uses the technical term "consideration" to describe what the promisor receives in the exchange from the promisee. Most typically, consideration is the money that one party gives to the other. In our Example 3, $25 is the consideration for the promise to supply a device that kills grasshoppers. But consideration need not be money, nor need it necessarily be something material. Consideration can be the *promise* of something material. For example, a farmer may promise to deliver his crop to a wholesaler in the fall and the wholesaler may promise to pay a certain price upon delivery. In this example, a promise of money is consideration for a promise to deliver crops, and *vice versa*.

There are, then, several forms of a bargain: money-for-a-promise, promise-for-a-promise, goods-for-a-promise, service-for-a-promise. Regardless of the form, in each case there is reciprocal inducement: each party gives up something in order to induce the other party to give up something. One side, the promisor, gives a promise, and the other side, the promisee, reciprocates by giving consideration. It is, according to the classical theory, consideration that perfects a bargain by making it legally enforceable. The classical theory holds that promises secured by consideration are enforceable and promises lacking consideration are unenforceable. As Justice Holmes put it, "The root of the whole matter is the relation of reciprocal

---

[1]An interesting question is, "Why did the classical theory confine enforcement to bargain promises?" A full answer to that would take us too far into the field of legal history. In section III below, we will return to this question and use economic analysis to answer the question of which promises should be enforceable.

conventional inducement, each for the other, between consideration and promise."[2]

The doctrine that consideration perfects a bargain has a celebrated and controversial consequence: in the classical theory a court asked to enforce a promise would not inquire whether the consideration was adequate. That is, the court would not ask if the amount of money paid was too little or too much, nor whether the promisor should have accepted the particular consideration given by the promisee. Hard bargains, even bargains that many ordinary people would regard as unfair, are enforceable under this theory. The court's only inquiry would be into the *presence or absence of consideration, not its adequacy*. It is enough for the court that the contracting parties found the consideration adequate at the time of their bargain.

Let us illustrate the bargain theory by applying it to the three examples at the beginning of this chapter. According to the bargain theory, the rich uncle's promise to give his nephew a trip around the world in Example 1 is enforceable only if there was consideration for the promise. Apparently the nephew did not give anything as inducement for the promise, so there was no consideration. Therefore, the promise is unenforceable according to the bargain theory. In general, the promise to give a pure gift, which is not induced by the promise of something in return, is not enforceable under the bargain theory. (See the box entitled "A Tomtit or a Peppercorn.")

In contrast, consideration was given in Example 2 in exchange for the promise to supply the used car. The question raised in Example 2 is whether there was offer and acceptance. If the seller thought they were discussing the rusty Chevy and the buyer thought they were discussing the immaculate Cadillac, then there was, as the law says, no "meeting of the minds." Without a meeting of the minds, there is no offer and acceptance, just a failure to communicate.

In Example 3, the seller offered a sure method for killing grasshoppers in exchange for $25, the buyer accepted the offer, and consideration took the form of paying $25, Therefore, the promise is enforceable according to the classical theory.

We used the classical or bargain theory to introduce the elements of a bargain: offer, acceptance, and consideration. To master these concepts requires practice in applying them in a variety of settings. Try to analyze the following cases in terms of the classical theory.

In the first case, *Batsakis v. Demotsis*, the order in which the facts are presented is confusing, so here is a summary to help you get started. Demotsis, finding herself in difficult circumstances in Nazi-occupied Greece, borrowed money from Batsakis. The Greek currency she borrowed was worth about $25 on the international market at the time, but she signed a promissory note to repay the loan in United States currency, specifically, to pay

---

[2]Oliver Wendell Holmes, Jr., THE COMMON LAW (1881).

A Tomtit or a Peppercorn

Situations arise in which people desire that a promise be enforceable even though the law would not ordinarily enforce such a promise. To illustrate, suppose the rich uncle in Example 1 wanted to give his nephew complete assurance that his promise of a trip around the world would be enforceable to the full extent. There is a problem. This is a promise to give a gift, which is unenforceable by the classical theory, and even in the practice of modern courts it is not fully enforceable. It is not fully enforceable because the nephew has not given anything to the uncle as inducement for the promise; that is, there has been no consideration.

Here's a solution: recast the promise to give a gift in the form of a bargain. If the uncle and his nephew followed a traditional method, the uncle would solemnly offer to give his nephew a trip around the world in exchange for, say, a tomtit (a small bird) or a peppercorn, and the nephew would solemnly give the uncle a tomtit or a peppercorn. More recently, people have not been willing to engage in the fiction of exchanging small birds or peppercorns. Instead they have achieved the same thing—attempting to disguise a gift promise as a bargain promise—by intoning the phrase "in consideration for which, I give you $1."

Should contract law go along with this charade and enforce the promise? (It used to. And that is what the parties wanted.) Or should the law "see through" the form and act on the substance? (That is what it does now. And that is not what the parties wanted.)

$2,000 plus interest. After the war the two parties met in America, and Batsakis sought repayment of the full amount of the note, whereas Demotsis offered to pay $25 plus interest. At the trial the jury awarded Batsakis $750 plus interest,[3] and the case was appealed by Batsakis.

Here is an excerpt from the appeals court's opinion:

Batsakis v. Demotsis, 226 SW2d 673 (Court of Civil Appeals of Texas, 1949)

McGILL, JUSTICE. This is an appeal from a judgment of the 57th judicial District Court of Bexar County. Appellant was plaintiff and appellee was defendant in the trial court. The parties will be so designated.

Plaintiff sued defendant to recover $2,000 with interest at the rate of 8% per annum from April 2, 1942, alleged to be due on the following instrument, being a translation from the original, which is written in the Greek language:

---

[3]How the jury computed this odd award is not explained in the opinion.

"Peiraeus
April 2, 1942

"Mr. George Batsakis
Konstantinou Diadohou #7
Peiraeus

"Mr. Batsakis:

I state by my present (letter) that I received today from you the amount
of two thousand dollars ($2,000.00) of United States of America money,
which I borrowed from you for the support of my family during these difficult days and because it is impossible for me to transfer dollars of my own
from America.

"The above amount I accept with the expressed promise that I will
return to you again in American dollars either at the end of the present
war or even before in the event you might be able to find a way to collect
them (dollars) from my representative in America whom I will write and
give him an order relative to this. You understand until the final execution
(payment) to the above amount an eight per cent interest will be added
and paid together with the principal.

"I thank you and I remain yours with respects.

"The recipient,

(Signed) Eugenia The. Demotsis."

Trial to the court without the intervention of a jury resulted in a judgment in favor of plaintiff for $750.00 principal, and interest at the rate of
8% per annum from April 2, 1942 to the date of judgment, totaling
$1163.83, with interest thereon at the rate of 8% per annum until paid.
Plaintiff has [brought this appeal.]

[The principal contention on appeal regards the allegations of the following paragraph from the defendant's answer to the plaintiff's
complaint:]

"*Plaintiff* [emphasis ours] avers that on or about April 2, 1942 she
owned money and property and had credit in the United States of
America, but was then and there in the Kingdom of Greece in straitened
financial circumstances due to the conditions produced by World War II
and could not make use of her money and property and credit existing in
the United States of America. That in the circumstances the plaintiff
agreed to and did lend to defendant the sum of 500,000 drachmae, which
at that time, on or about April 2, 1942, had the value of $25.00 in money
of the United States of America. That said plaintiff knowing defendant's
financial distress and desire to return to the United States of America,
exacted of her the written instrument plaintiff sues upon, which was a
promise by her to pay to him the sum of $2,000.00 of United States of
America money." . . .

Defendant testified that she did receive 500,000 drachmas from plaintiff. It is not clear whether she received all of 500,000 drachmas or only a
portion of them before she signed the instrument in question. Her testi-

mony clearly shows that the understanding of the parties was that plaintiff would give her the 500,000 drachmas if she would sign the instrument. She testified:

"Q. . . . Who suggested the figure of $2,000.00?

"A. That was how he asked me from the beginning. He said he will give me five hundred thousand drachmas provided I signed that I would pay him $2,000.00 American money."

The transaction amounted to a sale by plaintiff of the 500,000 drachmas in consideration of the execution of the instrument sued on, by defendant. It is not contended that the drachmas had no value. Indeed, the judgment indicates that the trial court placed a value of $750.00 on them or on the other consideration which plaintiff gave defendant for the instrument if he believed plaintiff's testimony. Therefore the plea of want of consideration was unavailing. A plea of want of consideration amounts to a contention that the instrument never became a valid obligation in the first place . . .

Mere inadequacy of consideration will not void a contract . . .

Nor was the plea of failure of consideration availing. Defendant got exactly what she contracted for according to her own testimony. The court should have rendered judgment in favor of plaintiff against defendant for the principal sum of $2,000.00 evidenced by the instrument sued on, with interest as therein provided. We construe the provision relating to interest at the rate of 6% per annum from April 2, 1942. The judgment is reformed so as to award appellant a recovery against appellee of $2,000.00 with interest thereon at the rate of 8% per annum from April 2, 1942. Such judgment will bear interest at the rate of 8% per annum until paid on $2,000.00 thereof and on the balance interest at the rate of 6% per annum.

Reformed and affirmed. ▬

Question 6.1:

a. The court states that "[m]ere inadequacy of consideration will not void a contract" and that is said to be the controlling rule in this famous case. What function did this rule serve in common law?

b. The sum of 500,000 drachmae supposedly had the wartime exchange value of $25 U.S. And yet the borrower agreed to pay the lender $2,000 in exchange for something objectively worth only $25. Can you think of reasons why the borrower might have *knowingly* been willing to make this extraordinary exchange? That is, suppose that she knew that the value of the loan was incredibly one-sided in favor of the lender. Under the circumstances given in the opinion, might she have agreed anyway?

c. Would your answer change if the borrower did not know the 1942 exchange rate between dollars and drachmae? Suppose she *could* have known, if only she had taken the time to ask someone. What then?

    d. What might you do if the testimony had revealed that Batsakis was the *only* person in 1942 Athens who had money to lend? Is that likely to have been the case?

    e. Did the borrower expect to be held to the loan? Should she have expected to be held to the loan's terms? Does she appear to be capable of repaying it? Why should we care about her expectations, or those of the lender, and her capability to repay?

    f. Suppose that the Court of Civil Appeals of Texas had upheld the trial court's finding that the loan was worth only $750? What effect might that holding have had on future contractual exchanges in Texas?

    g. What effect might there be on future contractual exchanges of the court's holding that it will not inquire into the adequacy of consideration?

The following case concerns whether a bargain has taken place or whether there has simply been an unenforceable gift. The situation is very much like that in Example 1 from the beginning of the chapter. Like *Batsakis v. Demotsis*, there are some complicated twists and turns in this case. Let's summarize the facts very briefly to help you appreciate what is at issue here.

At a family celebration and in the presence of family and invited guests, William E. Story, Sr., the uncle of William E. Story, 2d, promised his nephew that if the nephew would refrain from drinking, using tobacco, swearing, and playing cards or billiards for money until he was 21 years old, the uncle would pay him $5,000. The nephew agreed and abided by the terms of his uncle's promise. When the nephew asked for his money, the uncle replied that he fully intended to hand over the $5,000, but that he felt that he should keep the money until the nephew got his feet on the ground. The nephew never received the money; eventually he transferred his right to receive the $5,000 plus interest to another person named Hamer. Presumably Hamer was willing to give him immediate cash, say, $4,000. Before Hamer could collect the $5,000 plus interest from the uncle, the uncle died. So, in the opinion excerpted below, Hamer is suing Sidway, who is the executor of the uncle's estate, to recover $5,000 plus interest.

Hamer v. Sidway, 124 N.Y. 538, 27 N.E. 256 (Court of Appeals of New York, 1891)

[On his 21st birthday the nephew William E. Story, 2d, wrote to his uncle, William E. Story, Sr., to tell him that he had performed his part of the promise and thought he was entitled to the $5,000. The uncle shortly thereafter wrote the following letter to his nephew:]

"Buffalo, Feb. 6, 1875, W.E. Story, Jr.—

    Dear Nephew: Your letter of the 31st ult. came to hand all right, saying that you had lived up to the promise made to me several years ago. I have no doubt but you have, for which you will have five thousand dollars, as I promised you. I had the money in the bank the day you was [sic] twenty-one years old that I intend for you, and you have the money certain. Now Willie, I do not intend to interfere with this money in any way till I think you are capable of taking care of it, and the sooner that time comes the better it will please me. I would hate very much to have you start out in some adventure that you thought all right and lose this money in one year. The first five thousand dollars that I got together cost me a heap of hard work . . . This money you have earned much easier than I did, besides, acquiring good habits at the same time, and you are quite welcome to the money. Hope you will make good use of it. I was ten long years getting this together after I was your age . . . Truly yours, W.E. Story. P. S. You can consider this money on interest.''

The nephew received the letter, and thereafter consented that the money should remain with his uncle in accordance with the terms and conditions of the letter. The uncle died on the 29th day of January, 1887, without having paid over to his nephew any portion of the said $5,000 and interest. [Sometime after February, 1875, the nephew had transferred his entitlement to Hamer, who has presented the claim for the money to Sidway, the executor of the uncle's estate.]

PARKER, J. . . . The defendent contends that the contract was without consideration to support it, and therefore invalid. He asserts that the promisee, by refraining from the use of liquor and tobacco, was not harmed, but benefited; that that which he did was best for him to do, independently of his uncle's promise,— and insists that it follows that, unless the promisor was benefited, the contract was without consideration,—a contention which, if well founded, would seem to leave open for controversy in many cases whether that which the promisee did or omitted to do was in fact of such benefit to him as to leave no consideration to support the enforcement of the promisor's agreement. Such a rule could not be tolerated, and is without foundation in the law. . . . " 'Consideration' means not so much that one party is profiting as that the other abandons some legal right in the present, or limits his legal freedom of action in the future, as an inducement for the promise of the first.''

Now, applying this rule to the facts before us, the promisee used tobacco, occasionally drank liquor, and he had a legal right to do so. That right he abandoned for a period of years upon the strength of the promise of the testator that for such forbearance he would give him $5,000. We need not speculate on the effort which may have been required to give up the use of those stimulants. It is sufficient that he restricted his lawful freedom of action within certain prescribed limits upon the faith of his uncle's agreement, and now, having fully performed the conditions imposed, it is of no moment whether such performance actually proved a benefit to the promisor, and the court will not inquire into it; but, were it a proper subject of inquiry, we see nothing in this record that would permit a determination that the uncle was not benefited in a legal sense. . . .   ▬

Question 6.2:

a. The court held that the nephew should be paid the sum promised, even though the promise appeared to have been made informally at a family gathering where toasts and other gestures of goodwill were part of the celebration. How will courts decide which promises are made in earnest and which promises are frivolously made?

b. In this case the parties to the promise were uncle and nephew. Should courts be more reluctant to enforce promises between family members than between strangers?

c. The court indicates that its decision turns on the fact that the nephew had *relied* on the uncle's promise. Would *any* type of reliance make the promise of a gift into an enforceable promise? Or must the reliance be "reasonable" under the circumstances?

d. The court in this case indicates that the nephew's abstinence from liquor and tobacco was something of value foregone by the nephew in reliance upon the uncle's promise. Did the uncle benefit from his nephew's reliance? Did the court hold that the uncle must benefit from the reliance in order for his promise to be enforceable?

e. Suppose that instead of making demands on the nephew, the uncle simply promised to give the money, without conditions, as soon as the nephew turned 21 years old. This is the promise of a pure gift. Is there consideration? Would such a promise be enforceable under the bargain theory? Should courts enforce such promises?

These cases embody the elements of the bargain theory: offer, acceptance, and consideration. According to this theory, all three elements must be present to have a bargain, and only bargain promises are legally enforceable. We saw in *Batsakis v. Demotsis* that the court would not inquire into the adequacy of consideration; its presence was sufficient for the court to establish an enforceable bargain promise. And we heard the court in *Hamer v. Sidway* argue that the beneficiary of a gift promise must give up something, such as liquor and billiards, in return for the promise of a gift to make it enforceable. In these respects, the two courts followed the bargain theory.

B. What Should Be the Remedy for Breaking Enforceable Promises?

The bargain theory also had an answer to the question, "What should be the remedy for breaking enforceable promises?" The answer is that the victim should be compensated by the breaching party by the payment of a sum of money that is just enough to make him as well off as he would be if the promise had been kept. Computing compensation under this formula involves answering the counter-factual question, "How well off would the victim have been if the promise had been kept?" This question is answered by assessing the gain that the victim of the broken promise could reasonably expect from the promise. Consequently, the damage measure under the classical theory is usually called "expectation damages."

The plaintiffs in our three examples from the beginning of the chapter would not necessarily win in trials decided by applying the bargain theory, but we can still compute expectation damages in each dispute. In Example 1, the student's expectation damage is the value to him of a trip around the world. In Example 2, the expectation damage is the difference in market value between the rusty Chevy and the immaculate Cadillac. In Example 3, the expectation damage suffered by the farmer is the value of the crops destroyed by grasshoppers.

The answer of the classical or bargain theory to the question "What promises should be enforced?" is connected to the answer to the question "What should be the remedy for breaking enforceable promises?" The bargain theory holds that the answer to both questions is in the bargain. Promises should be enforced if they are part of a bargain, and the remedy for breaking enforceable promises is to award the value expected of the bargain. The fact of a bargain establishes enforceability, and the expected value of a bargain measures damages.

II. CRITICISMS OF THE CLASSICAL OR BARGAIN THEORY

The classical theory introduces the essential elements in a typical bargain, which is a good way to begin our investigation of contract law. The practice of the courts, however, has departed far from the guidelines of classical theory, so far that a leading scholar has pronounced the classical theory to be "dead."[4] Let's describe some of these departures and see if we can explain why they have occurred.

The legal enforceability of promises helps individuals to advance their private ends by cooperating together. One problem with the bargain theory is that there are promises whose enforceability helps individuals to achieve their private ends, even though these promises do not involve a bargain. In those circumstances, the parties might both desire legal enforcement of their promises, but if the law were to adhere strictly to the bargain theory, it would not give them that enforcement. Consider a promise to keep an offer open, a promise known as a "firm offer." Suppose, for example, that a car dealer promises to keep an offer open to sell a particular car at a stated price while a potential buyer considers it. The dealer makes the promise in order to induce the potential buyer to consider the offer carefully, thus increasing the probability of acceptance. The promise is more likely to have this effect if it is enforceable than if it is unenforceable. Thus, the dealer wants his promise to be enforceable in order to induce the buyer to consider the offer carefully. Also, the customer wants the promise to be enforceable so that he does not waste his time by considering it carefully and then finding that the dealer has reneged. In this example, however, the dealer gives the customer a promise, and the customer gives nothing in exchange. Because there is no exchange, there is no bargain, and the promise would, therefore, be unenforceable under the bargain theory.

---

[4]Grant Gilmore, THE DEATH OF CONTRACT (1974).

Strictly interpreted, the bargain theory implies that promises to keep an offer open are unenforceable. This result seems perverse in view of the fact that both promisor and promisee typically want the promise to be enforceable at the time it is made. Fortunately, courts usually enforce firm offers. Thus, contemporary courts help people to accomplish what they want, rather than adhering dogmatically to the bargain theory.

> **Question 6.3:** Suppose a computer company exchanges the following letters with a potential client. On May 10 the computer company mails a "firm offer" to sell a particular machine to the client at a specified price. On May 11 the computer company sells the machine to someone else and mails a letter to the original client withdrawing the firm offer. On May 12 the original client receives the firm offer, decides to accept, and mails back his check. On May 13 the client receives the notice of withdrawal, and he sues the computer company, alleging breach of contract. Should the court interpret the "firm offer" as an enforceable promise to keep an offer open? How would the bargain theory answer this question? When the offer was first made, would the parties—the computer company and the client—both want it to be enforceable?

A similar difficulty arises with gift promises. Recall our Example 1 in which a rich uncle promises to send his nephew around the world if he graduates from college with honors. This promise is probably unenforceable under the bargain theory because the nephew did nothing to induce the uncle to make the promise. It is likely, nevertheless, that both parties want the promise to be enforceable at the time it is made. To see why, consider that in order to win this reward, the student must incur the indirect costs of studying more and partying less. But he might also incur some direct costs, such as those of purchasing equipment: snowshoes for the Arctic and a pith helmet for the tropics. The student might buy these items in advance, but he may be reluctant to make the investment if his uncle's promise is unenforceable. The coordination of the student's behavior and the uncle's behavior would be facilitated by the enforceability of the promise, so both of them may want the promise to be enforceable. Despite the bargain theory, modern courts usually enforce gift promises if the promisee reasonably relied on the promise to his detriment; that is, the court will typically ask if a reasonable person would have incurred expenses in relying on the promise's being performed. If so, the court may require compensation for the promisee's reliance losses, even though the promise was unsecured by consideration. (See the box entitled "Humpty-Dumpty Jurisprudence" for a discussion of one way in which the law has attempted to avoid the strictures of the classical theory.)

Gift promises and firm offers are examples of promises that courts enforce even though the bargain theory instructs them not to. But there are also examples of promises that courts do not enforce even though they *should* be enforced under the bargain theory. Suppose that a smooth salesman induces an ignorant person to sign a complicated contract for financing the purchase of a consumer good such that the real price to be paid is 300% above the market value of the item. No fraud is involved, but the salesman's high pressure tactics take advantage of the buyer's weakness and ignorance. Should the court enforce the contract?

Humpty-Dumpty Jurisprudence:
The Life-History of the Word "Consideration"

"When *I* use a word, it means just what I choose it to mean—neither more nor less."—Humpty-Dumpty in Lewis Carroll, THROUGH THE LOOKING GLASS.

In the bargain theory of contracts, "consideration" means the thing the promisee gives the promisor to induce the promise. According to the bargain theory, the *effect* of consideration is to make the promise enforceable. American courts accepted the bargain theory in the early years of this century and adopted the legal principle that consideration makes a promise enforceable. Then, as the years passed, exceptions to the principle accumulated and eventually the courts were no longer prepared to adhere to it. Courts, however, are slow to adopt abstract principles and slow to discard them, so they were not prepared to *say* that they were abandoning the principle. Instead, the courts did something characteristic of them: they changed the meaning of the word "consideration." Instead of meaning "the thing the promisee gives the promisor to induce the promise," the word "consideration" as used by the courts came to mean "the thing that makes a promise enforceable."

A tautology is a proposition that is true by definition of the words, such as "All husbands are married." When the courts changed the meaning of "consideration," they reduced the legal principle of consideration to a tautology. If "consideration" means "the thing that makes a promise enforceable," the principle "consideration makes a promise enforceable" has no bite, no material implications. When a legal principle is reduced to a tautology, it merely draws our attention to the meaning of a word, rather than telling us something about the legal consequences of our actions. Having made the principle of consideration into a tautology, the courts could assert its truth without fear of being wrong. Hence we have an example of Humpty-Dumpty jurisprudence.

This example illustrates that individuals sometimes make contracts that are unreasonable or unfair to one of the parties. Such contracts create a tension between two conflicting goals of the court. On the one hand, the courts wish to help individuals pursue their private purposes. Respect for the ability of individuals to order their own lives requires the courts to enforce private agreements without prying into their contents. On the other hand, there are widely-shared standards of morality that condemn such things as high-pressure sales tactics, even though the tactics do not rise to the level of fraud. Enforcing a contract that violates these shared moral standards implicates the court in an injustice. A court is naturally reluctant to lend its authority to the victimization of someone. So the issue is, "Should the court respect the autonomy of the contracting parties and enforce the exchange, or should the court follow the dictates of conventional morality and refuse to enforce it?"

The unequivocal answer of the bargain theory to this dilemma was to respect individual autonomy and enforce the contract. There is no place in the bargain theory for refusing to enforce the contract on the grounds that the bargain violates conventional ethics. But this approach has proved too harsh for modern courts. Judges have refused to enforce contracts in which the price is outrageous on grounds that enforcement is "unconscionable." Unconscionability cases, which often involve credit buying by poor people, are examples of the tendency of modern courts to create novel doctrines in order to justify scrutinizing the content of contracts. Such innovations show more respect for group standards of fairness and less respect for individual autonomy than would result from strict adherence to the bargain theory.

Of course, the classical theorists knew that the courts would sometimes refuse to enforce bargains. For example, they knew that no one could legally contract to sell himself into slavery, to buy a vote, or to sell a pound of living flesh close to the heart, even if there were offer, acceptance, and consideration. Such cases are accommodated by the classical theory as special exceptions, but the appeal of any legal theory depends upon keeping the list of exceptions short and easily identifiable. This the bargain theory did not do.

III. THE PURPOSES OF CONTRACT LAW

The bargain theory was based upon a method that is often used in legal theory: identify and abstract the minimal elements of the typical event regulated by the law in question, and then raise these elements to the level of a legal principle. In contract law, the typical event is a bargain, and its minimal elements are offer, acceptance, and consideration. Raised to the level of a legal principle, the bargain principle asserts that these elements are necessary and sufficient for the enforceability of a promise. Later, when we consider tort law in a subsequent chapter, we will see this same method at work in the classical theory of torts.

The strength of this method is that it explains the typical case very well, which is why the bargain theory serves as a good introduction to contracts. The weakness with this method is that it does not explain the atypical case. Worse, it leads to a dogmatic dismissal of the atypical case. Thus, we offered two distinct criticisms of the bargain theory. First, there are many promises unsecured by consideration whose enforceability helps individuals to coordinate their pursuit of private goals but that are unenforceable under the bargain theory. Second, there are some promises secured by consideration whose enforceability violates widely-accepted standards of fairness. These two criticisms open up a long list of exceptions, so many that the bargain theory loses much of its appeal.

To handle atypical cases, we need to know more than the elements of the typical case; we need to know the *purposes* of the law. There is a tradition in contract theory, known as the "will-theory," that is helpful for understanding the purposes of contract law. The three elements of a bargain identified by the bargain theory, which are easy to observe, may be understood as the outward sign of a mental event, which cannot be observed. The mental event, which constitutes the agreement of the parties, is the joining of their wills. When the promisor and the promisee both will that the promise should be enforceable, there is a *meeting of minds*. The meeting of minds is the mental event that constitutes the real bargain, at least according to the will-theory.

Minds meeting, wills joining, mental events—the will-theory seems metaphysical at its core, and metaphysics is too ephemeral to be the stuff of the law. There is, however, an important truth in the will-theory. The truth is that *contract law's fundamental purpose is to enable people to achieve their private ends.* In order to achieve our ends, our actions must have effects. Contract law gives legal effect to our actions. *The enforcement of promises helps people to achieve their private ends by enabling them to rely upon each other and thus to coordinate their actions.* An aspect of a free society is the power of its citizens to enter into voluntary agreements to accomplish their private ends. Contract law provides a framework for private citizens to set the terms of voluntary association with each other.

There is an analogy between contracts and legislation. The constitution conveys upon legislators the power to make laws and prescribes the procedures for doing so. By making laws, legislators create legal obligations and effectuate policies: the obligation to pay a new tax, the construction of a new library, and so forth. Similarly, contract law conveys upon private citizens the power to make contracts and prescribes the procedures for doing so. By making contracts, private citizens create legal obligations to effectuate their goals. Contract law is like a constitution for voluntarily forming private relationships, and specific contracts are like the laws enacted under the constitution.

The purpose of contract law is to help people achieve their private purposes through the enforcement of promises. Promises should be enforceable when doing so helps the affected parties to achieve their ends, and not otherwise. We can think of contract law, then, as creating a sphere of private governance. This is a deeper purpose than the enforcement of bargains. According to our conception, a theory of contract law should concern itself with facilitating the pursuit of private purposes through voluntary agreements. Such a theory of contracts must draw upon a descriptive and normative account of the pursuit of private ends. Microeconomics contains such an account. Three fundamental concepts of microeconomics, which we discussed in our review of microeconomic theory in Chapter 2, are maximization (rational choice), equilibrium, and efficiency. The economic conception of rational choice is a descriptive tool for understanding purposive behavior; the concept of an equilibrium is useful for analyzing social interaction; and the concept of efficiency is useful for evaluating how effectively a law achieves its purposes. Armed with these microeconomic concepts, we now turn to the economic theory of contracts.

IV. AN ECONOMIC THEORY OF CONTRACT

Contracts is the area of the law with which economists are most likely to be at home. The heart of contract law is the exchange of promises, and one of the most important topics of the microeconomic theory of rational decision-making is exchange. The two major questions of contract law—What promises should be legally enforceable? How should they be enforced?—can be answered by viewing a promise as an instrument for achieving the ends of rational decisionmakers. To introduce the economic theory of contract, let us begin by asking why private individuals wish to exchange promises and why the *efficiency* of those exchanges can be improved through legally enforceable rules.

Microeconomic theory focuses on choices arising in instantaneous trans-actions. Should the decisionmaker study or go to a movie? Should she pur-chase an apple or a new paperback novel? This concentration on instantaneous exchange is well suited to convey the essentials of the theory of rational decisionmaking. But the exchange of promises is different from instantaneous exchange; indeed, there is not really much reason to promise anything in an instantaneous transaction. This observation leads to the reali-zation that the exchange of promises concerns *deferred exchange* or *exchanges that involve the passage of time for their completion.* An individual engaged in such an exchange must make a promise to another individual about what he will do and not do between the time that the promises are exchanged and the time that the exchange is completed. Promises are for-ward-looking; they are meant to limit the promisor's actions in the future. And rational decisionmakers willingly limit their future actions only when they expect to derive a greater benefit than cost from this limitation.

This unavoidable link between the passage of time and the exchange of promises creates problems that contract law must solve. Let us explore these problems by imagining a particular deferred exchange. Suppose that the Davies family has just signed a contract with the Wabash Construction Company to build a home. The floor plan, the materials to be used, the style and color of carpets and drapes, the landscaping of the front and back yards, the compliance with local zoning and building codes—all of this and more has been specified. Not least of the terms of the contract are the price that will be paid to the Wabash Construction Company by the Davies fam-ily and the date in the future by which the construction company promises to complete the home.

Because the future is involved, uncertainties arise, and whenever there are uncertainties, there are risks. Imagine some of the things that can go wrong in the construction of the Davies' home. A strike by the suppliers of the hardwood to be used in the flooring can delay the whole project. There could be political disruptions in the South American country that exports the copper necessary to fabricate electrical wire, sharply raising the price of wire. The Wabash Construction Company may be sued by a former employee for injuries suffered on the job, with the payment of the resulting judgment causing the firm to declare bankruptcy before the Davies' home is completed. Mr. Davies could lose his job or die, in which case the family would not want the home any more. The local government might change the zoning ordinances so as to make the landscaping plans unacceptable. The point is that these and numerous other contingencies can arise whenever time passes between the exchange of promises and their completion. Thus, one of the most important tasks in a deferred exchange is for the parties to *allocate responsibility for these contingencies.* As we will see, contract law can facilitate this risk allocation by establishing background rules. (The economic theory relating to risk and uncertainty was summarized in the appendix to Chapter 2, which you might like to review at this point.)

A deferred exchange often involves the exchange of information. For example, in our hypothetical transaction for the construction of a home, the Davies must convey to the Wabash Construction Company information about their ability to pay for the work that is to be done. The construction company must convey information to the Davies about its competence to perform this complex project, including any information about its past performance of similar projects and about its financial position. The rules of contract law can facilitate the exchange of this information by, for example, not allowing enforcement of a contract in favor of a party who has knowingly given false information. (Economic theories of information have already been discussed in several places in this book: the discussion of information asymmetries in Chapter 2; the discussion of several economic theories of information in Chapter 4; and the discussion of bargaining theory in Chapter 5.)

Let us summarize these introductory remarks. From an economic standpoint, the exchange of promises is most likely to arise in conjunction with a deferred exchange, one in which time must pass between the exchange of promises and their completion. Rational decisionmakers willingly promise to limit their future actions when the expected benefit of so doing exceeds the expected costs. Two of the most important economic problems that arise because of the passage of time between the formation of the contract and its performance are those of allocating the risk of contingencies and those of exchanging information. An economic theory of contract should propose rules for handling risk and information that will help the parties to accomplish their private ends.

A. Perfect Competition and Perfect Contracts

We begin by re-stating our assumption that the purpose of contract law is to help individuals achieve their private ends by enforcing their promises. Imagine a situation in which this purpose is fulfilled to perfection: every contingency is anticipated and the associated risk is allocated between the parties; all relevant information has been communicated. In such a situation, enforceability makes a contract into a perfect instrument for achieving the ends of both parties to it. Accordingly, we define a *perfect contract* to be *a promise that, if enforceable, is ideally suited to achieving the ends of the promisor and promisee.*

Naturally, the question arises, "Under what circumstances will this 'perfect contract' be achieved?" It turns out that the circumstances are already familiar to the economist as the ideal conditions of trade: the model of perfect competition. The model of perfect contracts is an adaptation of the model of perfect competition to take explicit account of the central concerns of contract law.

One of the most fundamental conclusions of modern welfare economics is that a perfectly competitive market leads to productive and allocative efficiency.[5] It follows that contracts formed in a perfectly competitive market will be productively and allocatively efficient.

This conclusion is fundamental to contract law because it implies that contracts formed under perfectly competitive conditions should be strictly enforceable. By "strictly enforceable," we mean that the terms in the contract should be enforced according to their accepted meaning, and no terms should be attributed to the contract that are not actually in it.

To see why this is so, let us develop an analogy between a perfect contract and a commodity, say, an automobile, produced in what we will assume to be a perfectly competitive market. First, we will explain the consequences of perfect competition for how producers and consumers match their decisions about which attributes cars will have. Then, we will show that government regulation of this perfectly competitive market will make auto consumers worse off. Finally, we will show how this analysis applies to a perfect contract: anything less than strict enforcement of a perfect contract will make the contracting parties worse off.

An automobile is a complex collection of many parts and attributes, including both standard parts (such as engine, transmission, brakes, and gears) and optional features (such as color, air-conditioning, and body configuration, e.g., 2-door, 4-door, station wagon, and truck). We know from microeconomic theory that a perfectly competitive market will produce an efficient quantity of cars and the efficient number and kinds of attributes of those cars.

Suppose that the government intervenes in the perfectly competitive automobile market and requires different parts in automobiles than the ones selected by the competitive market. For example, suppose that the competitive market has provided cars with both four-speed, five-speed, and automatic transmissions but that governmental regulation requires every automobile to have a five-speed transmission.

What are the effects of this intervention? First and foremost, we know that because the mix of automobile attributes under perfect competition was productively and allocatively efficient, the result under the government regu-

---

[5]See the discussion of these points in Chapter 2.

lation will be inefficient. Those buyers who had compared the value to them of the various transmissions available under perfect competition and had determined that they preferred a four-speed or automatic transmission cannot now select their most preferred automobile. As a result, some buyers are worse off under the governmental restriction than they were under perfect competition. It is important to recognize that this government regulation creates no offsetting benefit for sellers, at least not in the long run. Under perfect competition there are   no long-run profits because products are priced at marginal cost.[6] Thus, sellers cannot be hurt or benefited in the long run by a change like the restriction on the variety of transmissions.

Similarly, under perfect competition the parties to a contract assess the value of each term in it. Each promisee determines that the terms in the contract are exactly worth the price that he must pay the promisor for them. If every term is enforceable, then perfect competition enables the parties to make the contracts that they value the most.

By contrast, if the courts enforce contract terms selectively rather than enforcing all of them strictly, then the court rewrites the contract for the parties. It is as if the court were regulating contracts to require only certain terms in them. This is analogous to governmental regulation requiring all cars to have a 5-speed manual transmission. And the effects of these two kinds of regulation—one of acceptable contract terms, the other of acceptable transmission types—are the same: under perfect competition, selective enforcement of contracts will create inefficiencies, just as regulation creates inefficiencies for commodities. First, the parties whose contract terms are selectively enforced are, by definition, worse off because they had written the perfect contract. Secondly, future contracting parties, viewing the court's selective enforcement of the present contract, will try to take steps to avoid the disappointment of having their contract selectively enforced. But these steps will cause the parties to incur additional contracting costs, additional over what they would be if the court strictly enforced perfect contracts.

Let's consider an example. Suppose that a chef negotiates with a builder to construct a restaurant. The conditions of their contract are perfect: there are no relevant contingencies unthought of; all relevant information is exchanged. Initially, their contract requires the chef to pay $100,000 to the builder, who promises to complete construction by September 1st and, if he does not, to pay $100 per day for being late. But suppose that the chef, after further reflection, decides he would be willing to pay up to an additional $5,000 to increase the builder's liability to $200 per day for missing the target date of completion. The builder would accept this increase in his liability in exchange for increasing the purchase price by $3,000. Consequently, the initial contract can be modified so that both parties are better off. The revised contract imposes liability on the builder at $200 per day for being

---

[6]Recall from Chapter 2 that "zero profits" in economics means the same thing as "normal profits" in accountancy.

late; the contract price is revised to $104,000. The chef pays $4,000 more for a change in liability that he values at $5,000, and the builder receives $4,000 more for a change in liability that costs him $3,000. Thus, the revision in the contract increases its value to the parties by $2,000, with each party enjoying $1,000 of the gain.

In our example, the revised (perfect) contract is preferable to the original contract for both parties. However, as we will see in greater detail in the following chapter, courts scrutinize damage provisions in contracts with a skeptical eye. Suppose the court decided not to enforce the revised damage term, which sets liability at $200 per day, and instead reduced liability back to the original $100 per day. Refusing to enforce the damage term will reduce the value of the contract, just like forcing the buyer to accept a five-speed transmission in a car reduces the value of the exchange. Moreover, as we will see when we discuss remedies in the next chapter, the court's refusal will also impose extra (inefficiently high) costs on future contracting parties.

In general, enforceable promises create rights for the promisee and liabilities for the promisor. Whenever the promisee values the right more than the increase in liability costs the promisor, there is room for a mutually beneficial bargain. By adjusting the nonprice terms in the contract, the promisee can acquire the right; by increasing the price term in the contract, the promisor can be compensated an amount that exceeds the cost of his additional liability. Thus, the revision increases the value of the contract and the gain is split between the parties. Selective enforcement of competitive contracts by courts reduces their value by blocking such revisions.

The argument can be restated in terms of efficiency. If it is possible to revise a contract so that at least one party is better off and the other parties are not worse off, then the contract is inefficient. On the other hand, if such a revision is impossible, then the contract is efficient (to be precise, it is *Pareto* efficient). Perfectly competitive markets yield efficient contracts, provided that all the terms are enforced, whereas the selective enforcement of terms by the courts causes the contracts to be inefficient.

B. Contract Failure

Let's summarize the three points we have made thus far:

1. Perfect contracts should be strictly enforced according to their terms;
2. Perfectly competitive markets result in perfect contracts; and
3. Perfect contracts are efficient.

Few markets achieve the ideal of perfect competition, but many markets come close enough to be treated as if they were perfectly competitive. Similarly, promises seldom achieve the ideal of a perfect contract, but most contracts come close enough to be treated as if they were perfect. Specifically, most contracts are enforced according to their terms because doing so enables the parties to achieve their ends.

One piece of evidence that most contracts serve their purpose and are, therefore, close to being perfect contracts, is that few of them are disputed. However, some contracts *are* disputed; the implication that we may derive from our previous discussion is that those contracts are probably "imperfect." Because imperfect contracts are the most likely to be litigated, they are central to contract law. Recall our Example 2 at the beginning of the chapter. There the buyer's goal was to acquire the shiny Cadillac, but she actually got the rusty Chevrolet. So, this contract was not a good instrument for achieving her ends. In order to succeed in explaining the law, a theory of contracts must explain imperfect contracts as well as perfect contracts.

Once again the model of perfect competition provides a guide. The model of perfect competition is constructed from a set of assumptions about the structure of the market and the conduct of its participants. If these assumptions are satisfied, then the market is efficient. But if the market does not satisfy these assumptions, then it is usually inefficient. For example, the competitive model assumes that there are many sellers, but if there is only one seller, then a condition of monopoly may prevail, and the price will probably exceed the efficient level.

The term "market failure" describes a situation in which a market departs so far from one of the competitive assumptions that its performance is impaired. By determining which of the competitive assumptions is violated, the cause of the market failure can be identified. And once the cause is known, the next step for a policymaker is to determine whether government intervention is likely to correct the imperfection or to make it worse. For example, markets in which there is only one seller are either regulated by antitrust laws or, like public utilities, regulated by an administrative agency. Thus, the model of perfect competition provides the organizing principles for the economic theory of government regulation.

We may apply this line of reasoning directly to the theory of contracts. The model of perfect contracts specifies the assumptions under which a promise is strictly enforceable. The more closely a contractual setting satisfies these assumptions, the stronger the case for strict enforcement; the farther the contractual setting departs from these assumptions, the stronger the case for selective enforcement. Once the cause of the imperfection is identified, corrective measures can be specified. The court should correct an imperfect contract by restructuring its terms as the parties would have wanted it *if the contract were perfect.* Thus, the model of perfect contracts provides the organizing principles for the theory of contract enforcement.

C. The Assumptions Underlying Perfect Contracts

In order to develop a theory of imperfect contracts, we need to do two things. First, we need to have a guide for recognizing imperfect contracts. This will involve a review of the assumptions under which perfect contracts will be formed. We will see that when those assumptions are not fulfilled, parties are likely to form imperfect contracts. Second, we will want to know how courts should restructure imperfect contracts. This will require us to specify different remedies for different imperfections. What might be an appropriate restructuring under one form of imperfection might be entirely inappropriate under another.

1. Individual Rationality[7]

Three assumptions of rational individual decisionmaking can be isolated in the model of perfect competition. First, the rational decisionmaker can rank outcomes in order of preference. This ranking of outcomes by consumers is represented by each individual's utility function. In order to rank outcomes, it is necessary to have stable preferences.[8] Preferences that are too unstable to be represented by a utility function are irrational. As we will see, irrational preferences can vitiate a contract.

Second, the decisionmaker's opportunities are constrained so that he can achieve some, but not all, of his objectives. In the competitive model, the consumer's constraint is imposed by his income or budget. When contracts are made, the setting can impose a variety of constraints upon the promisor. In contract law, certain kinds of constraints can vitiate a contract. For example, certain constraints imposed by the other party to the exchange ("Your money or your life!") or by circumstances beyond either party's control (as in the necessity to have a heart transplant in order to live) may so substantially alter the conditions necessary for truly voluntary exchange that no court will enforce promises exchanged under those constraints.

Third, the decisionmaker who has ranked outcomes in order of preference and is constrained in his choice will naturally choose the best feasible outcome.[9]

In summary, three assumptions describe the economist's ideal of individual rationality:

1. Decisionmakers have stable preferences;
2. they are constrained in pursuing them, and
3. they advance their private purposes as far as the constraints permit.

When these conditions are satisfied, each party to a contract can be described as maximizing utility under conditions of certainty subject to the given constraints.

---

[7]Before reading this and the next section, you might want to review the material on the theory of consumer choice and the theory of supply in Chapter 2.

[8]In technical terms, the preferences must be transitive at any point in time, and they must not alter very quickly with the passage of time.

[9]The maximizing assumption is the crucial step for bringing contract law into contact with mathematical theories of optimization. See our review of this topic in Chapter 2.

2. Perfect Contractual Environment   In addition to the assumptions about individual rationality, the competitive model includes four important assumptions about the environment in which contracts are made. The first assumption is that such a contract does not harm anyone who is not a party to it. In other words, *there are no adverse third-party effects*. Third-party effects are incidental byproducts of the contract. We have already encountered this concept under a different name: externalities. In Chapter 4 we illustrated externalities by the example of pollution. If an electric utility generates power by a clean process such as by burning natural gas, then production will not directly affect third parties; but if the utility generates power by a dirty process such as by burning soft coal, then production of power may affect others adversely. So, a contract to supply electricity may have third-party effects, depending upon whether the current is generated by a clean process or a dirty process.

In order to bring suit in contract law, the plaintiff must ordinarily be the party to whom the promise was made (the promisee) or the party to whom the promisee's rights were transferred (the transferee).[10] Third parties are, by definition, not the promisee or the transferee. Thus, third parties can seldom sue for damages arising from breach of a contract. That does not mean that third parties are unprotected; they are protected by tort law, property law, and various statutes. It is as if contract law proceeds on the assumption that other branches of law will protect third parties.

The second important assumption about the environment of perfect competition is that each decisionmaker has *full information about the nature and consequences of his choice*. If information is incomplete rather than full, a decision that appears to be rational may prove to be irrational if the decisionmaker could only have viewed the decision with full information. In the perfectly competitive model, full information means that the buyers and sellers know the prices of all goods and their quality. Where contracts are concerned, full information means that one party does not unfairly surprise the other concerning the terms of the contract and its consequences. As we will see, contracts can be set aside when one of the parties lacks information of a significant type.

The third assumption about the environment of perfect competition is that there are enough buyers and sellers, both actual and potential, so that each person has alternative trading partners. This is the familiar requirement that no one has monopoly power over prices or quantities. The presence of

---

[10]Thus, an heir can sue for breach of promise made to the deceased. Similarly, when one firm takes over another, the acquiring firm can sue for breach of promise to the acquired firm by other parties.

monopoly power undermines the condition that the promise be voluntary in order for it to be enforceable.[11]

The final assumption concerning the competitive environment is that the process of carrying out a transaction has no cost. For example, when a car is purchased, the car itself is costly but, in the competitive model, the negotiating and bargaining over the car are assumed to be costless. Similarly, the process of forming a perfect contract is assumed to be costless. This process can be partitioned into several activities, such as locating contractual partners, negotiating contracts, drafting contracts, and resolving disputes about contracts. In reality these costs are not zero. Negotiating a contract takes time; drafting a contract requires legal expertise; and so on. But these costs are usually small relative to the value of the underlying transaction and assuming that these costs are zero is a useful beginning point for analysis.

V. THE RELATIONSHIP BETWEEN THE ASSUMPTIONS OF PERFECT MARKETS AND THE STRUCTURE OF CONTRACT LAW

The model of perfect contracts embraces three assumptions about individual rationality—ordered preferences, constrained choice, and maximization—and four assumptions about the contractual environment—no adverse third-party effects, full information, many available contractual partners, and zero transaction costs. Under these conditions, the promisor and promisee conclude a perfect contract; both prefer for all the terms in that contract to be strictly enforceable when the contract is made, as opposed to being selectively enforceable.

When these conditions regarding individual rationality and the market environment are not met, contracts are imperfect. The cause of the imperfection can be diagnosed by determining which one of the assumptions of perfect contracts is violated. Additionally, the contract imperfection weakens, but does not eliminate, the case for strict enforcement and strengthens the case for selective enforcement of the contract terms. In the next chapter we will discuss examples of contract imperfections that are so severe that selective enforcement might be an improvement over strict enforcement.

There are various legal doctrines that justify selective enforcement. In the remainder of this chapter, we will sort some of them out according to the type of failure in the competitive assumptions that they seek to correct. This chapter will not go beyond classifying doctrines of contract law, thus provid-

---

[11]The law has a pejorative term for monopoly contracts in which the unequal bargaining power of the parties undermines the voluntariness of the promise to such an extent that it is unenforceable. The term is *contracts of adhesion*. We will discuss these at length in the following chapter.

ing only an overview. A detailed analysis of some of these doctrines is carried out in the next chapter.

The first assumption is that the parties to the contract have stable, well-ordered preferences. If the promisor's preferences are unstable or not well-ordered, then he is unable to conclude a perfect contract. The law says that such people's promises are unenforceable because they are legally incompetent. For example, children and the insane do not have stable, well-ordered preferences, and, as a result, their promises are unenforceable. There are also special circumstances in which a person, who is ordinarily competent, may be temporarily incompetent, and during that incompetency she cannot conclude enforceable promises. For example, the ingestion of a prescription drug may make someone drowsy to the point of incompetency so that any promises given while in that state would be unenforceable. Consider a slightly more controversial example: if high pressure tactics are used to confuse a consumer and induce him to sign a contract, a court may be unwilling to enforce it. The consumer's failing is described by some lawyers as a *transactional incapacity*, that is, the incapacity to conduct this transaction rationally under these circumstances. Finally, reconsider Example 1 as a possible instance of temporary incompetence. Suppose the nephew raises his glass at the family reunion and proposes the following toast: "To my uncle, whose life is the inspiration of my college days." The uncle is deeply touched and responds by raising his glass and publicly promising his nephew a trip around the world. After the flush of enthusiasm and wine subsides, the uncle may regret his promise. The court may take these circumstances into account when deciding the extent to which the promise should be enforced.[12]

The second assumption of individual rationality is that the decisionmaker is constrained in such a way that he can obtain part, but not all, of what he would like. In contract law, a promise may not be binding if the constraints upon choice imposed either by the other party to the contract or by circumstances were too severe. There are three major doctrines that excuse promise-breaking on grounds that the promisor had no choice: coercion (or duress), impossibility, and necessity. If the beneficiary of the promise extracted it by threats, then promise-breaking is excused by reason of coercion or duress. Duress excuses the promise breaker because his freedom to choose was destroyed by the promisee. For example, in a famous movie the "godfather" of a criminal syndicate makes contract offers that "cannot be refused" because the victim signs the contract with a gun held to his head. Obviously, the courts would not enforce such contracts.

If a promise is made in good faith but fate intervenes to make performance impossible, then promise-breaking may be excused by reason of

---

[12]As we have already seen, a promise to give a gift is usually enforceable only to the extent that the promisee reasonably relied to his own detriment. If the nephew relied upon the promise to the extent of buying snowshoes and a pith helmet, the uncle may have to reimburse him, but the uncle will not have to pay for a trip around the world. Temporary incompetence is one reason cited for not enforcing donative promises to their full extent.

impossibility. For example, a manufacturer may be excused from fulfilling his contracts because his factory burned down. The doctrine of impossibility excuses promise-breaking when freedom to choose is destroyed due to no fault of either party.

If a promise is extracted when the promisor is in dire straits, then the court may excuse the promise-breaking on the grounds of necessity. For example, suppose a doctor runs out of gas on a seldom-used desert road. A passerby offers to sell him five gallons of gas for $50,000. Even if the doctor accepts the offer, the court will generally not enforce his promise to pay. The doctor will be excused from the promise on the grounds of necessity, regardless of whether he got into dire straits because of his own recklessness.[13]

The third assumption of individual rationality is that the parties to the contract are maximizing. As we noted in our discussion, this assumption does not add much to the first two, except to bring the decision into contact with mathematics. In the next chapter, where we use a mathematical analysis, this assumption will be used extensively.

Let us turn now to the connection between the four assumptions about the perfect contractual *environment* and the doctrines of contract law. The first of these assumptions is that there are no adverse third-party effects. In order to have standing to sue, the plaintiff must have been injured by the defendant. In contract law, it is usually impossible to show that a breach caused an injury to anyone other than the promisee or his heir, so that third-party effects do not figure prominently in contract law.[14]

The second assumption is full information. There are several doctrines in contract law that excuse promise-breaking on grounds that the promise resulted from misinformation: fraud, failure to disclose, frustration of purpose, and mutual mistake. If the beneficiary of the promise extracted it by lies, then breaking the promise is excused by reason of fraud. The doctrine

---

[13]Note that duress can be regarded as necessity caused by the promisee.

[14]Typically, third-party effects are alleged when a commercial contract threatens to harm one of the contractual partner's business rivals and is often discussed under the doctrine of "inducement to breach." Third-party effects of this sort also form part of what is known as an "economic tort."

A recent example comes from the world of professional sports. The professional baseball franchise in San Francisco, the Giants, was, until recently, not doing well, in no small part because Candlestick Park, where the Giants play their home games, is frequently subject to inclement weather. The City of San Francisco owns Candlestick and has leased it to the Giants under a long-term contract. The Giants are so unhappy with their present circumstances that they have considered moving elsewhere to play. Several cities that do not now have a professional baseball team, e.g., Denver, have expressed a strong interest in having the team. For the Giants to move, three-quarters of the current owners of National League baseball franchises must approve the change. An immediate move, however, would involve the Giants' breaching their lease with the City of San Francisco for Candlestick. The City Attorney of San Francisco has written to all the other owners of National League baseball clubs to tell them that if they vote to approve the Giants' move from San Francisco, the City will consider their vote to be an inducement to breach the Candlestick lease and will take appropriate action.

of fraud provides an excuse for breaking a promise that was premised upon misinformation supplied by the promisee. For example, the seller of the "sure method to kill grasshoppers" defrauded the farmer because the method provided was utterly impractical. The farmer in this case has a legal right to withhold or recover payment of $25 for the wooden blocks.

Fraud is a violation of the negative duty not to misinform the other party to a contract. Besides the negative duty, there are circumstances in which the parties have the *affirmative* duty to disclose information. In sales contracts, a seller has a duty to warn the buyer about hidden dangers associated with the use of the product, even though this information may cause the buyer to withdraw from the deal. For example, the manufacturer of a drug must warn the user about side effects. Similarly, by offering a good for sale, the seller is taken by the courts to imply that the good is fit for its intended use, something known as an "implied warranty of fitness." Thus, the manufacturer of a drug must be able to prove that it is effective in treating the ailment for which it is prescribed. On the other hand, there is apparently no duty to disclose disguised defects that lower the value of a good without making it dangerous or unfit for use.[15] For example, a used car dealer does not have to disclose the faults in a car offered for sale.

On the other hand, if someone makes a contract premised upon misinformation that he gathered for himself, then there is no legal principle releasing him from his contractual duties. Thus, a stock broker who promises to supply 100 shares of Exxon in six months at a predetermined price cannot escape his obligation just because the price of the stock rose when he expected it to fall.

We have discussed misinformation that one party supplies to another, and misinformation that a party supplies to himself. Another possibility is that both parties premise the contract upon the *same* misinformation. This is the basis of the promise-breaking excuse known as "frustration of purpose." Let's illustrate this by a famous example. In the early years of the 20th century, buildings situated along London streets were rented in advance for the day on which the new King's coronation parade was scheduled to pass by, but the heir to the throne became ill and the coronation was postponed. Some owners tried to collect the rent even though there was no parade on the day specified in the rental agreements. The courts refused to enforce the contracts on the grounds that the change in circumstances frustrated the purpose of the contracts.

Yet another possibility is that both parties premise the contract upon *different* misinformation. If promises are exchanged on the basis of contradictory, but reasonable, conceptions of what is promised, then the contract is said to rest upon a mutual mistake, which justifies setting it aside. In our Example 2, the court may nullify the contract because the seller genuinely

---

[15]We say "apparently" because the law is not perfectly clear on this point.

believed that he was negotiating to sell his rusty Chevrolet and the buyer genuinely believed that she was negotiating to purchase the immaculate Cadillac.

The third competitive assumption about the contractual environment is that there are many actual or potential trading partners. When this assumption is violated, there is monopoly power. There is no common law prohibition against monopoly,[16] but there are statutes—the antitrust laws—that prohibit many monopoly practices. The legal problems with contracts signed under conditions of monopoly thus belongs more to statutory law than to the common law of contracts.

Zero transaction costs is the fourth assumption about the competitive environment. Forming a contract often involves bargaining over the terms and drafting a formal document. Bargaining and drafting are costly, and these costs may prevent the parties from dealing with all the contingencies that a perfect contract would address. To illustrate, suppose that a retailer promises to deliver a new boat to a customer, but an unforeseen strike causes a long delay in the delivery of the boat. Let us assume that the contract between the retailer and the consumer did not allocate this risk explicitly. The question is, "Why not?"

Two answers are possible. One is that strike-delay delivery is such a rare event that the costs required to take this contingency explicitly into account cannot be justified. If so, then bargaining costs are so high that a perfect contract could not have been written by the retailer and the customer. If the parties are unable to resolve this imperfection, then a court must decide what terms the parties would have included if they had been able to agree upon a perfect contract. An alternative possibility is that a strike-delayed delivery is either not so rare or is foreseeable at such a low cost that the parties *should* have allocated the risk of that contingency. The bargaining costs are so low that a perfect contract could have been concluded but was not. In this circumstance it is highly likely that, because bargaining costs are so low, the retailer and the customer will revise the contract. But if for some reason they cannot, the court should again determine what the terms of the perfect contract between the retailer and the customer would have contained and enforce this hypothetical perfect contract. We will deal with concrete examples of this sort of situation in the next chapter.

The economic theory of contract thus evaluates the doctrines of contract law according to how well they fill in the gaps in contracts created by imperfections in individual rationality and market environment. Our classification of legal doctrines according to the market imperfection that they seek to remedy is summarized in Table 6.1.

---

[16]There are common law doctrines about freedom of choice that are relevant to some monopoly situations. We have already discussed this point in connection with constrained choice and the doctrine of necessity. For example, the doctor who ran out of gas in the desert purchased it from a monopoly supplier under conditions of necessity, so the contract was not binding.

Table 6.1   The Relationship between Contract Doctrines and Imperfections in Individual Rationality and Market Environment

Imperfection	Contract Doctrine
A. Individual Rationality	
1. Stable, well-ordered preferences	1. Incompetency
2. Constrained choice	2. Coercion; duress; necessity; impossibility
3. Maximizing behavior	3. Incompetency; transactional incapacity
B. Market Environment	
1. No adverse third-party effects	1. (Inducement to breach: a tort)
2. Full information	2. Fraud; failure to disclose; frustration of purpose; mutual mistake
3. Many trading partners	3. Necessity; antitrust laws
4. Zero transaction costs	4. All of the above

These doctrines address the first question of contract law, "What promises should be enforced?" Now we turn briefly to the second question of contract law, "What should be the remedy for broken promises?"

VI. THE ECONOMICS OF REMEDIES FOR BREACH OF CONTRACT

When a contract is perfect, the remedy will be explicitly stated as part of the contract. For example, we discussed above a contract in which a builder promised to construct a new restaurant for a chef and the contract explicitly stated that the builder must pay $200 per day for late completion. If damages are explicitly stated in a contract, then the court must decide whether to enforce these terms. When courts choose to enforce the damage clauses, they call them "liquidated damages clauses." In business jargon, "liquidate" means to convert into cash; so, liquidated damages state the cash amount to be paid as compensation for breach.

Typically, courts scrutinize the damage terms of contracts with a more critical eye than the other terms. Traditionally, setting damages for breach was considered the prerogative of the court, so the parties had to have special reasons for doing it themselves. For example, the parties were allowed to set damages if the harm caused by breach was uncertain, speculative, or difficult to prove in court.[17] In the absence of such special circumstances, the courts were reluctant to enforce damage clauses.

Damages are "compensatory" when they equal the actual harm suffered by the victim of breach. Damages that exceed the actual harm are called "penal" or "punitive." Common law courts are reluctant to enforce

---

[17]*See* Justin Sweet, *Completion, Acceptance and Waiver of Claims: Back to Basics,* 17 FORUM 1312 (1982).

terms in a contract calling for damages in excess of the actual harm because courts do not want to help one person punish another. When the courts choose not to enforce damage clauses, the reason they most frequently give is that the clauses are punitive, not compensatory. Instead of enforcing penalties, they lower damages to the level that they consider to be compensatory.

The question of whether a damage term is an enforceable liquidation clause or an unenforceable penalty does not arise when most contracts are litigated because most contracts do not contain explicit damage terms. When the contract is silent on damages for breach, the court must provide a remedy. A possible, but currently rare, remedy is for the court to issue an order requiring the promisor to perform as promised. This remedy is called "specific performance." As we will see, there is an economic case for making this remedy more widely available than it currently is.

The usual remedy for breach of contract is an award of money damages. How should they be set? If the contract were perfect, then the court should enforce its damage terms. When the contract is imperfect, the court should try to perfect it. Perfecting the contract involves setting the terms that rational parties would have agreed upon. In reality, the court usually computes damages at the level that compensates victims of breach for the harm they suffered. There is a broad variety of circumstances under which compensatory damages correspond to the damages that rational parties would have specified in a perfect contract. Thus, the economic approach provides a vindication of the court practice. The optimal level of damages, and its relationship to several measures of compensatory damages actually used by courts, is discussed in the next chapter.

Question 6.4: In Example 1, the rich uncle promised the student a trip around the world in exchange for the student's graduating with honors. The student bought supplies for the trip—a pith helmet and snow shoes. The student *expected* a trip around the world, and he *relied* to the extent of buying supplies. Consider three responses by the law for the uncle's breach of contract:

 a. no remedy: the student writes these events off to experience;
 b. reliance damages: the uncle must compensate the student for the expenditures he made in reliance upon the promise;
 c. expectation damages: the uncle must pay the student a sum of money equal to the cost of a trip around the world.

Which remedy do you think is best? Notice that reliance damages protect the student's reliance upon the promise, and expectation damages protect the expectation created by it. Reliance damages are the usual remedy for breach of a donative promise, and expectation damages are the usual remedy for breach of a bargain promise. Does it make sense for the law to have different remedies for breach of donative and bargain promises?

VII. A REFINEMENT: ARE THE ECONOMICS OF LONG-RUN CONTRACTS DIFFERENT?

We have been discussing how to organize the rules and doctrines of contract law. The reader should realize that the institution of contract involves more than its formal rules and doctrines. People fill out contracts every day without even knowing what the rules are. To illustrate, you probably have a checking account at a bank. When you opened your checking account, you filled out a deposit agreement. How much do you know about its terms? For example, are you obligated by this agreement to check your monthly statements for errors? If the bank debits your account without authorization, what are your remedies? Probably you have never even thought about these questions. Indeed, it may be rational for you not to have thought about these questions because a tiny fraction of bank customers ever have serious disputes with their banks over checking accounts.

Since many parties to contracts are ignorant about their contents and since few contracts are ever litigated, there must be important aspects of the institution of contracts that are informal, rather than being controlled by rules of law. There is a significant school of thought in law and economics that has devoted itself to the study of such informal institutions.[18] One important conclusion of this school of thought is that the informal understandings become more important than formal agreements when a contractual relationship is expected to endure over a long period of time. To illustrate long-run contracts, consider that coal companies often sign contracts stretching over many years to supply coal to industries that use it as a raw material. As another illustration, franchise contracts in retail businesses such as fast food restaurants or gasoline stations often establish long-term relationships between the franchisee (the person who puts up money to buy a local franchise) and the franchisor (the central corporation).

Any long-term human relationship, whether in business or in personal life, is unlikely to be tightly controlled by rules. Rules just do not allow sufficient flexibility for the parties to respond to changing conditions as they pursue their own interests through the relationship. Instead of looking to rules, the parties are likely to rely upon informal devices to control their relationship. Thus, if one party comes to regard the other as pressing his advantage too far or even cheating in the relationship, the recalcitrant party may be brought back into line by a warning or by a response in-kind rather than an appeal to legal rights in a court of law.

---

[18]Among lawyers, a leading representative of this line of thought is Ian Macneil, and among economists, leading representatives are Oliver Williamson, Ben Klein, and Victor Goldberg.

The End-Game Problem

One problem with long-term relationships is that the parties have an incentive to cheat when the relationship is coming to an end. This fact can be explained by an experimental game with the following rules. The full game will be played for one hour in discrete, repeated games lasting one minute each. During each one-minute game, you and another player have the opportunity to earn a dollar by dividing it between you. During each minute, you can discuss how to divide the money. At the end of the minute, each of you writes down the amount of the money that you want. If the two amounts sum to a dollar or less, each of you gets the amount that you wrote down. But if the two amounts sum to more than a dollar, the person who wrote the larger amount gets it, up to a maximum of $1.00, and the other person gets anything that is left. Thus the rules of the game allow a temporary advantage by "cheating." To illustrate, if you write $0.45 and the other person writes $0.45 on round 10, then each of you gets that amount; but if you write $0.45 and the other person writes $1.00 in round 10, the other person gets $1 in that round and you get nothing.

What is the best way to play this game? Should you cheat repeatedly, or should you cooperate? If you cheat, perhaps you can get the whole dollar a few times. If you cooperate, you will have to settle for less on each round, but perhaps your total will be larger than if you cheat on each turn.

In theory and practice, the best way to play this game is for each player to write down $0.50 on each of the early rounds and thus to divide the money equally. If either player cheats in one round, say, by writing $1.00, then the other player settles the score in the next round. This strategy is called "tit-for-tat." [The strategy and its implications for social policy are described in Robert Axelrod, THE EVOLUTION OF COOPERATION (1984).] But notice that a problem develops near the end of the game as the hour allotted for the full game draws to a close. On the last round, if

This policy of a response in-kind, called "tit-for-tat," can be modelled in game theory, which we reviewed briefly in Chapter 2, and a proof can be given that bargaining problems, which would be impossible to solve in a short-run relationship, can be solved in long-run relationships. (For an example of a game theoretic treatment of a long-run relationship, see the box entitled "The End-Game Problem.") In this respect, a long-run business contract is more like a partnership or a marriage than a one-shot exchange. In order to preserve the relationship, the parties restrain themselves and avoid sharp dealing. Sharp dealing is far more likely when the contractual partners never expect to see each other again than when they have an interest in continuing to trade.

One fruitful approach to long-term contracts is to study the informal mechanisms by which the parties try to protect themselves against the

the other player writes $.50 and you write $1.00, you get it all and the other player has no opportunity to retaliate. But the same logic applies to him as well as to you. So both of you are tempted to cheat on the last round. And if each of you thinks the other will cheat on the last round, both of you are tempted to cheat on the next-to-last round. And this reasoning also applies to the round preceding the next-to-last round. And so on clear through to the first round. Thus, there is a possibility that the whole game will unravel and cooperation will prove impossible, although in practice the real problem does not arise until near the end of the game. (In technical terms, this is an "end-game problem in a repeated prisoner's dilemma.")

Short-run contracts are like the last round of this game. Because the game is not repeated, the returns to cooperation are not large, and, therefore, cheating may be common. But for long-run contracts, cooperation may well dominate cheating as the better strategy. Whether this is the case is an empirical issue. Fortunately there is some evidence on this matter. There have been many experiments, many of them reported in Professor Axelrod's book, that suggest that cooperation—through informal relationships, like "tit-for-tat"—is the dominant strategy for long-run relationships.

This has important implications for the study of contract law. In long-run contracts where cooperation can usually be maintained, informal rules may be more common than strict adherence to the doctrines of contract law. But for short-term contracts, or near the end of long-term contracts, the formal rules of contract law may be more important in guiding relationships because cheating dominates cooperation and informal mechanisms do not have time to take hold.

other's breach. In an effort to find evidence of these informal mechanisms, David Teece studied contracts in the automobile industry. He found that large manufacturers like Ford often buy components from smaller companies through long-term contracts. Ford, however, typically owns the specialized equipment needed in the manufacturing process and rents these machines to the contractor. Teece found that this method of structuring the relationship is a good strategy for Ford to protect itself from being held hostage by its suppliers.

To see why, suppose that a small contractor supplied Ford with a vital part for its cars and, contrary to fact, the small contractor owned the specialized equipment. The small contractor would have the power to hold up Ford's manufacturing process for a long period of time by refusing to supply the vital parts. Ford could not obtain an alternative supply until the special-

How to Exchange Hostages

Medieval kings used to guarantee the peace among themselves by exchanging hostages. An economist, Oliver Williamson, has analyzed the logic of the exchange of hostages and applied it to modern contracts.[1] Ask yourself this question: suppose that a king wants to exchange hostages with another monarch to guarantee the peace. The king, who likes diamonds very much but does not care much for his children, values a diamond ring just as much—neither more nor less—as he values his own son. Would the king's diamond ring or his son make a better hostage, that is, a hostage who is more likely to guarantee a stable peace?

The better hostage is the one that deters both the hostage-giver and the hostage-taker from starting a war. If the hostage-giver starts a war, the hostage-taker will refuse to return the hostage. By assumption, the king values the diamond ring and his son equally, so the fear of losing the ring by starting a war is equal to the fear of losing his son by starting a war. They are equally good deterrents against the hostage-*giver's* starting a war. But they are not, however, equally good deterrents against the hostage-*taker's* starting a war. The hostage-taker would presumably like to have the diamond ring but presumably does not place much intrinsic value on having the son of the neighboring king. The hostage-taker, therefore, is more inclined to start a war and keep the hostage if it is a diamond ring than if it is the king's son. That is why the king's son is a better hostage than the diamond ring.

In general, a good hostage is something that the hostage-giver values highly and that the hostage-taker values little. It is the asymmetry in valuation that makes a good hostage.

Similarly, to guarantee a long-term contractual relationship from disruption, each party should give as a hostage something that the giver values highly and the receiver values little.

Question 6.5: What sorts of things can business corporations give as hostages in long-term contractual relations? Does hostage-giving in long-run relationships serve the same or a different function as consideration in a short-run contract?

[1]*See* Oliver Williamson, *Credible Commitments: Using Hostages to Support Exchange*, 83 AM. ECON. REV. 519 (1983).

ized machines were built and delivered. However, by retaining ownership of the specialized machinery, Ford protects itself against this possibility. If the contractor refuses to deliver the vital parts, Ford reclaims the specialized equipment and shifts it to another supplier and obtains the vital parts without undue delay. Thus, Teece explains the structure of this long-run contract by the informal bargaining power of the parties.[19] (See the box entitled "How to Exchange Hostages" for further suggestions on how long-term contracts might be structured.)

Before proceeding to the next chapter, a comment concerning the limits of the economic approach is appropriate. Contract law stresses individual autonomy; it sees that the obligation of the courts is to help individuals in the pursuit of their private ends by enforcing their agreements. Insofar as contract law is designed to facilitate the pursuit of private ends rather than to meddle in the affairs of individuals, an economic analysis that stresses the rationality of individual choices and the efficiency of court rules is bound to explain a lot. Insofar as contract law is designed to achieve *collective* purposes rather than to facilitate the pursuit of private ends, something will be omitted from the economic analysis.[20]

SUGGESTED READINGS ON THE ELEMENTS OF CONTRACTS

Eisenberg, Melvin, *The Bargain Principle and Its Limits*, 95 HARV. L. REV. 741 (1982).

Eisenberg, Melvin, *Donative Promises*, 47 U. CHI. L. REV. 1 (1979).

Farnsworth, E. Allan, *Contracts* (1984).

Freid, Charles, CONTRACT AS PROMISE (1981).

Goetz, Charles, and Robert Scott, *Enforcing Promises: An Examination of the Basis of Contract*, 89 YALE L.J. 1261 (1980).

Gordley, James, *Equality in Exchange*, 69 CAL. L. REV. 1587 (1981).

Kronman, Anthony T., *Contract Law and the State of Nature*, 1 J. L. ECON. & ORGANIZATION 5 (1985).

Macaulay, Stewart, *Non-Contractual Relations in Business: A Preliminary Study,* 28 AM. SOCIOLOGICAL REV. 55 (1963).

Macneil, Ian, THE NEW SOCIAL CONTRACT (1980).

Posner, Richard, & Anthony T. Kronman, eds., THE ECONOMICS OF CONTRACT LAW (1979).

Williamson, Oliver, THE ECONOMIC INSTITUTIONS OF CAPITALISM, Chs. 1–3 (1985).

---

[19]An excellent introduction to the economic theory suggested by Professor Teece's study is Benjamin Klein, Robert Crawford, and Armen Alchian, *Vertical Integration, Appropriable Rents, and the Competitive Contracting Process,* 21 J. LAW & ECON. 297 (1978).

[20]To illustrate a collective purpose in contract law, consider a situation in which a private contract conflicts with a public policy. Specifically, the courts may refuse to enforce a contract between a police officer and a private citizen to protect that citizen because the police officer already has a public duty to provide protection. Allowing private citizens to make private contracts of this kind with public officials would be corrosive of public law. This is called the "legal-duty rule."

CHAPTER 7

Topics in the Economics of Contract Law

In the preceding chapter, we saw that a theory of contracts must answer two questions: What promises should be enforced? And to what extent? To answer these questions, we reviewed and criticized the classical theory of contract, and then we sketched a microeconomic theory of perfect contracts. Recall that a perfect contract was defined as a promise whose strict enforceability at law makes it an ideal instrument for achieving the ends of the promisor and the promisee. When contracts are perfect, they should be strictly enforced; when contracts are imperfect, the law must correct for the deficiency by supplying an appropriate legal doctrine. Next we listed assumptions about individual rationality and market environment under which contracts will be perfect. The doctrines of contract law were viewed as correcting the failure of a promise to satisfy one of these assumptions.

In this chapter, we develop in much greater detail the economic theory of contracts we sketched in the previous chapter. Two important aspects of this development will be our attempt to provide *practical* guidelines for determining, first, when a contract is sufficiently imperfect that a court should selectively enforce its terms rather than enforcing them all, and, second, how that selective enforcement should be undertaken. In the first part of this chapter we try to answer the question "What promises should be enforced?" by examining some of the traditional defenses and excuses that are advanced when one party attempts to breach a contract. After concluding our discussion of defenses and excuses, we turn to the design of remedies for breach of contract in order to answer the question "What remedies should be available when a contract is broken?"

I. FORMATION AND PERFORMANCE DEFENSES: WHAT CONTRACTS SHOULD BE ENFORCED?

When a plaintiff sues for breach of contract, the arguments available to the defendant can be distinguished into two types. First, he may argue that a defect in the attempt to form a contract prevented its legitimate formation, so he owes no legal duty to the plaintiff. To illustrate, a person who refuses to give a promised gift may defend himself by arguing that his promise did not create a legal obligation (". . . the contract fails for want of consideration"). This sort of defense is called a *formation defense.* Second, he may admit that a contract was validly formed and a legal obligation created, but argue that, under the circumstances prevailing at the time he is to perform, he should be excused from his contractual duty. To illustrate, a manufacturer may argue that he should be excused from delivering the promised goods because his factory has burned down. This type of argument is called a *performance excuse.*

According to our economic theory, perfect contracts should be strictly enforced, and arguments against enforcement should be based upon alleged imperfections in the contract. Formation defenses are based upon imperfections in the circumstances and procedures that created the contract. Performance excuses are based upon the occurrence of contingencies that were not provided for in the contract. So the defenses and excuses recognized by law can be viewed as imperfections in the formation of a contract or in the contingencies contemplated by it that are best corrected by not enforcing the promise. We will evaluate the defenses and excuses against the standard of correcting the imperfection and enabling the parties to accomplish, as nearly as possible, the ends they sought in forming the contract.

A. Formation Defenses

The formation defenses that we will discuss are coercion or duress, incompetency, mutual mistake, fraud, and unconscionability. As we will see, the economic analysis of these defenses is diverse and rich.

1. Coercion or Duress   Most contracts are bargains for mutual advantage. We have already seen how central the idea of voluntary exchange for mutual advantage is in microeconomic theory. In Chapter 2 we discussed the Fundamental Theorem of Exchange, which holds that voluntary exchange is mutually beneficial, and then in Chapter 4 we analyzed exchange or bargains in more detail by using the economic theory of games. In discussing the formation defense of coercion or duress, we now turn to a further refinement in our analysis of bargaining. Specifically, we want to know what bargains are truly voluntary.

In bargaining over the price, the parties in an exchange are allowed by law to threaten each other only within very narrow limits. Indeed, the allowed threats are so mild that we hesitate to use the term "threat." The main threat, which is always allowed, is the threat to withdraw from the deal: "I absolutely will not sell for less than $4,300," or "My final offer is $3,500; take it or leave it." In contrast, threats of mental or physical harm—such as "Sell for $3,500 or I'll make harassing phone calls to your house," or

The Uniform Commercial Code, Restatements of Contracts, and Statute of Frauds[1]

Much of the common law of contracts has been codified in three important documents: the Uniform Commercial Code, the American Law Institute's Restatements of Contracts, and the modern state statutes based on the old English Statute of Frauds.

The Uniform Commercial Code was proposed in 1940 to the National Conference of Commissioners on Uniform State Laws. That group was founded in 1890 and consists of commissioners appointed by each state. The Conference drafts and recommends legislation to the states on subjects for which there is a desire for uniformity across state lines. After its initial proposal, the U.C.C. became a joint product of the Conference and the American Law Institute. The Code was adopted in 1952 by the Conference and the Institute and then extensively revised in 1956. It consists of nine articles covering all aspects of commercial transactions. For example, Article 1 sets out the general provisions of the code; Article 2 covers the sale of goods (services are not covered); and Article 9 covers secured transactions. Forty-nine states (all but Louisiana, which has a civil law tradition) and the District of Columbia have adopted the Uniform Commercial Code.

The Restatements of the law are a project of the American Law Institute, a private group of judges, lawyers, and law professors founded in 1923, that has sought to codify the common law in property, contracts, torts, and other subjects. The Institute's first project was the Restatement of Contracts, which was published in 1932. In the introduction to that Restatement, the Institute wrote, "The function of the Institute is to state clearly and precisely in the light of the decisions the principles and rules of the common law. The sections of the Restatement express the result of a careful analysis of the subject and a thorough examination and discussion of pertinent cases—often very numerous and sometimes conflicting.

"Sell for $3,500 if you want your kid-sister to come home safely from school"—are forbidden.

In extending our economic theory of contract to cover the case of coercion or duress, we need to explain how the law distinguishes between permitted threats, such as the threat to withdraw from the deal, and forbidden threats, such as threats of mental or physical injury.[1] Microeconomic theory

---

[1]In the preceding examples, the threatened acts are criminal offenses. It is not necessary, however, that a threat violate criminal law in order for the resulting contract to be void by reason of duress. There are a variety of situations in which courts will find that a promise was

The . . . statements of law made . . . may be regarded both as the product of expert opinion and as the expression of the law by the legal profession." In response to the adoption of the Uniform Commerical Code, the Institute began a second Restatement of Contracts in 1960 that was published in 1979.

The Statute of Frauds ("An Act for Prevention of Frauds and Perjuries") was passed by Parliament in 1677. The purpose of the act was to prevent fraud in the proof of numerous legal transactions: contracts, assignments, deeds to land, trusts, wills, and revocations of wills. So that there would be a trustworthy record of important transactions and, thus, less likelihood of perjury, the statute required a signed writing in certain contractual transactions. In some cases, the signed writing had to be supplemented by the attestation of witnesses. For example, the original statute required that "[N]o contract for the sale of any goods, wares or merchandises for the price of ten pounds sterling or upwards shall be allowed to be good, except . . .

> (c) that some note or memorandum in writing of the said bargain be made and signed by the parties to be charged by such contract or their agents thereunto lawfully authorized."

Although there are twenty-five parts to the original statute, covering a wide variety of matters, the requirement of a written record for contractual transactions whose value exceeds a certain minimum has become the most important feature in the modern revisions of the Statute. Nearly every state has adopted a revised Statute of Frauds.

[1]The following discussion comes from Fuller & Eisenberg, BASIC CONTRACT LAW (4th ed. 1981).

offers a means of making the distinction. First, we must recognize that part of the idea of a voluntary exchange is that the parties are free to decide whether to *participate* in the deal. The right to threaten non-participation is, then, an aspect of the voluntariness of the exchange. And recall that because it makes both parties better off, voluntary exchange is socially desirable. Contract law tries to lubricate the process of voluntary exchange by enforc-

---

extracted under duress even though no criminal threats were involved. One such case is discussed in great detail below. The point to note is that the distinction between permitted and forbidden threats in contracts does not correspond to permitted and forbidden acts under the criminal code.

ing private agreements and permitting the parties to threaten not to participate.

When the threat not to participate is exercised, the opportunity to create value (the surplus from cooperation) is lost, but existing value is not destroyed. However, when a destructive threat is excercised, *existing* value may be destroyed. As a result, society is generally less well off.[2] Suppose, for example, that someone offers to purchase your bicycle for $10 and informs you that unless you sell at that price, you'll be beaten within a hairsbreadth of your life. What *existing* values might be destroyed by this threat? Assume that the threat-maker values the bicycle less than you do. If, in the absence of fear for your physical well-being, you would not sell the bike for less than $100, then an exchange at $10 may make the threat-maker better off but it certainly makes you much less well off. Indeed, it is highly likely that there is a net decrease in value in the sense that the threat-maker's increase in well-being from acquiring the bike is less than your decrease in well-being from having to give it up for less than it is worth to you. It is not absolutely certain that this destruction in existing values will be the outcome of a coerced exchange. In fact, one can imagine circumstances in which existing values are *increased* by coercion. But those are such rare instances that they may be distinguishable from the general case of coercion. (For an example of an economic analysis of distinguishing those rare instances, see the discussion of the economics of imposing liability for failure to rescue in Chapters 8 and 9.) Coerced exchanges are so likely to be destructive of existing values that economic analysis argues for disallowing *any* of them.

A coerced or forced exchange can thus be defined as a trade extracted under the threat to destroy existing value. By contrast, a non-coercive exchange is extracted under the threat to block the creation of additional value (the surplus from cooperation). In economic jargon, threats to destroy value are forbidden, and threats not to participate in its creation are permitted. This economic analysis suggests this rule for dealing with coercion as a formation defense: *a promise extracted by a destructive threat is void for reason of duress, but a promise extracted by a threat not to participate is not void for reason of duress.*

> **Question 7.1:** Suppose that person *A*, while holding a loaded handgun, invites person *B* to exchange his wallet for his life. What existing values are at risk by this destructive threat?

We may develop these issues by examining the facts in the case of *Austin Instrument, Inc. v. Loral Corporation* [316 N.Y.S.2d 528 (1970); 324

---

[2]We are following widely-held community norms in ignoring the possibility that the threat-maker derives utility simply from the act of making a threat or of bullying others. No one contends that that source of utility should count as part of social well-being.

N.Y.S.2d 22 (1971)].[3] Loral had been awarded a general contract from the Navy for the production of radar sets, and Austin was one of its subcontractors. A year after the first contract was awarded by the Navy to Loral, the defendant was awarded a second contract from the Navy and solicited a bid from Austin to construct some of the component parts. This second bid was solicited at a time when Austin had not completed delivery on items prescribed in its first contract with Loral. Austin threatened non-performance on the remainder of its first contract unless Loral awarded the second contract on terms that favored Austin, including a retroactive price increase on the remaining items from the first contract. Austin was not the lowest bidder on some items covered by the second contract, so Loral did not want to award the second contract to Austin. But Loral needed Austin to deliver the promised items from the first contract to meet its delivery deadline with the Navy and escape the penalty clauses for late delivery in its general contract.

Loral could have refused to give Austin the second contract, and if, in retaliation, Austin acted on its threat to breach the first contract, Loral could have then sued Austin for breach. That would have been the traditional tactic. Instead, Loral capitulated to Austin's demand but made clear in a letter to Austin that it did so under duress. Deliveries proceeded on schedule, but after receiving all of the items specified in the two contracts with Austin, Loral withheld its last payment, and both parties sued.

The trial court in New York decided the case in favor of Austin on the grounds that Loral had access to the traditional legal remedy: Loral could have refused to give Austin the second contract and then sued for breach if Austin broke the first contract. So, in the first trial, the defense of duress failed, and Loral was ordered to make the final payment to Austin. On appeal, however, the higher court reversed the lower court's ruling and found in favor of Loral. The higher court held that duress was established by the fact that the threatened party could not obtain the goods from another source in the event of Austin's default.

How should this case have been decided under our theory distinguishing between destructive and permitted threats? According to our economic theory, duress occurs when a threat is made whose exercise would destroy existing value; duress does not occur when the threat is to refuse to cooperate in creating a surplus. In this case, Austin threatened to breach its first contract unless it was given both the second contract and a price increase on the initial contract. But breaching the first contract would have destroyed an existing value—the expected surplus already created by the agreement. By the economic standard, the appeals court was correct in finding duress.

In Chapter 4 we explained that the division of the surplus from exchange depends upon the bargaining power of the parties. The bargaining

---

[3]This analysis is found in Robert Cooter, *The Cost of Coase*, 11 J. LEGAL STUD. 1 (1982).

power of the parties in turn depends upon how much each will be harmed by failing to cooperate. It frequently happens that, after entering a contract, circumstances change in such a way that the bargaining power of one of the parties is augmented. It is a natural temptation on the part of the advantaged party to try to renegotiate more favorable terms.[4] This frequently happens to professional baseball and football players who, after a particularly good year, try to renegotiate their contracts. And that is what happened in *Austin v. Loral.* (For yet another example, see the box on the Bad Samaritans.) When Loral negotiated the original contract with Austin, Loral probably had other potential sources of supply of the needed parts. After awarding the subcontract to Austin, however, Loral became dependent upon Austin to perform on time. Austin tried to take advantage of its increased bargaining power to renegotiate the contract. In general, attempts to revise the terms of a contract solely because of a change in bargaining power are looked upon with disfavor by courts. There is an inefficiency aspect, which we discuss below, of allowing this change in bargaining power to control the terms of a contract. But there is also a feeling that this particular form of advantage-taking violates widely-shared social norms.

We have explained that enforcing contracts extracted under the threat of harm would provide an incentive for destructive acts. That is not the only social cost of destructive threats. Suppose the law changed and adopted the position that contractual promises elicited through threats of harm are legally enforceable. How might we expect people to behave? First, people would devote resources to protecting themselves from having promises dragged out of them; for example, they might avoid certain places, hire bodyguards, and acquire weapons or muscles. Second, some people would devote resources to waylaying others from whom they can badger promises to do the things they want done. In contrast, these wasteful uses of resources are unnecessary when the law refuses to enforce promises extracted under threat of harm. Since coercion is a valid formation defense, many of the resources that would be devoted to protecting oneself or to terrorizing others can be shifted to alternative, more productive uses.

Furthermore, if coercion were not a valid formation defense, there might be a large number of contracts that involved the transfer of resources from a higher- to a lower-valued use. Suppose that you are eager to have your house windows washed but are willing to pay no more than $20 to have it done by someone else. Suppose further that someone who specializes in window-washing is not willing to do the job for less than $40, that being the opportunity cost of the time it would take to wash the windows. In the absence of

---

[4]A threat to withhold payment unless the other party performs his half of the promise is not in itself objectionable. But a subcontractor's threat to withhold goods unless the contractor, who is in the middle of his construction and facing a deadline, pays more to the subconstractor is objectionable. This situation is known as "duress of goods," and is not generally allowed.

The Case of the Bad Samaritans

The famous case of *Post v. Jones,* 60 U.S. (19 How.) 150 (1857), concerns an instance of duress or necessity. The whaling ship *Richmond,* with a full cargo of whaling oil, ran aground on a barren coast in the Arctic Ocean and was slowly foundering. A few days later three other whaling ships came upon the *Richmond.* None of the three had a full cargo. They could take on some but not all of the *Richmond's* cargo of whale oil. These three ships might have left the *Richmond's* cargo to sink; or they might have taken as much of the cargo as they could hold, intending to hand that cargo over to the *Richmond's* owners, minus a salvage fee, when they returned to port. Instead, the three captains, while agreeing to save the crew, threatened not to take any of the *Richmond's* whale oil unless the captain of the *Richmond* agreed to hold an auction of his cargo. One of the three captains bid $1 per barrel for as much as he could take; the other two took as much of the remainder as they could hold at $0.75 per barrel. Both prices were well below the competitive price of whaling oil. When the three vessels returned to port with the *Richmond's* oil and crew, the owners of the *Richmond* sued, asking the court not to enforce the sale of the whale oil at the low auction prices.

Question 7.2: Did the captains who purchased the oil threaten to destroy existing value, or did they threaten not to participate in creating it? Does it matter to your answer whether sea captains have a legal duty to rescue ships and cargo in distress? (They do in fact have such a duty.) On economic efficiency grounds, should the auction be set aside? (That is what the court did.)

coercion on your part, the window washer is not going to wash your windows. But if you are legitimately allowed to threaten him unless he washes your windows for, say, $15, then he may agree to wash them, even though it would be more efficient (and more profitable to him) to accept other work. By not allowing coercion to enter into the formation of valid contracts, we are minimizing the occurrence of these inefficient transfers.

These arguments against enforcing coercive threats should sound familiar because they correspond to the thought experiment in Chapter 4 in which, beginning from a state of nature, a civil society with enforceable property rights was formed by bargaining. As part of that thought experiment we derived a principle (the Normative Hobbes Theorem) according to which law should be structured to minimize the harm caused by private disagreements. When applied to property law, this principle led to the conclusion that theft and destruction of property should be outlawed in order to maximize the value of the non-cooperative solution to bargaining. Our argument against enforcing promises extracted under coercion or duress is an application of this principle to contract law. In effect, the contract rules on coercion and duress help to maintain civil society and prevent a descent into the state of nature in which disagreements have disastrous consequences.

2. Incapacity or Incompetency The law presumes, as does economic theory, that individuals are the best judges of their promises. However, the law also recognizes that some people are incompetent to make contracts. Two general cases in which the law recognizes incapacity are immaturity and mental infirmity. Where the promisor or promisee is afflicted with either of these conditions, the promise that has been given is usually void.

Is there an *economic* argument to justify rescinding a promise made by an incompetent? What is it about those who are immature or mentally infirm that makes their transactions voidable? The heart of the economic answer is this: incompetents are not capable of making the sorts of calculations about subjective and objective value that microeconomic theory attributes to rational people. An immature or mentally infirm person cannot rationally compare his subjective valuation to objective values, such as prices, in order to decide what exchanges to make. Thus, there cannot be the presumption that exchange will make incompetent people better off. In short, these people do not have stable, well-ordered preferences. Thus, there can be no presumption that a bargain promise between a competent and incompetent person is mutually beneficial.

Additionally, a rule of not enforcing promises by incompetent people may improve the behavior of competent people. When you come to the chapter on torts, you will encounter the general principle that accident losses should be assigned to the party who can avoid them at least cost. This principle is applicable to contracts with incompetent people, who are prone to make costly mistakes. Since incompetent people cannot look after themselves, others must do so. Contract law, then, puts mature and sane people on notice that, in case of doubt, they should ascertain whether someone else is mature and sane before entering into a contract with them. By this assignment of responsibility, the cost of preventing harmful contracts by the immature and insane is placed upon the people who can avoid the harm at least cost.

> **Question 7.3:** A young girl found an attractive stone in the woods and sold it to a jeweler for $1. Later, her family discovered that the stone was a rough diamond worth $700. They attempted to void the contract on the grounds that the girl was incompetent to make a contract. Does the economic analysis of incompetency support this contention? Or was this just a "sharp" deal by the jeweler? (Re-analyze this problem after you have read the following section on mistake.)

> **Question 7.4:** Suppose that one party's incompetence is temporary, having been induced by excessive drinking or the taking of drugs. Would the efficient exchange of promises be fostered by a policy of generally enforcing these contracts? Who is the least-cost avoider of the harm, the party who could have foreseen the consequences of drinking or taking drugs, or the party who contracted with the person who was drunk or high?

3. Mistake: Mutual and Unilateral   In discussing the doctrine of consideration in the preceding chapter, we saw that the courts gradually redefined the word. Consideration originally referred to a definite aspect of a bargain, specifically the inducement offered by the promisee to extract the promise from the promisor. With time the term was emptied of its meaning and came to mean anything making a promise enforceable in the eyes of the judges. A similar shift in meaning is at work in the doctrine of mistake. Two kinds of mistakes are distinguished in contract law: mutual mistake and unilateral mistake. We will first explain the original, substantive meaning of these terms, and then we will explain the derivative, tautological meaning of them.

A *mutual* mistake arises when the parties to a bargain have no "meeting of the minds," that is, when both of them misunderstood what was being promised by the other. The transaction described at the beginning of the preceding chapter for the sale of a used car is an example. The seller thought that he was selling a rusty Chevy, for which $1,000 was a high price; the buyer thought she was buying a shiny Cadillac, for which $1,000 was a low price. Note that the mistake in this case is truly mutual: although each party has made no mistake about his or her own promise, he or she is mistaken about what it is that the other party has promised.

Mutual mistake is a valid formation defense in contract law, which makes sense in terms of simple economics. We have explained that law and economics favor voluntary exchange and disfavor involuntary exchange. When contracts are based upon mutual mistake, like the case of the rusty Chevy and the shiny Cadillac, there has been no agreement to make an exchange. Thus, if the courts were to force an exchange, it would be involuntary. There are many objections to involuntary exchanges, some of which we have already explained in detail by using bargaining theory. Instead of forcing an involuntary exchange, the courts set aside contracts based upon mutual mistake.

In contrast to mutual mistake, a *unilateral* mistake arises when only one of the parties to a bargain has misunderstood the exchange.[5] A contract based upon a unilateral mistake is usually enforceable. In other words, contract law permits people to trade on superior information. For example, if John knows that your old car has become a valued classic, and you are willing to sell it below market value because you do not know that it is a classic, the law will usually enforce a bargained agreement between the two of you. Even though you were mistaken about the car's value, John was not, so the mistake is unilateral and a contract between you is enforceable at law.

Question 7.5: In *Raffles v. Wichelhaus*, 2 Hurl. & C. 906, 159 Eng. Rep. 375 (Ex. 1864), the plaintiff sold the defendants 125 bales of cotton to arrive "ex *Peerless*

---

[5]Clearly, we are not here speaking of the sort of misunderstanding that was explained in the last section as due to incapacity or incompetence. Nor are we dealing here with the case in which the one-sided misunderstanding is due to some fraudulent misrepresentation.

from Bombay," that is, by way of the ship *Peerless* sailing from Bombay, India. A ship by that name sailed from India in December, but when it arrived, the defendants refused to take delivery of the cotton on the grounds that they had meant a second ship named the *Peerless* that had left Bombay in October. The Court of Exchequer gave judgment for the defendants on the argument that there had been no meeting of the minds.

How would you have decided this case?[6]

Because mutual mistake is a valid formation defense and unilateral mistake is not, there are strong incentives for a party who seeks performance of a contract to contend that any mistake was unilateral, and for a party who seeks to be excused from a contract to claim mutual mistake. There are, consequently, many cases in which the defense of mutual mistake is raised under conditions quite different from the case of the rusty Chevy and the shiny Cadillac. In that example, there was a misunderstanding about the physical identity of the object being exchanged. In other examples, which are more problematic, there is a misunderstanding about the *quality* of the object being exchanged, or there is a mistake about circumstances affecting the *value* of the object. In a famous example reproduced below, *Sherwood v. Walker,* these considerations are combined: a mistake about the quality of the object being exchanged affects its value. This is a case in which the seller promised to deliver a cow to the buyer. Subsequently, the seller learned that the cow was pregnant. A pregnant cow is far more valuable than a barren cow; after the seller found out the cow was pregnant, he refused to deliver the cow to the buyer as promised. He contended that the contract was premised on the mutual belief that the cow was barren, so he asserted the defense of mutual mistake.

In cases like this one, where the mistake concerns not the identity of the thing being exchanged but a quality of it that affects its value, the distinction between mutual mistake and unilateral mistake seldom provides reliable grounds for deciding the dispute. To see why, consider the beliefs of the buyer of the cow. Either he believed the cow was barren or he suspected that it was pregnant. If the buyer suspected the cow was pregnant, he would not point out his suspicions to the seller for fear that the seller would raise the price or withdraw from the bargain. One effect of this incentive structure is that a canny buyer like Sherwood may be unable to provide evidence in court that he suspected the object's true value, so a seller like Walker can mount an argument that the mistake was mutual.

In such disputes, the terms "mutual mistake" and "unilateral mistake" often become emptied of their original meaning. These terms originally referred to a fact about the bargain that the courts employed to decide whether to enforce the promise. Instead, the courts are likely to decide the case on other grounds and use these terms to announce their decision. Thus,

---

[6]Grant Gilmore suggested, in THE DEATH OF CONTRACT 35–39 (1974), that this case is "to the ordinary run of case law as the recently popular theatre of the absurd is to the ordinary run of theatre."

the term "mutual mistake" will be used to announce a decision not to enforce the promise, and "unilateral mistake" will be used to announce a decision to enforce the promise. What is required of legal theory under these circumstances is a criterion that tells how the courts should make such determinations.

Fortunately, economic theory has a more powerful analysis for solving this problem. Note that the problem of mistake is largely caused by the importance of information in the contemplated exchange. Information is a peculiar good that can create contract imperfections. Let's analyze mistake as a contract imperfection created by asymmetric information.

A useful distinction from which to begin is between *productive facts* and *redistributive facts*. By "productive facts" we mean information that can be used to increase wealth. To illustrate, the discovery of a vaccine for polio and the discovery of a water-route from Europe to China were productive. Incentives for discovery of productive facts are efficient when the discoverer is compensated at a rate commensurate with the increase in wealth yielded by her discovery. By "redistributive facts" we mean information creating a bargaining advantage that can be used to redistribute wealth in favor of the knowledgeable party but that does not lead to the creation of new wealth. To illustrate, knowing a week in advance of the public where a new highway will be located provides a powerful advantage in the real estate market. In contrast to productive facts, efficiency does not require compensating the discoverers of merely redistributive facts. Indeed, allowing the discoverers of redistributive facts to use them to transfer wealth to themselves induces defensive expenditures on the part of parties seeking to avoid losing their wealth to more knowledgeable people, and these defensive expenditures are wasteful from a social viewpoint.

This distinction can be applied to the doctrine of mistake. In certain settings where one party knows redistributive facts that the other does not know, the law will not enforce contracts. Consider the case of *Laidlaw v. Organ,* 15 U.S. (2 Wheat.) 178 (1815). The British blockaded New Orleans during the War of 1812 and, as a result, the price of export goods like tobacco plummeted. Organ, a buyer of tobacco, received private information that the war had ended by treaty, so he called on a representative of the Laidlaw firm and, having ascertained that the seller was ignorant about the peace treaty, Organ offered to buy tobacco from the Laidlaw representative. A contract was concluded between them at the depressed price; the next day public notice was given in New Orleans that peace was concluded and the price of tobacco soared. The mistake in this contract was obviously unilateral, not mutual—Organ knew about the treaty and Laidlaw did not—but the contract was apparently set aside by the court after a trial.[7]

---

[7]A verdict at trial for the buyer was appealed to the U.S. Supreme Court, who remanded it for retrial, but it is not entirely clear what happened upon retrial. *See* A. T. Kronman, *Mistake, Disclosure, Information and the Law of Contracts,* 7 J. LEGAL STUD. 1 (1978), and Kim Scheppele, "Efficiency and Equality in the Common Law: An Analysis of Nondisclosure as Fraud," (unpublished mimeo, Nov. 1985).

Organ intended this contract to transfer resources to him at less than its value under full information. The transfer did not serve any productive purpose. So the sale was apparently premised upon redistributive facts, as opposed to productive facts. If such contracts were enforced, commerce would be burdened by the need for sellers like Laidlaw to protect themselves against unfavorable wealth transfers. An economic interpretation of the controlling principle in the case is that *trades on private knowledge about purely redistributive facts may be set aside.*[8]

Productive facts and redistributive facts are pure types. Most new facts are mixed, not pure, in the sense that knowledge of them is both productive and redistributive. To illustrate, Eli Whitney's invention of the cotton gin in 1792 was enormously productive and it also provided a basis to speculate on increases in the value of land suitable for growing cotton. The law tends to enforce trades based on private facts that are mixed. To illustrate, when one dealer in a commodity like wheat or plywood trades with another on their own accounts, they disagree about the product's future price. One of them will be more right than the other, and the one with the better guess will redistribute wealth to herself through the transaction. It would be a costly error for courts to seize upon the redistributive element and refuse to enforce contracts between commodities dealers.[9] Trades on private knowledge of mixed facts (productive and redistributive) are usually enforceable.

---

[8]Kronman asserts that the contract should have been set aside because the facts known to Organ were acquired fortuitously, rather than being acquired through deliberate investment. This distinction is somewhat confusing because redistributive facts can be obtained fortuitously or by an investment, and the same can be said about productive facts. Nevertheless, our distinction between productive and redistributive facts is similar to the intent of Kronman's analysis, since both views are motivated by the insight that the law governing mistakes and disclosures should be controlled by efficiency considerations. In contrast, Scheppele rejects an efficiency explanation and reinterprets the line of cases similar to *Laidlaw* in terms of an "equal access" principle, according to which disclosure is mandatory if the marginal cost of information is much less for one party to the contract than for the other party. Thus, her analysis stresses that Laidlaw did not have equal access to information about the peace treaty because Organ could acquire it at lower cost through friends and relatives. See the preceding footnote for citations. For yet another view, see A. Rubinstein, "A Note on the Duty of Disclosure," Research Report No. 122, Hebrew University, June 1979.

[9]An additional, efficiency reason for enforcing the commodities dealers' contract is that speculators often perform two valuable functions: first, they shield producers from the risk of fluctuating prices, and second, they transmit valuable information to others by affecting prices. On the first point, traders in commodities futures are in effect insurance sellers, allowing risk-averse commodities producers to escape the risk that commodity prices will fluctuate before being extracted. To illustrate, commodities traders enable a farmer to sell his crop before he harvests it and thereby to escape the risk that the price will fall. Of course, the farmer may still feel rancor if, instead of the price falling, it rises. If the farmer studied economics, he might take comfort in the fact that commodities markets are highly competitive and, thus, futures prices are efficient and fair. On the second point, farmers (among others) will efficiently alter their production plans depending on the course of futures prices. If the price paid now for grain delivered next year (called "grain futures prices") rises, commodities traders thereby signal that they have reassessed upwards the price they expect to prevail next year. Farmers respond by plainning to plant more grain for harvest next year or to store less, and these actions ameliorate a potential shortage. This change in planting and storage plans then causes commodities traders to revise downward their expectation on prices at harvest time.

We have, then, arrived at two economic principles that should govern the analysis of contract cases in which the formation defense of mistake is raised:

1. trades on private knowledge of mixed facts (productive and redistributive) are enforceable;
2. trades on private knowledge of purely redistributive facts may be set aside;

These normative principles are based upon efficiency reasons that have weight in courts, so they are often useful for explaining cases.

You should now read the case of *Sherwood v. Walker* and apply this analysis to it.

Sherwood v. Walker, 66 Mich. 568, 33 N.W. 919 (Mich. 1887).

MORSE, J. . . . The main controversy depends upon the construction of a contract for the sale of the cow. . . . The Walkers are importers and breeders of polled Angus cattle. The plaintiff is a banker living at Plymouth, in Wayne county. He called upon the defendants at Walkerville for the purchase of some of their stock, but found none there that suited him. Meeting one of the defendants afterwards, he was informed that they had a few head upon their Greenfield farm. He was asked to go out and look at them, with the statement that they were probably barren, and would not breed. May 5, 1886, the plaintiff went out to Greenfield and saw the cattle. A few days thereafter, he called upon one of the defendants with the view of purchasing a cow, known as "Rose 2d of Aberlone." After considerable talk it was agreed that defendants would telephone Sherwood at his home in Plymouth in reference to the price. The second morning after this talk he was called up by telephone, and the terms of the sale were finally agreed upon. He was to pay five and one-half cents per pound, live weight, fifty pounds shrinkage . . . He requested defendants to confirm the sale in writing, which they did . . .

On the twenty-first of the same month the plaintiff went to defendants' farm at Greenfield, and presented the order and [confirmation letter to an employee of the Walkers,] who informed him that the defendants had instructed him not to deliver the cow. Soon after, the plaintiff rendered to Hiram Walker, one of the defendants, $80, and demanded the cow. Walker refused to take the money or deliver the cow. The plaintiff then instituted this suit.

[At the trial, t]he defendants introduced evidence tending to show that at the time of the alleged sale it was believed by both the plaintiff and themselves that the cow was barren and would not breed; that she cost $850, and if not barren would be worth from $750 to $1,000; that after the date of the letter . . . the defendants were informed by [an employee] that in his judgment the cow was with calf, and therefore they instructed him not to deliver her to plaintiff. . . The cow had a calf in the month of October following. . .

It appears from the record that both parties supposed this cow was barren and would not breed, and she was sold by the pound for an insignificant sum as compared with her real value if a breeder. She was evidently sold and purchased on the relation of her value for beef, unless the plaintiff had learned of her true condition, and concealed such knowledge from the defendants. . . The question arises whether the [defendants] had a right to [refuse to perform the contract]. . . I am of the opinion that the [circuit] court erred in holding [that the contract should have been performed at the agreed upon price]. I know that this is a close question, and the dividing line between the adjudicated cases is not easily discerned. But it must be considered as well settled that a party who has given an apparent consent to a contract of sale may refuse to execute it, or he may avoid it after it has been completed, if the assent was founded, or the contract made, upon the mistake of a material fact,—such as the subject-matter of the sale, the price, or some collateral fact materially inducing the agreement; and this can be done when the mistake is mutual. . .

If there is a difference or misapprehension as to the substance of the thing bargained for; if the thing actually delivered or received is different in substance from the thing bargained for, and intended to be sold,—then there is no contract; but if it be only a difference in some quality or accident, even though the mistake may have been the actuating motive to the purchaser or seller, or both of them, yet the contract remains binding. . . It has been held, in accordance with the principles above stated, that where a horse is bought under the belief that he is sound, and both vendor and vendee honestly believe him to be sound, the purchaser must stand by his bargain, and pay the full price, unless there was a warranty.

It seems to me, however, in the case made by this record, that the mistake or misapprehension of the parties went to the whole substance of the agreement. If the cow was a breeder, she was worth at least $750; if barren, she was worth not over $80. The parties would not have made the contract of sale except upon the understanding and belief that she was incapable of breeding, and of no use as a cow. It is true she is now the identical animal that they thought her to be when the contract was made; there is no mistake as to the identity of the creature. Yet the mistake was not of the mere quality of the animal, but went to the very nature of the thing. A barren cow is substantially a different creature than a breeding one. There is as much difference between them for all purposes of use as there is between an ox and a cow that is capable of breeding and giving milk. If the mutual mistake had simply related to the fact whether she was with calf or not for one season, then it might have been a good sale, but the mistake affected the character of the animal for all time, and for its present and ultimate use. She was not in fact the animal, or the kind of animal, the defendants intended to sell or the plaintiff to buy. . . The court should have instructed the jury that if they found that the cow was sold, or contracted to be sold, upon the understanding of both parties that she was barren and useless for the purpose of breeding, and that in fact she was not barren, but capable of breeding, then the defendants had a right to rescind, and refuse to deliver, and the verdict should be in their favor.

The judgment of the court below must be reversed, and a new trial granted, with costs of this court to defendants.

SHERWOOD, J. (dissenting) . . . There is no question but that the defendants sold the cow representing her of the breed and quality they believed the cow to be, and that the purchaser so understood it. And the buyer purchased her believing her to be of the breed represented by the sellers, and possessing all the qualities stated, and even more. He believed she would breed. There is no pretense that the plaintiff bought the cow for beef, and there is nothing in the record indicating that he would have bought her at all only that he thought she might be made to breed. Under the foregoing facts, . . . it is held that because it turned out that the plaintiff was more correct in his judgment as to one quality of the cow than the defendants, and a quality, too, which could not by any possibility be positively known at the time by either party to exist, the contract may be annulled by the defendants at their pleasure. . . If the owner of a Hambletonian horse had speeded him, and was only able to make him go a mile in three minutes, and should sell him to another, believing that was his greatest speed, for $300, when the purchaser believed he could go much faster, and made the purchase for that sum, and a few days thereafter, under more favorable circumstances, the horse was driven a mile in 2 min. 16 sec., and was found to be worth $20,000, I hardly think it would be held, whether at law or in equity, by any one, that the seller in such case could rescind the contract. . .

In this case neither party knew the actual quality and condition of this cow at the time of the sale. . . The defendants thought [Rose could not be made to breed], but the plaintiff says that he thought she could be made to breed, but believed she was not with calf. The defendants sold the cow for what they believed her to be, and the plaintiff bought her as he believed she was, after the statements made by the defendants. No conditions whatever were attached to the terms of sale by either party. . . It is not the duty of courts to destroy contracts when called upon to enforce them, after they have been legally made. . . There was no difference between the parties, nor misapprehension, as to the substance of the thing bargained for, which was a cow supposed to be barren by one party, and believed not to be by the other. As to the quality of the animal, subsequently developed, both parties were equally ignorant, and as to this each party took his chances. . . In this case the cow sold was the one delivered. What might or might not happen to her after the sale formed no element in the contract. . .

Question 7.6:

a. The knowledge that a cow is fertile, rather than barren, is productive, rather than merely redistributive. Why?

b. The possibility that Rose was fertile can be described as a beneficial risk—a risk that something good will occur. The contract did not allocate this risk explicitly. What facts would help to decide whether the contract allocated it implicitly?

c. Suppose the law imposed upon Sherwood the duty to disclose to Walker any evidence that the cow is fertile. Would there be an objection to such a duty on efficiency grounds?

d. Should it matter in this case that Walker was a professional cattle rancher?

Our analysis of *Sherwood v. Walker* does not begin to exhaust the types of mistakes that create contractual disputes. Two such examples follow in which the mistake is similar to the accidents that arise in tort law. In the next chapter we develop an economic theory for allocating accident costs but, for now, the analysis of these cases is up to you.

> **Question 7.7: The $3,000 Typographical Error.** Omega Corporation offers to sell a crane. The Alpha Company intends to bid $12,000 for the crane, but due to a typographical error, the bid is transmitted at $15,000. The Beta Company bids $13,000. There are no other bidders. Omega turns down the bid from Beta and accepts Alpha's bid. Subsequently, the mistake is discovered by Alpha, who offers to proceed only at the lower price of $12,000. Omega sues for the full $15,000. Beta is still prepared to pay $13,000 for the crane. The options before the court are: (i) declare that there was no contract ("mutual mistake"); (ii) declare that a valid contract was breached and award damages; or (iii) enforce the contract according to its terms.
>
> a. If the Coase Theorem applies to this case, which company will end up owning the crane?
> b. Has Omega relied on Alpha's offer in a way that was costly?
> c. What is the most efficient option before the court?

> **Question 7.8:** The Batchelors Peas Company hired an advertising agency to popularize its product. The agency then contracted with a pilot to tow a sign reading "Eat Batchelors Peas" over Manchester and other cities during a nine-month period. The pilot flew over Manchester on November 11, Armistice Day—a day of particularly poignant meaning to those who had lost relatives in the First World War—during a two-minute silence being held as part of a memorial service. The pea company suffered a considerable loss in reputation as a result. They received numerous complaints about the advertisement during the memorial service with such expressions as "You are beneath contempt" and "I will see that your goods never enter my house" being typical. The contract was silent on whether flying should take place on Armistice Day.
>
> On the grounds of economic efficiency and applying the tools of this section, should the advertising agency be held liable for damages to the Batchelors Peas Company? (See *Aerial Advertising Co. v. Batchelors Peas*, [1938] 2 All. E.R. 788.)

4. The Duty to Disclose, Misrepresentation, and Fraud

We analyzed the doctrine of mistake as an instance of asymmetric information about productive facts and redistributive facts. Misrepresentation and fraud are also problems that arise because of asymmetric information, but to analyze them, we need to distinguish a third category of information: *destructive facts*. By "destructive facts" we mean information that, if not disclosed, will cause harm to someone's property or person. To illustrate, failing to disclose the side effects of drugs can harm their users.

Another example of a destructive fact is provided by the case of *Obde v. Schlemeyer*, 56 Wash.2d 449, 353 P.2d 672 (1960). In this case one party bought a building from another, and not long thereafter, the buyer discovered that the property was infested by termites. There was conclusive evidence that the seller knew about the infestation and deliberately withheld the information from the buyer at the time of sale. The seller did not lie about the termites; he was never asked about them. The court awarded damages to the buyer because of the seller's failure to disclose the termite infestation.

In this case, the issue is one of both the unwarranted redistribution of wealth, as in *Organ v. Laidlaw,* and of the inefficient destruction of wealth. By not divulging the termite infestation, the seller is attempting to sell his building as if it were uninfested, thus causing the buyer to offer a price consistent with no infestation. The wealth redistributed to the seller by his not disclosing the presence of termites equals the difference between what the buyer offered believing there was no infestation and the lower price he would have been willing to offer had he known of the infestation. But considerations of efficiency are also relevant. To minimize termite damages, the termites should have been exterminated as soon as they were discovered. By not disclosing the infestation, the termites were given the opportunity to cause further destruction. The court imposed a duty to disclose in order to avoid such future losses. By enforcing a duty to disclose, the court diminished the need for future buyers to be wary or to undertake defensive expenditures against this sort of concealment by sellers. Additionally, because disclosure would prevent the seller from gaining anything by passing the costs of correcting the termite damage on to the buyer, a duty to disclose might also encourage sellers to discover and deal with termite infestation at an early date. These considerations suggest a third economic principle for contract cases involving asymmetrical information: *in bargaining there may be a duty to divulge facts whose nondisclosure is destructive.*

Question 7.9: Suppose that a seller does not truly know whether his home has termites. He simply has not bothered to investigate. When asked by a buyer if it does, he says, "I guess not." On efficiency grounds, should this statement be enough to void the contract?

Question 7.10: Prof. Schmidt, a geologist, has agreed to purchase McDonald's farm for a price of $2,000 per acre, which corresponds to the price of good quality farmland in the vicinity. However, Schmidt, on the basis of his own geological studies, is convinced that McDonald's farm contains valuable mineral deposits, which make the property worth $25,000 per acre. Schmidt's true motive is discovered by McDonald before Schmidt takes possession, and McDonald refuses to hand over the property. Schmidt sues for breach of contract. McDonald defends on the grounds that Schmidt had a duty to disclose the results of his studies.

According to the economic analysis, who should win? Suppose that instead of being a geologist, the buyer is someone who happened to overhear a geologist explaining his belief that McDonald's farm contained valuable minerals. Would this fact affect your analysis?

In *Obde v. Schlemeyer,* the seller did not claim that the property was free from termites. He simply failed to disclose information. At the worst, the seller's assertions about the property were misleading but not strictly false.

Under the traditional common law doctrine regarding the formation defense of fraud or misrepresentation, this would not have been enough to allow the buyer to recover damages from the seller. At common law, misrepresentation or fraud was a narrowly interpreted formation defense. The general rule was that a lie, an affirmative misrepresentation, either in the form of speech or act, had to be present in order to void the contract. Additionally, the person to whom the misrepresentation or lie was made had to have been reasonable in believing its truth. Thus, if the seller in *Obde*, rather than failing to disclose information, had been more ruthless and had actually claimed that the property was free from termites, the contract would have involved fraud, and under the traditional common law interpretation the buyer would have been entitled to damages. But at common law the concealment of some important fact about the contemplated exchange would lead to the court's failing to enforce a contractual promise; the rule was *caveat emptor*, "Let the buyer beware!"

This means that, to reach its result in *Obde v. Schlemeyer*, the court had to reject the traditional common law interpretation of this formation defense in order to impose an affirmative duty upon the seller to disclose destructive facts. The imposition of this affirmative duty is a relatively new development in the law. Of course, many misleading acts or statements are in the grey area somewhere between a lie and concealment—as in the ad for the grass-hopper killer noted at the beginning of the previous chapter—and it is these cases that are the source of most disputes.

Recently, courts and legislatures have extensively broadened the circumstances in which a contract may be voided where one party has misled or concealed facts from the other. For example, lenders are now required by law to divulge the annual percentage rate of interest on all consumer loans. Used car dealers are required in many states to reveal any major repairs done to their cars. In almost all states sellers of homes are required to tell prospective buyers of certain latent defects in the home, such as a cracked foundation. Producers of many products are required to list their ingredients in the order in which those ingredients make up the product. In some cases, manufacturers are required to notify consumers about energy use aspects or safety hazards of their output. The traditional common law rules on fraud and misrepresentation can be interpreted as preventing parties from profiting from redistributive facts or destructive facts, and the recent legislative extensions of the common law rules can be rationalized on similar grounds. But economists are keenly aware that these remedies tend to be costly and it is quite possible for legislation directed at a real abuse to cost consumers more than the damage they suffer from the unregulated abuse.

Question 7.11: Suppose that there is a misrepresentation by the *buyer*, not by the seller. Suppose that the seller is very attached to her home and wishes to sell only to someone who will maintain the property as a single-family dwelling. A prospective buyer says that he, too, wants to use the property as a single-family dwelling. The sale is completed, and the seller moves out. However, several days later, she learns that the buyer intended all along to demolish the home in order to put up a gas station. Has the buyer profited from a destructive fact that, on efficiency grounds, should lead to the recission of the contract to sell the home?

5. Unconscionability

The newest and most troubling formation defense is unconscionability. This defense is troubling because there is no precise definition of when a contract is unconscionable. (See the box concerning unconscionability.)

Lawyers frequently distinguish between *substantive* and *procedural* unconscionability. Substantive unconscionability usually refers to a price that is utterly disproportionate to market value. In contrast, procedural unconscionability consists of circumstances and procedures in the bargain that violate widely-accepted norms of fairness. Thus, substantive unconscionability refers to the *terms* or *results* of the contract whereas procedural unconscionability refers to the *circumstances* and *procedures* under which the contract was formed. Substantive and procedural unconscionability are often combined in actual cases because an unfair procedure frequently results in an unfair price. Instead of thinking of substantive and procedural unconscionability as two types of cases, it is better to think of them as different aspects of the same case.

As originally conceived, the doctrine of unconscionability had special application in cases involving buying on credit by the poor, where one of the parties is economically disadvantaged and lacking in bargaining skill. A famous case illustrating this situation is *Williams v. Walker-Thomas Furniture Co.,* 350 F.2d 445 (D.C. Cir. 1965), in which a contractual term called an "add-on" clause was held to be unconscionable.[10] Add-on clauses arise in consumer credit transactions. The circumstances are that a consumer wishes to purchase a durable good from a retailer and to borrow the money to make that purchase. Naturally, the lender-retailer wants some assurance that he will be repaid. To allay his fears on that score he takes some collateral or security for the loan from the borrower. In the event that the borrower defaults on the loan, the lender can take possession of the collateral, sell it, and use some or all of the proceeds of the sale to discharge the principal and interest due on the debt and any costs of collecting the debt.[11]

The add-on clause specifies that any goods that the borrower has previously purchased from the lender-retailer will serve as security or collateral for the current purchase. This is somewhat unusual in that in most consumer loans of this sort the lender requires only the currently purchased good as security. To illustrate, if the buyer previously purchased a refrigerator on an installment plan requiring 24 monthly payments, and the buyer, who is now

---

[10]The discussion follows the treatment of the add-on clause in Epstein, *Unconscionability: A Critical Reappraisal,* 18 J. L. & ECON. 293 (1975).

[11]By statute, the repossessor is limited to this recovery. For a fascinating discussion of the economics of repossession, *see* Schwartz, *The Enforceability of Security Interests in Consumer Goods,* 26 J. L. & ECON. 117 (1983).

Unconscionability: Rule or Blank Check?

The doctrine of unconscionability in contracts for the sale of goods was written into article 2 of the Uniform Commercial Code, which has been adopted by all but one of the United States. In addition, the semi-official Restatement of Contracts includes an account of this doctrine. Legal doctrines can prescribe a definite course of action in specified circumstances, or doctrines can authorize a broad exercise of discretion by the courts. Is the doctrine of unconscionability a rule or a blank check? Form your own opinion by reading these excerpts from the UCC and the Restatement of Contracts:

Uniform Commercial Code sec. 2-302 comment 1 (1977): "The basic test [of unconscionability] is whether . . . the clauses involved [in the contract]are so one-sided as to be unconscionable under the circumstances existing at the time of the making of the contract. . . The principle is one of the prevention of oppression and unfair surprise . . . and not of disturbance of allocation of risks because of superior bargaining power.

Restatement (Second) of Contracts (1979) sec. 208: "If a contract or term thereof is unconscionable at the time the contract is made, a court may refuse to enforce the contract, or may enforce the remainder of the contract without the unconscionable term, or may so limit the application of any unconscionable term as to avoid any unconscionable result.

Comment [These official comments are part of the **Restatement.**]: . . . c. **Overall imbalance.** Inadequacy of consideration does not of itself invalidate a bargain, but gross disparity in the values exchanged may be an important factor in a determination that a contract is unconscionable and may be sufficient ground, without more, for denying specific performance. . . Such a disparity may also corroborate indications of defects in

in the twentieth month, decides to purchase a new television on the installment plan, an add-on clause in the purchase agreement for the television entitles the seller to repossess both the television and the refrigerator in the event that the buyer fails to make timely payments on the television.[12]

---

[12]Here is how the contract accomplishes this result. The add-on clause typically provides that the lender may use his discretion in applying each installment payment made with respect to *any* item purchased against whatever outstanding balance he chooses. In our example, the consumer would pay off the refrigerator in the 24th month if he had not purchased the television as well. The creditor, however, does not apply all of the 24th payment to the refrigerator. Instead, he applies part of it to the refrigerator and part of it to the television. As a result, the consumer cannot pay off the debt on the refrigerator and then pay off the debt on the television. Instead, it is not until he makes the last payment on both of them that he removes the creditor's lien on either of them. The apportioning of payments allows the retailer-lender to retain his security interest in all the goods previously purchased until the debts with respect to all those items are finally discharged.

the bargaining process. . . Theoretically, it is possible for a contract to be oppressive taken as a whole, even though there is no weakness in the bargaining process and no single term which is in itself unconscionable. Ordinarily, however, an unconscionable contract involves other factors as well as overall imbalance. . .

d. **Weakness in the bargaining process.** A bargain is not unconscionable merely because the parties to it are unequal in bargaining position, nor even because the inequality results in an allocation of risks to the weaker party. But gross inequality of bargaining power, together with terms unreasonably favorable to the stronger party, may confirm indications that the transaction involved elements of deception or compulsion, or may show that the weaker party had no meaningful choice, nor real alternative, and hence did not in fact assent or appear to assent to the unfair terms. . .''

In the preceding sections of this chapter, we have met some forms of advantage-taking—coercion, incompetency, fraud and misrepresentation—that are so outrageous that nearly everyone agrees that in addition to their being inefficient, they are also inequitable. Moreover, we have seen that the trend is for modern courts to expand the traditional formation defenses to classify more kinds of advantage-taking as unacceptable. Unconscionability is clearly part of this trend, but no one is entirely clear what additional forms of advantage-taking are captured in the formation defense of unconscionability. For this reason, there is no settled body of cases or doctrine to which we may turn to discuss the economic issues in the formation defense of unconscionability. Instead, we must cull the reported cases to see the variegated circumstances and terms that the courts have deemed unconscionable in the last quarter century.

The court in *Williams* found the add-on clause to be unconscionable because it seemed to be so one-sidedly in favor of the retailer and because it worked a particular hardship on poor consumers. The court argued that poor consumers are unlikely to understand what they are letting themselves in for when they agree to something as complicated as an add-on clause. Because they probably did not fully understand the consequences of what they were signing, the court implied that the poor consumers might not be engaging in a truly beneficial transaction.[13] The court felt that the worst consequence of the add-on clause was the possibility that a single default with respect to a single payment for any of the goods bought from the retailer

---

[13]For a clearer idea of why they might not have understood the terms, see the quotation from the contract and the discussion of it below.

Small Differences and Large Consequences

As we saw in Chapter 3, precedents set in past cases influence subsequent decisions by courts. Depending on whether the precedent is with them or against them, lawyers try to demonstrate to the court that the facts in the case in dispute are the same as in previous cases or that they are different. When the demonstration succeeds in convincing judges that the facts are different, the precedential force of an earlier decision does not affect the case at hand.

One of the values of economic analysis in the law is that it can frequently help to provide a basis for making distinctions between similar and different cases. This is particularly important in an area of the law that is as vague as unconscionability. Three important California cases concerning unconscionability are sketched below. The first two have already been decided in favor of the plaintiff. In the third dispute, the Supreme Court of California has directed a lower court to try the case.[1]

Graham v. Scissor-Tail, Inc., 28 Cal. 3d 807 (1981).

Bill Graham, an experienced concert promoter, entered into four contracts with a successful musician, Leon Russell, whose wholly-owned corporation is called Scissor-Tail. The four contracts were all prepared on an identical form supplied by the American Federation of Musicians (AFM). AFM enjoys a virtual monopoly on such contracts, so all similar contracts use the same form. The contract did not explicitly allocate any losses that might occur, but provided that any disputes arising out of the contract should be resolved by the International Executive Board of the AFM.

The first concert took place as scheduled, but there was a net loss of $63,000. The second concert earned a net profit of $98,000. The final two concerts were not actually carried out under Bill Graham because of a dispute with Russell over the first two. Graham claimed that he was entitled by contract and industry custom to offset the loss from the first concert with the profits from the second concert. Russell claimed that the contract required Graham to segregate the funds from the two concerts, that Graham must absorb the entire loss on the first concert and divide the full profits on the second concert according to a formula contained in the contract.

Graham sued Scissor-Tail for breach of contract, and the court ordered arbitration by the AFM. The union issued a decision for Scissor-

---

[1]When the plaintiff originally filed a complaint, the defendant demurred, stating that the facts alleged by the plaintiff do not constitute legal grounds for action. The trial court accepted the demurrer, and the plaintiff appealed. The Supreme Court of California decided the appeal for the plaintiff and remanded the case to the trial court for trial. An appeal of that decision to the U.S. Supreme Court was lost by the defendant. So, after all this maneuvering, the plaintiff has won the right to a trial on the merits of the case.

Tail without a hearing. Graham protested and a hearing was held before a "referee" appointed by the union president. Scissor-Tail prevailed again. Graham then sued Scissor-Tail on the grounds of "procedural unconscionability." The specific allegation was that the provision in the contract designating one party's union as arbitrator fails to achieve the level of basic integrity required of a contractually structured substitute for a court trial. Graham won the suit.

A & M Produce Co. v. FMC Corp., 135 Cal. App. 3d 473 (1982).

A & M, a farming company solely owned by C. Alex Abatti, decided to try growing a new crop: tomatoes. For this purpose he required equipment, known as "weight-sizing equipment," to sort and pack the tomatoes. One supplier, Decco Equipment Company, told Abatti that, in addition to the weight-sizing equipment, he would need a hydrocooler to preserve the crop during processing, and the total cost would be $60,000 to $68,000. Another supplier, the FMC Corporation, said that a hydrocooler was unnecessary because their equipment would process the crop quickly. Abatti decided to buy the FMC equipment, paying $32,000. The contract of sale contained a "warranty disclaimer" denying FMC's liability for any losses that might occur as a consequence of defects in the equipment.

The machinery was installed but, when the tomatoes ripened, the result was a disaster: the entire crop was lost. A & M sued to recover the crop's value and the cost of the equipment. FMC defended on the grounds that the warranty limited their liability. The court accepted Abatti's argument that the warranty disclaimer was procedurally and substantively unconscionable.[2]

Perdue v. Crocker National Bank, 38 Cal. 3d 913 (1985).

Perdue maintained a checking account with Crocker Bank. He wrote a check that "bounced" because the funds in his account were less than the amount of the check. Crocker charged Perdue $6 for processing the bounced check. Perdue claims that it only costs Crocker 30 cents to process bounced checks. (The true cost of check-processing is difficult to determine.) Perdue sued Crocker on behalf of all checking account holders (this is called a "class action," with the class being all checking account holders) to recover damages on the theory that the discrepancy

---

[2]See the discussion of the economics of warranties in Chapter 9.

between the charge and its costs is unconscionable. The trial court decided for Crocker without a trial, but, on appeal, the California Supreme Court found that Perdue is entitled to a trial.

Question 7.12: Imagine that you are the lawyer defending Crocker against Perdue. How would you distinguish your case from *Scissor-Tail* and *A & M* on economic grounds? Approach the problem by considering the nature of the alleged market failure in each case.

could trigger the repossession of *all* the goods. So, if the consumer missed a payment on her television, she jeopardized not only her continued use of the television, but also that of the refrigerator, stove, couch, and so on. Because poor consumers are much more likely to be laid off from work, to become ill, and in other ways to default, the court thought this clause worked an unconscionable hardship on them.

There is a disagreement between lawyers and economists over cases like this one that is all too predictable. Courts identify a term of a contract or a condition of its formation as unconscionable. As soon as they have done so, an economist demonstrates that although the term or condition may sound harsh, nevertheless it makes perfect economic sense as, for example, a device for efficiently allocating some particular risk. In *Williams,* the consequences of a missed payment under the add-on clause are harsh. But the court gave very little weight to the benefits that the clause confers on consumers, especially on poor but creditworthy consumers. Nor did it consider the consequences to consumers of making the add-on clause unavailable in the future.

In seeking an economic explanation for the add-on clause, let us begin by asking why a retailer-lender would insert such a clause. The first step is to understand why the retailer-lender wishes previously-purchased goods to be part of the collateral for the current purchase. This is really two questions: first, why is some additional collateral needed? And, second, why the particular collateral of goods previously purchased from this retailer?

Consumer durables typically lose value faster than the purchase price is paid off. For example, it is a truism that a new car loses a significant fraction of its value the instant it leaves the dealer's lot. There are some plausible reasons for this rapid decline in value, not the least of which is that once the good leaves the dealer's hands it is subject to abusive use by the consumer. The lender requires some protection in these circumstances; in the event that he must repossess the good from a defaulting borrower, the rapid decline in the good's value makes it less likely that the lender can recover the full amount due him if his only recourse is to resell the used good. For that reason, consumer installment loans are usually for less than the full value of the good purchased. Consumers must come up with the difference between the amount of the loan and the purchase price—this difference is frequently called a "down payment"—from other sources.

But what about the consumer who has no other sources from which to get the down payment? This borrower must offer some other form of collateral in lieu of a down payment if the deal is to go through. Thus, the answer to the first of the two questions we posed is that additional collateral is needed because some consumers cannot offer the seller a down payment as a protection against the seller's risk of loss from borrower-purchaser default.

The second question asked why the retailer preferred the additional collateral to take the form of goods previously purchased from him. The simple answer is that these goods are likely to be the most valuable collateral the consumer has as security for a loan from this particular lender. Because he sells the items, the lender-seller has a good idea of their resale value. And because he knows their resale value, the risk he assumes from loaning the money to make the current purchase is less. That fact translates into a lower cost for the loan to the borrower. In that sense, then, the borrower benefits from the add-on clause: it lowers his borrowing cost when he has no money for a down payment or no other good security.

Finally, we may ask about the consequences of holding the add-on clause unconscionable. For the creditworthy poor who would prefer to offer previously purchased goods as collateral instead of making a large down payment in cash, the unavailability after *Williams v. Walker-Thomas Furniture Co.* of the add-on clause may make them worse off. Their borrowing costs may increase, and that may cause them to purchase fewer consumer goods than they otherwise would. Those retailers who offered the add-on clause in an attempt to lower the costs of consumer credit may also be made worse off by the D.C. Circuit's holding. Their sales may decline or their costs may rise, in either case reducing their profit.

We have explained why some poor consumers will be worse off as a result of the decision in the *Williams* case. But for those consumers who would not have understood the complexities of the add-on clause and would not make future purchases under it if they did, the holding that the clause is unconscionable may spare them some losses they might have suffered. How are these two considerations to be balanced? Lawyers tend to focus upon individual cases, and this may sometimes create a bias toward finding some form of relief. To illustrate, Mrs. Williams was a single mother of seven children with limited education who found the Walker-Thomas Furniture Company laying claim to most of the household goods she had purchased from it under fourteen contracts over a five-year period. In such individual cases, the consumer's situation is desperate, and the impulse to provide legal relief is powerful. In contrast, economists tend to focus upon statistics, not individuals, and it is clear that paternalistic protection of people like Mrs. Williams by legal restrictions on the credit market imposes high costs on poor consumers as a class.[14]

Unconscionability cases like *Williams* involve a buyer from a disadvantaged background who wishes to purchase a household item on a credit contract. There are, however, many cases in which the purchase is not on credit, nor is the buyer from a disadvantaged background. The State of California

---

[14]This same dispute has been replayed over many years with respect to usury laws, which economists oppose and much of the consuming public favors.

has been a leader in extending the unconscionability doctrine to such new areas. The box on "Small Differences" describes such extensions in three recent California cases and suggests an economic analysis of them.

Read the description of the cases and then put yourself in the position of a lawyer whose task is to distinguish the third case from the two previous cases on economic grounds.

Unconscionability is a doctrine without a clear set of rules. In an important recent article, Professor Eisenberg has attempted to provide a unifying set of rules by identifying four instances of unconscionable contracts that, he argues, should not be enforced on efficiency or equitable grounds even though they would survive scrutiny under the traditional common law formation defences.[15] We will examine these four instances to get a sense of how rules might be imposed in this area.

The first instance Professor Eisenberg calls "distress," which he distinguishes from coercion or duress by the fact that the promisor was not put into his distressful state by the promisee. Consider this example:

> *T*, a symphony musician, has been driving through the desert on a recreational trip, when he suddenly hits a rock jutting out from the sand. *T*'s vehicle is disabled and his ankle fractured. He has no radio and little water, and will die if he is not soon rescued. The next day, *G*, a university geologist who is returning to Tucson from an inspection of desert rock formations, adventitiously passes within sight of the accident and drives over to investigate. *T* explains the situation and asks *G* to take him back to Tucson, which is sixty miles away. *G* replies that he will help only if *T* promises to pay him two-thirds of his wealth or $100,000, whichever is more. *T* agrees, but after they return to Tucson he refuses to keep his promise, and *G* brings an action to enforce it.

There is apparently no efficiency argument for enforcing the contract to its full extent; but there is no efficiency argument for voiding the contract either. Professor Eisenberg suggests that instead of voiding the contract or enforcing it to its full extent, the court should enforce *T*'s promise to *G* but only for the value of the services *G* rendered—the opportunity cost of his efforts—plus a bonus, say 20%. The reason for including the bonus is that the fact that a court will award more than opportunity costs in these instances should provide a mild inducement to future rescuers to seek out and help stranded travelers.

The second instance of unconscionability that Professor Eisenberg identifies is "transactional incapacity." This, he argues, describes a situation beyond the traditional defense of incompetence. Here the focus is on a highly complex transaction for which an individual, even one of average intelligence, may "lack the aptitude, experience, or judgmental ability to make a deliberate and well-informed judgment concerning the desirability of entering into a given complex transaction." Consider an example from a case we have already discussed, *Williams v. Walker-Thomas Furniture Co.* This is the language in which the buyer learns of the aspect of the add-on

---

[15]Eisenberg, *The Bargain Principle and Its Limits*, 95 HARV L. REV. 741 (1982).

clause by which the seller can apply each installment payment against any outstanding balance he chooses:

> *"[T]he amount of each periodical installment payment to be made by [purchaser] to the Company under this present lease shall be inclusive of and not in addition to the amount of each installment payment to be made by [purchaser] under such prior leases, bills, or account; and all payment now and hereafter made by [purchaser] shall be credited pro rata on all outstanding leases, bills, and accounts due the Company by [purchaser] at the time each such payment is made."*

This is tough sledding, even when you already know what it means.

The third instance of unconscionability identified by Professor Eisenberg is "unfair persuasion." By this he means "the use of bargaining methods that seriously impair the free and competent exercise of judgment and produce a state of acquiescence that the promisee knows or should know is likely to be highly transitory." This may be illustrated by the facts in *Odorizzi v. Bloomfield School District*, 246 Cal. App. 2d 123, 54 Cal. Rptr. 533 (1966). The plaintiff Odorizzi was an elementary school teacher who had been arrested for violating criminal statutes against homosexual activity. He was questioned, booked, and released on bail, in the process going forty hours without sleep. Two school officials visited him immediately after he returned to his apartment and informed him that if he did not resign his teaching position immediately, they would publicize his arrest, thereby making it difficult for him to find a new teaching position elsewhere. If Odorizzi would agree to resign immediately, the officials promised that the arrest would not be publicized. Odorizzi resigned, and the criminal charges were later dismissed. He then brought an action against the school board to be reinstated, arguing, essentially, that unfair persuasion had been used to induce him to resign. The court held that he was entitled to reinstatement.

The final instance of unconscionability proposed by Professor Eisenberg is "price ignorance." An example is the case of *Toker v. Westerman*, 113 N.J.Super. 452 A.2d 78 (N.J.D.C., 1970), in which the defendant paid $899.98 for a refrigerator freezer whose sale value was apparently between $350 and $400. The reason for proposing this as an unconscionability defense is that one of the conditions for a perfectly competitive market and, therefore, for perfect contracts is that information about prices is readily and inexpensively available. Professor Eisenberg suggests that where sellers take advantage of buyers by exploiting their ignorance about alternative sources of supply, the contract of sale should be voided on the grounds of unconscionable behavior by the seller. An example would be the advantage sometimes taken of consumers by door-to-door salesmen. To combat this sort of high-pressure sales tactic, many states have statutes that grant consumers a "cooling off period"—typically three days—during which they may back out of a contract with a door-to-door salesman.

Eisenberg has proposed four grounds for unconscionability:

1. distress,	3. unfair persuasion, and
2. transactional incapacity,	4. price ignorance.

How successful these conditions would prove to be in practice is unclear, but at least Professor Eisenberg is trying to give specific content to the doctrine of unconscionability and to develop the doctrine by reference to an economic theory of market failures.

Question 7.13:

a. Suppose that Eisenberg's four conditions were adopted by courts as a complete theory of unconscionability. Apply those conditions to the following cases to see whether the contract was unconscionable by one or more of Eisenberg's standards: *Williams v. Walker-Thomas Furniture Co.; Graham v. Scissor-Tail; A & M v. FMC;* and *Perdue v. Crocker.*

b. Under what circumstances would you allow a consumer to void a contract as unconscionable because he was unfairly persuaded by a newspaper, circular, or television advertisement to purchase the good? Would you ever allow a consumer who had purchased a good or service on the basis of an advertised price to void the contract on the grounds of unconscionable price ignorance?

c. Suppose that you buy a new car and the automatic transmission—one of the "extras"—costs you an additional $450. Should you be able to sue the manufacturer and make him prove that $450 is not disproportionately above the actual cost of the automatic transmission? How costly would it be for manufacturers to have to document that their prices are in line with their costs? In the end, would these costs be paid by consumers or by manufacturers? How good are courts likely to be at deciding such disputes?

Conspicuously absent from Professor Eisenberg's list is the usual grounds for procedural unconscionability: grossly unequal bargaining power. In the model of bargaining developed in Chapter 4, we characterized bargains as agreements for mutual advantage. Eisenberg focuses upon the absolute value of the weaker party's threat point (distress), lack of bargaining skill (transactional incapacity), improper bargaining techniques (unfair persuasion), and asymmetric information (price ignorance), but not upon the relative bargaining power of the parties. The problem with focusing upon unequal bargaining power is that even unequal bargains are often mutually beneficial. By creating legal obstacles to unequal bargains, the court may hope to induce more equal bargains, but, in fact, the court may prevent any bargains of a particular type, thereby forcing many parties to forego the surplus from cooperation. It is an unfortunate fact that legal thinking about unequal bargaining is rife with confusion, as the box on contracts of adhesion illustrates.

Question 7.14: In a recent English case, the plaintiff, a 21-year old songwriter, had signed a contract in 1966 with the defendant, a music publisher. The contract was a standard form and assigned the copyrights of all the plaintiff's output to the defendant company in return for the defendant's agreement to pay 50% of the net royalties to the plaintiff. The contract was to run for five years and to be automatically renewed for another five years if the plaintiff's royalties during the first term exceeded 5,000 pounds sterling. The defendant company could terminate the contract on one month's notice and could assign the contract and any copyrights held under it without the plaintiff's consent. The plaintiff had no right to terminate and could assign his contractual interests with the defendant's consent. For signing the contract, the plaintiff received 50 pounds as an advance against future royalties. The plaintiff had become a successful songwriter and sought to be released from the contract on the grounds that it was unconscionably one-sided in the music publisher's favor. *Macaulay v. Schroeder Publishing Co. Ltd.,* [1974] 1 W.L.R. 1308 (H.L.).

Are the terms of this contract such that it must have resulted from grossly unequal bargaining power?

B. Performance Excuses

In the previous section we considered defects in the formation of contracts that can defeat the attempt to create a legal obligation. Now we turn from defenses to excuses. Here the defendant admits that a valid contract was formed, but he contends that changed circumstances since the formation of the contract should excuse him from his obligation to perform.

There are at least three types of changed circumstances that may excuse performance on a contract. First, the change in circumstances may *destroy the purpose* of the contract. To illustrate, as mentioned in the previous chapter, a coronation parade was planned for June, 1902 in London and many owners of property along the parade route leased rooms for the day to people wishing to observe the ceremony. However, illness in the royal family caused the parade to be postponed. Many who had rented the rooms overlooking the parade route refused to pay the rent, and some of the property owners sought to enforce the contracts. The courts held that the contracts were unenforceable because their purpose was destroyed by postponement of the ceremony.[16] Second, a change in circumstances may render performance *physically impossible.* An example arises when an opera singer develops laryngitis on the day of the promised performance. Third, a change in circumstances could render performance *commercially impracticable.* This might arise where a contractor who has been hired to dig a well runs into a sheet of rock that he could penetrate only at ruinous cost.

The economic question in performance excuses, as with many of the formation defenses, is the efficient assignment of risk. The law must determine, *ex post,* how to allocate the risk of a particular contingency that has arisen. In easy cases, there is an explicit allocation of the risk in the language of the contract and there is no market failure in the bargain, so the court can simply enforce the contract. In hard cases, neither the language of the contract nor the custom of the trade covers the allocation of risk for that contingency.

The court's problem in hard cases is, as it were, to fill in the terms missing from an incomplete contract. When a bargain is reached, the contract

---

[16]See, for example, *Krell v. Henry*, 2 K.B. 740 (1903).

Fill in a Form: Contracts of Adhesion

Most written contracts employ standard forms that limit the capacity of the parties to vary the terms. When a business insists upon a standard form contract, the other party's choice is to adhere to its terms or not have a contract. In an influential article, Friedrich Kessler criticized such bargains as being "contracts of adhesion."[1]

This phrase has worked its way into the fabric of law, especially in the area of unconscionability.

A contract of adhesion is a contract offered on a take-it-or-leave-it basis. We are invited to imagine a large corporation whose legal staff has prepared a form contract that is presented to consumers by its representatives, who lack the authority to vary the terms. Perhaps the terms are standard across an entire industry so that the disgruntled consumer has no alternative source of supply. Almost all automobile manufacturers, for instance, agree to repair certain problems with their new cars if those problems develop within the first five years or 50,000 miles of the car's life.

There are two opposing views of standard forms. On the one hand, they are said to be devices for raising costs to consumers by artificially restricting the consumer's choices. To the extent that the standard form contract is the result of collusion by the members of the industry, the standard form is inefficient for the same reasons that any monopoly is inefficient. The restriction benefits each producer in the industry by removing an area of competition. In the automobile warranty example, suppose that the technology of production is such that none of the warranted problems is likely to develop for seven years but that, thereafter, the probability of the sorts of problems covered by the warranty rises rapidly. By restricting the standard coverage to five years, the firms relieve themselves of the costs of making some repairs that, in a competitive market, might be covered under a warranty.

usually allocates some risks explicitly and omits mention of many other risks. How explicit is an efficient contract? Does it, for example, cover the allocation of every conceivable contingency? Clearly not. Inserting an additional contingency explicitly into a contract often improves the allocation of risk, which is a benefit. But greater explicitness requires additional drafting and negotiation, which is a cost. So, a contract is efficiently drafted when the benefit from the explicit allocation of risk from one more contingency is just offset by the cost of including the additional terms. This means that even in an efficient contract, there will be some risks that are not explicitly allocated.

When a risk materializes that is not explicitly allocated, the court must intervene. The question is, "In what way should it intervene?" To illustrate,

On the other hand, there are some powerful reasons for believing that this anti-competitive explanation for standard form contracts is inaccurate. First, *any* form of collusion among independent firms to establish a joint monopoly (that is, a cartel) is difficult. Moreover, even to the extent that independent firms are able to collude to offer an anti-competitive set of some contract terms, they may continue to compete over *other* contract terms, such as price, after-sale service, showroom accommodations, and so on. This competition may be so vigorous as to make the inefficiencies of the standard form contract insignficant. Second, standard form contracts in competitive industries may promote efficiency by saving both consumers and producers the transaction costs of designing special contracts on a sale-by-sale basis. One of the standard assumptions of a perfectly competitive market is that transaction costs are nil. Standard form contracts can, by greatly reducing transaction costs, move a market closer to the perfectly competitive ideal. Furthermore, under conditions of perfect competition there are many sellers offering the good on the same terms, so the fact that many firms use the same standard form may indicate a high level of competition.

The term "contract of adhesion" suggests that standard form contracts indicate monopoly power and market imperfections, whereas the same facts may indicate perfectly cornpetitive markets. That is why economists find this term unhelpful and misleading. To be specific, the fact that a contract was made on a standard form does not and should not establish a presumption that it is, or might be, unconscionable.[2]

[1]Friedrich Kessler, *Contracts of Adhesion—Some Thoughts About Freedom of Contract,* 43 COLUM. L. REV. 629 (1943).
[2]The economics of standard contract terms is pursued at greater length in our discussion of warranties in Chapter 9.

suppose that a contract to supply goods is silent, as most are, about the consequences of an increase in the cost of performance. Because the contract does not explicitly excuse the seller in the event of a modest increase in the cost of performance, such an increase will not provide him with a legal excuse for non-performance. When circumstances arise that are not explicitly contemplated by the contract, but the contract is enforced according to its terms, the contract is generally interpreted as if the omission were intentional. Allocations of risk that are intentional, but not explicit, may be called "implicit terms of the contract." This rule can lead to problems, especially if the contingency was not foreseeable at reasonable cost. But, in general, the rule of assuming that omissions were intentional is a good starting place for encouraging the efficient allocation of risk.

Sometimes the court can infer from the terms of the contract an implicit assignment of risk for the frustrating contingency. Consider a contract to drill for water on the buyer's property. Suppose that the driller runs into impenetrable rock and that the contract is silent on who should bear the cost of non-performance in the event of this contingency. Our rule of assuming an intentional allocation of risk when there is no explicit allocation in the contract would argue for not excusing the driller for non-performance. But there may be additional evidence, beyond our rule, that can be adduced for not excusing the driller. Suppose, for example, that the contract price is much higher than that offered by other, competing drillers. A plausible way to interpret this higher price is that the driller was selling to the buyer both his services as a driller and his guarantee, as an insurance underwriter, that he would be able to perform the contract in the event that rock or something else intervened. The part of the contract price attributable to the contractor's drilling services should be equal to that charged by his competitors, with the difference between the contract price and this competitive drilling price being interpretable as the premium on an insurance contract, underwritten by the driller. This arrangement will be the most efficient if the contractor is able to offer this insurance policy at a lower price than others. And there may be good reasons that he is a cheaper insurer than anyone else: he may have special expertise in well-drilling or be familiar with the subsurface rock in the area. In either case the driller has a competitive advantage that he is attempting to market by offering the buyer a joint drilling and insurance contract. Thus, in the event of non-performance by the contractor where the contract price is interpretable as above, the court may interpret the document as having assigned the risk to the driller and should, therefore, not excuse him from performing the contract.

In contrast, there are some contingencies that are not explicitly or implicitly allocated in the contract, which we call "missing terms." Sometimes the missing terms were contemplated by both parties but the cost of achieving agreement over them exceeds the perceived benefit. Sometimes the missing terms were contemplated by only one party and that party had reasons for not raising the issue with the other party. And sometimes the missing terms were contemplated by neither party. Some small probability events are not foreseeable at reasonable cost, so a reasonable investment in information will not bring these events to the attention of either party.

Whenever terms are missing, there was no agreement or understanding between the parties over allocating a risk. So the courts cannot assume an implicit allocation of risk by inquiring into the intentions of the parties. Instead, the missing terms must be filled in by the courts using some other considerations. When terms are missing from a contract, the defendant will typically seek to be excused from performance by invoking one of the performance excuses—destruction of purpose, impossibility, and commercial impracticability. The court must then fill in the contract by determining whether any of these excuses applies. To do so, the court must have some theory of the purposes of contract law. The theory that we will be developing is that courts should fill in the contract with performance excuses that achieve the efficient allocation of risk.

If the aim of the courts is to allocate the risk of the frustrating contingency efficiently, then the rule that they should apply in interpreting the performance excuses is this: *assign liability for the loss to the party that was the cheaper preventer of, or insurer against, the contingency that frustrated the contract.* This rule has the advantage of minimizing the burden such risks impose upon contracts and also of minimizing the total cost to society created by such risks. Besides this social goal, the rule can be defended as a reasonable reconstruction of the will of the parties. It is likely, but not absolutely certain, that the parties would have assigned the risk of the frustrating contingency, had they thought to assign it, to this cheaper party. This is because it was in the contracting parties' mutual interest to have done so. Therefore, this allocation corresponds to the putative intentions of the parties, where the imputation is based upon a rational reconstruction of their self-interest.

This rule, then, requires the court to inquire into the prevention and insurance costs of the two parties. This is a factual matter about which reasonable people can differ, but this interpretation of the defense of impossibility has the great virtue of focusing on the precise factual determination that the court should undertake. Let's consider that determination in more detail.

1. Impossibility   At common law, impossibility was not, in general, a valid excuse for not performing a contractual promise. Despite this general position, there were three commonly recognized exceptions that developed between the 17th and 19th centuries. The first is that the defendant would be excused, if between the time of the formation of the promise and its performance, the performance was declared to be illegal, either statutorily or by administrative or judicial decision. For example, during the Second World War a domestic railroad that had contracted to carry copra intended for export to the Norwegian government was excused from performing when the federal government, in response to the attack on Pearl Harbor, ordered the railroad to carry wood instead of the copra.[17] The second exception to the common law rule that impossibility was no excuse was that, where the contractual promise required performance by the promisor himself, then the promisee could not maintain an action for breach when the cause of nonperformance was the promisor's death.[18] Consider the example of a contract between a patron and a famous portrait painter to paint the patron's por-

---

[17]*L.N. Jackson & Co. v. Royal Norwegian Govt.,* 177 F.2d 694 (2d Cir. 1949), *cert. den.,* 339 U.S. 914 (1950).

[18]Note that this exception, as in the example given, most typically involves the promise to provide personal services. The law, both common and statutory, has frequently been reluctant to compel performance of personal service contracts under any circumstances. The reasons for this reluctance are discussed more fully in the section below on specific performance.

trait. That contract would be discharged by the painter's death or illness. However, a contract to paint a house would usually not be discharged because of the illness or death of the house painter. The usual explanation for this distinction is that there are numerous substitutes available to the promisee in the case of the house painter but that the personal services of the portrait painter are unique and, therefore, impossible to replace. The third exception was that, "if the existence of a particular thing is necessary for a party's performance, the party is excused if the destruction or deterioration of that thing prevents performance."[19] For example, a contract to deliver a corn crop is void if, because of horrible weather, the crop never matures. This list of three items has expanded in recent years as courts have generally become more willing to fashion remedies for plaintiffs.

To see how our rule for dealing with performance excuses might be applied to a concrete example, let's consider a modern case, *Tsakiroglou & Co. Ltd. v. Noble Thorl G.m.b.H.,*[20] in which impossibility was raised by the defendant. In October, 1956, a company in the Sudan signed a contract to sell a large quantity of peanuts to a West German firm. The parties used a standard form contract, one of the clauses of which read as follows:

> *In case of prohibition of import or export or war, epidemic or strike, and in all cases of force majeure preventing the shipment within the time fixed, or the delivery, the period allowed for shipment or delivery shall be extended by not exceeding two months. After that, if the case of force majeure be still operating, the contract shall be cancelled.*

On October 29, 1956, the Israelis invaded Egypt. Shortly thereafter the British and French moved into the area with the result that the Suez Canal was closed from November 2, 1956, till April 9, 1957. The sellers claimed that the contract was at an end because, following the clause above, the war and closure of the canal made shipment impossible. The West German buyers contended that shipment was not impossible, simply more costly, and that because the contract charged the seller with arranging insurance and freight, a so-called "c.i.f. contract," the seller was obliged to make good on the contract.

At an arbitration hearing it was determined that the peanuts could have been shipped from Port Sudan to Hamburg via the Cape of Good Hope, rather than via the more direct and customary route from Port Sudan through the Suez Canal. The distance via the Cape is almost 700 miles longer than the customary route. After the canal was closed, shippers adjusted by offering to carry trade from East Africa around the Cape of Good Hope. They based the rate for that alternative on the prevailing, but unavailable, Port Sudan-Suez shipping rate, imposing a surcharge as fol-

---

[19]RESTATEMENT (SECOND) OF CONTRACTS sec. 263 (1979). The rule holds if the thing necessary to performance never comes into existence.

[20]House of Lords, [1962] A.C. 93.

lows: 25 per cent of the Suez rate after November 10, 1956, and 100 per cent of that rate after December 13, 1956.

Under the terms of the contract, the seller (Tsakiroglou) was responsible for paying the shipping charges. Thus, because of the canal blockage and the surcharge on the alternative shipping route, he stood to make a great deal less on the contract than what he had anticipated making when the contract was formed. Naturally, he was eager to find a plausible reason for voiding the contract. The doctrine of impossibility presented such an opportunity.

Recall that the economic interpretation of that doctrine involves a multi-step process. First, the court must determine whether the risk of the frustrating contingency was *explicitly* allocated to one of the parties in the contract; if so, the contract is enforced according to those explicit terms. But second, if there is no explicit allocation, the court must determine whether the risk of the frustrating contingency was *implicitly* assigned to one of the parties in the terms of the contract (for example, by comparing the contract price with the competitive price); if such an implicit allocaton was made, the contract should be enforced according to that implicit allocation. But finally, failing either an explicit or implicit allocation of the risk, the court must determine which party was the cheaper preventer of, or insurer against, the frustrating contingency and allocate the risk, *ex post*, to that party. If the cheaper preventer of or insurer against the frustrating contingency was the *defendant*, the court should not excuse him from performance. If the cheaper preventer of or insurer against the frustrating contingency was the *plaintiff*, the court should excuse the defendant from performance.

In *Tsakiroglou* the contract, because it assigns cost, insurance, and freight to the seller, seems *implicitly* to assign to the seller the risk that any additional expenses of shipping the good to the buyer would fall on the seller in the event that the customary shipping route would be closed. This is in fact how the House of Lords interpreted the contract.

But suppose that it was not possible to find within the terms of the contract any help in determining how the parties assigned this risk. What should the court have done in those circumstances? The relevant question is, "Which of the parties was the cheaper preventer of or insurer against the frustrating contingency that the customary Suez route would be unavailable by reason of war?" Notice that there is nothing that either party could have done to prevent this contingency. Thus, the question boils down to one of determining which party was the cheaper insurer against this particular risk. And the answer would seem to be that the seller was the superior risk-bearer here. Consider these reasons why. First, the shipper-seller was a Sudanese firm and the shipment was to be made from Port Sudan, in his home country. Certainly, he would know far more about the alternative shipping routes from that port to Europe than would the buyer, a West German firm. Additionally, the seller was likely to have had extensive experience in the trade of shipping his output from East Africa to Europe and to have had, therefore, better information on the shipping market than the buyer would have had. Lastly, being located closer to the Middle East, the seller probably knew more about the volatile political conditions there than did the buyer; specifically, he might have been expected to have had a better idea about the possibility of war and of the closure of the Suez Canal in the event of war and, therefore, was more likely than the buyer to have had advance warning about the necessity to arrange an alternative delivery date or route. Therefore, if these parties had contemplated the contingency that has arisen, they probably would have assigned its risk to the seller. He could have been more cheaply insured against this cause of frustration of the contract, and so the cost of effecting this mutually beneficial exchange would have been lower—and thus, the contract more likely to have been formed—if the parties agreed to let the seller bear the risk.

> **Question 7.15:** What general factors enable one party to prevent a risk better than another? What general factors enable one party to insure against a risk better than another? Do these factors tend to converge, diverge, or is their association merely coincidental?

> **Question 7.16:** In the famous case of *Taylor v. Caldwell*, 3 B. & S. 826, 122 Eng. Rep. 309 (K.B. 1863), the plaintiff had leased the defendant's concert hall for four nights at 100 pounds sterling to be paid to Caldwell after each night's performance. Shortly after the first performance, the concert hall was destroyed by fire. Taylor sued Caldwell for breach of contract and asked the court to award him as damages the expenses he had incurred in preparation for the last three performances. The defendant sought to be excused from performing on the grounds that it was literally impossible for him to perform the contract after the fire.
>
> Using the economic analysis developed above, how would you decide this case?

2. Commercial Impracticability A newer version of the defense of impossibility is one called "commercial impracticability." This is not a common law defense; rather, it is one that has been codified in the Uniform Commercial Code, article 2, section 615.[21] The gist of this new performance excuse is to extend the impossibility excuse beyond physical impossibility to include *commercial* impracticability. In brief, commercial impracticability is meant to excuse a defendant from performing a contract when conditions have so changed since the contract's formation that the performance of the contract would threaten the commercial viability of the defendant.

This could be a sweeping extension of the performance excuses if there were not some constraints placed on a defendant who invokes this excuse for

---

[21]The relevant section reads as follows:

> Delay in delivery or non-delivery in whole or in part by a seller . . . is not a breach of his duty under a contract for sale if performance as agreed has been made impracticable by the occurrence of a contingency the non-occurrence of which was a basic assumption on which the contract was made. . . .

This formulation is distressingly vague. How difficult must performance be in order to rise to the level of the impracticable? What distinguishes the "basic" terms of a contract from the other terms?

non-performance. The official comments provided by the U.C.C. identify three conditions that must be met for a defendant to be excused from performance on the grounds of commercial impracticability:

1. the contingency must have been unforeseen and not within the contemplation of the parties,
2. "the risk of failure must not have been assumed either directly or indirectly by the party seeking excuse," and
3. the defendant must not have caused the changed circumstances that are his excuse.

The official comments also give examples falling within the scope of this defense—severe shortage of raw materials or supplies due to war, embargo, local crop failure, shutdown of major supplier—and examples falling outside the scope of this defense—a rise or collapse in the market. But the official comments stress the flexibility of the doctrine and the need to interpret it in light of its purposes. The commentators suggest that the purpose of the doctrine is, as we have said, to prevent performance under changed circumstances from threatening the commercial viability of the defendant. But to understand the economic logic of the doctrine, it is necessary to understand why the loss caused by a change in circumstances that renders performance of a promise commercially impracticable should fall upon the promisor rather than the promisee, and the U.C.C. gives no guidance at all on this point. The best that can be said is that the three constraints mentioned above on a defendant who invokes commercial impracticability restrict its use from a seemingly open-ended and vague set of circumstances to a potentially reasonable set of circumstances. But there still remains a distressing vagueness about the doctrine that is reminiscent of the vagueness surrounding the new formation defense of unconscionability.

The defense of impracticability figured centrally in a famous set of cases brought in the mid-1970s against the Westinghouse Corporation.[22] Westinghouse was one of several producers of nuclear reactors and was, in the early 1970s, attempting to persuade numerous public utilities to purchase reactors for the generation of electricity. The technology was new, and many of the utilities were not convinced that the nuclear generation of power was economically superior to the alternatives. In an effort to overcome these doubts among its potential customers and to out-compete other producers of nuclear reactors, Westinghouse hit upon the device of offering those utilities that purchased its reactors inexpensive uranium fuel. Specifically, Westinghouse agreed to supply those who bought its reactors with uranium at a fixed price of $8–10 per pound. This offer must been very attractive because by mid-1975 Westinghouse had sold enough reactors to public utilities that it had commitments to supply over 60 thousand tons of uranium to those utilities for the period 1975 to 1988.

---

[22]The following material is based on Joskow, *Commercial Impossibility, the Uranium Market, and the 'Westinghouse' Case,* 6 J. LEGAL STUD. 119 (1976).

Westinghouse's position as of January 1, 1975, was that, of the 60,000 tons promised, the company had an inventory of 6,000–7,000 tons and forward contracts to purchase another 14,000 tons. Thus, the company had a shortage of about 40,000 tons of uranium oxide, U_3O_8. Westinghouse first made this shortage public in July, 1975. By that time, the market price of uranium oxide had risen to more than $30 per pound. This meant that to cover its shortage Westinghouse would have had to incur losses of nearly $2 billion, which was more than half of the value of all of the company's assets. Completing the contracts to supply uranium at the price fixed in the early 1970s would, in essence, have led to Westinghouse's bankruptcy. Thus, it was not surprising that in September, 1975, the company announced that it would not honor its contracts to supply the uranium to the utilities at the announced price and was seeking to be excused for this breach on the grounds that, as specified in U.C.C. sec. 2–615, performance had become a commercial impracticability. Subsequently, most of the utilities filed actions for breach of contract and sought either specific performance or money damages from Westinghouse.[23]

If these actions had come to trial, should Westinghouse have been excused from its fixed-price contracts on the grounds of commercial impracticability? According to the U.C.C., the answer is apparently "No." A rise in the market is one of the conditions explicitly ruled out of the impracticability defense in the official comments.

This conclusion is reinforced by a scrutiny of some of the economic facts. First, Westinghouse's offer to supply the fuel to its customers at a fixed price was not, in itself, a bad idea. By serving as the central purchaser and distributor of so much uranium, the company could perhaps realize other economies of scale that individual utilities could not. And by specializing in this market, Westinghouse could achieve a better understanding of the risks than the individual utilities. In theory, the fixed price contracts for uranium may have been a good idea.

However, what is difficult to fathom is why Westinghouse took this good idea and managed it so poorly. At the heart of the matter is why the company left itself with so large a shortage by 1975. Its commitment to supply 40,000 tons of uranium that it did not have was an immense shortfall. In 1975 the total world production of uranium oxide was 13,000 tons, with the annual capacity of the world industry being 18,000–20,000 tons per year. Thus, Westinghouse had a shortage that was equal to two full years of the entire world's capacity or three years of its actual production. Moreover, the general expectation in the period 1970–72, when most of the fixed-price contracts were made, was that uranium prices would increase over the next decade or more. Almost no one believed that the price of uranium would fall. Of course, if it had fallen, Westinghouse's position to deliver at the fixed

---

[23]All of these actions have now been settled.

price would have meant extraordinarily large speculative profits for the company.

In view of the large size of this shortage, one wonders why the company did not take steps to protect itself against the disastrous consequences of a price increase in uranium oxide. There were several feasible actions that Westinghouse might have taken. First, it might have engaged in much more forward contracting for uranium; that is, it might have made many more contracts of its own with suppliers of uranium to purchase large quantities of the good in the future at fixed prices. Second, the company might have more intensively developed its own uranium reserves. Third, Westinghouse might have undertaken its own intensive price analyses to discover if the general market belief of an imminent price rise was reasonable. Lastly, the company could have originally negotiated, or subsequently renegotiated, its contracts with the utilities to include escalation clauses that, for example, tied the uranium prices to the general rate of inflation or to an index of commodity prices.

Westinghouse took none of these steps. This means that the three constraints that U.C.C. sec. 2-615 imposes on those seeking excuse by reason of commercial impracticability were not met in these cases. First of all, the contingency that gave rise to the defendant's claim of commercial impracticability—the rapid rise in the price of uranium—was not only *foreseeable*; it was widely *foreseen*. Secondly, the requirement that the defendant must not have willingly assumed the risk of the contingency that has come to pass is not met either. The only intelligible reason for the fixed-price contracts was to convince the utilities to buy Westinghouse reactors by agreeing to insure those utilities against upward fluctuations in the price of uranium. Thus, both parties knew or should have known who was bearing the risk of price increases for uranium. Finally, Westinghouse did nothing to lessen the adverse consequences of this foreseeable contingency, even after the company knew that its shortage was untenable. The only one of the U.C.C. conditions that the company satisfied was the one holding that the defendant cannot by his own actions have caused the event that made performance commercially impracticable.

Why did Westinghouse fail to take steps to protect itself from the disastrous consequences of a price increase? Professor Joskow suggests that Westinghouse may have failed to take these protective steps because it strongly believed a minority view about the future course of uranium prices. Under that view, the Atomic Energy Commission might decide to dump the considerable stockpile of uranium oxide that it was holding for purposes related to national defense, at the same time that the United States government ended its restriction on the importation of uranium. If both of these things had happened, then the resulting increase in the supply of uranium might have been sufficient to drive the price down much closer to the $8–10 per pound figure that Westinghouse had agreed to. But even if the company firmly believed this scenario, it still should have taken some steps to insure itself against losses from the scenario's not occurring.

None of the actions by the utilities against Westinghouse went to trial, perhaps because both sides recognized that the excuse of commercial impracticability would not prevail. The settlements between the utilities and Westinghouse generally involved an adjustment in the price at which Westinghouse agreed to supply uranium oxide such that Westinghouse and its customers shared the losses from the rise in the market price of uranium oxide.

The new doctrine of commercial impracticability is a distressingly vague extension of the traditional performance excuses. It is, like unconscionability among the formation defenses, a set of rules in search of justification. What is needed is an economic theory of this excuse that, beginning with the purpose of correcting market failure, attempts to develop a set of clear guidelines of commercial impracticability like those that Professor Eisenberg has proposed for unconscionability.

> **Question 7.17:** Suppose that the reason that the uranium oxide price rose was that the governments of the countries that were the leading producers of uranium had secretly formed a cartel and that that cartel effectively limited production and, thus, raised the price four-fold. Would the presence of this secret cartel excuse Westinghouse on the grounds of commercial impracticability?

II. THE ECONOMICS OF REMEDIES FOR BREACH OF CONTRACT

We turn now to a fuller economic consideration of the second great question that any theory of contracts must answer: What remedies should be available when a contract is broken? We will first briefly discuss the kinds of remedies available in law. Then we will develop an economic theory of these remedies.

A. An Overview of Remedies for Breach of Contract

When one of the parties to a contract fails to perform as promised, the contract has been broken or breached. The aggrieved party may go to court to have the contract enforced against the breaching party. The formation defenses and performance excuses that we discussed in the first part of this chapter will be raised and examined. If the court determines that the contract has been validly formed or that performance will not be excused, then it must proceed to fashion a remedy for the breach.

There are three broad remedies for breach that may be invoked. One is designed by the contracting parties; the other two are designed by the court that has been asked to adjudicate the breach.

The contracting parties themselves may have designated a remedy at the time the contract was formed and included that remedy as an explicit term in the contract. For example, party *A* may have agreed to pay party *B* $200 per day, up to a maximum of $5,000, for every day after September 1 that he failed to complete his performance of the contract. Alternatively, the parties, as in *Graham v. Scissor-Tail* discussed above, may have specified that in the event of non-performance by either of them, the matter is to be arbitrated by a designated person or group. In the event that the parties have designated their own remedy in the event of non-performance, the court's role may simply be to enforce that designated remedy.

The other two types of remedies for breach of contract are designed by the court. The first of the court-designed remedies is the payment of money damages, called "legal relief" or a "legal remedy," by the breacher to the innocent party. This is the usual court-designed remedy in breach cases. As we will see in much greater detail below, there are several different measures of money damages that the court may use in fashioning its award. The second of the court-designed remedies is specific performance, called "equitable relief." Specific performance is an order by the court to the breacher to perform the contractual promise. This is relatively rare as a remedy for breach of contract.

In the remainder of this chapter, we will develop an economic analysis of these remedies.[24]

B. Efficient Breach[25]

Before we analyze the remedies for breach of contract we need to develop a theory of what it is that we want a remedy for breach to accomplish. The notion of efficiency provides the benchmark that we will use to evaluate the remedies.

We may gain insight into the connecton between efficiency and breach of contract by relating breach to the bargaining costs we discussed in Chapter 4. Breach of contract can be regarded as something that happens as a consequence of the bargaining or transaction costs of forming contracts. If bargaining and drafting were costless, we could imagine that a contract would be created that explicitly provided for every contingency that could possibly arise. Included in the contract would be remedies for every type of

---

[24]It is worth mentioning, if only parenthetically, that society uses certain non-legal incentives to minimize the occurrence of breach of contract. Of these, one of the most powerful is the value of one's reputation. Because a reputation as a trustworthy contractual partner is sometimes valuable, a reputation as one who breaches contracts is detrimental and may restrain the impulse to engage in breach except in the most serious cases. Whether a regard for one's reputation induces breach only where it is efficient and not otherwise is not yet known. *See* Klein & Leffler, *The Role of Market Forces in Assuring Contractual Performance,* 89 J. POL. ECON. 615 (1981).

[25]Much of the materal in this and the next section is based on Ulen, *The Efficiency of Specific Performance: Toward a Unified Theory of Contract Remedies,* 84 MICH. L. REV. 358 (1984).

non-performance under every possible circumstance. Since every type of non-performance in every possible circumstance would have a remedy explicitly attached to it in the contract, there would be no occasion for the law to prescribe a remedy.

Because bargaining and drafting are costly, an efficient contract will not explicitly cover every contingency. In fact, the majority of contracts do not specify *any* remedies for breach. The existence of such gaps in contracts creates a need for the law to supply remedies.

One of the most enlightening insights of law and economics is the recognition that there are circumstances where breach of contract is more efficient than performance. We define an *efficient breach* as follows: *a breach of contract is more efficient than performance of the contract when the costs of performance exceed the benefits to all the parties.* We need to characterize the circumstances under which this will be true. The costs of performance exceed the benefits when a contingency arises such that the resources necessary for performance are more valuable in an alternative use. These contingencies come in two types. First, a *fortunate contingency* or *windfall* might arise that makes non-performance even more profitable than performance. Second, an *unfortunate contingency* or *accident* might arise that imposes a larger loss for performance than for non-performance.

To illustrate a windfall, suppose that *A* promises to sell a house to *B* for $100,000. Let us assume that *A* values living in the house at $90,000, and *B* values living in the house at $110,000. Thus, at *A*'s asking price, *A* realizes a seller's surplus of $10,000, *B* realizes a consumer's surplus of $10,000, and the total surplus from the exchange is $20,000. But suppose that before the sale is completed another buyer, *C*, appears on the scene and offers *A* $120,000 for the same house that he has contracted to sell to *B* for $100,000. *C*'s appearance is a windfall that has increased the total available surplus from $20,000 to at least $30,000.[26]

Economic efficiency will be served if resources are allocated to their highest-valued use, at the least cost of effecting the re-allocation. Thus, from an efficiency standpoint, contract law should specify a remedy for breach that will put the house in the hands of the person who values it the most, *C*, and effectuate this result at the lowest possible resource cost. For example, the law might require *A* to sell to *B*, in which case *B* would resell to *C*; or, alternatively, the law might permit *A* to breach the original contract, pay damages to *B* and sell the house directly to *C*. Later we will return to this example in order to consider whether the remedies actually provided in contract law achieve efficiency when breach is motivated by windfall gain.

Let's turn from breach motivated by windfalls to breach motivated by accidents. Suppose, as before, that *A*, who values his house at $90,000, contracts to sell it to *B* for $100,000. *B*'s purchase is motivated by the fact that

---

[26]The house is worth at least $120,000 to *C*, but we cannot infer from the amount he offers to pay exactly how much more it is worth to him.

his employer plans to relocate near A's house, and in light of this fact the house is worth $110,000 to B. Now suppose that after B has agreed to buy A's house, B's employer changes his plans and decides to relocate in a distant city. In view of this fact, the value of the house to B is much reduced, say to $75,000. Under these revised facts, there is no longer a surplus from exchange, so the deal should not be consummated. Instead of a windfall gain, there is an accidental loss whose cost would be minimized by non-performance on the contract. In these circumstances the law will allow B to breach the contract and pay damages; later we will return to this case to consider how high the damages are likely to be.

In summary, breach is efficient when, as a result of a windfall or an accident, the resources needed for performance are more valuable in an alternative use. Incentives for breach are efficient when the transfer of resources to the highest-valued use is accomplished at the lowest transaction costs and in such a way that no one is made worse off by the transfer and at least one person is made better off.

Let us refine this notion of efficient breach by briefly discussing the question, "Which court-designed remedy—the payment of money damages or specific performance—will induce only efficient breach?" Analyzing this problem in terms of bargaining theory is useful. Recall that transferring the house from A to B creates a surplus of $20,000. Furthermore, transferring the house from B to C creates an additional surplus of at least $10,000. (Alternatively, the house could be transferred directly from A to C; in that event, the surplus would still be at least $30,000.) If bargaining is costless, the house will eventually end up being owned by C, regardless of whether the court-designated remedy is damages or specific performance.[27] However, the distribution of the surplus from exchange is different under the two court-designed remedies.

To see why, assume that A has a binding contract to sell the house to B and the remedy for breach is damages. Further assume that the damages have been designed by the court so as to put B in the position he expected to be in if A had delivered the house, and B kept it. Because B anticipated a surplus of $10,000 from the performance of the contract, he is entitled to damages in that amount. Under this formulation of the damage remedy, A can breach the contract, pay $10,000 in damages to B, and sell the house to C for $120,000. As a result, A will enjoy $20,000 of the surplus and B will enjoy $10,000.[28]

But suppose that the court-designed remedy is specific performance. Under that remedy, the court requires A to sell the house to B as promised. Thus, A will have to deliver the house to B for $100,000, who will then resell

---

[27]This is an application of the Positive Coase Therem developed in Chapter 4.

[28]A makes $30,000 initially breaking the promise to sell to B for $100,000 and selling to C for $120,000. However, A has to pay $10,000 in compensation to B for breach. So, A's net gain is $20,000 and B's net gain is $10,000.

the house to C for $120,000. As a result, B will enjoy $20,000 in surplus and A will enjoy $10,000 in surplus, precisely the opposite shares of the surplus as occurred under court-designed damages.[29] The important point of this example is that when bargaining costs are zero, efficient incentives for breach are created under either court-designed remedy, but the surplus from exchange is distributed differently.

An implication of this analysis is that there is a distinction between the efficiency of the court-designed remedies only when bargaining or transaction costs are not zero as in the Positive Coase Theorem of Chapter 4. Moreover, the court-designed remedy that is best from an economic viewpoint minimizes the transaction cost of moving the good to its highest-valued use, as in the Normative Coase Theorem of Chapter 4. We will return to an examination of these costs in greater detail shortly; here we only want to hint at the relevant considerations regarding the bargaining costs in our example of breach induced by the opportunity to realize a windfall gain. First, recognize that the cost of buying and selling houses is not trivial. For example, the combined realtors' fees on the typical house sale are usually around 6% of the price. In addition, there are attorneys to be paid, title to be searched, and so on. In our example, the remedy of damages may save transaction costs, because it requires only one sale—from A to C—rather than the two sales required by specific performance—from A to B and from B to C. On the other hand, there is a different feature of this situation that argues that specific performance is the more efficient remedy. We assumed that B, who has agreed to pay $100,000 for the house, values it at $110,000. But A has no way of knowing exactly how highly B values the property. All A knows for sure is that B values it at $100,000 or more. It is possible, but unlikely, that buyer C who offers $120,000 does not really value it more than buyer B. If A breaches, pays damages to B, and sells the house to C, it could turn out that B values it more than C, so that B has to buy it back again from C. More importantly, we assumed in designing the amount of damages that the court knew B's reservation price ($110,000) on the house. In point of fact, that figure is extremely difficult for a court to determine. That being so, it may be very difficult for a court to compute correctly the amount of damages that will be efficient. How these competing considerations regarding damages and specific performance will compare depends on a more thorough analysis than we need engage in here. We will return to a more general discussion of the efficiency aspects of the two court-designed remedies shortly. Before we do, let's consider whether party-designed remedies are efficient.

---

[29]One important lesson of this example is that, in breach motivated by windfalls, the promissee (B) prefers the remedy of specific performance rather than damages, whereas the promisor (A) prefers the remedy in damages rather than specific performance.

C. Party-Designed Remedies: Liquidated Damages

At the time a contract is formed, the parties may specify what is to be done in the event that either of them breaches the contract. They might, for example, name a sum of money, called "liquidated damages," that the promise breaker will pay to the innocent party;[30] they may designate a manner, other than litigation, in which a dispute about performance can be resolved; or they may leave good faith deposits or performance bonds with a third party and specify that the breacher's deposit or surety bond is to be paid to the innocent party in the event of a breach. This stipulation forms a part of the contract, but there are special problems concerning its enforceability.

The courts have imposed limitations on the ability of contractual parties to stipulate their own remedies for breach of contract. There is a tradition that a court will not enforce a liquidated damages clause where the stipulation exceeds reasonably anticipated compensation and contains what appears to be a punitive aspect. In practice, this has meant that courts carefully scrutinized terms stipulating damages for breach that appeared to exceed the actual harm suffered, whereas courts routinely enforced terms stipulating damages that were less than, or the same as, the actual harm suffered.

Courts rationalized their traditional refusal to enforce penalty clauses on the grounds that the court's function in civil disputes is to compensate for injuries, not to punish wrongdoers.[31] There has been a great deal of reconsideration by economists and lawyers of these limitations on the ability of contracting parties to stipulate their own remedies. There are now sound theoretical reasons for believing that liquidated damages—and other forms of stipulated remedy—should be routinely enforced by the court, even if they appear to contain a punitive element. The reason for this is that a stipulation in excess of what appears to be reasonably anticipated compensatory damages may well serve two important functions and serve them more efficiently than will any alternative remedy that the court may design.

First, the punitive element may be considered as the payment on an insurance contract written in favor of the innocent party by the breaching party.[32] This situation arises where one party to the contract places a high subjective valuation on performance of the contract, and the other party is the best possible insurer of the loss of that subjective valuation.

---

[30]We saw an example of this in the previous chapter's case of a contract between a building contractor and a chef for the construction of a new restaurant. We will return to the economics of that particular contract below.

[31]This rationale contradicts the fact that courts often award punitive damages, especially in torts cases. We will discuss the economics of punitive damages in Chapter 9.

[32]See Goetz & Scott, *Liquidated Damages, Penalties, and the Just Compensation Principle: Some Notes on an Enforcement Model of Efficient Breach*, 77 COLUM. L. REV. 554 (1977).

Consider Professors Goetz and Scott's delightful example of the Anxious Alumnus. An alumnus of the University of Virginia is eager to follow the school's basketball team to what he believes will be a triumphal appearance at the Atlantic Coast Conference's post-season tournament. He intends to charter a bus to carry him and his friends from Charlottesville, Virginia, the home of the University of Virginia, to the tournament in Maryland. But he places such a high value on being at the games that he is extremely anxious about the possibility of not arriving there. Suppose the bus breaks down; suppose inclement weather prevents the bus from proceeding. If the bus company is unable to perform, the most the alumnus can reasonably expect to recover from the bus company in an action for breach of contract is the amount he paid to hire the bus. But this will undercompensate his true losses: he values performance of the contract to deliver him and his friends to the game at far more than the price he has paid to hire the bus; that is, he has a very high subjective valuation on performance. And yet that loss is far too speculative for a court to award him as money damages.

It is possible, Professors Goetz and Scott suggest, that the bus company would agree to pay the alumnus his subjective valuation of performance in the event of the bus company's breach in exchange for the alumnus's agreeing to pay the bus company a price for renting the bus that is above the competitive price. Suppose that the competitive price for hiring a bus to travel from Charlottesville to the tournament in Maryland is $500. Suppose further that the alumnus is convinced that if he does not get to the tournament, he will suffer $10,000 worth of anxiety and regret. In the course of negotiating the contract to hire the bus, suppose that the alumnus and the bus company agree to the following terms. The alumnus will pay $700 to hire the bus and in exchange the bus company will carry him and his friends to the tournament *and* will agree to pay him $10,500 in the event that they do not deliver him to the tournament. The difference ($200) between the negotiated contract price ($700) and the competitive price ($500) for hiring a similar bus to take a similar trip could then be considered as the premium on an insurance policy, written by the bus company in favor of the alumnus and protecting the alumnus against his losses in the event of his not attending the basketball games. By the same token, the seemingly punitive element of the liquidated damages—the difference between the stipulated amount to be paid in the event of breach ($10,500) and the competitive hire price ($500)—may be thought of as the face value of the insurance policy written by the bus company for a premium of $200.

The bus company may well be the cheapest underwriter available for such an insurance contract. And if it is, then efficiency argues for enforcing this liquidated damage clause: it protects the alumnus' subjective valuation on performance at the lowest possible price. Moreover, if the parties are convinced that the clause will be enforced, the contract will be breached only where it is more efficient to breach than to perform. Because this is precisely the result that one wants from a rule of contract law, this is a strong case for the routine enforcement of liquidated damage clauses.

A second reason for routinely enforcing stipulated damages clauses, even those containing a seemingly punitive element, is that these may be the most efficient means of one party's conveying information about his reliability and his ability to perform the contract. Consider a construction contract in which the buyer is especially eager to have the project completed by a specified date. Suppose that he is extremely doubtful of the contractor's ability to meet that deadline, but that the contractor is certain of his ability to complete performance by the specified date. It may be that the least expensive way for the contractor to convey to the seller his conviction about his ability to perform is for him to stipulate his willingness to pay seemingly punitive damages for each day beyond the deadline that the project remains uncompleted. In those circumstances, if courts are unwilling to enforce voluntarily agreed upon punitive liquidated damages, they force the parties to find a more expensive, less efficient way in which to exchange promises.

There is another reason why not allowing this particular punitive stipulation may foster inefficiency. In the construction example, suppose that the buyer's reluctance to believe the contractor was due to the fact that the contractor was new to the business. He could not, therefore, offer references or a record by which this or any other buyer could judge his ability to complete the project on time. He may be unable to offer a lower contract price because of the small size of his enterprise or because the construction industry is competitive enough to have driven price down to the level of costs. In that case, the contractor's only way of getting the contract may be his willingness to pay punitive damages to the buyer in the event of his breach. If the rule of law makes it impossible for a new contractor to compete in this manner, society will suffer higher than necessary construction costs. New contractors will find entry more expensive; hence, there will be fewer new contractors and, as a result, less competition. Those new contractors who do enter must find a more expensive and, therefore, less efficient way in which to convey to buyers their own estimate of their ability to perform.

Several economic defenses have been offered for the traditional reluctance of courts to enforce penalty clauses. One such defense is that penalty clauses may induce performance in circumstances where efficiency demands breach. To illustrate, suppose a construction contract imposes a penalty of $10,000 per week for late completion of a new office building, but the true loss to the purchaser from the delay is $5,000 per week. In that case the builder might spend, say, an extra $9,000 to avoid completing the building a week late, even though the saving to the purchaser is worth only $5,000. The contention is that if stipulations were limited to actual losses, the contractor would not inefficiently spend more than $5,000 to avoid delay in completing the office building.

Question 7.18: The alleged inefficiency can be avoided by bargaining. Use the Positive Coase Theorem of Chapter 4 to show how.

Another economic defense of non-enforcement of penalty clauses is that they create an incentive for one party to induce the other to breach the contract. To illustrate by the case of the Anxious Alumnus, suppose that between the time the bus is hired and the basketball tournament is played, the NCAA declares the starting five of his *alma mater* academically ineligible to play. Attendance at the tournament is now worth far less than $10,000 to him. Does the alumnus now have an incentive to induce the bus company to breach the contract? The answer is yes: if the bus company breaches, he will receive a sum that now far exceeds his (subjective) losses from non-performance. A partial solution to this potential inefficiency is to make inducement to breach a bar to recovery or a cause for mitigating the innocent party's award.[33]

> **Question 7.19:** Apply the concept of "market failure" to the case of the Anxious Alumnus in order to describe the conditions under which the penalty clause in the contract should be enforced and the conditions in which it should not be enforced.

> **Question 7.20:** Assume that it is efficient for liquidated damages in whatever amount to be routinely enforced. Does it follow that it would increase the efficiency of contractual relationships to *require* every enforceable contract to contain a liquidation clause? Why not?

D. Court-Imposed Remedies for Breach of Contract: Legal Relief

We now turn to a discussion of the remedies available through the courts. The subject of legal remedies for breach of contract is an extraordinarily broad and complex one; indeed, it is so broad and complex that, lengthy as our discussion will be, we can only touch on the issues here.

Let's begin with a review. The remedies available from a court for breach of contract are of two general types. First, the court may award the innocent party money damages, sometimes called "legal relief" or a "legal remedy." But there is no single measure of money damages that a court will award. In fact, there are three possibilities: reliance, expectation, and restitution money damages. As we will see, these different measures of money damages are computed differently, may create different incentives for breaching a contract, and may induce future contracting parties to structure their contracts differently. An important further issue that we want to discuss is how a court should measure these different money damage amounts.

---

[33]This solution works sometimes but not all the time. To see why, suppose the person hiring the bus is a meteorologist who knows that weather conditions will prevent the bus company from performing. He conceals this knowledge and pretends to be a devout alumnus with a high subjective valuation on performance. Thus, he insists on stipulating high damages for breach. The problem here is that, while there is no inducement to breach, there is a failure to disclose private information. In general, by enforcing the penalty clause, the court creates an incentive for one party to gamble on his superior information, whereas throwing out the penalty clause would remove this incentive and give the promisee a motive for revealing private information.

The second general category of remedy for breach of contract is specific performance, sometimes called an "equitable remedy." Under a decree of specific performance, the breaching party is instructed to perform the promise. We postpone a discussion of the efficiency of this remedy to a later section.

1. The Forms of Money Damages: Expectation, Reliance, and Restitution[34]

In a contract setting, the term "injury" can have two different meanings. One meaning is being worse off than if the contract had been performed. Another meaning is being worse off than if the contract had not been made. The interests invaded by these two injuries are known as the *expectation interest* and *reliance interest,* respectively.

The two distinct meanings of injury correspond to two distinct purposes of damages for breach of contract. *Expectation damages* are designed to protect the expectation interest, and have the purpose of placing the victim of breach in the position he would have been in if the other party had performed. If this purpose is achieved, the potential victim of breach is equally well off whether there is performance, on the one hand, or breach and payment of damages, on the other. In contrast, *reliance damages* are designed to protect the reliance interest, and have the purpose of restoring the victim of breach to the position he would have been in if the contract had not been made. If this purpose is achieved, the potential victim of breach is equally well off whether there is no contract with the breaching party, on the one hand, or contract, breach, and payment of damages, on the other.

We will use the term "perfect compensation" to mean a sum of money sufficient to make the victim of an injury equally well off with the money and with the injury as he would have been without the money and without the injury. In this sense, compensatory damages are the money equivalent of the injury. Expectation and reliance represent two different views of the injury. *Perfect expectation damages* are an award of money such that the injured party will achieve the level of satisfaction, if a consumer, or profits, if a firm, that would have been achieved if the contract had been performed. Similarly, *perfect reliance damages* are an award of money such that the injured party will achieve the level of satisfaction or profits that would have been achieved if the contract had never been made.

Let's illustrate this important difference by discussing the famous case of *Hawkins v. McGee*, 84 N.H. 114, 146 A. 641 (N.H., 1929). The plaintiff, George Hawkins, had a scar on his hand as the result of an injury suffered as a boy. Several years after the accident, when he was 18, Hawkins was persuaded by his family physician, McGee, to submit to an operation that the doctor claimed would restore the hand to perfection. In the operation, skin from the plaintiff's chest was grafted onto his hand, but the result was hide-

---

[34]Much of the material in this and the following section appeared in Cooter & Eisenberg, *Damages for Breach of Contract,* 73 CAL. L. REV. 1432 (1985).

Figure 7.1 Compensation in *Hawkins v. McGee*

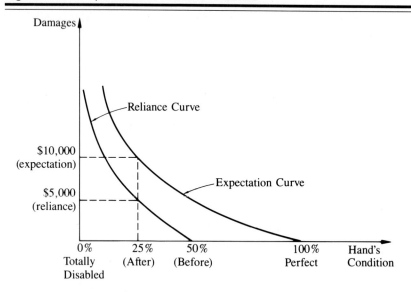

Expectation damages are the amount of money needed to compensate for the shortfall between the 100% perfect hand that Dr. McGee promised and the 25% perfect hand that was achieved. The expectation curve shows those combinations of money damages and disability that Hawkins finds equally as good as no damages and a perfect hand. Thus, under the expectation measure he is as well off with $10,000 in damages and a 25% perfect hand as with no damages and a 100% perfect hand. Reliance damages are the amount of money needed to compensate the deterioration of the hand from a 50% perfect hand, the pre-surgery condition, to the post-surgery 25% perfect hand. The reliance curve shows those combinations of money damages and disability that Hawkins finds equally as good as no damages and a 50% perfect hand. Under the reliance measure he is equally well off with $5,000 in damages and a 25% perfect hand as with no damages and a 50% perfect hand.

ous. The formerly small scar was now enlarged, covered with hair, and irreversibly worse. Hawkins sued the doctor for breach of his contractual promise to make the hand perfect. He prevailed and on appeal the question was, "What damages should be awarded to Hawkins?"

The damages issue in *Hawkins* may be illustrated in Figure 7.1. The horizontal axis in this figure indicates the range of possible conditions of the hand, which vary from total disability to perfect. The vertical axis indicates the dollar amount of damages. The curved lines on the graph indicate the relationship between the extent of the disability and the amount of money needed to compensate for it. The curves are constructed so that a change in the patient's condition from one point to another on the same curve leaves his welfare unchanged because a change in disability is exactly offset by a change in money compensation. Therefore, the curves are analagous to indifference curves in the microeconomic theory of consumer choice.[35]

---

[35]You might want to review the discussion of indifference curves in Chapter 2 before going on with this material.

First, consider expectation damages in *Hawkins v. McGee*, which are graphed by the curved line labeled "expectation." The physician promised to make the boy's hand perfect. Under the expectation conception, the uninjured state is the condition the patient would have been in if the physician had performed his promise. If the promise had been performed, the patient would have received a perfect hand and no compensation. Assume that after the operation the patient's hand was 25% perfect. Expectation damages are the amount of money needed to compensate for the shortfall between the 100% perfect hand that was promised and the 25% perfect hand that was achieved. To measure these damages, locate the 25% point on the horizontal axis, move vertically up to the curve labeled "expectation," and then move horizontally over to the vertical axis to determine the corresponding dollar amount of damages, which is $10,000. By construction, the patient is as well off with $10,000 in damages and a 25% perfect hand as with no damages and a 100% perfect hand. Thus, expectation damages equal $10,000 because this sum of money compensates for the shortfall between actual and promised performance. Note that the expectation curve and the resulting $10,000 figure illustrate the logic of compensation, not the damages actually computed in this case.

Now consider reliance damages, which are graphed by the curve labeled "reliance." Under the reliance conception, the uninjured state is the condition in which the patient would have been if he had not made the contract with the breaching party. Assume that if there had never been a contract, the patient would have had a 50% perfect hand, whereas after the operation the hand was 25% perfect. Reliance damages are the amount of money needed to compensate the deterioration of the hand from 50% to 25%. Like the expectation curve, the reliance curve is constructed to represent the relationship between the extent of the disability and the amount of money needed to compensate for it. The only difference is that the reliance curve touches the horizontal axis at the point where the hand is 50% perfect, rather than 100% perfect. By following the same steps as in expectation damages, we find that the patient is equally well off with $5,000 in damages and a 25% perfect hand as with no damages and a 50% perfect hand. Thus, reliance damages equal $5,000. In fact, Hawkins received $3,000 from the original jury; subsequently, after the appellate court ordered a new trial, the plaintiff settled for $1,400 plus lawyer's fees.

In short, the formal difference between expectation and reliance damages is the baseline against which the injury is measured, where "baseline" refers to the uninjured state. For the measurement of expectation damages, the uninjured state is the innocent party's position if the contract had been performed.[36] For the measurement of reliance damages, it is the position before the contract was signed.

---

[36]This proposition implicitly assumes that the rate of breach is low. When the rate of breach is high, it can be anticipated to some extent, and so the promisee can plan for breach, just as airlines and hotels plan for "no-shows." The phenomenon of statistically predictable breach creates a special set of problems for expectation damages.

The legal remedies discussed so far—expectation and reliance damages—seek to compensate the victim of breach for an injury. There is, however, another motive for awarding damages that occasionally arises in breach of contract disputes. Sometimes the promisor enjoys profits by breaching that the court considers unfair, so the court will require the injurer to disgorge them. Rather than compensating the victim for an injury, damages may be awarded to deny an unfair profit to the injurer. To illustrate, suppose A promises to sell a rare book to B for $10,000 and then C appears and offers A $15,000. A breaches the contract with B and sells to C, thereby earning an additional $5,000 in profits. However, the court may order A to give the $5,000 to B as restitution for breach of the contract. (Why would expectation damages be hard to compute in this case?) Thus, any benefits that the wrongdoer acquired are given to the innocent party as restitution for the wrong.[37]

2. How to Compute Damages for Breach of Contract   As we noted earlier, the practical implementation of the reliance and expectation principles is not straightforward. In the remainder of this section, let's look at several different methods of making the computation and relate them to some basic microeconomic concepts.

a. Substitute Price   When a party to a contract breaks his promise, the victim of breach may replace the promised performance with a substitute performance. The *substitute-price formula* awards the victim of breaches the cost of replacing a promised performance with a substitute performance. Suppose that Apex Ticket Agency offers cinema tickets at the price p_k and that a consumer orders x_k tickets. After Apex breaches, the consumer cannot get equivalent tickets except by paying the high price p_s to the Bijou Ticket Agency. The promised performance can be replaced at the cost $x_k (p_s - p_k)$. Accordingly, this is the amount of money that would be awarded as damages to the consumer under the substitute-price formula.[38]

---

[37]*See* Farnsworth, *Your Loss or My Gain?: The Dilemma of the Disgorgement Principle in Contract Damages*, 94 YALE L. J. 1339 (1985).

[38]If a commodity is homogeneous, a substitute performance may be identical to the promised performance. In that case, the substitute price is the actual price of a substitute transaction. The tickets promised by Apex may be identical to those sold by Bijou, in which case the substitute-price formula equals the actual cost of substitution. However, if the commodity is differentiated rather than homogeneous so that no perfect substitute exists, the substitute price must be computed by extrapolation from comparable market transactions. For the purposes of illustration, suppose that a contract for the sale of a four-door 1957 Chevrolet has been breached and that some measure of the value of the transaction is needed to award damages. However, the market price for that commodity is not available. Instead, we know the market prices of a four-door 1956 Chevrolet, and a two-door 1957 Chevrolet. From the price of the two-door 1957 Chevrolet and the relationship between the two- and four-door 1956 Chevrolets, we can compute a substitute price for the four-door 1957 Chevrolet.

b. Lost-Surplus Each party typically expects to gain from a contract. The difference between the value that a party places upon what he expects to receive and what he actually gives up is called "surplus." The *lost-surplus formula* awards the victim of breach the surplus that he would have enjoyed if the breaching party had performed.

The surplus that a seller enjoys on the sale of a commodity is normally the difference between the contract price of the commodity and its direct cost. To illustrate, if the cost c of tickets to the Apex Ticket Agency is their wholesale price, and if a consumer promises to purchase x_k tickets at the contract price p_k, then the surplus Apex expects on the contract is $x_k (p_k - c)$. This amount equals the seller's damages under the lost-surplus formula.

Now consider the lost-surplus formula when the roles of the parties are reversed. The surplus that the consumer enjoys on a purchase is normally the difference between the value of the good to him, which is called his "willingness-to-pay" or his "reservation price," and the amount he actually pays. Using the same illustration, assume the consumer would have been willing to pay as much as p_w for each of x_k tickets, and the contract price is p_k. The consumer's expected surplus from the contract with Apex is the difference between what he is willing to pay for the tickets and what the contract requires him to pay. Damages for Apex's breach under the lost-surplus formula therefore would be $x_k (p_w - p_c)$.

> **Question 7.21:** One problem with awarding the lost surplus as damages for breach is that the promise-breaker may be utterly surprised by the magnitude of his liability. An English court formulated a famous rule to limit such surprises in *Hadley v. Baxendale*, 9 Exch. 341 (Exch. 1854): the victim is entitled only to the *reasonably foreseeable* loss from breach of the contract. Judge Posner used the following example to justify the rule. A professional photographer buys film from a well-known producer in order to take spectacular pictures of the Himalayas for a National Geographic special. Unfortunately, the film is defective so that none of the shots comes out. Applying the rule of *Hadley v. Baxendale*, the photographer should be allowed to recover only the cost of the film, not the profits he expected from fulfilling his contract with the National Geographic Society. The economic justification for the rule is that the photographer is a better insurer against or preventer of these extraordinary losses than is the film producer.
>
> Things are slightly different if the photographer notified the film company of his intended use of the film. Why? How can a customer effectively notify such a company?[39]

c. Opportunity-Cost Making a contract often entails the loss of an opportunity to make an alternative contract. The *opportunity-cost formula* awards the victim of breach the surplus that he would have enjoyed if he had signed the best alternative contract to the one that was breached. To illustrate, assume

---

[39]In a recent decision, Judge Posner applied this doctrine limiting recovery to reasonably foreseeable losses to a torts case (although it is nearly a contracts case). *See Evra Corp. v. Swiss Bank Corp.*, 673 F.2d 951 (1982).

that a consumer foregoes the opportunity of buying x_k cinema tickets from Bijou at price p_o, and instead contracts to buy x_k tickets from Apex at price p_k. If he is then compelled to purchase at the higher price p_s after Apex's breach, the opportunity-cost formula sets damages equal to $x_k (p_s - p_o)$. In general, if breach causes the injured party to purchase a substitute performance, the opportunity-cost formula equals the difference between the best alternative contract price available at the time of contracting and the price of the substitute performance obtained after the breach.

We may show the opportunity-cost formula by adding a curve to the graph (Figure 7.1) we used to distinguish reliance and expectation damages. Our previous discussion of *Hawkins v. McGee* implicitly assumed that the operation performed by the defendant did not cause Hawkins to lose the opportunity of having another doctor perform the operation successfully. If such an opportunity were lost, its value would need to be included in the computation of reliance damages. The value of the foregone opportunity depends upon how close to perfection the hand would have been after an operation by another doctor. To illustrate, suppose that another doctor would have restored the hand to the 75% level. The injury from relying on Dr. McGee is then the difference between the 75% level that the other doctor would have provided and the 25% level achieved by Dr. McGee, not the difference between the 50% level before the operation by Dr. McGee and the 25% level after it. In general, when reliance causes an opportunity to be lost, the lost opportunity provides a higher baseline for measuring the injury than the actual state before the agreement, and the higher baseline in turn results in higher damages.

To depict reliance damages under the opportunity-cost interpretation, it is necessary to add another curve to Figure 7.1. The additional curve, depicted in Figure 7.2, touches the horizontal axis at the 75% point and, as with the first two curves, it is constructed so that every point on it represents the same level of welfare. Consequently, a change in the hand's condition represented by a move along the new curve is exactly offset by the corresponding change in damages. The value of the lost opportunity is read off the graph by moving vertically from the 25% point on the horizontal axis up to the "opportunity curve," and then horizontally to the intersection with the vertical axis. Following these steps, the opportunity-cost measure of damages is $8,000, which is less than expectation damages ($10,000) and more than reliance damages stripped of the opportunity cost ($5,000).

d. Out-of-Pocket-Cost   Action in reliance on a contract may involve an investment that cannot be fully recouped in the event of breach. The *out-of-pocket-cost* formula awards the victim of breach the difference between (1) the costs incurred in reliance on the contract prior to breach, and (2) the value produced by those costs that can be realized after breach. To illustrate, assume that a consumer breaches an agreement to buy x_k tickets from Apex at price p_k. In reliance on the contract, Apex purchased x_k tickets at the wholesale price c_i. At the time of breach, the spot price p_s, at which Apex can

Figure 7.2 Opportunity Cost in *Hawkins v. McGee*

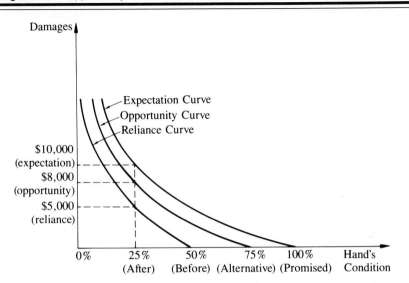

The expectation and reliance curves are defined just as they were in Figure 7.1. Suppose now that another doctor could have restored the hand to 75% perfection. The injury from relying on Dr. McGee is then the difference between the 75% level that the other doctor would have provided and the 25% level achieved by Dr. McGee, not the difference between the 50% level before the operation and the 25% level after it. This lost opportunity is represented by the opportunity curve. Points on that curve represent combinations of damages and disability that are equally as good as no damages and a 75% perfect hand. The opportunity-cost method of measuring damages is $8,000, which is less than expectation damages and more than reliance damages.

resell tickets, has fallen below the wholesale price c_i paid by Apex. Apex's out-of-pocket cost is $x_k (c_i - p_s)$.

Reversing roles, suppose the consumer contracts with Apex for theater tickets and then contracts with a baby-sitting service for the evening of the performance. Apex breaches, and the consumer therefore stays home that evening. The consumer's out-of-pocket cost is the cost of cancelling the baby-sitting contract.

e. Diminished-Value When performance of a contract is partial or imperfect, the value received is less than promised. The *diminished-value formula* awards the victim of breach the difference between (1) the post-breach value of a commodity that was to be received or improved under the contract, and (2) the value the commodity would have had if the contract had been properly performed. To illustrate, suppose that Seller promises Buyer to customize a boat with an Alpha compass, which will give the boat a market value of m_p. Instead, he delivers a boat with a Beta Compass, which causes the boat to have a lower market value of m_d. The amount that would be awarded to Buyer under the diminished-value formula is $(m_p - m_d)$, or the difference between the value of the boat promised and the value of the boat delivered.

Question 7.22: The Contracts: Buyer B pays $10,000 to New Orleans grain dealer D in exchange for D's promise to deliver grain to buyer B's London office on October 1. As a result of signing this contract, B decides not to sign a similar contract with another dealer for $10,500. D contracts with shipping company S to transport the grain. Buyer B agrees to resell the grain upon arrival in London for $11,000 to another party. B pays $100 in advance (non-refundable) as docking and unloading fees for the ship's projected arrival in London.

Breach: The ship begins taking water several days out of New Orleans and returns to port. Inspection reveals that the grain is badly damaged by salt water, and D sells it as cattle fodder for $500. D conveys the news to B in London, who then purchases the same quantity of grain for delivery on October 1 at a price of $12,000.

a. What is the substitute-price measure of damages for D's breach of contract with B?

b. What is the lost-surplus measure of damages for D's breach of contract with B?

c. What is the opportunity-cost measure of damages for D's breach of contract with B?

d. What is B's out-of-pocket cost due to D's breach?

e. What is the diminished-value damages for S's breach of the contract with D to deliver the grain to London?

E. Optimal Remedies

We have discussed two general conceptions of damages—expectation and reliance—and we have discussed specific formulas for implementing them—substitute price, lost-surplus, opportunity-cost, out-of-pocket-costs, and diminished-value. In this section of the chapter we will examine the incentive effects of different legal remedies for breach of contract against the standard of economic efficiency.

Many kinds of behavior are affected by the choice of remedies.[40] We cannot consider every type of affected behavior, so we will concentrate upon three: the promisor's decision to breach or perform (we have already introduced this under the definition of efficient breach), the promisor's precaution taken to reduce the probability that he will decide to breach, and the promisee's reliance upon the promise. To illustrate, when production costs rise precipitously, a manufacturer who promised to deliver goods to a buyer must decide whether to perform or breach. Before the rise in costs, the manufacturer had to decide whether to hedge against a possible rise in costs by signing futures contracts. Futures contracts are a form of precaution against

---

[40]Here is a partial list of affected behaviors: (i) searching for trading partners; (ii) negotiating exchanges; (iii) drafting contracts (explicitness); (iv) keeping or breaking promises; (v) precaution against events causing breach; (vi) reliance upon promises; (vii) the mitigation of damages caused by broken promises; (viii) resolving disputes caused by broken promises.

events that motivate breach. And the buyer must decide whether she should hedge against breach by lining up alternative sellers. Forbearing to line up alternative sources of supply is a form of reliance upon the contract. Because we have already discussed the incentive effects of alternative remedies upon breach, we will concentrate here on the incentive effects of alternative remedies upon precaution and reliance.

1. Precaution The promisor can usually take precaution against what we have called "accidents" that motivate breach.[41] But in doing so, he must balance the benefits of taking precaution against the costs. In general, the benefit from precaution is a reduction in the probability that the surplus from exchange will be lost. The cost of precaution is simply the cost of the actions taken or foregone to reduce the probability that the surplus will be lost. To develop the idea of precaution, we draw upon the following example:

> ### The Waffle Shop
>
> Yvonne is a chef who operates a restaurant for economists that is called the Waffle Shop because of what it serves and whom it serves. As the economy deteriorates and economists prosper, her business picks up to such an extent that she needs a larger facility. Yvonne enters into a contract with Xavier, a builder, who promises to construct the new restaurant for occupancy on September 1. Xavier knows that events could jeopardize completing the building on September 1 as promised; for example, the plumbers may strike; the city inspectors may be recalcitrant; the weather may be inclement; and so forth. He can reduce the probability of late completion by taking costly measures such as having the plumbers work overtime before the contract expires, badgering the inspectors to finish on time, rescheduling work to complete the roof before the rain starts, and so forth. These activities are the various forms of precaution by which Xavier can reduce the probability that he will break his promise.

The relationship between the probability that Xavier will perform as promised and his expenditure on precaution is graphed in Figure 7.3. The variable x denotes Xavier's expenditure on precaution, the variable p

---

[41]The design of incentives for precaution must focus upon the promisor because the promisor can often take precautions against events that would cause him to breach, but it is less often the case that the promisee can affect the contingencies that influence the promisor's decision to perform or breach. Sometimes an indirect influence operates. To illustrate, the promisee, by her reliance, may be able to affect the damages that will be awarded in the event of breach; and the promisee can sometimes affect the information available to the promisor concerning contingencies that will cause breach. But it is unusual for the promisee to be able to have a direct, material effect upon the circumstances that cause the promisor to breach. Recall the example of the Anxious Alumnus that we developed in our section on the economics of stipulated remedies. There, the bus company was the promisor, and the alumnus, the promisee. We concluded our discussion by pointing out that when circumstances change between the formation of the contract and its performance that lower the subjective value of performance to the promisee, the promisee has an incentive to induce the promisor to breach. For example, the promisee might attempt to place tacks on the highway or secretly drain the oil from the bus. These possibilities prompted us to argue that if the promisor's non-performance is attributable to the promisee's attempting to induce the breach, his non-performance should be excused.

Figure 7.3 Precaution and the Probability of Performance

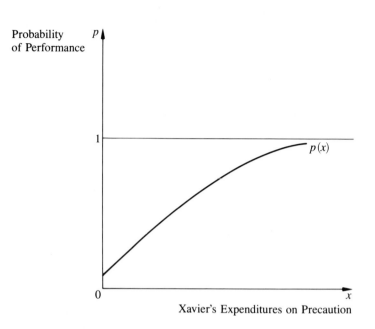

The vertical axis measures the probability of Xavier's performing the contract from 0, no chance that he'll perform, to 1, a certainty that he'll perform. The horizontal axis measures x, Xavier's precautionary expenditures that are designed to make performance more likely. The line $p = p(x)$ indicates that as precautionary expenditures, x, increase, the probability, p, of performance increases, but at a diminishing rate.

denotes the probability of performance, and the functional relationship between the variables is denoted $p = p(x)$. The probability of performance increases when Xavier spends more on precaution; so p is an increasing function of x. There is an intimate relationship between Xavier's precaution and Yvonne's reliance, which is our next topic.

2. Reliance

We have just seen that the promisor can often influence the probability of breach by taking precaution against the events that would cause him to breach. By contrast, the promisee can often influence the extent of the harm caused by breach through his control over the amount he spends in reliance upon the promisor's performance. The greater the promisee's reliance expenditures, the greater the harm that will result from breach. So there is an issue of designing remedies to induce efficient reliance. Let's see how this applies to Yvonne's behavior at the Waffle Shop.

Yvonne anticipates a surge in business when she opens the new facility. To accommodate the new business, she will have to order more food than

Figure 7.4   Promisee Reliance and the Probability of Promisor Performance

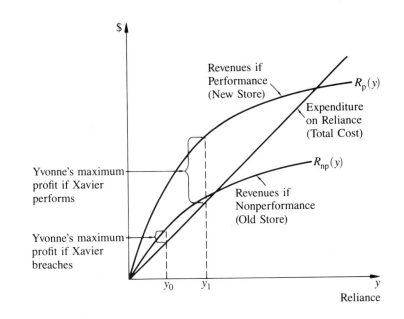

The amount that the promisee will spend in reliance on the promisor's performance is a function of the probability of performance. The vertical axis measures dollar amounts; the horizontal axis measures the quantity, y, of the promisee's, Yvonne's, reliance: specifically, y is the quantity of food ordered for the month of September in reliance that Xavier will have completed construction by the first of the month. Expenditures on reliance are measured by the straight line through the origin. The promisee's revenues are represented by one of two curves: by $R_p(y)$ if she is certain that Xavier will finish the building on time; by $R_{np}(y)$ if she is certain that Xavier will not finish the building on time. If she operates along $R_p(y)$, the profit-maximizing amount of reliance is y_1. If she operates along $R_{np}(y)$, the profit-maximizing amount of reliance is y_0.

she can use profitably in her old restaurant. She would like to place the orders for delivery on September 1, so that there will be no interruption in service. However, placing orders in advance creates the risk that she will lose money on the supplementary food orders if the building is not completed on time. The size of the order placed by Yvonne is a measure of her reliance upon Xavier's promise.

The relationship between Yvonne's reliance and her profits in September are graphed in Figure 7.4. For simplicity, we assume that the only costs that Yvonne can vary are those of her supplementary food orders. The variable y denotes her total variable costs for September, or, equivalently, her expenditure on food orders for that month. Total revenues in September are the income from meals sold during the month. Profit for the month equals the difference between total revenues and total variable costs, which is represented in Figure 7.4 by the vertical distance between the total revenue and total cost curves.

By assumption, Yvonne is a profit-maximizer; her aim is to rely on Xavier's completion of his promise at the level where the vertical distance between the total revenue and total cost curves is largest. However, there are two possible total revenue curves, depending upon whether Yvonne is in the new building or the old building. If Yvonne were certain that Xavier would finish the building on time, then she would choose the level of reliance y_1, where profits are maximized conditional upon Xavier's performance. If she were certain that Xavier would finish the building late and her reliance would be uncompensated, then she would choose the level of reliance y_0, where profits are maximized conditional upon Xaver's breach.

If Yvonne relies heavily on Xavier, Yvonne will choose a value of y close to y_1. But if Yvonne sets y close to y_1 and Xavier breaches, she will lose profits that she would have enjoyed by setting y close to y_0. So, reliance is risky. In general, if the probability were greater than zero and less than one that Xavier would finish the building late and her reliance would not be compensated, then Yvonne would choose a level of reliance between y_1 and y_0 in order to maximize her profits. (As we will see, the efficient level of reliance is between y_1 and y_0.)

Let's state the general characteristics of this specific example: the promisor (Xavier) can take costly precaution that increases the probability that he will be able to perform as promised. The more the promisee (Yvonne) relies upon the promise, the greater her profits if the promise is kept and the greater her losses if the promise is broken. What we now want to determine is how the remedies available for breach of contract can efficiently coordinate Xavier's precautionary behavior with Yvonne's reliance behavior.

3. Incentives for Efficient Precaution and Efficient Reliance

The remedies available for breach of contract create incentives for precaution and reliance in cases like the Waffle Shop. We will derive a simple measure of these incentives and explain its effect upon Yvonne and Xavier. You have already encountered this derivation in the chapter on property when we analyzed takings, and you will encounter it again in the next chapter on torts. This demonstrates that our model of the incentive effects of common law rules is general and arises in some form in each of the common law subjects.

The derivation of the optimal remedies to create efficient incentives for precaution and reliance is lengthy and employs both graphs and mathematical notation. For the benefit of the less mathematical readers, we will state the argument in simple prose; you can then decide for yourself whether to work through the full argument.

The promisor bears the full cost of the precaution he takes against the events that cause him to breach; incentives are efficient when he also receives the full benefit of this precaution. The benefit of precautionary expenditures against breach is the reduction in the risk that the surplus from cooperation will be lost. But, typically, part of the surplus accrues to the promisee. This seems to suggest that, because the promisor can never receive the full benefit of his precaution against breach, efficient incentives for precaution cannot be created, and therefore, promisors will always take too little precaution. However, this is precisely the point at which remedies can come to the rescue to create an efficient incentive for the promisor to take precaution. By creating a remedy that makes the promisor liable, in the event that he breaches, for paying the surplus that the *promisee* expects from performance, the law induces the promisor to internalize the full surplus. In most, but not all, cases, the surplus that the promisee expects from performance is measured by expectation damages. So, incentives for precaution by the promisor are usually efficient when he is liable to the promisee for expectation damages in the event of breach.

With regard to the promisee, the problem is to create a remedy that will induce her to take only efficient reliance and not to over-rely. If the promisor is liable for *all* the surplus that the promisee expects from performance of the contract, the promisee has an inducement to exaggerate this expectation by *over*-relying on the promisor's performance. At the other extreme, if the promisor is liable for *none* of the promisee's expected surplus from completion of the contract, then the promisee will bear the full cost of reliance and, consequently, take the efficient amount of expenditures in reliance on the promisor's performing.

These thoughts seem to create a paradox: efficient *precaution* will result from making the promisor liable for *all* the promisee's expected surplus from performance, but efficient *reliance* will result from making the promisor liable for *none* of the promisee's expected surplus. It appears to be the case that remedies for breach can create efficient reliance and inefficient precaution or, alternatively, efficient precaution and inefficient reliance, but not both efficient reliance and efficient precaution at the same time. The solution to this paradox is a legal remedy for breach of contract that makes the promisor liable only for *reasonably foreseeable* expectation damages.

4. An Optional Case: The Formal Analysis of Incentives for Efficient Precaution and Efficient Reliance

We turn now to the development of a more formal analysis of the incentives for efficient reliance and precaution created by legal remedies. If Xavier breaches and Yvonne sues, then the court must decide the questions of enforceability and remedy. If the court construes excuses broadly, usually finding that non-performance was permitted, then promises are seldom enforced. If the court construes excuses narrowly, usually finding that performance was required, then promises are usually enforced. Let q denote the probability of enforceability. Thus, q is the probability that Xavier will lose a suit for breach brought by Yvonne.

If Xavier loses a suit, then the court must provide a remedy for the breach. Obviously, the court cannot order Xavier to complete the building on time if the deadline has already passed. The remedy must take the form of money damages paid to Yvonne as compensation. Let m denote the money damages that Xavier must pay if he loses a suit.

If Xavier breaks his promise, then his expected liability for damages, denoted D, equals the probability, q, that he loses a suit times the money damages m, or $D = qm$. D is the simple measure of the incentives for precaution and reliance. The practice of the courts in determining D controls how much precaution it is rational for Xavier to take and how much it is rational for Yvonne to rely, as we will explain.

Notice that the two elements of D correspond to the two questions of contract law. Specifically, the question of enforceability concerns q and the question of remedy concerns m. The larger the value of q, the more likely that the contract is enforceable, and the higher the value of m, the larger the damages for breach. First, we will analyze how D affects precaution and reliance, and then we will turn to the analysis of the two components of D.

There are two kinds of costs that Xavier bears in connection with the risk that he will breach. When he enters a contract, he performs with probability $p(x)$, where x equals the extent of his precaution, and he breaches with probability $[1 - p(x)]$. (Recall that $p(x)$ is an increasing function of x.) Xavier's expected liability when he signs a contract is the probability of breach times the expected damages from breach: $[1 - p(x)]D$. Besides his expected liability, Xavier bears the cost of precaution x. The sum of these two elements equals the costs that Xavier expects to bear in connection with breach:

$$x + [1 - p(x)]D,$$

which is graphed in Figure 7.5. Note that, for the sake of simplicity, we are assuming that precaution costs $1 per unit. In a more general formulation we could put a price, p_x per unit of precaution, but our conclusions would not be changed. As the figure illustrates, Xavier's costs are high if he takes no precaution because his expected damages are large, and his costs are also high if he spends an excessive amount on precaution. Xavier minimizes the costs that he bears in connection with breach. His costs are minimized at the precaution level denoted x^* in Figure 7.5.

The point x^* can be described by a marginalist analysis. Precaution is cost-minimizing for Xavier when an additional dollar spent on precaution reduces his expected liability by a dollar. In other words, his costs are minimized when the marginal cost of precaution equals the marginal reduction in expected liability, that is, when marginal cost and marginal benefit are equal. The larger the expected damages D, the stronger is Xavier's incentive to take precaution against events that cause him to breach. This fact is

Figure 7.5 Promisor's Expected Costs of Precaution and Breach

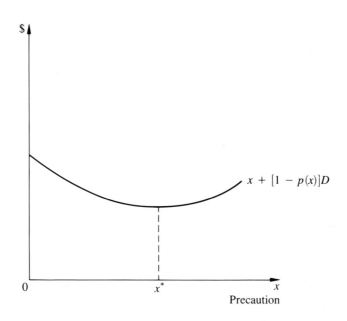

The vertical axis measures dollar amounts; the horizontal axis measures the quantity of x, the promisor's precaution. We assume that precaution costs \$1 per unit so that x equals the promisor's total expenditure on precaution against breach. Recall that the probability, p, that he will perform the contract is an increasing function of x, the amount of precaution. Thus, the probability that he will breach is $[1 - p(x)]$. If he breaches, the promisor is liable to pay D in damages so that his expected liability in the event of breach is $[1 - p(x)]D$. His total expected costs are the sum of these precautionary expenditures and expected costs of breach, or $(x + [1 - p(x)]D)$. These expected costs are minimized by taking precaution equal to x^*. This is the point for which the marginal cost of precaution, \$1 by assumption, equals the marginal reduction in expected liability for breach of contract.

depicted in Figure 7.6, where the cost-minimizing level of precaution x^* increases from x_0^* to x_1^* to x_2^* as expected damages D increase from D_0 to D_1 to D_2.

Having analyzed the effect of expected damages D upon Xavier's precaution, we now consider its effect upon Yvonne's reliance. The expected damages that Yvonne will receive in the event of Xavier's breach depend upon the amount of harm that she suffers, which in turn depends upon the extent of her reliance. For example, if Yvonne receives compensation for her supplementary food order, then the compensation will be larger if the order is larger. Thus, the total expected damages D may be an increasing function of reliance y, or $D = D(y)$.

Figure 7.6   Optimal Precaution and the Size of Damages

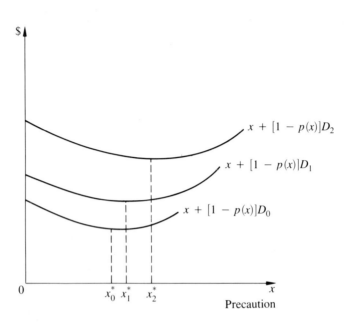

The three curves give the promisor's total expected costs for three different levels of money damages for breach: D_0, D_1, and D_2. The associated expected cost-minimizing levels of precaution are x_0^*, x_1^*, and x_2^*. Thus, the greater the level of money damages, the greater the promisor's level of precaution.

Suppose Yvonne is deliberating about how much to rely. The more she relies, the larger her loss in the event of breach by Xavier. However, a larger loss may be offset by larger expected damages. Insofar as Yvonne receives more expected damages for a larger loss, the risk associated with reliance is shifted from Yvonne to Xavier. Thus, the extent of Yvonne's reliance will depend upon the amount of risk-shifting that is created by the legal remedy for breach.

To illustrate, suppose the court awards damages equal to the full cost of the extra food ordered in reliance upon the contract. In that case, an increase in food orders by $1 would increase damages by $1 in the event of breach. This damage rule shifts *all* the risk of incremental reliance from Yvonne to Xavier, giving Yvonne an incentive to rely heavily.[42]

This argument can be restated in the marginalist language of microeconomics. A $1 increase in Yvonne's food order may be called "marginal reliance." Because expected damages are a function of reliance, $D = D(y)$, marginal reliance causes a change in expected damages. The change in

---

[42]There is an implicit assumption that $q = 1$, so that expected damages D equal money damages m.

expected damages caused by marginal reliance may be called "marginal expected damages" and is conventionally denoted $D'(y)$. If an increase in food orders by $1 causes expected damages to increase by $1 in the event of breach, then marginal expected damages equals marginal reliance: $D'(y) = 1$. All the risk of reliance is shifted from the promisee to the promisor when marginal expected damages equal marginal reliance, so the promisee relies heavily.

Now consider the opposite situation, in which there is no risk-shifting from the promisee to the promisor. This would be the case if expected damages are invariant with respect to reliance. To illustrate, suppose that Xavier must pay a fixed amount of money for each day's delay in completing the building, say $100 per day. As a consequence, Yvonne receives the same damages for each day's delay regardless of how much food she orders. Increasing her food order by $1 exposes Yvonne to the full risk that she will lose an additional $1 in the event of breach. In notation, marginal reliance has no effect upon expected damages; so marginal expected damages are nil: $D'(y) = 0$. When expected damages are invariant with respect to the promisee's reliance, the risk of marginal reliance is borne entirely by the promisee, instead of being shifted to the promisor. The promisee has an incentive to restrain her reliance. (Notice that this argument applies whether the contract called for damages of $100 per day or $1,000 per day. Can you see why?[43])

We have contrasted two types of expected damages and their incentive effects on reliance: expected damages that are an increasing function of reliance and expected damages that are invariant with respect to reliance. The more rapidly expected damages increase with respect to reliance, the more risk is shifted and the stronger is the promisee's incentive to rely. Thus, incentives to rely increase as marginal expected damages increase.

We have also shown that the promisor's precaution depends upon *total* expected damages and that the promisee's reliance depends upon *marginal* expected damages. The higher the total expected damages, the stronger the promisor's incentives for precaution. This is virtually equivalent to saying, "The higher the total expected damages, the stronger is the promisor's incentive to keep his promise." Similarly, the higher the marginal expected damages, the stronger the promisee's incentives for reliance. Having explained the incentive effects of expected damages, we now turn to the problem of discovering damage rules that create incentives for efficient reliance and precaution.

Let us call incentives efficient if they cause the promisor and promisee to behave in such a way that the value of the contract is maximized. The value of the contract will be reduced if there is too little or too much precaution or if there is too much or too little reliance. For example, suppose that expected damages D are initially too low to provide incentives for efficient

---

[43]If damages are invariant with respect to reliance, their total does not directly affect a rational promisee's incentives for reliance. There may be an indirect effect on the promisee's reliance due to the fact that higher invariant damages cause more precaution by the promisor.

precaution. By assumption, the cost of more precaution by Xavier is less than the resulting increase in Yvonne's expected profits. For concreteness, assume that an additional $1 spent on precaution by Xavier would increase Yvonne's expected profits by $3. Now suppose that expected damages D are increased. Xavier will respond by increasing his precaution x. To keep the arithmetic simple, suppose that Xavier increases precaution by $1, which is just enough to keep his expected liability constant. Thus, the value of the contract increases by $3 to Yvonne at a cost of $1 to Xavier, for a net increase of $2. This is a move in the direction of efficiency.

The move towards efficiency can benefit both parties. To illustrate, Xavier can recapture an equal share of the increase in value by a $2 increase in the price he charges Yvonne for completion of the contract. A $1 increase in expenditure in precaution, combined with a $2 increase in price, will cause each party to enjoy a net increase of $1 in the value of the contract. Thus, a $2 increase in total value of the contract is split equally between its parties.

As long as a change in expected damages increases the value of the contract, expected damages are not efficient. In this example an increase in expected damages increases the value of the contract and benefits both parties, so expected damages should be increased until further increases in the value of the contract are impossible. Efficiency is achieved when a small increase in expected damages imposes costs upon Xavier that equal the benefit to Yvonne.

A similar argument can be made about efficient reliance. If the contract gives Yvonne incentives to over-rely, then reducing her reliance by $1 will reduce her expected income by less than the reduction in Xavier's expected liability. Such a change increases the value of the contract.

Now let us evaluate the various damage measures we have discussed above with respect to their ability to achieve efficient reliance and precaution and thus to maximize the value of contracts.

To begin, it is helpful to describe efficient damage rules in the language of externalities. In the contract setting, precaution by the promisor benefits the promisee by reducing the probability of breach, and reliance by the promisee increases the promisor's liability for breach. Incentives are efficient when the benefits of precaution and the costs of reliance are internalized. We want to identify damage rules that have this property.

First, consider the promisor's incentives for precaution. Xavier bears the cost of his own precaution, which reduces the probability of breach. The reduction in the probability of breach causes two benefits: first, Xavier benefits from the reduction in his expected liability for expected damages, and, second, Yvonne benefits from the reduction in the harm that she expects to suffer from breach. If Xavier's reduction in expected damages equals Yvonne's reduction in expected harm from breach, then the benefits of precaution are fully internalized. So efficiency requires these two benefits to be equal. In brief, *the benefits of promisor's precaution are internalized when expected damages equal expected harm.*

What about the incentives for efficient reliance by the promisee? We discussed the fact that some damage rules transfer the risk of reliance from

Yvonne to Xavier, and others do not. Specifically, risk is transferred when expected damages are an increasing function of reliance, and risk is not transferred when expected damages are invariant with respect to reliance. Transferring risk externalizes the cost of reliance, whereas the cost of reliance is internalized when risk is not transferred. To achieve efficiency, the cost of reliance must be internalized. Therefore, *incentives for efficient reliance by the promisee are achieved by any invariant damage rule.* In other words, Yvonne internalizes the risk of reliance when *marginal* expected damages are nil (when $D'(y) = 0$).

The conditions for efficient reliance can be illustrated using Figure 7.4. If performance is likely, then heavy reliance is efficient, so the efficient value of y is close to y_1. If performance is unlikely, then little reliance is efficient, so the efficient value of y is close to y_0. Exposing Yvonne to the risk of breach causes her to rely at the efficient level, which is usually between y_0 and y_1.

The two propositions about efficient incentives may seem inconsistent. Efficient precaution requires expected damages to equal harm, which increases with reliance, whereas efficient reliance requires expected damages to be invariant with respect to reliance. How can both conditions be satisfied simultaneously?

This is an example of a general paradox afflicting compensation in all areas of the law. In fact, we have already seen this paradox in our discussion in Chapter 4 of the optimal policy for compensating regulatory takings, and we will meet it again in our exploration of compensation for tortious harm. In general, the incentives for precaution by injurers are efficient if they are liable for *all* of the damages that they cause, and the incentives for reliance by victims are efficient if they are compensated for *none* of the harm they suffer. When expected damages equal harm, the victim's incentives to reduce harm are eroded. When expected damages are less than harm, the injurer's incentives to avoid accidents are eroded. The problem of over-reliance is mathematically identical to the problem of under-precaution: a rule of compensation links them to each other in such a way that, seemingly, there must be either the one or the other. *The paradox of compensation is that making the injurer liable for the harm erodes the victim's incentives, whereas allowing the injurer to escape liability erodes the injurer's incentives.* In other words, compensation internalizes costs for the injurer by externalizing costs for the victim, and the absence of compensation does the opposite.

To illustrate the paradox, suppose Yvonne receives with certainty damages equal to the shortfall in her revenues caused by breach. Yvonne is guaranteed the same level of profits regardless of whether Xavier performs or breaches. All of the cost of breach is upon Xavier, so it is rational for Yvonne to act as if performance were certain. If Yvonne acts as if performance were certain, then she will over-rely by ordering too much food. Specifically, she will order y_1 in Figure 7.4, whereas efficiency requires her to order an amount less than y_1 and more than y_0. Yvonne's incentive to over-rely can be reduced by setting damages equal to a fraction of the harm that she suffers. However, setting damages below 100% of the harm will cause

Xavier to take too little precaution. Over-reliance or under-precaution, that is the choice offered by the paradox.

There is a solution to the paradox: make damages invariant and set them at a level equal to the harm caused by breach when reliance is efficient. In practice this means setting damages equal not to *all* the promisee's expected surplus from completion but rather to the promisee's *reasonably foreseeable* expected surplus from completion of the contract. In the ideal contract, this remedy will induce the parties to communicate to one another what their expectations on the surplus are, then to bargain about these expectations, and to include the promisee's reasonably foreseeable expected surplus as the liquidation term in the contract. To illustrate, suppose that efficient reliance by Yvonne and late completion of the restaurant by Xavier will cause a loss of $200 per day. Furthermore, suppose the contract specifies that Xavier will pay $200 per day for late completion of the restaurant. The full risk of marginal reliance rests upon Yvonne, as required for efficient reliance. Because Yvonne's reliance will be efficient, the actual harm caused by late completion will be $200 per day, so Xavier is liable for the actual harm suffered by Yvonne. In general, incentives for reliance and precaution are efficient when expected damages are invariant at the level of actual harm. In notation, letting y^* denote the efficient level of reliance, we conclude that

$$\left.\begin{array}{l} D = D(y^*) \\ 0 = D'(y) \end{array}\right\} \quad \begin{array}{l} \text{create efficient incentives} \\ \text{for reliance and precaution.} \end{array}$$

Question 7.23: In addition to requiring that a disappointed promisee engage in no more than reasonable reliance on the promisor's performance, the law also requires the promisee to *mitigate her damages*. That is, the innocent party in a breach must take reasonable actions to minimize her losses from the promisor's non-performance. In the Waffle Shop case, for example, Yvonne might be required to try to sell part of her supplemental food order to another restaurant.

Does the mitigation requirement create a further incentive for efficient reliance behavior on the part of promisees?

5. Application of the Model to a Case

Of the many types of behavior that contracts coordinate, we focused upon breach, precaution, and reliance. Read the following case and answer the questions to apply the analytical tools we have just developed.

Peevyhouse v. Garland Coal & Mining Company, 382 P.2d 109, *cert. denied*, 375 U.S. 906 (Okla. 1962)

JACKSON, J. In the trial court, plaintiffs Willie and Lucille Peevyhouse sued the defendant, Garland Coal and Mining Company, for damages for breach of contract. Judgment was for plaintiffs in an amount considerably less than was sued for. Plaintiffs appeal and defendant cross-appeals . . .

Briefly stated, the facts are as follows: plaintiffs owned a farm containing coal deposits, and in November, 1954, leased the premises to defendant for a period of five years for coal mining purposes. A "strip-mining" operation was contemplated in which the coal would be taken from pits on the surface of the ground, instead of from underground mine shafts. In addition to the usual covenants found in a coal mining lease, defendant specifically agreed to perform certain restorative and remedial work at the end of the lease period. It is unnecessary to set out the details of the work to be done, other than to say that it would involve the moving of many thousands of cubic yards of dirt, at a cost estimated by expert witnesses at about $29,000.00. However, plaintiffs sued for only $25,000.00.

During the trial, it was stipulated that all covenants and agreements in the lease contract had been fully carried out by both parties, except the remedial work mentioned above; defendant conceded that this work had not been done.

Plaintiffs introduced expert testimony as to the amount and nature of the work to be done. Over plaintiff's objections, defendant thereafter introduced expert testimony as to the "diminution in value" of plaintiffs' farm resulting from the failure of defendant to render performance as agreed in the contract—that is, the difference between the present value of the farm, and what its value would have been if defendant had done what it agreed to do. . . .

[T]he jury was at liberty to consider the "diminution in value" of plaintiffs' farm as well as the cost of "repair work" in determining the amount of damages.

It returned a verdict for plaintiffs for $5,000.00—only a fraction of the "cost of performance," *but more than the total value of the farm even after the remedial work is done.* [Emphasis in original.]

On appeal, the issue is sharply drawn. Plaintiffs contend that the true measure of damages in this case is what it will cost plaintiffs to obtain performance of the work that was not done because of defendant's default. Defendant argues that the measure of damages is the cost of performance "limited, however, to the total difference in the market value before and after the work was performed." . . .

[The court notes that if the remedial work were done, the market value of the Peevyhouse's farm would increase by only $300.]

We therefore hold that where, in a coal mining lease, lessee agrees to perform certain remedial work on the premises concerned at the end of the lease period, and thereafter the contract is fully performed by both parties except that the remedial work is not done, the measure of damages in an action by lessor against lessee for damages for breach of contract is ordinarily the reasonable cost of performance of the work; however, where the contract provision breached was merely incidental to the main purpose in view, and where the economic benefit which would result to lessor by full performance of the work is grossly disproportionate to the cost of performance, the damages which lessor may recover are limited to the diminution in value resulting to the premises because of the non-performance. . . .

Under the most liberal view of the evidence herein, the diminution in value resulting to the premises because of non-performance of the remedial work was $300.00. . . It thus appears that the judgment was clearly excessive, and that the amount for which judgment should have been rendered is definitely and satisfactorily shown by the record.

IRWIN, Justice (dissenting) . . . Although the contract speaks for itself, there were several negotiations between the plaintiffs and defendant before the contract was executed. Defendant admitted in the trial of the action, that plaintiffs insisted the [provisions regarding remedial work] be included in the contract and that they would not agree to the coal mining lease unless [those] provisions were included. . . .

The cost for performing the contract in question could have been reasonably approximated when the contract was negotiated and executed, and there are no conditions now existing which could not have been reasonably anticipated by the parties. Therefore, defendant had knowledge, when it prevailed upon the plaintiffs to execute the lease, that the cost of performance might be disproportionate to the value or benefits received by plaintiff for the performance. . . .

In the instant action defendant has made no attempt to even substantially perform. The contract in question is not immoral, is not tainted with fraud, and was not entered into through mistake or accident and is not contrary to public policy. It is clear and unambiguous and the parties understood the terms thereof, and the approximate cost of fulfilling the obligations could have been approximately ascertained. There are no conditions existing now which could not have been reasonably anticipated when the contract was negotiated and executed. The defendant could have performed the contract if it desired. It has accepted and reaped the benefits of its contract and now urges that plaintiffs under the contract be denied. . . .

Therefore, in my opinion, the plaintiffs were entitled to specific performance of the contract and since defendant has failed to perform, the proper measure of damages should be the cost of performance. . . .

[In a petition for rehearing, plaintiffs argued that the trial court had wrongfully excluded evidence that the diminution in the value of their farm was greater than $300, because the farm consisted not merely of the 60 acres covered by the coal-mining lease, but other lands as well. The court held, 5-4, that the evidence was properly excluded, because the complaint related only to the 60 acres covered by the lease, and the case had been tried and argued by plaintiffs on a cost-of-performance rather than a diminished-value theory.]

Question 7.24:

a. Is breach efficient or inefficient in this factual setting? Does the court's decision create incentives for efficient breach in future cases similar to this one?

b. What forms of precaution by the promisor (the coal company) and reliance by the promisee (the Peeveyhouses) might be relevant to this case? What are the incentive effects of the court's decision on precaution and reliance by future contracting parties?

c. The court asserts that the diminished-value measure of damages is more appropriate here than is the cost-of-performance measure. The reason they give is that the cost-of-performance theory will lead to something the court calls "economic waste." Do you agree?

d. Suppose that the costs of remedial work given in the opinion are accurate. What evidence does the court give as to the benefits of the remedial work? Is that evidence on the objective (market) value of the farm or on the subjective (personal) value of the farm to the Peevyhouses? Is it possible at this point to find any evidence on the Peevyhouses' subjective valuation on remedial work?

e. What about the effect of this decision on future contracting parties in Oklahoma? If you are a coal company that has signed a lease agreeing to perform remedial work after surface mining, would you restore the property? What if you were a coal company contemplating signing a lease with private individuals like the Peevyhouses? Would you agree to do remedial work after this decision? Would you include a discount in the price you paid for the lease to cover the anticipated costs of restoration? Suppose that you are a private property owner with a high subjective valuation on your property; perhaps your family has lived on this land for five generations. If a coal company offers to lease a portion of your property for surface mining, what would you do?

Question 7.25: A wealthy man contracted with a construction company to build him a "country estate." The contract specified numerous deadlines materials, and design details, including the buyer's insistence that all the pipes in the house be those manufactured by the Cohoes Pipe Company. The subcontractor who did the plumbing work instead used pipes manufactured by the Reading Pipe Company. The two kinds of pipe were indistinguishable, save for the raised letters along their side that read either "Cohoes" or "Reading."

When completion of the home was near, the buyer learned about the switched pipes and refused to pay the balance due on the contract to the building contractor. The contractor sued for that balance, and the buyer counter-claimed for damages or specific performance because of the switched pipe. [*Jacob & Youngs v. Kent*, 230 N.Y. 239, 129 N.E. 889 (1921).]

The court determined that the diminution in value of the property because of the mistaken use of Reading pipe was zero. The cost of doing the repair work was approximately $200,000, several times the market value of the house.

Assume that the contractor has breached the contract. Which of the measures of damages the court considers—diminution of value and cost of performance—creates efficient incentives for reliance and precaution by future contracting parties, especially in the circumstances where the promisee has a highly subjective—indeed, eccentric—valuation on performance, as did Mr. Kent? Which damages measure maximizes the value of the contract? Which of the measures of damages minimizes the costs of resolving this dispute?

F. Equitable Relief: The Award of Specific Performance[44]

Damage payments are the legal remedy for contract breach; specific performance is the equitable remedy. Specific performance is a judicial order requiring the promisor to perform his contractual promise or forbidding him from performing the promise with any other party. To return to our example of breach due to the possibility of a windfall gain, if *A* has promised to sell a house to *B* for $100,000 but breaches in order to sell to *C* for $120,000, *B* might seek relief in the form of a court order requiring *A* to sell to him. Alternatively, *B* might ask the court for an injunction forbidding *A* to sell to anyone but *B*.

The question that this section deals with is whether specific performance is an efficient remedy for breach of contract and how it compares with the forms of legal relief that we have been considering at creating efficient incentives for breach, precaution, and reliance.

1. The Efficiency of Specific Performance   As a general rule, in civil cases courts invoke equitable remedies only when they determine that legal remedies are likely to offer inadequate relief, that is, to be undercompensatory. In the case of breach of contract, the typical cases in which this undercompensation is said to arise are in the sale of "unique goods," the sale of land (considered by the law, largely for historical reasons, to be a unique good), long-term input contracts, and contracts for labor and other professional services. It is not hard to see why. For unique goods, the value to the buyer is determined by his subjective valuation, which can be much higher than the price others are willing to pay. For example, a collector of rare manuscripts may value the only manuscript copy of Faulkner's *The Sound and the Fury* far more than does anyone else. Because there is, for the collector, no substitute, an attempt by the seller to breach his contract to sell the manuscript to the collector cannot be easily resolved by the court's determining an amount of money damages that will protect the promisee's expectation interest. In contrast, when a good has a close substitute that is readily available in the market, no one is likely to value the good at much more than the price of the available substitute. In this respect manufactured goods, like bicycles or toasters, differ from one-of-a-kind goods like paintings. The remedy of specific performance gives the promisee the good itself, rather than its value, or allows the promisee to release the promisor from completing the contract only after the promisor has agreed to pay the promisee's expectation interest. By adopting the remedy of specific performance for breach of promise to deliver unique goods, rather than the remedy of damages, courts avoid the insoluble problem of trying to determine the promisee's subjective valuation of the breached good.

---

[44]This section is based on material in Ulen, *The Efficiency of Specific Performance: Toward a Unified Theory of Contract Remedies*, 84 MICH. L. REV. 358 (1984).

A case can be made that specific performance should be more widely available as a remedy, even in situations not involving unique goods. In our discussion of remedies for invasion of property rights in Chapters 4 and 5, we focused on the extent of bargaining or transaction costs between the affected parties in choosing between damages and the equitable remedy. We may apply that same theory to the determination of the efficient remedy for breach of contract.

Damages and specific performance, like damages and injunctive relief in nuisance law, should be seen as alternative means of achieving efficient resource allocation in the face of different transaction costs. When a contract has been breached, the question of utmost importance to the court should be the level of bargaining or transaction costs facing the defaulter and innocent party. If those costs are low, then private negotiations are possible and the most efficient relief for the court to order is specific performance. If, however, transaction costs are high, then the court should compel an exchange at a collectively-determined value; that is, it should assess money damages against the breacher.

And, in general, the post-breach transaction costs between contractual parties are not high. After all, they have established a relationship before breach, and the things that make for high transaction costs in other legal contexts are entirely absent here: the parties have identified each other; they have bargained, providing for many contingencies—including, possibly, breach; they may have had contact after formation and before full performance to clarify details, report progress, and the like. All of this is of utmost importance to recognize if the parties did not provide for some form of relief in the event of breach, for in that case the costs to them of dealing with the contingency that has arisen to frustrate the contract should be low. Certainly, the costs to the parties of resolving their dispute—for example, of determining what the innocent party's expectation interest is—would seem to be lower than they would be for a court. This is because the court, in order to resolve the dispute efficiently and, in doing so, to create an efficient rule to guide future contracting parties, would have to inform itself about all the relevant terms of the contract, the market for the commodity involved, the believability of each party's evidence on the victim's expectancy, the reasonableness of the risks assumed, and so on. This is a burdensome and expensive duty for the court to take on. On efficiency grounds, it can be argued that if courts wish to create efficient rules for those contemplating formation of contracts or breaching contracts, then they should routinely award specific performance: this will induce future parties most efficiently to stipulate their own remedies (or not to stipulate them if they would rather be specifically bound) and will induce only efficient breach. Thus, it can be argued that specific performance, the contractual counterpart of injunctive relief in nuisance law, should be the routine remedy for breach. It also follows that money damages should be reserved for those occasions on which the post-breach transaction costs of the contractual parties are high.

This argument can be developed in detail by reference to the components of costs in a contractual setting. To illustrate, the court costs attending specific performance may, in general, be less than those attending legal relief. Less must be demonstrated by the injured promisee, and the costs of determining the promisee's expectancy are left to negotiations between the promisee and promisor rather than being determined through evidentiary proceedings.

> **Question 7.26:** the *Peevyhouse* case that was discussed above. Would the efficiency problems with the court's decision disappear if the remedy in the case were specific performance rather than damages?

> **Question 7.27:** In the case of *Jacob & Youngs v. Kent*, would specific performance have been as efficient as the damages remedies that you discussed?

> **Question 7.28:** Show that specific performance can resolve the paradox of compensation by simultaneously creating incentives for efficient precaution and reliance.

2. Criticisms of Specific Performance   It is sometimes mistakenly said in criticism of specific performance that it does not have the flexibility that an award of money damages has. For example, one of the rules for awarding money damages is that the victim, to be entitled to his expectancy, must take steps to mitigate his losses from the breach. As you have by now demonstrated, this requirement creates efficient incentives for the promisee's reliance. It is argued that because the victim of a breach has no duty to mitigate under an award of specific performance, equitable relief is less efficient than is legal relief. Let's examine this criticism.

Consider a contract for the sale of a perishable product like tomatoes. Suppose that B agrees to purchase 1000 tons of fresh tomatoes from S, a wholesaler, at $10 per ton. S will realize a profit of $2,000 on the sale. S receives the produce from his supplier, but B, a restaurateur, has suffered a financial setback since the contract was formed (our *accident* contingency) and announces his intention to breach the contract. If the routine contract remedy is money damages, then S will be entitled to his expectancy, $2,000, plus any incidental costs incurred in trying to mitigate his losses by selling the tomatoes elsewhere. But if the routine remedy is specific performance, then there is a fear that S will simply allow the tomatoes to rot or that, more likely, his incentive to resell them will be less than is the case with money damages. Alternatively, specific performance may induce B to take delivery of the tomatoes, pay S $10,000, and attempt to resell them himself. If B is less advantageously placed to resell than is S, then it might be argued that specific performance has created an inefficiency by placing the duty to resell on the party with the higher costs of resale.

The inefficiency is illusory. B need not take delivery under specific performance, nor necessarily pay more in settlement to S than if a court awarded S his expectancy plus incidental expenses in reselling. If B would rather not be saddled with the costs of reselling the tomatoes, then he can purchase S's right to enforce the contract from S for $2,000 plus S's costs of resale. This will satisfy S since he is, by definition, doing as well as if B fully performed. *B* is better off in paying this sum than in taking delivery if his resale costs are greater than are *S*'s. Note that this is precisely the outcome that would have resulted under an award of money damages. This means that, even without a duty to mitigate under specific performance, the result of a buyer's breach is the same whatever the contractual remedy. Neither remedy is, on this score, more efficient than the other. The only requirement for the results to be the same under money damages and specific performance is that the bargaining costs between *B* and *S* must be low. For the reasons stated in the preceding section, this seems likely to be the case.

> **Question 7.29:** *R* has rented *L*'s premises for five years under the condition that he use the property only as a saloon; furthermore, the contract forbids him to sub-let the premises during the term of the lease. After two years, the county in which *R* has been operating his saloon suddenly and unexpectedly makes the sale of alcoholic beverages illegal. *R* breaches his contract with *L*, and *L* sues for specific performance. Under that remedy, might it not be the case that *R* will be inefficiently bound to pay *L* the remaining three years' rental? And would things not be more efficient if *L* had a duty to mitigate his losses by re-letting the premises if the routine award were money damages with a duty to mitigate?

> **Question 7.30:** In our discussion of money damages, we saw that the law imposes a further limitation on the award of money damages in the event of breach of contract. That is that the victim—recall the photographer whose pictures of the Himalayas were lost—can collect only his reasonably foreseeable damages. Consequential and extraordinary damages are excluded from the victim's recovery.
> Using the bargaining model and the Positive Coase Theorem, analyze whether specific performance will always allow the victim to collect direct and consequential damages and foreseeable *and* unforeseeable damages from the breacher. Or is the result under specific performance like that under the money damages: only reasonably foreseeable losses will be collected?

3. The Economics of the Special Defenses Available to the Breacher Under Specific Performance

When an innocent victim of breach asks for specific performance, the law allows the breacher to invoke special defenses that would not be available if the victim asked for money damages. He may claim an inadequacy of consideration, a lack of sufficient security for the promisee's performance, and that he was unilaterally mistaken. There is no sound efficiency reason for *any* of these defenses. None of them has found favor in our efficiency analysis of formation defenses, and there is, therefore, no good reason to offer them for the use of defendants to an action for specific performance.

However, there are two defenses against specific performance that make excellent economic sense. Additionally, these two defenses point out the circumstances in which bargaining costs may be so high that legal relief is more efficient than equitable relief for breach of contract.

The first of these defenses is impossibility. By this term we mean not only the circumstances contemplated in our discussion of performance excuses; we also mean the broader set of circumstances in which the contractual promise cannot be completed according to its terms. In the case of physical impossibility, a theater owner whose theater has just burned down cannot specifically perform his promise to provide that theater. In the broader sense, the owner of the Riki-Tiki-Tavi Beach Resort who promised to provide you two weeks of sunshine cannot specifically perform that promise if it rains. If there has been a breach, some form of legal relief will have to suffice. The point here is that specific performance should be the remedy only when performance is still possible.

The second defense for which there is a sound economic argument is difficulty of supervision. One of the most troubling issues in making specific performance the routine remedy for breach of contract is that there may be many circumstances in which the costs to the court of supervising the performance of the breacher may be inefficiently high. This is most likely to be the case in contracts for personal services. Consider this example. Suppose that *A* contracts with *B* to play Hamlet in a production of Shakespeare's play at *B*'s theater. Subsequently *A* breaches the contract by refusing to perform his role. Typically, a court will not grant *B* specific performance, that is, an order compelling *A* to perform Hamlet. This is because the costs to the court of judging whether *A* had discharged his contractual obligation to *B* are extraordinarily high. How should the court assure the quality of *A*'s performance as the Prince of Denmark? Perhaps because *A* is in such a pique about his dispute with *B* that without stringent and expensive supervision by the court he will seek to embarrass *B* by the shoddiness of his performance as Hamlet. When these supervisory costs are recognized, it may be more efficient for the court to award *B* money damages.

CONCLUSION

In this chapter we have used the economic theory of contracts to survey the rich fabric of contract law. The economic theory viewed the purpose of contract law to be to provide assistance to private parties in achieving their legitimate goals. To that end, rules of contract law facilitate the coordination of the activities of the contracting parties through encouraging mutually beneficial allocations of risk and efficient investments in precaution and reliance. The law can most efficiently intervene in these private activities when there are conditions that are likely to frustrate the exchange of perfect contracts.

Our discussion in this chapter attempted to provide the practical guidelines for designing the contract rules that follow from the economic theory of contract. We have discovered several ways in which the application of the economic theory may lead to different conclusions than those generally accepted in the legal literature, as in our interpretations of the formation defenses and performance excuses of the liquidated damages clauses. We have also seen instances in which the economic theory has provided a consistent and scientific justification for the practices that modern courts have adopted in contract disputes. The economic interpretations of duress, mistake, and unconscionability are notable examples.

However convincing or interminable, depending on your point of view, the economic analysis of contract rights and remedies may seem, it is merely the beginning of a remarkably fertile and exciting area of intellectual activity. There is still much more important work to be done in this important area of the law.

SUGGESTED READINGS ON CONTRACT LAW

Barton, John H., *The Economic Basis for Breach of Contract*, 1 J. LEGAL STUD. 277 (1972).

Burton, Steve, *Breach of Contract and the Common Law Duty to Perform in Good Faith*, 369 HARV. L. REV. 94 (1980).

Cheung, Steven, *Transaction Costs, Risk Aversion, and the Choice of Contractual Arrangements*, 12 J. L. & ECON. 23 (1969).

Farber, Daniel, *Reassessing the Economic Efficiency of Compensatory Damages for Breach of Contract*, 66 VA. L. REV. 1471 (1980).

Fuller, Lon & J. Perdue, *The Reliance Interest in Contract Damages*, 46 YALE L. J. 52 (1936).

Goetz, Charles & Robert Scott, *Measuring Seller's Damages: The Lost Profits Puzzle*, 31 STAN. L. REV. 323 (1979).

Goldberg, Victor, *An Economic Analysis of the Lost-Volume Retail Seller*, 57 SO. CAL. L. REV. 283 (1984).

Kronman, Anthony T., *Contract Law and Distributive Justice*, 89 YALE L. J. 472 (1980).

Kronman, Anthony T., *Contract Law and the State of Nature*, 1 J. LAW, ECON. & ORG. 5 (1985).

Kronman, Anthony T., *Specific Performance*, 45 U. CHI. L. REV. 351 (1978).

Perloff, Jeffrey M., *Breach of Contract and the Foreseeability Doctrine of Hadley v. Baxendale*, 10 J. LEGAL STUD. 39 (1981).

Perloff, Jeffrey M., *The Effects of Breaches of Forward Contract Due to Unanticipated Price Changes*, 10 J. LEGAL STUD. 221 (1981).

Polinsky, A. Mitchell, *Risk-Sharing Through Breach of Contract Remedies*, 12 J. LEGAL STUD. 427 (1983).

Posner, Richard A. & Andrew Rosenfield, *Impossibility and Related Doctrines in Contract Law*, 6 J. LEGAL STUD. 88 (1977).

Rea, Samuel, *Non-pecuniary Loss and Breach of Contract*, 11 J. LEGAL STUD. 35 (1982).

Schwartz, Alan, *The Case for Specific Performance*, 89 YALE L. J. 271 (1979).

Williamson, Oliver, *Assessing Contract*, 1 J. LAW, ECON. & ORG. 177 (1985).

CHAPTER 8

An Economic Theory of Torts

People often harm each other by doing something wrong: some drivers collide with pedestrians; the Dalkon shield, an intra-uterine birth control device, is alleged to make some women infertile; a newspaper inaccurately reports that a local businessman was arrested for soliciting a prostitute; Stagger Lee cheats on Billy; professors give unfair exams; and so forth. In none of these instances were the victim and the injurer in a contractual relationship. For that reason, if the victim sues for damages, he cannot look to contract law to resolve the dispute. Instead, the relevant body of law for resolving these disputes is tort law.

Tort law is in turmoil in the United States. The scope of harms for which plaintiffs have been allowed to bring actions and the size of the judgments they have received have been growing very rapidly. In fact, the growth has been so fast and expansive that there is a widespread belief among some thoughtful commentators that the tort system has broken down and needs to be extensively reformed.

Torts was one of the first bodies of the common law to which formal economic models were applied. As we will see, these models have provided valuable insights. As with all of our introductory chapters in this book, our focus here will be on theory, specifically a comparison between the traditional legal theory of torts and the economic theory. In the next chapter we apply economic theory to some specific areas of tort law, develop a more detailed analysis, and explore some dimensions of the alleged breakdown in and proposals for reform of the tort liability system.

I. THE ELEMENTS OF A TORT

The term "tort" is law-French, itself derived from the Latin word "torquere," to twist, and means a private wrong or injury. There is a classical theory that specified the essential elements of a tort, much as did the classical theory in contracts.[1] The classical theory enjoyed substantial acceptance in America at the turn of the century, although it never achieved the same degree of consensus as did the classical theory of contracts. This traditional or classical theory specified the elements of a tort that it regarded as essential. These elements, although no longer regarded as essential in torts, are a good starting point in our introduction to torts. It is easier to grasp these elements concretely, so we will present some examples before proceeding to the abstractions.

> **Example 1:** Joe Potatoes has been driven to drink by the escapades of his wife, Joan Potatoes. At the end of a hard night's work at the loading dock, Joe is approached by Bloggs. Suspecting that Bloggs has been romancing Joan, Joe insults Bloggs and strikes him, breaking Bloggs' nose. Bloggs subsequently sues for the injury to his reputation and his nose.

> **Example 2:** Three hunters go into the woods after pheasants. They are spread out in a straggling line and are about 25 yards apart when the hunter in the center flushes a bird that flies up, its wings pounding. The two hunters on the end of the line turn and fire simultaneously at the bird. The bird escapes, but the hunter in the middle is blinded by shot. One of the two hunters certainly caused the harm, but there is no way to determine which one of them it was. The victim sues both of them.

> **Example 3:** A manufacturer produces automobile fuel additives that demand careful control over quality. If quality control is maintained at a high level, the chemical mixture in the product is correct, and it never causes damage to automobile engines. However, if quality control is relaxed and allowed to fall to a low level, some batches of the chemical mixture will be flawed. A few of the cars using the flawed batch will be harmed; specifically, the engine will throw a rod and tear itself to pieces. After a rod is thrown, an alert mechanic can detect the cause of the harm by examining the car's fuel and other signs. In a lean year, the manufacturer relaxes its quality control and, subsequently, several owners of cars that throw rods bring suit.

In each of these examples, someone's person or property is harmed by someone else. The purpose of tort law, roughly speaking, is to protect the interests of people in their property and persons from damage by others. Implementing this purpose, however, is subtle and complicated. To understand the law, it is necessary to go beyond a general account of its purpose and understand its elements. Three elements, which we will illustrate by our examples, were distinguished in the classical theory of tort:

1. breach of a duty owed to the plaintiff by the defendant,
2. harm suffered by the plaintiff, and
3. the breach being the immediate or proximate cause of the harm.

A useful way to organize our introduction to torts is to explain these elements and then, in the second half of the chapter, to show their connection to economic analysis.

---

[1]For example, *see* Oliver Wendell Holmes, Jr., THE COMMON LAW (1881).

A. Breach of a Duty

A private wrong involves the breach of a duty that one person owes to another. The first element of a tort is, then, the breach of a legal duty owed to the plaintiff by the defendant. When such a breach occurs, it is said that the defendant was "at fault" or "negligent." To illustrate, Joe Potatoes in Example 1 breached a duty not to strike Bloggs, and one of the hunters in Example 2 breached a duty of care in handling guns. In Example 3 the manufacturer breached a duty to market a safe product.

The breach of a duty is wrong, but the character of the wrongs are quite different in the first two examples. Thus, Potatoes apparently intended to harm Bloggs, whereas the hunters presumably had no intention of harming anyone and were merely careless in handling their guns. This distinction between intentional and unintentional harm is an important one to which we will return. Here our focus is not on the mental state of the wrongdoer (or *tortfeasor*, as he is called in the law) but rather on the fact that a duty of care has been violated. Specifically, the intent of the tortfeasor does not affect the wrongdoer's duty to compensate the victim. The injury need not be intentional in order for the wrong to be a tort, the injurer to be liable, and the victim to recover damages. Thus, the fact that the hunters did not intend harm is not a sufficient defense.

This identification of the defendant's breach of a duty or obligation owed to the plaintiff leads directly to one of the most important questions that any theory of tort must answer: how are these duties determined? This is a vital question for any tort theory, but it is also an exceedingly difficult one because there are no easy generalizations. The most sweeping rule that we will dare to extract from the law is that potential tortfeasors are held to a duty of *reasonable* care. For example, Joe Potatoes, the offending hunters, and the manufacturer of fuel additives all have a legal duty to be reasonably careful. But exactly how much care is "reasonable"? The reasonable person standard is an *objective* standard that compares the precautionary activity of the defendant with what a reasonable person would have done *under the circumstances*. As this definition makes plain, the reasonable person standard for determining the defendant's duty is vague, but the concept of reasonable behavior is just as central to tort law as the concept of rational behavior is to economics. The reasonable person standard also has the virtue of being admirably flexible. (It is also subject to ridicule, as the box on Reasonable People indicates.) For example, an ordinary level of care is required for manufacturing fuel additives, whereas special care is required for handling dangerous objects like guns or poisonous drugs.

These standards—reasonable care, ordinary care, and special care—are left vague in law. For most actions, there is no statute that tells how much care is reasonable. Instead of precise specification in a statue, the legal standard usually depends upon the norms, practices, and values of ordinary people. As we will see, economics provides a systematic way of thinking about these legal standards and analyzing the social norms upon which they are based.

Let Us Now Praise Reasonable People

The following famous parody of the reasonable person standard is from an essay entitled "The Reasonable Man" by Lord A. P. Herbert:

"The Common Law of England has been laboriously built about a mythical figure—the figure of 'The Reasonable Man.' He is an ideal, a standard, the embodiment of all those qualities which we demand of the good citizen . . . It is impossible to travel anywhere or to travel for long in that confusing forest of learned judgments which constitutes the Common Law of England without encountering the Reasonable Man. . .

The Reasonable Man is always thinking of others; prudence is his guide, and 'Safety First' is his rule of life. He is one who invariably looks where he is going and is careful to examine the immediate foreground before he executes a leap or bound; who neither star-gazes nor is lost in meditation when approaching trap-doors or the margin of a dock; who records in every case upon the counterfoils of checks such ample details as are desirable, who never mounts a moving omnibus, and does not alight from any car while the train is in motion; who investigates exhaustively the *bona fides* of every mendicant before distributing alms, and will inform himself of the history and habits of a dog before administering a caress; who believes no gossip, nor repeats it, without firm basis for believing it to be true; who never drives his ball till those in front of him have definitely vacated the putting-green which is his own objective; who never from one year's end to another makes an excessive demand upon his wife, his neighbors, his servants, his ox, or his ass; who in the way of business looks only for that narrow margin of profit which twelve men such as himself would reckon to be 'fair,' and contemplates his fellow-merchants, their agents, and their goods, with that degree of suspicion and distrust which the law deems admirable; who never swears, gambles, or loses his temper; who uses nothing except in moderation, and even while he flogs his child is meditating only on the golden mean. [He] stands like a monument in our Courts of Justice, vainly appealing to his fellow-citizens to order their lives after his own example. . . ."

B. Damages

A second element in a tort suit is that the breach of duty must give rise to measurable damages. If the wrong does not result in harm, there are no grounds for a suit. Doing something dangerous that causes no harm does not constitute an actionable tort; indeed, carelessness that causes no harm is called, delightfully, "negligence in the air." To illustrate, suppose that the manufacturer in Example 3 sold a batch of fuel additives that were dangerous in, say, cars with turbo-charged carburetors but harmless to cars with conventional carburetors. A driver who bought the product might feel outrage when these facts became known, regardless of whether his car's carburetor is turbo-charged or conventional. Outrage, however, is not compensable. If the driver is one of the fortunate people with a conventional carburetor, he has not suffered harm and, therefore, has no grounds for a suit.

This fact sharply differentiates torts from morality. To illustrate, suppose that in Example 2, both of the hunters were equally reckless when they discharged their guns at the pheasant. Since they were equally reckless, they were on the same plane morally. It was a matter of luck, not moral desert or merit, that one of the hunters actually blinded the victim and the other hunter missed. They are equally culpable by the standards of morality, but in law the hunter who actually caused the harm is liable and the hunter who missed is not liable.

In the past the law circumscribed the types of harm for which compensation was allowed. For example, courts were willing to compensate for medical costs but reluctant to compensate for emotional harm, distress, and loss of companionship. Over the years, however, the courts have steadily expanded the categories of compensable harm. To illustrate, in addition to his physical injuries, Bloggs may have suffered emotional distress from being reviled and struck by Potatoes. In the past the law was reluctant to compensate for such intangible losses, because they are hard to measure; yet modern courts have entirely overcome this reluctance.

The expansion of the categories of compensable harm cuts two ways. It has allowed compensation for some tragically costly harms that would have gone uncompensated not long ago; for example, until the 19th century the legal maxim was that a person's action (if he had one) died with him. As a result, if B's carelessness caused A's death, A's family had no right of action against B; that action died with A. Only if A survived could there be a tortious claim for damages against B.[2]

This result struck most commentators as perverse, and so most states recognized, sometimes by statute, the tort of wrongful death, which allowed the victim's family, among others, to bring a civil action against the injurer for the harm they suffered because of the loss of their loved one. For example, suppose that the father in a family, who is employed, is killed in a tortious accident. Under wrongful death statutes, the surviving members of the family could ordinarily sue for their economic loss, which is conventionally calculated as approximately equal to the present value of the stream of future wages that the deceased would have earned.[3]

But this is not the only way in which the domain of compensable harms has been expanded. It has expanded in other ways that have created some

---

[2]Apparently the theory was that if death resulted, B had committed a crime and that a criminal action by the government would be brought against B. Thus, tort law protected the living injured and deterred wrongdoers; criminal law protected society and punished the criminal.

[3]To be strictly accurate, the amount that the father would have spent on his own personal consumption must be deducted from his future earnings to obtain the net loss to the surviving members of the family.

additional problems for the tort system. To see these, suppose that instead of the father dying, one of the dependent children is killed. The death of a dependent generally entails no loss of income to the rest of the family; on the contrary, the death of a child saves the family the expense of raising him or her. This fact once posed a difficult problem for courts: they wished to confine compensable damages to economic losses that are measurable, and yet there are usually no such losses for the death of dependent children. For the surviving members of the family to recover damages, it was necessary to allow compensation for emotional distress and loss of companionship. But this expansion of the categories of compensable losses, which was intended to solve one problem, has created another: how is the court to assign a dollar value to intangible losses? If someone destroys your antique vase, compensatory damages is an amount of money such that you would just as soon have the money as the vase. But the matter is much more problematic for intangible losses like loss of companionship or emotional distress. Are compensatory damages for the wrongful death of a child an amount of money such that the parents would just as soon have the money as their child? This way of speaking is callous and offensive to parents. It makes no sense to describe the damages given for the wrongful death of a child as "compensation."

It is painful for us to admit, but there are some controversial problems in tort law, like this one of computing intangible losses, that economics cannot solve. Still, let us not throw up our hands in complete despair: economics *can* suggest techniques of measurement that are accurate at least to a reasonable level of approximation, even for intangible damages, like the parents' loss from their child's wrongful death.

There is an additional, distinguishable problem that has arisen recently in the computation of damages. In some recent cases plaintiffs have won awards that are so large that they are alleged to have endangered the continued health of whole industries. An example is the recurrent medical malpractice crisis; the burgeoning size of medical malpractice awards and the resulting rise in liability insurance premiums has reportedly caused some doctors to switch their specialization from risky areas, like gynecology and obstetrics, to less risky areas, like internal medicine. These responses may have serious efficiency consequences in the delivery of health care, on the stability of the insurance industry, and on other important economic variables. We will examine these crises more thoroughly in the next chapter and consider some proposals for reforming the tort system to take account of them.

C. Causation

The third element of a tort concerns the connection between the wrong and the harm; the former must *cause* the latter. To illustrate, suppose that, just as Potatoes' fist was about to strike Bloggs' nose in Example 1, the floor board broke under Bloggs and he fell, thus avoiding Potatoes' fist, but, nevertheless, breaking his nose when he struck the ground. In this revised example, there is a wrong (throwing a punch), and there is damage (a broken nose), but the former did not cause the latter, so the wrongdoer is not liable.[4]

The idea of causation may seem simple—perhaps an image comes to mind of billiard balls colliding with each other—but this impression is misleading. To illustrate some complications, suppose a psychologist says that a young woman's suicide was *caused* by her childhood affair with her paternal uncle, or an economist says that devaluation *caused* inflation, or a minister says that God *causes* the sinful to suffer. These usages of "cause" are far more problematic than using "cause" to describe the consequences of colliding billiard balls. There is, in fact, a long philosophical tradition of distinguishing various types of causes. For example, Aristotle distinguished a hierarchy of causes, starting from the most immediate cause (the "proximate cause") and ending with the cause of all things (God or the "unmoved mover").

Courts and tort lawyers, however, are usually content to limit themselves to two types of causes. The first, and more comprehensive, of these is "cause-in-fact." Establishing that the defendant's act was a cause-in-fact of the plaintiff's harm is necessary but not a sufficient condition for the plaintiff's recovering. To illustrate this type of case, in Example 1 Potatoes' punch was the cause-in-fact of the injury to Bloggs' nose, whereas in the revised version of Example 1, where Bloggs fell through a weak floorboard before he could be struck, Potatoes' punch was not the cause-in-fact of the injury.

There is a simple criterion, called the "but-for test," that lawyers often use to decide whether action A was the cause-in-fact of event B: "But for A, would B (which *did* occur) not have occurred?" If the answer to this question is "Yes," then A is the cause-in-fact of B. If the answer to this question is "No," then A is not the cause-in-fact of B. Thus, in Example 3 an automobile owner cannot recover unless the defective fuel additive was the cause-in-fact of her engine's having thrown a rod. But for the defective fuel additive, would the car have thrown a rod? If the answer is "yes," then the defective fuel additive is said to be the cause-in-fact, but not otherwise.

The but-for test is adequate for determining cause-in-fact in most cases, but there are circumstances in which it is misleading or of little help. One circumstance in which this occurs is where there are multiple possible causes of a harm. To illustrate by another permutation of Example 1, suppose that Potatoes does in fact strike Bloggs and break his nose; however, suppose in addition that the floorboards were rotten and that, even if Potatoes did not strike Bloggs, Bloggs would have fallen and broken his nose. The punch fails the but-for test, and yet, even so, the punch was the cause-in-fact of the broken nose.

---

[4]Bloggs may, however, sue the company that owns the loading dock for not maintaining its floors. This alternative suit, however, may involve a special set of workers' compensation statutes, which have largely displaced the common law of torts for accidents occurring in the workplace.

Another problem is that there are circumstances in which the but-for test does not work and where any other imaginable test for cause-in-fact seems also to fail. In those circumstances, the plaintiff, although clearly injured, may fail to recover because of her inability to prove cause-in-fact, as illustrated by the hunters in Example 2. To win this case it is not enough for the plaintiff to prove that both of the hunters were negligent and that one of them fired the shot that caused the injury. To recover, the plaintiff must prove which one fired the harmful shot. But it is impossible to determine on available evidence which hunter that was; thus, the plaintiff cannot recover. (In the real case to which Example 2 corresponds, the court allowed the plaintiff to recover by holding each of the defendants 50% responsible.[5])

Upon reflection, it is not really surprising that the but-for test sometimes fails. The but-for test simply ascertains whether the defendant's wrongful act was a *necessary* condition for the plaintiff's injury. However, the concept of causation is much more complicated than the concept of a necessary condition, as philosophers have shown.[6]

Besides cause-in-fact, there is an additional causal requirement in most tort suits. The reason for the additional requirement is that the but-for test is not very discriminating. For example, Joe Potatoes' parents are a cause-in-fact of Bloggs' injury because, but for their having conceived Joe, Bloggs would not have had his nose broken by Potatoes. A further illustration can be seen in this famous verse from Mother Goose:

> For want of a nail, the shoe was lost;
> For want of a shoe, the horse was lost;
> For want of a horse, the rider was lost;
> For want of a rider, the battle was lost.
> For want of the battle, the kingdom was lost.
> And all for the want of a horseshoe nail.

This syllogism illustrates that "but-for" causes can be ordered from the remote to the proximate; furthermore, as the but-for causes become more remote, at some point the attribution of causation no longer makes sense.[7] Indeed, the conclusion that the downfall of a nation was caused by the want of a horseshoe nail is absurd. Tort law takes account of this fact that some causes-in-fact are remote and some close by requiring that causes be *proximate*, rather than remote, as a condition for recovering damages. In other words, for the plaintiff to recover, the defendant's breach of duty to the plaintiff must be, not just the cause-in-fact of the plaintiff's injury, but also the *proximate* (or *legal*) *cause*.

---

[5]*Summers v. Tice,* 33 Cal.2d 80, 199 P.2d 1 (1948). See the discussion of this case in Judith Thompson, *Remarks on Causation and Liability,* 13 PHIL. & PUB. AFFAIRS 101 (1984).

[6]Philosophers have tried to explain causality in terms of a complicated concatenation of necessary and sufficient conditions.

[7]This could be called the "principle of the decaying transitivity of causes."

Since proximity of cause to effect is a matter of degree, the question arises, "How close must the connection be in order to be 'proximate' in law?" As with the case of reasonable care, there is no hard and fast answer to the question of what constitutes proximate cause. One of the most famous examples of the problem of determining legal causation arose in *Palsgraf v. Long Island Railway Co.*[8] The relevant facts, as determined by the court, were these:

> Plaintiff [Mrs. Palsgraf] was standing on a platform of defendant's railroad after buying a ticket to go to Rockaway Beach. A train stopped at the station, bound for another place. Two men ran forward to catch it. One of the men reached the platform of the car without mishap, though the train was already moving. The other man, carrying a package, jumped aboard the car, but seemed unsteady as if about to fall. A guard on the car, who had held the door open, reached forward to help him in, and another guard on the platform pushed him from behind. In this act, the package was dislodged, and fell upon the rails. It was a package of small size, about fifteen inches long, and was covered by a newspaper. In fact it contained fireworks, but there was nothing in its appearance to give notice of its contents. The fireworks when they fell exploded. The shock of the explosion threw down some scales at the other end of the platform many feet away. The scales struck the plaintiff, causing injuries for which she sues.

The New York court determined that the railroad was not liable for Mrs. Palsgraf's injuries because the railroad guard's actions in pushing the passenger were too far removed in the chain of causes to be deemed the legal cause of the plaintiff's harm.[9]

Below, we will develop a theory about the connection between causal ralations in tort law and functional relations in economic analysis.

D. The Elements of a Tort in Perspective and Some Problems

The elements of a tort fit neatly into a coherent picture of social life and norms. In our daily interactions, we impose risks upon each other. To control these risks, society has developed norms that prescribe standards of rea-

---

[8]248 N.Y. 399, 162 N.E. 99 (1928).

[9]The majority opinion in this famous case is by Chief Justice Cardozo; there is a famous dissent by Justice Andrews that is well worth reading.

As is often true with famous cases, the facts are not as straightforward as generations of law students are led to believe. For example, in this case there was a strong possibility that the scales that fell on Mrs. Palsgraf may have been tipped not by the explosion but by the stampede of passengers on the platform that the explosion caused. Would the issue of proximate or legal cause be decided differently if the stampede was the cause of the injury? It also appears to be the case that Mrs. Palsgraf's principal injury was a stammer. She contended that the shock of the incident on the defendant's platform caused her to develop the stammer, but there is reason for believing that the trauma of the litigation may have contributed to the retention of the stammer. John Noonan, PERSONS AND MASKS OF THE LAW 127 (1976).

sonable behavior. These norms are, however, violated, and sometimes the violations result in harm. The cost of the harm must be borne by someone. In assigning responsibility for the harm, the courts trace events back to the violation of the duty and assign the cost to the party at fault. This picture, then, accounts for the elements of a tort: a breach of duty by the defendant that proximately causes harm to the plaintiff.

Most torts correspond to this picture. But as useful as this simplifying picture is, it distorts some aspects of tort law, especially its recent developments. Indeed, if our description of the elements of torts were left to stand on its own, it would be seriously misleading because there are major areas in modern tort law that lack at least one of these elements. In torts, as in contracts, the actual practices of the courts have departed far from the classical theory. We will illustrate the problems raised by recent developments for each of the elements of tort.

1. Liability Without Fault   Over the past forty years or so there has been a gradual movement away from the negligence or fault standard and toward a standard of liability without fault that is called "strict liability." This trend toward strict liability has been especially notable for harms arising from the use of commercial products, as we will see in detail in the following chapter. In the first section below we discuss the rise of strict liability and distinguish it from the negligence or fault standard. In the second section below, we discuss a different trend away from the classical theory of tort liability. This is the trend toward the imposition of liability for failure to rescue. Although it might be said that this is a broadening of the legal duty of care to include a duty to rescue others in distress rather than the imposition of liability without fault, this new liability is sufficiently distinct from negligence in the classical theory of liability to warrant placing it under the rubric of liability without fault.

a. Strict Liability   Under certain circumstances, an action that harms someone, but is not a breach of a legal duty, is sufficient for tort liability. To illustrate, a construction company that uses dynamite to clear rocks from the path of a road will be held liable for any harm caused by blasting even though they observe all the requisite standards of care and their handling of the dynamite is not at fault in any way. That is, if the use of dynamite causes harm to others, the user is liable, even though there was no misuse.

The rule of law for very dangerous activities like blasting is called "strict liability." Liability is strict in the sense that the defendant is held liable for causing the harm, regardless of whether he breached a legal duty to the plaintiff. Under this rule, moral opprobrium does not attach to liability because the defendant need not be at fault in order to be liable.

Like the moon, strict liability has gone through periods of expansion and contraction. Before the 19th century, the prevailing liability standard was that of strict liability: plaintiffs could recover by proving that the defendant caused the harm. There was no requirement that the defendant be at fault, that is, that he breached a duty of care that he owed to the plaintiff. This changed in the early and mid-19th century. Negligence or fault became the prevailing basis of tort liability while the rule of strict liability contracted to cover only harms arising from very dangerous activities or from commercial products like dynamite blasting or the sale of poisons. Interestingly, this change was instituted by common law judges in England and the United States, not by legislators.[10]

The rule of strict liability has enjoyed a renaissance in the 20th century, especially in the area of consumer product injuries. The contemporary manufacturer of a defective product is held strictly liable for the harm it causes, regardless of whether the defect was the manufacturer's fault. To illustrate by Example 3, some level of quality control is appropriate to manufacturing fuel additives. Even the best-designed system of quality control permits some defective products to slip through, so it is unlikely that a reasonable level of quality control will completely eliminate accidents. Under modern tort law, the manufacturer is liable for injuries caused by defective products even when quality control was adequate and the manufacturer was not at fault. The case for strict liability in consumer products cases is sometimes stated in terms of expectations: the buyer of a product does not expect to be injured by it. According to this view, tort law should protect the consumer's expectation just as contract law protects the promisee's expectation. A more satisfactory explanation can be given by the economic analysis of law, as we will see.

b. Liability for Failure to Rescue   The breaches of duty that we have identified as an element of the typical tort are, in general, breaches of duties to *refrain* from harming another person or his property. But what about liability for failing to take action that would prevent or minimize a harm? Suppose that as you are walking across a bridge you see a woman fall from the bank into the stream below. She screams for help. Suppose that there is a

---

[10]It has recently been argued that the common law judges made the change from strict liability to negligence in an effort to subsidize the development of new industries such as manufacturing and railroading. The central contention is that under strict liability, defendants are more likely to have to pay damages to plaintiffs than they are under negligence or fault-based liability. Because the new industries of the early and mid-19th century were more mechanical than previous production technologies and thus were more likely to cause harm to their operators, moving to fault and away from strict liability would lower the costs of introducing these new technologies and, therefore, increase their use. *See* Morton J. Horwitz, THE TRANSFORMATION OF AMERICAN LAW 1780-1860 (1977). This hypothesis, while intriguing, has generally not been accepted by legal historians. Their criticisms have been twofold: that Professor Horwitz has exaggerated the extent to which there were fundamental changes in the law in the early 19th century and that he has not adequately explained how the common law judges were able to pull off this fundamental change in the law without the help of legislators. *See* A. W. B. Simpson, *The Horwitz Thesis and the History of Contracts*, 46 U. CHI. L. REV. 533 (1979) and Gary T. Schwartz, *Tort Law and the Economy in Nineteenth-Century America: A Reinterpretation*, 90 YALE L. J. 1717 (1981).

rope with a lifesaving-ring beside you. If you fail to toss it to the woman, may she if she survives, or her family if she dies, bring a tort action against you for failure to rescue?

In general, tort law in England and the United States does not recognize a duty to rescue. (In most of the Continental European legal systems there is such a duty.) This is true even where, as in our example, the actions that you could have taken to render aid to the drowning woman were simple or, in economic terms, relatively costless. And yet despite this general absence of such a duty, there are two well-known exceptions in the common law countries: some professionals, principally doctors, have a recognizable legal duty (reinforced by their professional code, the Hippocratic Oath) to render aid; and in admiralty law—the law of the ocean—there is a duty to rescue persons and property of ships in distress.

The current trend is toward a relaxation of the traditional or classical theory's proscription against imposition of liability for failure to rescue. Two states, Vermont and Minnesota, have recently imposed liability for a failure to rescue by statute, and other states have considered a similar measure. The classical tort theory that we identified above has trouble explaining this tort. It cannot easily explain why the common law made the two exceptions for a duty to rescue; nor can the classical theory offer a satisfactory method of analyzing the more general issue of whether these or any other exceptions should be recognized. As we will see in the next chapter, the economic theory of torts proposes a far more coherent method of talking about expanding legal obligations to include a duty to rescue.

2. Punitive Damages In discussing the first element in a tort—the breach of a duty of care owed to the plaintiff—we noted that the harm need not be intentional in order for the victim to recover. This may seem counter-intuitive on first impression. A good parent does not punish a child for causing harm accidentally, so why should the law be different? The answer is to be found in the unavoidable fact that someone must bear the cost of the harm that was done. There are three parties upon whom the cost can fall:

1. the victim could be left to bear his own costs;
2. the injurer could be made to bear them; or
3. they could be borne by a third party, such as the government.

To many people it will seem fairer to charge the costs to the wrong-doer, even though no harm was intended, than to let the costs fall on the innocent victim or the innocent taxpayers. The institution of compensation forces the wrongdoer (or, when he is insured, the wrongdoer's insurance company) to restore the victim to the condition that would have prevailed but for the wrong, as nearly as this is possible. This strikes most people as fair, and later we will investigate at length whether it is also efficient.

We have pointed out that a successful plaintiff in a tort action can recover compensatory damages from the defendant. But it is also possible, in limited circumstances, to recover money damages that exceed the plaintiff's actual losses. These *punitive* (or exemplary) damages, as they are called, are reserved for those instances in which the defendant committed an *intentional* tort, that is, an instance in which he *meant* to cause harm.[11] Among the acts classified by the law as intentional torts are assault (in essence, a threat), battery (the actual striking of another person), false imprisonment (for example, trapping someone in his room), and intentional infliction of emotional distress. Punishment is allowed to enter the award of damages in these torts because it is far worse morally to harm someone intentionally than unintentionally. Thus, in our Example 1, Potatoes apparently intended to hit Bloggs, and that is a far worse thing than if he had struck him inadvertently. By striking Bloggs intentionally, Potatoes has exposed himself, not just to liability for compensatory damages to Bloggs but also to paying punitive damages.[12]

Besides intentionality, punitive damages may be awarded if the fault is gross or if there is reckless disregard for the safety of others. Once again, the fact giving rise to punishment is far worse morally than negligence.

Punitive damages are one of the most perplexing and controversial institutions of modern tort law. As we will see in greater detail in the following chapter, juries in the last decade or so have been increasingly willing to give plaintiffs punitive damages. More than that, the size of these punitive awards is unpredictable and sometimes huge. For example, in a recent case involving two corporations, Texaco and Pennzoil, the jury awarded the plaintiff $11.12 billion in damages, of which $1 billion was punitive damages.[13] Damage awards of this magnitude, which are without precedent, could disrupt and fundamentally alter the conduct of business in the United States. We will argue that an economic case can be made for punitive damages but the current practices of courts are difficult to justify.

---

[11]For example, the California Civil Code, Article 3, Section 3294, recognizes oppression, fraud, and malice as grounds for punitive damages, and each of these acts is defined in the code in terms of intentional harm.

[12]As we will see in our discussion of criminal law, punishment is also one of the distinguishing characteristics of the criminal law. The common theme in crime and intentional torts is the defendant's intent. Once this connection is recognized, it is not surprising to learn that in the history of law in England, crimes were originally regarded as private disputes, just like torts. Crimes originally belonged to the common law. Over the centuries, however, the government replaced the victim in the role of prosecutor, and statutes replaced custom in the role of specifying punishments.

[13]The case is still on appeal. The issue in the case was whether the defendant, Texaco, had improperly induced Getty Oil Corporation to breach an agreement for it to be acquired by Pennzoil. Texaco subsequently acquired Getty. See the discussion of the size of the award in this case in R. Epstein, *The Pirates of Pennzoil*, REGULATION (May/June 1986).

3. Liabiltiy Without Causality   Recall that in Example 2 both the hunters were equally at fault but only one of them actually caused the injury, and it is impossible to say which one it was. According to traditional tort law, the plaintiff could not recover because he could not establish cause-in-fact. But that result has struck some courts and commentators as unfair: someone who has been injured through no fault of his own and through fault of someone else should not have to bear his losses solely because he cannot identify the wrong-doer. An alternative to the traditional causality proof has been fashioned by one modern court. Since there is a 50% chance that each of the hunters caused the injury and since they were equally at fault, why not hold them both liable and make them split the cost of compensating the victim? This solution, which represents a fundamental break with the traditional requirement of proving cause-in-fact, has actually been adopted by the courts for a small class of cases.

One instance in which this theory of assigning liability has been adopted involved the injury of an anesthetized patient; there was no doubt that someone in the operating room caused the injury, but it was impossible for the plaintiff to say who.[14] Another famous illustration of the principle of liability without causality is *Sindell v. Abbott Laboratories.*[15] Between 1941 and 1971 several drug companies produced a product called diethylstilbestrol (DES) that was prescribed by doctors as a miscarriage preventative for expectant mothers. In the late 1960s DES was discovered to cause a fast-spreading and deadly vaginal and cervical cancer in women whose mothers had taken DES, and in 1971 the Food and Drug Administration ordered Abbott and other manufacturers to stop marketing and promoting the drug. Many women sued the manufacturers of DES for the harms they suffered because their mothers took the drug. However, because there was such a long interval between the time the mothers took DES and the illness manifested itself in their daughters, there were extreme problems in establishing which among the 200 companies that made DES had produced the particular pills taken by the plaintiff's mother and was, therefore, responsible for the plaintiff's injuries. Much like the victim of the hunters in Example 2, plaintiffs could establish that the drug harmed them but they could not establish which brand or brands their mothers had used. Thus, under the traditional tort theory, the plaintiffs could not establish cause-in-fact and could not, therefore, recover.

The California Supreme Court allowed the plaintiffs in *Sindell* to recover from the manufacturers by crafting a novel theory of liability without causation. The court reasoned that when there is an innocent plaintiff and negligent defendants and when the defendants are better able to bear

---

[14]This liability without causality is distinguishable from "joint and several liability," a standard that we discuss briefly in the next chapter.

[15]26 Cal. 3d 588, 607 P.2d 924 (1980).

the losses arising from the accident than are the plaintiffs, it would be unjust not to allow the plaintiffs to recover simply because they cannot establish who precisely caused the harm. Instead, the court urged the lower court to assign liability among the defendants in proportion to company market shares in the production and sale of DES at the time the plaintiff's mother took the drug. To illustrate, if firm A had 50% of the market for DES, firm B had 30%, and firm C had 20%, then 50% of the damages would be paid by firm A, 30% by firm B, and 20% by firm C.

4. Conclusion   Recall that in our first chapter on contracts we noted that the classical theory of contracts could not easily accommodate modern notions of enforceable promises. However, the economic theory of contracts offered an alternative that covered the circumstances envisioned in the classical theory as well as the anomalies that the traditional theory could not easily explain. Similarly, the three anomalies of modern tort law that we have just discussed cannot easily be accommodated in the classical theory of tort law. The economic theory of torts that we will outline in the remainder of this chapter and detail in the next can handle these problems of modern tort law. For that reason, we believe that it is a better theory.

II. ELEMENTS OF THE ECONOMIC ANALYSIS OF TORTS

We argued that the purpose of tort law is to protect the interests of people in their property and persons from involuntary damage by others. To effectuate this definition, the law typically grants relief when the breach of a legal duty by the defendant causes measurable damage to the plaintiff. This account of the elements of tort law had to be qualified, however, to take account of the full range of the contemporary torts, and the qualifications proved so severe as to jeopardize the usefulness of the classical theory. In the remainder of this chapter we will use economics to arrive at a more comprehensive theory by reinterpreting the elements of a tort, beginning with causation. First, however, we will set the stage for the theory by using economic analysis to draw a distinction between the domains of tort and contract law.

A. Distinguishing Between Tort Law, Property Law, and Contract Law

The common law of property, contract, and tort law may be distinguished from one another by the extent to which they intervene in private relationships. At one extreme is contract law, whose purpose could be viewed as assisting individuals to conclude more perfect private relationships. At the other extreme is tort law. As we noted in the opening pages of this chapter and discuss further below, tort law supplements contract law by devising rules for apportioning losses in situations where it is too costly for potential injurers and potential victims to enter into a contractual relationship to make that apportionment. The result is that tort law requires the most explicit intervention into private behavior by the law. In between these extremes is property law. In this section, we wish to make this distinction among the three principal areas of the common law in explicit economic terms, specifically, in terms of bargaining costs. Our discussion will be framed in terms of distinguishing tort and contract because those areas appear to be at the extremes in terms of bargaining costs. As an exercise, you might see how property law fits into this framework.[16]

Both tort law and contract law speak of a defendant's *breach* of a duty to the plaintiff. In the traditional theories of those areas, formalities of procedure and substance drew a sharp line between those breaches that were tortious and those that were contractual. But from the mid-19th century on, when extreme formalities began to disappear from the law, the line between tort and contract began to grow fainter. In fact, one prominent scholar recently argued that one of the most distinguishable trends of modern law was the disappearance of contract law into tort law.[17]

This state of affairs has led to a certain amount of confusion. Although, as Professor Gilmore argued, the two areas may be converging, they are still sufficiently distinguishable in terms of procedures and elements that many suspect that there is an important distinction worth preserving. One of the salutary results of the development of the economic theories of contracts and of torts is that economic theory makes the boundary between these two areas somewhat clearer. The distinction is explained by bargaining theory and the notion of transaction costs we introduced in the first chapter on property. Its essence is this: *the rules of contract law concern relationships between people for whom the ex ante costs of bargaining are low and who have, as a result, entered into a contractual relationship; the rules of tort law concern relationships between people for whom the ex ante costs of bargaining about the harm are high and who cannot, therefore, enter into a contractual relationship.* Thus, we do not use the rules of contract law to deal with the harms arising in an automobile accident because it is clearly not feasible for every driver to reach a contractual relationship with every other driver regarding the apportionment of risk that they will harm one another. Nor can every driver enter into a contract with all pedestrians to assign the risk of their inadvertently colliding. The transaction or bargaining costs are too high.

---

[16]That there is just as much overlap between tort and property as there is between tort and contract should be plain from the fact that nuisance and trespass are treated as topics in courses in tort law and in property law. A more formal method of showing the relationships between property, tort, and contract may be found in Cooter, *Unity in Tort, Contract, and Property: The Model of Precaution*, 73 CAL. L. REV. 1 (1985).

[17]Grant Gilmore, THE DEATH OF CONTRACT (1974).

One of the virtues of this distinction between the two areas of the law on the basis of bargaining costs is that it also explains why there are circumstances in which contract and tort law seem unavoidably to merge. Let us consider two instances, which we will explore in greater detail later.

First is the area known as "products liability," an area of tort law that deals with harms arising from commercial products. The typical claim arises when a customer is harmed while using a manufacturer's product. On our definition of the distinction between tort and contract, should this be treated as a tort or as a breach of contract? It all depends on the level of bargaining costs. These are not exceedingly high here because the customer and the manufactuer are not strangers in the same way that those involved in an automobile accident are likely to be strangers. On the other hand, the bargaining costs are not so low that there is an individual contract between each customer and manufacturer assigning responsibility for various risks and exchanging information. The level of bargaining costs is somewhere between being low enough to be treated as a contractual relationship and high enough to be treated as a tortious relationship. This being so, it should not be surprising to learn that the area of products liability is a hybrid of those two areas of the law. The nature of this hybridization will become clearer in the next chapter when we discuss the history of products liability law.

Second is an area sometimes known as "implicit contract." The paradigm case is one in which a physician happens upon an unconscious woman who needs medical aid. If the physician renders aid, should he later be compensated by the unconscious woman as if he had had a contract with her? Or is the physician's aid to be understood as his fulfilling a duty to rescue? If so, then he can seek no compensation for doing what he should have done anyway; in fact, if there is a duty to rescue, then he could be held liable for compensatory damages if he should fail to give aid to the unconscious woman.

This confusing situation may be clarified by applying our notion of the importance of bargaining costs. The bargaining costs between the unconscious woman and the physician are very high. This would seem to suggest dealing with the situation under the rules of tort law. However, it makes more sense to say that although the bargaining costs are high because of the patient's unconsciousness, if she were conscious and aware of her need for medical care, she and the physician would probably have entered into a contract to render medical care. Thus, on the bargaining cost theory distinguishing torts from contracts, this is an example of a contract and should, therefore, be dealt with under the rules of contract law. (In the next chapter we will re-examine the case of the physician and the unconscious patient when we discuss the economics of assigning liability for failure to rescue.)

Finally, we want to stress that although the distinction in terms of bargaining costs is helpful, there remain some ambiguities between the various areas of the common law. Two examples are doctor-patient relations and employer-employee relations. These would seem to be areas of private relationships ideally suited for regulation through the rules of contract law, and yet they are, by and large, regulated through other regulatory policies: labor law, tort law, administered compensation systems such as workers' compensation, and statutes. Whether it would be better to deal with these areas through contract rules is a matter of some dispute these days.

We have used bargaining theory to distinguish a tort from a contract and to explain why there may be some situations that are intermediate between tort law and contract law. With this distinction in hand, we now turn to the explicit development of an economic theory of tort liability.

B. Causation and Externalities

In a well-known essay on causation, the philosopher Bertrand Russell argued that this concept tends to disappear from science as it advances. According to Russell, a mature science formulates the relationship among variables in precise mathematical terms. When scientists present an explanation, they refer to precise mathematical concepts rather than the vague concept of a cause. The concept of causation thus tends to be submerged in mathematics as a science advances.[18]

Russell's argument is an accurate description of the economic analysis of torts. An economic model includes variables and equations. As we saw in Chapter 2, the equations are usually functions relating the variables to each other. Our first task is to connect the idea of causality in torts to functional relations in economic models.

The link is provided by the idea of an externality, which we introduced in Chapter 2 and discussed in some detail in the second chapter on property. Recall that we defined an externality as a cost that the voluntary actions of one person impose on others without their consent. To give mathematical expression to this idea, we explained that externalities imply the interdependency of utility or production functions, which we illustrated by a two-person example. Let us review that interdependency briefly. Suppose that person A consumes goods x_1 and x_2 in the quantities x_{a1} and x_{a2}. A's utility from these quantities consumed can be represented by $u_a = u(x_{a1}, x_{a2})$. Similarly, person B's utility depends upon his consumption of goods 1 and 2, denoted x_{b1} and x_{b2}. Suppose, however, that good 1 is tobacco, which A smokes (and B chews), and suppose that B is allergic to tobacco smoke. Under this assumption B's utility depends not just upon his consumption of the two goods but also upon the extent of A's smoking. Consequently, B's utility function is written $u_b = u(x_{b1}, x_{b2}, x_{a1})$. The third term in B's utility function, x_{a1}, creates a direct dependency of B's utility upon A's consumption. This direct dependency is the mathematical representation of an externality.

---

[18]There is no such relationship in mathematics as "causality." It is, however, true that the mathematical formulation of a scientific theory can often be regarded as a rigorous account of particular causal relations. There is, thus, a connection between causal relations and functional relations, but the precise connection is beyond the scope of this book.

The externality that we represented mathematically is called a "consumer-on-consumer" externality. We could, however, change the injurer from a person into a factory and thereby illustrate a "producer-on-consumer" externality. Specifically, suppose that factory A burns coal, denoted x_{a1}, to produce electricity, denoted x_{a2}, according to the production function $x_{a2} = f(x_{a1})$. Factory A's consumption of coal produces smoke that harms person B; B consumes coal (for heat) and electricity (for lights); thus, B's utility is given, as before, by the equation $u_b = u(x_{b1}, x_{b2}, x_{a1})$. The third term in B's utility function establishes a direct dependency of B's utility upon A's production.

This analysis permits us to clarify the element of causality in torts. The causality requirement in torts—one person's behavior proximately causes harm to another—implies that their utility or production functions are interdependent. *For a causal relationship to exist in tort law, there must be a functional relationship of the type that economists call an externality.*[19]

This statement should not be misunderstood. All we are saying is that an externality is a necessary condition for the existence of a causal relationship in tort law. It does not follow that the presence of an interdependence in utility or production functions is a *sufficient* condition for establishing legal causation. Mrs. Palsgraf's utility function and the production function of the Long Island Railway Company were interdependent, yet she could not collect for her injuries. Bo's utility may be adversely affected to the point of nausea by Ted's choice of what necktie to wear, but it does not follow that Bo can recover compensatory damages from Ted.

Does economics provide a way of distinguishing those externalities that cause *compensable* harm from harms that do *not* give rise to tort liability? The general prescription from economics is that external harms should be compensable when creating a legal right to compensation is efficient. We will be exploring the conditions under which such rights are efficient in much of the remainder of this chapter.

C. Damages and Utility

We are tracing the connection between economic analysis and the elements of a tort. Having discussed the relationship between causality in torts and externalities in economics, our next task is to connect the concept of damage

---

[19]Some recent writing on these issues may be found in Richard A. Posner, TORT LAW: CASES AND ECONOMIC ANALYSIS 585–588 (1983); W. Landes & R. Posner, *Causation in Tort Law: An Economic Approach*, 12 J. LEGAL STUD. 109 (1983); S. Shavell, AN ANALYSIS OF ACCIDENT LAW (1986); and Shavell, *An Analysis of Causation and the Scope of Liability in the Law of Torts*, 9 J. LEGAL STUD. 463 (1987).

in torts with a parallel concept in economics. This link can be found by examining the consequences of interdependent utility and production functions. A harmful externality causes a downward shift in the victim's production or utility function. This downward shift indicates that material harm has been done.

By way of illustration, recall that in the preceding example person B's utility function was represented by the equation $u_b = u(x_{b1}, x_{b2}, x_{a1})$. The term x_{a1} creates the direct dependence of B's utility upon A's economic activity. The larger the value of x_{a1}, the greater the harm suffered by B. It is useful to illustrate this fact in a graph. Most students, however, are accustomed to graphing "goods," not "bads." To make the graph more familiar, we will use a mathematical trick so that we can represent the "bad" as if it were a "good." x_{a1} indicates the amount of smoke-producing good used by A. Smoke is a bad, and pure air is a good. So let z indicate air purity, and assume that z is an inverse function of A's use of the smoke-producing good. Thus, $z = z(x_{a1})$, and as x_{a1} increases, z decreases. Now we rewrite B's utility function as $u_b = u(x_{b1}, x_{b2}, z)$.

B's utility is shown in Figure 8.1. The horizontal axis represents air purity z, which varies from 0% to 100%. The vertical axis represents B's consumption of the second good x_{b2}. The curved lines represents B's indifference curves over air purity and x_{b2}.[20] We will hold constant the units of x_{b1} consumed. Suppose that B initially consumes 10 units of the second good, x_{b2}, and that the initial level of air purity is 80%. B's initial position is (80%,10), which lies on the indifference curve labelled u_0. Now suppose that A's smoking causes the air's purity to fall from 80% to 50%. As a result, B finds himself at the point (50%,10), which is on the lower utility curve labelled u_1. A's smoking thus causes a fall in utility equal to $(u_0 - u_1)$. This is the damage caused by A's smoking as measured in units of utility.

If this were a property dispute, B might ask for injunctive relief, and if an injunction were granted and enforced, A would stop smoking near B (or purchase from B the right to enforce his injunction), allowing B's utility to return to its initial level, u_0. The traditional remedy in torts, however, is money damages, not an injunction, so let us assume that A continues smoking and pays money damages to B. The courts award damages in dollars, not in utils, so it is necessary to convert the utility loss $(u_0 - u_1)$ into a dollar loss. Notice that an increase in B's consumption of the second good, x_{b2}, from 10 units to 15 units would restore B to the initial indifference curve, u_0. 5 units of the 2nd good are required to compensate B exactly for the reduction in air purity caused by A.

Instead of interpreting x_{b2} as B's consumption of some good, it is convenient at this point to interpret it as the money that B spends on consumer

---

[20]Chapter 2 explains indifference curves.

Figure 8.1   Damages and Utility

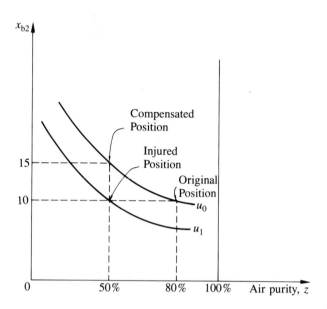

Person *B*'s indifference curves for the commodity x_{b2} and air purity are shown. *B* initially consumes 10 units of x_{b2} and 80% pure air, a combination that lies on the indifference curve u_0 at a point labeled "original position." Then someone else's smoking causes the air purity to fall to 50%. *B* is then at the point labeled "injured position" on the lower indifference curve, u_1. To compensate *B* for this injury the utility loss from u_0 to u_1 must be converted into dollars. An award of money damages that would allow *B* to purchase 5 units of x_{b2} would put *B* back onto the original indifference curve u_0 at the point labeled "compensated position."

goods rather than as units of some particular consumer good. This interpretation is convenient because, if x_{b2} is money, the compensatory damages would be exactly 5 units of money. Thus, if money were measured in hundreds of dollars in the graph, compensating damages would equal $500.

This account of compensatory damages in torts is identical to the account of compensatory damages in the case of *Hawkins v. McGee*, which was presented in the second chapter on contracts. Recall that in *Hawkins v. McGee* a surgeon promised to restore a boy's defective hand, but the operation made the boy irrevocably worse. Compensatory damages was the amount of money needed to restore the boy to the level of utility that he would have enjoyed if the doctor had not injured his hand.

Question 8.1: What was the advantage to the plaintiff in *Hawkins* of bringing his suit in contract rather than in tort?

Question 8.2: With this economic interpretation of damages in tort law in mind, show the impact on the victim's utility of allowing him to recover *punitive* damages from the tortfeasor.

D. Fault[21]

In the classical theory, a tort involves defendant's breach of a duty of care owed to the plaintiff, and the law says that the defendant who breaches this duty is "at fault" or "negligent." We have already seen that the law defines this duty by reference to a "reasonable" level of care and that there is an unavoidable vagueness in this criterion.

The economic analysis of tort law offers a seemingly more precise notion of the defendant's duty, that is, a more precise method of determining when a defendant has been at fault. However, there are normative and positive aspects of the economic notion of fault that must be clearly distinguished. The *positive* aspect of the economic analysis stresses the *behavioral consequences* of whatever duty of care the law imposes on potential tortfeasors. This type of analysis does not make claims that the legal standard is necessarily *efficient*; instead, it merely treats the prevailing legal duty as creating an implicit price on various levels of precautionary behavior and then investigates how rational decisionmakers are likely to respond to that implicit price. By contrast, the *normative* economic theory of tort law seeks to offer a method for determining what the defendant's obligation or duty to the plaintiff *should* be in order to achieve a well-defined economic goal. The normative efficiency goal of tort law most widely accepted in law and economics is that first proposed by Dean Calabresi: *that the rules of tort liability should be structured so as to minimize the sum of precaution, accident, and administration costs.*[22]

As should be clear by now, it is sometimes difficult in law and economics to keep these normative and positive aspects separate. In the economic theory that we summarize below, we will be dealing most extensively with the normative theory. In the next chapter, where we extend the theory and discuss some applications of it to prominent public policy problems, we will be relying more on a positive analysis.

We begin the economic analysis of the legal duty of care with a set of simplifying assumptions. Assume that someone engages in an activity that may impose external costs upon others. External costs can usually be reduced by the injurer at some expense to himself; for example, the potential tortfeasor can incur the opportunity costs of driving more slowly or the direct costs of paying closer attention to lane markings, traffic lights, stop signs, and so on. A polluter can reduce the external harm he inflicts by installing pollution abatement equipment and by reducing the level of pollution-causing output. This relationship between precaution and external costs is summarized in Figure 8.2.

Taking precaution often involves spending money, losing time, or bearing inconvenience. The costs of precaution increase as more of it is taken.

---

[21]This section is based upon Cooter, *Prices and Sanctions*, 84 COLUM. L. REV. 1523 (1984).

[22]G. Calabresi, THE COSTS OF ACCIDENTS: A LEGAL AND ECONOMIC ANALYSIS (1970).

Figure 8.2   Optimal Precaution Against Injury to Others

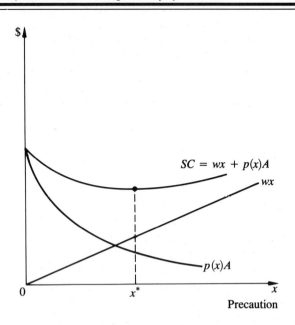

The straight line labeled *wx* indicates the actor's private costs of precaution on the assumption that precaution costs $*w* per unit. The probability of the actor's inflicting costs on others is represented by the line labeled *p(x)A*. *A* represents the costs that might be imposed on others, and *p* represents the probability of those costs being imposed as a *decreasing* function of the amount of precaution, *x*. The injurer's total expected costs are the sum of these two elements: [*wx* + *p(x)A*]. The curve labeled *SC* shows the sum of the *wx* and *p(x)A* curves. The cost-minimizing level of precaution is *x**, where the cost per unit of precaution, *w*, equals the reduction in the probability of an accident from taking an additional unit of precaution, *p'(x)*, times the accident costs, *A*.

Figure 8.2 contains a simple representation of these facts. On the horizontal axis, the quantity of the actor's precaution, *x*, is shown. Dollar amounts are measured along the vertical axis. We assume that precaution costs *w* per unit and that *w* is constant. Thus, *wx* is the amount spent on precaution. The straight line in Figure 8.2, labeled *wx*, indicates the tortfeasor's private costs of precaution as a function of the amount of precaution he purchases.

The cost of precaution, *wx*, constitutes the first component of the tortfeasor's costs. The second component is the cost that the tortfeasor's actions impose on others. To draw that relationship between the tortfeasor's level of precaution and the costs he imposes on others, we can make either or both of the following assumptions:

1. The probability of an accident is a declining function of the tortfeasor's level of precaution; thus, the greater is *x*, the lower the probability that someone will be harmed and, therefore, the lower the external cost.

2. The amount of harm imposed on others in the event of an accident is a declining function of the tortfeasor's level of precaution.

If we let A represent costs that will be imposed on others and p represent the probability of those costs' being imposed, then we can write the relationship between the expected external costs and the tortfeasor's level of precaution as

$$p(x)A(x).$$

These costs may be called the "expected" external costs because of the introduction of the probabilistic element. The external element of the tortfeasor's costs are indicated by the downward-sloping curve in Figure 8.2 labeled $p(x)A$.

To keep the math clean, we will usually write the expected external costs in the simplified form $p(x)A$. Furthermore, we assume that the curve $p(x)A$ is convex, as depicted in Figure 8.2, because, as seems reasonable, a small increase in precaution reduces external costs by a large amount when precaution is low, while a small increase in precaution reduces external costs by a small amount when precaution is high.

We may now combine the two components of the tortfeasor's costs—the cost of precaution, wx, and the expected external cost, $p(x)A$—to obtain the social cost. The social cost curve in Figure 8.2 is thus obtained by adding the two curves vertically at every level of precaution. The result is the U-shaped curve whose value equals $[wx + p(x)A]$.

Notice that because of our assumptions, there is a level of precaution, denoted x^*, that minimizes social costs. It is worth taking a moment here to characterize this socially optimal amount of precaution in mathematical terms. Social costs are minimized when the actor chooses the level of precaution that makes $[wx + p(x)A]$ as small as possible. Those of you who are familiar with calculus will recognize that we can solve for the optimum, x^*, by setting the first derivative of SC with respect to x equal to zero. (If you do not know calculus, stick with us! We'll make this intelligible after only two more sentences of mathematics.) Thus,

$$SC' = 0 = w + p'(x)A.$$

Or re-writing terms,

$$w = -p'(x)A.$$

The level of precaution, x, that solves this equation and thus minimizes social costs is x^*. Note what this equation for x^* says: at the socially optional level of precaution, the cost per unit of precaution, w, equals the reduction in the probability of an accident from taking an additional unit of precaution, $p'(x)$, times the accident costs, A. (Because we have assumed that the probability of an accident's occurring is a declining function of the amount of precaution, $p'(x)$ is negative. Therefore, the negative sign in front of $p'(x)A$ makes the right-hand side of that equation a positive number.) If we characterize the left-hand side of this equation as the marginal cost of precaution and the right-hand side as the marginal (social) benefits of precaution, then we may say that the social-cost minimizing level of precaution for a potential tortfeasor to take occurs at that level of precaution for which the marginal costs of taking an additional unit of precaution are just equal to the marginal benefits of that additional unit of precaution. This way of stating the social optimum is the familiar one that recurs repeatedly in microeconomic analysis.

One of the most important points we made in our summary of welfare economics in Chapter 2 is that in the absence of regulatory mechanisms, rationally self-interested decisionmakers will tend to ignore any external costs they impose on others and to consider only their private costs in making their utility- or profit-maximizing decisions. We now wish to explore how the rules of tort liability can be used to minimize the social costs that arise because of externalities. In terms of our Figure 8.2, we wish now to see how the rules of tort liability might induce the actor to choose x^* as his level of precaution so as to minimize the social costs of his actions.

Note that in the absence of any liability rule (or a rule of no liability) the rationally self-interested decisionmaker operates only along the straight line wx. His precaution costs, wx, are minimized by choosing $x = 0$. This is represented graphically by the fact that the line wx in Figure 8.2 achieves its lowest value at the graph's origin, where $x = 0$. Thus, a rule of no liability does not provide incentives for an adequate level of precaution: *there will be too many accidents and the external costs inflicted on others will be very large.*

Suppose, instead, that there is a rule of tort liability—let us call it Rule *A* for the time being—that imposes an obligation to take a specified amount of precaution. Rule *A* partitions levels of precaution into a permitted zone and a forbidden zone by creating a legal standard of precaution x^*. Decisionmakers who take precaution as great or greater than the legal standard ($x \geq x^*$) escape liability for another person's harms. Those who take less precaution than the legal standard ($x \leq x^*$) may have to pay compensatory damages for another person's harms.

Figure 8.3 illustrates Rule *A*. It shows precaution on the horizontal axis and the actor's costs on the vertical axis. Because of the possibility of sanctions imposed on the actor for violating Rule *A*, the two components of the tortfeasor's cost—his private costs of precaution and the external costs he imposes on others—are combined. When his level of precaution is below x^*, the actor bears the cost of his precaution and he must also pay for the harms he causes; when the actor's precaution is above x^* he pays only for his own precaution and is absolved of responsibility for any external costs his actions impose on others. Thus, his costs jump abruptly at the legal standard x^*. To the left of the discontinuity that occurs at x^*, the potential injurer's expected costs are $[wx + p(x)A]$; to the right of the discontinuity, the potential injurer's costs are wx.

To keep Figure 8.3 simple, we have assumed that if he violates the legal standard by taking less than x^* in precaution, the injurer must pay the external cost of the act. This means that the tortfeasor is liable for the full harm

Figure 8.3   Expected Liability Under a Negligence Rule

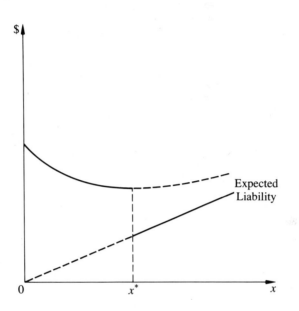

The discontinuous line labeled "Expected Liability" shows the expected costs facing an injurer when a negligence rule establishes x^* as the legal standard of care. To the left of x^*, the Expected Liability curve corresponds to the SC curve of the previous figure and is the sum of the private costs of precaution, wx, and the expected liability for harm to others, $p(x)A$. If the actor takes less precaution than x^*, he bears the cost of his precaution and must also pay for the harms he causes. To the right of x^* the actor is absolved of liability so that his costs fall back to the costs of precaution, wx.

that he causes. Additionally, we have assumed that x^* has been set equal to the social-cost minimizing level of care. Thus, the curve in Figure 8.3 is identical to the social cost curve in Figure 8.2 at values of x below x^*. We will explore shortly the implications of relaxing these assumptions.

What will be the effect of this rule upon the behavior of a person who is rationally self-interested? A self-interested person will choose his level of precaution to minimize his private costs. If he faces costs like those created by Rule A, then he will search for the lowest point on the expected cost curve. This occurs when his precaution equals the legal standard x^*. Thus, a self-interested person subject to Rule A will take just enough precaution to satisfy the legal standard and escape liability.

An important implication of this model is that, despite our assumption that the legal sanction imposed for being in the forbidden zone equals the actual harm caused, this equality is not essential to induce the actor to take the social cost-minimizing amount of precaution x^*. Rather, it is only essential that the sanction be large enough so that his private costs are minimized by conforming to the legal standard x^*. This point is illustrated in Figure

Figure 8.4   Damage Levels and the Negligence Rule

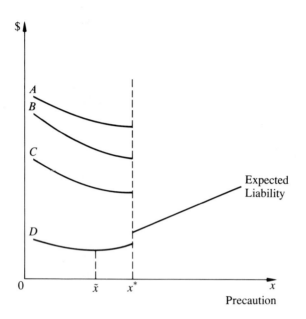

x^* represents the legal standard of care: to the left of the standard, the actor is responsible for the harms he causes and his own precautionary expenditures; to the right of the standard he is not liable for harms and incurs only his own precautionary expenses. Thus, the Expected Liability line to the right of x^* corresponds to wx from the previous figures. To the left of x^* four different curves represent four different levels of expected liability. These different levels can result from two different sources: (1) the accident costs that are inflicted may differ depending on the person and property that are injured; and (2) the court may make a mistake in calculating the level of harm. The first source corresponds to the levels marked A, B, and C. Notice that the cost-minimizing level of precaution is x^*, regardless of the extent of the harm inflicted. The second course *may* correspond to curve D, where damages have been set much too low. Notice that where this happens, the cost-minimizing level of care falls below its "true" level of x^* to $\tilde{x}$. This error might cause future injurers to take too little precaution: they believe that $\tilde{x}$ will absolve them of liability. (Not all errors in measuring damages have adverse consequences. An error that says damages correspond to curve C when in fact they should be B does not lead to underprecaution by future injurers.)

8.4, which shows the actor's private costs under four different assumptions about the level of the expected sanction. The crucial feature of Figure 8.4 is that the lowest point in the graph is at x^*, regardless of whether the expected sanction corresponds to the high level A, the medium level B, or the low level C. Any one of the three expected sanctions will induce conformity with the legal standard x^*. However, if the expected sanction falls to the very low level indicated by D, then $\tilde{x}$, not x^*, is the lowest point on the cost curve, so the actor will minimize his private costs by taking less precaution than the legal standard.

Our Rule A is really the tort liability standard known as negligence, which, by establishing a duty to take reasonable care, partitions a potential tortfeasor's precautionary decisions into permitted and forbidden zones. To understand the incentive effects of a negligence rule, consider the effect that such a rule would have on the manufacturer in Example 3 from the beginning of the chapter. (We are making the counterfactual assumption that the liability rule for defective consumer products is negligence rather than strict liability.) In our example, some defective batches of fuel additives inevitably slip through quality control and may subsequently injure the property or persons of consumers. Precaution against these accidents is costly. We assume that effective precaution is possible by the manufacturer and impossible by consumers. Social costs are the sum of the costs of the manufacturer's precaution and the cost of the harm caused by defective products. Thus, Figure 8.2 can be interpreted as a graph relating the social cost of manufacturing defects to precaution against them. As we saw, social costs are minimized at the point x^* in that graph, making that level of precaution socially efficient. If the manufacturer's precaution is below the legal standard x^*, then he is liable for any external costs that result. If liability covers the full cost of the harm suffered by the victim, the injurer's private costs will equal the social cost in the zone of liability, as depicted in Figure 8.3. However, when the manufacturer's precaution satisfies the legal standard, he escapes liability under a negligence rule, so he only bears the cost of his own precaution in the zone of nonliability.

This means that there is a jump or discontinuity in the manufacturer's costs at the legal standard of care because his liability plummets from 100% to 0% at the point where his precaution satisfies the legal standard. The size of the jump is determined by the amount of damage caused by defective products when precaution exactly satisfies the legal standard.[23] As a consequence of the jump, it is far cheaper for the injurer to be nonnegligent than to be negligent.[24]

---

[23]In law it is sometimes said that a person who is negligent is only liable for the harm that would have been avoided by nonnegligent care. This statement is misleading for many types of accidents because nonnegligence just reduces the probability of an accident, rather than eliminating its possibility. To illustrate by a famous example, suppose that railroad trains emit sparks that sometimes set fire to farmers' fields. Suppose that nonnegligent operation of the train requires the use of spark arresters, which reduce, but do not eliminate, spark emissions. Under a negligence standard, a railroad using spark arresters would escape liability from fires caused by its trains, whereas a railroad failing to use spark arresters would be liable for fires caused by its trains. The point to notice is that failing to use spark arresters increases the probability of fires but makes the railroad liable for all the fires, including the fires that spark arresters would not have eliminated. This fact gives rise to the discontinuity in the railroad's cost function.

[24]In economic jargon, the level of care that minimizes the manufacturer's private net costs is a corner solution in the choice set where marginal private costs of a change far exceed marginal private benefits.

What happens if we relax the assumption that the legal standard of care equals the social-cost-minimizing level of precaution, x^*? Will the level of precaution taken by potential tortfeasors change? The answer is yes. Because it is far cheaper to be nonnegligent than negligent, changes in the legal standard will induce equivalent changes in the potential tortfeasors' precaution. Thus, the potential injurer will satisfy the legal standard even if it is pegged at a level above or below the socially efficient level x^*.

E. Forms of the Negligence Rule

We have explained that a negligence rule imposes the obligation to satisfy a legal standard of care, which is usually defined as a reasonable level of care, and, under ordinary circumstances, it pays to conform to such a standard. We developed this general discussion in order to bring out the essential economic aspects of the negligence standard. Now we wish to introduce several forms of the negligence rule and to distinguish them from each other. The distinction can be made with the help of some mathematical notation. Assume that person A engages in an activity that risks harming person B. Person A is, then, the potential injurer and person B is the potential victim. Suppose that, in contrast to what we have previously assumed, *both* parties can take precaution to reduce the probability and severity of accidents. Let x denote precaution taken by the potential injurer A, and let y denote precaution taken by the potential victim B. Furthermore, let x^* and y^* denote the legal standards of precaution for the injurer and the victim.

The simplest form of the negligence rule, which we call "simple negligence," imposes liability for accidents on the injurer if, and only if, his precaution is below the legal standard, regardless of the level of precaution by the victim:

simple negligence:
$$x < x^* \Rightarrow \text{injurer liable}$$
$$x \geq x^* \Rightarrow \text{injurer not liable}$$

This rule is graphed in Figure 8.5. Along the vertical axis we have measured the victim's level of precaution. Note that because the rule of simple negligence does not evaluate the victim's precaution by reference to a legal standard of care, there is no legal standard y^* for the victim. Along the horizontal axis we have measured the injurer's precaution, with x^* representing the legal standard of care. The zone of injurer's liability is the shaded rectangle; outside of this rectangle, the victim bears responsibility for accident costs, which we will refer to as "residual responsibility."

An alternative form of the negligence rule is one in which both parties' precautionary behavior is evaluated *vis-à-vis* a legal standard. The difference with respect to the rule of simple negligence is that we now allow a defense of contributory negligence, under which the plaintiff's negligence is a complete bar to her recovery. To illustrate, suppose that a person dived into a

Figure 8.5 Simple Negligence

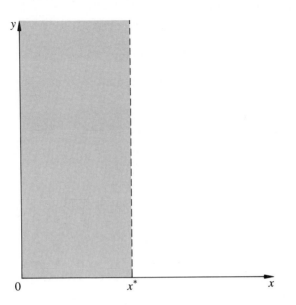

Under a rule of simple negligence, only the injurer's behavior is evaluated by a legal standard of care, x^*: if $x < x^*$, the injurer is liable; if $x \geq x^*$, he is not liable. The shaded area represents the combinations of injurer and victim precaution under which the injurer is liable for the victim's losses. Outside the shaded rectangle, the victim bears residual responsibility for losses.

swimming pool and sustained an injury by striking her head on the bottom. She sues the owner of the pool. At the trial the jury finds that the owner of the pool was negligent for not posting signs warning about the pool's depth. But the jury also finds that the victim was negligent in not checking the depth of the water before diving. Under a rule of simple negligence, the owner is liable, but under the rule of negligence with a defense of contributory negligence, the owner escapes liability. The mathematical representation is as follows:

negligence with a defense of contributory negligence:

$$x < x^* \text{ and } y \geq y^* \implies \text{injurer liable}$$
$$x \geq x^* \text{ or } y < y^* \implies \text{injurer not liable.}$$

This rule is graphed in Figure 8.6. Again the vertical and horizontal axes represent precautionary behavior by the victim and the injurer, and y^* and x^* indicate the legal standards of care for the two parties to the accident. Notice that the shaded rectangle indicating the zone of the injurer's liability has shrunk relative to its size in Figure 8.5.

Figure 8.6 Negligence with a Defense of Contributory Negligence

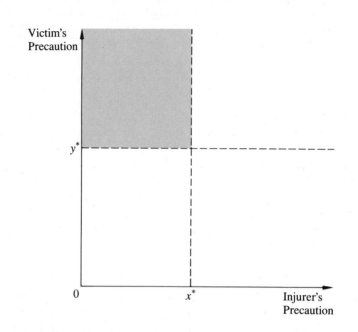

Under a rule of negligence with a defense of contributory negligence, both the victim and the injurer are subject to a legal standard of care, y^* and x^* respectively: if $x < x^*$ and $y \geq y^*$, the injurer is liable; if $x \geq x^*$ or $y < y^*$, the injurer is not liable. The shaded rectangle indicates the area of victim and injurer precaution in which the injurer is liable for the victim's losses. Outside the shaded rectangle, the victim bears residual responsibility for losses. Notice that the area of injurer liability is less than under a rule of simple negligence.

Under the rules of simple negligence or negligence with a defense of contributory negligence, one party is responsible for *all* the costs of an accident, even though both parties are at fault. The third form of the negligence rule, called comparative negligence, is identical to negligence with contributory negligence when only one party is negligent. However, when both parties are negligent, the accident costs are divided between them in proportion to how their negligence contributed to the accident. For example, if both parties are deemed negligent and the plaintiff is said to be 20% responsible for her own losses, then she may recover only 80% of her losses from the defendant. Under comparative negligence, contributory negligence is a *partial* not a complete bar to recovery. Thus:

comparative negligence:
$$x < x^* \text{ and } y \geq y^* \implies \text{injurer 100\% liable}$$
$$x \geq x^* \text{ and } y < y^* \implies \text{victim 100\% liable}$$
$$x < x^* \text{ and } y < y^* \implies \text{liability proportional to negligence.}$$

An important point about comparative negligence is that there are practical problems in determining how to calculate relative fault. This makes it somewhat difficult to talk about comparative negligence in the same way that we have talked about the other versions of the negligence rule. However, for the sake of illustrating the comparative negligence rule in the same way that we have illustrated the other forms of the negligence rule, we will explain one method of measuring relative fault. Let us make the simplifying assumptions that the victim and the injurer are engaged in the same activity and that they are held to the same standard of care. For example, suppose that both parties are driving their automobiles in a residential area where the posted speed limit is 30 miles per hour. The cars collide, but only one of the cars is damaged. The driver of the damaged car was going 35 miles per hour and the other driver was going 40 miles per hour. Both drivers are at fault. A simple measure of their fault is the difference between their actual speed and the posted speed limit: $(40-30)$ and $(35-30)$. The ratio of these numbers is a simple measure of their relative fault: $(40-30)/(35-30)$, which equals $2/1$. If this were the measure of relative fault, the injurer would bear $2 in accident damages for each $1 borne by the victim. Thus, if the damaged car cost $1,000 to repair, the injurer would pay $667 and the victim would pay $333.

In general, the relative difference between the party's actual levels of precaution and the legal standard of precaution provides a simple measure of comparative negligence: $(x^*-x)/(y^*-y)$. This measure is illustrated graphically in Figure 8.7. In Panel a, the legal standards of care for the injurer, x^*, and the victim, y^*, are shown, as are the actual levels of precaution taken, x and y. The slope of the line depicted in this figure indicates the ratio $(x^*-x)/(y^*-y)$. The steeper this line, the greater the fault of the *victim* relative to the fault of the injurer; the flatter the line, the greater the fault of the *injurer* relative to the fault of the victim. This is shown in Panel b. As the victim's precaution y increases from y_0 to y_1 to y_2 and approaches the legal standard y^*, her relative fault falls and the share of the accident costs borne by the injurer increases. When the victim satisfies the legal standard y^* her relative fault is zero, and all the accident costs fall upon the injurer.

Question 8.3: Suppose that A, the driver of a car, has been seriously injured in an accident that was caused by the fault of B, the driver of the other car. A was not at fault in her driving. However, she was not wearing her seat belt. If she had been, her personal injuries would have been trivial. Which form of the negligence rule might you use to evaluate A's act of not wearing a seat belt in order to create an incentive for her to take efficient precaution to reduce the probability or severity of an accident?

Naturally, the question arises whether one or more of these various forms of the negligence rule are more efficient than the others. Economists have examined this question and have reached the somewhat surprising conclusion that *when the legal standard is set at the efficient level of precaution,*

Figure 8.7 Comparative Negligence

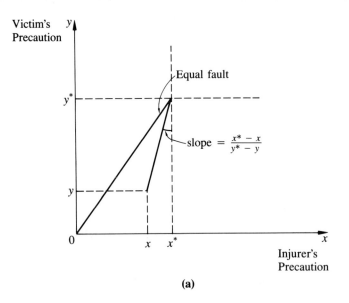

(a)

In Panel a, under comparative negligence, there are legal standards of care imposed on both the victim, y^*, and the injurer, x^*. When $y < y^*$ and $x < x^*$, comparative negligence apportions liability for the victim's losses according to the formula: $(x^* - x)/(y^* - y)$. For the actual levels of precaution shown, y and x, the share of fault is given by the slope of the line between the points (y^*, x^*) and (y, x). The steeper this line, the greater the fault of the *victim* relative to the fault of the injurer; the flatter the line, the greater the fault of the *injurer* relative to the fault of the victim. For reference a line marked "Equal Fault" has been drawn to indicate those combinations of victim and injurer precaution for which they will be held equally responsible; that is, along that line each will bear responsibility for 50% of the victim's losses. This line

every one of the negligence rules creates incentives for efficient precaution by potential victims and potential injurers. The reason for this is that *rationally self-interested decisionmakers are led by considerations of self-interest to choose the legal standard of care under any of the negligence rules.*[25]

The proof of this conclusion is an important example of how economists construct a proof of an efficient equilibrium. Recall that one of the parties can escape responsibility for accident costs by satisfying the legal standard of precaution. Once responsibility is avoided, there is no incentive for that party to take any additional precaution. As a consequence, one party will

---

[25]Strictly speaking, the efficiency equivalence of simple negligence, negligence with contributory negligence, and comparative negligence is true only under the assumptions we have made previously. If we relax those assumptions—e.g., if we assume that the evaluation of a party's precaution with respect to the legal standard of care is subject to uncertainty—then some forms of the negligence rule are more efficient than others. We discuss this matter at greater length in the following chapter.

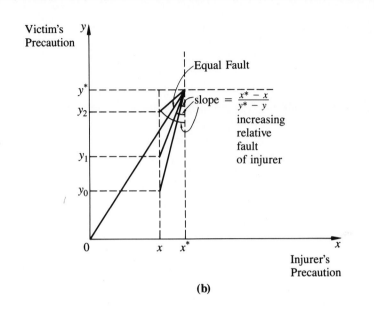

(b)

indicates that for the actual x and y shown, the victim is relatively more at fault than is the injurer. In Panel b, the effect of varying the degrees of fault of victim and injurer are shown. The (negligent) level of precaution of the injurer, x, is held constant, while the (negligent) level of precaution of the victim is varied. The ratio $(x^* - x)/(y^* - y)$ measures the share of fault. Again, an Equal Fault line has been included to show the combinations of precaution for which the parties are 50% responsible for the victim's losses. Notice that as the victim's precaution increases from y_0 to y_1 to y_2, the slope of the line $(x^* - x)/(y^* - y_i)$, where $y_i = y_0, y_1, y_2, \ldots$, grows flatter to indicate that the fault of the injurer relative to the fault of the victim is increasing.

exactly satisfy the legal standard in order to escape responsibility for accident costs, so that party's behavior will be efficient provided that the legal standard is set at the efficient level of care. That leaves residual responsibility for accident costs on the other party. The party that bears responsibility for accident costs has an incentive to balance the cost of additional precaution against the resulting savings in accident costs, and we have already seen that this calculation will lead the decisionmaker to choose that level of precaution for which the marginal cost of precaution equals the marginal social benefits of precaution. And, of course, this occurs at the social-cost-minimizing level of care. Thus, the party who bears residual responsibility internalizes the cost of accidents and takes efficient precaution.

Put somewhat differently, we are suggesting that a rationally self-interested decisionmaker will assume that other potential parties to an accident, victims or injurers, have chosen to take efficient precaution as required by the legal standard of care and, that being so, it makes sense for the rational decisionmaker also to take efficient precaution. We conclude that both parties—potential victims and potential injurers—will take precaution at the efficient level.

> **Question 8.4:** Assume that both the victim and the injurer in an accident could have taken precautionary action to reduce the probability and severity of the accident. Show that both simple negligence and negligence with contributory negligence induce an efficient level of precaution by both parties. Reevaluate your answer to Question 8.3 in light of your answer to this question.

We have just shown that any form of the negligence rule creates incentives for efficient precaution provided that the legal standard is set at the efficient level of care. But can courts, legislatures, and administrative agencies in fact identify the efficient level of care to establish it as the legal standard? In torts cases, courts often enforce standards of reasonableness and community norms. To some extent, the courts discover the level of reasonable precaution by hearing evidence on how people actually behave. On the other hand, the courts to some extent make up their own minds about the reasonable level of precaution based upon evidence about relative costs and benefits. There is, thus, a deep issue about the extent to which community standards and norms of reasonableness correspond to efficient levels of precaution.

It can be argued that reasonable care is identical to efficient care. The essence of the argument is that reasonableness requires the decisionmaker to give similar weight to the cost of more precaution, which he bears, and the benefit of more precaution in terms of the reduced frequency and severity of accidents, which others enjoy. His behavior is unreasonable and his precaution is faulty when he gives more weight to the costs he bears than to the benefits it creates for others. This interpretation of reasonableness in effect requires the decisionmaker to act as if all costs and benefits were internalized, as required for efficiency. Whether this is an accurate interpretation of the actual reasoning employed in the courts is a difficult empirical question.

In the following famous case, a judge set the legal standard of care by explicitly balancing the benefits and costs of precaution, just as an economist would have done in order to discover the efficient level of care. Moreover, as you will see, he proposed a practical method of determining the social-cost-minimizing level of care in any given tort case. Read the case with an eye for the economic analysis used in reaching the decision and then think about the questions that follow the opinion.

United States v. Carroll Towing Co., 159 F.2d 169 (2d Cir. 1947).

[The facts in this case concern the loss of a barge and its cargo in New York Harbor. A number of barges were secured by a single mooring line to several piers. The defendant's tug was hired to take one of those barges out of the harbor. In order to release that barge, the crew of the defendant's tug, finding no one aboard any of the barges, re-adjusted the mooring lines themselves. The adjustment was not done properly so that later one of the barges broke loose, collided with another ship, and sank with its cargo. The barge's owner sued the tug owner and others for negligently causing his losses. The defendant tug owner attempted to avoid his share of the liability by showing that the barge owner's agent, called a ''bargee,'' was contributorily negligent in not being on the barge at the time the tug's crew sought to adjust the mooring lines.]

L. HAND, J. . . . It appears from the foregoing review that there is no general rule to determine when the absence of a bargee or other attendant will make the owner of a barge liable for injuries to other vessels if she breaks away from her moorings. However, in any cases where he would be so liable for injuries to others, obviously he must reduce his damages proportionately, if the injury is to his own barge. It becomes apparent why there can be no such general rule when we consider the grounds for such a liability. Since there are occasions when every vessel will break away from her moorings, and since, if she does, she becomes a menace to those about her; the owner's duty, as in other similar situations, to provide against resulting injuries is a function of three variables: (1) The probability that she will break away; (2) the gravity of the resulting injury, if she does; (3) the burden of adequate precautions. Possibly it serves to bring this notion into relief to state it in algebraic terms: if the probability be called P; the injury, L; and the burden, B; liability depends upon whether B is less than L multiplied by P; i.e., whether $B < PL$. Applied to the situation at bar, the likelihood that a barge will break from her fasts and the damage she will do, vary with the place and time: for example, if a storm threatens, the danger is greater; so it is, if she is in a crowded harbor where moored barges are constantly being shifted about. On the other hand, the barge must not be the bargee's prison, even though he lives aboard; he must go ashore at times. We need not say whether, even in such crowded waters as New York Harbor a bargee must be aboard at night at all; it may be that the custom is otherwise, . . . and that, if so, the situation is one where custom should control. We leave that question open; but we hold that it is not in all cases a sufficient answer to a bargee's absence without excuse, during working hours, that he has properly made fast his barge to a pier when he leaves her. In the case at bar the bargee left at five o'clock in the afternoon of January 3rd, and the flotilla broke away at about two o'clock in the afternoon of the following day, twenty-one hours afterwards. The bargee had been away all the time, and we hold that his fabricated story was affirmative evidence that he had no excuse for his absence. At the locus in quo—especially during the short January days, and in the full tide of war activity—barges were being constantly ''drilled'' in and out. Certainly it was not beyond reasonable expectation that, with the inevitable haste and bustle, the work might not be done with adequate care. In such circumstances we hold—and it is all that we do hold—that it was a fair requirement that the [barge owner] should have had a bargee aboard (unless he had some excuse for his absence), during the working hours of daylight. ▬▬▬

Question 8.5:

a. The equation for liability proposed in this case is known as the "Hand Rule" and is one of the most famous formulations in the economic analysis of law. The rule says that if the expected injury, PL [what we called above "$p(x)A$"], exceeds the costs of precaution, B [what we called above "wx"], and the defendant did not take the precaution, then the defendant is negligent. (Precaution that costs less than expected accident costs is sometimes referred to as "cost-justified" precaution. Thus, negligence can be said to be the failure to take cost-justified precaution.)

In order for the rule to be consistent with our analysis of the social-cost-minimizing standard of care, how should B, P, and L be interpreted? Are they, for example, to be considered as *marginal, average,* or *total* quantities? Do you see any problems with its calculation?

b. Suppose that the value of the barge and its cargo are $100,000. The probability that the barge would break loose if the bargee is *not* present is 0.001. If the bargee is present, then the probability of the barge's breaking loose is reduced by half, to 0.0005. However, in order to realize the reduction in the probability of accident, the barge owner must either induce the bargee to give up his scheduled time ashore by offering him a higher wage or by policing the bargee's behavior more closely. Either increase in precaution will cost the barge owner $25. If the barge owner does not incur this $25 expense, is his behavior negligent?

c. In making the calculation of expected costs, should the accident costs be "reasonably expected" accident costs or the worst possible case? For example, in the previous question we stated that the value of the barge and its cargo were $100,000. When making his calculations about precautionary behavior, the owner of the tug, the *Carroll,* would probably use an *average* figure for the expected losses in the event of an accident. Thus, he would implicity be assuming that the barge was an average barge with an average cargo. If, however, the barge contains a cargo that is far more valuable than average, won't the tug owner have taken too little precaution if he used the average figure?

d. Does the Hand Rule formulation assume a particular attitude toward risk on the part of the defendant? For example, would a risk-averse defendant be more or less likely than a risk-neutral defendant to take precaution if the marginal cost of precaution is just equal to the expected marginal benefits of precaution? Does that make any difference, in the sense that to apply the rule the court should determine the defendant's attitude toward risk before making the Hand calculation? (Recall that attitudes towards risk are discussed in the appendix to Chapter 2.)

F. The Economics of Strict Liability

The major alternative to some form of the negligence rule is a rule of strict liability. Strict liability makes the injurer bear the cost of accidents that he causes, regardless of the extent of his precaution. Under strict liability, there is no legal standard of precaution that is relevant to the assignment of costs. Is it possible to create incentives for efficient precaution under this liability rule? How do negligence and strict liability compare with respect to these incentives?

We can give a complete answer to these questions: strict liability creates efficient incentives for the injurer's precaution provided that damages are *perfectly compensatory* and that the situation between injurer and victim is one of *unilateral precaution*.

By the term *perfectly compensatory damages* or *perfect compensation*, we mean a level of damages such that the victim is indifferent between there being no accident and there being an accident with compensatory damages. (We illustrated perfectly compensatory damages in Figure 8.1 above.) As we will see, perfect compensation is a central concept because it characterizes the level of damages at which the injurer fully internalizes the cost of accidents. *Under strict liability, any amount of damages different from those that perfectly compensate the victim creates an inefficient incentive for the potential injurer and, thus, leads to inefficient levels of precaution.*

By the term *unilateral precaution* we mean that only one party may be looked to for precaution that reduces the severity or likelihood of an accident. Let us discuss these conditions—perfect compensation and unilateral precaution—in turn.

Recall that in Example 3 from the beginning of the chapter the manufacturer is strictly liable for the actual harm caused by defective products. This means that she must bear the social costs of accidents caused by her products, regardless of any level of precaution that she might have taken. We can demonstrate the impact of this rule by reproducing Figure 8.2 and re-labeling it as Figure 8.8. Both the curves representing the private costs of precaution, wx, and the expected accident costs, $p(x)A$, are shown and have been summed vertically to represent the expected social costs, $SC = [wx + p(x)A]$. The level of precaution for which these expected social costs are minimized, x^*, is also represented. Under strict liability there is no standard of care, compliance with which will excuse the manufacturer from liability for the costs her actions impose on others. Thus, she is liable for all the social costs caused by her products. This means that the full expected social cost curve, SC, becomes the expected private cost curve of the manufacturer. Being a rational decisionmaker, she will choose that level of precaution that minimizes her expected private costs. Because social costs are borne by the manufacturer, minimizing her private costs is equivalent to minimizing social costs; she "internalizes" those external costs. And because there is no discontinuity in the private cost function of the manufacturer under strict liability as there was under negligence, the manufacturer minimizes private costs at a level of precaution where marginal benefit equals marginal cost, namely, at x^*.

Question 8.6: Suppose that the level of damages is less than perfectly compensatory. The injurer is held strictly liable for these less-than-perfect damages. Can you illustrate the impact of this on the incentives for precaution of the injurer? Would the level of precaution be greater or less than x^*, the social-cost-minimizing level of precaution under perfect compensation?

Question 8.7: What if the damages are greater than perfectly compensatory? What incentives does that create for potential injurers under strict liability?

Figure 8.8 Expected Liability Under Strict Liability

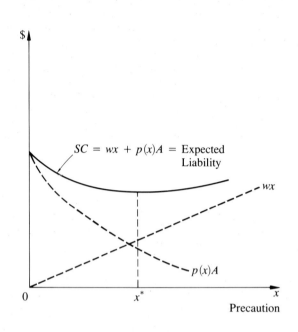

The straight line labeled *wx* indicates the actor's private costs of precaution on the assumption that precaution costs $w per unit. The probability of the actor's inflicting costs on others is represented by the line labeled $p(x)A$. A represents the costs that might be imposed on others, and p represents the probability of those costs' being imposed as a *decreasing* function of the amount of precaution, x. The injurer's total expected costs are the sum of these two elements: $[wx + p(x)A]$. The curve labeled SC shows the sum of the *wx* and $p(x)A$ curves. The cost-minimizing level of precaution is x^*, where the cost per unit of precaution, w, equals the reduction in the probability of an accident from taking an additional unit of precaution, $p'(x)$, times the accident costs, A. These are exactly the cost curves that face the injurer under a negligence rule. However, under strict liability there is no legal standard of care, compliance with which absolves the actor of liability. The injurer is liable for any harm that he causes.

Would the level of precaution be greater or less than x^*, the social-cost-minimizing level of precaution under perfect compensation?

The discussion above has shown that the rule of strict liability provides efficient incentives for injurers provided that damages are set at the perfectly compensatory level. But what about the second condition for efficient incentives under strict liability—that precaution is unilateral? This is a question about how the rule of strict liability takes account of the *victim's* ability to reduce the probability or severity of an accident. In fact, when we do take victim precaution into account, the efficiency of strict liability becomes problematic. The reason is that although strict liability creates the right incentives for potential injurers, it may create an incentive problem for potential victims. To appreciate this point, it is useful to distinguish between situations that call for *bilateral* precaution and those that call for *unilateral* precaution. Bilateral precaution simply means that efficiency requires *both* parties to take precautions against accidents, whereas unilateral precaution means that efficiency requires *only one* of the parties to take precaution against accidents. The distinction is relevant because, when efficient precaution is bilateral, it is impossible to achieve incentives for efficient precaution through a rule of strict liability.

To explain this point, we will contrast negligence and strict liability. Remember that we showed that each form of the negligence rule is efficient because, while one party has incentives to take efficient precaution to avoid liability, the other party also has incentives to take efficient precaution because she bears residual responsibility. The various forms of the negligence rule thus create efficient incentives for both parties by setting a standard for each of them, and, when the standard is met by one, requiring the other party to internalize the social costs of accidents. For this reason, bilateral precaution creates no insurmountable difficulties for a negligence rule.

In contrast, strict liability imposes all accident costs on the injurer, regardless of the victim's precaution. Since the injurer bears the costs of accidents, the victim's incentives for precaution are undermined. Where precaution can be taken only by the injurer, this is not a problem. And typically the circumstances in which the classical theory imposed strict liability were those of unilateral precaution—dynamite blasters, those who dispensed poisons, and those who kept dangerous animals were all held strictly liable.[26]

But in circumstances where precaution is bilateral, strict liability creates inefficient incentives for the victim to take precaution. To illustrate, suppose that automobile manufacturers are strictly liable for failures in car transmissions. Some car owners would be tempted to shift gears roughly or to spend less to maintain their car's transmission than they would if they had to bear the repair costs themselves. And this is clearly inefficient because this is a situation of bilateral precaution: there are some actions that car owners, as well as car manufacturers, can take to reduce the likelihood of transmission failure.

---

[26]Typically in strict liability the actions of the plaintiff are not examined; the only issue is whether the defendant proximately caused the victim's harm. However, in some older strict liability actions, the defendant was allowed to mount certain "affirmative defenses," whose thrust was that the plaintiff was not entitled to compensation even though the defendant's actions caused him harm. For example, under the older interpretation of strict liability for product-related harms, the defendant could escape (strict) liability by demonstrating that the plaintiff had willingly assumed the risk of harm (for example, if the defendant clearly warned the consumer of the potential harm from use of the product) or that the plaintiff had misused the product in a manner for which it was clearly not intended to be used (for example, by using a stick of dynamite as a hammer). These are not exactly instances of bilateral precaution and so fall outside our rule for distinguishing situations in which negligence is preferable to strict liability. We will return to these affirmative defenses under strict liability in our extended discussion of products liability in the following chapter.

We can identify this problem more sharply by recognizing that strict liability is the mirror image of no liability. Under a rule of no liability, as we saw above, self-interested injurers have no incentive to take any precaution because they are not led to internalize any social costs they impose; their private cost-minimizing precaution level is at the origin of Figure 8.2 or 8.8 where $x = 0$. In contrast, the rule of strict liability with perfect compensation creates no incentives for precaution by self-interested *victims*. Their cost-minimizing level of precaution may well be $y = 0$. The incentive effects of no liability upon the *injurer* are thus the same as the incentive effects of strict liability with perfect compensation upon the *victim*.

The rule of no liability gives efficient incentives for victim's precaution and no incentives for injurer's precaution; similarly, strict liability with perfect compensation gives efficient incentives for injurer's precaution and no incentives for victim's precaution. Thus, neither of these rules can provide efficient incentives under conditions of bilateral precaution.

Would the fact that, in reality, the rule of strict liability seldom results in perfect compensation change this conclusion? If, for example, victims are usually undercompensated, this might create for them a sort of residual liability. Remember that insurance companies deal with the problem of moral hazard (see the appendix to Chapter 2) by making the insured responsible for a residual amount of loss from an accident through a deductible or co-insurance provision. Would systematic undercompensation of victims under a rule of strict liability accomplish the same thing? Unfortunately, undercompensation cannot solve the problem of efficient incentives in a situation of bilateral precaution. To see this, start from perfect compensation under strict liability and allow the level of compensation to become more and more inadequate; it is true that this creates stronger and stronger incentives for precaution for the victim, as required for efficiency. Unfortunately, however, as the level of damages becomes more and more inadequate, the *injurer* has weaker and weaker incentives for precaution. We conclude, then, that the rule of strict liability cannot solve the problem of providing efficient incentives to both parties, regardless of the level at which damages are set, but the rule of strict liability can provide efficient incentives to the injurer provided that damages are set at the perfectly compensatory level.[27]

---

[27]Finally, we wish to define rules that are the mirror image of simple negligence and negligence with a defense of contributory negligence. These rules have formed part of the literature in this area and are sometimes said to describe the behavior of some courts. Many legal commentators, however, contend that strict liability, as understood by modern courts, comprehends neither of these variants:

strict liability with a defense of contributory negligence:
$$y < y^* \implies \text{injurer not liable},$$
$$y \geq y^* \implies \text{injurer is liable}$$

where y^* is the legal standard of care to which the victim is held. The defendant is still held strictly liable; that is, there is no legal standard of care on the defendant's care.

G. Comparing Negligence and Strict Liability

The incentives created by negligence and strict liability work in different ways. Under strict liability, the actor balances the cost of additional precaution against the resulting reduction in accident costs for which he is responsible; he minimizes his private costs when the benefits and costs of a small change in precaution are equal.[28] By contrast, under a negligence rule, the benefits and costs of a small change in precaution are not usually equipoised, because the actor's private costs are much lower when he just satisfies the legal standard than they would be if he just failed to satisfy it.[29]

We have shown that when efficient precaution is bilateral, a negligence rule can create efficient incentives and a rule of strict liability cannot. Thus, where incentives for precaution are concerned, bilateral precaution favors a negligence rule and unilateral precaution favors strict liability. There are, however, some other important considerations in comparing these rules. (See the box "You Can't Kill Two Birds with One Stone.")

Unlike negligence, strict liability makes the potential injurer very responsive to imperfections in assessing and computing damages. If the courts sometimes allow an injurer to escape liability for harm that he caused, or if the courts sometimes award damages that are less than the harm caused by the injurer, or if some victims do not bring suit, then it will be profitable for potential injurers to reduce their precaution below the efficient level. (This conclusion could be illustrated using Figure 8.8, where shifting the private cost curve below the social cost curve causes the cost-minimizing level of precaution to fall.)

There are other important differences between negligence and strict liability. One difference is that strict liability applies continuing pressure upon injurers to discover new technologies that will reduce accident losses. In contrast, a negligence rule removes the injurer's incentive to innovate insofar as he can completely escape liability by taking precautions that are reasonable given the existing technology.

Another difference that has proved important in the history of torts is the problem of proof and the costliness of trials. Proving negligence is some-

---

strict liability with a defense of dual contributory negligence:

$$x \geq x^* \text{ and } y < y^* \implies \text{injurer not liable}$$
$$x < x^* \text{ or } y \geq y^* \implies \text{injurer liable}$$

Notice that "strict liability" in these rules simply throws residual liability onto the injurer, rather than leaving it on the victim.

[28]In technical economic language, the actor under strict liability is at an interior solution where marginal private benefit equals marginal private cost. Thus, a tangent line to his cost curve in Figure 8.8 has zero slope at x^*.

[29]In technical language, the actor under Rule A is at a corner on the cost function where the cost of an incremental change exceeds the benefit. For an interesting discussion of the peculiarities in behavior caused by discontinuous cost functions, *see* John M. Marshall, *Gambles and the Shadow Price of Death*, 74 AM. ECON. REV. 73 (1984).

You Can't Kill Two Birds with One Stone

Whenever you drive your car, there is a risk that you will injure someone else. One way to control this risk is to impose liability on you for any injuries caused by your negligent driving. We have shown that it pays for you to respect the legal standard of care and conform to it. So, the law can affect the care with which you drive by imposing a negligence rule upon you.

But what about the *amount* that you drive? The risk of injury that you impose upon others depends upon the care with which you drive and also on the amount that you drive. Under a negligence rule, by conforming to the legal standard of care, you will always escape liability for tortious accidents, no matter how much you drive. To illustrate, by driving 10,000 miles a year, the probability that you will injure someone in an accident is approximately 10 times higher than it would be if you drove only 1,000 miles per year. So long as your driving is nonnegligent, so that your liability is zero, you do not bear any portion of the ten-fold increase in expected harm from accidents when you increase your driving from 1,000 miles per year to 10,000 miles per year.

In general, a negligence rule can create incentives for efficient *precaution*, such as safe driving, but not incentives for an efficient *activity level*, such as the number of miles driven.[1] The effects of activity level upon risk are externalized with a negligence rule.

times difficult and costly; the plaintiff must demonstrate by a preponderance of the evidence that the defendant legally caused his harm and that he violated a legal standard of care in doing so; under strict liability all that must be proved is legal cause. As a result, it is fair to say that strict liability has generally lower administration costs than does negligence.[30] Because these costs should be included in the social-cost-minimizing calculation, we must, in our overall assessment of the liability standards, take these costs of proof and of trials into account.

These thoughts on the differences between negligence and strict liability should help point out the pitfalls in applying the economic theory of liability to actual cases. Where there is bilateral precaution, some form of the negligence rule creates efficient incentives for both parties but is costly to administer. Strict liability creates efficient incentives for precaution where there is unilateral precaution and is, moreover, relatively inexpensive to administer. Potential pitfalls arise where the inefficiencies from imposing strict liability in a situation of bilateral precaution are nearly offset by the

---

[30]This conclusion is even stronger for those forms of the negligence rule that also investigate the *plaintiff*'s compliance with a legal standard of care. Because strict liability usually does not involve investigation of the plaintiff's actions, it does not involve these additional costs.

The incentive structure is quite different under a rule of strict liability. If a driver is strictly liable for the harm he causes, then he internalizes accident costs. When accident costs are internalized, he has an incentive to set every variable affecting the probability of an accident at its efficient level. So, the rule of strict liability can induce both efficient precaution and an efficient activity level by potential injurers.

But we have already seen that strict liability has a different problem: it undermines the incentives for precaution by the victim.

There is a general principle at work here: two policy targets cannot be controlled with one variable. Specifically, precaution and the activity level cannot both be controlled by a negligence rule that imposes a standard of precaution. An additional control variable is needed for the activity level, such as a gasoline tax. Similarly, the precaution of the injurer and the precaution of the victim cannot both be controlled by a rule of strict liability that imposes costs upon only one of them. To hit two policy targets, two controls are required, just as two stones are usually needed to hit two birds. On the other hand, if costs are fully internalized by private decisionmakers, then public officials need not worry about controlling any variables since the economy will achieve efficiency on its own.

[1]This conclusion and much of the material in this box was first clearly stated by Steven Shavell in *Strict Liability versus Negligence*, 9 J. LEGAL STUD. 1 (1980).

savings in administration costs of that standard over any form of the negligence rule. It is also possible that there are situations of unilateral precaution where determining perfect compensation is so difficult that strict liability creates seriously inefficient incentives, although it is to be recommended on the grounds of lower administration costs. No one has yet made a thorough investigation of all these tradeoffs.

One final caveat should be made. All of our conclusions about the efficiency aspects of the various liability standards are subject to re-evaluation when we relax the assumptions of the model we have been using. We leave refinements such as these to the following chapter.

Question 8.8: Using the economic theory, explain which liability standard—negligence or strict liability—creates superior incentives for efficient precaution in the following situations:

a. Dynamite-blasting by a construction company causes the mink on a nearby commercial mink ranch to go berserk and to attack and kill each other, causing a nearly total loss to the ranch owner. Should the construction company be strictly liable for the mink rancher's losses? Or should the injurer's actions be judged on a fault basis? With what result?

b. Some consumers of a leading non-prescription cold remedy become seriously ill as a result of taking that remedy. It is later learned that the pills were adulterated, probably after they left the manufacturer. If the consumers sue the manufacturer, should his actions be judged on the basis of strict liability or negligence? With what result?

c. A pedestrian, who was crossing the street against the light, was struck by a speeding driver. The pedestrian sues the driver for her harm. What liability standard should you apply?

1. What if the pedestrian is a blind woman with a cane?
2. What if the driver is a famous heart surgeon speeding to the hospital to operate on a gravely ill and publicly prominent patient?
3. What if the pedestrian is a child?
4. What if the driver is a minor?

CONCLUSION

According to the classical theory, a tort is a breach of a duty that harms someone else. The elements of a tort are, accordingly,

1. breach of a legal duty owed to the plaintiff by the defendant,
2. measurable harm suffered by the plaintiff, and
3. establishment that the defendant's breach proximately caused the plaintiff's harm.

Although contemporary tort law has created many exceptions to the classical theory, these elements are still a useful starting point for the economic analysis of torts. Proximate cause in torts is similar to an external bad in economics—a direct dependence of one person's utility or production upon the choice variables controlled by someone else. Harm consists in a fall in utility or profits, which is compensated by an amount of money that restores utility or profits to the level that would have been achieved but for the injury. A legal duty partitions the set of actions into permitted and forbidden zones, and attaches a sanction to being in the forbidden zone. The partition creates a discontinuity in costs, so usually it pays to conform to the legal standard, even if there are many imperfections in its application. The various forms of the negligence rule are obligations backed by sanctions. All of them create incentives for efficient behavior when the legal standard is pegged at the efficient level, regardless of whether efficient precaution is bilateral or unilateral. With a negligence rule, it is crucial that the legal standard should be set correctly.

In contrast, the rule of strict liability merely prices the external cost of the harmful or dangerous actions. Because strict liability does not impose a legal standard of care, there is no problem of errors in setting a legal standard. On the other hand, strict liability cannot provide efficient incentives for both the injurer and the victim to take precaution; it creates efficient incentives only where precaution is unilateral to the injurer. Finally, strict liability cannot provide efficient incentives for the injurer to take precaution unless damages are perfectly compensatory.

To gain perspective on this account, we relate it to our theory of property. We argued that the purpose of property law is to create a zone of private discretion over material things. Discretion consists of a bundle of rights that owners can exercise or not exercise, as they see fit. The owners' discretion is protected when they can obtain an injunction to prevent others from interfering with the exercise of their rights.

Protecting property rights, which involves preserving discretion, must be distinguished from protecting the interests of owners. The owner's interests are protected when he can obtain compensation from someone who diminishes the value of his property rights. To illustrate, if you borrow a family heirloom and accidentally destroy it, the owner's discretion over its use is lost, but if you pay him compensation, his interest in it is protected. The purpose of torts is, then, to protect the interests of people in their property and persons from damage by others. This protection is, however, quite costly. The amount of protection that one person must provide to another is bounded by concepts of reasonableness and community standards of behavior. Tests of reasonableness and community standards of behavior arise from balancing the costs of precaution against the benefits. The power of the economic analysis of torts is its ability to offer a systematic account of how to strike this balance.

SUGGESTED READINGS

Brown, John P., *Toward an Economic Theory of Liability*, 2 J. LEGAL STUD. 323 (1973).

Calabresi, G., THE COSTS OF ACCIDENTS: A LEGAL AND ECONOMIC ANALYSIS (1970).

Calabresi, G., and A. Hirschoff, *Toward a Test for Strict Liability in Torts*, 81 YALE L. J. 1055 (1972).

Epstein, Richard, *A Theory of Strict Liability*, 2 J. LEGAL STUD. 151 (1973).

Fletcher, George, *Fairness and Utility in Tort Law*, 85 HARV. L. REV. 537 (1972).

Grady, Mark, *A New Positive Economic Theory of Negligence*, 92 YALE L. J. 799 (1983).

Polinsky, A. Mitchell, *Strict Liability v. Negligence in a Market Setting*, 70 AM. ECON. REV. 363 (1980).

Posner, Richard A., *A Theory of Negligence*, 1 J. LEGAL STUD. 29 (1972).

Posner, Richard A., *Strict Liability: A Comment*, 2 J. LEGAL STUD. 205 (1973).

Posner, Richard A., TORTS: CASES AND ECONOMIC ANALYSIS (1983).

Prosser, William L., A HANDBOOK OF THE LAW OF TORTS (4th ed. 1971).

Rabin, Robert, ed., PERSPECTIVES ON TORT LAW (2d ed. 1983).

Shavell, Steven, AN ANALYSIS OF ACCIDENT LAW (1987).

CHAPTER 9

Topics in the Economics of Tort Law

The preceding chapter introduced the fundamental concepts of tort law by comparing the classical theory to the economic analysis. We saw that there was a correspondence between the classical elements of a tort and some familiar economic concepts: the element of causality in the traditional theory corresponds to a material externality in economics; the element of damages corresponds to a fall in utility or profits caused by the externality; and the element of fault corresponds to a partition of the decisionmaker's choice set into permitted and forbidden zones with a discontinuity in costs at the boundary. We also saw that the economic analysis provided a purpose for tort liability—the minimization of the social costs (defined as the sum of the precaution, accident, and administration costs associated with those harms) of tortious harms—and, in principle, a method of calculating the social-cost minimizing level of precaution—that for which the marginal cost of a unit of precaution equals the expected marginal benefit (in terms of the reduced probability and severity of the harm). Furthermore, we saw that the economic analysis, by viewing the harm suffered by the victim as the sum necessary to return him or her to his or her original indifference curve or isoquant, can assist in the determination of the amount of compensatory damages. Finally, we saw that the economic model can help lawmakers choose the best form of the liability rule for particular circumstances, such as the choice between strict liability and negligence. To illustrate, a negligence rule is usually preferable from an economic viewpoint to a rule of strict liability when precaution is bilateral: that is, when efficiency requires both injurers and victims to take precaution to reduce the probability or severity of an accident. In contrast, strict liability will minimize social costs when there is unilateral precaution, that is, when efficiency requires only the injurer to take precaution to reduce the probability or severity of an accident.

In this chapter we apply the economic analysis to some selected topics that are especially important in contemporary tort law. Many people believe there is a crisis afflicting the tort liability system. The examples that can be offered of this crisis are legion. Here are a few. The largest and most profitable asbestos-manufacturing company in the United States, the Manville Corporation, was forced to seek the protection of bankruptcy law when the company's anticipated liability for harms attributable to asbestos exposure over the last fifty years exceeded $2 billion, the value of the company's assets. A teenager, who was crossing a school building's roof late at night in order to burglarize the school, fell through a skylight, was paralyzed, and threatened to sue the school district. The district's insurance company, fearing the sums that a jury might award the plaintiff if the suit went to trial, settled with the teenager for $260,000, plus $1,500 per month for the rest of the teenager's life. The G. D. Searle Company, frightened by the bankruptcy of the A.H. Robins Company because of that rival's liability arising from its Dalkon shield, recently announced that it would no longer produce intrauterine birth control devices. This decision was taken despite the fact that Planned Parenthood and other experts believe the Searle product to be the safest IUD on the market. Vaccines for such devastating childhood diseases as whooping cough and polio are in short supply owing to manufacturers leaving the industry because of their fear of tort liability. Some doctors have become so fearful of medical malpractice suits that they have changed their specialties, moving from high-risk areas such as obstetrics-gynecology to lower-risk areas such as internal medicine. Volunteer youth soccer coaches in most cities receive an orientation session in which they are instructed by Park District attorneys not to take an injured young athlete to the hospital in their own car for fear of their or the district's being held liable for any injuries the athlete may have suffered.

The perceived crisis in the tort liability system has given rise to a secondary crisis in the liability insurance industry. Because of the widening scope of liability, insurers have had to increase their premiums dramatically and rapidly. It is routinely asserted today that a surgeon practicing in a major metropolitan area pays $100,000 per year in medical malpractice insurance premiums. In some instances, insurance companies have quit underwriting liability policies altogether, forcing the insured either to self-insure or to take more drastic steps. For example, some municipal park districts have cited the unavailability of liability insurance as the cause of their discontinuing summer sports programs for youth and of their dismantling public play structures like slides and swing sets.

This catalogue of horrors suggests that tort liability is too extensive and that the rights of victims should be reduced. But the opposite conclusion can be reached from the same facts. It can be argued that in the past, people who were maimed, killed, or lost their property due to the fault of others often had no recourse. Instead of the tort crisis being a bad thing, it can be regarded as a long overdue vindication of victims' rights.

In this chapter we will focus on one of the most rapidly growing areas of tort liability—products liability—to examine the roots of these crises, to assess widely different evaluations of it, and to see what reforms might be recommended. The economic analysis of torts of the previous chapter, and a few extensions that we will introduce in the next section of this chapter, should prove to be very helpful in understanding the liability and insurance crises and in evaluating proposed reforms.

These perceptions of a crisis have given rise to a broadly supported call for federal legislation to abolish the current state systems of tort liability. In the final section of this chapter we will look at various suggestions for replacing the current tort liability system with what are known as "administered compensation" systems. One such reform is no-fault automobile insurance. We will explore the theoretical arguments for such a system and see how it has been implemented and discuss the case for expanding no-fault beyond automobile accidents.

I. APPLYING THE ECONOMIC MODEL AND SOME FURTHER TOPICS

In this section we want to apply the economic model we developed in the previous chapter to some concrete examples. First, we will discuss a few cases to see how efficiency standards may be applied. Then we will extend the economic analysis to explain such topics as comparative negligence, joint and multiple tortfeasors, vicarious liability, and liability for failure to rescue. Later in this section, we will take a critical look at some of the less realistic assumptions of the economic analysis. For example, the simple model assumed that litigation was costless and that decisionmakers could accurately estimate the risk of uncertain events. Both assumptions are, at best, questionable. How would our policy conclusions of the previous chapter about the economic efficiency of different liability standards be altered if we relax those assumptions?

A. Negligence

The following case is complex. We want to assist your reading of it by alerting you to a fundamental issue it raises, specifically industry custom as a defense to a charge of negligence. The opinion suggests that compliance with industry custom with regard to precaution should not be accepted as a defense to a charge of negligence. The defendant had contended that it was not negligent because only one company in the coastwise tug industry had radio receiving sets for checking on the weather; everyone else took precaution against foundering at sea by towing close to the shore and keeping a lookout with binoculars for storm warnings posted on the shore. An additional benefit of staying close to shore was that if a storm warning were cited, a safe harbor could be found relatively quickly.

The T. J. Hooper, 6 F.2d 737 (2d Cir. 1932).

L. HAND, J. The barges No. 17 and No. 30, belonging to the Northern Barge Company, had lifted cargoes of coal at Norfolk, Virginia, for New York in March, 1928. They were towed by two tugs of the petitioner, the "Montrose" and the "Hooper," and were lost off the Jersey Coast on March tenth, in an easterly gale. The cargo owners sued the barges under the contracts of carriage; the owner of the barges sued the tugs under the towing contract, both for its own loss and as bailee of the cargoes; the owner of the tugs filed a petition to limit its liability. All the suits were joined and heard together, and the judge found that all the vessels were unseaworthy; the tugs, because they did not carry radio receiving sets by which they could have seasonably got warnings of a change in the weather which should have caused them to seek shelter in the Delaware Breakwater en route. He therefore entered an interlocutory decree hold-ing each tug and barge jointly liable to each cargo owner, and each tug for half damages for the loss of its barge. The petitioner appealed, and the barge owner appealed and filed assignments of error.

Each tug had three ocean going coal barges in tow, the lost barge being at the end. The "Montrose," which had the No. 17, took an outside course; the "Hooper" with the No. 30, inside. The weather was fair with-out ominous symptoms, as the tows passed the Delaware Breakwater about midnight of March eighth, and the barges did not get into serious trouble until they were about opposite Atlantic City some sixty or seventy miles to the north. The wind began to freshen in the morning of the ninth and rose to a gale before noon; by afternoon the second barge of the Hooper's tow was out of hand and signalled the tug, which found that not only this barge needed help but that the No. 30 was aleak. Both barges anchored and the crew of the No. 30 rode out the storm until the after-noon of the tenth, when she sank, her crew having been meanwhile taken off. The No. 17 sprang a leak about the same time; she too anchored at the Montrose's command and sank on the next morning after her crew also had been rescued. The cargoes and the tugs maintain that the barges were not fit for their service; the cargoes and the barges that the tugs should have gone into the Delaware Breakwater, and besides, did not handle their tows properly. [The court confirmed the findings of the court below that the barges were not seaworthy in fact and that had the masters of the tugs received radio broadcasts from the weather bureau at Arlington indicating an approaching storm they would not have pro-ceeded to sea, since "prudent masters . . . would have found the risk more than the exigency warranted."]

To be sure, the barges would, as we have said, probably have with-stood the gale, had they been well found; but a master is not justified in putting his tow to every test which she will survive, if she be fit. There is a zone in which proper caution will avoid putting her capacity to the proof; a coefficient of prudence that he should not disregard. Taking the situation as a whole, it seems to us that these masters would have taken undue chances, had they got the broadcasts.

They did not, because their private radio receiving sets, which were on board, were not in working order. These belonged to them personally, and were partly a toy, partly a part of the equipment, but neither furnished by the owner, nor supervised by it. It is not fair to say that there was a general custom among coastwise carriers so to equip their tugs. One line alone did it; as for the rest they relied upon their crews, so far as they can be said to have relied at all. An adequate receiving set suitable for a coastwise tug can now be got at small cost and is reasonably reliable if kept up; obviously it is a source of great protection to their tows. Twice every day they can receive these predictions, based upon the widest possible information, available to every vessel within two or three hundred miles and more. Such a set is the ears of the tug to catch the spoken word, just as the master's binoculars are her eyes to see a storm signal ashore. Whatever may be said as to other vessels, tugs towing heavy coal-laden barges, strung out for half a mile, have little power to manoeuvre, and do not, as this case proves, expose themselves to weather which would not turn back stauncher craft. They can have at hand protection against dangers of which they can learn in no other way.

Is it then a final answer that the business had not yet generally adopted receiving sets? There are, no doubt, cases where courts seem to make the general practice of the calling the standard of proper diligence . . . Indeed in most cases reasonable prudence is in fact common prudence; but strictly it is never its measure; a whole calling may have unduly lagged in the adoption of new and available devices. It never may set its own tests, however persuasive be its usages. [A section of the U.S. Code required coastwise vessels to carry a transmitting set in order to facilitate calling for help; there was no statutory requirement to carry a receiving set.] Courts must in the end say what is required; there are precautions so imperative that even their universal disregard will not excuse their omission . . . But here there was no custom at all as to receiving sets; some had them, some did not; the most that can be urged is that they had not yet become general. Certainly in such a case we need not pause; when some have thought a device necessary, at least we may say that they were right, and the others too slack. . . . We hold the tugs liable therefore because, had they been properly equipped, they would have got the Arlington reports. The injury was a direct consequence of this unseaworthiness.

Decree affirmed.

Question 9.1:

a. Suppose that the coastwise tug industry between New York and Norfolk, Virginia, is very highly competitive; there are lots of different companies; entry and exit are relatively easy; also alternative shipping modes—e.g., trains—exist and charge only a slightly higher price than the tugs. In those circumstances would you accept compliance with industrial custom—e.g., not having a radio receiving set—as a complete defense to a charge of negligence?

b. What if the coastwise tug industry was either monopolized or cartelized? Would you accept custom as a defense in those circumstances? Why not? What if the industry is somewhere between perfectly competitive and monopolistic so that some firms have receiving sets and others do not? Would you simply conclude that there is no industry custom? How would you then determine fault?

c. Would you find information about insurance rates for cargo carried on the tugs with and those without radio receivers of interest? What if the rates were the same? What would you infer about the customary precaution of staying close to shore without a radio to receive weather reports?

d. Fifteen years after he wrote this opinion Judge Hand proposed the famous Hand Rule in another case having to do with tugs and barges. (See *U. S. v. Carroll Towing* in the previous chapter.) Here he seems to stress the insufficiency of the tug owners' precaution by referring to the fact that radio receiving sets are inexpensive. If he could have applied the Hand Rule, to what would he have compared that cost in determing whether the owners were at fault in not requiring those sets?

e. In a much broader context, what is the most effective societal instrument for determining optimal precaution—court testimony, the forces of supply and demand in a competitive market, administrative agency regulation (e.g., recall that the U. S. Code required tugs to have radio transmitting sets; why was there no requirement for receiving sets?), or governmental subsidization of research and development into safety? Is one policy *always* the best guide to optimal precaution, or does the determination of the most effective social instrument depend on circumstances? Which circumstances?

The following case raises some of the same issues raised in *The T. J. Hooper* but in the context of a serious injury to person, not to property. Additionally, the case directs our attention to the fine line that sometimes exists between torts and contract law.

Helling v. Carey, 84 Wash.2d 514, 519 P.2d 981 (Wash. 1974).

HUNTER, ASSOCIATE JUSTICE. This case arises from a malpractice action instituted by the plaintiff (petitioner), Barbara Helling.

The plaintiff suffers from primary open angle glaucoma. Primary open angle glaucoma is essentially a condition of the eye in which there is an interference in the ease with which the nourishing fluids can flow out of the eye. Such a condition results in pressure gradually rising above the normal level to such an extent that damage is produced to the optic nerve and its fibers with resultant loss in vision. . . . The disease usually has few symptoms and, in the absence of a pressure test, is often undetected until the damage has become extensive and irreversible.

The defendants (respondents), Dr. Thomas F. Carey and Dr. Robert C. Laughlin, are partners who practice the medical specialty of ophthalmology. Ophthalmology involves the diagnosis and treatment of defects and diseases of the eye.

The plaintiff first consulted the defendants for myopia, nearsightedness, in 1959. At that time she was fitted with contact lenses. [She consulted the defendants several times over the next nine years.] Until the October 1968 consultation, the defendants considered the plaintiff's visual problems to be related solely to complications associated with contact lenses. On that occasion, the defendant, Dr. Carey, tested the plaintiff's eye pressure and field of vision for the first time. This test indicated that the plaintiff had glaucoma. The plaintiff . . . was then 32 years of age.

Thereafter, in August of 1969, after consulting other physicians, the plaintiff filed a complaint against the defendants alleging, among other things, that she sustained severe and permanent damage to her eyes as a proximate result of the defendants' negligence. During trial, the testimony of the medical experts for both the plaintiff and the defendants established that the standards of the profession for that specialty in the same or similar circumstances do not require routine pressure tests for glaucoma upon patients under 40 years of age. The reason the pressure test for glaucoma is not given as a regular practice to patients under the age of 40 is that the disease rarely occurs in this age group. Testimony indicated, however, that the standards of the profession do require pressure tests if the patient's complaints and symptoms reveal to the physician that glaucoma should be suspected.

The trial court entered judgment for the defendants following a defense verdict. The plaintiff thereupon appealed to the Court of Appeals, which affirmed the judgment of the trial court. . . .

We find this to be a unique case. . . . The issue is whether the defendants' compliance with the standard of the profession of ophthalmology, which does not require the giving of a routine pressure test to persons under 40 years of age, should insulate them from liability under the facts in this case where the plaintiff has lost a substantial amount of her vision due to the failure of the defendants to timely give the pressure test to the plaintiff.

The incidence of glaucoma in one out of 25,000 persons under the age of 40 may appear quite minimal. However, that one person, the plaintiff in this instance, is entitled to the same protection as afforded persons over 40, essential for timely detection of the evidence of glaucoma where it can be arrested to avoid the grave and devastating result of this disease. The test is a simple pressure test, relatively inexpensive. There is no judgment factor involved, and there is no doubt that by giving the test the evidence of glaucoma can be detected. The giving of the test is harmless if the physical condition of the eye permits. The testimony indicates that although the condition of the plaintiff's eyes might have at times prevented the defendants from administering the pressure test, there is an absence of evidence in the record that the test could not have been timely given. . . .

Under the facts of this case reasonable prudence required the timely giving of the pressure test to this plaintiff. The precaution of giving this test to detect the incidence of glaucoma to patients under 40 years of age is so imperative that irrespective of its disregard by the standards of the ophthalmology profession, it is the duty of the courts to say what is required to protect patients under 40 from the damaging results of glaucoma.

We therefore hold, as a matter of law, that the reasonable standard that should have been followed under the undisputed facts of this case was the timely giving of this simple, harmless pressure test to this plaintiff and that, in failing to do so, the defendants were negligent, which proximately resulted in the blindness sustained by the plaintiff for which the defendants are liable. . . .

The judgment of the trial court and the decision of the Court of Appeals is reversed, and the case is remanded for a new trial on the issue of damages only.

Question 9.2:

a. The opinion suggests most of the data necessary for deciding negligence in this case on the basis of the Hand Rule. Suppose that a tonometry test, which will detect glaucoma, costs $5. Suppose further that the average jury verdict for total or legal blindness in the period 1973–1977 was $678,000.[1] Given that the likelihood of glaucoma in a person under 40 is "one in 25,000," does the failure to give a tonometric exam to the 32 year-old plaintiff pass the Hand Test? That is, on the basis of the Hand Test, was the defendant negligent in not giving the exam?

b. Subsequent to this famous case, an empirical study showed that most of the ophthalmologists in Washington were routinely giving glaucoma tests as part of an ordinary examination for people in the age range of Barbara Helling. What does this fact reveal about the economic rationality of ophthalmologists?

c. If your answer in part a is that the doctor is negligent, how do you explain the fact that the custom of the medical profession was *not* to do tonometry on those under 40? Is the profession uncompetitive? What influence on the profession's choice of custom with regard to tonometry might these other factors have:

1. Most patients under 40 who contract glaucoma and should have had tonometry do not sue.[2]

2. Traditionally, doctors would not testify against one another; that is, one doctor would not comment on another doctor's actions.

B. Computing Damages

In the previous chapter we noted that the ability of liability rules to induce efficient precaution depends in part on the ability of the court to award truly compensatory damages to the victims of a tort. In this section we turn to an examination of how microeconomics can help to determine the amount of damages necessary to compensate a victim. Additionally, we use microeconomics to discuss the efficiency aspects of punitive damages in tort awards.

1. Compensatory Damages   In the preceding chapter we explained that compensatory damages are intended to make the victim whole, and the immediate economic interpretation of compensation is restoring the victim to the same utility curve or profit curve that he or she would have enjoyed but for the injury. There are circumstances, however, in which the victim of a tort is awarded damages that the court calls "compensatory," yet the very idea of compensation is objectionable. For example, when a child is killed in

---

[1]The figures are drawn from the excellent analysis of medical malpractice in William B. Schwartz and Neil Komesar, *Doctors, Damages, and Deterrence: An Economic View of Medical Malpractice,* NEW ENGLAND JOURNAL OF MEDICINE (June 8, 1976) 1282–1289.

[2]See the discussion of enforcement error in the section on punitive damages below.

a tortious accident, damages *cannot* be computed on the formula, "Find a sum of money such that the parents are indifferent between having the money and a dead child, or not having the money and having their child alive." The same difficulty arises in a more attenuated form for irreparable physical injuries, such as a crippling accident.

There are, in fact, two distinct concepts of compensatory damages in tort law. One concept is the standard economic concept of *indifference: compensation is perfect when the victim is indifferent between having the injury plus the damages and having neither.* Compensatory damages are thus perfect when the potential victim is indifferent about whether there is no accident or an accident with compensation. This concept is relevant for injuries in which a substitute for the lost good is available in the market. When a substitute is available, the market price of the substitute measures the value of the good to the plaintiff. This concept is also relevant for goods that are bought and sold from time to time but for which there is no regular, organized market. For example, a hand-written letter by James Joyce and a 1957 Chevy convertible are sold from time to time, but these items are too rare for a regular market to exist. The owners of these rare goods usually have prices at which they are prepared to sell them, and these prices measure perfectly compensatory damages.[3]

This concept of perfect compensation, based on indifference, is fundamental to an economic account of incentives. When the potential injurer is liable for perfectly compensatory damages, he internalizes the external harm caused by accidents. As we saw in the previous chapter, perfect compensation, when enforced, thus creates incentives for efficient precaution by the potential injurers.

There is no price, however, at which a good parent would sell his child. The idea that a person could be "indifferent" between a sum of money and a child is repugnant. And, for some people, there may be no price at which they would sell an arm or a leg.[4] So, for injuries involving the loss of a child or a limb, compensation simply cannot be perfect. Juries must, nevertheless, award injuries for the wrongful death of a child or for personal injuries. Our problem, then, is to provide a more satisfactory understanding of their computation.

Although no proper parent would trade a child's death for money, a necessary part of living is being exposed to the risk of death or serious injury. For example, flying on an airplane or driving down the expressway involves such a risk. These risks can often be reduced, but doing so is costly. To illustrate, airplanes must be inspected and repaired at regular intervals,

---

[3]Economists use the term "reservation price" to refer to the minimum price at which the owner of a good is willing to sell it. Determining the owner's reservation price for a unique good is a difficult practical problem, but it is not a problem conceptually.

[4]For some people, there may be an amount of money at which selling, say, an arm is an attractive bargain, but their concept of morality would not permit them to do it.

"Fortunately for my client, the victim died."

Would you rather be dead or crippled? In most tortious accidents, the victim and his family usually prefer the person alive and crippled rather than dead. It is, consequently, worse to cause someone's death in a tortious accident than to cause them to be crippled. Yet, the death of the victim can be fortunate for the injurer, because the damages awarded by courts are often greater when the victim of a tortious accident is crippled than when he dies.

Question 9.3: Does this seem to be an anomaly to you? Does it violate the economic idea that value is to be determined by individual preferences? Does it create incentives that are inefficient or even perverse?

---

which is costly, but the shorter the intervals, the fewer the accidents. Similarly, heavy cars with special safety features provide extra safety to passengers. When a parent decides what features of a car to buy or an air carrier decides how frequently to inspect planes for safety, a decision is being made that balances the cost of additional precaution against reductions in the probability of injury.

A rational decision about these risks involves balancing the costs and benefits of precaution. By reasoning in this way, it is possible to impute a value to the loss of life. To illustrate, suppose that the probability of a fatal automobile accident falls by 1/10,000 when an additional $100 dollars is spent on automotive safety. If expenditures on automotive safety are rational, then the reduction in the probability of a fatal accident, multiplied by the implicit value assigned to a life, equals the marginal cost of care:

$$(1/10,000) \times \text{(implicit value of life)} = \$100,$$

$$\text{or}$$

$$\text{(implicit value of life)} = \$100 \ / \ (1/10,000),$$

which implies that the implicit value of a life is $1,000,000. (See the box entitled "Fortunately for my client, the victim died.")

In order to apply the risk-equivalent method in a legal dispute, the court would consider situations in which the risk is reasonable by general agreement. In these circumstances, there will be some value p for the probability of a fatal accident, and some value B for the burden of precaution. Efficiency requires taking additional precaution until the burden equals the change in probability p multiplied by the loss L, or $B = pL$. (This is the Hand Rule.) Thus, the court would compute the risk-equivalent value of a life by solving the equation for L, yielding $L = B/p$.

The preceding method illustrates the computation of the *risk-equivalent* value of an accident. This same method could be used for accidents resulting in personal injuries, say loss of a limb, as well as for death. The basic idea is to determine the cost of an accident by finding the implicit value assigned to it in risky situations comparable to the one in which the accident in question actually occurred. We may use the term *risk-equivalent compensation* to refer to this method of computing compensatory damages.

We have described two distinct methods for computing compensatory damages: the indifference method and the risk-equivalent method. The first method is appropriate for market goods; the second method is appropriate where not only is there no market for the good at risk but there are legal and moral barriers to such markets. It is only when the indifference method is appropriate that damages are perfectly compensatory. However, both methods—the indifference method and the risk-equivalent method—when applied without enforcement error, provide incentives for an efficient level of precaution.

2. Measuring Compensation If utility functions could be observed, computing perfect compensation would be unproblematic. After an injury, the utility curves of the victim would be sketched as in Figure 8.1 of the previous chapter and damages would be read off the graph. Utility curves, however, are not observed directly. Instead, economists impute a preference ordering to a decisionmaker on the basis of the choices that he makes. It is the choices, not the ordering, that are directly observed. So part of the problem of computing damages is to infer the preference ordering from the decisionmaker's choices.[5]

Unlike utility, demand and supply are observable. The utility theory of compensation can be operationalized by linking it to demand and supply. In general, demand for a good by an individual, or by an aggregate of individuals, is a function of many variables, including price, income, and tastes. The demand curve picks out one of these variables, specifically price, and depicts its relationship to the quantity of the good demanded. The other variables affecting demand, which are not represented explicitly in the demand curve, are implicitly being held constant while the price varies. The variables held constant are the prices of other goods, the income of the buyers, and the tastes of the buyers.

When the price falls, and all the other variables in the preceding list are held constant, consumers move down the demand curve. The fact that consumers can obtain the good at a lower price implies that their utility has increased. Thus, moving down the demand curve corresponds to an increase in utility caused by a fall in price.

As explained, the fall in the price of the good causes the consumer's utility to rise as he moves down the demand curve. For conceptual purposes, it is possible to imagine that just enough income is taken away from the buyer as he moves down the demand curve to offset the effect of the fall in price. In other words, the fall in the price of the good, which makes him better off,

---

[5]The technical name for the theory of such imputations is "revealed preference theory."

could be offset by taking some income away from him, which makes him worse off, so that the net effect is to make him no better off and no worse off. Of course, offsetting the lower price by a fall in income is a conceptual exercise, not a real event.

In welfare economics, a special type of demand curve is frequently used for conceptual purposes that has just this characteristic: as the consumer moves down the demand curve, the fall in price is exactly offset by a fall in income, so that his utility remains constant. Like an indifference curve, every point on this special demand curve represents the same level of utility. The constant-utility demand curve is fundamental to the theory of compensation and, more generally, to applied welfare economics.

To see why, think of the constant-utility demand curve as the relationship between the maximum amount that a person can pay for a good without affecting his utility. In other words, the constant-utility demand curve describes the decisionmaker's willingness-to-pay for the good. When applied to law, the willingness-to-pay for a good equals the amount of compensation that must be paid for depriving him of it. In other words, perfect compensation for harm consisting in the fall in the quantity of a good equals the corresponding area under the constant-utility demand curve.

To illustrate, assume that the demand curve in Figure 9.1 is drawn by holding utility constant as the quantity x_2 and the willingness-to-pay p_2 vary. Let the initial quantity be denoted x_{02} and let harm reduce the quantity to x_{12}. The shaded area in the figure, which lies under the demand curve and inside the interval between x_{02} and x_{12}, indicates the amount the person could pay for receiving the quantity of the good $x_{02} - x_{12}$ without any change in his utility. Consequently, the shaded area also indicates the amount that must be paid in compensation for taking away from him the quantity of the good $x_{02} - x_{12}$ in order to restore him to his initial level of utility. Thus, perfectly compensatory damages for depriving someone of a quantity of a good that he cannot replace in the market equals his willingness-to-pay for it, which in turn equals the area under the constant-utility demand curve.

From a formal standpoint, goods and bads are the same but for sign. Thus, the preceding argument about compensation for depriving someone of a good also applies to imposing a bad upon someone. Specifically, the harm caused by imposing the bad equals the victim's willingness-to-pay to be free from it. The willingness-to-pay to be free from a bad can be represented as a constant-utility demand curve and the area under it will indicate the perfectly compensatory damages for imposing a bad upon someone.

Instead of depriving someone of a good or imposing a bad upon him, sometimes a person is wrongfully prevented from buying a good at a particular price. The preceding analysis can easily be extended to such cases. The difference between a person's willingness-to-pay for a good and what he

Figure 9.1 Perfect Compensation, Utility, and Demand

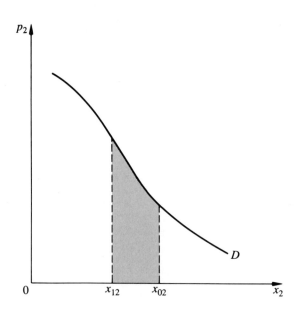

The curve D is a constant-utility demand curve for commodity x_2, whose price is measured along the vertical axis. A constant-utility demand curve measures the decisionmaker's willingness-to-pay for each unit of a commodity and can be used to measure compensation for tortious harms: perfect compensation for harm consists in the fall in the quantity of a good equal to the corresponding area under the constant-utility demand curve. Suppose that the consumer's original quantity of x_2 is x_{02} but tortious harm has reduced this to x_{12}. The shaded area under D indicates the amount of money the person would be willing to pay in exchange for the quantity of the good $(x_{02} - x_{12})$ without any change in utility. Thus, the shaded area also indicates the amount that must be paid in compensation for taking away from him the quantity $(x_{02} - x_{12})$ in order to restore him to his initial level of utility.

actually pays is called the "consumer surplus" that he enjoys from the transaction. Perfectly compensatory damages for wrongfully preventing someone from buying at a particular price equals the loss in consumer surplus caused by the act.

To illustrate, suppose that someone is wrongfully prevented from buying good x_i at price p_{0i}, as a result of which the person has to purchase the good at the higher price p_{1i}. At the low price p_{0i}, the person would buy x_{0i}, whereas he only buys x_{1i} at the higher price p_{1i}. A rough approximation to compensatory damages is the additional cost of the purchase, which could be computed to equal the overcharge on the goods purchased, $x_{1i}(p_{1i} - p_{0i})$, or else it could be computed to equal the overcharge on the goods that would have been purchased at the lower price, $x_{0i}(p_{1i} - p_{0i})$. These measures, which are not exact, are usually good enough for practical purposes. (An

Figure 9.2 Perfect Compensation for Economic Harm

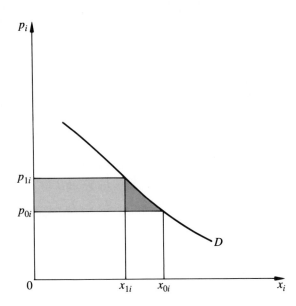

Our previous analysis has concerned compensation for depriving someone of a good or inflicting a bad. But sometimes a person is wrongfully prevented from buying a good at a particular price. How should he be compensated? The curve D is a constant-utility demand curve for commodity x_i, whose price is measured along the vertical axis. Suppose someone has wrongfully been prevented from purchasing x_i at the price p_{0i} and must instead purchase it at the higher price p_{1i}. If the price had been p_{0i}, he would have purchased x_{0i} of x_i, but because the price is actually p_{1i}, he purchased only x_{1i} units. Two approximate forms of compensation for the victim are the overcharge on the goods purchased, $x_{1i}(p_{1i} - p_{0i})$, or the overcharge on the goods that would have been purchased at the lower price, $x_{0i}(p_{1i} - p_{0i})$. A more exact compensatory amount—but one much more difficult to compute—is the shaded area in the figure, consisting of two elements. The heavily shaded area equals the consumer-surplus foregone on the $(x_{0i} - x_{1i})$ that could not be purchased at the lower price. The lightly shaded area equals the actual overcharge on the goods purchased: $x_{1i}(p_{1i} - p_{0i})$.

---

exact determination is represented by the shaded areas in Figure 9.2 and explained in a footnote.[6])

---

[6]Relative to perfect compensation, the first of these measures undercompensates and the second measure overcompensates. Perfect compensation can be computed by considering the constant-utility demand curve. The willingness-to-pay for the additional good is the area under the constant-utility demand curve between x_{0i} and x_{1i} in Figure 9.2. The price that would have been paid, but for the wrongdoing, is p_{0i}. Thus, the surplus enjoyed by the consumer on this incremental quantity of the good is the difference between the area under the constant-utility demand curve and the total price that would have been paid, $p_{0i}(x_{0i} - x_{1i})$, as indicated by the heavily shaded area in the figure. The overcharge on the goods actually purchased is $x_{1i}(p_{1i} - p_{0i})$, as indicated by the lightly shaded area. Thus, the perfectly compensatory damages

Perfect compensation as measured by the area under the constant-utility demand curve exactly equals perfect compensation as measured graphically in Figure 8.1 of the previous chapter using indifference curves. The purpose of passing from the utility representation to the demand representation was to operationalize the damage measure by passing from unobservable variables to observable variables. The reader's first impression may be that this task has not been accomplished because, like indifference curves, the constant-utility demand curve is not readily observable. Specifically, the demand curves that are actually estimated for markets are not constant-utility demand curves.

Rather than being unique to compensation for a tort, this problem arises in all areas of applied welfare economics, including cost-benefit analysis. Over the years economists have worked out a solution that is reasonably satisfactory. It can be proven that, for purposes of measuring welfare changes caused by small changes in quantities and prices, the constant-utility demand curve is the same, or nearly the same, as the ordinary demand curve. Thus, in practice, the ordinary demand curve can be estimated econometrically or by some rougher means, and welfare changes can be measured by proceeding as if it were a constant-utility demand curve.

Besides demanding goods, individuals supply them, including capital and labor. The analysis of demand can be repeated for supply by constructing constant-utility supply curves. Instead of carrying out this exercise, supply will be treated with reference to firms.

The profit-maximizing firm can be analyzed as if it were a consumer with a very simple utility function. To illustrate, the supply curve for a firm is drawn in Figure 9.3. The supply curve shows the relationship between the quantity of the good that the firm will supply and the market price.[7] Equiva-

---

equal the loss in consumer's surplus on the goods that would have been purchased at the lower price and were not purchased at the higher price, as indicated by the heavily shaded area, plus the overcharge on the goods that were actually purchased, as indicated by the lightly shaded area.

[7]In a more formal treatment of supply, economists draw a distinction between supply curves for an industry and for an individual firm and between supply curves for the short run and the long run. For our purposes it is sufficient to concentrate on the short-run supply curve for a firm. That supply curve is the marginal cost curve of the firm above the minimum point on the firm's average variable cost curve. Marginal cost is the increment in the firm's total cost caused by producing and marketing one more unit of output. In the short run some of the firm's inputs, usually capital goods such as machines, are assumed to be fixed. Output levels can be changed only by altering levels of *variable* inputs, such as labor and materials. Fixed costs are those associated with the fixed inputs and cannot be changed in the short run. These costs must be paid regardless of the amount of output that the firm produces and markets. As a result, the level of fixed costs does not matter in the determination of the short-run profit-maximizing level of output. In the short run only variable costs matter. If the market price per unit of the firm's output is below the minimum point of the firm's average variable cost curve, then it is cheaper for the firm to close down and produce nothing and to incur a loss equal to fixed costs rather than to produce and market any output. For that reason, the firm's short-run supply curve is equal to its marginal cost curve but only when marginal cost exceeds the minimum point on the average variable cost curve.

Figure 9.3   Perfect Compensation for a Supplier

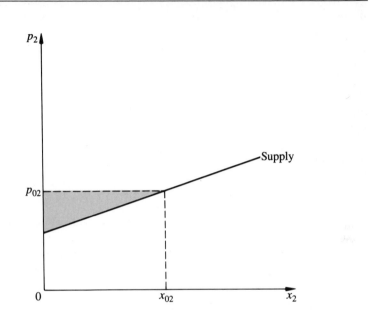

Sometimes a profit-maximizing firm is wrongfully excluded from selling a good. How should perfectly compensatory damages be computed in this instance? Suppose that a firm that produces and sells commodity x_2 and has the supply curve noted in the figure has been wrongfully excluded from the market for this good. If the firm had been permitted to participate in this market on equal terms, suppose that it would have supplied quantity x_{02} at the prevailing market price of p_{02}. The resulting profits would have been the shaded area in the graph, which is the area between the price line p_{02} and the supply curve. (The economic profit of the firm is equal to the difference between the price received for its output and the costs of producing that output, as represented by the supply curve.) Consequently, that amount is the perfectly compensatory amount of damages for the firm.

lently, the supply curve can be interpreted as the relationship between the quantity of the good and the cost of supplying it, including the ordinary return to capital. Profit net of the ordinary return to capital is sometimes called "economic profit," as opposed to accounting profit. When a good is supplied at cost, there is no effect upon the firm's economic profits. Thus, the supply curve shows the minimum prices at which a firm can supply a good without any change in its economic profit, just as the constant-utility demand curve shows the maximum prices that a consumer can pay for a good without any change in his utility.

For purposes of illustration, the supply curve will be used to compute perfectly compensatory damages for wrongfully excluding a firm from selling a good. The profit that a firm enjoys from selling a good equals the difference between the price received for it and its cost where the cost is indicated by the supply curve. Suppose that a firm with the supply curve depicted in Figure 9.3 is wrongfully excluded from a market for good x_2

Organizations as Victims

Economists routinely impute utility functions to individual consumers and workers, but what if the victim who seeks compensation is an organization, such as a partnership, a corporation, a government, or a club? Like individuals, organizations can be regarded as decisionmakers and their choices can be regarded as revealing organizational preferences. Like an individual, the preferences of a rational organization can usually be represented by a well-ordered utility function. So the question arises, "Can the utility analysis of the idea of compensation be extended to organizations?"

In applied welfare economics, benefits or harms to institutions are traced through to individuals, at least in principle. For example, the loss in profits suffered by a business is traced back to a loss in income to the business's owners. A common practice is to assume a one-to-one relationship between the loss in profits to the organization and the loss in income to individual owners, and to assume that the owners are interested in the business only for the sake of profits.[1] Under these assumptions, the company's profits "stand in" for the utility of affected persons. Since the changes in profits to the business equal changes in income to its owners, compensating the organization is equivalent to compensating its owners.

In the case of business firms, the conventional assumption in economics is that they maximize profits. Thus, when a utility function is imputed to a business within the usual domain of choice, it has a simple form: profits are the only thing that they care about. For a business, the fall from a higher indifference curve to a lower indifference curve corresponds to a fall in profits, which can be compensated by paying damages to the business equal to the lost profits.

In general, when there is a one-to-one relationship between the loss as measured by the institution's preferences and the losses to individuals, the institutional preferences can be used as a surrogate for the welfare of affected individuals. However, the extension of the utility analysis of compensation to organizations that are not profit-seeking, such as govern-

where the price is p_{02}. If the firm had been permitted to participate in this market on equal terms, it would have supplied the quantity x_{02}. The resulting profits would have been the shaded area in the graph, which is the area between the price line p_{02} and the supply curve. (See the box entitled "Organizations as Victims.")

3. Punitive Damages Punitive damages are, by definition, damages given to the plaintiff as a way of punishing the defendant. We must begin our economic analysis of punitive damages by answering two questions:

ments, clubs, and non-profit corporations, is problematic because there is less agreement about the behavioral theories for describing them.[2] In the absence of an accepted behavioral theory, there cannot be agreement about how to trace the consequences of harm suffered by these organizations back to its effects upon the welfare of individuals.

[1]This is clearly a strong assumption. Among other things, the assumption implies that the owners of a firm directly control the firm's actions. But in practice and in theory, this direct control is a rarity. The owners (the shareholders) of a firm typically delegate the control of the firm to a management team, over whom the owners have imperfect control. This imperfect control gives rise to what is known in the literature as a "principal-agent" problem. In that literature, the principals (the owners of the corporation) hire agents (the firm's management) to implement their program, but because of the high cost of monitoring the agents' compliance with the principals' desires, the principals' goal (maximum profits) may not be achieved. Where this problem arises, some of the loss in profits of the organization may fall on the agents.

Additionally, the assumption in the text implies that other employees of the firm may also escape losses when the organization loses profits. Because of imperfections in the labor market (e.g., strongly asymmetrical information about alternative employment opportunities), the workers of an ailing company may also suffer.

The thrust of these two points is that damages when an organization is the victim of a tort may well spread out beyond the owners to include the management and other employees. The time is ripe for an investigation of the extent to which efficiency considerations can guide a court in determining the extent to which these consequential damages should be compensable.

[2]Here are some citations to economic theories of non-business and non-profit institutions. For non-business entities, *see* William Niskanen, *The Peculiar Economics of Bureaucracy in* THE ECONOMICS OF PROPERTY RIGHTS (Petovich and Furbotn eds. 1974); Kaushik Basu, REVEALED PREFERENCE OF GOVERNMENT (1980); Robert Cooter and Gregory Topakian, *Political Economy of a Public Corporation: The Pricing Objectives of BART,* 13 J. PUBLIC ECON. 299 (1980). For non-profit organizations, *see* Henry Hansmann, *The Role of Nonprofit Enterprise,* 89 YALE L. J. 835 (1980); Robert Cooter and Janet Landa, *Personal Versus Impersonal Trade: The Size of Trading Groups and Contract Law,* 4 INTERNATL. REV. LAW & ECON. 15 (1984).

1. Under what conditions are punitive damages awarded?
2. How is the amount of punitive damages computed?

In most states there is a statute describing the conditions under which punitive damages are to be awarded. These are usually attempts to state the common law practices actually followed by the courts. According to the usual formulation, punitive damages can be awarded when the defendant's behavior is malicious, oppressive, gross, willful and wanton, or fraudulent.[8] These statutes merely provide guidelines for awarding punitive damages. Since the guidelines have not been formulated into exact rules, there is much uncertainty about when punitive damages can be awarded.

There is even more uncertainty concerning how punitive damages are to be computed. Statutes typically contain no instructions for computing the actual amount of punitive damages. Punitive damages are supposed to bear a reasonable relationship to compensatory damages and to the ability of the defendant to pay, but the courts have not specified what "reasonable" or "ability-to-pay" means in any detail. It is uncertain, for example, whether punitive damages may be only double the amount of compensatory damages or up to ten times compensatory damages. Judges apparently have an idea of how much is enough, and jury awards have often been reduced by judges, but there are currently no rules regarding the computation of punitive damages.

When rules are sparse, the jury has wide scope to use its discretion. In the typical case involving punitive damages, the jury is asked to decide whether punitive damages should be awarded and, if so, how much to award, but the jury is not given definite instructions for answering either question. When law is thin, the jury's intuitions prevail, and these are an uncertain and unstable foundation upon which to base such an important element of the tort law. Thus, there is a compelling need in torts for more law to control punitive damages, and economic analysis can provide guidelines for its development.

To begin the economic analysis of punitive damages, let's supply some numbers to the situation described in Example 3 of the preceding chapter.

> **Facts:** A manufacturer of fuel additives is keeping a careful eye on costs. If quality control is maintained at a high level, which costs $9,000 per year, the chemical mixture in the product is correct and it never causes damage to automobile engines. However, if quality control is relaxed and allowed to fall to a low level, $9,000 is saved but some batches of the chemical mixture will be flawed. A few of the cars using the flawed batch will be harmed; specifically, the expected damage to cars is $10,000 per year [$1,000 in expected damages to each of 10 cars].

From an economic viewpoint, the company can expect to save consumers $10,000 per year by spending $9,000 per year on quality control, so efficiency requires the manufacturer to make the expenditures.

---

[8]To illustrate, here is the section on "Exemplary Damages" from the California Civil Code, sec.3294:

"For Oppression, Fraud or Malice.

(a) In an action for the breach of an obligation not arising from contract, where the defendant has been guilty of oppression, fraud, or malice, the plaintiff, in addition to the actual damages, may recover damages for the sake of the example and by way of punishing the defendant."

That is not much detail to govern actions upon which millions of dollars turn. Notice that nothing is said about how to compute punitive damages.

Will making the manufacturer strictly liable for compensatory damages produce this result? The answer is "yes" if the tort liability system is perfect, "no" if it is imperfect. Suppose that the tort liability system is perfect in the sense that disputes between the manufacturer and consumers can be resolved costlessly and without error, and damages are perfectly compensatory (swallow hard!). With a perfect tort liability system and a rule of strict liability, every car owner harmed by the product will recover from the manufacturer without having to spend anything to resolve the dispute. The manufacturer thus faces $10,000 in expected liability if he does not take precautions costing $9,000. A rational manufacturer maximizes profits net of expected tort liability, so he will set quality control at the high level.

Now consider the change in behavior that occurs when we make the realistic assumption that the tort liability system works imperfectly. Specifically, suppose that for every two consumers whose cars suffer damage, only one of them actually brings suit and recovers. Call the ratio of compensated victims to total victims, which is 1/2 in this example, the "enforcement error." Given an enforcement error of 1/2 and assuming the successful plaintiff only receives compensatory damages, the manufacturer's expected liability will be $5,000 if he adopts the low level of quality control. He can, however, save $9,000 by reducing his quality control from high to low. So, enforcement error in this example creates a situation in which a profit-maximizing manufacturer, whose expected liability is limited to compensatory damages, will choose the low level of quality control, which is inefficient.

The enforcement error can be offset by augmenting compensatory damages with punitive damages. Total damages equal the sum of compensatory damages and punitive damages. Let the "punitive multiple" be the number that, when multiplied by compensatory damages, equals the total damages. To illustrate, if the punitive multiple is 2, and compensatory damages are $1,000 per car, then total damages are $2,000 per car. Hence, the punitive damages are also $1,000 per car. In our example, assuming every consumer receiving compensatory damages also received punitive damages, a punitive multiple of 2 exactly offsets the enforcement error of 1/2 and restores the manufacturer's liability to the level that would have prevailed under perfect enforcement.[9]

We have shown that enforcement errors create an incentive for a rationally self-interested decisionmaker to take precaution that is inefficient, but that this incentive can be removed by awarding enough punitive damages to

---

[9]Implicit in this argument is the assumption that the rate at which consumers successfully bring suit against the manufacturer does not change when punitive damages are added to compensatory damages. This is a strong and unrealistic assumption. When damage awards are high, victims and their attorneys have a stronger incentive to bring an action against those who injured them. This then causes a second-round effect in that as the number of actions increases, the enforcement error falls and the punitive multiple should fall. It is an open question whether the existence of a punitive multiple can increase the number of actions just enough to correct for the inefficiency caused by enforcement error or whether it leads to over-enforcement.

offset the enforcement error.[10] To develop this line of thought further, we will amend our example to make it more general and more congenial to mathematical analysis.

> **Facts:** The facts are the same as in the preceding question, except that now the manufacturer can continuously adjust his quality control. That is, the quality of the fuel additive is an increasing, continuous function of the amount spent on quality control. (Before we assumed a *discontinuous* function. Only two levels of quality control were available: low, at a cost of $0, and high, at a cost of $9,000.)

Under this assumption, efficiency requires the manufacturer to take precaution out to the point where an additional $1 spent on quality control reduces the expected damage to cars from defective fuel additives by $1. This is the level of precaution at which the marginal cost of quality control equals its marginal (social) benefit.

The fact that precaution is continuous, rather than discrete, does not change our conclusions. If the tort liability system is perfect, the manufacturer internalizes the harm caused by defective products, so he takes precaution to the point where its marginal cost equals the marginal reduction in expected damages suffered by consumers.

But now suppose that the tort liability system works imperfectly. Specifically, suppose as before that only one in two of the car owners who suffer damage actually bring suit and recover, so the enforcement error is 1/2. Given this level of enforcement error, the profit-maximizing manufacturer will undertake quality control at a level at which an additional $1 spent on quality control reduces expected losses to consumers by $0.50. Recall our definition of the "punitive multiple":

$$\frac{\text{compen. damages } + \text{ punitive damages}}{\text{compen. damages}} = \text{punitive multiple}$$

An enforcement error of 1/2 can be offset by a punitive multiple equal to 2. In general, *allowing each injured consumer to recover punitive damages and setting the punitive multiple equal to the inverse of the enforcement error restores incentives for efficient precaution.* (For a formula demonstration of this proposition, see the box entitled "The Punitive Multiple: Restoring Efficient Incentives by Punitive Damages.")

This rule is potentially useful as a guide to setting punitive damages. If such a rule were written into the law, either by statute or by judges, juries would have some guidance in setting the punitive multiple. There are, however, some difficulties with institutionalizing this rule. One of them is that the enforcement error is not always observable. This problem, however, is not insurmountable, as we explain in the box entitled "Observability and the Punitive Multiple."

According to our theory, punitive damages are appropriate to offset enforcement error, either real or imagined on the part of the decisionmaker.

---

[10]In general, this illustrates the substitutability between the frequency and magnitude of punishment, a point we pursue in the chapters on crime.

Observability and the Punitive Multiple

We have shown that efficient incentives can be restored by setting the punitive multiple equal to the inverse of the enforcement error. The enforcement error, however, may be unobservable or observable only with error. When the enforcement error is difficult to observe, the decisionmaker's subjective beliefs about its magnitude may depart from objective reality. Under these conditions, achieving efficient incentives depends upon setting the punitive multiple according to the decisionmaker's subjective beliefs about the enforcement error. In this box we describe how that can be accomplished.

In the preceding box we explained that the selfish actor minimizes the sum of the costs of precaution and expected liability:

$$\min_{x} \ [wx + p(x)L].$$

Furthermore, if the decisionmaker expects to escape punitive damages, his liability equals the harm times the enforcement error: $L = Ae$. Substituting into the preceding relationship yields the minimization equation we labeled (2a):

$$\min_{x} \ [wx + p(x)Ae]. \tag{2a}$$

Costs are minimized when the marginal cost of precaution, w, equals the marginal reduction in the probability of an accident p' times the liability Ae:

$$0 = w + p'(x)Ae.$$

(Here we are assuming that A and e do not vary with x; that assumption can easily be relaxed, but the conclusions do not change.) Rearranging the terms in this equation yields

$$e = w \ / \ [- \ p'(x) \ A].$$

According to this equation, the enforcement error as perceived by the decisionmaker equals the unit cost of precaution divided by the reduction in compensatory damages from additional precaution. Furthermore, the optimal punitive multiple equals the inverse of the enforcement error: $m = 1/e$. Hence,

$$m = (A/w) \ [-p'(x)].$$

We have thus proved the following proposition: if we assume that precaution is continuous and taking it reduces the probability of an accident and that the marginal injurer thinks he will escape punitive damages, then *to internalize social costs for such a class of actors, the punitive damages multiple should equal the ratio of compensatory damages to the cost of precaution, multiplied by the marginal probability of averting an accident.*

We used this approach to suggest a definite rule for computing the punitive

The Punitive Multiple:
Restoring Efficient Incentives by Punitive Damages

Here is an account of how to compute the punitive multiple so that punitive damages exactly offset the enforcement error and efficient incentives are restored. The notation is as follows:

x = precaution, whose cost is w per unit;
p = probability of an accident;
= $p(x)$, with $p' \leq 0$, $p'' > 0$ (that is, the probability of an accident declines as precaution increases but declines at a decreasing rate);
A = harm caused by an accident;
L = injurer's liability conditional on an accident's actually occurring;
m = punitive damages multiple; and
e = enforcement error.

Assume that precaution x, whose unit cost is w, is continuous and taking it reduces the probability p of an accident. The socially responsible decisionmaker takes precaution to minimize the sum of its costs and the expected cost of harm:

$$\min_{x} [wx + p(x)A]. \tag{1}$$

By contrast, the purely selfish actor is not concerned with the harm, A, suffered by others, but rather his concern is with his own expected liability L. The purely selfish actor thus takes precaution to minimize the sum of its cost and his liability times the probability of an accident.

$$\min_{x} [wx + p(x)L]. \tag{2}$$

multiple. Our approach can also be used to clarify the existing legal rules that specify the conditions under which punitive damages can be awarded. In order for the plaintiff to win punitive damages, he must prove that the defendant was at fault and that the fault was especially serious: gross, malicious, deliberate, or the like. (The proof of serious fault is required even where plaintiffs seek punitives in consumer product liability cases, where the manufacturer is strictly liable for the harm caused by defective products.) In the preceding chapter we showed that making a sanction conditional upon fault creates a discontinuity in the decisionmaker's cost function. As a result of this discontinuity, it is far cheaper for most decisionmakers to conform to the legal standard. Recall our important finding that most decisionmakers will conform to the legal standard *even if there are enforcement errors*, for example, if damages are too small or if consumers seldom pursue their legal remedies.

Consider first the consequences of an enforcement error e and no punitive damages. The decisionmaker's liability is limited by assumption to compensatory damages, A, which are imposed with enforcement error e in the event of an accident. Thus,

$$L = Ae.$$

Substituting into the preceding relation yields

$$\min_x [wx + p(x)Ae]. \tag{2a}$$

By comparing the optimization equations (1) and (2a), it is apparent that they differ by the term e; the enforcement error represents the externalization of social costs that causes the decisionmaker to take too little precaution.

To make the selfish actor internalize social costs, compensatory damages must be augmented by punitive damages. When punitive damages are allowed, liability equals the punitive multiple times the compensatory damages net of the enforcement error:

$$L = Aem.$$

The minimization equation (2a) becomes

$$\min_x [wx + p(x)Aem]. \tag{3}$$

If the punitive multiple equals the inverse of the enforcement error, $m = 1/e$, then the last two terms in (3) cancel and (3) reduces to (1). Thus, the minimization equation in step 3 is equated with the minimization equation in step 1, as required for incentives to be efficient.

We illustrated this fact in Figure 8.4, where we showed that changes in the level of the sanction imposed generally did not result in a change in precaution. However, recall that in that figure, if the enforcement error is large enough, the expected cost curve will fall the full distance of the discontinuity, which creates a situation where the injurer's costs are minimized by taking less precaution than that specified in the legal standard.

Because of the discontinuity created by the fault standard, it will never pay to fall a little bit short of the legal standard.[11] Either it pays to conform

---

[11]In technical terms there is a nonconvexity in the cost function at the legal standard. There may be two local minima, one at the legal standard and one far below it.

to the legal standard, or it pays to fall *far* short of it. When precaution is far short of the legal standard, the fault is serious (gross, deliberate, malicious, etc.). This is exactly the condition under which the law allows punitive damages. A decisionmaker who is far below the legal standard has probably made a rational decision to disobey the law, which is grounds for punitive damages, whereas a decisionmaker who is a little below the legal standard has probably attempted to comply with the law but made a mistake, which is grounds for liability but not punishment. We conclude that, while punitive damages can correct for the enforcement error by restoring the cost function to its initial height, punitive damages should not be imposed unless actual care is far below the legal standard.

We have offered an account of punitive damages that is addressed to potential injurers who behave irresponsibly for their own material advantage. Punitive damages can also arise in quite different settings, for example, in the area known as intentional torts, which covers cases of assault, battery, and false imprisonment, where the parties are emotional and malevolent. This issue, and many others, will have to be omitted from this introduction to the fascinating and troubling topic of punitive damages. Here are a couple of problems on punitive damages that you should try to solve.

Question 9.4:

Facts: Mr. Worthy sets up a trust fund for his son and names Sleazy Savings and Loan as the trustee. SS&L is to manage the trust's $100,000 principal and continue re-investing its earnings for five years. After 5 years, the trust will be dissolved and its entire value turned over to the son.

After 2 years Worthy discovers that SS&L used $10,000 of the trust's principal to buy stock in a construction company that has gone bankrupt. The loss to the trust from this bankruptcy was the full $10,000. These things happen, and so long as SS&L was managing the trust lawfully, Mr. Worthy has no grounds for a legal complaint.

However, Mr. Worthy has irrefutable proof that SS&L's management of the trust and its loss of the trust's $10,000 were, well, sleazy. It turns out that the construction company maintained a checking account at SS&L and that the company had deposited in that account the $10,000 it had received when the Trust Department at SS&L had purchased stock on behalf of Mr. Worthy. Moreover, the Loan Department at SS&L had independently given the construction company a loan. Because it feared that the bankruptcy of the construction company would mean that its loan would not be repaid, SS&L seized the $10,000 from the stock purchase as soon as it appeared in the construction company's checking account.

Mr. Worthy alleges intentional breach of fiduciary duty and sues to recover $10,000 in compensation plus punitive damages. SS&L defends on the grounds that it had engaged in sound fiduciary practices: the trust portfolio was diversified, the other stock in it earned more than the average rate of return on the market, the investment was prudent in the circumstances, and the Trust Department at SS&L did not know about the construction company's debt or the seizure of the funds.

Expert testimony for the plaintiff was provided at trial by an economist who astounded the court with the power of his science and the brilliance of his insights (although he modestly declined to predict tomorrow's Treasury bill rate). His equations proved that SS&L had made a rational calculation of the benefits and costs of violating its fiduciary duty. According to SS&L's computation, the probability of Worthy's bringing suit and winning was 0.2, which would result in SS&L's returning the $10,000 as compensation; the probability of SS&L's avoiding a suit or prevailing in court was 0.8, in which case it would gain $10,000.

a. Breaching its fiduciary duty was a gamble for SS&L. How much did SS&L expect to gain from this gamble? (Notice that this computation includes the element of compensatory damages.)

b. Suppose that SS&L figured that if they lost the suit, they would have to pay punitive damages. What is the smallest amount of punitive damages that would deter them from breaching their fiduciary duty?

c. Remember that the ratio of total damages to compensatory damages is called the "punitive multiple":

$$\frac{\text{compen. damages} + \text{punitive damages}}{\text{compen. damages}} = \text{punitive multiple}$$

What is the punitive multiple in this case?

Question 9.5: This is a question based on Example 1 from the previous chapter and involves what is known as a dignitary tort.

Facts: Joe Potatoes has been driven to drink by the escapades of his wife, Joan Potatoes. At the end of a hard night's work at the loading dock, Joe is approached by Bloggs. Suspecting that Bloggs has been romancing Joan, Joe insults Bloggs and strikes him, breaking Bloggs' nose. Bloggs subsequently sues for the injury to his reputation and his nose. Assume that the "true" compensation would be $2,000 for injury to the nose, $1,000 for injury to reputation, and $500 for emotional distress.

a. Suppose that damages for emotional distress are not allowed as a matter of law. Is it appropriate for the court to award $500 in punitive damages?

b. If there are no obstacles to awarding $3,500 in compensatory damages, is there any reason to give punitive damages as well?

c. If $3,500 is truly compensatory and if Bloggs receives punitive damages as well, will Bloggs be grateful that he was assaulted?

C. Comparative Negligence[12]

In the previous chapter we discussed the several forms of the negligence rule: simple negligence, negligence with contributory negligence, and comparative negligence. For most of the last two hundred years negligence with

---

[12]The material in this section draws on Cooter & Ulen, *An Economic Case for Comparative Negligence*, N.Y.U.L.REV. (1986).

contributory negligence has been not only the dominant form of the negligence rule but the dominant tort liability rule in the common law countries. However, within the last fifteen years all this has changed. Today all but 13 states and the District of Columbia have altered their law of accidents so that the prevailing standard is one of comparative negligence for non-product-related torts. The change has been effected principally by statute with a minority of states adopting the rule by judicial decision. In this section we will explain briefly how the comparative negligence rule works and how it differs from the rule of negligence with contributory negligence. We will also summarize the academic literature on the economic analysis of comparative negligence.

The simple reason for the rise of comparative negligence is an increasing dissatisfaction with the rule of contributory negligence. Recall that a contributorily negligent plaintiff could not recover anything from the defendant, even from a negligent defendant. This rule struck most people as exceedingly harsh. To see why, imagine that an automobile accident has occurred; both the plaintiff and the defendant were driving. Suppose also that violation of the speed limit constitutes negligence and that the evidence shows that the plaintiff was going 35 miles per hour in the 30 mile-per-hour zone while the defendant was going 65 miles per hour in that same zone. Under the rule that bars recovery for a contributorily negligent plaintiff, the plaintiff will not be able to recover. This seems harsh in that the plaintiff's negligence was trivial by comparison to the defendant's.

To avoid this sort of harsh result, most jurisdictions found a means of limiting the scope of the rule of contributory negligence—e.g., by means of the last clear chance doctrine we discussed in Chapter 3.[13] But eventually these limitations on the application of the rule of contributory negligence gave way to comparative negligence.

The principal difference between comparative negligence and the rule of negligence with contributory negligence is that under comparative negligence plaintiff's contributory fault is a *partial* but not a *complete* bar to his recovery from a negligent defendant. Thus, under comparative negligence the negligent injurer owes *something*, but not *full* compensation, to the negligent victim.

Today in the United States there are three, or perhaps four, distinguishable forms of comparative negligence: pure comparative negligence, two versions of modified comparative negligence, and the slight-gross rule of comparative negligence.

Pure comparative negligence entails the sharing of damages among the parties to the accident in the same proportion as their negligence contributed to the accident. Suppose that *A* and *B* are involved in an automobile

---

[13]Each of these limitations allowed an otherwise contributorily negligent plaintiff to recover *all* his losses. Note how this differs from the result under comparative negligence described below.

accident in which A's car, worth $200, and B's car, worth $12,000, are both totally destroyed. Assume for convenience that the cars have no salvage value. A sues B for negligence and asks for compensation for the loss of his car. B counterclaims for his losses. Let us assume that the jury, at a consolidated trial, assigns 10% of the negligence that caused the accident to A and the remaining 90% to B. Thus, A recovers 90% of his $200 losses, or $180. B, under his counterclaim, recovers 10% of his loss of $12,000 or $1,200. Note that, on net, A owes B $1,020, a result that may strike many as unfair: A, whose fault was minimal, seems to be bearing the far larger burden of the losses arising from the accident. This conclusion would be incorrect, as can be seen by comparing the total losses and the shares of those totals borne by each party under pure comparative negligence. The total losses arising from the accident are $12,200. Of that total, A's share is 10% or $1,220, made up of the loss of his car—worth $200—and his obligation to pay B $1,020. Similarly, B's share of the total losses is 90% or $10,980.

But suppose that the rule is not pure comparative negligence but rather the old rule of negligence with contributory negligence. Let's compare the apportionment of damages under those two different systems. Suppose that the facts are exactly as those given above but that the rule of law bars recovery for a negligent plaintiff. Thus, when A sues B, his contributory negligence precludes his recovering any of his $200 losses. Similarly, B's contributory negligence forces him to bear all of his $12,000 losses. Thus, of the total losses arising from the accident, $12,200, A's share, $200, under the standard of negligence with contributory negligence is only 1.6%. B bears the remaining 98.4% of the total losses.

This comparison of the share of losses under the two rules seems to suggest that comparative negligence is more *equitable* than is negligence with contributory negligence. That is in fact the major argument that has been made in favor of comparative negligence. We will postpone for a moment an inquiry into the relative *efficiency* of the two forms of the negligence rule.

The second form of comparative negligence is *modified* comparative negligence. This is by far the most popular form of comparative negligence, having been adopted in 25 of the 37 states that have abandoned the rule of negligence with contributory negligence for some form of comparative negligence. In point of fact, there are two varieties of this rule. The first (referred to as the "Wisconsin rule") retains contributory negligence as a complete bar to plaintiff's recovery where plaintiff's negligence is greater than or equal to the defendant's negligence. The second form (known as the "New Hampshire rule") allows the plaintiff to recover if he is 50% at fault but not if his fault exceeds the defendant's. Thus, the difference between the two forms of modified comparative negligence is that, under the Wisconsin rule, the plaintiff's recovery is barred if his negligence is greater than or equal to the defendant's and, under the New Hampshire rule, the plaintiff's recovery is barred only if his negligence is greater than the defendant's.

In terms of the example discussed above under pure comparative negligence, the apportionment of damages under either of the varieties of modified comparative negligence would be different. Let us assume that each party's losses and the jury's apportionment of fault between them are as above. Thus, A has suffered losses of $200, and B of $12,000. A is held to be 10% responsible for the accident; B, 90%. In A's action against B, A will recover $180 under modified comparative negligence, just as he did under pure comparative negligence. But under either form of modified comparative negligence, B's recovery of 10% of $12,000 will be barred since his percentage of responsibility for the accident is strictly greater than is A's. Thus, of the total losses—$12,200—A's share is reduced, under modified comparative negligence, to 1.5% with B bearing the remaining 98.5% of the total losses. Note that this is, from A's point of view, slightly better than he did under the old rule of negligence with contributory negligence.

The final form of comparative negligence, called the "slight-gross" rule, is in general force in only two states, Nebraska and South Dakota. Here the plaintiff's contributory negligence will bar recovery unless his negligence is slight and the defendant's is gross. The statutes allow for apportionment of damages so that the plaintiff's recovery is reduced, where his contributory negligence is slight, by the percentage of fault that the jury attributes to his actions. Thus, the actual implementation of the slight-gross system is very much like that under either form of modified comparative negligence.

Despite this sweeping trend away from contributory negligence and toward comparative negligence, there has been relatively little efficiency analysis of comparative negligence by economists and lawyers familiar with economics. The reason for this is probably that, because they have reached a consensus that negligence with contributory negligence is efficient in cases of bilateral precaution, the commentators have generally concluded that comparative negligence must be less efficient. Still, almost everyone concedes that comparative negligence is *fairer* than the negligence with contributory negligence rule that it has largely replaced.

D. Uncertainty and Comparative Negligence

A recent article on the economics of comparative negligence has reached some novel conclusions about the fairness and efficiency aspects of that liability standard. Explaining the argument of this article provides an occasion for discussing how uncertainty about the court system affects incentives. We said in the preceding chapter that all forms of the negligence rule, including the new rule of comparative negligence, are equally efficient under the standard assumptions of the economic analysis that we made in the previous chapter. To differentiate among the forms of the negligence rule, the authors introduce uncertainty into the operation of the tort liability system, specifically in the sense that a potential victim or injurer cannot be certain how a court will evaluate his precaution by comparison to a legal standard of care. It is possible, for example, that the court will determine that the party was negligent when in fact he was not negligent; alternatively, the court may find the party non-negligent when in fact he was violating the legal standard of care. We may call this condition "evidentiary uncertainty."

The costs faced by the injurer are represented as a function of his precaution in Figure 9.4. The high curve in both panels in the figure represents the injurer's costs when he is held liable, and the straight line represents his costs when he is not held liable. x^* denotes the legal standard. Under conditions of certainty, as shown in Panel a, his costs jump abruptly from the high-cost curve to the low-cost curve as his precaution reaches x^*. This discontinuity in costs, which occurs at the point where his precaution reaches the legal standard and he becomes non-liable, was discussed at length in the preceding chapter.

However, under conditions of evidentiary uncertainty, as shown in Panel b, he cannot be certain that the jury will perceive the true relationship between his precaution and the legal standard. The effect of uncertainty is to smooth the big jump in costs at the legal standard. Smoothing occurs because the injurer's expected costs are a weighted average of his costs when liable and his costs when not liable, with the weights given by the probability that he is found liable. We assume that the probability that he is found non-liable increases as his precaution increases. Based upon this assumption, the standard diagram can be modified to show how uncertainty smooths the discontinuity. The modification is indicated in Panel b of Figure 9.4 by the sloping curve that connects the high-cost curve and the low-cost line.

Uncertainty about the court's assessment of a party's precautionary level *vis-a-vis* the legal standard of care induces most injurers to take *more* precaution than prescribed in the legal standard of care. In effect, they give themselves a margin of error to be sure that they avoid liability. This behavior is represented in Panel b of Figure 9.4 by the fact that costs are minimized on the smoothed curve at x^+, which is a higher level of precaution than the legal standard x^*.

We have presented a variety of reasons why the legal standard might be set at the efficient level of care. For example, that is the result of setting the legal standard by the Hand Rule. When the legal standard is set at the efficient level, it represents an ideal level of precaution that people are expected to achieve. However, evidentiary uncertainty causes potential injurers to exceed the legal standard. So, when the legal standard is set at the efficient level, evidentiary uncertainty will cause over-precaution relative to the efficient level.[14]

Under certain conditions, this *over*-precaution is less under comparative negligence than it is under any other form of the negligence rule, including negligence with contributory negligence. The simple reason is that under comparative negligence if either party makes a mistake in choosing the level

---

[14]This could be avoided by setting the legal standard at the minimum level of care that the community regards as appropriate, rather than setting the standard at the social cost-minimizing level of precaution.

Figure 9.4 Precaution under Evidentiary Uncertainty

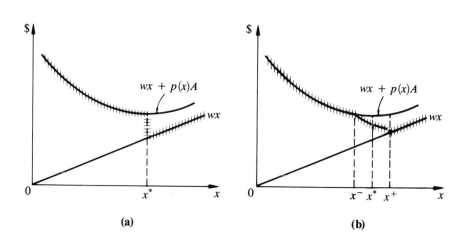

(a)   (b)

Panel a shows the decisionmaker's decision about precaution when there is certainty in the court's evaluation of his level of precaution, *x*, *vis-a-vis* the legal standard of care, *x**. The cross-hatched line represents the decisionmaker's expected costs for different levels of precaution. Under certainty, as we saw in the previous chapter, there is a sharp vertical discontinuity in the expected costs at the legal standard of care, *x**.

Panel b shows the same decisionmaker's decision about precaution when he is uncertain how a court will evaluate his precaution *vis-a-vis* the legal standard of care. It is possible that the court will hold him liable even though $x > x^*$, and it is also possible that the court will exonerate him from liability even though $x < x^*$. We call this a condition of "evidentiary uncertainty." If we assume that the levels of precaution x^- and x^+ represent upper and lower bounds on the levels of precaution within which this evidentiary uncertainty occurs, then the decisionmaker's expected cost curve no longer has the sharp discontinuity at *x**, the legal standard of care, but rather declines gradually between x^- and x^+. To prevent being held liable because of evidentiary uncertainty, a risk-averse decisionmaker may minimize his expected costs by taking more precaution than prescribed in the legal standard of care. In Panel b, x^+ is the level of precaution that minimizes the decisionmaker's expected costs.

of precaution to satisfy the legal standard of care (that is, if there is evidentiary uncertainty), the losses are shared between the two parties rather than being concentrated on one or the other party, as is the case in any other form of the negligence rule.

One frequent criticism that is made of comparative negligence is that its administration costs are too high. The rules to use in apportioning fault are vague, even where the parties are engaged in the same activity: no one is quite sure how to apportion fault where *A* was going 45 in a 30 mile-per-hour zone and *B* was going 60. But things are even worse when the parties are engaged in different activities. How, for instance, would you have apportioned fault in *Butterfield v. Forrester*, the case in Chapter 3 involving an obstruction in the road left by Forrester and a negligent horseman, Butterfield, who crashed into the obstruction? Given this difficulty, it is alleged that litigants and juries will spend inordinately large amounts of effort trying to establish exact percentages of fault where such exactitude is impossible to achieve. Until recently, admiralty law solved this vexing problem by apportioning fault on a 50%-50% basis whenever there was contributory fault by the plaintiff. In point of fact, because there have been no empirical studies of the matter, no one knows for certain what the administration costs of the various liability standards are. This is, of course, an important fact about which to have information. Apparently, however, the feeling that comparative negligence is fairer than negligence with contributory negligence is so strong that nearly every jurisdiction in the country has opted for the new rule, regardless of its alleged adverse efficiency consequences or high administration costs. If the argument that under situations of evidentiary uncertainty and assuming certain other conditions are satisfied, comparative negligence is more efficient than any other form of the negligence rule is correct, then the inefficiency objection to comparative negligence fades. That leaves only the matter of administration costs to be dealt with in a more systematic way.

All these conclusions are, however, rather breathtaking in their reliance upon pure theory. Empirical testing of the theories is needed to inspire confidence in their policy implications.

E. Applying the Economic Model

We have developed various arguments about compensatory damages, punitive damages, and negligence rules. As an exercise, we invite you to bring these arguments to bear upon one of the most famous recent tort cases—the criminal prosecution of the Ford Motor Company for deaths and other injuries resulting from the explosion of the gas tank in its Pinto—to see what it can tell us about the economic analysis of tort liability.[15]

In August, 1978, three young women were driving in northern Indiana in their 1973 Ford Pinto. After putting gas in the car at a self-service station and resuming their drive, they noticed that the gas tank cap was resting on the rear of the car. No sooner was the cap spotted than it blew off the car. The driver turned the car around to go back for the cap and had just stopped in the right-hand lane of a four-lane highway in order to get out and retrieve the cap when the Pinto was struck in the rear by a speeding van. The Pinto burst into flames, killing two of the young women instantly; the third died in the hospital shortly thereafter, but not before telling an orderly at the hospital the facts above.

Shortly after these tragic deaths, the grand jury of Pulaski County, Indiana, handed down an indictment of the Ford Motor Company on criminal charges. The indictment contained two counts: first, that Ford "did through

---

[15]The discussion that follows draws heavily on Richard Epstein, *Is Pinto a Criminal?* REGULATION (March/April 1980).

the acts and omissions of its agents and employees ... recklessly authorize and approve the design of the 1973 Ford Pinto, and did recklessly design and manufacture the 1973 Pinto in such a manner as would likely cause said automobile to flame and burn upon rear-end impact"; second, that Ford did "recklessly create a substantial risk of bodily harm" to the three young women.

The novel aspect of this famous case is that it is a *criminal* complaint. We have not yet dealt with the economic theory of crime, and so we are not yet fully equipped to determine the relative merits of a civil and a criminal complaint. However, there were also several highly publicized civil suits for wrongful death arising from rear-end accidents involving the Pinto. Let us analyze the facts above in the following way: first, let's suppose that there was no criminal complaint; instead let us ask what would have been the most likely outcome in a *civil* suit for the tort of wrongful death by the families of the three young women against the Ford Motor Company;[16] and then, having done this, let us see what role there might have been for a criminal complaint against the Ford Motor Company. This inquiry into the basis of a criminal complaint will serve to introduce some critical issues in the assessment of punitive damages.

Until the late 1960s, if the successors (for example, their parents, spouses, and children) of the three decedents had a cause of action in a civil suit, it would have been an action only against the driver of the van that struck the Pinto. And the theory under which the driver's liability, if any, would have been determined was negligence. It is not at all clear how such a suit against the driver of the van would have been resolved; there are important factual questions about the van driver's and the decedents' behavior (were they contributorily negligent and thus barred from recovery? all of them? only the driver?) that were not developed and that bear critically on the issue. At the worst, the van driver would probably have been held to be negligent, not grossly (or recklessly, wantonly, or willfully) negligent. That means that at the most he would have been held liable for *compensating* the decedents' successors. There would probably not have been an issue of assessing punitive damages against him.

If you ask yourself whether the Ford Motor Company might have been sued by the decedents' successors, you might answer that the company should be liable only if the car was defective and if that defect proximately

---

[16]In fact there have been numerous civil liability actions against Ford for injuries suffered because of gas tank explosions in the Pinto. As noted in the text, these tort actions were brought on a theory of defendant's strict liability, not negligence as we will assume in our discussion. In the most famous of these civil cases, Ford "was accused of intentional and willful disregard of safety." The jury returned a verdict for plaintiffs in the amount of $125 million in punitive damages and $3.5 million in compensatory damages. The judge reduced the punitive amount to $3.5 million. The amended judgment was affirmed on appeal—*Grimshaw v. Ford Motor Co.*, 174 Cal. Rptr. 348 (Ct. App. 1981).

caused the harm.[17] One way of putting this is to contend that the car was not "crashworthy." Let us postpone for a moment how we might make a determination of "crashworthiness" and instead ask what the law was on this matter. Until the late 1960s courts in the United States, in general, rejected the theory that automobile manufacturers should be liable for harms arising from the "uncrashworthiness" of their products. Those harmed in automobile collisions could recover only from other drivers who had negligently caused the harm, but not from the manufacturer of their car. This exclusion from common law liability did not mean that there might not be statutory regulation of the crashworthiness of automobiles, and, indeed, there was. The National Highway Traffic Safety Administration imposed some safety requirements on automobile manufacturers, and, as we will see, one of these requirements played a part in the criminal prosecution of Ford in Pulaski County, Indiana.

In 1968 in *Larson v. General Motors Corp.*, the traditional rule against common law liability for uncrashworthiness fell. The basis of the judgment, which was widely accepted, was the seemingly sensible observation that collisions are statistically foreseeable and that, therefore, manufacturers could and should be required to participate in minimizing the resulting costs of collisions by providing such precautions as padded dashboards, collapsible steering wheels, and safety glass.

The *Larson* holding came in 1968 and so was available in the later 1970s after the Pinto crash near Elkhart, Indiana. That meant that, in theory, the decedents' successors in the Pinto case could have proceeded against the Ford Motor Company.[18] In fact, they did not do so. But let us change our hypothetical civil suit to consider the plaintiff's civil suit against the Ford Motor Company for recovery under a theory of Ford's having produced an uncrashworthy car.

The particular defect complained of in the Pinto cases was the design and location of the car's gas tank. The testimony of the plaintiffs' expert witness at the criminal trial was that the tank was located too close to the cosmetic rear bumper and was surrounded by sharp metallic objects. As a result, he argued, the tank was particularly susceptible to rupture and explosion and thus to cause injury to the occupants. Moreover, the plaintiffs' expert testified that for an additional production cost of $11 per car Ford could have either moved the tank or surrounded it with its own rubber buffer so that the danger would have all but vanished.

Ford's engineers testified that the design and location of the gas tank were not defective. Ninety per cent of all United States-manufactured auto-

---

[17]These are precisely the questions that would be asked in a products liability suit against any manufacturer. We will discuss these sorts of actions in more detail below.

[18]One great advantage of this option was that the corporate defendant was much more likely than was the van driver to have enough wealth to pay a judgment in the plaintiffs' favor. Such a defendant is said to have a "deep pocket."

mobiles–including all of General Motors' cars–had the gas tank in the same general location as did the Pinto and, in some cases, the surrounding environment was even more hostile than the Pinto's. The most important safety reason for placing the gas tank over the rear axle was that that design placed the tank as far as possible from the driver. Ford and other manufacturers believed that that design was safer than any alternative because most accidents were front-end or side collisions. Rear-end collisions were relatively infrequent. Thus, a re-design of the placement of the gas tank to minimize the costs arising from rear-end collisions would inevitably raise the likelihood of increased harms from front-end and side collisions.

An important part of Ford's decisionmaking process was a cost-benefit calculation for redesigning the location of the gas tank.[19] The following table indicates the gist of these calculations:[20]

Benefits of Re-designing the Gas Tank Location

Savings	180 burn deaths; 180 serious burn injuries; 2,100 burned vehicles.
Unit Cost	$200,000 per death; $67,000 per injury; $700 per vehicle.
Total Benefit	180 x ($200,000) + 180 x ($67,000) + 2100 x ($700) = $49.5 million.

Costs of Re-designing the Gas Tank Location

Sales	11 million cars, 1.5 million light trucks.
Unit Cost	$11 per car, $11 per truck.
Total Cost	11,000,000 x ($11) + 1,500,000 x ($11) = $137 million.

Question 9.6: How would the Hand Rule evaluate this evidence? What must the probability of these rear-end accidents be in order for Ford to be deemed negligent under the Hand Rule?

Question 9.7: Using our discussion of the measurement of compensation, how might the actual numbers used in the cost-benefit study have been arrived at?

---

[19]Ford contended that its reason for making the cost-benefit analysis was that the National Highway Traffic Safety Administration required them to do so. Moreover, Ford said that the NHTSA supplied them with $200,000 as the figure for the value of a lost life.

[20]The figures are taken from Richard A. Posner, TORTS: CASES AND ECONOMIC ANALYSIS 725 (1983). Notice that they are made with figures for 1978.

These cost-benefit calculations are projections from studies done by Ford on the hazards from rolling cars over. Thus, the 180 deaths represent an estimate of the number of people whose lives could have been saved in *roll-over accidents* by relocating the gas tank away from the rear of the car. The data do not indicate how many additional lives would have been lost from other types of accidents, such as front-end and side collisions, as a result of relocating the gas tank. The cost-benefit data was not admitted as evidence in the Indiana case because the cause of death was not roll-over. However, the cost-benefit calculations have received a great deal of publicity as exemplifying a particular way of thinking about safety.

The prosecutor and much public opinion felt that making such a calculation of whether to incur an $11 expense to save statistically foreseeable harm was, at the least, callous and, at the worst, criminal. What is your view?

Question 9.8: Using our theory of punitive damages, do you think that Ford should have been punished? What additional information might you require to answer this question?

Question 9.9: Apply the rule of comparative negligence to this case. How much liability do you think belongs with Ford? What difference do you think the uncertainty about the legal standard will have on Ford's precaution in the future?

F. Expanding the Economic Model of Liability: Topics and Questions

The economic model that we have been exploring in this and the previous chapter is not a final product. Rather, it is a beginning of an important body of legal and economic analysis that some of you will help to complete. In this section we provide a series of special topics to which the model can be applied. Much of the work is left for you.

1. Vicarious Liability   There are circumstances in which one person may be held responsible for the torts committed by another. Where this happens, the third party is said to be "vicariously liable" for the tortfeasor's acts. Vicarious liability may extend from an agent to his principal, or from a dependent child to a parent, but by far the most common instance of vicarious liability is that of employer responsibility for the tortious wrongs of their employees under the doctrine of *respondeat superior*, "let the master answer." For this to happen, note that the employee must have been "acting within the scope of [his] employment." This is an elastic concept and has recently been stretched further and further, but it clearly does not cover instances where the employee is engaged in what is known as "frolic and detour." Another restriction is that the employer's liability extends only to the unintentional torts of his employee, not to any intentional torts. That distinction has also been blurred in recent cases so that employers are increasingly held liable for their employee's intentional torts.

The economic analysis of *respondeat superior* focuses on two aspects of the rule.[21] The first is that allowing the plaintiff to proceed against the employer (or the employee to receive indemnification from his employer) increases the likelihood of the victim's recovering, as does any form of strict liability. Employees are, generally, not as wealthy as are their employers, or,

---

[21]For a full discussion of the economics of this issue, *see* Alan Sykes, *The Economics of Vicarious Liability*, 93 YALE L.J. 1231 (1984).

more pertinently, they are less likely to have liability insurance. Thus, the doctrine makes it less likely that a plaintiff will go away empty-handed because of the insolvency of the injurer. But there must be more to *respondeat superior* than that because no one seriously believes that liability should be determined solely on the principle of ability-to-pay. The second, and more important, economic reason for *respondeat superior* is that making the employer strictly liable for his employees' torts creates an incentive for him to take optimal precaution in selecting his employees, in assigning them various tasks, and in deciding with what tools to equip them. These seem to be circumstances of unilateral precaution because the employer, not the employee or those injured, chooses and supervises the employees. We have previously identified situations of unilateral precaution as being appropriate for strict liability. Because *respondeat superior* is, in essence, employer's strict liability for the unintentional torts of his employees, it may be more efficient than a negligence alternative.

Question 9.10: What if the victim is a fellow employee who was injured on the job? Should *respondeat superior* hold in that instance?

Question 9.11: The common law did not hold parents liable for their children's unintentional torts unless the parents' negligent supervision led directly to the child's tort. But the common law did hold husbands vicariously liable for their wives' torts, a rule since abrogated by statute.

Can you provide an economic explanation for these rules that makes them consistent with *respondeat superior*?

Question 9.12: In many states, a bartender (under so-called "dram shop" laws), friend, party host, or other person who serves liquor to an already intoxicated person is held vicariously liable for any damages that that person subsequently inflicts on another person or his property. Does this form of vicarious liability make economic sense?

2. Joint Tortfeasors   Recall Example 2 from the previous chapter in which a hunter was injured when both of his two hunter companions fired birdshot toward him. Let us modify the facts and imagine that he was hit by birdshot from *both* of his companions. This sort of situation has been treated in the common law as one of "joint and several liability." This phrase means that the plaintiff may proceed jointly against both injurers or the plaintiff may elect to recover all damages from only one of them. That is, each defendant is individually responsible for all the plaintiff's losses. Although he may choose from which of his injurers to collect, the plaintiff may not recover more than his total losses.

The common law recognized two circumstances in which joint and several liability would hold:

1. if the defendants acted together to cause the victim's harm, or
2. even if the defendants acted independently, the victim's harm was indivisible.

An example of the first is where two cars driven by A and B are racing down a street and one of them hits C, a pedestrian. An example of the second circumstance is our case of the pheasant hunters.

Suppose that the plaintiff chooses to recover from only one of several injurers. May the defendant then force the other injurers to contribute to paying the damages? At common law, the defendant did not generally have a right to contribution, as this is called, from other joint tortfeasors. This was true even if the plaintiff's selection of which tortfeasor to sue was malicious or totally capricious. This harsh rule against contribution has been abrogated, usually by statute but sometimes by judicial decision, in almost all the states. (This is true only for unintentional torts; for intentional torts, such as a violation of the antitrust statutes, there is still no right of contribution among joint tortfeasors.)

The doctrine of joint and several liability is used to get to the "deep pocket." To illustrate, suppose that an uninsured motorist is going at high speed, strikes a pothole in the road, loses control of his car, and hits another passenger car, seriously injuring its driver. Assume for the sake of argument that 90% of the fault lay with the speeding driver and 10% of the fault lay with the city government for not filling the pothole. The victim will have difficulty recovering anything from the speeding driver because he lacks insurance. However, if the victim can prove that the city was negligent in maintaining the road, then the victim can recover 100% of his loss from the state, even though the pothole only contributed 10% to the accident.

Naturally, the question arises whether joint and several liability and contribution or no contribution make economic sense.[22] Just as was the case in distinguishing between negligence rules and strict liability, here the crucial distinction is between situations where the optimal precaution is unilateral by one of the defendants or joint among all of them. Where the optimal precaution involves joint action by multiple defendants, the no-contribution rule, by imposing residual liability on each defendant, creates the optimal incentive for each of them to take precaution. Thus, in the example where A and B are racing their cars and C, a pedestrian, is struck and injured by one of them, optimal precaution requires both parties, not just one, to take care. If there is no contribution, both of them are liable for the plaintiff's entire losses. In terms of the Hand Rule, the rule of no contribution increases the expected accident costs that each must use in computing the amount of precaution to take. Note that the efficiency argument for the no-contribution rule among joint or multiple tortfeasors is precisely analogous to our efficiency argument for the imposition of some form of the negligence rule in situations of bilateral precaution. Recall that where there is the possibility for bilateral (or joint) precaution by injurer and *victim* (rather than by joint

---

[22]*See* Landes & Posner, *Joint and Multiple Tortfeasors: An Economic Analysis,* 9 J. LEGAL STUD. 517 (1980); and Polinsky & Shavell, *Contribution and Claim Reduction Among Antitrust Defendants: An Economic Analysis,* 33 STANFORD L. REV. 447 (1981).

injurers, as we have been discussing), a form of the negligence rule induces optimal precaution by both parties through the creation of residual liability: if the victim fails to satisfy the legal standard of care, she is responsible for *all* her losses; if the injurer fails to satisfy the legal standard of care, he is responsible for *all* the victim's losses. This is precisely the result reached by a rule of no contribution where there is bilateral precaution among joint tortfeasors. Moreover, the no-contribution rule saves on the administration costs of apportioning fault among joint tortfeasors.

3. Liability for Failure to Rescue

Recall our discussion in the previous chapter of the fact that the common law did not impose liability for failure to rescue. Thus, for example, someone who failed to throw a rope from the bank to a drowning man, even if this could have been done easily, could not be held liable by anyone on the drowned man's behalf.

It was suggested early in this century that the common law's failure to embrace a Good Samaritan rule was not easily defensible. In fact, in a famous article Professor Ames proposed such a rule in the following form:

> One who fails to interfere to save another from impending death or great bodily harm, when he might do so with little or no inconvenience to himself, and the death or great bodily harm follows as a consequence of his inaction, shall be punished criminally and shall make compensation to the party injured or to his widow and children in case of death.[23]

At first blush, the rule requiring an easy rescue seems perfectly straightforward and laudable. The benefits of the rescue are large; the costs to the rescuer are small. But on further reflection, Ames' rule presents some vexing problems. Foremost among these is the fact that it is difficult to know where to draw the line between inaction that has and has not resulted in great harm to another. As one recent commentator has put it, "Once one decides that as a matter of statutory or common law duty, an individual is required under some circumstances to act at his own cost for the exclusive benefit of another, then it is very hard to set out in a principled manner the limits of social interference with individual liberty. . . . Once forced exchanges, regardless of the levels of payment, are accepted, it will no longer be possible to delineate the sphere of activities in which contracts (or charity) will be required in order to procure desired benefits and the sphere of activity in which those benefits can be procured as of right."[24]

By way of illustration, consider this case, originally from Macaulay's discussion of the Criminal Code he drew up for India. A man who is dying sends across the Indian subcontinent for the services of a surgeon who is the only man in India who can save his life. If the surgeon refuses to go, should

---

[23]Ames, *Law and Morals*, 22 HARV. L. REV. 97 (1908).

[24]R. Epstein, *A Theory of Strict Liability*, 2 J. LEGAL STUD. 151, 199 (1973). This same article raises some other important shortcomings of Ames' Good Samaritan rule as well as of the economic theory of negligence.

he be liable for the losses that follow from the sick man's death? Ames suggests that he should not be liable because his duty to rescue contemplates situations where the cost to the rescuer are trivial by comparison to the benefit to the rescued. The Indian surgeon case is one where the costs to the rescuer are large. But Professor Epstein asks us to consider this further hypothetical: suppose that a friend of the dying man offers to pay all the surgeon's expenses, for example, by flying him to the sick man in his private jet and paying him his usual fee. If the doctor accepts, then it must be the case that the benefits to the friend and sick man of the surgeon's services, as expressed in their willingness-to-pay, exceed the costs to the doctor. But if this is so, then these are precisely the circumstances under which a voluntary contractual exchange would take place, and if such an exchange can be concluded, there is little to be said for a Good Samaritan law.

But suppose that after the friend's offer to pay all his expenses, the doctor still refuses to come. What then? One possible conclusion is that the friend's offer was not high enough to offset the doctor's opportunity costs and provide a reasonable return on his time and effort. And if that is the case, then one might heartlessly conclude that it is economically efficient for the surgeon *not* to take the trip. However, we do not need to go that far; the point, Professor Epstein suggests, is not to be callous about the victim's benefits and the potential rescuer's costs but rather to point out that Ames' rule is not as straightforward as it sounds. For example, it requires the court to make fine-tuned calculations of cost and benefit for which courts may not be very well-suited. The line distinguishing Ames' easy rescue from a more difficult one is not, after all, an easy one to draw.

Can economic analysis provide some additional insights on the issue of liability for failure to rescue? The fundamental economic fact about rescue is that this is a situation in which the rescuer can confer an external *benefit* on the potential victim.[25] Note how this economic perspective brings out the unusual nature of the duty to rescue. As we noted in the previous chapter, tort law is by and large concerned with attempting to get potential injurers to internalize external *costs* they might impose on others. Thus, the issue of whether there should be a legal duty to rescue might be framed as whether the law should require certain persons to confer an external benefit involuntarily on others in addition to requiring a legal duty not to impose costs involuntarily on others.

When an external benefit is present, voluntary exchange fails in the sense that the benefit-creator engages in a socially sub-optimal amount of the benefit-generating activity. A commonly cited example of this sort of benefit is elementary education. All of society, not just students and their

---

[25]If the rescuer and rescued person *could* have entered into an contractual relationship (even if they did not), is there an external benefit? If there is no external benefit, should this be treated as a tortious or as a contractual relationship? Consider this question in light of the question about professionals and maritime salvors on page 413.

immediate families, benefits from having all its members receive elementary education. However, it is very difficult for students or their families to induce those third-party beneficiaries to help pay for privately provided schooling. Some students, concluding that the private costs of elementary education exceed the private benefits, will not go to school. Thus, in the absence of some public intervention in the market for elementary education, there will be too few students. So, the state makes provision for its supply, rather than leaving supply entirely to the market. The usual policy prescription for external benefits is to subsidize the benefit-generating activity. This might be done in one of three general ways: (1) by lowering the costs of those (privately) supplying the beneficial activity, e.g., through direct subsidization from governmental revenues, (2) by direct public provision of the benefit-generating good or service, e.g., public primary schools, or (3) by encouraging the demand for the beneficial good or service, e.g., by lowering income tax liability by a fraction of each dollar spent on the beneficial activity.

Do the standard policy prescriptions apply to rescue? If so, there should be rewards for rescuers out of public or private funds or subsidies of the rescuer's activities or even public provision of rescuing activities. And, in fact, society does all of those things. First, rescuers are sometimes given pecuniary awards from private or public groups for their actions, and perhaps even more importantly, they are highly praised. For example, federal, state, and local governments as well as private groups, such as churches and clubs, often hold ceremonies honoring those who engage in dramatic rescues. Second, society undertakes both the direct and indirect lowering of the costs of rescue. For example, at public beaches and other public areas where swimmers may get into trouble and need rescue, lifeguards are provided at public expense, as well as ropes, boats, and telephones that make rescue cheaper and, therefore, more likely.

Given that these policies for increasing the amount of the external benefit-generating activity of rescue already exist, does it make economic sense to add (or possibly substitute) a policy of holding persons liable for failing to make easy rescues?[26] There is no clear cut answer. First, we have already seen that there may be large costs to distinguishing easy and hard rescues in legal disputes. A second economic factor to consider is that the fear of exposure to liability for failure to rescue may cause potential rescuers to avoid situations in which they will be called on to rescue someone. And this may *reduce* the number of rescues. For example, strong swimmers may avoid public beaches for fear of being held liable for failing to rescue those in difficulty. Whether this result of the change in liability will follow is somewhat doubtful; nonetheless, it is worth considering. And finally, it is important to

---

[26]*See* W. Landes & R. Posner, *Altruism in Law and Economics,* 68 AM. ECON. REV. 417 (1978) and Landes & Posner, *Salvors, Finders, Good Samaritans, and Other Rescuers: An Economic Study of Law and Altruism,* 7 J. LEGAL STUD. 83 (1978). *See also* E. Weinrib, *The Case for a Duty to Rescue,* 90 YALE L.J. 247 (1980).

consider whether, if there is liability for failure to rescue, the non-pecuniary motivation for rescue may begin to wither, leading to undesirable results. Instead of praising rescuers, people may well begin to say that the action was not, after all, selfless but rather motivated by fear of liability.

> **Question 9.13:** Suppose that there is no liability for failure to rescue, but that courts hold that, once a potential rescuer begins a rescue, he can be held liable for doing it negligently. For example, suppose that *A* falls unconscious on the sidewalk. *B*, who is not a doctor and does not know the techniques of cardio-pulmonary resuscitation, nonetheless feels bound to try to do something and starts pounding on *A's* chest and blowing into his mouth. Suppose further that it turns out that *B* did these things with such imprecision and violence that there is a strong likelihood that she contributed to *A's* severe injuries. In light of the discussion above, examine the consequences of holding *B* liable for negligent rescue.

> **Question 9.14:** Suppose that in the course of rescuing *B, A* is herself harmed. Should she be allowed to recover the costs of her harm from *B*? Or should the defense of assumption of the risk preclude *A*'s recovery?

> **Question 9.15:** There are two clear situations in which the law allows rescuers to bring an action for a reward from the rescued person. The first allows professionals, such as doctors, to receive their usual fee from those whom they rescue. For example, a doctor who comes upon an unconscious man will not have liability imposed upon him for failure to render aid; however, if he does help, he may bring an action against the person he has aided for his usual and customary fee. The second anomaly arises in admiralty law, the law of the oceans. A salvor, one who "salvages" vessels or cargo, is entitled to a reward for a successful rescue at sea. Using the analysis of the text, can you suggest why the common law countries make these two exceptions?

> **Question 9.16:** In *Hurley v. Eddingfield*, 156 Ind. 416, 59 N.E. 1058 (1901), the plaintiff brought an action against the defendant Dr. Eddingfield for $10,000 in damages for failing to prevent the death of Hurley's intestate. "At and for years before decedent's death appellee was a practicing physician at Mace[, Indiana], in Montgomery County, duly licensed under the laws of the state. He held himself out to the public as a general practitioner of medicine. He had been decedent's family physician. Decedent became dangerously ill, and sent for appellee. The messenger informed appellee of decedent's violent sickness, tendered him his fee for his services, and stated to him that no other physician was procurable in time, and that decedent relied on him for attention. No other physician was procurable in time to be of any use, and decedent did rely on appellee for medical assistance. Without any reason whatever, appellee refused to render aid to decedent. No other patients were requiring appellee's immediate service, and he could have gone to the relief of decedent if he had been willing to do so. Death ensued, without decedent's fault, and wholly from appellee's wrongful act. The alleged wrongful act was appellee's refusal to enter into a contract of employment." The court affirmed the lower court's judgment absolving the defendant. Is this a case in which Ames' rule could have been fruitfully invoked to impose a liability for failure to rescue where the costs of doing so were trivial? Or is the case of the Indian surgeon more appropriate?

4. Costly Litigation   The models we have been discussing have implicitly assumed that litigation is costless. Of course, nothing could be further from the truth: litigation is expensive and sometimes ruinously so. A more complete analysis of the efficiency of the various liability rules we have discussed should introduce these costs explicitly. Some recent articles have done so.[27]

One obvious conclusion is that litigation costs introduce enforcement errors into the legal process. Consider an extreme case in which litigation costs exceed the expected compensatory damages. There, victims will not bring suit and so the potential injurers will not receive the signal from the tort system that what they are doing is unacceptable. (We already encountered a similar problem under the name "enforcement error" in our discussion of punitive damages.)

Another consideration is not so obvious. In the preceding chapter, we explained that a rule of strict liability or negligence could be used to provide efficient incentives for precaution. However, even though both rules can provide incentives for efficient precaution, one rule will usually result in higher transaction costs of redistributing money from injurers to victims than the other. (The transaction costs of redistribution consist of the cost of settlement negotiations and trials.) A rule of strict liability will enable more victims to recover, so there will be a need for more redistributions, which will mean more negotiations or more suits, with the result that there may be a greater total cost of redistributing money from injurers to victims. On the other hand, a negligence rule will result in fewer redistributions (recall that most injurers will satisfy the legal standard and escape liability), but those trials and negotiations that occur will be more lengthy. On balance, it is difficult to say whether strict liability or negligence will result in greater total redistributive expenditures.

> **Question 9.17:** Use the economic theory of bargaining to characterize the kinds of torts in which the transaction costs of settling disputes are likely to be large. (Hint: recall the distinction between public bads and private bads.)

These considerations open up a host of other interesting issues. What role, if any, is there for a contingent fee system to correct the inefficiencies that costly litigation imposes? (A "contingent fee" occurs when an attorney takes a client's case under the terms that, if the client wins, the attorney receives a fixed percentage of the award as his fee, and if the client loses, the attorney receives nothing from the client.) What role does competition among attorneys play in lowering the cost of litigation to its competitive level? Should American courts adopt the English rule that the loser in litigation pays his and the *other party's* lawyer's fees?

---

[27]Janusz Ordover, *Costly Litigation in the Model of Single Activity Accidents,* 7 J. LEGAL STUD. 243 (1978); and Polinsky & Rubinfeld, *The Welfare Implications of Costly Litigation in the Theory of Liability* (mimeo, 1986).

Unfortunately, a discussion of these fascinating questions is beyond the scope of this text. Indeed, the economic analysis of these issues has only just begun. It promises to be one of the more interesting extensions of the basic economic model we have discussed in this work.

5. Decisions Under Uncertainty An additional topic that needs to be expanded in the economic theory of liability is a more complete discussion of how people make decisions about uncertain outcomes. The models we have been developing in this book have generally assumed that decisionmakers dealt with uncertain events by applying the expected utility model, which we outlined in the appendix to Chapter 2. But there is now an extensive literature, mostly by psychologists but also by economists and finance specialists, that suggests that there are circumstances in which the expected utility model neither describes nor predicts how people make decisions under uncertainty.

Recall that the expected utility model posits that decisionmakers calculate the probability of an event's occurring and assign utility to each possible outcome. The expected utility model then assumes that decisionmakers combine this information about utility with the information about probabilities to take the action that maximizes their expected utility. Most decisionmakers are thought to be risk-averse, and we have seen that the model predicts that risk-averse people protect themselves against uncertain events by self-insuring, by purchasing market insurance, or by reducing (or discounting) the price they are prepared to pay for the risky asset.

The academic criticism of this model of how people make decisions under uncertainty has been based on the findings of a large number of empirical tests. The thrust of these findings is that there are many circumstances in which the expected utility model of decisionmaking under certainty neither describes accurately nor predicts accurately how people respond to risk. There are two distinguishable aspects to this criticism of the expected utility hypothesis. First, the critics contend that while some people intuitively use the expected utility model to make decisions under uncertainty, most people cannot do so unless they have been explicitly trained in the use of that model. Thus, the decisions of corporate managers may well conform to the expected utility hypothesis because they learned about the model in business school. But the decisions of the sole proprietor of a small business may not conform because she has never heard of the model and has not discovered its use on her own. In instances like this latter case, ignorance of the expected utility model may induce decisionmakers to use *ad hoc* rules of thumb to make decisions under uncertainty. And it may well be the case that these rules of thumb lead to sub-optimal decisions about precaution. Where ignorance of the expected utility model is the source of these sub-optimalities, one possible corrective public policy is to inform these decisionmakers of the expected utility model.

Second, there may be a more complex problem that the critics of the expected utility hypothesis have identified; that is the possibility that there are some risks that human beings are simply incapable of examining correctly. For instance, Kahneman and Tversky report that most people simply cannot accurately estimate low probability events; they seem to deal with them by assuming that low probability means that the event will never happen—that the probability of the event's happening is zero. In other instances, such as accidents from nuclear power plants, people seem systematically to exaggerate the probability of an accident's occurring, regardless of objective information to the contrary. It may be that no matter how lurid and convincing the evidence that cigarette smoking causes lung cancer, some people simply cannot translate that objective information into the appropriate action. Where people cannot accurately estimate risks, the problem is not necessarily one of lack of information but rather one of an inability to process the information. Moreover, the problem here is not ignorance of the expected utility model. The implication is that even if decisionmakers knew of that model, they would make wrong decisions because the probability figure they use would be inaccurate. The public policy response to the presence of some risks that cannot be accurately estimated cannot simply be to provide more information about those risks or about the benefits of using the expected utility model. Instead, public policy must in these instances be directed at identifying the optimal level of precaution and directly requiring decisionmakers to take it. Naturally, these are highly complex issues that raise nearly as many questions as they answer. Still, the literature critical of the expected utility hypothesis is important enough that you should be aware of it.

Professors Kahneman and Tversky have identified several rules of thumb or "heuristics" that people frequently use for dealing with uncertainty and have suggested that people may be systematically misled by these rules of thumb in certain situations.[28] Let's identify one of these heuristics and see how its systematic misuse may lead to inefficiencies.

The "availability" heuristic posits that in making decisions about uncertain future events, people tend to ignore statistical data in favor of evidence that seems relevant to them or is easily available. For example, despite all the statistical evidence published over the last 25 years (and the warnings on cigarette packs), someone might underestimate the risk of getting cancer because she had an uncle that smoked till the day he died of a heart attack at age 95. This example suggests a systematic *under*-estimate of the *true* (or objective) risk of contracting cancer. Consequently, the consumer is likely to take too little precaution (i.e., to smoke too much) or to under-insure against this contingency. Notice that the problem is not a lack of information on the part of the consumer. Statistically accurate information is widely available on the probability of contracting cancer from smoking cigarettes. The problem arises because the consumer uses what is to her *more believable* informa-

---

[28]Kahneman & Tversky, eds., JUDGMENT UNDER UNCERTAINTY: BIASES AND HEURISTICS (1981).

tion, what happened to her uncle, rather than that available from a more distant source.[29]

A different example of the misuse of the availability heuristic might show that people systematically *over*-estimate the probability of some harms and, consequently, take too much precaution or over-insure. For example, information is easily "available" today on television, over the back fence, and in magazines about the risk of harm from nuclear power, from the disposal of hazardous wastes, and from recombinant DNA research. This "availability" has caused people to ignore the statistical fact that the true probability of these harms occurring is very, very low. Despite this unassailable statistical information, there is no doubt that some people are far more frightened of radiation from a nuclear power plant than from other, statistically more risky, acts such as driving a car. In general, negative evidence has more impact than positive evidence. For example, the thousands of hours of trouble-free commercial airline service are systematically under-valued by customers by comparison to the relatively infrequent crashes.

One especially important misuse of the availability heuristic is the fact that people systematically underestimate the risks of low probability events. A plausible explanation of this is that these events happen so rarely as to present few people with direct experience. For example, few of us enter into enough large contracts to estimate the risk of breach accurately. This may apply to tortious harms, too.

These criticisms of the expected utility model could prove very important to the economic analysis of law. Much of the economic analysis of property, contract, and tort rules is directed towards encouraging the efficient allocation of risk. If the model that underlies much of the current analysis is not an accurate guide to how people actually deal with uncertainty, then many of the conclusions of the economic analysis are suspect. For example, if the efficiency justification for a particular rule is that it places the liability for loss on the cheaper preventer of or insurer against some uncertain event but that person is incapable of performing the expected utility calculation that the rule presumes, then inefficiencies (and inequities) are sure to result.

It should be noted that this is only one aspect of the potential problems that a full discussion of uncertainty presents for the basic economic model of tort liability. There are many others, one of which we touch on briefly in the following section.

---

[29]It is worth mentioning that the woman may be right. Predicting the probability of a particular person's getting cancer is in its infancy and is determined by so many subjective facts—such as family history, lack of stress, diet, and so on—that the woman may be correct in basing her decision to smoke on her family's history rather than on statistical averages. This observation raises the more general problem of when it is appropriate to apply statistical averages to particular persons or situations.

Question 9.18: Even though seat belts are an effective precaution against harm in an automobile accident, only about 10% of drivers and passengers routinely wear them. Is this an example of the misuse of the availability heuristic?

6. Probabilistic Causation[30]

In the previous chapter we noted that there are some well-known problems in determining causation in tort law. However, in some recent cases the traditional requirement that the plaintiff establish that the defendant proximately caused the harm by a preponderance of the evidence has been waived. Recall that in the *Sindell* case the plaintiffs' mothers had taken a drug while the plaintiffs were *in utero* and that that drug caused cancer in the plaintiffs some twenty years later. It was not possible to prove which of the numerous producers of DES had manufactured the drug taken by the plaintiffs' mothers. Nonetheless, the California Supreme Court allowed the plaintiffs to collect without proof of proximate cause. The formula adopted was that each of the manufacturers would pay a share of the compensatory damages equal to the firm's market share of the drug at the time of the harm.

One reason for the California Supreme Court's novel abandonment of the important causation aspect of tort liability[31] is that modern society has given rise to harms that were never dreamed of when the common law was being developed and for which, therefore, the categories of the traditional tort law were unsuited. The most troubling of these modern torts are referred to as "traumatic" or "time-delayed" torts. The essential aspect of these new torts is the long period of time that passes between the defendant's tortious action and the victim's harm. Recall that in the *Sindell* case a full generation passed between the time the drug was ingested and the harm appeared. Another example of a time-delayed tort are the asbestos cases, where typically twenty years elapsed between the exposure to asbestos and the harm. (We will discuss these cases in more depth below.) Similarly, the disposal of hazardous wastes is likely to cause harms for decades into the future. Many of the instances of carcinogens that have been reported are examples in which there will be a long lag before the tortious harm arises.

The passage of time creates some special problems for tort law. First is the fact that the longer the lag, the more likely it is that numerous intervening and complicating causes can arise. And these additional complications make the determination of proximate cause all the more problematic. For example, during the generation that the daughters of mothers who had taken DES were developing cervical cancer, some of those same daughters were

---

[30]This section draws on Mario Rizzo & Frank Arnold, *Causal Apportionment in the Law of Torts: An Economic Theory*, 80 COLUM. L. REV. 1399 (1980); William M. Landes & Richard A. Posner, *Tort Law as a Regulatory Regime for Catastrophic Personal Injuries*, 13 J. LEGAL STUD. 417 (1984); David Rosenberg, *The Causal Connection in Mass Exposure Cases: A "Public Law" Vision of the Tort System*, 97 HARV. L. REV. 851 (1984); Glenn Robinson, *Multiple Causation in Tort Law: Reflections on the DES Cases*, 68 VA. L. REV. 713 (1982); and Glenn Robinson, *Probabilistic Causation and Compensation for Tortious Risk*, 14 J. LEGAL STUD. 779 (1985).

[31]Most jurisdictions have chosen not to follow the California precedent in this sort of case.

smoking cigarettes, working in classrooms whose walls were treated with asbestos paint, and in other ways being exposed to other things that might cause cancer. The more of these alternative explanatory variables there are, the less confidence the law can have in pointing to *one* of them as the legal cause of the victims' harms. A second problem that a long lag between the defendant's act and the victim's harm creates for the tort liability system is that the evidence for establishing liability may be unavailable, as was the case in *Sindell*.

These troubling possibilities have given rise to a proposal for allowing certain *probable* victims to recover from a *probable* injurer before any physical harm has manifested itself. The proposal is that where the probability of harm's developing in the future is above a minimum threshold—for example, 0.60 or 60%—the potential victim should be allowed to recover the expected damages in the event that the harm manifests itself *discounted* by the probability that the harm will arise. Let's consider an example.

Suppose that after the *Sindell* case and its publicity numerous women who had not yet developed cervical cancer or any other physical ill but whose mothers had taken DES learned of the strong likelihood that they too would develop cancer at some unspecified time in the future. For the sake of making the appropriate calculation, suppose that the probability of these women developing cervical cancer, given that their mothers took DES, is 0.75. In the event that they contract cervical cancer, they will incur damages of $400,000 each. Finally, suppose that the most likely time for the cancer to develop is when the woman is 30 or older. Under the theory that would allow recovery *today* for the strong probability that harm will be inflicted in the distant future, the actual recovery of any given plaintiff will depend in part on her age. Imagine a woman who is 20 years old on the day she wins a judgment against the drug companies that supplied her mother's DES. Because her damages are both probabilistic and suffered, if at all, in the future, the calculation of the damages under the theory of recovery for what might be called *tortious risk* is a bit complicated. The $400,000 harm must first be discounted by the probability of 0.75 and then discounted a second time to convert it back to a present value.[32] Thus, the judgment for this woman will be

$$J = 0.75 (\$400,000) / (1.03)^{10}$$
$$= \$223,228.$$

The argument in favor of recovery for tortious risk is that it gets around the largest of the problems of time-delayed torts. By allowing recovery shortly after the defendant's act rather than requiring the victim to wait until

---

[32]Recall that A invested at an annual interest rate of r will have a value of
$$V = A(1 + r)^t$$
after t years.

We may reverse the formula to discover what the present value of V is, where V is realized t years hence and the interest rate for those t years is r. Call that present value A and
$$A = V / (1 + r)^t.$$

the manifestation of harm, as would be the case under the traditional tort theory, the evidentiary and causation problems of litigation twenty years after the tortious act become much less significant. It has been argued that there is an efficiency aspect of this new tort. By allowing probable victims to bring actions quickly, the signal about the unacceptability of the defendant's (or *probable* tortfeasor's) action is conveyed quickly. It may well be the case that a signal transmitted to a wrongdoer 20 or more years after the harmful act has very little incentive effect on other potential tortfeasors. However, this is an empirical issue about which there is very little evidence.

While there are benefits to allowing actions based on probabilistic causation, there are also problems, some related to efficiency, others to morality. With regard to efficiency the question must be asked whether there might not be alternative methods of regulating these long-term harms and of compensating victims that are more efficient than creating an action for tortious risk. For example, it might be altogether better not to allow recovery for probabilistic harm but instead to preserve the right to recover once the harm manifests itself and in the meantime to rely on administrative agency regulation of those activities that might cause harm at some distant time in the future. We largely do this today with regard to hazardous wastes. Those are potentially very dangerous substances, but their harm, if any, is not likely to manifest itself for many years. Instead of relying on recovery for probabilistic harm or waiting till those harms in fact occur and allowing recovery under the traditional tort theory, both the federal and state governments closely regulate the generation and disposal of hazardous wastes.

There are other problems with allowing recovery for probabilistic harm. First, there is no insurance available to potential tortfeasors for the imposition of risk in the absence of actual harm. Given that fact, potential tortfeasors who face liability for probabilistic harm will have to take some steps to self-insure if they are exposed to this form of liability. That self-insurance may be so expensive as to cause some otherwise valuable products and activities not to be produced. Second, there are problems with determining the threshold level for allowing an action for probability of harm. Even the advocates of the action for recovery of probabilistic harm have not provided guidelines for distinguishing those harms that are sufficiently likely to occur from those that are not. Any time a legal threshold of any kind is established there are problems, as we saw in the previous chapter's analysis of the effect of altering the legal standard of care. Third, there are deep philosophical and practical problems in dealing with the inevitable situation in which a probabilistic victim recovers and then never suffers the harm. Should the damages be returned to the probabilistic injurer? Fourth, the person who actually suffers the harm needs the *un*discounted compensation. To illustrate by the preceding numbers, the woman who actually develops cancer may need $400,000 to cover her expenses, whereas her risk-discounted compensation amounts to $223,228. Lastly, we do not have sufficient theoretical or empirical knowledge of firm and individual behavior to be confident of predicting what the consequences of exposure to probabilistic harm are likely to be. Taken all together, these problems constitute a strong case against allowing recovery for exposure to the mere risk of harm.

> **Question 9.19:** Suppose that there is no action for recovery of probabilistically caused harm. After the *Sindell* case women whose mothers took DES understandably easily suffer emotional distress from the discovery that they too are likely to contract cancer in the distant future. On efficiency grounds, should they be allowed to recover from the drug companies for the emotional distress they feel today from exposure to this risk?

II. MODERN PRODUCTS LIABILITY LAW: THE EVOLUTION OF PRODUCTS LIABILITY DOCTRINES

Products liability law was formerly a minor part of tort law, but within the last two decades it has become a large and important specialty. Indeed, it is fair to say that this area has emerged from being an obscure legal specialty to a public policy issue of national prominence. Many observers of tort law today believe that the area of products liability is in crisis and should serve as a case study of all that is wrong with the entire system of tort liability.[33] For example, manufacturers contend that juries are holding them liable for harms resulting from product use on theories that defy understanding and are occasionally awarding punitive damages of unprecedentedly high level. Although there are no specific figures available, the strong impression is that the million dollar judgment has become more common in products liability judgments than in other areas of the private law. To protect themselves against these awards, manufacturers and others at risk currently pay $3 billion per year in premiums for products liability insurance, a sum undreamt of just a few years ago. And in some cases, insurers have decided that the products liability area is so uncertain that they have withdrawn from the market entirely. Some of the manufacturers and others who have been left without insurance coverage have decided to quit producing their products. In other instances, otherwise profitable and productive manufacturers have sought the protection of the federal bankruptcy laws to protect themselves against mounting judgments from employees and customers who claim to have been injured by their product.

All of these examples seem to indicate that, at the least, there is turmoil in the products liability system and that, at the worst, the system is in need of far-reaching reform. In this section we will explore this important area of tort law in order to see what contribution microeconomic theory can make to this debate. We will use the economic model to suggest how reform might

---

[33]Naturally, those who represent the victims of accidents involving products contend that the system is working well and that all the cries of gloom and doom from manufacturers and products liability insurers should be ignored.

be undertaken and then compare this reform with several other recent proposals for new legislation.

Today products liability law is the most prominent example of strict liability in the entire area of torts. But this is a relatively recent development.

The history of products liability law may be divided roughly into three periods. The first extends from a famous case in the mid-19th century, *Winterbottom v. Wright*, 10 M. & W.109, 152 Eng. Rep. 402 (Ex. 1842), to the equally famous case of *MacPherson v. Buick Motor Co.*, 217 N.Y. 382, 111 N.E. 1050 (1916), and is characterized by the fact that recovery for injuries from commercial products was available, if at all, only under *contract* principles. The second period stretches from *MacPherson* to the Second Restatement of Torts in 1965 and is characterized by the slow disappearance of contractual principles from the law of products liability and the emergence of a negligence standard for determining producers' liability for product-related harms. The final period of products liability law stretches from 1965 to the present and is characterized by the complete absence of contractual principles, the emergence of strict liability as the basis for recovery for harms arising from product use, and the trend toward a standard of absolute liability for manufacturers.

A. The Privity Requirement, Contract Principles, and Warranties

Today when goods are sold to a buyer, the seller will be held liable if he has caused a defect in the goods that makes them dangerous. But under 19th century common law principles, this liability arose out of the contractual relationship between the parties. There were, however, serious difficulties with this doctrine: the consumer has a contract with the retailer, but most defects are caused by the manufacturer, not by the retailer, and the consumer did not have a contract with the manufacturer, at least according to the traditional analysis. In the language of the law, there is "privity of contract" between consumer and retailer, but not between consumer and manufacturer. So, when a consumer in the 19th century was injured by a defect in a manufactured product, the consumer could rarely recover from the manufacturer. Privity of contract was a very effective barrier to recovery by consumers for injuries caused by defective products.[34]

To see this argument, consider an example, based on the case *Winterbottom v. Wright* that initiated this period in products liability law. Suppose that a manufacturer of wagon wheels has, unknown to him, produced several wheels that are defective because the wood from which they were made was not properly seasoned. As a result of the defect, the wheels are likely to

---

[34]There were some exceptions to this traditional rule. If the product, such as a poison, was "inherently dangerous," then the victim might be able to recover from a remote party who caused the defect. However, this doctrine was inconsistent and capricious in its application. For a discussion, *see* Edward Levi, AN INTRODUCTION TO LEGAL REASONING 20–27 (1948).

buckle while being used, creating the possibility of persons and property being thrown from the wagon and injured. The manufacturer distributed his product to a wholesaler who stocked wagon parts. In turn, the wholesaler then distributed some of the defective wheels to retailers, who then sold them to consumers. Suppose that one of the consumers is thrown from his wagon and severely injured. Under the rule of privity of contract, the injured consumer can look only to the wagon parts retailer for recovery, and because the retailer had probably not violated the implicit or explicit terms of his contract with the consumer, the injured party was unlikely to recover.

The privity requirement for recovery for product injury has almost invariably been argued to have been a harsh and antiquated doctrine whose hidden purpose was to penalize consumers and favor wealthy manufacturers. Seen in another light, the privity requirement was not an insidious doctrine meant to favor one class of citizens over another but rather the common law's subtle method of achieving a desirable economic goal: the efficient allocation of the risk of product failure and harm among customer, retailer, and manufacturer. By severely limiting the availability of common law tort remedies for product-related harms, the privity requirement implied that if manufacturers, retailers, and consumers wanted to have a common law remedy for losses arising from product failure and personal injury, they would have to look to contract principles. Of course, this diversion away from tort law and toward contract law would be efficient only if the allocation of the risks of failure and personal injury arising from product use could efficiently be included as part of the contract of sale and if the manufacturing and retailing industries were sufficiently competitive to lead to competition in contract warranty terms. We will try to answer this important question, but we can only do so indirectly. For some time now, contracts of sale have not generally contained such terms, largely because several decades ago the law rejected the notion that customers and businesses would be allowed to allocate risk of product-related harms contractually. (They do contain terms regarding injury to *property*.) Thus, we cannot simply look to the terms of the typical contract of sale to see how or how well this allocation is made. However, we can look at the terms of these contracts between customers and sellers regarding allocation of risk of *other* product failures— such as those requiring repair and those causing damage to property—to see how well contractual principles achieve an efficient allocation of that risk. If manufacturers and consumers allocate those other risks in an efficient way, perhaps they can also allocate the risk of personal injury from product failure. Let's review the empirical literature on risk-allocation between manufacturers and consumers and then, based on the conclusions of that literature, speculate on what role contract principles such as those relied upon in the first period of the evolution of products liability law could play in an efficiency-based products liability law.

An important attribute of any good sold is its warranty. A warranty is that part of the contract of sale that states the manufacturer's and seller's promises as to various qualitative aspects of the commodity. The terms of the warranty typically cover such characteristics as the product's durability, responsibility for labor and parts repairs, and the uses to which the good may and may not be put for the warranty to remain in force.[35]

Several important economic questions that arise with respect to warranties are these: Why do some manufacturers offer them and others do not? Why do manufacturers' warranties contain the particular terms that they do and not other terms? Why is it the case that within the same product class the terms of warranties may differ? In large part, the answers to these and related questions are directed at determining whether warranties are more typically a method of exploiting consumer ignorance or a method of efficiently satisfying consumer desires.

Before turning to these issues, let us distinguish between *express* and *implied* warranties. Express warranties are written, form a part of the bargain for the contract of sale, and are, or should be, evident to both parties to the transaction. An implied warranty is not a part of the contract itself; rather it is a term of warranty that has been read into the contract by a court or legislature. For example, the Uniform Commercial Code states that for many goods there is an implied warranty of merchantability, which means that the product is fit for its intended use. To a limited extent, buyers and sellers may disclaim these implied warranties, but current thinking is that some of these implicit warranties are so fundamental that no party to a transaction may lawfully disclaim them.

There are two general theories that seek to explain why express warranties exist and why they typically have the terms they do. The first is the *signaling* theory. The theory begins with the assumption that for many goods— for example, so-called "hard goods" such as appliances and other consumer durables—it is costly for buyers to obtain information about many important qualities of those goods. Somehow, buyers of these goods arrive at a view of the average quality of all the products in a particular market, and they determine that they will not pay more than what the average quality is worth to them. In these circumstances, a seller who knows that the quality of his product is greater than the average that consumers expect must find some way to convince them of his product's superior quality. The seller's motivation for wanting to communicate this information is his belief that if consumers can accurately distinguish his product's superior quality and if they are willing to pay for it, then his sales, and, therefore, his profits, will increase.

Two things stand in the way of effectively communicating this information to consumers. First, consumers cannot appreciate the superiority of this seller's product by direct observation. And second, a mere assertion of superior quality is not likely to be believed because other sellers can make the same, but false, claims. The seller can surmount these limitations by

---

[35]This section relies heavily on Alan Schwartz & Robert Scott, COMMERCIAL TRANSACTIONS 189–94 (1982).

expressly warrantying the high quality of his product. A claim of superior quality backed up by the warranty's guarantees is believable because, if the claim is false, the seller will have to spend large sums in order to conform to the warranty, which might, for example, require giving disaffected consumers double the purchase price ("double your money back"). Moreover, a claim of superior quality is difficult for a competing seller whose output is of mediocre quality to emulate because, again, the inferior product's claims are false and expose the seller to high expenses to make good on the warranties. This theory, then, treats the terms of express warranties as signals to consumers from the sellers about the true quality of the product.

While the signaling theory is logically consistent, it does not seem to fit the empirical facts very well. The most noticeable fact about warranties for similar products is their similarity. Indeed, it is not uncommon for all the sellers of a particular kind of product to make precisely the same warranties. Moreover, sellers of widely different products make nearly identical warranties. And yet there is no doubt that product quality varies greatly within an industry and across industries. The signaling theory of warranties is difficult to maintain because it predicts variation in warranty coverage as product quality varies, which the facts disconfirm.

The second theory of the express warranty is referred to as the *investment* or *comparative advantage* theory.[36] The gist of this theory is that the terms of express warranties are to be understood as the result of an efficient allocation of risk of loss from product defects between manufacturer and consumer. Manufacturers assume responsibility for those losses for which, by comparison to consumers, they have a comparative advantage in prevention or correction. For example, the manufacturer of refrigerators has a comparative advantage over most consumers in making repairs on a defective refrigerator compressor. Therefore, we should expect the competitive process of bargaining over responsibility for losses arising from a defective compressor to be assigned by the parties to the manufacturer, who can more cheaply prevent or repair those losses. On the other hand, consumers assume responsibility for those losses for which *they* have a comparative advantage. For example, the consumer is better placed to see to it that the refrigerator door is used carefully. Therefore, one would expect the bargaining process to lead to consumers, rather than manufacturers, being assigned responsibility for repairing dents and other use-related harms to the door.

The comparative advantage theory seems to conform to the facts better than does the signaling theory. Specifically, it accounts for the following common terms in the "standard warranty" in a way that the signaling theory cannot:

---

[36]*See generally* Priest, *A Theory of the Consumer Product Warranty,* 90 YALE L. J. 1297 (1981); Priest, *The Best Evidence of the Effect of Products Liability Law on the Accident Rate: Reply,* 91 YALE L. J. 1386 (1982); and Schwartz & Wilde, *Imperfect Information in Markets for Contract Terms: The Examples of Warranties and Security Interests,* 69 VA. L. REV. 1387 (1983).

1. a disclaimer of all implied warranties;
2. an express warranty that the goods are "free from defects in material and workmanship";
3. a remedy limitation that limits (a) the time within which warranty claims can be made and (b) the seller's obligation with regard to the repair or replacement of defective parts; and
4. an exclusion of seller liability for consequential damages.[37]

Let us see to what extent the comparative advantage theory can explain the last three of these standard warranty terms. Recall that the gist of this theory of warranty terms is that consumers and sellers will allocate responsibility for losses from product defects according to their comparative advantage in preventing or insuring against those losses.

How would the comparative advantage theory explain the standard express term warranting the product to be "free from defects in material and workmanship"? That is, why does the manufacturer assume responsibility for losses arising from "defects in material and workmanship"? There are several reasons. First, sellers are better placed than are consumers to predict and to prevent the occurrence of these sources of product defect. Second, the seller may be able to take advantage of economies of scale in his repair process. Labor may be specialized in repairing defective products. For example, most of us take our cars to auto mechanics for repairs rather than do it ourselves for the simple reason that the mechanic is a specialist and can, therefore, do the job much more quickly and thoroughly than can we. Capital, too, may be specialized and bulky, making the repair process subject to economies of scale. For example, the diagnostic machine that the auto mechanic uses on your engine to spot trouble is far too expensive for any one consumer to purchase himself. Because of these economies, the seller, by assuming responsibility for repairs on material- and assembly-related defects, can offer his product for sale for a lower price than would be the case if consumers had to assume responsibility for this source of loss. Third, the seller can carry a large inventory of parts necessary for a wide variety of repairs. Any single consumer would find it prohibitively expensive to stock all the parts that might be needed for repairs. Again, the seller can pass on

---

[37]"Consequential" damages are to be distinguished from "direct" damages. An example will illustrate the difference. Suppose that a consumer has just bought a new set of tires. They come with a warranty that limits the buyer's recovery to direct damages and disclaims responsibility for consequential damages. Shortly thereafter as he is driving on the new tires, one of them blows out because, let us say, there is a defect in its manufacture. As a result of the blowout, the driver loses control of his car and crashes into a storefront, suffering severe injuries and causing great damage to the store. The direct damages of the defective tire are the costs of replacing it with a new tire. The consequential damages of the defective tire—those costs that arose as a *consequence* of the defect—are the driver's injuries to himself and his car and the damage to the store. By the assumed terms of the warranty, the tire manufacturer is not liable for these latter costs.

this savings on inventory costs to his customers by assuming responsibility for this source of loss from the use of his product.

The second substantive term of the standard warranty typically limits the buyer to a period of six months to a year (or, as in new car warranties, to a fixed number of miles or years) within which warranty claims can be brought and also limits the seller's obligation to the repair or replacement of defective parts. How does the comparative advantage theory explain these remedy limitations? First, recognize that the seller has an incentive to preserve good will and a good reputation among consumers. Such a reputation is likely to increase sales and, therefore, profits. At the same time, however, the seller wishes to minimize the number of warranty claims, either by making his product defect-free or by screening out spurious claims. The time limitation is set so that most of the claims brought within that period are likely to be for defects due to the seller's defective workmanship or materials. Thus, those defects discovered only after the warranty period has expired are likely to be ones resulting from the *buyer's* misuse or from greater-than-average wear and tear. Clearly, consumers have a comparative advantage over sellers in minimizing losses arising from misuse, and on the comparative advantage principle it therefore makes good economic sense to assign liabilities regarding the timing of warranty claims between the two parties in the manner that the standard warranty adopts. To the extent that this differentiation is accurate, the seller minimizes the number of spurious warranty claims and can, therefore, offer his product at a lower price than would be the case if he were not able to distinguish defectively produced from defectively used products in this way.

The third substantive term of the standard warranty is closer to the nub of the products liability issue. That is the term excluding the seller's liability for *consequential* damages arising from product failure. The law today is suspicious of this warranty term, but the comparative advantage theory suggests that the term may be an efficient assignment of risk from product loss. The reason is that buyers are, in general, better able than are manufacturers to estimate both the probability of suffering consequential damages and their extent. For example, only the buyer knows whether he intends to drive his car recklessly or under the influence of alcohol and, in either of those cases, to suffer extraordinarily large losses in the event of product failure. Moreover, the buyer is in a better position to estimate his lost earnings in the event he is incapacitated by an accident that is the consequence of product failure. He knows whether he is a corporate executive or an unemployed hod carrier; he knows better than the seller whether he has familial obligations that must be met in the event of an accident. For all of these reasons, buyers can make more accurate estimates of the probability and extent of consequential damages than can sellers. As a result, buyers can, in general, minimize or insure against these losses at lower cost than can sellers. This means that it is generally in the interests of both parties for consumers rather than sellers to bear responsibility for the consequential losses due to product failure.

One way to see the efficiency of this standard warranty term is to demonstrate that inefficiencies would result if the term were disallowed: this would be the case, for example, if the law required sellers to compensate their customers for consequential damages arising from product defects. Under that alternative rule, sellers would include in the cost of their merchandise an implicit insurance premium for underwriting the consequential damages arising from product failure. But because sellers' knowledge of their customers' likely losses from product failure is less than complete, this insurance premium will have to be high enough to cover the worst imaginable cases. The total price of merchandise will be higher than if the law allowed sellers to disclaim liability for consequential damages. Thus, under the standard warranty term excluding liability for consequential damages, sellers would be able to reduce the price that they charge for their output. Customers who had little risk of extraordinary losses would pay a much lower price for the commodity. Customers who faced high consequential losses from product defects would have to take their own steps to prevent losses or to insure against those losses. For example, if a business customer faces large lost profits from a defective machine tool, he can purchase enough business-interruption insurance to cover that risk. If the buyer is a consumer whose lost earnings or familial obligations would be large in the event of a product defect that hospitalized him, he can purchase the proper amount of medical and disability insurance.

The weight of the empirical evidence favors the comparative advantage theory of the standard warranty's terms. Nonetheless, it is worth mentioning two alternative hypotheses about the standard warranty. The first of these alternatives has greatly influenced modern product liability law's rejection of a warranty-based solution to the problem of product-related harms. The second alternative has not yet been fully researched but is a sophisticated critique of the comparative advantage theory.

A popular explanation for these standard warranty terms is that the seller has greater bargaining power than does the buyer, and, therefore, *imposes* these terms on the buyer. The implication is that the terms of the standard warranty are one-sidedly in favor of the seller and impose an unwanted cost on the buyer. The consumer is said to be the victim of a situational monopoly in which he must accept what to him are undesirable terms solely in order to get his hands on the underlying commodity. Note that if the warrantor's market is competitive, this hypothesis is unacceptable.

A different explanation of the standard warranty terms focuses on the fact that most consumers do not read the fine print on a contract of sale. As a result, the typical consumer has little idea of what his rights and obligations relative to product defects are. Rather, the explanation continues, most consumers have some vague notion that they are protected against major defects in a product. (For the extent to which legislative action has provided that protection, see the box entitled "Statutory Regulation of Warranty Terms.") This fact, the argument goes, allows producers to impose one-sided terms on consumers. This hypothesis may be related to the criticisms of the

Statutory Regulation of Warranty Terms

The view that consumers may easily be bamboozled by the terms of warranties has given rise to federal regulation of certain warranty terms in the Magnuson-Moss Warranty Act, passed by Congress in the mid-1970s. The Act imposes restrictions on a seller's ability to disclaim implied warranties and also imposes certain labeling and disclosure requirements.

Under the Magnuson-Moss Warranty Act any firm offering a written warranty or service contract to consumers is forbidden to disclaim any of the legally implied warranties, such as that of merchantability. Recall that an implied warranty of merchantability holds that the product is "fit for the ordinary purposes for which such goods are used." (The Uniform Commercial Code allows the seller to disclaim the implied warranty of merchantability.) However, the Act does allow the manufacturer, under certain circumstances, to limit the time period during which the implied warranties are to run so long as the written warranty makes this limitation clear and easily understood.

The labeling and disclosure requirements of the Act impose three principal restrictions on a firm's written warranty:

1. The firm must declare and clearly post whether the warranty is a "full warranty" or a "limited warranty." A full warranty is much more comprehensive and must contain certain terms. For example, the full warranty cannot allow the exclusion or limitation of consequential damages; the manufacturer must agree to remedy defects promptly and without charge; a defective product must be replaced or a refund given within a certain time period after several attempts to repair the defect; and there can be no time limitations on implied warranties.
2. The written warranty must "fully and conspicuously disclose in simple and readily understood language the terms and conditions [of the warranty.]"
3. The warrantor must make the warranty available to the consumer before the product is sold.

To the extent that these restrictions improve the efficiency of the information about warranty terms transmitted between sellers and consumers, the Magnuson-Moss Warranty Act should improve the ability of warranties to allocate risk. However, to the extent that the Act restricts the range of warranty terms to a set that is less preferrable to consumers and sellers, it imposes inefficiencies on the exchange process.

expected utility model we mentioned above. Recall that empirical evidence shows that people do not estimate low-probability events well; they tend to under-estimate the probability of those contingencies and, as a result, to take too little precaution or to under-insure against them. If product failure (especially that causing large losses) is rare, consumers may under-estimate their probability and may, therefore, agree to inefficient warranty terms. This is a potentially important alternative to the comparative advantage theory of the standard warranty, but there is not yet sufficient evidence to justify its acceptance.

The comparative advantage theory of the consumer product warranty has implications beyond the acceptance of that theory over the alternatives. It also suggests that products liability law should draw upon contract principles, not just torts, to achieve efficiency. As a result, the older common law, by basing recovery for product-related harms on contract principles through the requirement of privity, may have had strengths that are not generally appreciated today.

> **Question 9.20:** Suppose that a consumer purchased a wagon wheel from a retail merchant and that the contract of sale contained an express waiver of the manufacturer's liability for consequential damages arising from the wheel's failure. Suppose the wheel fails, causing the wagon to swerve and crash into an oncoming horseman. The wagon owner is injured but cannot recover under the old theory from the wheel's manufacturer. But what about the horseman? Under the old theory, may he recover from the manufacturer? From the wagon owner?

B. From Privity to Negligence to Strict Liability

The famous *MacPherson* decision in 1916 ended the privity requirement. Thereafter, products liability became a subset of tort law rather than of contract law. Specifically, the negligence rule was applied to cases of product-related injuries for the next half century. A defendant manufacturer or retailer could be held liable for the injuries resulting from the plaintiff's use of his product if the manufacturer was at fault, and, typically, fault was found if the manufacturer had failed to include reasonable safety features or warnings of danger.

At the same time that the negligence rule for product-related harms was being elaborated, there were two other important trends in the law of products liability. First, warranty terms—particularly those providing for exclusion of liability for consequential damages—continued to exist and to be important. This meant that contract and tort principles for dealing with injuries arising from product use co-existed, causing a certain amount of confusion. This confusion came to an end toward the end of this second period in the evolution of products liability law in the highly influential case of *Henningsen v. Bloomfield Motors, Inc.*, 32 N.J. 358, 161 A.2d 69 (1960). Mr. Henningsen had purchased a new Plymouth from the defendant retailer and then had given the car to his wife as a gift. The contract of sale with the retailer and manufacturer contained an express limitation of liability of the defendants to the *original purchaser*, i.e., Mr. Henningsen, and only for the repair or replacement of defective parts within 90 days or 4000 miles. The seller expressly waived liability for consequential damages. Well within the time limitation, Mrs. Henningsen, the plaintiff, was driving the car when the steering mechanism failed, causing the car to crash and injuring her. She sued the retailer and manufacturer, and the New Jersey Supreme Court held for her: "We are convinced that the cause of justice in this area of the law can be served only by recognizing that [Mrs. Henningsen] is . . . a person who, in the reasonable contemplation of the parties to the warranty, might be expected to become a user of the automobile. Accordingly, her lack of privity does not stand in the way of prosecution of the injury suit against the defendant Chrysler."

> **Question 9.21:** Does the comparative advantage theory offer a reason why both the purchaser and the retailer and manufacturer benefit from the sort of warranty term seen in *Henningsen* in which the terms of the warranty apply only to the *original purchaser* and not to someone to whom he loans the car, nor to someone who steals the car, nor to another family member?

The second great development of the half century after *MacPherson* was the gradual replacement in products liability law of the tort liability standard of negligence with that of strict liability. The process was relatively gradual but was completed by 1965 when the Second Restatement of Torts explicitly accepted strict products liability. One of the first important decisions proposing strict liability for all product-related injuries was a concurring opinion by Justice Traynor of the California Supreme Court in a 1944 case involving an exploding Coke bottle. The relevant parts of the opinion speak eloquently for a strict liability standard.

Escola v. Coca-Cola Bottling Co., 24 Cal. 2d 453, 150 P.2d 436 (1944).

[The plaintiff was a waitress in a restaurant. While she was placing bottles of Coca-Cola into the restaurant's refrigerator, one of them exploded in her hand, causing her to be severely injured. The plaintiff alleged that the defendant had been negligent in selling "bottles containing said beverage which on account of excessive pressure of gas or by reason of some defect in the bottle was dangerous . . . and likely to explode." However, she could not show any specific acts of negligence on the part of the defendant and announced to the court that she relied on the doctrine of *res ipsa loquitur* exclusively. That doctrine—literally, "the thing speaks for itself"—is invoked where the action of the defendant is so obviously faulty that simply pointing out the action is proof enough of fault. Here the plaintiff uses *res ipsa loquitur* because only a defective Coke bottle will explode. The California Supreme Court, speaking through Gibson, C.J., affirmed the judgment for the plaintiff below. What has come to be famous is the following concurring opinion by Justice Traynor.]

TRAYNOR, J. I concur in the judgment, but I believe the manufacturer's negligence should no longer be singled out as the basis of a plaintiff's right to recover in cases like the present one. In my opinion it should now be recognized that a manufacturer incurs an absolute liability when an article that he has placed on the market, knowing that it is to be used without inspection, proves to have a defect that causes injury to human beings. *MacPherson v. Buick Motor Co.* established the principle, recognized by this court, that irrespective of privity of contact, the manufacturer is responsible for an injury caused by such an article to any person who comes in lawful contact with it. . . .

Even if there is no negligence, however, public policy demands that responsibility be fixed wherever it will most effectively reduce the hazards to life and health inherent in defective products that reach the market. It is evident that the manufacturer can anticipate some hazards and guard against the recurrence of others, as the public cannot. Those who suffer injury from defective products are unprepared to meet its consequences. The cost of an injury and the loss of time or health may be an overwhelming misfortune to the person injured and a needless one, for the risk of injury can be insured by the manufacturer and distributed among the public as a cost of doing business. It is to the public interest to discourage the marketing of products having defects that are a menace to the public. If such products nevertheless find their way into the market it is to the public interest to place the responsibility for whatever injury they may cause upon the manufacturer, who, even if he is not negligent in the manufacture of the product, is responsible for its reaching the market. However intermittently such injuries may occur and however haphazardly they may strike, the risk of their occurrence is a constant risk and a general one. Against such a risk there should be general and constant protection and the manufacturer is best suited to afford such protection. . . .

The liability of the manufacturer to an immediate buyer injured by a defective product follows without proof of negligence from the implied warranty of safety attending the sale. Ordinarily, however, the immediate buyer is a dealer who does not intend to use the product himself, and if the warranty of safety is to serve the purpose of protecting health and safety it must give rights to others than the dealer. In the words of Judge Cardozo in the *MacPherson* case: "The dealer was indeed the one person of whom it might be said with some approach to certainty that by him the car would not be used. Yet, the defendant would have us say that he was the one person whom it was under a legal duty to protect. The law does not lead us to so inconsequent a solution." . . . Judge Cardozo's reasoning recognized the injured person as the real party in interest and effectively disposed of the theory that the liability of the manufacturer incurred by his warranty should apply only to the immediate purchaser. It thus paves the way for a standard of liability that would make the manufacturer guarantee the safety of his product even when there is no negligence.

As handicrafts have been replaced by mass production with its great markets and transportation facilities, the close relationship between the producer and consumer of a product has been altered. Manufacturing processes, frequently valuable secrets, are ordinarily either inaccessible to or beyond the ken of the general public. The consumer no longer has means or skill enough to investigate for himself the soundness of a product, even when it is not contained in a sealed package, and his erstwhile vigilance has been lulled by the steady efforts of manufacturers to build up confidence by advertising and marketing devices such as trade-marks... Consumers no longer approach products warily but accept them on faith, relying on the reputation of the manufacturer or the trade-mark... Manufacturers have sought to justify that faith by increasingly high standards of inspection and a readiness to make good on defective products by way of replacements and refunds... The manufacturer's obligation to the consumer must keep pace with the changing relationship between them....

The manufacturer's liability should, of course, be defined in terms of the safety of the product in normal and proper use, and should not extend to injuries that cannot be traced to the product as it reaches the market.

Note that there are three important and separate arguments being made here for strict liability over negligence for product-related harms:

1. **Unilateral precaution.** Justice Traynor suggests that the manufacturer is nearly always in a better position to take precaution against losses arising from product failure.
2. **Risk- or loss-spreading.** The manufacturer can pass on the costs of providing an insurance contract with his product or of compensating those harmed through the use of his product much more easily than can the typical individual victim. The increase in the unit cost of the product would be pennies.
3. **Lower administration costs.** Justice Traynor notes that the burden on the plaintiff in a strict liability action—to show legal causation by a preponderance of the evidence—is much less than in a negligence action—to show legal causation *and* fault by a preponderance of the evidence.

These three arguments have always formed the theoretical basis for strict products liability and for the move toward absolute liability that we will discuss shortly. At this point, you should begin to think whether these three arguments square with the efficiency analysis of the previous chapter of situations in which strict liability is more efficient than alternative liability standards.

C. Strict Products Liability and the Trend Toward Absolute Liability

Justice Traynor's concurring opinion in *Escola* was unusually forward-looking. It would be another two decades before strict products liability became the rule. The beginning of the third and present period in the development of products liability law may be dated from the publication of section 402A of the Second Restatement of Torts (1965) by the American Law Institute. That section, and a caveat, are as follows:

Sec. 402A. SPECIAL LIABILITY OF SELLER OF PRODUCT FOR PHYSICAL HARM TO USER OR CONSUMER

(1) One who sells any product in a defective condition unreasonably dangerous to the user or consumer or to his property is subject to liability for physical harm thereby caused to the ultimate user or consumer, or to his property, if

    (a) the seller is engaged in the business of selling such a product, and

    (b) it is expected to and does reach the user or consumer without substantial change in the condition in which it is sold.

(2) The rule stated in Subsection (1) applies although

    (a) the seller has exercised all possible care in the preparation and sale of his product, and

    (b) the user or consumer has not bought the product from or entered into any contractual relation with the seller.

CAVEAT:

The [American Law] Institute expresses no opinion as to whether the rules stated in this Section may not apply

  (1) to harm to persons other than users or consumers;

  (2) to the seller of a product expected to be processed or otherwise substantially changed before it reaches the user or consumer; or

  (3) to the seller of a component part of a product to be assembled.

In the two decades since the Second Restatement strict products liability has become the norm. For a defendant manufacturer to be held liable under this form of strict liability, his product must be determined to be *defective*. A defect can take three different forms: (1) the defect may have occurred in the *manufacturing* process, as would be the case if a bolt were left out of a lawnmower during its assembly, causing a piece of the mower to fly off and injure a user; (2) the defect may have occurred in the *design* of the product, as was alleged against the Ford Motor Company's design of the Pinto gas tank; and (3) the defect may consist of the manufacturer's *failure to warn* of dangers in the use of the product.

The determination of whether a certain action or product is defective is often made in the same way that fault is determined in a negligence action, especially where the defect is in design rather than manufacture. Thus, there is some dispute about whether strict products liability is really strict liability at all or a special version of the negligence rule applied only to product-related harms. For our purposes, how we classify the products liability standard is not as important as examining how it complies with the economic analysis of various liability standards of the previous chapter. Let us now turn to that issue.

Recall that our discussion of negligence and strict liability suggested that a central issue in determining which standard is more efficient in a given circumstance is whether precaution for reducing the likelihood and severity of the accident is unilateral or bilateral. If it is bilateral—that is, if both parties can take precautionary action to reduce the probability and severity of an accident—then a form of the negligence rule is the appropriate standard. If precaution is unilateral—that is, if only the injurer can be looked to for actions to reduce the probability and severity of an accident—then strict liability is the appropriate liability standard. If it were to be based on this economic analysis, what would modern products liability law look like?

The more efficient standard would seem to be strict liability. This is because most instances of product-related harms are those in which precaution lies unilaterally with the manufacturer. It is he who is in control of the design of the product, of the manufacturing process, and it is he who is most likely to be aware of any special dangers that the product presents and, therefore, can most efficiently convey information about those dangers through warnings.

However, there are defenses available under strict liability that also form a part of the efficiency analysis. In a products liability action there used to be two such defenses: *assumption of the risk* and *product misuse.* A defendant manufacturer who is otherwise strictly liable for harms arising from the use of his product may escape liability by a convincing demonstration that the plaintiff voluntarily assumed the risk of such injury or has misused the product in a way for which it was obviously not designed or intended. There are many complex legal issues involved in determining whether someone has voluntarily assumed a risk or misused a product. For an efficiency analysis of products liability, the importance of these defenses is that they encourage the efficient allocation of risk of loss from product-related injuries between the consumer and manufacturer. In fact, the defenses should achieve the same sort of allocation of risk between consumer and manufacturer as would be reached in warranty terms reached by exchange in a competitive market. Thus, just as the standard warranty term would exclude manufacturer's responsibility for repairing a product that the consumer had misused, so, the argument goes, should strict liability exclude recovery for harms arising from the plaintiff's misuse of the product. For example, if a consumer picks up his lawnmower to use it to trim his hedge, then he has either employed the product in a use for which it was never intended or has voluntarily assumed the risk that harm will come to him from this misuse. The lawnmower manufacturer would almost surely not have assumed liability in a warranty for injuries resulting from this misuse. Most consumers would not use his product in that way and would willingly have agreed to a warranty term that allocated responsibility to them for losses arising from this misuse. However, if, for whatever reason, the lawnmower manufacturer were not allowed to exclude liability for consumer misuse or for voluntarily assumed risk in a warranty, he would be forced to write an insurance policy for each of his consumers for these losses. To cover the cost of this insurance policy, the manufacturer would have to raise his product price in order to cover the costs of the insurance policy. The difficulty with this consequence of not allowing consumer and manufacturer to allocate risk in an efficient way is that the price of the product is higher than it need be for almost all the product's consumers. Those who had no intention of misusing the product must purchase something, the insurance policy, to which they attach very little value. They might, therefore, substitute away from the product in favor of a different product. Even those who may misuse the product are probably paying more for the product plus insurance than they would if they were aware of the possibility of misuse and purchased insurance against loss from a specialist in underwriting such policies. Neither of these situations is efficient.

The conclusion we draw is that strict liability with the defenses of assumption of the risk and product misuse is an efficient standard for minimizing the social costs of product-related injuries.

The trend in modern products liability law is, however, toward a less efficient standard: absolute liability, or what is sometimes called "enterprise liability." Under that theory manufacturers would be held liable for almost every injury resulting from the use of their outputs. Indications that products liability is moving in that direction come from recent trends in the interpretation of the elements of strict products liability actions by prominent courts. Consider, for example, a recent decision by the New Jersey Supreme Court. In *Beshada v. Johns-Manville Prods. Corp.,* 90 N.J. 191, 447 A.2d 539 (1982), the defendant asbestos manufacturer was held liable for having failed to warn of the dangers of asbestos even though the Court found that those dangers were not known to science at the time the duty to warn was breached. The implication of this ruling is that the failure to warn of dangers that cannot be known will constitute a defective warning. Because this implies that there is almost no way to avoid liability, the *Beshada* decision may be taken as a step toward manufacturers' absolute liability.

There have been other indications of this trend. In many important jurisdictions the defense that the consumer assumed the risk of loss from product use has been greatly curtailed, and in a few states it is not available at all. Similarly, the defense of product misuse has been weakened. In Iowa the Supreme Court has held that consumer misuse is no longer available as a defense in a strict products liability action. In other jurisdictions consumer misuse has become so pale a defense that manufacturers are held liable if they have not reasonably foreseen consumer misuse of their products. For example, since it is reasonably foreseeable that someone will drive an automobile at very high speed while drunk and that a crash in which the car rolls over may result, a manufacturer may be held liable for not providing safety precautions that will minimize losses in the event of this reasonably foreseeable consumer misuse. (See the box entitled "Two Theories of the Evolution of Products Liability Law" on why products liability has evolved as it has.)

D. An Optional Case Study: The Economics of the Duty to Warn[38]

This section presents a detailed economic analysis of one of the possible defects in a products liability action: failure to warn the user of dangers.

Some beneficial products, such as dynamite and some pesticides, are inherently dangerous. When a product is inherently dangerous, the law imposes upon the manufacturer a duty to warn those who use the product. For purposes of theory, the warning issued by the manufacturer of an inherently dangerous product can be thought of as a statement concerning the ranking of the product along a single dimension of product safety.

A reasonable consumer will not use a product unless the expected benefits of use outweigh the inherent risks. The manufacturer's warning is one of the consumer's sources of information concerning the product's dangerousness. When warnings are effective, a stronger warning causes fewer consumers to buy the product and those who do take more precaution; conversely, a weaker warning causes more consumers to use the product and to take less precaution. Consequently, the accident costs caused by an inherently dangerous product will diminish with the strength of the warning and a reasonable warning will avert some, but not all, harm to consumers.

This relationship between the warning and accident losses is depicted in Figure 9.5. In this figure the inherent dangerousness of the product is constant, so that the extent of accident losses is determined by the extent of the product's use and the care with which it is used, which in turn depend upon the strength of the warning. The strength of the warning is shown on the horizontal axis, and the accident costs are shown on the vertical axis. Moving to the right, accident costs rise as the warning becomes weaker.[39]

A possible legal rule is to hold the manufacturer liable for the harm caused by inadequate warnings. For purposes of illustration, assume that x^* in Figure 9.5 represents the ideal warning. (We postpone until later a discussion of the standard with respect to which x^* is ideal.) If the manufacturer issues this warning, the accident costs that lie to the right of x^*, labeled areas B_1 and B_2, will be averted. In contrast, an ideal warning will not avert the accident costs that lie to the left of x^*, labeled area A in Figure 9.5. Averting the accident costs corresponding to area A would require a warning that is too strong because it drives away customers who ideally should use the good. Going to the opposite extreme, a warning like $\bar{x}$ is too weak because it attracts consumers who ideally should not use the good, and this results in excessive injuries, indicated by area B_1.

A rule that holds sellers liable for accidents attributable to a lax warning can be described in either of two ways. First, a lax warning can be described

---

[38]This section is based on Cooter, *Defective Warnings, Remote Causes, and Bankruptcy: Comment on Schwartz,* 14 J. LEGAL STUD. 727 (1985).

[39]Technically, the height of the curve in Figure 9.5 indicates the marginal loss from accidents as the warning varies, and the area under the curve indicates the total losses from accidents.

Two Theories of the Evolution
of Products Liability Law

A natural question to ask of products liability law is why it has evolved in the way it has. Has the change from contract principles to tort and within this century from negligence to strict liability and recently to enterprise liability been a natural evolution from a confused, inaccurate standard toward a better, more coherent standard? Or is the evolution a response to changing objective economic circumstances? Or has the evolution away from contract principles and more recently away from strict products liability been a mistake?

Two recent articles provide important insights into these questions. Professor Priest of the Yale Law School has contended that the evolution of enterprise liability is the result of the assiduous promotion of a mistaken theory of products liability by a few prominent legal scholars. (George L. Priest, *The Invention of Enterprise Liability: A Critical History of the Intellectual Foundations of Modern Tort Law*, 14 J. LEGAL STUD. 461 (1985).) Beginning in the 1940s these scholars convinced the profession that strict products liability was preferable to any alternative method of dealing with product-related injuries for three reasons: (1) manufacturers possessed market power that gave them bargaining power over consumers; this power allowed manufacturers to dictate unfair terms in warranties and led to under-investment in product safety technology; (2) manufacturers are always better placed than are consumers to spread the losses from product-related injuries; and (3) because manufacturers are generally better placed than are consumers to minimize the losses from product accidents, strict liability will induce manufacturers to internalize the expected costs from product accidents and, therefore, to invest in precaution and in research into superior technology. Professor Priest believes that the first two of these premises are mistaken, a conclusion supported by our examination of the economics of products liability law above. Moreover, Professor Priest argues that these mistaken views have been used to justify converting products liability actions into a system whose principal aim is to ensure that victims of product-related injuries are compensated, without much regard for the incentive effects for precaution and insurance created by the results.

as a negligent act: the failure of the manufacturer to observe his duty to warn. Second, a lax warning can be described as a defective consumer product: the producer is held strictly liable for the injuries caused by the warning's inadequacy. The two verbal formulations are materially equivalent because the scope of responsibility and the extent of liability are the same: the manufacturer is only responsible when the warning is too weak and his liability is limited to the harm that an ideal warning would have averted.

A completely different view of the evolution of products liability law is that of Professor Landes of the University of Chicago Law School and Judge Posner of the United States Court of Appeals for the Seventh Circuit. (William M. Landes & Richard A. Posner, *A Positive Economic Analysis of Products Liability,* 14 J. LEGAL STUD. 529 (1985).) They contend that the prevailing view that modern products liability law is inefficient is incorrect and that the evolution from contract to negligence to strict liability is, in general, efficient. (They do not contend that the movement toward absolute liability is efficient.) Landes and Posner stress that they are not suggesting that each individual decision is economically sound, but rather that the broad trends of products liability law of the last century are economically sound. The change in the doctrinal basis of the law of product-related injuries may be explained, they contend, by changing underlying economic variables. For example, the increasing mechanization and complexity of products raised the costs to consumers of informing themselves about the risks associated with product use. This development meant that the relative costs of manufacturer *versus* consumer insurance or precaution against losses from product failure shifted in favor of manufacturers always being the cheaper insurer or provider of safety. Similarly, the increasing urbanization of American society physically separated manufacturers from consumers, making the bargaining costs of a contractual solution (through warranties) to the problem of allocating the risk of loss from product failure prohibitively high. Landes and Posner confronted this hypothesis with data in several empirical tests. For example, they tested the hypothesis that the year in which a state abandoned the privity requirement was a function of the rate of urbanization in the state, the per capita income of its citizens, the stock of automobiles, and other social, economic, and demographic factors that are taken to be related to product complexity. Their hypothesis was that the greater the rate of urbanization, the greater the per capita income in the state, and the greater the product complexity, the earlier the state would abandon the privity requirement. They found that only urbanization was a significant determinant of the date at which privity was dropped.

Thus, the warning $\bar{x}$ in Figure 9.5 can be described as negligent or as defective, but in either case liability corresponds to the area B_1, representing the injuries that the warning x^* would have averted.

Another question of language concerns whether to describe the rule portrayed in the figure as limiting liability to harms that are proximately caused by lax warnings or as including remotely caused harms. The harms represented by B_1 can be called "proximate" because an adequate warning would

Figure 9.5 Manufacturer's Warning and Accident Severity

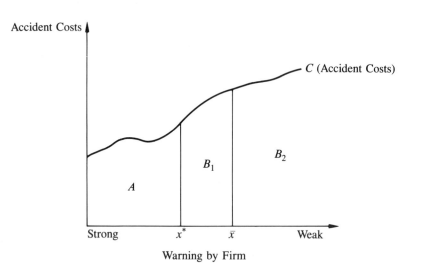

The line labeled C (Accident Costs) shows that accident costs rise as the warning becomes weaker. Suppose that x^* represents the ideal (the most efficient) warning. If the manufacturer issues a warning of that strength, the accident costs labeled B_1 and B_2 will be averted, but accident costs in the amount A will occur. A stronger warning would be inefficient because, although it would avert more accident costs, it would do so at the high cost of driving away customers who should, ideally, use the product. A weaker warning, like $\bar{x}$, would be inefficient because it would attract consumers who ideally should not use the good with the result that accident costs increase by B_1.

---

have averted them, whereas the harms represented by A can be called "remote" because they would occur even if the warning were adequate. Thus, the rule of liability represented by the figure may be taken to restrict liability to harms proximately caused by lax warnings.

1. Ex Ante and Ex Post Standards   So far we have discussed the ideal warning x^* as if it were known by the manufacturer. In reality, an investment of costly resources is usually required to discover the inherent dangers of a product. The level of information about the product's dangers is efficient when the expected social benefit from further investment in research equals its cost. Sometimes the expected social benefit from further research is different from the actual benefit, as discerned after the passage of time. To illustrate, it is now clear that the actual benefit from research on the connection between asbestos and various illnesses was larger than most experts believed forty years ago. Consequently, there is a distinction between *ex ante* efficient research, which appeared optimal relative to what was known at the time, and *ex post* efficient research, which proved optimal relative to subsequently discovered facts.

A similar distinction can be made for warnings: a warning is *ex ante* efficient if it is optimal relative to the information obtained from an *ex ante* efficient level of research; a warning is *ex post* efficient if it is optimal relative to the information obtained from *ex post* efficient research. Thus, an *ex ante* efficient warning appears best prospectively, whereas an *ex post* efficient warning proves best retrospectively. To illustrate by the preceding figure, interpret $\bar{x}$ as the *ex ante* efficient warning and interpret x^* as the *ex post* efficient warning, in which case B_1 represents the accident costs caused by the prospectively best warning and averted by the retrospectively best warning.

For purposes of assigning liability, the *ex ante* and *ex post* standards for the adequacy of warnings are different, but, regardless of which standard is adopted, negligence and strict liability are materially equivalent verbal formulations. Liability for the harm caused by an *ex ante* [*ex post*] unreasonable warning can be described as strict liability for the harm caused by an *ex ante* [*ex post*] defective warning.

This is not to say that there is nothing in a name. Negligence may carry with it a higher burden of proof than strict liability. In addition, an allegation of negligence carries with it imputations of fault that are not present under strict liability. In an area in which conscious choice is present, a finding of fault becomes the opening wedge for punitive damages. Moreover, finding fault in a warning judged by an *ex post* standard amounts to blaming a manufacturer for not knowing the future. (Recall the *Beshada* opinion noted above.) Hindsight may be an exact science, but prophecy is religion. If courts insist upon holding manufacturers liable for being bad prophets, they ought not to be blamed for it, so the phrase "*ex post* defective warning" should be used instead of "*ex post* negligent warning".

2. Efficiency, Absolute Liability, and Liability for Inadequate Warnings

The preceding section described a rule of liability for the consequences of inadequate warnings. Alternatively, the manufacturer might be held absolutely liable for all the harm caused by the use of his product, regardless of the warning that he gives to buyers. We will now show that under plausible assumptions a rule of liability for inadequate warnings is more efficient than a rule of absolute liability. Specifically, in order for a rule of absolute liability to induce efficient warnings, producer's liability and victim's compensation both must be perfect. In contrast, a rule of liability for inadequate warnings induces efficient warnings if the standard of adequacy is correctly set, even though liability and compensation are imperfect. Proving these propositions requires a detailed explanation of consumer behavior, producer behavior, and efficiency.

a. Consumer Behavior When a consumer buys an inherently dangerous good, he pays a price to obtain it, he enjoys its intrinsic value, and he may make expenditures on safety precautions when using it. Insofar as the intrinsic value exceeds the price and the cost of precaution, the buyer enjoys an immediate net benefit from the transaction. However, he exposes himself to the risk of consequential losses because he may be injured by the product. In the event of injury, he may receive damages. To the extent that the damages do not fully compensate him, there is risk of uncompensated harm. Using economic jargon, the elements of value affecting consumers are:

consumer = willingness-to-pay − price − precaution − risk of uncompensated
surplus   harm

$$\underbrace{\hspace{5.5cm}}_{\substack{\text{immediate}\\\text{net benefits}}} \qquad \underbrace{\hspace{2.5cm}}_{\text{risk}}$$

Since potential consumers differ according to their propensity to be harmed and according to their ability to benefit from the good, they can be ranked according to the extent of the anticipated consumer surplus from buying the good. To aid in visualizing this point, assume that each consumer either buys exactly one unit of the good or does not buy any of it. By definition, the marginal consumer is indifferent between buying the good and not buying it, so his expected consumer surplus is nil, or, equivalently, his immediate net benefits equal his perceived risk. The marginal consumer represents the tipping point between users and nonusers. Every consumer ranked above the marginal consumer buys the good because he expects to enjoy positive surplus, and every consumer ranked below the marginal consumer does not buy it because he would expect negative surplus.

If consumers had perfect information about the inherent dangers of the product, perceived risk would equal actual risk. However, instead of having perfect information, consumer beliefs about risk are influenced by the manufacturer's warning. If the warning is strong, a consumer will not buy unless his immediate net benefits from use are high relative to his propensity to be harmed. Thus, the strength of the manufacturer's warning affects how far down in the ranking of consumers by immediate net benefits it is necessary to go before coming to the marginal buyer. The weaker the warning, the more consumers buy the good and the lower are the immediate net benefits of the marginal consumer, as represented by line B_1 in Figure 9.6.[40]

b. Behavior of Manufacturers Besides the consumer's surplus, the sale of the product generates profits for manufacturers. A manufacturer's immediate profit equals the difference between the revenue from sales and the cost of production. A weaker warning by the firm attracts more buyers, which increases immediate profits, as represented in Figure 9.6 by line

---

[40]The height of the line B_1 indicates the immediate net benefits enjoyed by the marginal consumer at different levels of the warning, and the area under the curve (integral) indicates their sum. The downward slope of the curve reflects the fact that the immediate net benefits of the marginal buyer probably diminish as the warning becomes weaker, but the propositions explained in the text are true even if it slopes up.

Figure 9.6 Determining the Ideal Manufacturer's Warning

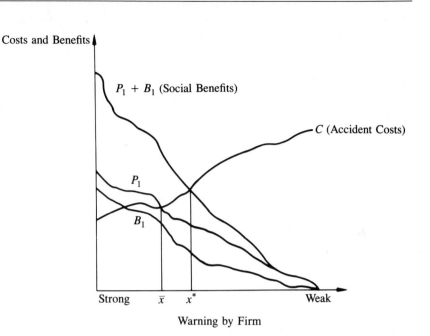

Costs and Benefits

$P_1 + B_1$ (Social Benefits)

C (Accident Costs)

P_1

B_1

Strong $\bar{x}$ x^* Weak

Warning by Firm

The curve labeled C (Accident Costs) indicates that as the firm's warning becomes weaker, the accident costs increase. The downward-sloping curve labeled P_1 represents the firm's net profits as a function of the strength of the warning: a weaker warning increases sales and, therefore, profits but may increase tort liability, which must be subtracted from the profits from increased sales to get net profits. The downward-sloping curve labeled B_1 indicates the immediate net benefits of purchasing the product as a function of the strength of the warning: a weaker warning attracts more consumers with the marginal consumer getting less and less immediate benefit from consuming the product. The highest downward-sloping line, labeled "$P_1 + B_1$ (Social Benefits)," is the vertical sum of P_1 and B_1. The ideal warning, x^*, is the one for which the marginal accident costs are equal to the marginal social benefits. Note that the warning $\bar{x}$, which is determined where the marginal accident costs equal the marginal *private* benefits (the firm's marginal profit), is, socially speaking, too strong.

P_1.[41] However, additional sales may give rise to additional tort liability, which must be netted out of immediate profits to give total profits:

total profits = revenue − production cost − damages

immediate profits   liability

A profit-maximizing firm will choose its warning by balancing immediate profits against liability; specifically, the warning is issued at the point which the marginal immediate profit equals the marginal liability.

---

[41]The height of P_1 indicates the marginal value of immediate profits and the area under the curve (integral) indicates the sum of immediate profits.

 c. Efficient Warnings and Absolute Liability   The social benefits from the production and sale of the good equal the sum of the consumer's immediate net benefits and the manufacturer's immediate profits, or, graphically, $(B_1 + P_1)$ in Figure 9.6. Against these social benefits must be balanced the social costs of accidents indicated by line C in the figure. Starting with a strong warning, efficiency requires weakening it until the social benefits curve $(B_1 + P_1)$ intersects the accident cost curve C, which yields the efficient warning denoted x^*.

 An efficient liability rule causes the profit-maximizing warning to equal the socially efficient warning. To compare the efficiency of the rule of absolute liability and the rule of liability for inadequate warnings, we need to introduce two technical terms. "Perfect liability" means that the damages paid by the injurer exactly equal the full cost of the harm suffered by the victim. If the damages equal the full cost of the harm suffered by the victim, but the victim must use part of the damages to pay lawyers and court costs, perfect liability results in under-compensation. Consequently, we use the term "perfect compensation" to mean that the injured consumer receives damages that exactly make him whole. We will show that absolute liability results in inefficient warnings unless there is both perfect liability and perfect compensation, whereas a rule of liability for inadequate warnings can result in efficient warnings even though liability and compensation are both imperfect.

 If the manufacturer is absolutely liable and if liability is perfect, the liability cost curve in Figure 9.6 will be identical to the accident cost curve. Thus, the manufacturer will find the profit-maximizing warning by equating immediate profits and accident costs (his liability) at the margin, which occurs at $\bar{x}$ in the figure. Since $\bar{x} < x^*$, the profit-maximizing warning is stronger than the efficient warning.

 It is not hard to see why absolute liability results in warnings that are too strong. Recall that social benefits equal the sum of manufacturer's immediate profit and consumer's immediate net benefits. In choosing the warning, the manufacturer looks to his profits, not to the effects upon consumers. Consequently, for the manufacturer's self-interested behavior to be socially efficient, the marginal consumer's immediate net benefits must be nil, so that social benefits and manufacturer's immediate profits are equal at the margin. As already explained, the marginal consumer equates the immediate net benefits to the risk of uncompensated harm, so the marginal consumer's immediate net benefits will be nil if there is no risk of uncompensated harm. For inherently dangerous products, there is no risk of uncompensated harm when compensation is perfect. Thus, efficient warnings under a rule of absolute liability require perfect liability for producers and perfect compensation of injured consumers. Furthermore, when liability is absolute and perfect but compensation is imperfect, the producer's warning will be too strong relative to an efficient warning.

 Perfect liability and perfect compensation are, however, seldom combined. First, compensation for personal injuries is so problematic in theory and practice that actual jury awards appear highly imperfect. Second, even if the jury awarded perfectly compensatory damages, a substantial portion of damages are soaked up by lawyers' fees and uncompensated court costs. Actual estimates indicate that plaintiffs' costs in the typical tort case amount to between 29% and 44% of the damages awarded.[42] As has been said, "When the pig of a tort claim is run through the python of the legal process, there is not much left for the accident victim." The consumer routinely faces the risk of uncompensated harm, resulting in warnings that are too strong.

This result can be explained in terms of externalities. When the manufacturer is absolutely liable for the full harm caused by his product, he fully internalizes the risk of accidents. However, when the consumer is imperfectly compensated for accidents, he demands an immediate surplus from buying the good. The manufacturer does not internalize this element of social benefits. Since some social benefits of consumption are externalized by the firm, the profit-maximizing warning discourages more consumers than is socially efficient.

d. Efficient Warnings and Liability for Inadequate Warnings   A rule limiting liability to the harm caused by inadequate warnings overcomes this difficulty. Under such a rule, there is no liability until the warning crosses the threshold of inadequacy and becomes too weak, but once that threshold is crossed the liability costs to the manufacturer jump sharply. The situation is depicted in Figure 9.7 where the arrows point to the line indicating the manufacturer's liability costs, which jump up at the legal standard x^*. The profit-maximizing manufacturer will choose his warning to avoid the zone where his liability costs jump up; specifically he will conform to the legal standard or slightly exceed it in order to allow for a margin of error by courts. Because the jump in costs is so precipitous, the manufacturer will continue to conform to the legal standard even if liability is imperfect in the sense that some costs are externalized. In general, if the legal standard is efficient, a rule of liability for inadequate warnings causes efficient behavior, even though some benefits are externalized due to imperfect liability and imperfect compensation.

This point can be seen by examining Figure 9.7. To the left of the legal standard, x^*, immediate profits exceed liability, whereas to the right of the legal standard, liability exceeds immediate profits. Since the zone of profitability is where the immediate profit curve is higher than the liability curve, the profit-maximizing firm chooses the weakest warning at which its immediate profits are at least as large as its liability. Thus, since the immediate profits curve intersects the liability curve at its discontinuity in Figure 9.7, the profit-maximizing warning equals the legal standard.

---

[42]Gary Schwartz, *Directions in Contemporary Products Liability Scholarship*, 14 J. LEGAL STUD. 763 (1985). His figures are obtained from studies of automobile insurance company records and records on asbestos litigation.

Figure 9.7   Liability for Failure to Warn

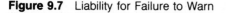

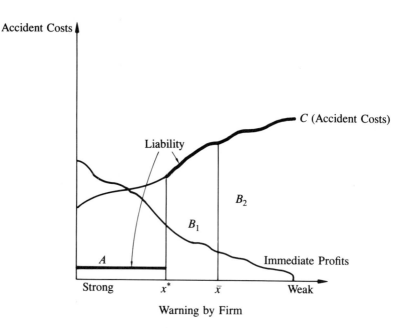

Warning by Firm

If the firm will be held liable for failing to issue a warning at least as strong as x^*, then its expected liability costs are given by the segments denoted by the arrows: to the left of the legal standard, x^*, the liability costs are negligible, but to the right of x^* they equal the accident costs. (x^* has been determined by the process described in the previous graph.) Note that these liability costs are discontinuous at x^*. To the left of the legal standard, immediate profits exceed liability, whereas to the right of the legal standard, liability exceeds immediate profits. Since the zone of profitability is where the immediate profit curve is higher than the liability curve, the profit-maximizing firm chooses the weakest warning at which its immediate profits are at least as large as its liability. Thus, since the immediate profits curve intersects the liability curve at its discontinuity, the profit-maximizing warning equals the legal standard.

From the viewpoint of allocative efficiency, the relevant legal standard is the *ex ante* measure. If the legal rule is liability for harm caused by *ex ante* inadequate warnings, the manufacturer's warning will maximize expected net social benefits. In contrast, the *ex post* standard will cause manufacturers to issue warnings that are too severe.

Several remarks are in order about these conclusions. First, it is likely that manufacturers will escape legal liability in some instances because of imperfections in the legal system, or they will be found liable for damages from which some of the true costs of the accident are excluded by law. (See the box entitled "Insurance and Bankruptcy" to see how those possibilities affect our conclusions.) Under a rule of absolute liability, imperfect liability of manufacturers tends to cause warnings to be too weak, and, as explained, imperfect compensation of victims tends to cause warnings to be too strong. It is an empirical question which tendency is weightier.

Second, rather than considering incentives to innovate, our argument assumes that technology is unchanging. Strict liability provides a constant pressure towards accident-reducing innovation by manufacturers. In contrast, insofar as the manufacturer escapes liability by issuing an adequate warning, he has little incentive to invest in innovations that would reduce accident costs. One way to overcome this problem is by applying the negligence standard to the investment in innovation, so that a manufacturer is held liable unless he makes adequate efforts to discover unknown dangers and avoid them through redesigning the product.

Third, unlike strict liability, the rule of liability for inadequate warnings requires setting an efficient legal standard. Errors in setting the legal standard will disrupt the efficiency of this rule. To illustrate, if the legally required warning is weaker than the socially efficient warning, manufacturers will usually conform to the legal warning, not the efficient warning. This problem does not arise with strict liability because it does not involve a legal standard. In view of this fact, the relative desirability of strict liability and negligence depends upon the kinds of errors that courts are likely to make. On the one hand, if the courts are likely to make large errors in setting the legal standard for warnings, then strict liability is preferable to negligence. On the other hand, if absolute liability exposes the consumer to a large risk of uncompensated harm, which will be the case when the transaction costs of dispute resolution are large, liability for inadequate warnings is superior to absolute liability.

E. Proposals for Reforming the Products Liability System

We began our discussion of products liability law by noting that the system is in turmoil. This crisis in products liability is part of a larger perceived crisis in the tort system, one that extends beyond product-related accidents to automobile accidents, malpractice actions against doctors and other professionals, and newer causes of action. In this section we will consider several reforms that have recently been suggested for correcting the specific crisis in products liability, not in the general tort system. Later we will discuss some proposals for a more general reform of the tort liability system.

Before we turn to that subject, it is worth taking a moment to ask why there is perceived to be a crisis in products liability law. Of all the evidence of turmoil that we noted above when we first introduced the subject of products liability law, two events of the last several years stand out as the most dramatic indications to the general public of a crisis in this area of the law: the bankruptcy of otherwise profitable firms because of adverse products liability judgments, and the inability of those at risk to purchase liability insurance.

Of the bankruptcies alleged to be attributable to products liability, the most dramatic was that of the Manville Corporation in the late summer of 1982. That company was the leading producer of asbestos in the country and

Insurance and Bankruptcy

Many firms do not insure enough to ward off bankruptcy or reorganization in the event of mass tort claims. Like the death of an individual, dissolution of a firm usually extinguishes tort claims that would arise in the future. Consequently, corporate reorganization and bankruptcy externalize some accident costs imposed by the firm's activities. The problem of cost-externalization can be reduced by extending the insurance coverage of firms. This box concerns the legal policies that create incentives for more extensive insurance.

Figure 9.8 relates the amount of insurance to the magnitude of possible tort claims. Along the forty-five degree line, insurance increases at the same rate as tort claims, so this line represents full coverage. Along the horizontal axis, insurance remains nil as tort claims increase, so this line represents no insurance. An actual firm will usually not insure against small losses but will take policies with deductibles. The actual insurance line therefore corresponds to the no-insurance line for small tort claims. As the tort claim rises, the firm begins to purchase insurance. However, most firms have an upper limit on their insurance coverage, so, when the possible tort claim becomes very large, the actual insurance line eventually drops down to the no-insurance line.

It is easy to see why most firms have an upper limit on insurance. Suppose that a decisionmaker has wealth equal to $100,000, which he wishes to protect against liability claims, and suppose that the insurance premium is 25 cents per dollar of coverage. It costs $25,000 to insure against a $100,000 tort claim, $50,000 to insure against a $200,000 tort claim, and $100,000 to insure against a $400,000 tort claim. Just paying the premium on $400,000 of coverage uses up his entire wealth, so it is not profitable to insure against losses that are this large. Better to run the risk of a suit than to use up all wealth to insure against it. Consequently, there is an upper limit on the coverage, short of $400,000, that it is rational to buy.

In Figure 9.8, the slope of the insurance line represents the intensiveness of insurance, and the upper limit, denoted U, represents extensiveness of insurance. As depicted, the upper limit U occurs beyond the value of the decisionmaker's wealth W, and short of the largest possible tort claim K.

The risk of losses larger than U is externalized. A problem for policymakers is to discover ways of extending U farther to the right, reducing externalized risk. Two general types of policies will accomplish this result.

was, by all the usual indications, a very profitable enterprise. But that surface profitability hid a severe financial crisis that the company faced because of the numerous judgments awarded and anticipated against Manville for deaths and injuries resulting from exposure to asbestos. At the time that it

Figure 9.8 Insurance and Bankruptcy

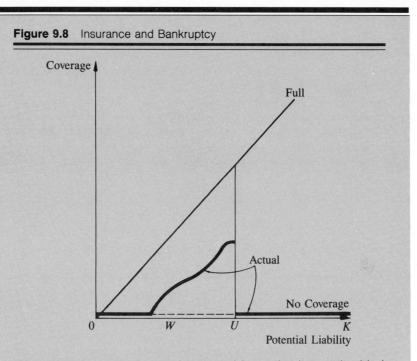

When a firm declares bankruptcy, future tort claims against it are extinguished. Thus, bankruptcy allows some accident costs inflicted by the firm to be externalized. Is there a way to induce firms to take enough insurance coverage so as to minimize this externalization of future tort claims? The figure relates the amount of the firm's insurance to the magnitude of possible tort claims against it. The firm is likely to purchase less than full coverage. For very small tort claims the firm will either have no coverage or large deductibles. Therefore, for small tort claims the actual insurance line corresponds to no-insurance along the horizontal axis. As the tort claims rise, the firm begins to purchase insurance, as indicated by the rise in the line marked "Actual." But the firm typically has an upper limit on its coverage, here marked U, so that when the possible tort claims become very large, the actual insurance line eventually drops down to the no-insurance line. W indicates the wealth of the firm, which, note, is less than the upper limit of its insurance coverage. K indicates the largest possible tort claim, for which the firm is uninsured. Thus, the risk of losses larger than U is externalized. The public policy problem is to devise a way to extend U farther to the right. One possibility is to put more of the firm owner's personal wealth in jeopardy in the event of the firm's bankruptcy. Another is to narrow the successor doctrine so that a new firm acquiring the assets of a bankrupt firm also acquires the old firm's past and future tort liabilities. A third possibility is to cap liability by limiting the maximum that victims can recover to a figure less than K but slightly more than U.

filed for the protection of the bankruptcy code, Manville was defending itself against 16,500 asbestos claims, with an additional 500 claims being filed every month. The anticipated cost of each claim was $40,000, making the discounted value of all those and reasonably anticipated future claims in

First, increasing the amount of wealth W at risk makes the safe strategy of insuring relatively more attractive than the risky strategy of not insuring, which pushes U to the right. At least two legal devices extend the amount of wealth at risk. First, the amount of the decisionmaker's wealth that survives bankruptcy can be reduced. This end could be accomplished by narrowing the protection of personal wealth afforded by limited liability corporations. Second, the scope of the successor doctrine can be expanded, so that a new firm acquiring the assets of a dissolved firm also acquires the old firm's past and future tort liabilities. As a result, the new firm's entire wealth is potentially jeopardized by a tort claim. When the successor doctrine does not apply, corporate reorganization extinguishes some possible tort claims or shields the new firm's wealth from them.

Besides increasing the wealth in jeopardy, the second legal strategy for extending insurance coverage is to reduce liability for very large losses. Specifically, putting a cap upon the upper limit of the firm's liability, so that maximum liability is just above the firm's initial upper bound of insurance coverage, will cause the firm to extend its coverage. To see why, let K in Figure 9.8 represent the upper bound (cap) on liability. Capping liability at a value just above U does not affect the expected utility of the risky strategy of not extending insurance beyond U, because, in spite of the cap, a liability claim anywhere in the range above U forces the firm into bankruptcy. However, capping liability does increase the expected utility of the relatively safe strategy. Specifically, the cap increases the probability an increase in insurance from U up to the new value of K will enable a firm to avoid bankruptcy brought on by tort claims. Since the cap causes the safe strategy to become relatively more attractive than the risky strategy, the upper bound of insurance coverage expands. In summary, moving W to the right or moving K to the left can in principle increase the extent of insurance.

Of course, capping liability will not increase the extent of insurance unless the right cap is used. In the preceding discussion, the cap occurred just beyond the firm's upper bound of insurance coverage.[1] If the cap occurs below the firm's upper bound of insurance coverage, lowering the cap will reduce the extent of insurance coverage because there is no need to insure against losses for which the firm will not be liable.

[1] If the cap occurs well above the firm's upper bound of insurance coverage, the extent of its insurance will be unchanged.

excess of $2 billion. The company's assets were worth slightly more than $1 billion.[43]

Although the bankruptcy of Manville and other asbestos manufacturers is a dramatic event, it should not necessarily be concluded that products lia-

[43] An excellent treatment of the economic and legal issues in the Manville bankruptcy is Richard Epstein, *Manville: The Bankruptcy of Modern Products Liability Law*, REGULATION

bility law is in a crisis simply because it forces some firms to go out of business. As we argued above in our discussion of the contractual doctrine of commercial impracticability, bankruptcy may be an optimal response to a failure to internalize external costs. But that is not the usual contention with regard to bankruptcy resulting from adverse products liability judgments. Most critics have pointed to these instances of bankruptcy as the otherwise avoidable social costs of a products liability system gone mad. Recall that in the *Beshada* case an asbestos manufacturer was held liable for not having discovered the dangers of exposure to asbestos and warned of those dangers at a time when it was impossible for the manufacturer to have made that discovery. To the extent that the standards applied in products liability actions are not optimal, as Professor Epstein and others have argued, then the bankruptcies should never have occurred and constitute a dramatic example of the costs of an inefficient legal system. (For a discussion of how tort liability has affected another industry, see the box "Vaccines and Products Liability.")

Another dramatic event that has seemed to many to speak volumes on the necessity for products liability reform is the liability insurance crisis. The argument is that the vast expansion of liability and the rapid increase in the size of awards has caused insurance companies to take drastic measures: either the liability insurance premiums skyrocket or liability policies become unavailable. For example, Specialty Systems, Inc. of Richmond, Indiana—a company that specializes in removing asbestos and that has not yet been sued for product-related harms—last year purchased a $500,000 liability insurance coverage for a $9,361 premium. This year the premium rose 4,900% to $460,000. The company purchased the policy because its customers will not hire Specialty Systems without proof of such a policy. The result is that the insured either passes on to his customers as much of this phenomenal increase as demand elasticity will allow or changes his line of business.

Some commentators allege that this insurance crisis is, like the bankruptcy examples, dramatic testimony to how seriously amiss products liability law has become. The argument is that if products liability law were sensible, liability insurance premiums would be much lower so that the inefficiencies of high product prices and of substitution away from high-risk activities and products would be reduced. Other commentators say the fault is not with products liability but rather with the poor business practices and cyclical nature of the insurance industry. The principal contention is that insurers generate much of their profit by re-lending at interest a large fraction of the receipts from selling policies. When interest rates are high, as they were in the late 1970s and early 1980s, the insurance companies cut premiums in order to increase the sale of policies so as to have more to invest at the elevated interest rates. In fact, the argument continues, during periods of high interest rates insurers may sell policies at prices that are well below

(September/October, 1982). A more recent book that takes the view that Manville and other asbestos companies' behavior was inexcusable is Paul Brodeur, OUTRAGEOUS MISCONDUCT: THE ASBESTOS INDUSTRY ON TRIAL (1985).

Vaccines and Products Liability

An adverse consequence of an inefficient products liability regime that is less well publicized than bankruptcy is the effect of the system on the availability of beneficial products. Consider the result of the liability crisis on the availability of various vaccines against serious diseases.

Many recent products liability cases have involved the duty that pharmaceutical manufacturers and doctors have to warn those taking drugs of the potential risks the drugs involve. These cases teach us something important about the consequences of extending the reach of products liability law too far.

One such case involved polio vaccine. Some background about that vaccine is helpful. The first vaccine against this crippling disease was the Salk vaccine or IPV, which is a so-called killed-virus vaccine. Because the vaccine is made from a killed virus, it prevents polio in the person who receives it without presenting the risk that the recipient will contract polio. The second vaccine was the Sabin vaccine or OPV, a live-virus vaccine. The Sabin vaccine has several advantages over the Salk vaccine. First, it is administered orally and is, therefore, easier to use. Secondly, and more importantly, because the Sabin vaccine is made from a *live* virus, the recipient retains the virus in her system and can pass it to others. Because the virus is very weak, those who receive it through contact with someone who has taken OPV are themselves immunized against polio. Thus, the OPV has an external benefit: it immunizes the recipient and some of the people with whom she comes in contact. This benefit is so considerable that public health authorities strongly recommended that young children take the Sabin vaccine instead of the older Salk vaccine. Before the switch, there were still 2,500 cases of polio a year. After the switch to the live-virus vaccine, polio virtually disappeared.

However, the live-virus vaccine presents a risk.[1] Approximately one of every 4 million who take the vaccine or come in close contact with those who have taken OPV contract polio and are either permanently crippled or die.

Is there is a method by which products liability law can deal with the risks presented by OPV without sacrificing its benefits? In *Reyes v. Wyeth Laboratories* (1974) a young lady who contracted polio after taking the Sabin vaccine sued the vaccine's producer on the grounds that the defendant company had not properly warned the child's parents of the small risk that taking OPV could lead to permanent crippling or death from polio. The jury returned a verdict for the plaintiff that was upheld on appeal by the United States Court of Appeals for the Fifth Circuit. There can be little doubt that the defendant should be required to warn consumers of such a risk, however minute. And after the *Reyes* decision it became standard practice to include package inserts warning recipients of the OPV of the risks of the vaccine. Manufacturers of the vaccine, and

---

[1] *See* Edmund Kitch, *Vaccines and Product Liability: A Case of Contagious Litigation*, REGULATION (May/June 1985).

by implication, of other pharmaceuticals, were on notice—and rightly and efficiently so—that they had a duty to warn recipients of the risks of their pharmaceuticals. One efficiency reason for preferring this conclusion is that it allows the benefits of the live-virus vaccine to continue so long as the information about the costs of the vaccine are conveyed to those taking it. (One may doubt whether the typical decisionmaker is capable of evaluating the risk of one-in-four-million, but that is a different matter.)

However, anyone familiar with the trends in modern products liability law would be shocked if the matter stopped at this sensible conclusion. No one really expects courts to allow a child who had contracted polio to leave the court without an award, regardless of how proper and extensive the warning of the vaccine's risks had been. And indeed that is what has happened. In several recent cases involving children whose parents have been properly warned in accordance with *Reyes*, large awards have been returned, some including punitive damages presumably meant to induce the company to return to the killed-virus vaccine instead of the live-virus vaccine.

These awards are likely to lead to a severe inefficiency in that they preclude any private mechanism for the benefits of these superior vaccines to be given the same weight as the costs. Under the absolute liability of the recent cases, the manufacturers of polio vaccine and other drugs understandably focus only on the expected risks created by their products. Without the defense of assumption of the risk after an adequate warning, there is no mechanism by which the manufacturer is allowed to give the benefits equal consideration.

This is not mere speculation. There is ample evidence that pharmaceutical manufacturers are so fearful of products liability awards that they have become reluctant to manufacture and distribute beneficial drugs. In 1976 after an outbreak of swine flu, a very dangerous illness, manufacturers of a vaccine against that disease refused to market it because private insurers, fearful of the products liability consequences of 100 million or more injections, would not issue liability insurance. The companies offered the innoculations only after the federal government agreed to be the exclusive defendant in any actions for harms arising from the swine flu vaccine.[2] The DPT vaccine against whooping cough is in short supply in this country because the largest manufacturer, Eli Lilly & Company, has quit producing the drug because of the fear of adverse products liability judgments. Only one manufacturer of that vaccine is willing to gamble that he will not be held liable for the side effects of the vaccine despite conveying an adequate warning. Currently in the United States the follow-

---

[2]The vaccine's manufacturers proved particularly astute on this matter. The vaccine seems to have caused a potentially paralyzing or fatal disease called Guillain-Barré syndrome in a small fraction of those who were innoculated. Numerous plaintiffs brought actions against the federal government, as the sole defendant, on a theory of inadequate warning. The federal government relatively quickly stopped the program of innoculation for swine flu.

ing vaccines that were once manufactured by a number of firms are now produced by a single firm: measles, mumps, Sabin polio, Salk polio, and rabies. Worse still, the threat of products liability suits may well critically reduce the incentive of pharmaceutical companies to invest in research and development of potentially beneficial new drugs.[3]

[3]*See* Peter Huber, *Safety and the Second Best: The Hazards of Public Risk Management in the Courts*, 85 COLUM. L. REV. 277 (1985).

actuarially sensible levels. But when interest rates fall, the insurers cannot make profits from re-lending premiums; instead their profits must come from their insurance underwriting business. This necessitates a very rapid increase in policy premiums. The corrective, it is alleged, is closer regulation of the business practices of the insurance companies, e.g., restrictions on the amount by which they may raise premiums in a given time period and tighter reserve requirements. Such facts as are available about these various crises are represented in Figure 9.9.

1. A Federal Products Liability Statute   In view of the crisis in products liability law and its manifestation in the liability insurance crisis, there have been numerous proposals for reform. One of the most recurrent of these is for the creation of a federal products liability statute. Currently products liability law is the preserve of the states. Although we have frequently written in this chapter as if the states are in complete agreement on the doctrines of products liability, there are important differences among the states regarding products liability law.

There are two distinguishable reasons why manufacturers have urged a uniform federal products liability law. First, many manufacturers contend that the differences among the states are so significant that they must incur excessive costs of tailoring their products to accommodate these differences. These costs would be saved, with consequent savings to consumers, if there was a uniform federal products liability law. Secondly, and probably more importantly, many believe that the products liability law that has become the norm in the states is seriously flawed and getting worse. All this could be corrected by starting all over with a sensibly drafted uniform federal products liability law.

There have been several efforts to accommodate this desire for uniformity in products liability law. In 1975 the Department of Commerce developed a Uniform Product Liability Act in the hope that each of the states would adopt it in much the same way that they have adopted the Uniform Commercial Code. The Act had very little impact. Very few states adopted the Act in its entirety, and only a few more states used the Act to re-write their products liability law.

Beginning in the early 1980s, Congress adopted the more direct route to products liability reform of proposing federal legislation to create a uniform products liability act that, under the rule of federal pre-emption, would over-ride any state law on the matter. The various bills that have been proposed share the same general characteristics. The central definitions of liability for product-related harms are not really controversial. They are as follows:

> The manufacturer will be liable to the victim of a product-related accident if the victim can establish by a preponderance of the evidence that
> 1. the product was unreasonably dangerous in construction; or
> 2. the product was unreasonably dangerous in design; or
> 3. the product was unreasonably dangerous in that the manufacturer failed to provide adequate warnings or instructions about a danger connected with the product or about the proper use of the product; or
> 4. the product was unreasonably dangerous because the product did not conform to an express warranty made by the manufacturer with respect to the product.

These provisions simply capture the central aspects of existing products liability law, such as Sec. 402A of the Second Restatement of Torts. However, it is the following constraints and restrictions that constitute the real reforms and have excited the most controversy:

1. Expert opinion *alone* will not constitute sufficient evidence of defect as defined above; there must be corroborating *objective* evidence.
2. The theory of "market share" liability [the holding of the *Sindell* case discussed above] is rejected. This is the theory by which firms are held liable in proportion to their market share of the product that has produced injury where it was impossible to identify which producer supplied the product that caused the victim's injury.
3. The proposed bills restrict the ability of plaintiffs to use previous actions against the defendant to determine issues of fact.
4. Punitive damages may be awarded to the victim of a product-related accident only where the defendant has shown "reckless disregard" for the safety of product consumers. Moreover, the amount of punitive damages is to be determined by the trial court judge, not by a jury.
5. Retailers and distributors are exonerated from liability except where their fault has contributed to the victim's harm or the manufacturer is unavailable (because, e.g., he has left the business) or is judgment-proof (because, e.g., she has filed for bankruptcy).
6. The rule of no contribution among joint or multiple tortfeasors is replaced by a rule of proportional contribution.
7. The present value of some collateral payments that the victim might receive for his injuries, e.g., a workers' compensation award, would be deducted from a damages award.
8. The unreasonableness of the product defect would be judged by the contemporary technology, not by subsequent improvements that could not have been known by the manufacturer at the time of production. However, the manufacturer would continue to be liable, as under current law, for failure to warn if dangers are discovered

Figure 9.9 The Crisis in Tort Liability

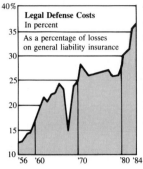

Legal Defense Costs
In percent

As a percentage of losses on general liability insurance

Source: Insurance Services Office Inc.

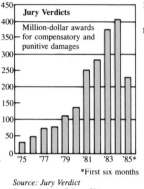

Jury Verdicts

Million-dollar awards for compensatory and punitive damages

*First six months

Source: Jury Verdict Research Inc., Solon, Ohio

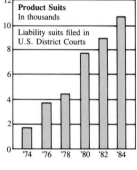

Product Suits
In thousands

Liability suits filed in U.S. District Courts

Source: Administrative Office of U.S. Courts

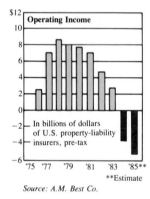

Operating Income

In billions of dollars of U.S. property-liability insurers, pre-tax

**Estimate

Source: A.M. Best Co.

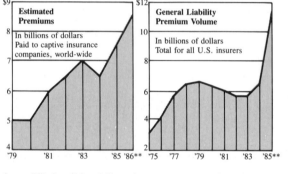

Estimated Premiums

In billions of dollars
Paid to captive insurance companies, world-wide

**Estimate

Source: Tillinghast, Nelson & Warren Inc.

General Liability Premium Volume

In billions of dollars
Total for all U.S. insurers

Source: A.M. Best Co.

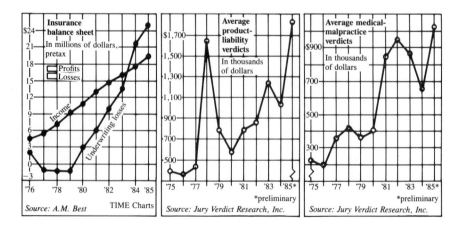

Insurance balance sheet
In millions of dollars, pretax

☐ Profits
☐ Losses

Income

Underwriting losses

Source: A.M. Best   TIME Charts

Average product-liability verdicts

In thousands of dollars

*preliminary

Source: Jury Verdict Research, Inc.

Average medical-malpractice verdicts

In thousands of dollars

*preliminary

Source: Jury Verdict Research, Inc.

after production. A related point has to do with the manufacturer's subsequent correction of a product after production and distribution. In most of the proposed bills, the manufacturer's subsequent corrective measures could not be used as evidence of a defect to establish liability.

9. Finally, the traditional strict liability defenses of the consumer's assumption of the risk and of consumer misuse or alteration would be restored.

These central provisions of a proposed uniform products liability act by and large conform with the liability standard for product-related injuries recommended by our economic analysis of the subject. However, the debate on the various bills dealing with products liability reform proposed to Congress in the 1980s have been lengthy and at times rancorous, and unfortunately, the prospects for the enactment of a fundamental reform like the one proposed in these bills are not bright.

2. Bandages, Chewing Gum, and Bailing Wire: Caps on Awards and Other Quick-Fix Cures

At the same time that Congress has been debating fundamental reforms in the products liability system, the states have been responding to the products liability crisis and the associated liability insurance crisis in a much more expedient manner. While a few states have debated some fundamental reforms in their products liability standards, the majority of the states have responded to the crises by focusing on the symptoms of the products liability malaise rather than on its causes. They are, in essence, treating cancer with aspirin and footrubs.

A common example of the sort of products liability reform that the states have embarked upon is to put a cap or upper limit on the amount that victims can recover. Sometimes the states place this cap only on what is perceived to be the offending element in recent damage awards, typically those for pain and suffering. The other elements of a damage award are not capped. For example, Missouri has capped awards for pain and suffering in medical malpractice awards at $350,000. In other cases, the states have limited the total amount that can be recovered. For example, New Mexico has recently limited to $50,000 the amount that can be recovered from a tavern-owner for serving alcohol to drivers who subsequently cause accidents. In South Dakota the total amount that can be recovered in a medical malpractice action is limited to $1 million.

Table 9.1 summarizes the reforms that the states have passed in 1986 to address the perceived wrongs in the tort liability system.

Recently, Congress and the White House have joined this quick-fix bandwagon. Although it has not been able to agree on a more fundamental treatment for the products liability crisis, Congress has been able to pass legislation dealing with the symptoms. For example, in 1981 Congress passed the Risk Retention Act, which allowed firms in the same industry to form insurance pools as an alternative to the high cost of commercially obtained products liability insurance. The Act gave these pools valuable exemptions

Table 9.1 Liability Reform in the States in 1986

State	Legislative Reform
Alaska	Non-economic damages limited to $500,000 in all cases; joint and several liability limited; periodic payments approved instead of a lump sum payment.
Arizona	Liquor establishment liability limited.
California	Joint and several liability for non-economic damages abolished by referendum.
Colorado	Joint and several liability abolished; punitive damages limited; liquor establishment liability limited to $50,000.
Connecticut	Joint and several liability, lawyers' fees, and municipal employees' liability limited; periodic payments approved.
Delaware	Liability immunities expanded.
Florida	Non-economic damages limited to $450,000; punitive damages limited; joint and several liability abolished for non-economic damages and limited for economic damages; periodic payment required for total awards exceeding $500,000 if the economic component exceeds $250,000.
Hawaii	Awards for pain and suffering limited to $375,000; joint and several liability limited for defendants found 25% at fault or less, except in auto, property damage, or environmental cases.
Illinois	Joint and several liability limited for defendants found less than 25% at fault, except in medical malpractice or pollution cases or awards covering medical expenses; local government liability limited.
Indiana	Liquor-establishment liability limited; directors of non-profit corporations given immunity for acts not covered by insurance; judges may impose sanctions against frivolous suits or defenses.
Iowa	Punitive damages limited; periodic payments permitted at judge's discretion; liquor-establishment and municipal-employee liability limited; standards for expert witnesses tightened in medical and dental malpractice cases.
Kansas	Non-economic damages limited to $250,000; total damages in medical malpractice cases limited to $1 million, with limits to be adjusted annually for inflation.
Maine	Medical malpractice suits screened; three-year statute of limitations set for professional negligence; wrongful birth and wrongful life actions prohibited; periodic payments required for awards exceeding $250,000; lawyers' fees in medical malpractice cases limited, and mediators under contract to the state made immune from liability.
Maryland	All non-economic damages limited to $350,000.
Massachusetts	Non-economic damages limited to $500,000 in medical malpractice cases except where a jury finds substantial impairment or disfigurement; sliding cap applied to lawyers' fees.
Michigan	Non-economic damages capped at $225,000 in medical malpractice cases, except in cases of injury to the reproductive system or loss of a "vital bodily function"; joint and several liability limited in other cases except product liability.

State	Legislative Reform
Minnesota	Damages for "intangible losses" limited to $400,000, except for pain and suffering; punitive damages made more difficult to seek.
Mississippi	Local governments are immune from liability.
Missouri	Medical malpractice damages capped at $350,000.
New Hampshire	Punitive damages eliminated; non-economic damages limited to $875,000.
New Mexico	Liquor-establishment liability damages capped at $50,000.
New York	Joint and several liability for non-economic damages limited for defendants found less than 50% liable; does not apply to cases involving automobiles or construction, or to certain product-liability cases; periodic payments required for awards exceeding $250,000.
Oklahoma	Punitive damages cannot exceed compensatory damages.
South Dakota	All damages in medical malpractice cases capped at $1 million; awards for loss of consortium (usually the loss of a sexual relationship in marriage) limited to $100,000; periodic payments required for all awards exceeding $50,000; separate trial required on punitive damages in all liability cases.
Tennessee	Liquor establishment liability limited; liability for board members of governments and non-profit entities limited.
Utah	Joint and several liability abolished; liquor-establishment liability limited; non-economic damages in medical malpractice cases capped at $250,000; periodic payments permitted in medical malpractice cases when requested by either party.
Virginia	Liability of transportation districts limited to $25,000 or amount of insurance coverage; punitive damages and prejudgment interest cannot be collected from the districts.
Washington	Joint and several liability abolished; all non-economic damages limited, based on average wages; lawyers' fees may be reviewed by judges; periodic payments approved; liquor-establishment liability limited; school-board members and hospital directors given immunity.
West Virginia	Non-economic damages capped at $1 million in medical malpractice cases, and statutes of limitations in such cases shortened; non-economic damage awards against municipalities limited to $500,000; punitive damages in municipal liability cases eliminated; joint and several liability modified in such cases and for defendants found less than 25% at fault.
Wisconsin	Non-economic damages capped at $1 million in medical malpractice cases; lawyers' fees limited in such cases.
Wyoming	Joint and several liability abolished; liquor-establishment liability limited.

Source: Alliance of American Insurers and *Wall Street Journal*, August 1, 1986, p. 14, col. 5.

from insurance, antitrust, and tax regulations. More recently, a task force of the Department of Justice proposed a federal limitations on awards for pain and suffering and punitive damages and on the use of contingent fees by attorneys in products liability actions.[44]

From an efficiency standpoint what is distressing about these caps and limitations is that they are likely to have adverse consequences without providing the sort of relief that their sponsors anticipate. In this regard, the economic analysis of these proposals is very much like that of any other price ceiling, for example, rent control, whose inefficiencies we discussed in Chapter 2. All of the cap figures, whether on an element of damages, such as pain and suffering, or on the total amount that may be recovered, are arbitrary. There is no reason to believe that, for example, $1 million will adequately compensate all or even most victims of medical malpractice or of a product-related injury. Those for whom that would be more than perfect compensation are not likely to be affected by such a limitation. However, where $1 million will be less than perfect compensation, the incentive created for the behavior of both potential victims and potential injurers may be changed for the worse. For example, if potential victims are aware of the limitation and are risk averse, then they may purchase inefficiently large amounts of first-party insurance. Or they may inefficiently consult "too many" doctors before a major medical operation. But worse is the likely inefficiency the cap creates for the behavior of potential injurers. If they are aware of the ceiling, they may take too little precaution against accidents that are likely to result in losses that exceed the ceiling.

We can make this point in terms of the graphical analysis of liability of the previous chapter. This cap limits the expected accident cost of some accidents, and this causes the expected liability curve to fall. This, in turn, makes the minimum point on the expected liability curve fall to the left of the true social-cost minimum. This effect is reproduced in Figure 9.10. Note that, when compensation is capped at A, the potential tortfeasor's cost-minimizing level of precaution is less than it would be if there was no cap and the potential tortfeasor could expect to face the full social costs of accidents.

> **Question 9.22:** If the liability standard in product-related accidents were changed to negligence and a cap were imposed on the total amount recoverable from a negligent defendant, would there be a lessening of the amount of precaution taken by potential tortfeasors?

> **Question 9.23:** One element of the proposals for dealing with the perceived escalation of punitive damages is not to limit their amount or the circumstances in which they can be awarded but rather to require that any punitive damages be

---

[44]Outside the products liability area, the White House has recently proposed a bill to Congress to limit awards for pain and suffering, mental anguish, emotional distress, and the loss of consortium (the loss of a spouse's companionship) in all tort actions against the federal government to $100,000. An additional aspect of the proposal is that the Government would be allowed to make its damage payments in periodic installments, rather than in a lump sum, as is the current rule.

Figure 9.10   Damage Limitations in Products Liability Actions

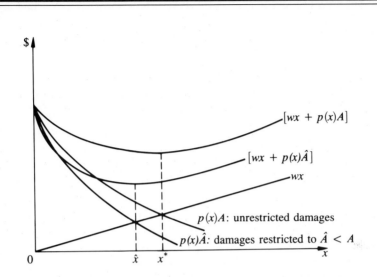

Many states have imposed limitations on the total amount that those injured in product-related accidents may recover. These limitations may cause potential injurers to reduce their precautionary expenditures, leading to more product-related accidents. The amount spent by the actor on precaution is given by the line marked *wx*. There are two expected-accident costs lines. Both indicate that the probability of an accident, $p(x)$, is a declining function of the amount of precaution, *x*. But they differ in the amount of accident costs: when damages are unrestricted, expected accident costs are $p(x)A$; when victims are limited to recovery of $\hat{A}$, expected accident costs are $p(x)\hat{A}$, which is less than unrestricted coverage. As a result, there are two total expected cost curves for the potential injurer with two different cost-minimizing levels of precaution. If damages are unrestricted, total expected costs are $[wx + p(x)A]$ with costs minimized at x^*. If damages are restricted, total expected costs are $[wx + p(x)\hat{A}]$ with costs minimized at $\hat{x}$.

paid not to the plaintiff but to, for example, a charity designated by the plaintiff or the court. How might plaintiffs' incentives to seek punitive damages be affected by such a scheme? How might the jury's disposition to award punitives be affected?

3. An Assessment of the Proposed Reforms of the Products Liability System   Economic analysis can help to assess the various reforms of the products liability system that we have just discussed. We were critical of those reforms that rely on caps and ceilings on the amount that victims can recover or on how lawyers are compensated. Economists disagree about some important public policy issues, but one issue about which there is near unanimity in the profession is that artificial price floors and ceilings do more harm than good. Thus, there is very little an economist might say in favor of the sorts of schemes that the states have recently debated and in some cases enacted to solve the products liability crisis.

An economic analysis of the products liability system suggests that the problem is not with attorneys, juries, victims, insurance companies, or injurers; nor is the problem that each of these bears a small share of the responsibility but no one bears a large share. Plaintiffs' attorneys cannot be blamed for bringing actions for recovery. They are simply responding to incentives created by awards in previous cases. Indeed, it would be surprising if large awards in products liability cases did *not* cause a subsequent increase in the number of actions filed. Nor can juries be faulted for their generosity toward victims of product-related accidents. Juries follow a judge's instructions: if he tells them that they may find the defendant liable even though the plaintiff blatantly misused the product or even though the defendant, as in *Beshada*, could not possibly have known what he was doing was going to be deemed unsafe, we cannot blame the jury for following the judge's instructions. Nor can we blame juries for the size of the awards returned; those are subject to appellate review, and as we saw earlier in this chapter in our discussion of punitive damages, there is very little clear guidance for a jury on the size of punitive damages. Similarly, it is difficult to blame the products liability crisis on insurance companies. The insurance business is so highly competitive that the presumption should be that the premium level accurately reflects the actuarially fair risk of loss. Thus, if insurance premiums rise, the presumption should be that the risk of loss has risen. To blame insurance companies for this rise is to blame the messenger for bringing bad news. And finally, there is nothing at all to suggest that injurers have become less safe or more reckless.

Rather, the problem with the products liability system is that the liability standard has gone awry. In short, the intellectual underpinnings of this important area of the law are flawed. The most efficient liability standard for this area is strict liability with the defenses of product misuse and assumption of the risk. Briefly put, this standard would duplicate the sort of standard that would have been achieved by the consent of manufacturer and consumer through voluntary exchange if the costs of bargaining were low. The current system has evolved beyond this standard and toward absolute manufacturer liability. It is this extension beyond strict liability with the usual defenses that is at the root of the current crisis.

The more fundamental reforms of the products liability system that have been proposed to Congress in the last several years seem to recognize the underlying flaws of the current system. Those fundamental reforms offer some hope of significant correction without any of the inefficient results of the quick-fix proposals. If only our crystal balls were less cloudy than they are, we would be able to predict whether the treatment of product-related injuries will be significantly reformed or some hasty tourniquet will be applied to stanch the bleeding.

III. NO-FAULT ALTERNATIVES TO THE TORT LIABILITY SYSTEM

There is an influential school of thought that holds that *all* of the tort liability system—not just that dealing with product-related injuries—is in crisis. The central complaints of the members of this school against the tort liability system are that it is an inefficiently expensive method of compensating the victims of tortious acts and that it does not adequately deter potential tortfeasors. To correct these shortcomings, the critics have proposed that most of the tort liability system be replaced by a system of no-fault compensation for the victims of accidents.[45] The gist of these systems is that a *bona fide* victim will receive *partial* compensation either from his own insurance company or from a governmental unit without regard to his own or a third-party's fault in causing the accident. In nearly all of the states, a no-fault system now governs compensation for nearly all job-related injuries through workers' compensation plans. (See the box "Workers' Compensation.") In about half of the states, a no-fault insurance system governs compensation for personal injuries arising from automobile accidents. There have been proposals for introducing no-fault principles into products liability and medical malpractice. And at the farthest extreme, New Zealand has abolished tort liability for *all* accidental personal injuries and replaced it by a government-administered system of compensation.[46]

In this section we will focus on the no-fault insurance systems for automobile accident victims with much briefer consideration of proposals for extending no-fault to other forms of accidental losses. As we will see, this is one of the few areas in law and economics where empirical investigation has supplemented theoretical discussions.

A. No-Fault Automobile Insurance Plans

The area of accident law upon which the search for an alternative to the tort liability system has gone the farthest is that concerning automobile accidents. Automobile accidents represent one of the highest risks of injury that the ordinary citizen faces. Moreover, disputes arising from those accidents account for a large fraction of all civil complaints. This has been true since the 1920s when the automobile became affordable to most Americans. Thus, it is not surprising that dissatisfaction with the tort liability system's method of dealing with losses arising from automobile accidents is of long standing.

---

[45]The systems are sometimes referred to as "administered (or administrative) compensation" systems.

[46]The New Zealand Accident Compensation Act (as amended by the Accident Compensation Amendment (no. 2) Act 1973) abolished almost all tort actions for personal injury or death and replaced it with a comprehensive insurance plan that provides benefits to anyone who suffers "personal injury by accident." Unlike the employer-financed workers' compensation system or the insurance-based no-fault automobile systems, the New Zealand system is financed from general tax revenues. Note that the system covers only personal injuries; harm to property is still governed largely by the common law principles of tort liability. G. Palmer, COMPENSATION FOR INCAPACITY: A STUDY OF LAW AND SOCIAL CHANGE IN NEW ZEALAND AND AUSTRALIA (1979). The scheme has not been accepted in Australia. The bulk of the litigation under the Act has been regarding injuries arising from medical services. The Accident Compensation Commission has had to decide whether an injury was an accident or the result of sickness or disease.

Workers' Compensation

Among the most common accidents are those that occur at the work-place. It has been estimated that in any given year 10% of all industrial workers will be injured while on the job, although only one-third of these accidents results in lost work time. The average risk of on-the-job accidents is slightly higher than the risk of accident off the job, for example, in the home, but is about half the risk of injury in an auto-accident.

Given the pervasiveness of job-related accidents, the question arises, "How does the tort liability system determine who bears the costs of on-the-job accidents?" Until the late nineteenth century an employee who had been injured on the job was unlikely to recover anything from his employer. The common law of job-related accidents created three defenses for the defendant-employer that were extremely difficult for the plaintiff-employee to surmount. These defenses were

1. common employment (also known as the "fellow servant rule")—the employer could escape liability by noting that the proximate cause of the plaintiff's harm was the negligence of another *employee*. For example, those injured in a train crash could not recover from their employer if the crash was due to the negligent throwing of a switch by another employee. The injured employee's only cause of action lay against the negligent employee. In practical terms, this defense meant that the plaintiff would not be compensated because the negligent employee was not likely to have sufficient resources to compensate the victim.
2. assumption of the risk—the employer could argue that the employee willingly assumed the risk of a job-related injury. For example, a fireman, who is subject to very high risk of job-related harm, is paid a wage premium for assuming that risk.[1] Having voluntarily assumed a risk and, in some cases, having been compensated for that assumption of risk, the employee cannot recover for resulting job-related harms.
3. contributory negligence—the employer might concede his own negligence but escape liability by noting that the employee's own negligence had contributed to his harm.

Because the mechanization and complexity of production increased in the 19th century, the incidence of job-related accidents increased. And yet because the three common-law defenses generally insulated employers from liability, employees bore the brunt of these accidental losses.

By the end of the 19th century, this state of affairs had caused almost every western country but the United States to seek an alternative to tort liability for dealing with on-the-job accidents. The most common alternative was a system of compulsory compensation of injured employees without regard to fault and financed by a levy on employers and adminis-

---

[1]For an excellent discussion of this point in labor economics, see Kip Viscusi, RISK BY CHOICE (1983).

tered by the government. The United States soon followed suit; almost every state enacted some form of non-fault compensation between 1911 and 1920. At first, these workers' compensation systems, as they were known, were elective and confined only to very dangerous occupations. But by 1950 workers' compensation systems in this country had spread so that today all but three states have a compulsory system for nearly all workers. The result is that 90% of the United States labor force is covered by workers' compensation systems. The systems are state-based and differ slightly from state to state. Some states still have elective coverage; others have size-of-firm restrictions that exempt small firms from joining the system; and most states exclude farm workers from coverage. The role of the federal government is confined to offering special workers' compensation for employees who are excluded under state laws, e.g., coal miners and railroad employees.

Although the various state workers' compensation systems have some important differences, they share some common characteristics. The purpose of the system is to guarantee the injured employee *partial* compensation for his harms, including occupational diseases, but to spare him and his employer the costs of seeking (or defending against) full compensation in the tort liability system. The employer contributes a sum to the state workers' compensation system based on the dollar amount of his payroll. These contributions are then used to compensate injured employees in the state. To this end, an injured employee files a claim with the state governmental agency that administers the system. If the agency determines that the harm is job-related, then it awards him compensation according to a statutory schedule of benefits. This schedule of benefits is calculated for either partial or total disability and depending on whether the disability is temporary or permanent. For some injuries the benefits paid are invariant to the actual losses of the employee. Thus, the benefit for a lost arm may be $5,000 regardless of whether the worker was a professional typist or a receiving clerk. For other injuries, the benefits are scaled to the injured employee's actual losses. For example, the recovery of lost income is typically limited to two-thirds of lost wages. Similarly, most states offer full compensation without restriction on medical and rehabilitation expenses. In the event of a dispute between the employee and the workers' compensation commission, the matter may be adjudicated. Every system provides for the exclusion of some harms from coverage, generally those that are attributable to willful misconduct, aggressive assault, and drunkenness.

Some of the important differences between the state workers' compensation systems turn on the relationship between the workers' compensation and the tort liability system. In some states workers may collect workers' compensation benefits *and* sue their employer for recovery on a negligence theory. In other states, the employee must elect one or the other of these alternatives with statutory restrictions on when workers' compensation will be the exclusive remedy.

The economic consequences of the workers' compensation systems have not been thoroughly studied. In theory, there are some potentially inefficient consequences. For example, making some of the scheduled benefits invariant to the employee's actual losses may distort the employee's and the employer's decisions about the amount of precaution to take. To illustrate, because some benefits are not sensitive to the age and career stage of the employee, some (generally young) employees are under-compensated by workers' compensation while others (generally older) employees are over-compensated. This may distort the decisions of employees about how much precaution to take and of employers about the age-structure of their labor force.

There is very little empirical work on whether the workers' compensation system has altered the safety of the workplace to a greater or lesser extent than would have the tort liability system. We know, for example, that the trend in this century has been toward fewer job-related injuries and deaths. Would this trend have been different in the absence of workers' compensation? Recently there has been an increase in the number of job-related injuries. To what is this attributable: alterations in the workers' compensation systems in the 1970s or to other, underlying changes in the labor force and workplace, e.g., in the percentage of women in the labor force? Has there been a discernible impact of the workers' compensation system on the choice of technology in the workplace as between labor- and capital-intensive production functions?[2]

[2]Some additional research worth consulting on this important but neglected topic are the following: Lawrence Friedman, A HISTORY OF AMERICAN LAW (2d ed. 1985); R. Epstein, *The Historical Origins and Economic Structure of the Workers' Compensation Act*, 16 G.A. L. REV. 775 (1982); G. Schwartz, *Tort Law and the Economy in Nineteenth-Century America: A Reinterpretation*, 90 YALE L. J. 1717, 1768–1771 (1981); H. Demsetz, *When Does the Rule of Liability Matter?* 1 J. LEGAL STUD. 13 (1972); and L. Darling-Hammond & T. Kniesner, THE LAW AND ECONOMICS OF WORKERS' COMPENSATION (Santa Monica, CA: The Rand Institute on Civil Justice, 1980).

From the Columbia Report of 1932 through the publication of a highly influential work by Professors Keeton and O'Connell in 1965 (BASIC PROTECTION FOR THE TRAFFIC VICTIM), there has been a strong call to replace the tort liability system for automobile accidents with a no-fault system.

Beginning in 1970 several states began to adopt the no-fault alternative for compensating the victims of automobile accidents. These plans, like those for workers' compensation, share some core characteristics and yet have some important differences. In general, the no-fault plans for automobile accident victims deal only with *personal injuries*, not with harm to property.[47] The victim is to be compensated for his losses by his own insurance

[47]Massachusetts tried no-fault insurance for property damage, too, but abandoned that experiment after six years. The principal shortcomings of the no-fault insurance scheme for property damage were that the legislation forbade insurance companies from refusing to insure anyone and required a $250 deductible in every policy. Both were extremely unpopular. There is an excellent discussion of these matters in R. Epstein, C. Gregory, & H. Kalven, CASES AND MATERIALS ON TORTS 973–980 (4th ed. 1984).

company, regardless of his or anyone else's fault in causing the accident. There is no schedule of benefits for these personal injuries; no-fault benefits are closely tied to the victim's actual losses. An important exception to this general statement is that the victim will not receive compensation for his pain and suffering. He might have received such compensation from the defendant in a tort action, but because his insurance policy is not likely to cover such losses and because his losses will be compensated only according to the terms of his insurance contract, the victim is confined to insurable losses. The fact that no-fault relies on first-party insurance as the method for compensating automobile accident victims suggests two important points:

1. A no-fault system requires an increased amount of state govenmental regulation of the insurance market. For example, the state government must specify many of the terms of the standard first-party insurance contract. Additionally, the state may heighten its requirement of evidence of insurability before granting a drivers' license.

2. An important consequence of the switch to no-fault will be the impact on insurance rates. Those who favor no-fault have argued that the system is much less expensive at compensating victims than is the tort liability system. If so, an important piece of corroborating evidence would be a decline in automobile insurance rates after the introduction of no-fault. The critics have predicted a dramatic and intolerable increase in insurance rates after the switch to no-fault. As we will see, much of the debate on no-fault has centered on whether insurance rates have increased or decreased as a result of the switch.

To appreciate the arguments that were made in favor of no-fault, it is important for us to examine the arguments that were made in criticism of the tort liability system's handling of losses arising from automobile accidents.[48] One of the most thorough and influential modern criticisms of the tort liability system and auto accident losses was a 1971 report by the United States Department of Transportation entitled MOTOR VEHICLE CRASH LOSSES AND THEIR COMPENSATION IN THE UNITED STATES. Some of the most important findings of that report are the following:

Only 45% of all those killed or seriously injured in auto accidents benefited in any way under the tort liability system.

When the economic loss was small (less than $500), victims recovering under tort received an average of 4 1/2 times their economic loss. However, at the other end of the loss spectrum when loss was $25,000 or more, even successful tort claimants averaged a net recovery of only 1/3 of their economic loss.

---

[48]Much of the following discussion draws heavily on the material in AUTOMOBILE NO-FAULT INSURANCE: A STUDY BY THE SPECIAL COMMITTEE ON AUTOMOBILE INSURANCE LEGISLATION (Am. Bar Assn. 1978). The preface to that study indicates that Judge Richard A. Posner was the principal author.

> *Final tort settlement took on the average 1/2 year longer for seriously injured victims with economic losses of $2,500 or more than it did for persons with small losses.*

> *Tort liability insurance would appear to cost in the neighborhood of $1.07 in total system expenses to deliever $1.00 in net benefits to victims.*

> *Motor vehicle accident litigation in the court system was estimated to occupy 17% of the system's available resources.*

Each of these points would seem to constitute a significant indictment of the tort liability system's treatment of automobile accidents. However, each of these findings is misleading. Therefore, the basis of the agrument against the tort liability system is seriously flawed. Let us look more closely at some of the Department of Transportation's findings.

The fact that only 45% of those seriously injured or killed in auto accidents receive benefits from the tort liability system is misleading. First, not all auto accidents in which there is serious injury or death are the result of an injurer's fault. Some of those accidents were single-vehicle accidents, and in others, the victim was contributorily negligent. Moreover, if one uses the DOT's data and calculates the percentage of all those seriously injured in auto accidents who received some benefits from collateral sources (such as insurance policies, disability pay, workers' compensation, sick leave, and so on), 90% of all those seriously injured in auto accidents recover some of their losses. Second, the criticism that only a fraction of seriously injured automobile accident victims are compensated by the tort liability system rests on the misperception that the tort liability system is or should be a system of insurance, something tort liability was never meant to be. We have stressed the efficiency aspect of the tort system, specifically its ability to encourage the internalization of external harms. Clearly this does not mean that all those harmed by the actions of another will be compensated *by that other person*. But it does not mean that the victim will not receive compensation from some source. In fact, despite the criticism of the DOT report, there is no inherent incompatibility between the fault system and universal victim compensation. The current system is a well-crafted combination of the two: tort liability recovery plus first-party insurance against losses not likely to be compensable. But to ask the tort liability system to serve as an efficient internalizer of illegitimate external costs *and* as a system of universal compensation is to ask the impossible. As the American Bar Association's study of automobile no-fault systems so aptly put it: "This illustrates the dilemma of tort liability, when evaluated as if it were an insurance system: if a low percentage of victims recover, this fact can be used as evidence that liability provides inadequate compensation; but if a high percentage recover, this fact can be used as evidence that liability has been converted into, and hence should be replaced by, explicit insurance."

The DOT report's second statistic—that those with small losses are generally overcompensated by the tort liability system while those with large losses are generally undercompensated—is similarly misleading. Those with small lost earnings may well be those—such as college students—who have large lost future earnings as a result of the accident. Thus, they *should* recover more than their actual losses. Those with large lost earnings are likely to be those who are able to afford large amounts of life, medical, disability, and accident insurance. Because no-fault insurance places a relatively low monetary cap on awards, those with small lost earnings are likely to be *under*-compensated by the no-fault insurance system. Similarly, those with large losses are not likely to be aided by no-fault insurance because the cap placed on no-fault awards is usually far below what they need for compensation.

The contention that the administration costs of the tort liability system exceed the benefits it confers is also misleading in that it greatly understates the benefits that the tort liability system may generate. We have stressed repeatedly in this book that one of the most important economic functions of legal rules is to create incentives for efficient behavior *in the future*. Thus, one of the most important functions of the tort liability system is to put potential victims and potential injurers on notice about the costs they may not legitimately impose on others. The resulting internalization of those forbidden externalities is one of the great efficiency accomplishments of the tort system. Indeed, there is some suggestive evidence that the tort liability system is achieving this deterrence goal. For example, it appears to be the case that increases in liability insurance premiums reduce the number and severity of automobile accidents.[49]

This suggests that in making a cost-benefit assessment of the tort liability system one must count as a benefit the net accident costs foregone because of the safety rules established by that system. In most instances this will be a positive figure and may even be a large positive figure. The shortcoming of the DOT figure is that it ignores these future social benefits by counting as a benefit of the tort system only the dollar value of the award to the current plaintiff.

Finally, the report finds the tort liability system to be inefficient because litigation regarding automobile accidents occupies such a large fraction (17%) of the court system's limited resources. The difficulty with that contention is that the report offers no measure by which one is to judge that 17% is inefficiently high. In the absence of a measuring device, there is no method of determining what the optimal amount of litigation is.

These thoughts suggest that the criticisms of the tort liability system are not proven, and that, therefore, the need to find an alternative to that system is not established. Be that as it may, in the early 1970s twenty-four states adopted some form of no-fault for automobile accidents, as indicated in Table 9.2. Since the late 1970s no additional states have adopted no-fault for automobile accidents.

---

[49]*See* Richard W. Grayson, *Deterrence in Automobile Liability Insurance* (unpublished Ph.D. diss., U. Chi. Grad. Sch. of Bus., 1971).

Table 9.2   State No-Fault Statutes

Year	No. of States	States
1971	1	Massachusetts
1972	5	Delaware, Florida, Oregon, South Dakota, Virgina
1973	7	Connecticut, Hawaii, Maryland, Michigan, Nevada, New Jersey, Texas
1974	7	Arkansas, Colorado, Kansas, New York, Pennsylvania, South Carolina, Utah
1975	3	Georgia, Kentucky, Minnesota
1976	1	North Dakota

The statutes in the states differ considerably but may nonetheless by placed in three broad categories:

1. Those no-fault plans that provide modest benefits and interfere minimally with the tort system.[50] Typically these systems place no restriction on the victim's access to tort liability other than to require that any no-fault benefits be deducted from a tort judgment. For example, in Delaware mandatory first-party personal injury benefits are available up to $10,000 per person and $20,000 per accident, if more than one person is injured, to cover medical expenses, lost earnings, loss of service, and funeral expenses.

2. Those no-fault plans that provide limited no-fault benefits and restrict or prohibit some tort claims.[51] For example, Massachusetts allows a maximum of $2,000 in benefits, to cover medical expenses, lost wages, death, and funeral expenses. No-fault benefits are not available if workers' compensation benefits are available, and for those not covered by workers' compensation, the statutory benefits for lost wages are reduced by the extent of any collateral benefits the victim receives. A tort action may be brought only where the victim is killed, sustains a statutorily defined serious injury, or has medical expenses in excess of $500.

3. Those no-fault plans that give broad no-fault benefits and restrict or prohibit some tort claims.[52] For example, in Michigan medical and hospital benefits are not limited; the victim may recover 85% of lost earnings, up to a limit of $100 per month for three years and funeral expenses up to $1,000. Tort actions involving an automobile accident are allowed only where the injury was intentional, the victim's losses

---

[50]Examples are the no-fault statutes in Arkansas, Delaware, Maryland, Oregon, South Carolina, South Dakota, Texas, and Virgina.

[51]Examples are the no-fault statutes in Colorado, Connecticut, Florida, Georgia, Hawaii, Kansas, Kentucky, Massachusetts, Minnesota, Nevada, New York, North Dakota, and Utah.

[52]Examples are the no-fault statutes in Michigan, New Jersey, and Pennsylvania.

exceed the no-fault benefits to which he or she is entitled, or where there is a statutorily defined serious injury or the victim is killed.

What has been the result of no-fault insurance on insurance rates and the number and severity of accidents? Despite the fact that there have been numerous studies of the matter, the record is not clear. The opponents of no-fault have discovered some unexpected adverse consequences while the proponents have found some of the beneficial results they had predicted. If we were to venture an opinion, it would be that the anticipated benefits of the switch to no-fault have not been great enough to warrant the switch and the unexpected adverse consequences have been serious enough to question the entire experiment.

Consider the results, admittedly controversial, of the no-fault insurance system in the Commonwealth of Massachusetts. In the first four years of the no-fault system, there was a dramatic 87% reduction in the number of suits filed that alleged negligent bodily injury in an automobile accident. This sounds like precisely the sort of efficient consequence that the proponents of no-fault had predicted. However, almost all of the suits that were dropped were those for minor bodily injury, and although the drop in the number of suits filed was dramatic, the savings were not. Minor bodily injury cases are usually settled before trial, and when they are tried, they are not expensive; thus, a reduction in the number of these actions is not much of a savings of the resources of the court system. Worse still, in the years after the introduction of no-fault, the fraction of auto complaints filed that subsequently went to trial doubled, and the average damage award in these suits increased by 125%. Four years after the statute had been enacted automobile accident cases still accounted for 25% of the civil caseload of the Massachusetts trial courts, far above the national average before no-fault was passed.

There were some other unanticipated consequences of the Massachusetts no-fault insurance system. By comparison to the pre-no-fault system, a much larger proportion of those receiving no-fault benefits were involved in single-vehicle accidents and rear-end collisions. Why should this be? One possibility is that the expanded coverage offered by no-fault encouraged victims who would have previously borne their own losses (because of the fear of being dropped by their insurance company) to approach their insurance company for compensation (in the belief that the universal coverage requirement of the no-fault statute meant the insurance company would not drop them). A more ominous possibility is that drivers are less cautious under no-fault.

What happened to Massachusetts insurance rates under no-fault? As could have been predicted, first-party insurance rates rose while liability insurance rates fell. But what is of crucial interest is whether the decline in the liability insurance was greater or less than the rise in first-party insurance rates. Overall, it appears that the rate for the total insurance policy (covering bodily injury, property damage, collision, and comprehensive liability) doubled between 1970 and 1977. However, there is some dispute about whether the general inflation of the 1970s or the no-fault insurance system is to blame for this increase.[53]

Finally, what about the number and severity of accidents under no-fault? There has only been one economic study of this effect, and the conclusion of that study was that the adoption of no-fault statutes increased the number of fatal accidents and that the more stringent the no-fault statute, the greater the increase in fatal accidents.[54] There are several reasons for doubting this conclusion. First, the theoretical connection between no-fault and fatal road accidents is not at all clear; indeed, a sensible working hypothesis would be that there is no connection between no-fault insurance and automobile fatalities because all the no-fault statutes left tort actions intact for deaths and very serious injuries. An alternative hypothesis, one not contemplated in the study but one that might be important, is that the compulsory liability insurance provisions of most no-fault laws may have led to a general lowering of the quality of drivers with a resulting increase in fatal accidents. Second, the study did not adequately control for the influence of other important determinants of the number of fatal accidents. For example, throughout the 1970s most states lowered the drinking age; more young drunk drivers would certainly increase the number of fatal auto accidents.

> **Question 9.24:** Comment on this contention: "Hence, the no-fault principle seems to involve a choice between higher premium costs and even less adequate compensation than under the tort system."

> **Question 9.25:** Does the no-fault system deter faulty driving? Does it matter that under no-fault insurance some will be allowed to recover who would not have recovered under the fault system because of contributory negligence or would have had their award restricted under comparative negligence?

B. Elective No-Fault for Product-Related Injuries and Medical Malpractice

The proponents of no-fault insurance for automobile accident injuries have proposed extending no-fault to other troubled areas of the tort liability system, specifically to products liability and medical malpractice.[55] With regard to product-related injuries, the proposal is that the manufacturer could elect to offer with his product—presumably as part of the contract of sale, much

---

[53]*See* O'Connell & Beck, *An Update of the Surveys on the Operation of No-Fault Auto Laws,* 1979 INS. L. J. 129, where it is maintained that there has been a significant drop in insurance rates as a result of the switch to no-fault.

[54]*See* Elizabeth Landes, *Insurance, Liability, and Accidents: A Theoretical and Empirical Investigation of No-Fault Accidents,* 25 J. LAW & ECON. 49 (1982). For a criticism, *see* Jeffrey O'Connell & Saul Levmore, *A Reply to Landes: A Faulty Study of No-Fault's Effect on Fault?* 48 MO. L. REV. 649 (1983).

[55]*See* J. O'Connell, ENDING INSULT TO INJURY (1975).

like an express warranty—a schedule of benefits that he would pay in the event that the consumer was injured while using the product. In the event of an injury, there would be no inquiry into the product's defect or the user's fault; benefits would simply be paid to the injured consumer according to the contractual schedule. Pain and suffering would not be compensable, collateral benefits would be deducted, and a few other restrictions would apply. The system would be financed from a fund established by the manufacturer; presumably the manufacturer would include a premium as part of his product's price to cover his anticipated liability.

Those manufacturers who chose not to offer elective no-fault would still be strictly liable for product-related injuries under the current system. The argument is that if the elective no-fault system is more efficient than the current system, then manufacturers have an incentive to opt out of the tort liability system and into the elective no-fault system. Currently, the total price charged by manufacturers includes a component to cover the material and labor and other costs of producing the output and a separate component to cover the expected liability costs under the current products liability system. If the limitations for pain and suffering and the savings on settlement and litigation under the elective no-fault regime are great enough, then the component of the product price included to cover anticipated liability will be lower under the elective no-fault system than under the current products liability system. The result is that total product prices may fall under an elective no-fault system for dealing with product-related injuries.

The proposal for elective no-fault for products liability and for medical malpractice has not been favorably received. There are problems with the proposed system, as the following excerpt from a review of the initial proposal amusingly points out:

> The following illustration may be useful in illuminating this pioneering proposal for an elective [no-fault system for product-related injuries]. Smith bought at retail a soundly constructed household ladder manufactured by a company that had opted for the [elective no-fault system]. At another store he purchased sport shoes that fit him poorly, and, not long ago, pursuant to an examination, he acquired new eyeglasses that blur his vision slightly. On a fair day Smith, fortified by a few beers, tries out the ladder. Upon reaching the top his foot slips out of the new sport shoe; he then tries to wiggle his foot back into the shoe but is impeded by the distortion of vision attributable to the new eyeglasses and perhaps by an impairment in motor response attributable to drinking the beer; in the end he falls off the ladder and sustains very serious injuries. Under present law Smith would have no possibility of recovering from the manufacturer or retailer of the ladder, he would probably not be able to recover from the shoe store, and his prospects of recovering from the optometrist or the local tavern would be equally remote.[56] Under the proposed new regime, however, Smith

---

[56]This review was written in 1975. Today under the prevailing rules of products liability, Smith would probably be able to recover from any or all of the following: the ladder manufacturer, the shoe store, the optometrist, the local tavern, the beer manufacturer, and the publisher of the do-it-yourself book that gave him (defective) instructions on how to mount a ladder.

could get compensation for his injuries from the insurance funded by the pro-ducer of the ladder—a company that made and marketed a product that was sound in design and construction.[57]

However bad the current system for dealing with product-related inju-ries is, this excerpt points out that the inefficiencies of the elective no-fault scheme are probably larger still.

CONCLUSION

In this chapter we have applied the economic theory of tort liability of the previous chapter to some leading issues in tort law. Our feeling is that the economic theory allows us to understand some rules of tort law—e.g., the principles of vicarious liability and of joint and multiple tortfeasors—that the traditional theory of tort liability was not able to explain satisfactorily. Moreover, the economic analysis of tortious harm allows a more thorough analysis of some matters, such as liability for failure to rescue, than does the traditional theory. We have also examined from an economic standpoint the current crisis in products liability law and the various proposals for its reform. The more thorough proposals to replace the tort liability system with a no-fault system of administered compensation do not bear up very well when judged on an economic efficiency standard.

Despite the length of this chapter, we stress it is truly only an introduc-tion to a very complex and fascinating topic. Not only have we had to ignore important further details and complexities in each of the areas we have examined in this chapter, but we have also had to ignore some other areas entirely. We have not even attempted to discuss the economics of such important torts as defamation (libel and slander), the invasion of privacy, and misrepresentation. (A question below invites you to apply the economic theory of tort liability to one of these torts.) Nor have we had time or space to discuss the economics of such intriguing issues as medical malpractice or the liability of handgun manufacturers or that of tobacco manufacturers for the harms arising from the use of their products. We are certain that you will find that when you learn the central legal issues in those further areas, you will be able to discern the important efficiency aspects of different legal rules in those areas by applying the economic analysis of the last two chapters.

Question 9.26: Consider the following famous case on the right of privacy, *Melvin v. Reid*, 297 P.91 (1931):

"It is alleged that [Mrs. Melvin's] maiden name was Gabrielle Darley; that a number of years ago she was a prostitute and was tried for murder, the trial resulting in her acquittal; that during the year 1918, and after her acquittal, she

---

[57]W. Blum, *Review of O'Connell's Ending Insult to Injury*, 43 U. CHI. L. REV. 217 (1975).

abandoned her life of shame and became entirely rehabilitated; that during the year 1919 she married Bernard Melvin and commenced the duties of caring for their home, and thereafter at all times lived an exemplary, virtuous, honorable, and righteous life; that she assumed a place in respectable society, and made many friends who were not aware of the incidents of her earlier life; that during the month of July, 1925, the defendants [Reid and others], without her permission, knowledge, or consent, made, photographed, produced, and released a moving picture entitled *The Red Kimono*, and thereafter exhibited it in moving picture houses in California, Arizona, and throughout many other states; that this moving picture was based upon the true story of the past life of the appellant, and that her maiden name, Gabrielle Darley, was used therein; that defendants featured and advertised that the plot of the film was the true story of the unsavory incidents in the life of the appellant; that Gabrielle Darley was the true name of the principal character; and that Gabrielle Darley was appellant; that by the production and showing of the picture, friends of appellant learned for the first time of the unsavory incidents in her early life. This caused them to scorn and abandon her, and exposed her to obloquy, contempt, and ridicule, causing her grievous mental and physical suffering to her damage in the sum of $50,000. . . ."

Has there been a tort here? On what theory would you analyze this tort—neglience or strict liability? In deciding on this issue, does it matter whether the person whose past is revealed is a public figure—say, a United States senator—or, as here, a private individual? For example, would you allow a private citizen to recover under a tort theory but not allow a public figure to recover? Why? What sort of incentives for behavior are created by allowing recovery for invasion of one's solitude or privacy? How would the economic theory of this tort apply to an employer's inquiries into a potential employee's past life?

SUGGESTED READINGS

Calabresi, Guido, THE COSTS OF ACCIDENTS: A LEGAL AND ECONOMIC ANALYSIS (1970).

Calabresi, Guido, *First Party, Third Party, and Product Liability Systems: Can Economic Analysis of Law Tell Us Anything About Them?* 69 IOWA L. REV. 833 (1984).

Cooter, R., Lewis Kornhauser, and David Lane, *Liability Rules, Limited Information, and the Role of Precedent*, 10 BELL. J. ECON. 366 (1979).

Craswell, Richard, and John Calfee, *Some Effect of Uncertainty on Compliance with Legal Standards,* 70 VA. L. REV. 965 (1984).

Danzon, Patricia M., MEDICAL MALPRACTICE: THEORY, EVIDENCE, AND PUBLIC POLICY (1985).

Dewees, Donald N., CONTROLLING ASBESTOS IN BUILDINGS: AN ECONOMIC INVESTIGATION (1986).

Eads, George, and Peter Reuter, DESIGNING SAFER PRODUCTS: CORPO-

RATE RESPONSES TO PRODUCT LIABILITY LAW AND REGULATION (1983).

Epstein, Richard, MODERN PRODUCTS LIABILITY LAW (1980).

Haddock, David, and Christopher Curran, *An Economic Theory of Comparative Negligence*, 14 J. LEGAL STUD. 49 (1985).

Landes, William, and Richard A. Posner, *The Positive Economic Theory of Tort Law*, 15 U. GA. L. REV. 851 (1981).

Landes, William, and Richard A. Posner, THE ECONOMIC STRUCTURE OF TORT LAW (1987).

Note (Jennifer Arlen), *An Economic Analysis of Tort Damages for Wrongful Death*, 60 N.Y.U.L. REV. (1986).

O'Connell, Jeffrey, THE LAWSUIT LOTTERY (1979).

Posner, Richard A., ECONOMIC ANALYSIS OF LAW 147–198 (3d ed. 1986).

Rabin, Robert, ed., PERSPECTIVES ON TORT LAW (2d ed. 1983).

Rolph, J., and J. Hammett, R. Houches, & S. Polin, AUTOMOBILE ACCIDENT COMPENSATION, vs. I–IV (Santa Monica, CA: The RAND Institute on Civil Justice, 1985).

Ross, H. Laurence, SETTLED OUT OF COURT: THE SOCIAL PROCESS OF INSURANCE CLAIMS ADJUSTMENT (2d ed. 1980).

Rottenberg, Simon, ed., THE ECONOMICS OF MEDICAL MALPRACTICE (1978).

Symposium: *Alternative Compensations Schemes and Tort Theory*, 73 CAL. L. REV. 548 (1985).

Symposium: *Catastrophic Personal Injuries*, 13 J. LEGAL STUD. 415 (1984).

Symposium: *Critical Issues in Tort Law Reform: A Search for Principles*, 14 J. LEGAL STUD. 459 (1985).

Symposium: *The Law and Economics of Privacy*, 9 J. LEGAL STUD. 621 (1980).

Wittman, Donald, *The Price of Negligence under Differing Liability Rules*, 29 J. LAW & ECON. 151 (1986).

CHAPTER 10

The Economic Efficiency of the Common Law Process

Suppose that after years of marriage Joan Potatoes and her husband, Joe, decide to divorce. Their common property and, possibly, their future income, will have to be divided. They will probably proceed by consulting lawyers, and, having clarified their rights, they will bargain in an attempt to reach a settlement. Most such bargaining succeeds and most legal disputes are settled without a trial, but, if they cannot agree, they may land in court. After the case is argued, the judge and jury (if there is a jury) will deliberate. Eventually a decision will be reached and the results announced. If Joan is disgruntled with, say, the share of the property awarded to her, she may appeal, in which case there may be another trial before a higher court.

As this example illustrates, there are at least the following stages in a full-blown legal dispute, regardless of the substantive issues:

1. bargaining in an attempt to settle,
2. trial, and
3. appeal.

Each stage in the process raises important questions of law and policy. The preceding chapters have applied economics to the *substantive* common and statute law of property, torts, and contracts. This chapter, instead, applies economic analysis to the *procedural* aspects of civil disputes. We will try to answer such questions as: Why does most bargaining between legal disputants succeed? Why do some disputes end in trials? Do the procedural rules followed in a civil trial satisfy the requirements of rational decisionmaking? Does the process of appeal cause the common law to evolve toward economically efficient rules of property, tort, and contract?

I. LAWSUITS: AS AMERICAN AS APPLE PIE
(AND A LOT MORE EXPENSIVE)

Americans are more litigious than other peoples. There are 20 times as many lawyers per capita in America as there are in Japan, 5 times as many as there are in West Germany, and almost 4 times as many as there are in England.[1] American trial courts disposed of over 4 million civil cases in 1981, over 2.5 million criminal cases, and 0.6 million juvenile cases.[2] In per capita terms, there were about 3 dispositions by courts per 100 American residents. For the civil cases, the data suggest that contract disputes produce about 10 times as many trials as tort disputes, with property disputes somewhere in between.[3] Historical data reveal an upward trend in civil cases filed as a percentage of the population in many American jurisdictions over the course of the 20th century.[4] Fortunately, most cases are disposed of without resort to trial. Estimates suggest that 5–10% of civil disputes filed actually require the commencement of a trial in order to resolve them.[5]

No one knows how much legal disputes cost society. Combined federal, state, and local spending on civil and criminal justice was put at $39.7 billion dollars in 1983, or $170 per capita. The three elements were $88 per capita on police protection, $44 on correctional services (e.g., prisons and jails), and $37 on judicial services. This amounts to about 3 percent of all government spending for the fiscal year 1983.[6] The expenditures on police protection are mostly devoted to deterring crime, the expenditures on correctional services are mostly devoted to punishing criminals, and the expenditures on judicial services are mostly concerned with resolving disputes.

---

[1]Administrative Office of the United States Courts, MANAGEMENT STATISTICS FOR THE UNITED STATES COURTS (1981) at 13, 129, as reported in Table 3 of Marc Galanter, *Reading the Landscape of Disputes: What We Know and Don't Know (And Think We Know) About Our Allegedly Contentious And Litigious Society,* 31 UCLA L. REV. 40, 52 (1983).

[2]National Center for State Courts. *State Court Caseload Statistics: Annual Report 1981* (Court Statistics and Information Management Project, April, 1985) table 12 at 47.

[3]These numbers should be treated with caution because of wide variance across states and because of errors in the variables. National Center for State Courts, STATE COURT CASELOAD STATISTICS: ANNUAL REPORT 1981 (Court Statistics and Information Management Project, April, 1985) table 20 at 84–86.

[4]The upward trend is not, however, smooth or unwavering. See Galanter, *supra* note 1, at 39–40.

[5]See Galanter, *supra* note 1, at 44. However, a more careful disaggregation of data reveals a complicated picture. Erhard Blankenberg found that the ratio of settlement to judgment in Germany was 10 to 1 for traffic accidents, but only 2.7 to 1 for debt collection, 2.4 to 1 for disputes over service contracts, and 1.7 to 1 for disputes about rental contracts. See *Legal Insurance, Litigant Decisions, and the Rising Caseloads of Courts: A West German Study,* 16 LAW & SOC. REV. 619 (1981–82).

[6]The data are reported in "Cost of Justice System Is Put at $39.7 Billion in U.S. Study," *New York Times,* 14 July 1986, at 11. The article is a report on a study by the Bureau of Justice Statistics, Department of Justice.

It is the latter that concerns us in this chapter. Direct government expenditures on judicial services, as represented by the $37 per capita figure quoted above, is only a small fraction of the true cost of resolving disputes by the courts because most of the costs are borne by private parties rather than by government. Exact data on the full cost are unavailable, but it is possible to make a back-of-the-envelope computation. When a court conducts a full-blown trial, the parties involved in the procedure at any point in time are typically a judge, a 12-person jury, the plaintiff and the plaintiff's lawyer (or prosecutor in a criminal case), the defendant and the defendant's lawyer, a court stenographer, and a court guard. In addition, someone is usually presenting testimony, possibly an expert witness. Counting heads, that adds up to 20 people. To get an idea of the labor cost of a trial, we need to make an estimate of the values of these 20 people's time. But the labor of these participants is valued at widely different rates. For example, if the lawyers work for large firms, they may bill at around $200 per hour, whereas the jurors are usually reimbursed by the state at around $10 per day (which is far less than the opportunity cost of a juror's time). The value of most people's time is in between these extremes. If we make the conservative estimate that the average value of the labor of all 20 participants in the trial is, say, $20 per hour, then the labor value of a full trial would be around $400 per hour. But these are not the total costs of a trial; we must also include such costs as those of supplying a court room. Although we have no firm idea what these additional costs are, it is clear that the total cost of a trial would be over $400 per hour (our estimated labor cost). The point of this back-of-the-envelope computation is that the costs showing up in government statistics are only a fraction of the total cost to society. (These high costs of litigation have given rise to a search for other methods of settling disagreements. For one example, see the box entitled "Alternative Dispute Resolution: The VISA Arbitration Committee.")

Various theories have been advanced to explain the high rates of litigation in contemporary America. The most cheerful view, favored by the plaintiff's bar (i.e., those lawyers who specialize in representing plaintiffs), is that underprivileged Americans, who previously suffered indignities in silence, are finally asserting their legal rights. According to this view, litigation protects rights that were formerly invaded, so high litigation rates are evidence of more social justice.[7] If there is more litigation in the United States than in other countries, this line of thought suggests that we are protecting the underprivileged better. A more dreary view is that lawyers, especially some "ambulance chasers," are manufacturing suits in order to make a profit from litigation. ("When I was the only lawyer in Shinbone, I almost

---

[7]For example, John Coffee argues against the theory that economic incentives cause too many civil suits. See *Understanding the Plaintiff's Attorney: The Implications of Economic Theory for Private Enforcement of Law Through Class and Derivative Actions*, 86 COLUM. L. REV. 669 (1986).

Alternative Dispute Resolution: The VISA Arbitration Committee

Many contracts contain terms stipulating procedures for resolving disputes. These procedures characteristically bypass the public courts and substitute streamlined alternatives. To illustrate, many health maintenance organizations stipulate that disputes between patients and doctors will be resolved by compulsory arbitration. This is an attempt to reduce the cost of medical malpractice insurance. As another illustration, many contracts for the delivery of goods specify that disputes will be resolved by compulsory arbitration according to the rules of the American Arbitration Association, and that arbitration will occur in the home city of the seller. This is an attempt by sellers to avoid the high cost of defending themselves in disputes over breach of contract.

Another interesting example is provided by the VISA credit card corporation. VISA provides a network connecting banks who issue cards to consumers and enroll merchants to accept VISA cards as payment for goods. Consumers sometimes refuse to pay a disputed bill. ("The goods were never delivered." "It broke as soon as I got it home.") When this happens, the bank that issued the card to the consumer will try to charge the item's cost back to the bank that enrolled the merchant who sold the disputed goods. Naturally, this action could result in a legal dispute between the two banks about the responsibility for the item's cost. Such disputes are handled by VISA's Arbitration Committee. The "plaintiff" has to pay a fee for originating a complaint and both parties submit written accounts of the facts. The Arbitration Committee decides on the basis of these documents, without ever meeting with the disputants. When the Arbitration Committee announces its decision, the loser pays the judgment and also the costs of arbitration. There are no lawyers, no detailed legal procedures, no face-to-face encounters between disputants.

The burdensome procedures followed by public courts are designed to ferret out the truth while protecting the rights of the parties. The VISA members could have adopted these procedural rules for resolving their disputes but chose not to. The fact that VISA members voluntarily abandon most procedural rights suggests that their costs exceed their benefits to VISA members. In general, the institution of contract permits people to abandon many of their procedural rights in order to streamline dispute resolution by substituting a private forum for public courts. Should courts encourage this substitution? What limits should courts place upon a person's power to contract out of the public court system?

starved, but now that another lawyer has come to town, I eat steak, and I'm building a new house.")

These rival theories warrant careful scrutiny. We will begin by examining the logic of bargaining in order to understand why rational people press disputes and sometimes end up in court. Our examination should provide a finer understanding of the causes of high litigation rates.

II. WHY SUE?

Many disputes are settled without the filing of a legal complaint. Indeed, it seems safe to say that most disputes are settled this way, even though there is no data on the frequency of informal disputes. The question is, "Why sue?"

Game theory explains why some disputes result in suits and others do not. A civil dispute typically involves disagreement over how to divide a sum of money (what we could call the "stakes" or, in the terms of the bargaining theory we developed in Chapter 4 and in Chapter 7, the surplus). Thus, a divorce may involve dividing the wealth that the parties accumulated while married. And in a dispute about the performance of a contractual obligation, the stakes or surplus might be the gain that the breacher anticipates from being allowed to breach. In bargaining, self-interested parties will press for a share of the stakes, but their demands will be moderated by the fact that failure to settle results in a costly trial that destroys part of the stakes. The elements of the bargain are, then, the stakes to be divided, demands by the parties, and the possible destruction of part of the stakes by noncooperation.

If the expected judgment in a certain class of cases is less than the cost of a trial, potential plaintiffs who are rational will not ordinarily bring suit. For example, suppose an automobile, worth $1,000, is the disputed item in a divorce. Let us suppose that the plaintiff believes that the probability of the court's awarding him the car is 0.5, so the plaintiff's expected value of the trial judgment is $1,000(0.5) = $500.

Whether the case is worth pursuing depends upon the cost of a trial. Suppose the trial will cost the plaintiff $750. The expected judgment at trial is $500 and the expected cost of trial is $750, so the plaintiff expects to suffer a net loss of $250 from trial. This dispute is not worth pursuing. These numbers illustrate that plaintiffs normally will not press disputes when the expected judgment is small relative to the cost of trials.

Even when the expected judgment is relatively large, there is another mechanism that may prevent suits. Potential defendants are often in the position of being able to avoid disputes by taking precaution against the events that give rise to them. If the expected judgment is very large relative to the cost of precaution, potential defendants will seldom give potential plaintiffs the opportunity to bring an action. As we saw in the previous two chapters, a manufacturer will spend large sums on quality control to avoid defects that would expose him to massive liability claims by injured consumers, and the larger his precautionary expenses, the less likely is an accident involving his product. Similarly, owners of property can avoid creating nuisances, drivers can use care, and promisors can perform on their contracts.

We have shown that the number of suits will be small if the expected damages are small relative to trial costs or large relative to precaution costs. Clearly, then, as the expected judgment rises above a trivial amount, the number of suits must increase, and as the expected judgment becomes very large, the number of suits must decrease. This proposition is illustrated in Figure 10.1, where the number of suits, which is read off the vertical axis, is

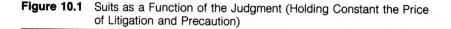

Figure 10.1 Suits as a Function of the Judgment (Holding Constant the Price of Litigation and Precaution)

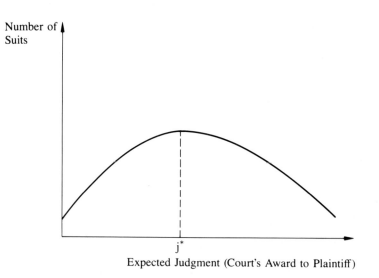

Expected Judgment (Court's Award to Plaintiff)

The curve shows that the number of suits depends on the plaintiff's expected judgment. When that expected judgment is small, the number of suits is small, largely because the costs of trial exceed the expected benefits of a trial. As the expected judgment rises, so does the number of suits, up to point j^*. For high levels of expected judgment, the defendant is likely to take sufficient precaution to make a dispute unlikely. As a result, the number of suits declines for expected judgments larger than j^*.

largest when the expected judgment, which is read off the horizontal axis, equals a value denoted j^*, which is neither very small nor very large.

There is some dispute about the extent to which the money value of judgments awarded to plaintiffs has increased in recent years.[8] The commonly held view is that the (average) value of judgments has increased. If this is true, would this necessarily lead to more suits? That depends upon whether the trial judgments are on the upward-sloping portion of the curve in Figure 10.1 or the downward-sloping portion. It is only in the increasing zone, which lies to the left of j^*, that higher (expected) judgments cause more suits. The belief that increasing judgments have caused more suits rests upon the implicit assumption that the increased willingness of potential plaintiffs to bring suit more than offsets the increased precaution by potential defendants to avoid disputes. (A special kind of case that has increased

---

[8]Systematic comparisons of awards are difficult to make, but data clearly suggest that compensation for the small number of tort cases that involve unusually severe injuries grew in recent years. Mark A. Peterson & George Priest, THE CIVIL JURY: TRENDS IN TRIALS AND VERDICTS, COOK COUNTY ILLINOIS, 1960–1979 (1982).

Class Actions

Did you ever write a check for more money than was in your account? Such a check usually "bounces," and your bank (and perhaps the merchant) charges you a fee called an "NSF charge" (not sufficient funds charge). In 1975 Mr. Perdue was charged $6 by Crocker Bank for writing an NSF check. He sued the bank in a case that eventually went to the California Supreme Court.[1] It costs a lot more than $6 to pursue a case that far. Mr. Perdue and his lawyers never would have carried this case so far if there had not been more to the matter than $6. In fact, Mr. Perdue brought this action not merely on his own behalf but as a *class action* on behalf of a *class of plaintiffs*, viz., all those account holders at Crocker Bank who paid NSF charges. If successful, Mr. Perdue would recover his $6 and all the other alleged overcharges (which, after deducting his attorney's fees, he would then have been obliged to attempt to distribute to the other members of the class).

When a plaintiff attempts to bring an action on behalf of a class of plaintiffs, the court must decide whether to "certify" a class action and permit someone like Mr. Perdue to sue on behalf of everyone else. This is a delicate problem because a successful suit by Mr. Perdue will extinguish everyone else's claims. Once the court has decided that the action may proceed as a class action, the members of the class, most of whom were not even consulted about the case, will have lost their right to sue individually.

When should a class be certified? Economics suggests that class actions are appropriate when the stakes are large in aggregate and small for any individual plaintiff. In our example, the sum of NSF charges to all account holders at the Crocker Bank roughly measures the stakes in dispute. The full value of the stakes are at risk for the defendant bank, but only a tiny fraction of the stakes are at risk for any individual plaintiff. So the certification of a class seems appropriate.

Once a class is certified, if the plaintiff agrees to a settlement, or if the plaintiff succeeds at trial, damages will be paid by the defendant. These damages must be distributed in such a way that the whole class of plaintiffs benefits, rather than merely benefiting the active plaintiff and his lawyers. The active plaintiff and his lawyers are naturally inclined to grab a large share for themselves. The courts must decide whether a proposed remedy in a class action is fair. For example, should the plaintiff's lawyers, who are often responsible for organizing and initiating the suit, be compensated at their standard billing rate? Or should they receive more than their usual fee in order to compensate for the high risk of losing the suit? Distributing small sums of money to everyone in the class is usually prohibitively expensive. What should be done with the money to which the members of the class are entitled? Try to answer these questions by using economic principles.[2]

[1]This case has already been discussed in the section on unconscionable contracts in Chapter 7.

[2]For an economic model of remedies for class actions, see Lewis Kornhauser, *Control of Conflicts of Interest in Class Action Suits*, 41 PUBLIC CHOICE 145 (1983).

recently is the class action. For a brief discussion, see the box entitled "Class Actions.")

Another change that would cause more suits is a decrease in litigation costs. There has been a rapid increase in the number of lawyers in recent years that should increase competition among them. More competition means lawyers are more willing to sell their services for less and to devote greater effort to identifying potential clients.

To illustrate, plaintiff's lawyers in tort cases usually earn a "contingency fee," which means that they get about one-third of the judgment if their client wins and nothing if their client loses. Suppose that the stakes in the suit are $1,000, the probability of winning is 0.5, and the contingency fee is 0.3; then the expected value of the case to the plaintiff's lawyer is $1,000(0.5)(0.3) = $150. If the case takes 2 hours to prepare and try, then the plaintiff lawyer's expected remuneration is $75 per hour. Whether the case is worth taking depends upon whether more lucrative opportunities are available; that is, the lawyer must determine the *opportunity cost* of the time spent on this case. If there is little competition, the lawyer may be unwilling to take the case, but if competition is severe, he or she may be eager to take it. So, as competition among lawyers increases, cases will be brought on a contingency fee that no lawyer would previously take.[9]

We have explained why economic theory suggests that more suits will occur when there are more lawyers competing for clients. This conclusion is merely an application of the usual demand and supply analysis, as depicted in Figure 10.2. An increase in the supply of lawyers causes the supply curve to shift to the right, as a result of which the quantity of lawyers' services sold in the market increases from q_1 to q_2 and the price of lawyers' services falls from p_1 to p_2. The proposition that more lawyers causes more suits is little more than the proposition that the demand curve for lawyers' services slopes down and the supply curve slopes up. The interesting question is whether, or to what extent, the observed changes in rates of litigation can be explained by changes in the number of lawyers. In spite of some research on lawyers' remuneration,[10] there is no good empirical evidence on this question.

III. SETTLEMENT OR TRIAL?

So far we have investigated why plaintiffs file complaints and commence a suit. But most legal disputes are settled without a trial. For example, a study of divorces found that about 90% are settled without a trial and only 10% are

---

[9]One way to test whether this has occurred is to determine whether the product of the contingency fee and the expected judgment has decreased for tort suits.

[10]See, e.g., Ronald Gilson & Robert Mnookin, *Sharing Among the Human Capitalists: An Economic Inquiry into the Corporate Law Firm and How Partners Split Profits*, 37 STAN. L. REV. 313 (1985); see also Peter Pashigian, *Comment on Gilson and Mnookin*, 37 STAN. L. REV. 393 (1985).

Figure 10.2   The Effects of More Lawyers

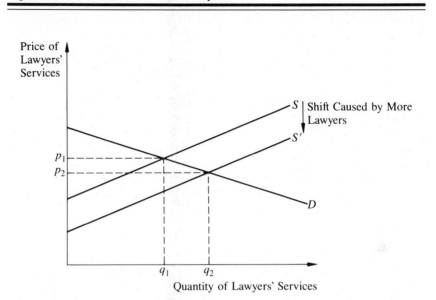

An increase in the number of lawyers causes the supply curve to shift to the right, from S to S'. Assuming that the demand for lawyers' services is constant, the result of the increase in the supply of lawyers' services is two-fold: the compensation of lawyers falls from p_1 to p_2, and the equilibrium quantity of lawyers' services rises from q_1 to q_2.

actually tried.[11] Why do some complaints end up being tried rather than settled out of court? It might seem on first impression that trials, being so costly, would not occur unless someone behaves irrationally. Like many first impressions, this one is wrong.

Game theory explains why rational bargainers sometimes fail to settle their disputes and end up in trial. There are several strands of argument to be developed. The simplest answer is that trials occur because the sum of the expected value of trial to each of the parties exceeds the value of a settlement.

For the purposes of illustration, suppose that in the initial situation one party possesses a car and the other party feels entitled to a share of its value. The value of the car is $1,000. Thus, the stakes in the dispute are $1,000. In the event of a suit, the party in possession of the car will be the defendant, and the party pressing for a share of its value will be the plaintiff.

To keep the example simple, imagine that the parties begin bargaining over dividing the car's value. How hard each party will press his demands

---

[11]R. Cooter & S. Marks, *Settlement Rates in Divorce: Evidence from Michigan* (University of California, Berkeley, School of Law, 1980).

Nuisance Suits

Developers in New York City sometimes face suits that they settle in order to avoid construction delays. These suits are an example of "nuisance suits." They have no merit in the sense that the plaintiff does not expect to win anything in the event of a trial. Rather, the plaintiff expects to be "bought off" by the defendant in a settlement.

What conditions make a nuisance suit possible? Our bargaining theory can easily answer this question. Suppose a trial would cost the plaintiff $1,000 and the defendant $1,000, and the plaintiff expects to win $0 at trial. It is not hard to show that, under these conditions, the rational solution is for the plaintiff to receive nothing in settlement. The plaintiff's threat value is $-\$1,000$. The cooperative surplus (here, the total amount that the parties would save from not going to trial) is $2,000. In a settlement the plaintiff should receive his threat value plus half the cooperative surplus, or $-\$1,000 + 0.5(\$2,000) = \$0$. So the defendant should offer the plaintiff nothing. That is, the defendant should call the plaintiff's bluff and refuse to settle.

Now change the numbers. Suppose a trial would cost the plaintiff $1,000 and the defendant $5,000, and the plaintiff expects to win $0 at trial. The large cost of the trial to the defendant could be due to the fact that he is a developer in New York City and that the $5,000 cost of the trial in part represents the indirect or opportunity costs to him if construction is delayed until the trial ends. Under these new numbers, a rational defendant should pay off the plaintiff and settle the nuisance suit. How much should he pay off? The plaintiff's threat value is still $-\$1,000$, but the cooperative surplus of not going to trial is now $6,000 (the plaintiff's savings of $1,000 plus the defendant's savings of $5,000). Thus, the defendant's payoff to the plaintiff should be $2,000, which equals the plaintiff's threat value plus half the cooperative surplus, or $-\$1,000 + 0.5(\$6,000) = \$2,000$.

In general, nuisance suits are possible between rational plaintiffs and defendants only when a trial is more costly to the latter than to the former.

depends upon how well he thinks he can do at trial. Thus, one source of trials is optimism: when parties think they will win at trial, neither will concede when bargaining.

The way in which optimism causes trials can be explained by the bargaining theory developed in Chapter 4. According to that theory, bargaining is controlled by the threats of the parties. The threat of the parties in our example is to refuse to settle the dispute and to force a trial. In order to compute the value to the parties from acting on their threats, it is necessary to know their expectations about trial. To keep the analysis simple, suppose that each one thinks that the probability of being awarded the car after trial is 50%, so the expected value of the judgment is, as before,

0.5($1,000) = $500. Furthermore, suppose each party's litigation costs will be $200. Thus the expected value of trial for each party is $500 − $200 = $300. The combined value of trial for both of them is thus $300 + $300 = $600. However, if they can settle, the combined value will be $1,000. So, there is a surplus from cooperation equal to $1,000 − $600 = $400. (Notice that this is the amount equal to the sum of the parties' litigation costs.)

In most circumstances the parties will settle and enjoy the surplus from cooperation. Our interest, however, is not in cooperation so much as the breakdown of cooperation and the failure to settle. By a slight modification of the numbers, it is easy to explain why optimism can cause a breakdown in bargaining and lead to a trial. Suppose that both parties are unreasonably optimistic and both of them expect to win at trial. False optimism might be caused by lack of information or by the natural inclination to believe that fault lies with someone else. Whatever the reason, assume that each party believes that his probability of winning the car at trial is 80%, in which case the expected judgment is 0.8($1,000) = $800. By subtracting litigation costs, we get the expected value of trial for each party: $800 − $200 = $600. This is what we called the *threat value* of each party in our development of bargaining theory in Chapter 4. It is impossible to divide the stakes of $1,000 so that each party receives his threat value of $600. Because neither party perceives an advantage from settling, a trial is certain.

In this example, the total (subjectively) expected value from trial is $1,200, and the value of cooperation is only $1,000. So, instead of a surplus from cooperation, there is an expected loss of $200 from cooperation. In general, optimism causes trials by making the subjectively-expected value of trial so large that there is no surplus from cooperation. To see how these ideas can explain the unscrupulous use of the threat of litigation to extract a settlement, see the box on nuisance suits.

IV. STRATEGIES

We have explained how irrational optimism can cause wasteful trials. It is possible, however, to have wasteful trials between parties who are not overly optimistic. Such trials occur because of the strategic nature of bargaining, which can be explained by more game theory.

Bargaining strategies are complicated in reality, but their logic is revealed by an extreme simplification. It is sufficient for representing the strategic aspects of bargaining to assume that the players must choose between two strategies, one hard and the other soft. If the hard strategy is adopted, the player demands, say, 60% of the stakes. Alternatively, if the soft strategy is adopted, he demands, say, 40% of the stakes. (Intermediate strategies are not allowed here in order to keep the analysis simple.)

The outcome of bargaining is determined by the choice of strategies by plaintiff and defendant. The consequences of these bargaining strategies are depicted in the payoff matrix below. In order for the parties to settle, it must be possible to satisfy their demands by dividing the stakes. Thus, if one party bargains hard and the other bargains soft, they settle and each player receives his demand, with the hard bargainer receiving 60% of the stakes and the soft bargainer receiving 40%. This fact is represented in the matrix by the northeast cell and the southwest cell. For example, in the northeast cell, the plaintiff bargains soft and receives 40% of the stakes (or, to use the figures of our example above of the dispute over a $1,000 car, $400), whereas the defendant bargains hard and receives 60% (or $600).

Payoff Matrix for Litigation Bargaining

		Plaintiff	
		Hard	Soft
Defendant	Hard	0 0	.4 .6
	Soft	.6 .4	.5 .5

These strategies and payoffs are reversed in the southwest cell. There the plaintiff bargains hard and receives the larger share of the stakes in the settlement, whereas the defendant bargains soft and receives the smaller share.

In the southeast cell, in contrast, neither party adopts a hard strategy. If both parties adopt a soft bargaining strategy, both demand 40% of the stakes. These demands can be satisfied with something left over, which, by assumption, they split equally. Thus, when both strategies are soft, as represented by the southeast cell, each one gets 50% of the stakes.

In the three cells discussed so far, at least one player adopts a soft strategy and a settlement results. However, settlement is impossible when both parties adopt hard strategies because it is mathematically impossible to give 60% of the stakes to each of the disputants. In the absence of a settlement, a trial must occur. Assume for the sake of simplicity that the expected outcome of a trial is an equal division of the stakes, so each party expects to receive $500. In the event of a trial, however, each party must also pay litigation costs. To keep the analysis simple, assume that each party's litigation costs are $500. Thus, the expected value of a trial for either player is his expected share of the stakes less his share of litigation costs, or $500 − $500 = 0. This fact is represented by the northwest cell of the payoff matrix.

The payoff matrix represents the essence of bargaining: if both parties press too hard, they get nothing. If only one party presses hard, he gets a lot and the other gets a little. So, what should they do? By examining the payoff matrix, it is possible to figure out the strategies that rational players would pursue. Suppose that the defendant is committed to a hard bargaining strategy and this fact is known by the plaintiff. The plaintiff can either adopt a hard strategy, in which case a trial occurs and the value of the game to him is 0, or the plaintiff can adopt a soft bargaining strategy, in which case he and the defendant settle in the northeast cell, and the value of the game to him is .4. Given these options, it is obviously best for the plaintiff to adopt a soft strategy and receive 40% of the stakes. And this outcome would please the defendant since he would receive the large payoff of 60%.

The preceding argument began with the assumption that the defendant could commit himself to his hard strategy. The result was to force the plaintiff to accept a settlement giving him a smaller share of the stakes. It is clear, then, that the defendant would like to commit himself to a hard strategy, communicate this fact to the plaintiff, and thus force the plaintiff to adopt the soft strategy.

This argument illustrates that the art of bargaining involves eliminating your own ability to compromise so that your opponent is compelled by his rational self-interest to give in. The ability to commit irrevocably to a position that eliminates compromise is represented in game theory by sequential choice of strategies. Thus, in the preceding example, if the defendant gets to choose his strategy first, and the plaintiff must choose second in the full knowledge of the defendant's prior choice, the defendent will choose the hard strategy, with the result that the plaintiff maximizes his payoff by choosing the soft strategy.

Notice that the ability of the party who chooses first to commit to a hard strategy forces the party who chooses second to adopt a soft strategy. So long as the party who chooses second is rational, trials never occur. But this assumes that irrevocable commitments are possible. There are many real world situations in which irrevocable commitments are impossible. The means for irrevocably committing to a particular strategy are usually denied by law[12]—it is not the business of the law to prevent someone from compromising in a dispute. If commitment to a hard position is impossible, neither party can rid himself of the ability to compromise. Furthermore, even where commitments are possible, bargaining occurs in such a haze of uncertainty that the committing party may be unable to convince his opponent that his commitment is irrevocable.

When irrevocable commitments are impossible, each player remains uncertain about his opponent's strategy. Neither knows for certain whether the other will compromise until they actually reach a settlement or find themselves at trial. Therefore, to model uncertainty, we must assume that each player chooses his strategy without knowing his opponent's strategy. Uncertainty exists because neither party knows for certain the other party's strategy at the time he makes his choice.

If the parties choose their strategies sequentially, the party choosing second knows the strategy of the party choosing first. If, however, they choose strategies simultaneously, neither knows the other's strategy for certain. Thus we model uncertainty by assuming that the players choose strategies simultaneously.

---

[12]"I promise not to compromise beyond this stated value in bargaining with you" is not an enforceable contract at law.

We can work out the optimal strategies of the players when choosing simultaneously, and thus find the "solution" to this bargaining game, including the frequency of settlements and trials. Let us continue to use the payoff matrix and dollar figures from before as representing the choices (a hard or a soft bargaining strategy) open to the parties. Some plaintiffs will adopt hard strategies and others will adopt soft strategies. Let p denote the proportion of plaintiffs adopting hard strategies; consequently, $(1 - p)$ equals the proportion of plaintiffs adopting soft strategies. Our specific assumption about uncertainty is that the defendant who bargains with a plaintiff only knows the probability p that the plaintiff will adopt a hard strategy. (Even this information may be unavailable, but let's keep things simple by assuming that this fraction p *is* known.) The defendant does not know the strategy actually pursued by the particular plaintiff with whom he is dealing until after the dispute is resolved by settlement or trial.

If the defendant chooses a hard strategy, he will receive $0 with probability p, and he will receive $600 with probability $(1 - p)$. Thus, the defendant's expected value from choosing a hard strategy is

$$0 \cdot p + 600(1 - p). \tag{10.1a}$$

Similarly, by choosing a soft strategy he receives $400 with probability p, and $500 with probability $(1 - p)$, so his expected value from choosing a soft strategy is

$$400p + 500(1 - p). \tag{10.1b}$$

The plaintiff in this dispute is in an analogous situation. Let q denote the proportion of defendants adopting hard strategies; consequently, $(1 - q)$ equals the proportion adopting soft strategies. In the presence of uncertainty, a plaintiff only knows the probability q that the defendant will adopt a hard strategy. Given these facts, the plaintiff's expected value from choosing a hard strategy is

$$0 \cdot q + 600(1 - q), \tag{10.2a}$$

and his expected value from choosing a soft strategy is

$$400q + 500(1 - q). \tag{10.2b}$$

Economic theory provides a way to "solve" this bargaining game. An equilibrium is a situation in which the proportion of plaintiffs and defendants adopting each type of strategy remains constant, instead of tending to change. Constant proportions will be achieved when no player can improve upon his expected payoff by changing his strategy, given the distribution of strategies adopted by his opponents. Thus, in equilibrium no one can do better so long as the others do not change.[13]

If the expected value of a hard strategy is the same as the expected value of a soft strategy, there will be no reason for a player to change from one

---

[13]The strict name for the solution concept being used is a "Bayesian Nash equilibrium."

strategy to another. In other words, an equilibrium is achieved when the expected value of either strategy is the same for every player (given the proportion of the opposition choosing hard strategies).[14] The defendant's expected value of a hard strategy is the same as his expected value of a soft strategy when equation (10.1a) equals equation (10.1b):

$$0 \cdot p + 600(1 - p) = 400p + 500(1 - p) \tag{10.1}$$

Likewise, the expected values of the two strategies are the same for the plaintiff when (10.2a) equals (10.2b):

$$400q + 500(1 - q) = 0 \cdot q + 600(1 - q) \tag{10.2}$$

Solution of these two equations for p and q gives the following equilibrium values for p and q in this bargaining game: $p = q = 0.2$.[15]

We have found an equilibrium frequency with which plaintiffs and defendants choose hard strategies. A trial occurs when both parties adopt hard strategies, which occurs with probability $p \cdot q = 0.2 \cdot 0.2 = 0.04$. Thus, in equilibrium in our example, 4% of the disputes will be resolved by trial and 96% will be settled without a trial.

We have used a payoff matrix and an equilibrium concept, much simplified,[16] to show that adopting hard bargaining strategies may be rational for a percentage of disputants even though their unwillingness to compromise sometimes results in trials. To acquire a better understanding of this strategic theory of trials, try to answer the following questions. And for a brief discussion of how the decision to go to trial might be affected by different rules of assigning liability for litigation expenses, see the box entitled "Should the Loser Pay All?"

---

[14]Strictly speaking, this is the definition of a "mixed strategy equilibrium," in which some plaintiffs and some defendants choose each type of strategy. There are also "pure strategy equilibria" to this game in which all defendants choose the same strategy and all plaintiffs choose the same strategy. This seems less realistic and, therefore, less interesting than the mixed strategy case.

[15]Here is the solution for p:

$$0 \cdot p + 600(1 - p) = 400p + 500(1 - p)$$
$$600 - 600p = 400p + 500 - 500p$$
$$600 - 600p = 500 - 100p$$
$$500p = 100$$
$$p = 100/500 = 0.2$$

This is one of three "Bayesian Nash equilibria" for this game. The game would have to be more complicated to yield a unique, stable equilibrium.

[16]The bargaining model represented by our payoff matrices has some disadvantages created by its extreme simplicity. One problem is that the equilibrium values we found above are not unique. Besides the mixed equilibria, in which both strategies are played with positive frequency, there are pure equilibria in which each class of player always adopts the same pure strategy, e.g., defendants bargain hard and plaintiffs bargain soft. Furthermore, the mixed strategy equilibria in the simple linear model are not generally stable. To obtain unique, stable equilibria, the payoff functions would have to be concave rather than, as here, linear.

Question 10.1:

a. Suppose the relative value of playing a hard strategy increases from 0.6 to 0.8, and the relative value of playing a soft strategy falls from 0.4 to 0.2, as illustrated in the following revised matrix:

		Plaintiff	
		Hard	Soft
Defendant	Hard	0 0	.2 .8
	Soft	.8 .2	.5 .5

The frequency of trials will increase in equilibrium. By how much?

b. Suppose the cost of litigation decreases from $500 to $400. The revised matrix looks like this:

		Plaintiff	
		Hard	Soft
Defendant	Hard	.1 .1	.4 .6
	Soft	.6 .4	.5 .5

The frequency of trials will increase in equilibrium. By how much?

c. Let s denote the value of the stakes s, and let t (for "trial") denote the cost of litigation per player. The revised payoff matrix is

		Plaintiff	
		Hard	Soft
Defendant	Hard	$.5s-t$ $.5s-t$	$.4s$ $.6s$
	Soft	$.6s$ $.4s$	$.5s$ $.5s$

Solve for the equilibrium values of p and q as a function of s and t.

V. DOES THE COMMON LAW TEND TOWARD EFFICIENCY?

The goals of foreign policy cannot be achieved unless government strives to do so, but other social purposes can be achieved without government consciously striving to do anything. In one of social science's most famous metaphors, Adam Smith described the participants in a competitive market, who consciously pursue their private interests, as directed by an "invisible hand" to serve the public good. According to Smith, government does not have to give directions to businesspeople competing in perfect markets;

Should the Loser Pay All?

In Britain fewer disputes go to trial than in the United States. And in Britain the loser of a lawsuit must pay the litigation costs of the winner, whereas in the United States each party ordinarily pays his own litigation expenses. Some people believe that the British rule of "loser pays all" causes fewer trials than the American rule of "each pays his own."[1]

Many United States courts recognize an institution called "offers to compromise," which, in effect, adopts part of the British rule. To explain the institution, consider an example: suppose Joan Potatoes demands $600 as her share of the car valued at $1,000 in her divorce with her husband, Joe. Her offer to compromise for $600 will be recorded at the courthouse. If after this recordation there is a trial, Joan will pay most of Joe's court costs if the trial judgment awards Joan more than $600, whereas Joe will pay most of Joan's court costs if the trial judgment awards Joan less than $600. The effect, then, is to penalize hard bargaining. (To test whether you understand "offers to compromise," figure out how it would modify the preceding payoff matrix.)

We have developed several explanations of why trials occur. To see their consequences for the dispute about whether the loser should pay all, try to answer the following questions:

Question 10.2: Suppose trials occur because both parties are optimistic about winning. Will there be more trials under the British or the American rule?

Question 10.3: A nuisance suit has no merit in the sense that the plaintiff's expected judgment is nil. (See the box on nuisance suits.) Will there be more nuisance suits under the British rule or the American rule?

Question 10.4: Suppose trials are caused by strategic behavior. Which rule, British or American, will result in fewer suits?

[1]There are other important differences between British and American trial practices besides this rule for allocating litigation expenses. For example, contingency fees are not allowed in Britain, and all civil trials are bench trials. These and other differences may also contribute to the fact that fewer disputes go to trial in Britain than in the United States.

rather, government merely has to restrain itself from interfering and competitive markets will achieve efficiency on their own.

A competitive market is a kind of social machine whose laws of operation allocate resources efficiently without anyone consciously striving for that goal. Common law adjudication has some elements of a competitive market: plaintiffs and defendants compete with each other to advance their own ends. Deciding when to litigate and how much to invest in preparing the case is often motivated by self-interest, just as the decisions to buy or sell a commodity are. Litigants try to win their cases, not increase the law's efficiency, but does the former result in the latter? Are common law courts like markets in the sense that they tend toward efficiency without anyone consciously striving for it?[17]

The economic analysis of law has investigated the inspiring possibility that litigation can improve the common law—in the sense of making the law more economically efficient—without the conscious help of judges. Several mechanisms have been proposed to explain how competition would drive courts toward the adoption of economically efficient common law even without judges consciously adopting that goal. One such mechanism is *selective litigation*. Suppose that inefficient laws are more likely to be litigated than efficient laws. (In a moment we will explain why that is likely to be the case. When we speak of "law" here, we are referring to the common law system of judge-made law, not statutory or administrative law.) A consequence of this assumption is that inefficient laws will be repeatedly challenged in court, whereas efficient laws will be less frequently challenged. Under these circumstances, inefficient laws may be overturned, whereas efficient laws will persist unchallenged. This process of selective litigation works like a strainer that catches inefficient laws while allowing efficient laws to slip past. The residue, being repeatedly sieved, becomes more efficient with the passage of time.

The process of filtering out inefficient laws could operate without judges consciously favoring efficiency; indeed, it would be sufficient for judges not to *dis*favor efficiency. If efficient laws are not favored or disfavored, the probability of a law surviving a court test is independent of whether it is efficient or inefficient. But we are assuming that inefficient laws are challenged in court more often than efficient laws. The two assumptions—efficiency is negatively correlated to the probability of a court test, and efficiency is not negatively correlated to the probability of a law surviving such a test—are sufficient to cause the law to evolve towards efficiency.[18]

We have explained that selective litigation, like natural selection, can cause evolutionary change in the common law. In order for selective litigation to cause the law to evolve toward efficiency, selection must be biased against inefficient laws. Is there any reason to think that inefficient laws will be challenged in court more often than efficient laws?

The answer is "Yes," but this is not a very strong yes—more like a "Probably." We have already seen that a rational plaintiff will not sue unless the expected judgment is large relative to litigation costs. Inefficiency in the

---

[17]This problem was first raised by Paul Rubin in *Why Is the Common Law Efficient?*, 6 J. LEGAL STUD. 51 (1977). See also George Priest, *The Common Law Process and the Selection of Efficient Rules*, 6 J. LEGAL STUD. 65 (1977) and John Goodman, *An Economic Theory of the Evolution of the Common Law*, 7 J. LEGAL STUD. 393 (1978).

[18]A consideration of the conditions under which differential litigation will cause the legal system to evolve towards efficiency is in Robert Cooter & Lewis Kornhauser, *Can Litigation Improve the Law Without the Help of Judges?*, 9 J. LEGAL STUD. 139 (1980). Their conclusions are pessimistic.

law tends to increase the value of the expected judgment. To see why, consider what it means for a law to be inefficient: inefficient laws allocate entitlements to the wrong parties. To illustrate this proposition, return to our example of the division of property in a divorce. Suppose that Joan Potatoes and Joe Potatoes place different valuations upon their house: Joan values it at $150,000 and Joe values it at $100,000. Efficiency requires the allocation of legal entitlements to the party who values them the most, so efficiency requires Joan to get the house. If Joan gets the house, the value to Joe of overturning that allocation is $100,000.[19] In contrast, if Joe gets the house, which is inefficient, the value to Joan of overturning that allocation is $150,000. Since Joan has more at stake than Joe, Joan would be more likely than Joe to challenge an unfavorable legal allocation.

In general, the party who values a legal entitlement the most will spend more on a suit to obtain it than anyone else, so an inefficient allocation of the entitlement will provoke more expenditure on litigation than will an efficient allocation. This point can be seen by contrasting distribution and efficiency.[20] The allocation of legal entitlements affects both the quantity of wealth (i.e., efficiency) and its distribution. When legal entitlements are allocated inefficiently, the plaintiff who overturns the misallocation stands to gain from both the increase in wealth and from its redistribution. In contrast, when legal entitlements are already allocated efficiently, the plaintiff who overturns the allocation stands to gain from the redistribution of wealth and to lose from the decrease in its quantity. So, the value of overturning inefficient laws exceeds the value of overturning efficient laws.

We have explained why more money will be spent challenging inefficient laws than challenging efficient laws. More will be spent extensively and intensively: more *extensive* litigation means more frequent challenges in court; more *intensive* litigation means that the plaintiffs hire more expensive lawyers and spend more on preparing the case. Insofar as these expenditures improve the quality of the argument in court and insofar as courts are influenced by higher quality arguments, litigation against inefficient laws will tend to be more successful than litigation against efficient laws.

We have argued that litigation selects against inefficient laws, resulting in more frequent court challenges and better preparation of the plaintiff's case. There is, apparently, a mechanism at work in the common law that is similar to the work of the "invisible hand" in markets.

Unfortunately, the grip of the invisible hand on courts is far weaker than on markets. To understand why, consider an analogy between legal precedents and scientific discoveries. Some scientific advances, including the discovery of basic principles, are unpatentable. Insofar as scientific advances

---

[19]If, instead of a house, the good were a homogeneous commodity with a perfect replacement available in the market, both parties would place the same value on the good, specifically, the market value. A house, however, may be unique, not homogeneous.

[20]See our discussion of this point in Chapter 2.

are unpatentable, investors in research cannot capture the full value that it creates. Part of the value spills over, which constitutes an externality. Markets for basic scientific discoveries may fail because value spills over, unlike, say, the market for bananas where the grower captures the product's full value.[21]

Trials have more in common with basic scientific research than with bananas. A law is, by its nature, general in the scope of its application, so challenging a law affects everyone who is or will be subject to it. The effects of a new, more efficient precedent spill far beyond the litigants in the case where it is set. Consequently, most plaintiffs appropriate no more than a fraction of the value that a new precedent creates and redistributes.

> **Question 10.5:** The plaintiff who brings a case in which a more efficient rule is established enjoys only a fraction of the social benefit of the more efficient rule. Does this fact argue that the bringing of lawsuits should be subsidized by the government, perhaps by society bearing some of the costs of resolving legal disputes? Without such a subsidy will the socially optimal amount of litigation be brought by plaintiffs?
>
> Conversely, the plaintiff who brings an action that imposes social *costs* (such as a nuisance suit or one to preserve an inefficient rule that enriches him) bears only a fraction of the full costs of his action (specifically, his own litigation expenses). Does the law have a mechanism for discouraging this sort of behavior, e.g., by forcing such a plaintiff to bear the full social *costs* of his action?

We have argued that plaintiffs are more inclined to challenge inefficient laws because overturning them increases the quantity of wealth instead of merely redistributing it. This bias toward efficiency, however, may well be overwhelmed by the inclination of plaintiffs to challenge laws when they can capture a large share of the precedent's value. Thus, regardless of a law's efficiency or inefficiency, plaintiffs may bring suit when they expect the redistributive gains of a successful suit to be large. In those circumstances, plaintiffs have no regard for the social costs that the continuation of an inefficient rule will impose on other parties. An example of just this sort of process is the crisis in products liability law that we described in detail in the previous chapter. We argued that the prevailing liability rules in product-related harms were not efficient; clearly, those inefficiencies encourage some plaintiffs to look to the courts for substantial redistributive gains and thus encourage excessive litigation of product-related injuries. Notice here that the inefficient rule has encouraged more litigation, as the selective litigation model suggests, but that this increased litigation is not likely to lead to social benefits (i.e., an increase in the quantity of wealth) but rather to a decline in efficiency and a redistribution of wealth. The problem with viewing a court as a market is that redistributive gains are frequently more important than inefficiencies in channeling litigation.

---

[21]See the discussion in Chapter 5 of the economics of information and how the law can encourage an efficient amount of investment in information discovery and transmission.

VI. JUDICIAL PREFERENCE FOR EFFICIENCY

We have asked whether common law tends toward efficiency without any-one consciously striving for it. The answer seems to be that the unconscious forces favoring efficiency are present but weak. What about conscious forces? Do judges consciously adopt efficiency as a goal?

There are a variety of philosophical views about whether a judge can properly decide a case on the grounds of efficiency. It can be argued, for example, that judges should allocate legal entitlements *fairly* and that the fair allocation has no systematic connection to an efficient allocation.[22] Alternatively, it can be argued that efficiency is one of several important rea-sons that properly influence adjudication.[23]

This philosophical debate raises issues that are far beyond this book's domain, but there is one aspect of the dispute that is worth a moment's con-sideration here. A striking fact about the economic analysis of law is that it seems to explain the logic of some laws even where common law judges have not explicitly discussed efficiency in their opinions. One possible explana-tion, which we have examined and largely dismissed, is that selective litiga-tion drives the law towards efficiency without the help of judges. Another possibility, which we believe to be accurate, is that judges consciously prefer more efficient rules but that their own descriptions of what they are doing employ terms other than "efficiency." Our hypothesis is that efficiency prin-ciples are embedded in the law under other names.

We cannot here develop this theory systematically, but we can provide some suggestive examples. We have argued repeatedly in this book that one requirement for efficient incentives is the internalization of costs and bene-fits by the private decisionmaker. That is, private decisionmakers face effi-cient incentives (and will, therefore, take actions that are socially optimal) when social costs and social benefits become part of their private profit- or utility-maximizing decisions. There are certain conditions under which the law seems to prescribe the internalization of costs. To repeat the general thrust of Chapter 8, suppose that an injurer can avoid harming someone else by taking precaution against accidents. Internalization requires the injurer to proceed as if the harm were his own (i.e., that the harm were part of his expected costs). When the injurer internalizes the cost of the harm, he will balance it against the cost of precaution, as required for economic efficiency. (See the box entitled "Is the Best Path Straight and Narrow?")

It can be argued that cost internalization is exactly what negligence rules in the law of torts require of injurers. The negligence standard requires the

---

[22]For example, Ronald Dworkin has developed a jurisprudential theory according to which utilitarian arguments are improper in court. See, e.g., *Law's Ambitions for Itself*, 71 VA. L. REV. 173 (1985) and LAW'S EMPIRE (1986).

[23]For example, Melvin A. Eisenberg argues that common law judges should be influenced by social values about which there is a consensus. Efficiency is, presumably, such a value but only one of several. See M. Eisenberg, A THEORY OF ADJUDICATION (forthcoming).

Is the Best Path Straight and Narrow?

Suppose the courts face a novel issue and they must make a new common law rule. Should they frame the rule to be straight and narrow, or vague and broad? Two economists have analyzed the issue as a tradeoff between underinclusion and overinclusion.[1] If the law is too narrow, it will exclude factual situations that ought to fall under it. If, however, the law is too broad, it will include factual situations that ought not to fall under it. The optimal width of the law's compass thus depends upon which danger is greater, overinclusion or underinclusion.

Question 10.6:   Common law courts traditionally preferred the straight and narrow, whereas legislators traditionally favor broad laws that leave administrative details to regulators. Can you explain these preferences by differences in the information available to judges and legislators, and consequently, by differences in the risk of underinclusion and overinclusion?

[1]Mario Rizzo & Frank Arnold, *An Economic Framework for Statutory Interpretation,* LAW & CONTEMP. PROB. (forthcoming).

injurer to take reasonable precaution in the circumstances. It can be argued that precaution is reasonable when its costs are in line with its benefits. So, under this interpretation, tort law requires the injurer to balance the costs and benefits of precaution by proceeding as if the harm to others were his own. The law chooses to phrase this "a requirement that injurers show equal concern for the harms suffered by others as for themselves." But this is simply cost internalization under another name.

Here is another example of courts using alternative terminology to decide cases on efficiency grounds. Each dollar the plaintiff receives in a law suit must be paid by the defendant, so the immediate effect of dividing the stakes is pure redistribution. Self-interested disputants may have diametrically opposite preferences concerning the distribution of the stakes. But suppose they look beyond the immediate division of the stakes and consider the future effects of the rule. Even though they disagree about *this* case, they may agree over the rule that they would like to use to resolve new disputes that arise in the future.

Let's consider an example. Negligence rules as they used to operate were all-or-nothing: either the plaintiff was entitled to full compensation for the injury, or the defendant was not liable. In recent years many states have abandoned all-or-nothing rules in favor of comparative negligence. Under the rule of comparative negligence, each party is responsible for accident costs in proportion to the harm he caused. Thus, if the defendant was twice as negligent as the plaintiff, the defendant is liable for two-thirds of the harm.

Suppose that everyone who lives in a jurisdiction governed by an all-or-nothing rule favors changing to comparative negligence. Furthermore, suppose that someone is injured under circumstances in which the current rule puts all the costs on the other party, whereas comparative negligence would split the costs between them. The accident victim will want this dispute resolved by using the current law, even though he, and everyone else, favors resolving future disputes by the new rule of comparative negligence.

A court may take such a case as the occasion to change the law from the old all-or-nothing rule to the new rule of comparative negligence. Good arguments can be made that judges have the power to abandon a rule in favor of an alternative that makes everyone better off in the future. Certainly a court that made such a change would justify it by pointing to the future benefits that everyone will enjoy. The retrospective application of the new rule can be defended on the grounds that everyone prefers its prospective application.

An important normative standard in economics is Pareto efficiency. An improvement by this standard is a change that makes someone better off without making anyone worse off. When an appeals court adopts a new precedent, one party to the dispute wins and the other loses. A change in which there are some losers is not an improvement by the Pareto standard. So, the Pareto standard in its simplest interpretation does not provide a guide to adjudicating disputes. We have explained, however, that people who disagree about the best rule for resolving their current dispute may yet agree about the best rule for resolving future disputes. In other words, people who disagree about the best rule to apply retroactively may yet agree about the best rule to apply prospectively. If the prospective application of a new rule makes some people better off and no one worse off, we will say that the new rule is an improvement by the *ex ante Pareto standard.*

This modified concept of Pareto efficiency is very valuable in the economic analysis of law. When appeals courts adopt a new rule whose prospective application is better for everyone, the court may be arguing in different language that the new precedent is ex ante Pareto efficient.[24] (See the box entitled "Rent-A-Judge" for a brief description of how a novel method of dispute resolution might induce judges to behave in a fashion different from that postulated in this section.)

VII. STANDARDS OF PROOF

Economic theory has developed an elaborate calculus for making decisions under uncertainty. The theory combines probabilistic reasoning with util-

---

[24]This proposition is used to argue in favor of the change to comparative negligence in Robert Cooter & Thomas Ulen, *An Economic Analysis of Comparative Negligence,* N. Y. U. L. REV. (forthcoming).

Rent-A-Judge

In Los Angeles, as in most major cities, it can take several years before disputes are tried in a public court. There is, however, an alternative route to trial. Instead of a public trial, the parties can agree to "rent" a retired judge to decide their case. The resulting private trial is usually held in a mutually convenient place, such as a hotel suite. The retired judge usually conducts the trial in an informal manner, without the concern for procedure shown in public trials. The case is decided by application of the relevant state law. The judge's final decision is, furthermore, registered with the state court and has the full effect of law, just as in a public trial.

Critics say that "rent-a-judge" is unfair to the poor because only the rich can use it. Proponents say that everyone benefits—people who rent judges benefit from a speedy trial and others benefit indirectly from relieving the congestion in the public courts. Can microeconomic analysis help to sort out these positions?

Suppose you were a retired judge. In your former role as a public judge, you were supposed to be "disinterested." That is, the income that you enjoyed as a public judge was unrelated to how you decided cases. Now that has changed. Your income is directly determined by how often you are "rented." To be rented, both parties to a potential dispute have to agree to choose you. Do you think a "rent-a-judge" who sought to maximize his income would decide cases any differently from a disinterested public judge?[1]

[1]Cooter, *The Objectives of Private and Public Judges,* 41 PUBLIC CHOICE 107 (1983). Would you expect a higher quality of judging from disinterested judges or income-maximizing judges? The Constitution gives federal judges lifetime tenure (i.e., once appointed, they remain in office for life unless removed by impeachment proceedings) and forbids Congress from cutting the pay of federal judges. Do these rules tend to increase the quality of the performance of federal judges?

itarian value theory. The basic idea is that a rational decisionmaker proceeds in three steps: first, she determines the probability of each possible state of the world; second, she attaches utility to each possible state; and finally, the probabilities are multiplied by the utilities to give the expected utility. To illustrate, suppose Joan and Elizabeth agree to flip a coin for the last piece of pie. Joan will get the remaining piece of pie if, and only if, the coin lands heads. The probability of a coin toss landing heads is 0.5, so the expected utility from the gamble is 0.5 times the utility value of a piece of pie.[25]

Flipping a coin for a piece of pie is a choice involving uncertainty. So is insuring a house or purchasing a portfolio of stock. In general, choices under uncertainty are gambles. The theory of economic decisionmaking under

---

[25]See the appendix to Chapter 2 for a full discussion of the economics of decisionmaking under uncertainty.

uncertainty prescribes rules for rational gambling. If gamblers fail to conform to these rules, they will use contradictory evaluations of the stakes or behave in ways that enable their opponents to win.

A trial is an uncertain event that requires a decision by the court. The basic question in the economic analysis of legal procedure is, "Do court procedures correspond to the logic of economic decisionmaking under uncertainty?" If the answer is "Yes," then courts make uncertain decisions like rational gamblers. If the answer is "No," then courts are irrational by the standards applicable to gambling and insurance.

A striking feature of legal procedure is that rules of evidence prohibit inferences that a rational gambler would make. For example, evidence that is based upon mere rumor or hearsay is excluded from trials. Thus, an economist performing as an expert witness cannot base his testimony on what he was told by another economist.[26] Although second-hand evaluations are excluded in court, this kind of evidence might be used to purchase stock and to make other decisions about uncertain future events. In general, rumors, hearsay, and any other information affect the probabilities a rational gambler assigns to events, even though such evidence is excluded from courts. Indeed, one can go so far as to say that the rational gambler would be irrational to ignore evidence that courts exclude.[27]

Another example of a conflict between legal procedure and rational gambling concerns the standard of proof. In civil suits, the plaintiff must prove his case by a preponderance of the evidence. To see how probabilities affect this burden, consider an example:

> **The Gate Crasher's Paradox:** A rock concert is sold out. The auditorium holds 1,000 people. Ticket holders file through the front doors and occupy 400 seats. Then, before any more legitimate ticket holders can get in, some rude youths break down a back door and crash in, occupying all 600 of the remaining seats. There are so many gate crashers that the concert's organizer cannot eject them, so he proceeds with the music.
>
> The concert organizer photographs the crowd and succeeds in identifying 100 who were in the audience. Of the 100, he does not know which ones bought tickets and which ones crashed the gate, so he names all of them in a law suit. By the time the suit is brought, tickets stubs have long been discarded, so few defendants can prove that they purchased tickets. At trial the plaintiff's lawyer points out that civil suits are decided according to the preponderance of the evidence. Furthermore, he shows that 600 out of 1,000 people in the audience were gate crashers, so the chances are at least 0.6 that any defendant is a gate crasher. Therefore, the lawyer concludes that the plaintiff deserves to win and the defendants deserve to lose.

---

[26]The legal theory is that the expert who is the source of the evidence must be present to undergo cross examination.

[27]We have already seen the law's difficulties with probabilities in our discussion of probabilistic causation in the previous chapter.

This use of probabilistic reasoning is sound for betting on whether any particular defendant crashed the gate, but it is unacceptable in court. Let us change the facts to make the evidence more acceptable:

> One of the guards at the back door purportedly recognized 100 of the gate crashers. The concert organizer sues them and the guard testifies in court that he saw them crash the gate. The guard admits that his memory is imperfect. The plaintiff's lawyer asks the guard to perform some recall experiments and he succeeds about 60% of the time. The plaintiff's lawyer points out that civil suits are decided according to the preponderance of the evidence; the guard's eyewitness identifications are more likely to be correct than incorrect; therefore, the lawyer argues, the plaintiff deserves to win.

The first example of evidence was based upon pure correlation, which courts view unfavorably. The second example of evidence was based upon eyewitness reporting, which courts view favorably. This example was constructed so that the pure correlation equals the reliability of the eyewitness testimony. Even though the correlation equals the reliability of the eyewitness, the former evidence would be excluded in court and the later evidence would probably be allowed, so the plaintiff would lose the case under the first set of facts and probably win the case under the second set of facts. To a rational gambler, however, if a pure correlation equals the reliability of an eyewitness testimony, they would receive equal weight in reaching a decision. When betting whether the defendant crashed the gate, a 60% correlation is just as good as a 60% reliable eyewitness testimony.

Procedural rules thus impose constraints upon court decisionmaking that rational gamblers would not respect. A jury is not being asked to give its betting odds on whether the defendant did what the complaint alleges; rather, the jury is being asked to decide whether the complaint is supported by the facts as admitted by the rules of legal procedure.

Although the rules of procedure sometimes contradict the economic rules of decisionmaking under uncertainty, there may yet be broad areas of agreement. For example, it can be argued that while procedural rules impose constraints upon courts, within these boundaries juries and judges reason just like rational, economic decisionmakers. Procedural rules prescribe a framework whose justification is not necessarily economic, but within that framework the economic logic may operate.

An economically rational decisionmaker begins with some prior beliefs and updates them in light of new evidence by conforming to certain rules of inference. Evidence is, perhaps, processed in much the same way in trials. To illustrate, the judge instructs the jurors at the beginning of a trial to rid themselves of all prior beliefs concerning the case. They are to begin as if they knew nothing factual pertaining to this dispute. Starting from this position of no prior evidence, they are to revise their beliefs exclusively in light of the evidence allowed to enter the trial, and evidence will be excluded unless it conforms to the rules of evidence. Furthermore, the judge explains that one of the parties has the burden of producing evidence proving his position in the dispute. Thus, the plaintiff in a civil suit usually must prove by a preponderance of the evidence that he was injured by the defendant and that the defendant was acting unreasonably; in a criminal trial, the prosecutor must prove the defendant's guilt beyond a reasonable doubt.

This framework can be recast in the language of decision theory. A rational gambler begins with prior beliefs based upon his hunches and instincts and upon whatever information he has gleaned about the event in question. A juror is asked by the judge to construct a hypothetical prior (i.e., probability estimate) that conforms to the rules of evidence. The constructive prior assumes no knowledge of particular facts pertaining to the case. Furthermore, the constructive prior favors the defendant because the plaintiff has the burden of proof. The constructive prior is updated in light of the evidence allowed to enter the trial. At the trial's end, the decisionmaker, whether juror or judge, will have a *posterior* probability (i.e., a probability of the defendant's liability formed after hearing the evidence presented at the trial) concerning the facts of the case. This posterior probability is not his betting odds, but rather a constructive posterior probability formed by conforming to the rules of evidence. If the constructive posterior exceeds 50%, the plaintiff has proved his case by the preponderance of the evidence and deserves to win; otherwise, the plaintiff deserves to lose. Reasoning in the courtroom may thus be described as constrained rational choice under uncertainty, where the constraints are formed by rules of evidence that confine betting behavior within legal limits. (See the box "Why Unanimity Among Twelve Jurors?")

CONCLUSION

In this chapter we have analyzed the economics of the legal process using game theory and some of the economics of legal procedure using the economic theory of decisionmaking under uncertainty. The economic analysis of legal process and procedure is powerful because the economic conception of the rational man overlaps with the legal conception of the reasonable man. Indeed, the economic conception provides a more explicit account of some attributes of decisionmakers upon which the law is premised.

In general, economic theory has contributed to the analysis of law, but the law has so far contributed little to economics. The legal process is an avenue that can accommodate two-way traffic. All legal disputes, regardless of their substance, follow common processes that can be described by bargaining theory. Bargaining theory has been developed by economists, but there is a real problem with obtaining data from markets to test its hypotheses. Most markets are sufficiently competitive that bargaining is restricted; some bargaining is prohibited by antitrust laws; and some permitted bargaining is episodic, as with collective bargaining. In contrast, legal disputes occur repeatedly in sufficiently large quantities to generate usable data. As the quality of the data that is available on litigation bargaining improves, the study of the legal process can contribute to economics by providing empiri-

Why Unanimity Among Twelve Jurors?

Juries in the common law countries have traditionally consisted of 12 people, who are conscripted and not paid much for their services. Suppose that juries were reduced from 12 to, say, 6 in routine civil trials or that the rule of unanimity among 12 jurors was changed to a requirement of a 10-2 vote. Clearly, these changes could reduce the social costs of litigation by conserving on conscripted time. But would these changes result in less justice? This is not merely an intriguing intellectual exercise. The United States Supreme Court has held constitutional the use of 6-member juries and of non-unanimous 12-member juries in certain criminal trials and of 6-member juries in federal civil cases.

Lawyers and economists have investigated the effects of moving to 6-member and non-unanimous 12-member juries. In a seminal theoretical article, Professors Klevorick and Rothschild explored the effects of replacing the unanimity rule with one requiring at least a 10 to 2 decision from a 12-member jury. They found that such a change would not lead to any discernible effect on the decision reached by the jury. That means that given the same facts, a 12-member jury will reach the same conclusion as to guilt or innocence, liability or not, whether they are required to be unanimous or to reach a 10-2 result. However, the authors did discover a striking reduction in the time of jury deliberation after a trial under the 10-2 rule. At a minimum, the deliberations were 25% shorter and in some cases the time saving was 100% (because the jury's initial ballot was 10-2, 11-1, or 12-0). Klevorick and Rothschild tentatively concluded that there are considerable efficiency gains to be had with no sacrifice in the quality of justice from replacing the unanimity rule for 12-member juries with a 10-2 rule.[1]

---

[1]See A. Klevorick & M. Rothschild, *A Model of the Jury Decision Process*, 8 J. LEGAL STUD. 141 (1979) and A. Klevorick, M. Rothschild, & L. Winship, *Information Processing and Jury Decisionmaking* (Civil Liability Working Paper, Yale Law School, 1982.)

Other studies of the 6-member and non-unanimous 12-member jury include Richard O. Lempert, *Uncovering 'Non-discernible' Differences: Empirical Research and the Jury-Size Cases*, 73 MICH. L. REV. 643 (1975) and Hans Zeisel & Shari Seidman Diamond, *'Convincing Empirical Evidence' on the Six-Member Jury*, 41 U. CHI. L. REV. 281 (1974). The seminal empirical study of the jury is Harry Kalven, Jr. & Hans Zeisel, THE AMERICAN JURY (1971).

---

cal tests for hypotheses from bargaining theory. All we need to make significant gains in our understanding of this area of law and economics is a new generation of legal scholars who know how to test bargaining theory and of economists who are familiar with the legal process.

SUGGESTED READINGS

Bebchuk, Lucien, *Litigation and Settlement Under Imperfect Informaton,* 15 RAND J. ECON. 404 (1984).

Danzon, Patricia M., *Contingent Fees for Personal Injury Litigation,* 14 BELL J. ECON. 213 (1981).

Feeley, Malcolm, COURT REFORM ON TRIAL: WHY SIMPLE SOLUTIONS FAIL (1983).

James, Jr., Fleming, and Geoffrey C. Hazard, Jr., CIVIL PROCEDURE (3d ed. 1985).

Landes, William, *An Economic Analysis of the Courts,* 14 J. LAW & ECON. 61 (1971).

Posner, Richard A., THE FEDERAL COURTS: CRISIS AND REFORM (1985).

Posner, Richard A., *An Economic Approach to Legal Procedure and Judicial Administration,* 2 J. LEGAL STUD. 399 (1973).

Priest, George, and Benjamin Klein, *The Selection of Disputes for Litigation,* 13 J. LEGAL STUD. 1 (1984).

Priest, George, *Selective Characteristics of Litigation,* 9 J. LEGAL STUD. 399 (1980).

Ross, H. Laurence, SETTLED OUT OF COURT: THE SOCIAL PROCESS OF INSURANCE CLAIMS ADJUSTMENT (2d ed. 1980).

Shavell, Steven, *Suit, Settlement, and Trial: A Theoretical Analysis Under Alternative Methods for the Allocation of Legal Costs,* 11 J. LEGAL STUD. 55 (1982).

Symposium on the Allocation of Attorney Fees in Litigation, 47 LAW & CONTEMP. PROB. 1 (1984).

CHAPTER 11

An Economic Theory of Crime and Criminal Law

Crime, which was once a rarity in the typical person's life, has become a pervasive social phenomenon in the last several decades. Nearly one in three households is directly affected by a crime each year. As a result, passionate arguments are made on behalf of a radical reform in the criminal law to make punishment more certain, more swift, and more severe. And equally passionate arguments are made that such a reform would involve a disastrous interference with personal freedoms. These and other complex matters regarding crime and punishment are among the most important public policy issues of the day.

In this and the next chapter we will define crimes and distinguish them from civil offenses, explore the broad statistics on the crime wave, examine economic models of criminal behavior and of the behavior of law enforcement agencies, and survey such important empirical issues as the deterrent effect of criminal sanctions, including capital punishment, and the effects of handgun control legislation. We approach these issues through two questions: What acts should be punishable? And to what extent? The first question, which we address in this chapter, requires an exploration into the nature of crime and punishment. The second question, which is the central focus of the next chapter, concerns the calibration of punishments.

I. WHAT IS A CRIME?

A person commits a crime by violating a criminal statute. Are these statutes coherent, and do they have a systematic purpose, or are crimes a heterogeneous collection of acts with no unifying purpose, the detritus of legislative history? This is the problem that this chapter seeks to solve with the help of economics.

In the previous chapters we have concentrated upon judge-made law. Judges must explain their opinions in written documents that are scrutinized by their peers. As we have seen in the previous chapter, this requirement, plus the other constraints under which judges operate in the common law system, imposes an efficiency rationale on the rules that emerge from the common law process. In contrast, when legislators make laws, they do not have to explain their actions in official documents, nor are their reasons subjected to official scrutiny by their peers. A collection of statutes is, consequently, more diverse and less reasoned than most bodies of common law. This fact makes a unified account of crimes difficult.

In our introductory chapters on contracts and torts, we began by explaining the minimal elements in the typical contract and tort suit, even though the account of these elements was riddled with exceptions. Similarly, we begin this chapter with an account of the minimal elements in the typical crime, even though the exceptions here are also numerous.

Fault is the failure to fulfill an obligation. In every crime there is fault: doing what ought not to be done or failing to do what ought to be done.[1] Fault is not, however, sufficient to justify criminal prosecution in many cases.[2] In our discussion of torts, we found that a fault that causes injury makes the injurer liable for compensatory damages. The intention to harm is unnecessary for tort liability, but it is necessary to justify criminal prosecution in most cases involving personal injury. When fault is combined with the intention to harm, and the harmful act is proscribed in a criminal statute, the actor is guilty of a crime. The first element of the typical crime is, thus, *criminal intent*.

Mens rea (Latin for "a guilty mind") is the legal term for criminal intent.[3] To develop this idea, consider the following ranking of potentially dangerous acts along a continuum:

Probability of Harm

$$0 \overline{\hspace{9cm}} 1$$

careful		negligent	reckless		intentional	cruel
(blameless)		(fault)			(guilt)	

legal	line separating
standard	civil wrongs
of	from criminal
precaution	wrongs

---

[1]Hence the Anglican prayer, "We have done what we ought not to have done and left undone what we ought to have done, and there is no help in us."

[2]There are crimes in which fault with intentionality is sufficient for prosecution. There are even crimes in which fault is unnecessary for prosecution—so-called "strict liability" crimes. We discuss these crimes later in this chapter after developing the four central characteristics of crimes.

[3]Guilt in criminal law should not be confused with guilt in psychiatry. In psychiatry, guilt is the feeling that one is blameworthy; it is usually accompanied by regret and remorse. In law, guilt concerns the intention to commit a crime. A guilty intent often causes guilty feelings, but not always. To illustrate, a criminal may be guilty in the legal sense, but not feel guilt in the psychiatric sense.

A person who is careful about a potentially dangerous activity like, say, driving a car, is unlikely to harm anyone. And a careful actor satisfies the legal standard and is not at fault. A negligent actor imposes greater risk on others and violates the legal standard. Mere negligence, however, is a lesser degree of fault than recklessness. A reckless person departs far from the legal standard in disregard for the safety of others. To rise to the level of guilt, however, the actor must do something still worse: *intentionally* harm someone. The intent to harm, not mere recklessness, is a necessary part of criminal intent in the typical case involving personal injury.

There are further gradations in criminal intent that are sometimes relevant to guilt and punishment.[4] To illustrate, harming someone intentionally to gain a personal advantage is not as bad as harming them cruelly and taking pleasure in their pain. There is, thus, a continuous gradation in the moral evaluation of the actor from blameless on the good end to cruel on the bad end.[5] It is the boundary on this continuum between fault and guilt that is crucial to the criminal law.

The second element of a crime concerns the nature of the harm. In torts, the harm is private, whereas with crimes the harm is *public*. This difference is represented by the contrast between the active parties in a tort and a criminal suit. A tort suit is brought by the victim (the plaintiff), whereas a criminal prosecution is brought by the state (the public prosecutor or the attorney general). Sometimes it is said that a crime threatens the peace and security of the state. When we distinguished public and private goods in an earlier chapter, we used peace and security as an example of a public good: there is little rivalry among citizens for the enjoyment of peace and security, and it is costly to exclude non-paying citizens from enjoying this good. A crime, then, harms the public, which often involves a threat to peace and security, which is a public good. Let's consider two examples.

> **Example 1:** Atlee is an independent businessman who sells cocaine. While he is engaged in a seemingly mutually beneficial exchange with Gantner, a regular customer, the police arrive and arrest them. Should both of them be released if they can demonstrate that their exchange was a valid contractual transaction?

This is an example of what is frequently called a "victimless" crime. For many of these crimes—such as gambling, prostitution, and the sale of drugs—

---

[4]The Model Penal Code [2.02(2)] has thus reduced the matter to four basic types of crimes that require fault:

1. crimes requiring intention (or *purpose*) to do the forbidden act (or omission) or cause the forbidden result;
2. crimes requiring *knowledge*;
3. crimes requiring *recklessness*; and
4. crimes requiring only *negligence*.

Wayne LaFave & Robert Scott, CRIMINAL LAW 194 (1st ed. 1977).

[5]We could, of course, extend the line and fill in the gaps; indeed, fine distinctions of this kind are essential to criminal law. To illustrate, off the scale to the left lie meritorious acts, and off the scale to the right lie sadistic acts.

the parties to the crime are engaged in what appears to be a mutually beneficial exchange that is no different, in this respect, from a legitimate contract.[6]
However, one might maintain that there is in fact a victim in these transactions, viz., society, whose peace and security are threatened by these actions.
It is true that this "victim" is vague. Nonetheless, some crimes are defined
for actions perceived to be harmful to society or to the social fabric. No
doubt the actions that are so perceived change from time to time so that
there are variations in the kinds of actions that are believed to threaten the
public at large. For example, today there are almost no crimes attached to
wearing certain kinds of clothes. But in the late Middle Ages dress was a
frequent indicator of social standing, and as a result, there were *sumptuary
laws* providing for criminal sanctions for those who wore items of clothing to
which their station did not entitle them. Members of society clearly
belonged to classes, and peace and security were supposedly threatened
when citizens sought to disguise themselves as members of a higher class.
Sumptuary laws have largely disappeared, and, similarly, the enforcement of
laws against such victimless crimes as gambling, prostitution, marijuana use,
and homosexuality has been much less vigorous than it was twenty years
ago.

> **Question 11.1:** Using the economic explanation for "victimless" crimes, can you
> explain why counterfeiting is considered a crime? Is there an alternative or addi-
> tional economic explanation?

Now consider this second example, which might be entitled "Is a Miss
as Good as a Hit?":

> **Example 2:** Montgomery is an inveterate gambler and has recently incurred
> some extremely large gambling debts that he is unable to pay. His spinster aunt,
> Miss Maxwell, has a fortune that she intends to leave to Montgomery at her
> death. But that death is distant. In order to get the money sooner, Montgomery
> has purchased a lethal poison. He is about to place it in his aunt's bedtime milk
> when he is discovered. Should he be criminally liable for this unsuccessful
> attempt to commit a crime?

This is an example of what is called an "inchoate," or uncompleted,
crime. It is clear that Miss Maxwell has no cause of action in tort against her
nephew—saving possibly intentional infliction of emotional distress—
because she has not suffered a legally compensable harm. Behavior that
causes no actual harm but merely has the potential for causing harm does
not typically confer a private cause of action. And yet no one doubts that a
person who tried to seriously injure another and failed should be punished.
A failure to do so would surely encourage dangerous behavior.

This is an argument that we ought to impose criminal sanctions on
attempts to harm. If the success or failure of an attempt is purely a matter of

---

[6]Note that we are excluding from consideration a contract between Atlee and Gantner
that *clearly* involves harm to third parties, e.g., a contract to kill Atlee's employer.

luck, then the attempt is morally as bad as the successful crime. Yet is is usually the case that unsuccessful attempts to harm are punished less than successful attempts. Is there an economic reason for this practice? The answer is yes. If the failed attempt is punished the same as the successful attempt, then a person who fails in his first attempt to commit a crime might as well have another go. Suppose a thief who is fleeing the police shoots at them and misses. If a miss carries as much penalty as a direct hit, he has nothing to lose by shooting again.

Question 11.2: Does the argument in the text provide a justification for punishing speeding or for punishing the act of running a red light when no one has been harmed?

The two elements discussed so far—criminal intent and public harm—are characteristic of the criminal act. Now we turn to two elements that characterize, not the act itself, but its legal consequences. The person who commits a crime exposes himself to the risk of *punishment*. Punishment can take several forms: the criminal's freedom may be curtailed through imprisonment, his movements restricted by being placed on probation, or a fine in excess of compensation may be imposed. In a serious enough case, the defendant faces the possibility of being executed by the state for what he has done.

Punishment in criminal law is quite different from compensation in civil law. Compensation in civil law aims to make the victim whole at the expense of the injurer. Punishment in criminal law makes the injurer worse off without directly benefiting the victim. Since the motivation is different, the issues of compensation and punishment are often independent of each other in a particular case. Thus, punishment may be imposed on top of compensation, as when recovery in tort is followed by criminal prosecution, or in lieu of compensation, as when, say, a person is prosecuted for attempted murder but there is no cause for a civil suit because the attempt was frustrated before anyone got hurt.

Question 11.3: In *State v. Garoutte,* 95 Ariz. 234 (1964), the defendant was charged with manslaughter in the driving of a car. Before the criminal trial began, Garoutte filed a motion to dismiss under Arizona's "compromise" statute. That statute, which is similar to those in most states, provides that a defendant accused of a misdemeanor—but not a felony[7]—may be excused from prosecution by the state if the act constituting the misdemeanor has a remedy in a civil action and the party injured appears before the court to say that he has received satisfaction.

The widow and children of the man killed by Garoutte were paid a sum of money in settlement of their civil complaint. They then appeared before the court to testify that they were satisfied. On the basis of this testimony, the trial

---

[7]Both misdemeanors and felonies are crimes, but felonies are more serious than misdemeanors. A typical distinction between the two classes of crime is that a misdemeanor is any crime punishable by up to one year in prison and a felony is any crime punishable by more than a year in prison.

court dismissed the criminal complaint against Garoutte. The State of Arizona appealed.

Keeping in mind the discussion above about the nature of a crime, should the criminal complaint against Garoutte be dismissed?

The fourth element of a crime is the standard of proof required by law. The prosecutor in a criminal case bears a far greater burden of proof than the plaintiff in a civil case. In a civil action the plaintiff must prove his case by the preponderance of the evidence: that is, his case must be more believable than his opponent's. In a criminal action the plaintiff must prove his case *beyond a reasonable doubt*. Although these phrases are vague, it is clear that proof beyond a reasonable doubt is a much higher standard than the preponderance-of-the-evidence standard that prevails in civil actions.

To summarize, these are the four elements of a crime:

1. Criminal intent.
2. Public harm.
3. Punitive sanctions, and
4. Proof beyond a reasonable doubt.

II. DISTINGUISHING A CRIME FROM A PRIVATE LAW ACTION

Why is there a class of offenses called "crimes" with these four attributes and a different class called "civil actions" to which a different set of rules applies? To put the same question in another way, why is there anything other than a civil action? For example, why is it that when someone is intentionally killed there is, first, a wrongful death action in tort and, second, a criminal complaint of murder? Answering these questions turns out to be a more difficult task than one might have imagined. But it is essential that we come to grips with the reasons for the existence of criminal law: if we are not agreed about why it exists, then we cannot speak sensibly about what that criminal law ought to be, nor of what the limits and limitations of the civil law are.

Consider this example:

Example 3: Jonny was walking down the sidewalk when he was struck and seriously injured by a car driven by Frankie. Jonny has sued Frankie in tort seeking compensation for the harms he has suffered. Suppose that Frankie hit Jonny because she had aimed her car at him in a conscious attempt to hurt him. Is it enough to hold Frankie liable only for the amount necessary to compensate Jonny for his losses?

All of us have the feeling that in these circumstances it will not do to hold Frankie liable only for the damages she has inflicted on Jonny. The question is, "Why not?"

In this example, Frankie *intended* to cause harm, so her action goes beyond fault to guilt: she is guilty of doing something that is morally and legally wrong. The requisite *mens rea* required for criminal prosecution is apparently present. Perhaps it will be possible to prove these facts beyond a reasonable doubt. One answer to our question, "Why punish Frankie?" is that punishing those who are proven guilty is *morally right*, just as punishing the innocent is *morally wrong*.

In addition to this moralistic reason, an instrumental reason can be given. If there were no criminal prosecution, fear of being intentionally hit by drivers might spread among pedestrians. The spread of fear among pedestrians is a loss of peace and security, and because those are public goods, it is appropriate that the state should take an interest in punishing those who spread fear and insecurity. Thus, a second answer to our question, "Why punish Frankie instead of merely holding her liable?" is that the injury caused by her crime was suffered by the public, not merely by Jonny.

> **Question 11.4:** Suppose that Frankie is a famous heart surgeon speeding to administer a terribly important operation to the President of the United States. In her haste to get there, she is greatly exceeding the speed limit, loses control of her car, and runs over pedestrian Jonny, causing him great harm. Should Frankie be *criminally* liable for the harm she has caused to Jonny? Or does the reason for her harming Jonny excuse her from criminal (but not from civil) liability?

> **Question 11.5:** We discussed the example of Frankie intentionally running her car into Jonny. In Chapter 9 we discussed the example of Ford setting safety standards with the knowledge that making the car safer would save lives. By failing to make safer cars, is Ford guilty of murder? What is the difference between Frankie's intent and Ford's intent? In framing standards of conduct, why should society give weight to Ford's profits and give no weight to the pleasure Frankie gets from running over Jonny?

So far we have tried to explain why a consideration of the elements of a crime points to punishment rather than compensation as the remedy for crime. Now we take a different tack and look to the limits of compensation. In the second chapter on torts, we distinguished between two bases for compensation: indifference and risk-equivalence. We said that compensation is perfect when the potential victim is indifferent about accidents in the sense that he would just as soon have the injury and the damages as have no injury and no damages. Now, let's consider a similar thought experiment regarding a crime. How much money would be required for you to consent to having someone murder you or lop off an arm? As we saw in Chapter 9, this question does not make much sense because the concept of indifference is difficult to apply to death or bodily harm. We argued that it is impossible, even in principle, to set damages in tort at a level such that potential victims are indifferent about being struck by cars. The potential victims prefer drivers not to hit them, even though compensation will be paid. But clearly the solution is not to ban driving. Most people are willing to accept the risk of living in a society with automobiles rather than doing without their cars. Part of the solution is to prohibit people from *intentionally* running into others and to back this prohibition by punishment.

This argument can be stated in narrowly economic terms. When perfect compensation is impossible, it is also impossible to use compensatory damages to internalize the external harm caused by tortious acts. If the harm is imperfectly internalized, rationally self-interested actors will commit more than the efficient number of torts. This difficulty can be overcome by creating a legal standard and punishing those who violate it. Stated in narrowly economic terms, our argument is that *when perfect compensation is impossible, revoking the criminal law and replacing it with torts, so that punishment is replaced by compensation, may be inefficient.*

Even if perfect compensation is possible in principle, it may be impossible in fact. Let us suppose, for example, that a level of compensation exists that makes Jonny indifferent about whether Frankie lops off his arm. It would still be almost impossible to prove what this level is in court. The obstacle to proof is that arms are not bought and sold in a market, so there is no *objective* way to know how much the loss is worth to Jonny. (The best we can do in court is to ask Jonny or his heirs what amount he or they feel would compensate them for the loss. And the answer to that question simply cannot be accepted without comparing it to some *objective* standard.) When there is no objective market to induce people to reveal their subjective valuations, economists say that there is a "problem or preference revelation." When perfect compensation is possible in principle, it may be impossible in fact because of the problem of preference revelation.

Suppose that perfect compensation is possible in principle and in fact. Do more objections remain? The answer is yes, because permitting the injurer to harm the victim infringes upon the latter's liberty. In the first chapter on property, we distinguished between protecting an interest and protecting a right. Recall that if trespass is allowed by law on the condition that the trespasser compensates the owner for any harm he causes, the *interest* of the owner in his property is protected, but the owner's *right* to use his property as he chooses, without interference from others, is infringed. Similarly, if the victims of car accidents were perfectly compensated, their interests in their persons and property would be protected, but their right to go about their business without interference from others would be infringed. Protecting interests secures wealth, but allowing the infringement of rights diminishes liberty.

We have argued that there are two difficulties with compensation that stand as obstacles to substituting it for punishment: first, perfect compensation may be impossible, and, second, even if it is possible, the law may seek to protect the potential victim's rights rather than his interests. There are some additional reasons to prefer punishment over compensation that can be explained by a final example.

Example 4: Willeford has stolen Leonard's television set worth $1,000, but he has been caught. Is efficiency served if Leonard can recover the set or its value ($1,000) from Willeford in a civil action for the tort of conversion?

The difficulty with leaving this matter to compensation in a civil action is that such an award will not adequately deter potential thieves from attempting to acquire goods through theft rather than through market transactions. This is because the probability of the thief's being apprehended and convicted is considerably less than one. Suppose that this probability is 0.5 in our example, which is much higher than the actual rate, and that a thief is considering whether to acquire a $1,000 television set through theft or by acquisition from a legitimate retailer. The expected cost of the legal acquisition is $1,000, but, assuming civil liability and no punishment, the expected cost of illegal acquisition of the same good is 0.5($1,000) = $500. If the moral imperative not to commit the theft is not very strong in the thief, then his perception that the television can be had for much less through thievery will induce him to steal.

In order to dissuade the potential thief from this course of action, the law must impose punitive sanctions on the criminal such that the expected cost of illegal activity exceeds the expected cost of legal activity. In this instance, a punishment with a monetary value of, say, $2,500 is enough to induce only legal transactions on the part of potential thieves who are rational and informed.

Theft is, of course, an infringement upon the liberty of property owners, and that is bad in its own right. In addition, permitting theft is likely to reduce society's total wealth. In earlier chapters we saw that society is, in general, better off if goods are acquired through voluntary exchange because, *ceteris paribus*, such exchange guarantees that goods move to those who value them the most. As we saw in the first chapter on contracts, goods that change hands without the consent of both parties—as by theft—do not carry this same guarantee. The stolen good may be more valuable to its owner than to the thief, but the theft occurs because the thief need not pay the owner's asking price. This is an argument that remedies in criminal law should, in part, be set so as to protect and encourage voluntary exchange through markets.

III. STRICT LIABILITY CRIMES

We distinguished two characteristics of the criminal act—criminal intent and public injury—and two of its legal consequences—punishment and a high standard of proof. These are the common elements for most crimes. In previous chapters of this book, we have seen that one method for constructing a legal theory is to identify the minimal elements shared by almost all the acts regulated by a particular body of law, and then to raise those elements to the level of a principle: the principle that every act must have these elements in order to be regulated by the body of law in question. We found that this method of theory-building provided a useful introduction to the subject but that the law in practice usually burst the bounds imposed by the principle.

The same can be said about the relationship between the four elements of a crime and the criminal law. After reading the previous chapters in this book, you will not be surprised to learn that criminal law has burst the bounds imposed by these elements, as we will illustrate by reference to criminal intent.

There have always been some crimes for which criminal intent is unnecessary. For example, statutory rape occurs when a man has sexual intercourse with a girl who is below the age at which she can legally consent. Even though the girl was willing and the man believed, wrongly, that she was above the legal age of consent, he is still guilty of rape. In such circumstances the man might not have intended to have intercourse with a girl below the legal age of consent, so he did not intend to do what the statute forbids. Since he did not intend to do what the statute forbids, he did not have criminal intent or *mens rea*, yet this fact is not a defense against prosecution for statutory rape.

As economic regulations accumulated in the 20th century, many crimes were added to the list that do not require *mens rea*. Examples are adulterating food, installing unsafe wiring in violation of building codes, possessing a federally proscribed narcotic without a doctor's prescription, and selling a potentially dangerous medication without an adequate warning. Like statutory rape, each of these crimes can be committed even though the actor did not intend to violate a law. Unintentional violations of regulations typically occur when the actor is ignorant about the legal requirements of the activity in which he is engaged. The law in effect imposes an obligation to know the relevant regulations on those who engage in these activities.

Crimes without criminal intent are called *strict liability crimes*, just as torts without fault are called strict liability torts.[8] With the flourishing of economic regulations, the list of strict liability crimes has grown rapidly. (See the box entitled, "Are There Corporate Criminals?") This fact has called into question the centrality of *mens rea* as an element in crimes.

IV. AN ECONOMIC ACCOUNT OF THE DECISION TO COMMIT CRIME

We began this chapter by discussing the elements of the typical crime. We found that criminal intent is an important characteristic of criminal acts. Our discussion of strict liability crimes, however, shows that criminal intent is not a necessary element in every criminal prosecution. To understand

---

[8]A further distinction can be drawn between two kinds of crimes that do not require criminal intent: those that do not require criminal intent but do require fault and those that require neither criminal intent nor fault. The term "strict liability" crimes is sometimes reserved for the latter class, those crimes requiring neither intentionality nor fault. *See* W. LaFave & R. Scott, CRIMINAL LAW 190 (1st ed. 1977).

Are There Corporate Crimes?

Corporations regularly commit torts, and when they do, liability is imposed upon the organization, not upon its individual members. But what about crimes? Can a corporation commit a crime? For many years there was a legal obstacle to convicting corporations of crimes: *mens rea*. An individual can have a guilty mind, but it is not clear that organizations can. How, it was asked, can an organization have criminal intent?

So long as it was thought that organizations could not have criminal intent, the crimes that corporations could commit were limited to strict liability crimes, such as selling uncertified drugs or transporting explosives by forbidden routes. Other crimes, like manslaughter, fraud, or assault could be committed by the *members* of the corporation, but not by the corporation itself.

There is now an effort to overcome this obstacle and prosecute corporations for acts requiring criminal intent. For example, we have seen that the Ford Motor Company has been prosecuted, so far unsuccessfully, for manslaughter in connection with manufacturing the Pinto with an allegedly unsafe gas tank, which is said to cause the car to explode when struck from the rear.

Question 11.6:
a. Does it make sense to allow victims to collect punitive damages from corporations for committing torts, and not to allow the prosecution of corporations for the crime corresponding to the tort?
b. Can corporations be punished beyond the value of their assets? Or does bankruptcy impose an absolute limit on the extent of punishment?
c. Suppose an employee commits a crime in order to benefit her employer. Should her boss bear any share of the criminal responsibility?

crimes we need to go beyond a list of elements and develop a theory to elucidate the purposes of criminal law.

As a first step toward such a theory, we will develop an economic account of the criminal mind. As represented in economic theory, decisionmakers are rational, and that includes criminals. So we begin with an account in this section of the most rational type of crime: a crime deliberately committed for material gain.

Crimes can be ranked by seriousness, and punishments can be ranked by severity. The schedule of punishments is such that the more severe punishments attach to the more serious crimes. We represent these facts in Figure 11.1.

The seriousness of the crime is measured on the horizontal axis; the severity of the punishment can be read off the vertical axis; the curved line

Figure 11.1   Severity of the Offense and Severity of the Punishment

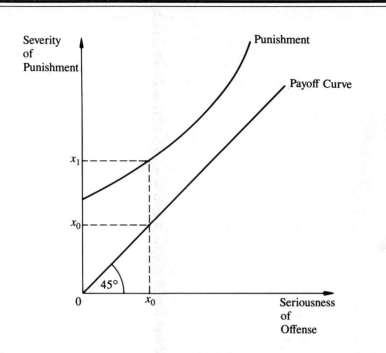

Crimes can be ranked by seriousness, and punishments can be ranked by severity. More severe punishments attach to more serious crimes. Clearly, punishment involves a fine that is greater than the dollar amount of the crime, as when a fine of x_1 is imposed for an offense of amount x_0. Therefore, the curve labeled "Punishment" lies above the Payoff Curve (45°-line); it slopes up to indicate that the punishment becomes more severe as the crime becomes more serious.

labeled "punishment" slopes up to indicate that the punishment becomes more severe as the crime becomes more serious.

To give this graph more concrete meaning, consider a property crime with a simple metric: embezzlement. Assume that the seriousness of the crime can be measured by the amount that is embezzled. Under this assumption, the metric for the horizontal axis in Figure 11.1 is dollars. Similarly, assume that the punishment at issue is a fine, so that a more severe punishment corresponds to a higher fine. Under this assumption, the metric for the vertical axis is also dollars. Since both metrics are dollars, they are easy to compare. Note that the punishment for a given level of severity of embezzlement is always greater than the dollar value of the amount embezzled. For example, the punishment for the crime of embezzling x_0 is x_1 and $x_1 > x_0$. Thus, if the criminal embezzles $1,000, so that $x_0 = $1,000$, the fine might be $2,000, so that $x_1 = $2,000$. The fact that $x_1 > x_0$ reflects our previous discussion about the inadequacy of mere compensation for criminal wrongs. In the graph, the fact that the punishment curve lies above the 45° line indicates that the fine always exceeds the amount embezzled.

Figure 11.2   The Effect of Uncertainty in Punishment

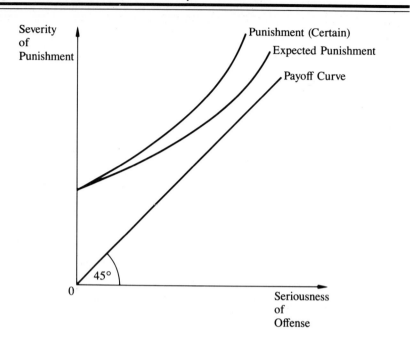

The "Punishment (Certain)" curve reproduces the punishment curve from the previous figure and makes explicit the assumption that the punishment will be imposed with certainty. If there is some uncertainty about apprehending or convicting the criminal, then punishment becomes probable but not certain. If, for example, the fine for embezzling $1,000 is $2,000 and the probability that an offender will be apprehended and convicted is 0.75, then the *expected* fine is 0.75($2,000) = $1,500. To represent this element of uncertainty, the figure shows a curve labeled "Expected Punishment," which is the Punishment (Certain) curve rotated downward.

Question 11.7: What is the significance of the fact that the severity-of-punishment curve in Figure 11.1 intersects the vertical axis at a positive value?

Punishment of the offender is, however, uncertain. The offender may escape apprehension, or she may be apprehended but not convicted. A rational decisionmaker takes this fact into account when contemplating embezzlement. Recalling the terminology of the appendix to Chapter 2, we may say that the rational embezzler calculates an expected value for the crime by discounting for uncertainty. To illustrate, if the fine for embezzling $1,000 is $2,000, and the probability that an offender will have to pay the fine is 3/4, then the expected fine is $1,500. To represent this element of uncertainty, Figure 11.2 is drawn with the punishment curve from the previous graph rotated downward to reflect the uncertainty of punishment, thus yielding the *expected punishment curve.*

Let us consider how a person who is utterly amoral and perfectly rational would respond to this uncertain punishment schedule. Recall that the seriousness of the crime is measured by the amount of money that is embezzled. Consequently, the 45° line in Figure 11.2 indicates the amount of money that the embezzler can obtain as a function of the seriousness of the offense that she commits, which we call the *payoff curve*. A rational and amoral decisionmaker will embezzle money so long as the payoff exceeds the expected punishment. The expected punishment is always above the payoff in the graph, so embezzlement is irrational in these circumstances. The graph is presumably the situation in which most people find themselves.

The situation is different in Figure 11.3. In this case, the expected punishment dips below the payoff curve for embezzlement at least as serious as x_1 and no more serious than x_2. Under these circumstances, a decisionmaker who was rational and amoral would embezzle some money. We can read off the graph exactly how serious the offense must be in order to be most profitable. The expected profit from the offense is the difference between the payoff and the expected punishment, which is represented on the graph by the vertical distance between the payoff curve and the expected punishment curve. The vertical distance is maximized when the seriousness of the offense is x^*. In conclusion, the rational and amoral decisionmaker will embezzle the amount x^*.

The rational criminal's behavior can be explained by using mathematical notation corresponding to the graphical analysis of Figure 11.3. Let the seriousness of the crime be indicated by the variable x. Let the amount embezzled be indicated by the variable y. The amount embezzled is the criminal's payoff for committing the crime. We have assumed that the seriousness of the offense is measured by the amount that is embezzled: thus, $x = y$. Consequently, the criminal's payoff as a function of the seriousness of the crime is given by the equation $x = y$, whose graph is the 45° line.

Let the punishment f, assumed to be a fine, for committing a crime of seriousness x be given by the function $f = f(x)$. Furthermore, let the probability of being punished for committing a crime of seriousness x be given by the function $p = p(x)$. Thus, the expected punishment is the product of the amount of punishment and its probability: $p(x)f(x)$.

The rationally self-interested criminal chooses the seriousness of his crime x to maximize his net payoff, which equals the payoff minus the expected punishment:

$$y - p(x)f(x) \text{ where } y = x.$$

The marginal values of the functions $p(x)$ and $f(x)$ give the change in the probability of punishment and its severity when the seriousness of the crime, x, changes slightly—specifically, when the criminal embezzles an additional dollar. We denote these marginal values p' and f'. The criminal maximizes net benefits by embezzling an amount of money such that an additional dollar embezzled would cause the expected fine to increase by one dollar:[9]

---

[9]Using the calculus to find the maximum, choose x to set the derivative of $[x - p(x)f(x)]$ equal to zero.

Figure 11.3 Expected Punishment and the Decision to Commit a Crime

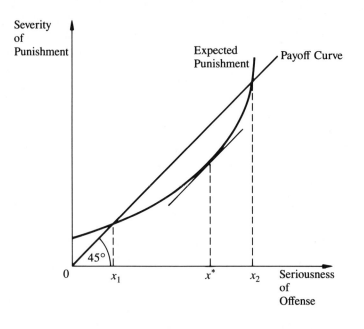

Where the probability of apprehension or conviction is sufficiently low, the Expected Punishment curve dips below the Payoff Curve, with the result that the payoff for crimes of value between x_1 and x_2 is greater than the expected punishment. Under these circumstances, a rational and amoral decisionmaker will contemplate committing a crime. The optimal crime to commit, given the curves in the figure, is one of size x^*; the expected profit for that crime (the vertical distance between the Payoff Curve and the Expected Punishment curve) is the greatest.

$$1 = p'f + pf'$$

marginal payoff   marginal expected punishment

The increase in the expected punishment from embezzling an additional dollar has two components: the change in the probability of punishment, p', and the change in the severity of punishment, f'. The probability of punishment usually increases with the seriousness of the crime because more serious crimes attract greater enforcement effort by the authorities. Furthermore, the severity of the punishment almost always increases with the seriousness of the crime. Thus, p' and f' are ordinarily positive numbers.

For many crimes, even embezzlement, the seriousness depends upon factors other than the amount that is stolen, and the payoff may also be measured by considerations other than wealth. For example, the embezzler may derive considerable non-pecuniary satisfaction from being known in his circle of hoodlum friends as a successful embezzler. Similarly, there are powerful non-criminal justice system elements that may enter into the expected punishment—for example, shame, social disapproval, and subsequent difficulty in getting a job.

When we abandon the simple assumption that payoffs and punishments are measured in dollars, the rational criminal's calculations, as represented by the preceding graphs, are more complicated in fact but they remain the same in principle. To illustrate, the criminal justice authorities must rank offenses to establish schedules of punishment. Let the horizontal axis in Figure 11.4 indicate the rank that authorities assign to offenses. (The metric here is pure rank order, like the location of names in the telephone book, not a natural measure like dollars or meters.) Let the vertical axis be denominated in units of utility. The expected punishment curve represents the expected loss in utility from being punished. The payoff is also given in utils, which may consist in, say, money and pleasure. The rational, amoral decisionmaker will commit a crime if the payoff exceeds the expected punishment; specifically, in Figure 11.4 he or she will commit the crime corresponding to x^*, where the marginal payoff in utility equals the expected marginal disutility of the punishment. Changing the metric changes the details of the curves, but not their significance.

At this point the reader may be wondering whether these abstractions actually have anything to do with the motives of criminals. Certainly the economic model of rational choice has limitations when applied to criminal law. Economists usually describe this model as an account of *behavior*, not as an account of subjective reasoning processes. Thus, consumers are said to act *as if* they were reasoning in this manner. However, in criminal law there is a direct concern with *reasons*, not just behavior, because the commission of most crimes requires criminal intent, which is a characterization of subjective motives. It is not enough for a conviction that the accused acted *as if* she had criminal intent; it must be proved that she actually had it.

Despite its focus on behavior rather than reasons for behavior, the economic model of rational choice is still useful as an account of the criminal mind. Criminal intent is often distinguished according to the level of deliberation. To illustrate, a crime may be committed spontaneously in the sense that the criminal did not make any plans in advance, nor did he search out an opportunity to commit a crime, but when an opportunity fell into his lap, he availed himself of it. At the opposite extreme, a crime may be carefully planned out in advance and all the possibilities weighed. Thus, a premeditated crime shows a greater degree of deliberateness than a spontaneous crime.

The economic model may be understood as an account of the *deliberations* of a rational, amoral person when deciding in advance whether to commit a crime. In the case of premeditated crimes, the economic model may correspond to the actual reasoning process of the criminal. In the case of spontaneous crimes, where there is no time for deliberation, the economic model may be understood as an account of the criminal's *behavior*. For spontaneous crimes, the criminal may not actually reason as in the economic model, but she may act as if she did. By acting "as if" she had deliberated,

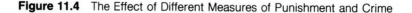

Figure 11.4 The Effect of Different Measures of Punishment and Crime

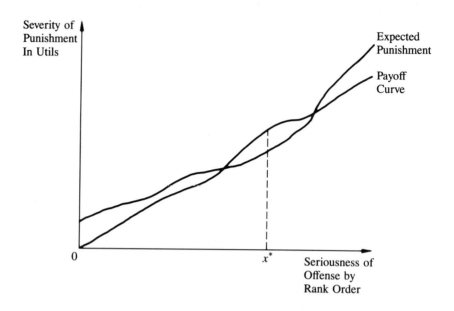

We now ask what difference it makes if, instead of measuring punishment and the seriousness of crime in dollar amounts, we measure them in more realistic units. Suppose that along the vertical axis we measure the severity of punishment in utils and that along the horizontal axis we measure the seriousness of criminal offenses according to pure rank order, with seriousness increasing as one moves to the right. The advantage of these changes is that they allow more general analysis. Punishment can take any of the forms it actually might take: a fine, probation, jail, or some combination of these. Crimes can be ranked from, say, public indecency to premeditated murder. The Expected Punishment curve now represents the expected loss in utility from being punished in whatever form. The Payoff Curve represents the points for which the expected loss in utility from punishment equals the seriousness of the crime. This change in the measures of crime and punishment changes the shapes of the curves but it does not change the analysis or conclusions of the previous figures. Where the Expected Punishment curve falls below the Payoff Curve, a rational and amoral decisionmaker may decide to commit a crime and will choose the level of crime for which the expected benefit (the vertical distance between the two curves) is the greatest. In the figure that is a crime of seriousness equal to x^*.

we mean that, when presented with the opportunity to commit a crime, she responds immediately to benefits and risks as if she had deliberated about her choice. If she responds in this way, her behavior can be explained by the economic model, even though her reasoning process is only a fragment of it.

Even when interpreted as a behavioral model, the model of rational choice is valuable in the study of criminal law. To see why, consider another difference between the application of the rational choice model to markets and to a criminal prosecution. When economists study markets, they are concerned with *aggregate* behavior. When studying markets, the statistical outliers—eccentric and erratic behavior—wash out by being aggregated with the mass of ordinary people. In contrast, criminal prosecutions focus upon *individuals*, and individual criminals are often statistical outliers. Seen in this perspective, the economic model of rational choice does not seem applicable to the criminal law.

But this is not the only perspective on criminal law. Criminal law involves more than the prosecution of individuals. General policies toward crime must be set by legislators and officials in the criminal justice system. General policies must be formulated with an eye to their aggregate effects, such as their ability to minimize the social costs of crime. At this level of inquiry, the economic model, with its close relationship to statistics and econometrics, is very valuable. In the next chapter we will discuss issues of legal policy, such as the calibration of punishment, that involve predicting aggregate behavior.

But that is jumping ahead. We have claimed that the economic model of choice describes the deliberation of rational criminals when their crimes are premeditated, and we have claimed that rational criminals behave as if guided by the economic model when they commit spontaneous crimes. If this claim is true, empirical investigations should demonstrate that crime rates are responsive to the considerations identified in our model, specifically, that crimes rates respond to risks (punishments) and benefits (payoffs). This is an empirical question; that is, it must be answered by an appeal to facts, thus going beyond the logical consistency of our economic model. Fortunately, there is a great deal of evidence on this matter, and we now turn to a summary of the literature on deterrence.

V. DOES PUNISHMENT DETER CRIME?[10]

The proposition that crime rates respond to risks and benefits is called the "deterrence hypothesis." This hypothesis is an application of the theory of demand to one of the most important issues in criminal justice. Recall that the law of demand states that because of the inverse relationship between price and quantity demanded, demand curves slope downward. Applied to matters of crime and punishment, this theory suggests that crime goes down when the expected punishment of criminals goes up. Few people seriously dispute this contention. The real issue in question is, "By how much?" The essence of the dispute is, then, *how elastic is crime with respect to the expected punishment?*

In answering this question, it is possible to distinguish two broad and important competing hypotheses with vastly different consequences for the

---

[10]Much of the material in this section is drawn from James Q. Wilson, THINKING ABOUT CRIME (2d ed. 1983) at 117–44 (ch. 7, "Penalties and Opportunities").

public policy of reducing the costs of crime. The first, which may be called the *deterrence hypothesis*, asserts that people respond significantly to the deterring incentives created by the criminal justice system. If so, then increasing the resources that society devotes to the arrest, conviction, and punishment of criminals may be the best policy prescription for reducing the amount, and social costs, of crime.

The second hypothesis holds that criminals are not deterred by variations in the certainty and severity of criminal justice system variables. Rather, this hypothesis holds that crime is caused by a complex set of socio-economic and biological factors and that the appropriate way to reduce the amount of crime and thus to lower the costs of crime is to divert resources into channels that attack these root causes of crime: for example, into job-creation, income maintenance, family counseling, mental health, and other programs designed to alleviate the biological, economic, and sociological origins of crime.

Although recent public debate has tended to frame these two hypotheses as mutually exclusive, it could well be true that they are both correct, in which case the optimal public policy for reducing crime may be a *mix* of criminal justice system and sociological programs. Nonetheless, the empirical literature has implicitly assumed the mutual exclusivity of the two hypotheses. We will examine the relevant literature for each of the two hypotheses and then, at the end of this section, mention the latest thinking on crime that seems to point toward a synthesis of the two hypotheses.

A. General Deterrence

There is a statistical problem about the empirical studies of the deterrence hypothesis that must be addressed at the beginning. One cannot draw inferences about the deterrent effect of sanctions by looking *solely* at those who did *not* respond to those sanctions. For example, one cannot conclude that punishment for murdering another human being cannot deter murder solely because murders continue to occur, notwithstanding the presence of punishments for doing so. Rather, what we should like to know is how many murders were *not* committed because the potential murderer was dissuaded from his act by the fear of punishment. A deterrent effect of this sort is called *general* deterrence. The statistical and econometric problems that arise in attempting to measure how many offenses were not committed are large. We will discuss some of these problems briefly in this section and others much more fully in the following chapter in the course of our examination of the deterrent effect of capital punishment.

The usual statistical study of deterrence seeks to explain the incidence of a certain kind of crime—say, robbery—as a function of certain independent variables. These explanatory variables cover, first, certain aspects of the criminal justice system—e.g., the probabilities of being arrested and convicted and the average prison sentence for that crime—as proxies for the expected punishment; second, certain labor market conditions—e.g., the unemployment rate and the income level of the state—as measures of the opportunity cost of crime; and third, certain socio-economic variables—e.g., the racial and age composition of the population and the percentage of the state's population living in urban areas—that are believed to have an impact on the decision to commit a crime.

All statistical studies of the deterrence hypothesis are subject to two kinds of problems. First are those associated with the quality of the data. If it is the case that the number of crimes reported by victims differs significantly among jurisdictions or that the accuracy of police data on crimes varies widely across crimes and jurisdictions, then a study that assumes that the quality of the data is the same in all jurisdictions will derive spurious results.[11] Second, the estimated model may omit some important but difficult to measure variables—e.g., the quality of family life the criminal had as a child—and, as every student of econometrics knows, if these omitted variables are correlated with some of the included variables, the estimated relationship will be biased and, therefore, unhelpful.

There have been numerous empirical studies of the deterrent effect of criminal sanctions, some better than others at avoiding the problems just noted. All that can be accomplished here is an attempt at an even-handed summary of a few especially noteworthy studies.

A famous study by the economist Isaac Ehrlich used data on robbery for the entire United States in 1940, 1950, and 1960 to estimate the deterrence hypothesis, and concluded that when all other variables were held constant, the higher the probability of conviction for robbery, the lower the robbery rate. Interestingly enough, Ehrlich also found that there seemed to be no deterrent effect attributable to the severity of punishment, as measured by the average length of a prison sentence for robbery, in the years 1940 and 1960 but that there was such a deterrent effect in 1950.[12]

Alfred Blumenstein and Daniel Nagin studied the relationship between draft evasion and penalties for that evasion. The reason for focusing on that particular crime was that the statistical problems associated with more familiar crimes are largely absent in the case of draft evasion. Their conclusion was that evasion rates were negatively correlated with the

---

[11]Of course, one way of avoiding this problem is to use alternative sources of information about crime, for example, the Census Bureau's interviews with the victims of crime. See I. Goldberg, "A Note on Using Victimization Rates to Test Deterrence," Technical Report CERDCR-5-78, Center for Econometric Studies of the Justice System, Stanford University (December, 1978).

[12]Ehrlich, *Participation in Illegitimate Activities: A Theoretical and Empirical Investigation*, 81 J. POL. ECON. 521 (1973).

probability of conviction for draft evasion—that is, the greater the probability of conviction, the lower were draft evasion rates. Thus, this crime is deterrable.[13]

A study by Kenneth Wolpin used time-series data from England and Wales over the lengthy period 1894–1967 to determine whether there was a deterrent effect for certain crimes arising from changes in the probabilities of being arrested, convicted, and punished. The data were better than any comparable data from the United States and, because of the length of the time period covered, allowed for considerable flexibility in the hypotheses tested. Wolpin found that crime rates in the United Kingdom were an inverse function of the probability and severity of punishment.[14]

Finally, the National Research Council of the National Academy of Sciences established a Panel on Research on Deterrent and Incapacitative Effects in 1978 under the chairmanship of Alfred Blumenstein to evaluate the studies of deterrence. The panel concluded that the evidence in favor of a deterrent effect of criminal sanctions was slightly stronger than the evidence of no deterrent effect: "the evidence certainly favors a proposition supporting deterrence more than it favors one asserting that deterrence is absent."[15]

B. Deterrence of Those Most Likely to Commit Crimes

Perhaps one of the reasons the evidence on the general deterrent effect of punitive sanctions is weak is that all investigators had been using aggregate data: state-wide or nation-wide data that included a wide range of non-violent crimes committed by a disparate group of offenders. In order to capture the number of crimes that were *not* committed, the aggregate data in the studies noted above included the vast majority of the population, who, because of strong internal controls, fear of loss of reputation, and the like, are never likely to commit a criminal offense. Deterrence, if it is to work, must principally deter that subset of the population that is most likely to commit crimes. Although we do not know all the members of that subset, we do know some of them, for example, young males and previously convicted

---

[13]Blumenstein & Nagin, *The Deterrent Effect of Legal Sanctions on Draft Evasion*, 28 STAN. L. REV. 241 (1977).

[14]Wolpin, *An Economic Analysis of Crime and Punishment in England and Wales, 1894–1967*, 86 J. POL. ECON. 815 (1978).

[15]Blumenstein, Cohen, and Nagin, eds., DETERRENCE AND INCAPACITATION: ESTIMATING THE EFFECTS OF CRIMINAL SANCTIONS ON CRIME RATES (1978). A critique of that report may be found in Ehrlich & Mark, *Fear of Deterrence*, 6 J. LEGAL STUD. 293 (1977).

and imprisoned offenders.[16] If possible, it would be helpful to know the extent to which this subset of potential criminal offenders was deterrable.

There have been two studies of this sort. Ann Witte followed the post-release behavior of 641 men over a three-year period in North Carolina. She gathered information on whether the men were arrested again during that period (about 80% were), on their previous convictions and imprisonments, on their labor market experience after release (what jobs they were able to get and at what wage), and on whether they were addicted to alcohol or drugs. On the basis of this information, Professor Witte tested the hypothesis that previous conviction and imprisonment induces these high-risk potential offenders to engage in fewer crimes in the future. Her conclusions were that the higher the probability of conviction and imprisonment, the lower the number of subsequent arrests per month free from prison—that is, that "deterrence works." Additionally, she discovered that the strength of the deterrent effect varied between different classes of potential offenders. The effect of a *severe* (as opposed to a *certain*) prior punishment seemed to have had the strongest impact on those who had engaged in more serious, including violent, crimes. For those whose *metier* was the less serious property crime, certainty of arrest and conviction seemed to have a stronger deterrent effect than did the severity of punishment. The deterrent effect of any criminal justice system variable was weakest for drug addicts. Lastly, ease of subsequent employment had no significant effect on future criminal offenses.[17]

The men in the Witte study had an average age of 32. It could well be the case that for younger males, who are well known to be a more crime-prone group, the deterrent effect is weaker or, as with older drug addicts, almost entirely absent. The second major study of individuals who are more

---

[16]There has been an intriguing recent attempt by students of crime to predict what demographic groups are most likely to commit crime. The most famous of these is Peter Greenwood's study for Rand entitled SELECTIVE INCAPACITATION (1982). Greenwood found that high-rate criminal offenders could be predicted as having seven characteristics: (1) conviction while a juvenile; (2) use of illegal drugs as a juvenile; (3) use of illegal drugs during the last two years; (4) employed less than 50% of the time in the previous two years; (5) incarcerated in a juvenile facility; (6) imprisoned more than 50% of the last two years; and (7) had a previous conviction for the current offense. A possible public policy implication of this identification is that those with these characteristics are especially likely to commit crimes in the future and, therefore, should be incapacitated in prison for a longer period than other criminals. See, also, M. Moore, S. Estrich, D. McGillis, and W. Spelman, DANGEROUS OFFENDERS: THE ELUSIVE TARGET OF JUSTICE (1985). The authors give "qualified endorsement" to a policy of "selective incapacitation." Of course, decisions about whether to grant bail, about the severity of punishment, and about parole are all currently made on the basis of predictions about the criminal disposition of the offender. Interestingly, in Barefoot v. Estelle, 463 U.S. 880 (1983), *reh. den.* 464 U.S. 874 (1983), the United States Supreme Court allowed psychiatric testimony on an individual's likely future dangerousness to be put before a jury deciding on whether the defendant should be executed.

[17]Witte, *Estimating the Economic Model of Crime with Individual Data,* 94 Q. J. ECON. 57 (1980).

highly likely than the population at large to commit crimes focused on this younger group. Charles Murray and Louis Cox, Jr., tracked the record of 317 Chicago males with an average age of 16 who had been imprisoned for the first time by the Illinois Department of Corrections. Despite their youth, this was a hardened group of young men: before receiving their first prison sentence, they had averaged 13 prior arrests, including being charged with 14 homicides, 23 rapes, more than 300 assaults, over 300 auto thefts, almost 200 armed robberies, and more than 700 burglaries. The average sentence for their first offense was 10 months. Murray and Cox followed these 317 young offenders for about 18 months after their release and found that during that period the group's arrest record fell by two-thirds. The authors concluded that imprisonment served as a deterrent to future crime for this high-risk group.[18]

There are two alternative explanations for the Murray-Cox finding. Perhaps the reduction in the frequency of arrest is due to the increasing skill of the criminals at avoiding arrest. Or it may be due to the subjects' simply "maturing out" of crime. Neither possibility seems likely. For the first alternative to be true, it must be the case that prisons are such good schools of crime for these juveniles that they taught these delinquents enough skills to reduce their probability of arrest by two thirds. No educational institution is that good. The second possibility may also be doubted, but only after we have made a further comparison. If juveniles mature out of crime, then the frequency of later arrest should be the same for those juvenile delinquents who were arrested and put on probation but not imprisoned and for those who *were* imprisoned. Murray and Cox made this comparison and found that the reduction in the frequency of re-arrest held only for those juvenile delinquents who had been imprisoned. Thus, they concluded that the deterrent effect could be attributed to the form of punishment and not to the aging of juvenile offenders.

C. Economic Conditions and Crime Rates

Recall that competing with the deterrence hypothesis is the one that contends that economic and other social factors, not criminal justice system variables, are the principal determinants of crime rates and that, therefore, the optimal policies for reducing the amount of crime are those that ameliorate economic and social conditions. There have been important empirical studies of the extent to which improvements in employment and other income-related policies reduce the amount of crime. And there have also been important studies of the influence of other, non-economic factors—such as early family life and heredity—on crime rates. In what follows we

---

[18]C. A. Murray and L. A. Cox, Jr., BEYOND PROBATION: JUVENILE CORRECTIONS AND THE CHRONIC DELINQUENT (1979).

concentrate on the economic factors. This is not because we believe that economic factors are more powerful explanatory variables than are other factors but because a consideration of those non-economic factors is beyond the scope of this book. (In fact, we believe that the non-economic factors are the most important causes of crime.)[19]

First, the evidence on a simple relationship between income levels and crime is inconclusive. There may be those who are poor because they have adopted a life of crime (and are not very good at it); there may be others who have turned to crime because they are poverty-stricken; and there may well be a third group who commit crimes and are poor because of some third, unknown factor. But even if there is no clear relationship between income levels and crime, perhaps there *is* a relationship between cyclical fluctuations in economic conditions and crime.

The conventional wisdom is that a worsening of employment conditions leads to an increase in the amount of property crimes. Unemployed workers commit crimes either to gain income or to deal with the idle time and frustration of their position. But there is not a great deal of statistical support for this conventional wisdom. In a 1975 survey of the literature on this point, Robert Gillespie found three studies that discovered a significant relationship between unemployment and crime but seven that did not.[20] In a 1981 update of that survey, Thomas Orsagh and Ann Witte also found little evidence of a significant relationship.[21]

The most recent analyses of the relationship between cyclical fluctuations and the crime rate have, in general, agreed that there is no significant relationship. Cook and Zarkin found that there was a small increase in the number of burglaries and robberies during recent recessions.[22] However, they found no connection between the business cycle and homicides. The authors found a curious relationship between economic fluctuations and auto theft. Those thefts apparently move counter-cyclically, going down during a recession and up as the economy rebounds. Interestingly, Cook and Zarkin find that long-term trends in crime rates are independent of the business cycle.

These results should not be surprising. On reflection, it is evident that the relationship between unemployment and crime is an exceedingly com-

---

[19]We highly recommend the magisterial inquiry into the causes of criminal behavior in James Q. Wilson and Richard Herrnstein, CRIME AND HUMAN NATURE (1985).

[20]Gillespie, ECONOMIC FACTORS IN CRIME AND DELINQUENCY (1978).

[21]Orsagh & Witte, *Economic Status and Crime: Implications for Offender Rehabilitation,* 72 J. CRIM. L. & CRIMINOLOGY 1055 (1981).

[22]Philip J. Cook and Gary A. Zarkin, *Crime and the Business Cycle,* 14 J. LEGAL STUD. 115 (1985). This is, perhaps, surprising given their correlation between the business cycle and less serious property crimes and the usual belief that there is a correlation between those property crimes and homicides. *See also* Richard Freeman, *Crime and Unemployment,* in CRIME AND PUBLIC POLICY (James Q. Wilson, ed., 1983), and James Q. Wilson and Philip J. Cook, *Unemployment and Crime—What Is the Connection?* 79 PUB. INTEREST 3 (1985).

plex one. Consider, for example, how we might explain a finding that as unemployment increased so did the crime rate. Unemployment may compel some people to commit crimes as their only source of income, but an economic downturn may also reduce the opportunities for profitable crimes that are available to potential thieves. To illustrate, unemployment may give a person a motive to sell cocaine, but general unemployment may also reduce the number of potential customers with enough money to buy cocaine from a would-be dealer.

An additional complicating factor to consider is that when crime is profitable it may draw some people out of the legitimate work force. This may be especially true for sub-groups in the labor force. For example, suppose that young men determine that they can derive greater immediate net benefits from selling cocaine or robbing suburban homes than from pursuing legal employment opportunities. As a result, these young men leave their jobs and are, therefore, usually counted as having left the labor force or, perhaps, as being unemployed. Also, there could be some other factors causing a simultaneous, but otherwise independent, increase in unemployment and crime.[23]

D. A Conclusion About the Deterrence Hypothesis

This brief survey of the literature on deterrence may be summarized as follows: increases in the probability of arrest, conviction, and punishment, and increases in the severity of punishment, appear to have a deterrent effect on the population at large as well as on that small portion of the population that is most likely to commit crime; improvements in labor market opportunities appear to have no significant impact on the aggregate level of crime. Thus, improvements in the employment opportunities of the high-risk group of potential offenders does not seem to deter future crimes as effectively as do increases in the criminal justice system variables. These conclusions are reasonably firm; a more tentative conclusion is that an improvement in

---

[23]An excellent discussion of the literature on deterring crime through increasing the benefits of legal alternatives may be found in Wilson, THINKING ABOUT CRIME (rev. ed. 1983) at 137–42. Wilson's summary of the literature is that policies directed at increasing job skills or employment opportunities are most likely to be successful in deterring first-time, novice offenders and least likely to succeed for those who have already embarked on a career in crime.

A wonderful anecdotal bit of evidence that captures the thrust of this section (that there is more to the explanation of variations in crime rates than variations in economic variables) comes from Wilson & Herrnstein, CRIME AND HUMAN NATURE:

"During the 1960s, one neighborhood in San Francisco had the lowest income, the highest unemployment rate, the highest proportion of families with incomes under $4,000 per year, the least educational attainment, the highest tuberculosis rate, and the highest proportion of substandard housing. . . . That neighborhood was called Chinatown. Yet in 1965, there were only five persons of Chinese ancestry committed to prison in the entire state of California."

labor market conditions reduces the likelihood of crime only among novice, first-time offenders.

CONCLUSION

We distinguished two characteristics of the typical crime (criminal intent and a public injury) and two legal consequences (punishment and a high standard of proof). We contrasted these four elements of the typical crime with the corresponding elements of the typical tort. Next we contrasted the purposes of criminal law with the purposes of tort law. We concluded that criminal law aims to protect our rights, not merely to compensate us for injuries to our interests. A variety of reasons were adduced for protecting rights rather than compensating for injuries to interests, such as the non-compensability of death and some physical injuries, the desire to preserve discretion over the use of property, and the need to preserve a structure of voluntary exchange.

After this discussion of the elements of crimes, we pointed out that modern law has burst the confines of this theory. Specifically, strict liability crimes have become numerous as economic regulation has proliferated. To respond to this challenge to the doctrine of *mens rea,* we reinterpreted criminal intent in light of an economic theory of rational choice. One implication of the economic model of the criminal mind is that crime rates should be responsive to changes in the expected punishments. We surveyed the empirical literature on the deterrence hypothesis and found support for the economic model.

Having developed an economic model of the criminal mind and offered some empirical evidence in support of it, our next task is to show its use in formulating policy in the area of criminal law. That is the task of the next chapter.

SUGGESTED READINGS

Anderson, R., THE ECONOMICS OF CRIME (1976).

Becker, Gary S., *Crime and Punishment: An Economic Approach,* 76 J. POL. ECON. 169 (1968).

Block, Michael, and Robert Lind, *An Economic Analysis of Crimes Punishable by Imprisonment,* 4 J. LEGAL STUD. 479 (1975).

Fletcher, George P., RETHINKING CRIMINAL LAW (1978).

Fletcher, George P., *A Transaction Cost Theory of Crime?,* 85 COL. L. REV. 921 (1985).

Hart, H.L.A., PUNISHMENT AND RESPONSIBILITY (1968).

Heineke, John M., ed., ECONOMIC MODELS OF CRIMINAL BEHAVIOR (1978).

Jevons, Marshall, THE FATAL EQUILIBRIUM (Cambridge: The MIT Press, 1984). [This is a murder mystery solved by the application of microeconomic theory. Kenneth Elzinga and William Breit are Marshall Jevons. See also, his (their?) MURDER AT THE MARGIN (1979).]

Klevorick, Alvin, *On the Economic Theory of Crime*, in NOMOS XXVII: CRIMINAL JUSTICE (J. Pennock & J. Chapman eds. 1985).

LaFave, Wayne, and A. Scott, HANDBOOK ON CRIMINAL LAW (2d ed. 1986).

Luksetich, William, and Michael White, CRIME AND PUBLIC POLICY: AN ECONOMIC APPROACH (1982).

Perkins, R., and R. Boyce, CRIMINAL LAW (3d ed. 1982).

Posner, Richard A., THE ECONOMIC ANALYSIS OF LAW 201–226 (3d ed. 1986).

Posner, Richard A., *An Economic Theory of the Criminal Law,* 85 COL. L. REV. 1193 (1985).

Wilson, James Q., and Richard H. Herrnstein, CRIME AND HUMAN NATURE (1985).

CHAPTER 12

Topics in the Economics of Crime and Punishment

We have distinguished two questions that a theory of the criminal law must answer: What acts should be punished? And to what extent? The first question was addressed in the previous chapter, primarily through a discussion of the elements of a crime. We found that criminal statutes typically proscribe the intentional inflicting of harm upon the person or property of others. In the usual instance, a crime represents a threat to the peace and security of society as a whole; perfect compensation of the victim is often impossible both in principle and in fact; compensatory damages are an inadequate deterrent to the criminal; and the crime threatens the victim's rights, not merely his interests, and also threatens the voluntary structure of exchange.

In this chapter we apply these insights to some important public policy issues in criminal justice. For example, how should society determine the level of punitive sanctions? As we will soon see, this is a very difficult topic that involves important factual issues, such as the relative effectiveness of alternative forms of punishment, as well as important normative issues, such as the fact that some people regard some punishments, e.g., the death penalty, as immoral, regardless of its effectiveness as a deterrent. We will address the extensive economic literature on the death penalty. We will also investigate the connection between crime and drug addiction. Finally, we will look at the economic issues of handgun control. First, let's see whether there has been an alarming increase in the amount of crime.

I. IS THERE A CRIME WAVE?

In recent years the cry for harsher treatment of criminals in America has grown louder and has been translated into legislation. For example, the State of California has moved rapidly from a system of broad judicial discretion in criminal sentencing to a system of determinant sentencing whose explicit purpose is to treat criminals more harshly. The move towards harsher punishment is in part motivated by the public's perception that crime has reached unprecedented heights. To begin our inquiry into the policy issues of this chapter, we explore the extent to which the public's perception of a crime wave is accurate.

The contention that crime has increased rapidly in the recent past is only partly true. The general pattern of recent decades is that the amount of a wide variety of crimes declined from a peak in the mid-1930s to a low point in the early 1960s; then began a rapid and unprecedented increase from the early 1960s till the mid- or late 1970s; and has begun to decline slowly in the 1980s.[1] For example, between 1937 and 1946 the homicide rate in the United States was roughly constant at 6.9 murders per 100,000 population but, thereafter, began a steady decline to 4.5 murders per 100,000 in 1962. But then after 1962 the rate increased to 4.8 in 1964, to 5.6 in 1966, and to 9.1 in 1972.

A similar pattern is observable for robbery. In 1946 the robbery rate was 59.4 per 100,000, which represented a slight increase over the rate of the mid-1930s. The rate then declined steadily to a low of 51.2 in 1959, and then, inexplicably, and in the single year 1960, it rose to 59.9. It remained at that high level for the next several years and then, in 1962, began a steady *increase* through 1968 till the rate had *doubled* to 131 per 100,000 population.[2]

A full discussion of the reasons for these variations in the crime rates is beyond the scope of this work, but there are a few broad and important points that will figure in our later exposition and so are worth mentioning here. First is the curious paradox that at the same time that there was a rapid increase in all sorts of crime, there was the beginning of one of the longest sustained periods of economic growth in our history. Why should the members of an increasingly wealthy society take to crime in record numbers? It has been suggested that an answer may lie in the way in which that increasing wealth was distributed in society, but this is unlikely to be a helpful explanation because there is little doubt that the equality of wealth and income distribution in the 1960s was improving.

A second interesting point about the crime wave of the 1960s arises from observations about the changing age distribution of the population during that decade. The discernible jump in all crimes in the early 1960s coincided with the maturing into adolesence—roughly ages 14 to 24—of the "baby boom" generation that had been born just after World War II. In

---

[1]The principal sources for statistical information on crime are the United States Federal Bureau of Investigation's *Uniform Crime Reports* (annual) and the United States Department of Justice, Bureau of Justice Statistics, *Sourcebook on Criminal Justice Statistics* (annual).

[2]There is a strong suspicion that these figures *under*state the actual numbers of property crimes. This is because it is believed that approximately 75% of all larcenies, 50% of all burglaries, and 30% of all auto thefts are not reported to the police.

1950 there had been 24 million people aged 14 to 24, and by 1960 that figure had increased only marginally to 27 million. However, within the next decade the number increased by 13 million, or by 1.3 million per year. The subsequent impact on United States society was profound.[3] But for our purposes the special interest in this rapid increase in young people lies in its potential ability to explain the rapid increase in crime in the 1960s. It is well known that young people are far more likely to commit criminal offenses than is any other age group. Indeed, judging from arrest statistics, which may be biased, two-thirds of all street crime is committed by people under age 25; 80%, by those under 30. Thus, an absolute and relative increase in the number of adolescents will, all other things equal, increase the amount—and perhaps the seriousness—of crime. Additionally, the increase in the number of adolescents in the 1960s may have been so large that secondary consequences, such as the loosening of traditional familial and community bonds and constraints, may have further contributed to the rise in crime. Testimony to this secondary impact comes from the fact that the increase in crime in the 1960s was so large that the increase in the number of 14-to-24 year olds can explain only a fraction of the rise in crime. For example, one study found that the rise in the murder rate during the 1960s was more than ten times greater than what one could have predicted from the changing age distribution of the population.[4]

These figures may seem somewhat unsatisfying in that they lure one into believing that an explanation for the variation in crime rates exists, but then further investigation reveals that the story is not so simple. Anyone attempting to study the economics of crime should try to become accustomed to this feeling. This is a terribly complex area in which simple explanations and solutions are rare.

II. OPTIMAL PUNISHMENT

Concern over the crime wave is motivated by widespread fear of criminals and the urgent wish of ordinary people to avoid being victimized. These considerations bring the matter of deterrence to the forefront of the policy debate. In the preceding chapter, we developed an economic model of the decision to commit a crime and found that the empirical evidence generally confirms the theory's prediction that punishment deters crime. Now we

---

[3]For a discussion of these far-ranging consequences, *see* R. Easterlin, BIRTH AND FORTUNE: THE IMPACT OF NUMBERS ON PERSONAL WELFARE (1980).

[4]A detailed discussion of these figures and of alternative explanations for the crime wave of the 1960s may be found in James Q. Wilson, THINKING ABOUT CRIME (rev. ed. 1983), 13–25 (ch. 1, "Crime Amidst Plenty: the Paradox of the Sixties,") and 223–49 (ch. 12, "Crime and American Culture").

want to take the next step and show the optimal level of punishment for purposes of deterrence.

Suppose that there is a particular crime that we wish to deter, say, as before, embezzlement. It might be possible to eliminate embezzlement, or very nearly eliminate it, by having severe punishment imposed with a high probability upon offenders. However, deterring embezzlers in this way may run into two kinds of difficulties. First, very harsh penalties may violate the moral and constitutional rights of the criminals. For instance, a law imposing the death sentence for embezzling petty cash would be immoral and, in America, unconstitutional, principally because of the large disparity between the severity of the punishment and the seriousness of the offense. The second kind of constraint, which *is* our direct concern, is cost. Apprehending, prosecuting, and punishing embezzlers can be expensive. Policymakers will, naturally, want to balance these costs against the advantages of reducing embezzlement when making policy decisions about crime. This balancing has two distinct aspects. First, policymakers will want to determine a target for the total amount of deterrence. As we will see, the optimal amount of deterrence is not to erase crime altogether. The reason for this is that eradicating crime is costly and has a declining social benefit. Second, policymakers will want to allocate their limited resources so as to achieve their deterrence target at the least cost; that is, they will seek to achieve their goal efficiently. We will use economic theory to clarify how these two computations should be made.

A. The Efficient Level of Deterrence

To begin, let us consider how the criminal justice system should formulate its overall goal with regard to crime; that is, how should the authorities determine to what extent to enforce the criminal law? This economic way of putting the matter can be informally stated as follows: because crime imposes costs on society and because deterring crime uses resources, there is an "optimal amount of crime" (or an optimal amount of deterrence). We may determine that amount abstractly with the help of Figure 12.1.

In the figure, the horizontal axis measures reductions in the amount of criminal activity, ranging from no reduction at the origin up to a complete absence of crime at the amount 100%. Dollar amounts are measured along the vertical axis. The curve MSC_D represents the marginal social costs of achieving a given level of crime reduction. MSC_D slopes upward because it becomes increasingly more costly to achieve given levels of reduction in the amount of crime. For example, it is not very costly to achieve initial reductions in the amount of crime—from, say, a 5% reduction to a 7% reduction—but is much more costly to reduce the amount of crime from, say, 95% to 97%. Notice further that MSC_D rises at an increasing rate to represent the fact that the marginal social cost of achieving ever greater reductions in the amount of crime is increasing. An important reason for this is that the

Figure 12.1   The Efficient Level of Deterrence

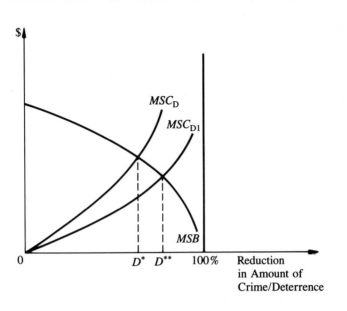

To what extent should government enforce the criminal law? The curve MSC_D represents the marginal social costs of achieving a given level of crime reduction and slopes upward to indicate that it becomes increasingly costly to achieve reductions in the amount of crime: it costs much more to achieve a 2% reduction in crime from 95% to 97% than from 5% to 7%. The curve labeled MSB measures the marginal social benefit of achieving various levels of crime reduction or deterrence and slopes downward because the marginal benefits of further reductions in the amount of crime decline: a 2% reduction in the amount of crime from 5% to 7% confers greater benefits than a 2% reduction from 95% to 97%. The socially optimal amount of deterrence occurs at the point where the marginal social cost of reducing crime equals the marginal social benefit, at point D^* in the figure. Note that if the cost of achieving a given level of deterrence should fall to MSC_{D1}, the optimal amount of deterrence would increase to D^{**}.

opportunity cost of resources devoted to deterring crime increases as society achieves ever larger reductions in the amount of crime: those resources could have been used for other worthy public goals, such as education, health care, welfare, and the like.

The curve labeled MSB measures the marginal social benefit of achieving various levels of crime reduction or deterrence. These benefits include reducing the harmful effects of crime. MSB slopes downward because the marginal benefit to society of further reductions in the amount of crime declines. Thus, the benefit of the first units of reduction—from, say, a 5% reduction to a 7% reduction—is large, but the benefits of reducing the amount of crime from a level of 95% to 97% are relatively small.

The socially optimal amount of deterrence occurs at the point where the marginal social cost of reducing crime further is equal to the marginal social benefit. In Figure 12.1 that occurs at the level of deterrence marked D^*. Notice that for any level of reduction in crime less than that amount—that is, to the left of D^*—the marginal social benefit of a further reduction in the amount of crime is greater than the marginal social cost so that it would be in society's interests to reduce crime further, that is, to deter more crime. Similarly, to the right of D^* the marginal social costs of more deterrence exceed the marginal social benefits so that allowing more crime to go undeterred would actually make society better off.

Although we have not said anything definite about the exact shape or location of MSC_D and MSB, it should be obvious that changes in those costs and benefits can affect the optimal level of deterrence. For example, suppose that the opportunity cost of resources devoted to deterring crime fell, the marginal social benefits of deterrence remaining the same; MSC_D would fall to MSC_{D1} and the optimal level of deterrence would increase to D^{**}.

1. The Mathematics of Optimal Deterrence   In this section we derive the intuitive results of the previous section on the optimal amount of deterrence using the formal tools of microeconomic theory.

Let z represent the expenditure by government on deterring crime. Thus, z includes expenditures on police, courts, prosecutors, probation officers, prisons, and so forth. For now we assume that expenditures are efficiently allocated among these various factors in the production of deterrence. (The following section explains how to make such an efficient allocation.) The frequency of crime, p, is a decreasing function of expenditures on deterrence: $p = p(z)$.

When a crime—remember that we are considering embezzlement—is committed, it has a direct cost d to the victim, which includes, say, the monetary loss from being swindled. In addition, the crime has an indirect cost i suffered by society, which includes, say, the cost of the fear of future swindles spread among potential victims. The harm caused by a crime is the sum of the direct cost and the indirect costs: $(d + i)$. Thus, the total harm caused by crime rate p equals $(d + i)p(z)$. The social cost of crime is the sum of the harm it causes and the expenditures taken to deter it:

$$\text{social cost} = (d + i)p(z) + z.$$

The question of whether crime has social benefits is complicated. To illustrate, the embezzler described in the preceding chapter enjoyed a net benefit from his crime,[5] and perhaps it should count as a social benefit of the crime. (Maybe he needed the money very badly.) On the other hand, the pleasure enjoyed by someone who intentionally harms another person (if it is a pleasure) is so thoroughly immoral that it should not be given any weight in determining criminal policy, and so there are no social benefits

---

[5]Specifically, his net benefit equals the difference between the amount swindled and the expected punishment, or in our notation $[x - p(x)f(x)]$.

from that action. We do not need to resolve the complex issue of whether crime has social benefits in order to develop our example.

Let b indicate the social benefit from crime, which may be positive or it may be zero. The net harm of crime is the sum of the direct and indirect harm less the benefit; thus,

$$\text{net harm} = d + i - b.$$

Now we can formulate society's deterrence objective: choose the level of deterrence, z, to maximize the net social benefits:

$$bp(z) - (d + i)p(z) - z;$$

or equivalently, minimize the net social costs of crime:

$$(d + i)p(z) + z - bp(z).$$

Let p' denote the marginal decrease in the crime rate from an additional unit of deterrence. The marginal conditions for an optimum are

$$1 = -(d + i - b)p'.$$

This equation is easy to interpret. It says that, at the social optimum, one dollar spent on additional deterrence (the marginal cost of deterrence) equals the product of the resulting fall in the crime rate $(-p')$ times the net harm of crime.

It is easy to derive some consequences about efficient deterrence from this mathematical formulation of the problem. First, if deterrence were free and the benefit of crime was small, optimal deterrence would be perfect, and no crimes would be committed. But so long as deterrence is costly, optimal deterrence is unlikely to be perfect deterrence.[6] Second, if the cost of deterrence rises, the optimal amount of it falls. Third, if the net harm from crime rises, optimal deterrence increases.

B. The Efficient Allocation of Resources for Deterrence

Having shown in a general way how the optimum amount of deterrence is determined, we next turn our attention to an analysis of the allocation of funds among the different means of deterring crime. There are many allocation decisions to be made, such as the choice between foot patrols and car patrols by police, the choice between more police or more prosecutors, the choice between more use of fines or more use of jails. We will examine several of these choices to bring out some underlying principles.

---

[6]Perfect deterrence would only be efficient if

$$\min (d + i)p(z) + z - bp(z) \text{ given } p(z) \leq 1$$

had a solution at the corner where $p(z) = 1$.

Figure 12.2   Deterrence Lines

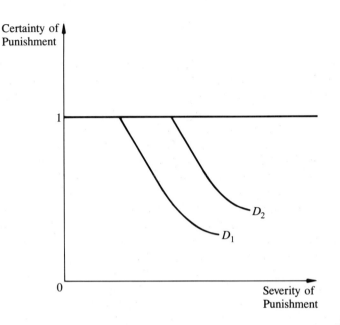

The product of the probability of punishment and the severity of punishment is *expected punishment*. The lines labeled D_1 and D_2 in the figure represent combinations of certainty and severity where the expected punishment is constant; for example, as one moves down D_1, reductions in the certainty of punishment are exactly offset by changes in its severity. But moving from any point on the line D_1 to any point on D_2 represents an increase in the expected punishment. If we assume that the amount of crime is constant when the expected punishment is constant, then D_1 and D_2 can each be interpreted as lines of constant deterrence or deterrence isoquants, that is, lines along which the amount of crime is constant. Thus, the total amount of crime deterred along D_1 is less than that deterred along D_2. (An alternative, but consistent, view of D_1 and D_2 is that they are the indifference curves of the typical criminal defined over certainty and severity of punishment.)

First, suppose that there is a choice between allocating resources to make punishment more certain or more severe. To see how this choice is made, we will refer to Figure 12.2. The certainty of punishment is measured on the vertical axis in that figure as a probability, specifically, the probability of the criminal's being apprehended and convicted; the severity of punishment is measured on the horizontal axis. When the probability of punishment is multiplied by its severity, the result is the *expected punishment*. The straight lines in Figure 12.2, which slope downward, represent points for which the expected punishment is constant. The expected punishment is the same along any one line, because changes in the probability of punishment from moving along the line are exactly offset by changes in its severity. However, moving from any point on the line D_1 to any point on the line D_2 represents an increase in the expected punishment.

Deterrence of crime is closely related to the expected punishment. To keep the analysis simple, let us assume that the amount of crime is constant when the expected punishment is constant, and the amount of crime decreases when the expected punishment increases. Consequently, the lines D_1 and D_2 in Figure 12.2 can each be interpreted as lines of constant deterrence, that is, lines along which the amount of crime is constant.[7] Thus, the total amount of crime deterred by the combinations of certainty and severity along D_1 is less than that deterred along D_2. In technical language, these lines are *deterrence isoquants*.

Now we introduce cost considerations. A move to a higher level of expected punishment in Figure 12.2 will deter more crime; a move to a lower level will deter less; however, a movement *along* the deterrence-isoquant will have no effect upon deterrence. But it may be the case that some points along a particular deterrence-isoquant represent combinations of certainty and severity that are cheaper than others. By moving from an expensive point on an isoquant to an inexpensive point, the criminal justice system will save money without any change in deterrence.

Whatever level of deterrence society settles upon—e.g., D^* in Figure 12.1—efficiency requires the criminal justice system to find the point on the isoquant where that level of deterrence is achieved at least cost. The argument corresponds exactly to the standard argument in the theory of production that an efficient firm uses the factors of production in combinations such that any given level of output is produced at least cost.

The computation of the efficient combination of certainty and severity is illustrated in Figure 12.3. As in Figure 12.2, the straight line D_0 in Figure 12.3 is a line of constant deterrence. The curved line represents the combinations of certainty and severity that can be obtained with a given expenditure on deterrence. To illustrate, the curve labeled "high" indicates the combinations of certainty and severity that a locality can achieve by spending a high amount on deterrence, say, $10 million. The curve labeled "low" indicates the combinations that the locality can achieve by spending a low amount on deterrence, say, $5 million. Notice that the points (x_1, y_1) and (x^*, y^*) are both on the same isoquant, so they represent different combinations of certainty and severity that achieve the same level of deterrence, D_0. However, the point (x_1, y_1) is on the high cost curve, and the point (x^*, y^*) is on the low cost curve. Efficiency requires policymakers to choose (x^*, y^*) rather than (x_1, y_1). In general, the efficient combination of severity and certainty is found at the point where the cost curve is tangent to the deterrence-isoquant, as at (x^*, y^*).

---

[7]In effect, these lines are the indifference curves of the typical criminal. In a more general treatment, these indifference curves would be convex to the origin. The assumption that they *are* straight lines is a matter of convenience. Our conclusions do not depend on it.

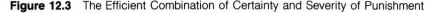

Figure 12.3 The Efficient Combination of Certainty and Severity of Punishment

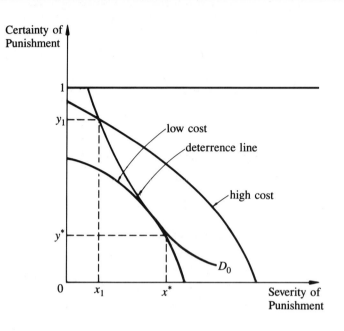

Once the authorities have chosen the optimal level of deterrence, D^* or D^{**} in Figure 12.1, how should they allocate resources between certainty and severity of punishment? Efficiency requires that the criminal justice system find the point on the deterrence isoquant that involves the least cost. The straight line D_0 is the deterrence isoquant that corresponds to the socially optimal amount of deterrence. Any point on that line represents combinations of certainty and severity of punishment that achieve the same level of deterrence. The curved lines represent combinations of certainty and severity of punishment that can be achieved by a given expenditure. For example, the curve labeled "high" indicates the combinations of certainty and severity of punishment that the authorities can achieve by spending, say, $10 million per year on deterrence. The curve labeled "low" indicates the combinations that the authorities can achieve by spending a low amount on deterrence, say, $5 million per year. The combination (x_1, y_1) is the intersection of the high cost curve and D_0; the combination (x^*, y^*) is the intersection of the low cost curve and D_0. Both points are on the same deterrence isoquant and so achieve the same amount of deterrence. Efficiency requires policy-makers to choose the combination (x^*, y^*) on the low cost curve. In general, the efficient combination of severity and certainty of punishment is found at the point where the lowest cost curve is tangent to the deterrence isoquant.

To make this abstract exercise more concrete, let us consider some real examples. Suppose that the certainty of the punishment depends upon expenditures for police and prosecutors and that the punishment for the relevant crime is a fine. Police and prosecutors are costly, whereas fines are cheap to administer, at least so long as the fine is not too large relative to the

Figure 12.4 Allocating Resources to Deterrence When Certainty of Punishment Is Expensive

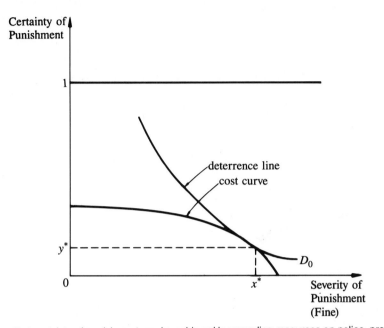

Assume that certainty of punishment can be achieved by spending resources on police, prosecutors, and the like, which are very expensive, and that severity is achieved by a system of fines, which is a very inexpensive system to administer. Thus, the cost of severity is low relative to certainty. The cost curve in the figure indicates this. When certainty is costly and severity is cheap, efficient deterrence requires severe punishment administered with a low probability of apprehension and conviction. This is represented in the figure by the tangency of the cost curve and deterrence line at the combination (y^*, x^*), where the probability of apprehension and conviction, y^*, is small relative to the fine x^*.

offender's income.[8] Thus, certainty of punishment is costly for the state to achieve relative to severity of punishment by a fine. Figure 12.4 represents this fact by drawing the cost curve so that it is almost horizontal for modest fines. When certainty is costly and severity is cheap, efficient deterrence requires severe punishment administered with low probability of apprehension and conviction. This fact is represented in Figure 12.4 by the point (x^*, y^*); the probability y^* is small relative to the fine x^*.

In contrast, suppose that the punishment is imprisonment, which we assume to be very expensive. In that case, efficiency may require certainty of punishment but not severity. This possibility is illustrated in Figure 12.5, where the optimal point, (x^*, y^*), corresponds to a certain, but short, jail sentence.

---

[8]Indeed, fines are a source of income to the state, not a cost to the taxpayers.

Figure 12.5 Allocating Resources to Deterrence When Severity of Punishment Is Expensive

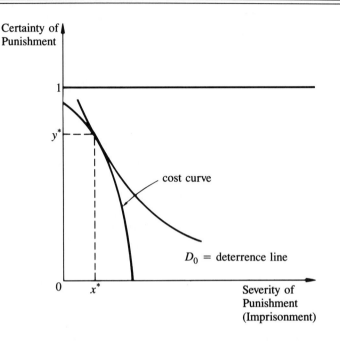

In contrast to the assumptions of the previous figure, assume that certainty of punishment is now relatively less costly than severity of punishment because, say, the contemplated punishment is imprisonment, which is very expensive. The cost curve in the figure indicates this. When certainty is cheap and severity is costly, efficient deterrence requires a relatively light punishment but a high probability of apprehension and conviction. This is represented in the figure by the tangency of the cost curve and deterrence line at the combination (y^*,x^*), where the probability of apprehension and conviction, y^*, is high relative to the severity of punishment (say, length of imprisonment) x^*.

There is another immediate consequence of this argument concerning combinations of fines and jail sentences. The previous figures represented the tradeoff between certainty and severity of punishment. In contrast, Figure 12.6 represents the tradeoff between fines and imprisonment. In Figure 12.6, Panels a and b, we represent the severity of imprisonment on the horizontal axis and the severity of the fine on the vertical axis. The deterrence isoquant, labeled D_0 in the figure, connects combinations of fines and imprisonment that deter equal amounts of crime. In other words, D_0 indicates how much fines must increase to offset a decrease in imprisonment in order to hold constant the amount of crime. It seems safe to assume that imprisonment is far more costly to the state than collecting fines. The relative cost of imprisonment and collecting fines is represented in the graph by the "price line."

Total expenditures on punishment are the same everywhere along the price line. At what point on the price line is deterrence greatest? Deterrence is greatest where the price line touches the highest deterrence line, which occurs at point y^* in Panel a of Figure 12.6. Furthermore, point y^* is on the vertical axis. This means that the state achieves the greatest deterrence at given cost by relying exclusively on fines and not using imprisonment.

There is another line in the figure that we have not discussed, the line S_a in Panel a of Figure 12.6. S_a represents the offender's financial solvency constraint: he or she is not capable of paying a fine greater than S_a. Fortunately, the optimal fine of y^* lies below S_a, which indicates that the offender can pay the fine.

Suppose the offender cannot pay the full fine? In Panel b the curves are the same as in Panel a, but note that this offender's solvency constraint, S_b, is considerably below that of the offender depicted in Panel a. As a result, the optimal fine, y^*, for achieving D_0 in deterrence is greater than S_b. Thus, D_0 can be achieved here only by a combination of a fine and a jail sentence, specifically, by a fine of S_b and a jail sentence equal to x^*. Notice that this combination is achieved at a cost to society that is higher than in Panel a: the optimum is at the intersection of D_0, S_b, and the higher cost curve, which is parallel to the low cost curve reproduced from Panel a.

This is a highly abstract model of the decision regarding the optimal amount of deterrence and of the most efficient means of achieving it. It is now time for us to apply it to see the extent to which the model describes the actual operation of the criminal justice system or might suggest ways in which that system could be operated more efficiently.

III. THE FORMS OF PUNISHMENT

If we accept the conclusions of the previous chapter about deterrence and are mindful of the discussion just concluded about the efficiency aspects of the alternative forms of punishment, a natural question to raise is, "What form does the punishment of criminals actually take?" Is the use of fines and incarceration efficient in the current criminal justice system?

While we will concentrate in what follows on the punishment imposed on criminals, it is important to remember that the criminal justice system is a complex set of organizations that embraces much more than the prison system. The police, public prosecutors, the grand jury system, courts of general criminal jurisdiction, parole officers—all play an important role in achieving the goals of the criminal justice system.[9] There is a great deal to be

---

[9]In addition to the increase in crime noted at the beginning of this chapter, there is a widespread feeling that the criminal justice system has broken down, too. We are not referring to the largely unsupported contentions that murderers and other serious offenders are "getting off too lightly," but rather to such disturbing facts as that only three out of 100 felonies results in someone being imprisoned and that this imprisonment may occur only after a year's delay in trying and sentencing the offender.

Figure 12.6 The Tradeoff Between Fines and Imprisonment

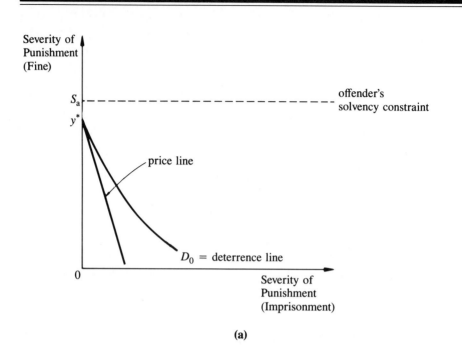

(a)

Which form of punishment should the authorities use, fines or imprisonment? In the panels of this figure the severity of imprisonment is measured along the horizontal axis and the severity of a fine is measured along the vertical axis. The deterrence lines indicate the combinations of fine and imprisonment that achieve the same (socially optimal) level of deterrence. Assume, as is genuinely true, that fines are cheaper for the authorities than jail sentences. This fact is represented in both panels of the figure by the steep slope of the cost curves. The general conclusion of the figure is that the authorities should punish by using fines, not jail sentences, so long as the criminal is financially solvent. Jail sentences should never be used until the capacity of the criminal to pay fines is exhausted.

said about the economics of each of these components of the system. (For example, see the box on plea-bargaining.) Our focus on the forms of punishment does not necessarily reflect the relative importance of that element of the system but rather the fact that this issue is one on which the law and economics literature has spent the most time.

A. Imprisonment

Let us take our goal in criminal law to be the minimization of the direct and indirect costs of crime and the costs of administering a criminal justice system. As we have seen, "direct costs" refer to the physical and psychic harm, the lost and destroyed property, and other costs of criminal activity. "Indirect costs" refer to those private costs that are incurred to protect against

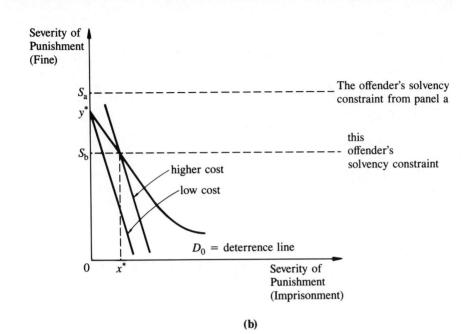

Severity of Punishment (Fine)

S_a — The offender's solvency constraint from panel a

y^*

S_b — this offender's solvency constraint

higher cost

low cost

D_0 = deterrence line

0   x^* Severity of Punishment (Imprisonment)

(b)

In panel a, S_a represents the offender's financial solvency constraint: he or she cannot pay a fine greater than S_a. The optimal level of deterrence, D_0, can be achieved by a fine of y^* and no jail sentence because $y^* < S_a$, the limit of the offender's solvency.

In panel b, the offender's solvency constraint, S_b, is considerably below that of the offender depicted in panel a. As a result, the optimal fine, y^*, for achieving D_0 in deterrence is greater than S_b. Thus, D_0 can be achieved here only by a combination of a fine and a jail sentence, specifically, by a fine of S_b and a jail sentence equal to x^*. Notice that this combination is achieved at a cost to society that is higher than in panel a: the optimum is at the intersection of D_0, S_b, and the higher cost curve, which is parallel to the low cost curve.

crime—such as the costs of indelibly marking property for identification purposes or the costs of installing an alarm system—or costs that are passed on to the customers of legitimate businesses in order to make up for the losses due to such crimes as theft, embezzlement, and fraud. The costs of the criminal justice system include the costs of police, prosecutors, defense lawyers, the courts, and prisons and jails. The economic issue is, "What form of punitive sanction minimizes the costs of crime?" The principal choices available for non-capital crimes—we will return to a discussion of capital crimes shortly—are monetary fines and incarceration. The conclusion of the economic literature is that, on the criterion of efficiency, the current criminal justice system relies too much on incarceration and far too little on fines. The argument in brief is that fines are a much less costly method than imprisonment of achieving a given level of deterrence. In a previous section we summarized the logic of this argument. Here we want to be more intuitive about the costs and benefits of these alternative forms of punishment.

Plea-Bargaining

Among the scarce criminal justice resources are court and prosecutorial time and effort. Resources spent by public prosecutors preparing criminal complaints against embezzlers cannot be spent preparing for cases against more serious offenders. Court time devoted to hearing a trial against petty criminals delays the trial of more serious criminals. One of the common practices developed to save time and effort of prosecutors and courts is *plea bargaining*. We develop some economic aspects of that practice from the following situation and associated questions:

Facts: The owner of a small bar closed for the night and began counting the money. He was surprised by a masked armed robber. As the thief was leaving the scene, one of the bar's patrons, who was loitering in the parking lot, got a look at him. Using solid circumstantial evidence, the police arrested a well-known hood called Lefty, and after he was chosen from a lineup by the patron, Lefty was charged with the crime.

After working on the case, the public prosecutor is uncertain about her ability to win a conviction at trial. A conviction will depend in part upon the testimony of the eyewitness, who, besides being an unstable character, was drinking in the bar just before the robbery. It is difficult to foresee how well the eyewitness will perform on the stand. The defendant, through his lawyer, begins plea-bargaining with the prosecutor. The prosecutor and the defendant's lawyer, who have access to much the same facts, both conclude that there is a 50% chance of acquittal at trial and a 50% chance of conviction.

If convicted, the sentence would depend upon several contingencies, but the most important one is the identity of the judge. There are two judges in this jurisdiction, "hanging Judge Grim" and "lenient Judge Smiley." If the case is tried and a conviction secured before Judge Grim, the probable sentence is 3 years, whereas with Judge Smiley, the probable sentence is 1 year. The assignment of the case to either judge is equally likely.

The facts relevant to the decision of the prosecutor and the defendant may be represented in this decision tree:

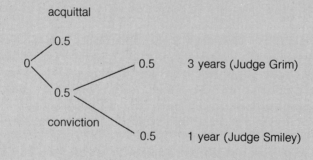

acquittal

0.5

0

0.5

conviction

0.5   3 years (Judge Grim)

0.5   1 year (Judge Smiley)

Question 12.1 (and More Facts):

a. In the event of a trial, what punishment is "expected," in the mathematical sense, by the attorneys? (multiply punishments by probabilities)

b. The prosecutor has such a busy schedule that she is not eager to try this case. She would be willing to reduce the punishment by as much as 6 months, relative to the expected punishment, to avoid a trial, but not by more than 6 months. What is the minimum sentence that the prosecutor would accept in exchange for a bargained plea of guilty?

    Similarly, the defendant, who is terrified by the possibility of a severe sentence from Judge Grim, is willing to add as much as 6 months to his expected sentence in order to avoid the uncertainty and cost of a trial. What is the maximum sentence that the defendant would accept in plea bargaining?

c. What is the surplus from cooperating and settling, rather than trying the case, as measured in prison time? (The cooperative surplus, which we discussed in Chapter 4, is the sum of the benefits to each of the two parties from cooperating.)

d. What is the most reasonable sentence for the parties to agree upon in plea bargaining? (The reasonable solution to a bargaining game, as discussed in Chapter 4, is for each person to receive his threat value plus an equal share of the cooperative surplus.)

    Suppose that materially identical cases to this one arise frequently. Assume that all the material facts concerning prison time are the same as in the preceding example.

    Further, suppose that the prosecutor may be tough or lenient. If the prosecutor is tough, she drives such a hard bargain that the defendant is driven to the margin of indifference between pleading guilty and demanding a trial. If the prosecutor is lenient, the defendant receives the full advantage of the bargain.

e. Assuming the parties settle these materially identical cases by plea bargaining, what is the range in outcomes for the defendants?
    1. _____ = most severe punishment (tough prosecutor).
    2. _____ = most lenient punishment (lenient prosecutor).

f. If the prosecutor is tough, the average prison time per case under plea bargaining is _____ .

g. The mathematically expected prison time when every case is tried is _____ .

    Questions f and g reveal a curious fact. By hypothesis, the accused is indifferent between a plea bargain for 18 months in prison, which is a certain outcome, and a trial in which the expected punishment is 1 year. These are equally-punishing prospects to him. Presumably, equally-punishing prospects deter crime equally. To hold the punishing prospect and deterrence constant, plea-bargaining requires 18 months of prison time and trying every case results in only 1 year of prison time, on average. Thus, plea bargaining requires an additional 6 months of prison time for cases such as this one. Is it possible that trying every case is cheaper for the state than plea bargaining? Does the reduced prison time more than compensate for the expense of trials?

h. Now assume that plea bargaining is forbidden and all these cases are tried. What is the range in outcomes?
   1. _____ = most severe punishment.
   2. _____ = most lenient treatment.

Questions e and h reveal another curious fact: the range of outcomes is far greater under trials than under plea bargains. Does the difference in the range of outcomes between bargains and trials represent superior justice or undesirable disparity? Is it possible that plea-bargaining is more just because it reduces disparity in treatment by narrowing the dispersion in outcomes due to chance, such as drawing Judge Grim rather than Judge Smiley?

In principle, there are at least four benefits to incarceration: it incapacitates the criminal; it provides a form of retribution for society; it offers an opportunity for rehabilitation of the criminal;[10] and it deters the imprisoned criminal and other potential criminals from committing future crimes. We have already touched on the deterrence function of punishment and will return to it again shortly. Here let us take up the first three of the four benefits of incarceration.

First, society perceives the denial of freedom that results from imprisonment as, in part, a suitable and just form of retribution for the crime. For the law-abiding citizen the shame and personal cost of imprisonment loom large in his considerations, and it therefore strikes many people as inadequate punishment when a criminal is either relieved of any obligation to go to prison or is imprisoned for too short a time. However, although society derives benefits in seeing retribution effected on criminals by placing them in prison, it is difficult to estimate the amount of that retributive benefit. Therefore, one cannot say whether that benefit is large or small, nor how it compares with the retributive benefit from alternative forms of punishment.[11]

The second benefit derived from imprisonment is rehabilitation, but this is a slippery concept. At times it simply means "deterrence" so that the criminal who no longer commits crimes has been, in this sense, "rehabilitated." We have already seen that rehabilitation as deterrence works. But at other times rehabilitation means that the prison has taught the criminal something of social value, such as marketable job skills, or has persuaded him of the error of his ways. Rehabilitation typically implies that a soul has

---

[10]In some states prisons are called "houses of correction."

[11]It is worth noting, too, that this retributive benefit of incarceration may be more keenly felt in some parts of the United States than in others, that it may be stronger for more heinous crimes, or that it may be strong for less serious crimes committed by prominent people.

been reclaimed. There is no doubt that this second, more positive sense of rehabilitation has fallen out of favor.[12] In recent years expenditures in prisons on counseling, job training, and general education have been declining in real terms. Whether this means that rehabilitation in a positive sense has not worked or has simply become too expensive is not clear.

The third benefit of incarceration is incapacitation, and this aspect of imprisonment has recently received a great deal of favorable attention. Incapacitation refers to the fact that while a person is confined to prison, he cannot commit crimes against people outside prison. One of the great advantages of focusing on incapacitation is that it does not require for its justification that the criminal be a rational calculator of costs and benefits. For punishment to deter, it must be true to a greater or lesser degree that the criminal weighs the costs of getting caught and subjected to that particular form of punishment against the benefits of committing the crime. (As we saw in Chapter 11, it is probably true that most people, including hardened criminals, *do* take such considerations into account.) By contrast, incapacitation almost *always* works, regardless of the degree to which criminals and others make the appropriate calculations, so long as four conditions are satisfied. The evidence suggests that each condition is met.

The first of the four conditions that must be met for incarceration to provide incapacitating benefits is that some offenders must be repeat offenders. That condition guarantees that incapacitation will lead to fewer total crimes being committed because, during their prison stay, repeat offenders will be prevented from committing crimes, which, by assumption, they would do if they were not in prison. If all criminals were single-time offenders, then there would be no incapacitating benefit to incarceration. The most recent studies indicate that about two-thirds of all current prison inmates had criminal records before their current stay in prison. Additionally, it appears to be the case that between 25% and 50% of all offenders are re-arrested within a very short time—six months to one year—of their release from prison. Therefore, we may conclude that whatever other benefits may accrue from imprisoning criminals, it certainly protects law-abiding citizens from those who would likely commit crimes if they were free to do so.

Second, incapacitation must reduce the total number of crimes committed by repeat criminals (called "recidivists") over their criminal career. To illustrate, suppose that the punishment for repeat offenders is scaled so that the punishment grows more severe for each conviction for the crime. Suppose that a particular criminal keeps repeating a crime until he is convicted enough times so that the punishment for another conviction is so high that he stops. Specifically, suppose that after the third conviction the prospect of a very severe punishment for a fourth conviction causes him to stop committing the crime. For this person, incarceration in prison slows him down and

---

[12]For an illuminating discussion of why the value of rehabilitation may have declined, see Francis Allen, THE DECLINE OF THE REHABILITATIVE IDEAL (1981).

delays the time it took for him to reach three convictions. But incapacitation in prison does not influence how many crimes he commits over his entire criminal career. Substituting another punishment for imprisonment, providing the alternative was equally severe, would not alter the fact that he will be convicted of three crimes before abandoning his criminal career. To reduce crime, incapacitation must *cause* fewer repetitions of the crime. This could well happen because a person ages while incapacitated in prison and the propensity to commit crime declines with age. There is considerable evidence for this proposition.

Third, those criminals incapacitated by imprisonment must not be immediately replaced by new criminals taking their vacated positions. There is good reason to suspect that this condition is met, too. There are certain crimes that are organized as continual businesses—drug trafficking and prostitution are examples—and, because they do not have to abide by the antitrust laws, those criminal businesses very effectively exclude others from entering their line of business. Moreover, even if there is no barrier to entry erected by existing practitioners, it may be so costly for new entrants to participate in some crimes as to forestall their entry. For both of these reasons, there may well be crimes for which it is the case that entry occurs only when an offender is sent to prison.[13] Thus, an incapacitated practitioner of these crimes *is* replaced. But most criminal businesses do not follow this model of easy excludability. Indeed, for the most common crimes—burglary, robbery, and auto theft—entry is very inexpensive, and the possibility of excluding new entrants is remote. Thus, an entrant does not have to await the removal of an established practitioner to prison.

The fourth condition that must be satisfied in order for incarceration to provide incapacitating benefits is that prisons must not be "schools for crime," such that offenders commit more crimes upon release—or commit the same number of crimes more effectively—than were foregone during their stay in prison. There is no systematic evidence that imprisonment makes criminals more effective at crime, nor that it leads to the criminal's committing more or worse crimes after release. Most evidence suggests that imprisonment deters some offenders from future crimes, as we have seen in detail above. This deterrence is especially marked for young male offenders, but because the propensity to commit crimes declines with age, the incapacitation through imprisonment of young males may deter future crime simply by keeping those offenders in prison until they are older and, thus, less likely to commit crimes. (See the box on determinate sentencing.)

Because these necessary conditions for incapacitation to confer benefits on society are met, we may conclude that imprisonment provides a benefit to society even if it does not deter, even if it does not rehabilitate, and even if it does not confer strong retributive feelings for law-abiding citizens. How-

---

[13]The result is analytically the same if the response to the disappearance of an offender is the expansion of an existing criminal business territory or enterprise.

Determinate Sentencing

When it was widely believed that imprisonment could help to rehabilitate the criminal offender (in the soul-reclaiming sense), sentences frequently read something like "for not less than five years, nor more than 10 years." This is called *indeterminate sentencing*. The actual time served would be determined by the prison authorities and the parole board depending on the prisoner's behavior and rehabilitative progress. One of the noticeable results of society's disillusion with the rehabilitative aspects of imprisonment is the demise of the system of indeterminate prison sentences and parole.

An alternative method of punishment is *determinate sentencing*. This involves a mandatory sentence—say, 15 years in prison for committing crime *X*—with the offender eligible for parole only after having served some fixed amount of time. Some states, such as Minnesota, Washington, and California, have recently replaced the system of indeterminate sentencing and parole with one providing for determinate sentences. In the states of Minnesota, Washington, and several others a "grid" system is used. The grid is constructed as a table by ranking down the vertical side of the table the seriousness of the criminal offense from a minor felony to first-degree murder on a scale from, say, 1 to 14. Then, along the top of the table the history of the offender is scaled from 0 (a first-time offender) to 9 (a violent career criminal). Entries in the table increase in severity as one goes down or across. The actual sentence imposed on a given offender is simply read off the grid. Parole boards will be abolished. However, in order to preserve discipline in the prison, the prison authorities have the ability to reduce the sentence by up to one-third.

Question 12.2:

Do hardened criminals respond to changes in punitive sanctions? Is it possible to explain the existence of laws—called "good time" laws—that give prisoners reduced sentences for good behavior in prison using the deterrence hypothesis of the previous chapter?

ever, to the extent that prisons also succeed in deterring, rehabilitating, and providing retribution, then the benefits to society of imprisoning criminals are increased.

Of course, in measuring the most efficient manner in which to punish criminals we must offset the costs of imprisonment against these benefits. The evidence on the costs of imprisonment is more specific than that on the benefits. We know, for example, that to keep one prisoner in a maximum security prison for one year costs more than $10 thousand. But this figure understates the true cost of imprisonment because it fails to take account of the opportunity costs of the prisoner's time and other productive talents.

Inmates frequently devote the bulk of their time to the making of highway signs, doing one another's laundry, preparing meals, and the like. There is little doubt that a more productive use of their time can be found. To the extent that these productive uses of prisoners' time are foregone, the costs to society of their imprisonment are greater than they need to be. If, for example, prisoners were organized to produce output efficiently, then this element of the cost of imprisonment could be reduced. (On how this might be done, see the box entitled "Prisons for Profit and 'Factories with Fences'.")

Note that even if the costs of the prison system are high, that fact alone is not enough to evaluate the efficiency of that form of punishment. To make that assessment, we need two additional pieces of information. First, we need an estimate of the (marginal) benefits to society of imprisonment so that we can calculate the (marginal) net benefits of imprisonment. Second, we need to know the net benefits of alternative (and equally deterring) methods of punishing criminals in order to compare the prison figure with that of the alternatives. Thus far, neither of these figures has been estimated. The public policy debate about the efficiency of imprisonment *versus* the alternatives has, therefore, been conducted without the appropriate facts in hand.

B. Fines

The leading alternative method of punishing criminals is the imposition of punitive monetary fines. We have already seen the theoretical arguments in favor of fines so that our focus here can be on the benefits and problems of implementing a system of fines for deterring crime.

Let us compare the use of fines and of incarceration in several Western nations and in some United States jurisdictions by looking at Table 12.1. Minor regulatory offenses—e.g., driving violations and game law violations—were not included in this tabulation so that the comparison is made across those traditional crimes for which imprisonment and monetary fines are viewed as appropriate alternative sanctions.

Note, in general, the much greater reliance in Western Europe on monetary fines as the sanction for traditional crimes. Naturally, the question arises as to why there should be such a marked discrepancy in the use of these alternative sanctions among countries that are remarkably similar in a wide number of economic, cultural, and political dimensions.

There are, however, some plausible explanations for the differences. For example, the United States' criminal population could differ in significant ways from the European criminal population. For example, in committing assaults, Americans may more frequently use a gun or other dangerous weapon that merits stronger punishment than the imposition of a monetary fine. Or a higher percentage of the United States' criminal population may be repeat offenders, for whom imprisonment may be the preferred sanction, while European criminals may tend to be first-time offenders, for whom

Table 12.1* Selected Traditional Crimes—Comparative Sentencing Patterns, 1977

Country	Total of Selected Defendants	Percent of All Defen- dants	Incarceration	Fine Only	All Other
England, Wales	293,580	69%	14%	56%	30%
Germany	191,329	77%	10%	77%	13%
Sweden	29,121	67%	13%	43%	44%
U.S. Federal District Courts	16,057	56%	39%	5%	56%
Washington, D.C. Superior Court, 1974	1,847	38%	32%	4%	64%

*The table and accompanying textual information are from R. Gillespie, *Sanctioning Traditional Crimes with Fines: A Comparative Analysis,* 5 INTERNATL. J. OF COMP. AND APPL. CRIM. JUSTICE 197 (1981).

fines may be the preferred sanction. And it could be that European criminals are more responsive to the threat of punishment than are criminals in the United States. Thus, more severe penalties are required in this country in order to achieve the same level of deterrence that a less severe sanction would generate in Europe.[14] Finally, lower levels of unemployment in some Western European countries may leave European criminals with a greater ability to pay fines.

Alternatively, the differences between Europe and the United States in sentencing for traditional crimes may be due to a philosophical or cultural difference, rather than to differences in the criminal populations. There is some evidence of such a philosophical divide. Europeans exhibit a distrust of imprisonment[15] while Americans exhibit a distrust of fines.[16] The greatest reason for this difference appears to be the long-standing commitment of the United States criminal justice system to rehabilitation of the criminal combined with the strong feeling that, although fines have the ability to punish and perhaps to deter, they cannot rehabilitate.[17]

Perhaps because we have not been disposed to use them, the existing structure of monetary fines in this country may not be well developed. The

[14]There is no empirical evidence on any of these matters. *Id.* at 201.

[15]G. Mansell, *Comparative Correctional Systems: United States and Sweden,* 8 CRIM. L. BULL. 748 (1972).

[16]AMERICAN BAR ASSOCIATION PROJECT ON STANDARDS FOR CRIMINAL JUSTICE, STANDARDS RELATING TO SENTENCING ALTERNATIVES AND PROCEDURES (1971), and NATIONAL ADVISORY COMMISSION ON CRIMINAL JUSTICE STANDARDS AND GOALS, PROCEEDINGS OF THE NATIONAL CONFERENCE ON CRIMINAL JUSTICE (1973).

[17]This statement should be taken with the cautionary note, referred to above, that "rehabilitation" is a slippery concept. A fine that deters an offender from committing future crimes has, on the broad definition noted above, "rehabilitated" the offender.

Prisons for Profit and "Factories with Fences"

Most of us presume that the prisons in which criminals are detained are operated by the state or federal government. But one of the most interesting trends of the last ten years is a move towards privatization of the prison system. The move is still in its infancy—there are only about 12 privately-operated prisons in the country—but there is a strong belief that the trend will broaden.

In a sense, privatization of punishment is not new. From an early date in this century, private employers in many states were allowed to hire gangs of convict labor. Additionally, several non-profit organizations like the Salvation Army and the Volunteers of America have long operated halfway houses in which criminals, especially juvenile delinquents, were housed, worked, and, to a degree, rehabilitated.

The largest private corporation in this new field is Corrections Corporation of America, Inc. CCA thus far operates mainly minimum security prisons and centers meant for the temporary detention of, say, illegal immigrants awaiting deportation. CCA contends that its costs are 6% below those of similar facilities operated by governmental bodies. Recently, CCA has made an offer to pay $250 million for a 99-year lease to operate the Tennessee state prison system. The company would then run the prisons for a fee based on the number of prisoners.

There are economic arguments to be made both for and against the privatization of prisons. The principal argument for *public* involvement of some sort is that prisons provide a public good. As we saw in Chapter 2, private profit-maximizing businesses will, in general, provide too little of a public good because it is impossible for them to extract a price for the benefits that the public good provides. For example, prisons incapacitate criminals, which provides some benefit, however small, to all of us.[1] But note that this public good aspect of imprisonment does not necessarily argue for the public *ownership* of prisons. A private profit-maximizing firm can often be induced to provide the optimal amount of a public good if its costs are subsidized directly out of the public fisc or by lenient tax treatment of its profits or costs.

The principal argument for the purely *private* ownership and operation of prisons is that, in general, private profit-maximizing businesses are more efficient than are governmental bodies. The incentive to return a normal rate of profit to the private owners spurs cost-cutting, technological innovation, a superior quality of output, and numerous other benefits valued by society. For example, the new, privately-operated detention center of the U.S. Immigration and Naturalization Service in Houston was financed and constructed by the Corrections Corporation of America for one-half the cost of comparable facilities and in one-third the time. Additionally, a private company on the West Coast, Behavioral Systems Southwest, operating on behalf of the state prison system, incarcerates 600 to 700 prisoners per day in leased hotels and large houses. The company deals only with low-risk prisoners and manages to detain them in its leased facilities for about $25 per day, compared with the $75-to-$100 per day cost of detention in a conventional facility. Lastly, it must be admitted that, as noted above, there is widespread dissatisfaction with the criminal justice system today and a consequent willingness to experiment with new solutions, such as private prisons. Given these arguments for and against, a careful accounting of the costs and benefits of the alternatives is in order.

The opposition to the privatization movement is formidable. The National Sheriffs Association and the American Federation of State, Country and Municipal Employees, which represents 40,000 corrections employees, are strongly opposed. However, the John Howard Association, a private, non-profit group that lobbies for prisoners' rights, is not yet sure that private prisons are a bad idea. Their position is that government-operated prisons have not done such a good job so that the alternative of private operation deserves serious consideration. The American Correctional Association, the professional organization in the field, is also adopting a wait-and-see attitude.

Many of the critics are concerned that the cost-cutting actions of the private organizations may lead to a sacrifice in the quality of prisoner care, with consequent abuses in the quality of food, shelter, and other material conditions for the prison population. Their other major concern is how far this private contracting will go. There may be few problems in a private corporation's dealing with non-violent and other minimum security criminals. But as the seriousness of the crime escalates, the potential problems increase.[2] Think, for example, whether it makes sense for the government to delegate to a private corporation the power to execute criminals. Yet another concern raised by the private profit-maximizing operation of prisons is the inducement this may create for the prison companies to lobby for strong law enforcement and stiff prison sentences and against other criminal sanctions, such as halfway houses, probationary programs, and the imposition of fines.

An interesting intermediate solution to the problems of the current system—and one not so radical as privatization—is what former Chief Justice Burger has called the creation of "factories with fences." The proposal is to invite private industry to hire prisoners to produce marketable goods in the hope that the inmates will thereby learn skills by which to live when released. To a limited extent, there are already such programs operating. At Attica State Prison in New York a metal shop that manufactures file cabinets showed a profit of approximately $1.3 million in 1984.[3] In Minnesota, Stillwater Data Processing, Inc., a private, non-profit corporation, employs 16 inmates of a maximum security prison as computer programmers; thus far, the program is breaking even. The federal government has established 27 pilot projects in its prison system for the production of marketable output. The output is exempt from the operation of a federal law that makes it illegal to transport prison-made goods in interstate commerce. Similar laws, called "State Use Statutes," forbid the sale of prison-made goods to the state government. Several states, eager to take advantage of the "factories with fences" idea, have repealed their state-use statutes, despite predictable opposition from organized labor.

An additional development spurring this search for alternatives to traditional government-financed and operated prisons is the move toward limitations on government spending. Debt limitations, referendum requirements, and administrative delays have all made it difficult for local and state authorities to use general obligation bonds, the usual method of financing prison construction. In many cases these restrictions have led to little or no new prison space being built to accommodate the increasing criminal population. The resulting overcrowding has become acute, threatening the well-being and health of some prisoners and prompting the federal courts to take jurisdiction over the prisons in parts of 40 states and 155 counties.

The search for cheaper or more efficient methods of sanctioning crime is likely to lead beyond experiments with industry in prison and the private ownership of prisons to even more novel methods of detention and sanction. For example, Nimcos, Inc., of Boulder, Colorado, has introduced an electronic surveillance system that will allow authorities to put criminals under house arrest. The system consists of an ankle bracelet holding a transmitter that allows a receiver and a computer to keep track of the prisoner's movements. If, as a condition of parole, an offender is told he must not leave his home after 8 p.m., the bracelet can inform the authorities whether the parolee is complying with the condition. Nimcos estimates that the system costs about $10 per day per offender, far below the $75-to-$100 per day figure for incarceration.

[1]An interesting inefficiency of the prison system is that the capacity is inflexible in the short and medium run. Thus, it cannot very well respond to increases in the number of convictions or an increase in the average length of sentence.

[2]For example, a lawsuit has been brought against the private company that operates the U.S. Immigration and Naturalization Service facility in Houston because a guard at the facility accidentally killed one of the detainees. The legal questions raised by this incident are thorny.

[3]*Can Our Prisons Become 'Factories with Fences'?* 40 THE RECORD OF THE ASSOCIATION OF THE BAR OF THE CITY OF NEW YORK 298 (1985). This article is a report by a committee assigned to explore the feasibility of prison industries. The committee gave qualified approval to the idea.

typical structure of fines here is for a fixed fine per offense, independent of the offender's wealth, with statutorily-defined absolute maximums. By contrast, Sweden and other Scandinavian countries combine the use of the fixed fine-per-offense system with a more flexible system of monetary fines known as the "day-fine" system. Under this scheme, the prosecutor determines the offender's recent daily income and recommends that he be punished, if guilty, by being responsible for paying that daily income times a certain number of days. For a trivial crime, such as a traffic offense, the figure may be 5 or 10 days. For a serious crime, the number of days may rise to the maximum of 120. Note that the system allows the amount of the fine to vary

both by the income of the criminal and the seriousness of the crime.[18] Moreover, because the day-fine is calibrated to the offender's income or wealth,
day-fines may be assessed much more widely than the United States' *flat*
fine, which is independent of the offender's income or wealth.

> **Question 12.3:** Several states have established victims' compensation funds,
> which provide for the payment of most of a crime victim's losses out of general
> tax revenues. Other states have, instead, moved to replace the nearly automatic
> imprisonment of criminal offenders with a system under which the criminal—
> typically, only those who have committed less serious crimes against property—
> is paroled to a job in order to pay both his victims and society. Are both pro-
> grams recommended by an efficiency analysis?

IV. THE DEATH PENALTY

The ultimate sanction that a society reserves for the worst crimes is death.
Until recently the clear trend in the world and in this country was away
from the use of this sanction or toward an outright abolition. But, at least in
this country, that trend has been reversed. Between 1976 and 1985 there
have been 46 executions in the United States, with the vast majority of those
occurring in the South.

After a brief period in the 1960s during which executions, although still
legal, virtually ceased, the Supreme Court held the death penalty to be
unconstitutional, when capriciously and discriminatorily applied, in 1972 in
Furman v. Georgia.[19] The vote was five to four. Justices Marshall and Bren-
nan felt that the death penalty was cruel and unusual punishment under any
circumstances and, thus, would *always* be unconstitutional. The other three
justices of the majority were not prepared to go so far, holding instead that
capital punishment was unconstitutional only when it was, as they thought it
to be, capriciously and discriminatorily applied, and, therefore, violated the
equal protection interpretation of the Fourteenth Amendment.

This flaw is one that could, in principle, be corrected, and after 1972
state legislatures amended their death statutes to take account of the Court's
concerns. For example, the new statutes allowed for the imposition of death
only for the most serious crimes[20] and only where the rules for doing so were
fair and objective. Additionally, the procedures for selection of the jury that

---

[18]For details on how the system works, see H. Thornstedt, *The Day-Fine System in Sweden*,
(1975) CRIM. L. REV. 307.

[19]408 U.S. 238 (1972).

[20]For example, in *Coker v. Georgia*, 433 U.S. 584 (1977) the Supreme Court held that capital punishment for rape is a "grossly disproportionate" punishment for a crime that does not
involve the loss of the victim's life. In other cases decided about the same time, the Court struck
down state statutes that imposed a mandatory death sentence for certain other crimes.

might impose death must not be biased toward imposition of the death penalty through, say, automatic exclusion of jurors who are opposed to capital punishment.[21] Then in 1976 the Court upheld three state statutes that met the criteria it had laid down over the past four years.[22] The constitutionality of death statutes has continued to be the subject of litigation since 1976, but the Court appears to be determined to hold statutes constitutional so long as they pass the tests established in *Furman* and subsequent cases. If there is a discernible trend in the most recent opinions on capital punishment, it is a growing dissatisfaction among the justices on the ever-lengthening delays between sentencing and executions.

There are extremely important and complex ethical issues involved in a thorough discussion of the death penalty. And, as can well be imagined, passions have run very high in the literature on this topic. Our focus here will be on the issue of whether executions deter homicides. We certainly do not mean to suggest that deterrence is necessarily more important than the ethical, philosophical, and other analyses of capital punishment.[23] Deterrence is simply the issue that economists have studied.

Most of the debate on the economics of capital punishment has centered on statistical issues, such as the specification of the model to be estimated or the adequacy of the data. It is worth noting at the outset that this emphasis on statistics is inevitable because economic theory alone cannot answer the underlying question of whether and to what extent the threat of execution deters homicides. Economic theory is perfectly consistent with the view that the death penalty deters and with the view that it does not deter. Thus, if there is to be an answer to the public policy question involved, it must be an answer returned from statistical analysis.[24]

The first major study of the deterrent effect of the death penalty was by the sociologist Thorsten Sellin.[25] Sellin, used four tests to detect a deterrent

---

[21]*Witherspoon v. Illinois,* 391 U.S. 510 (1968).

[22]*Profitt v. Florida,* 428 U.S. 242 (1976); *Jurek v. Texas,* 428 U.S. 262 (1976); and *Gregg v. Georgia,* 428 U.S. 153 (1976).

[23]An excellent introduction to some of the moral issues involved in the death penalty debate may be found in Kaplan, *The Problem of Capital Punishment,* 1983 U. ILL. L. REV. 555 at 565–570.

[24]We have already discussed the empirical evidence for the deterrent effect of minor punitive sanctions and have discovered that there is support for the proposition that criminals and potential criminals respond to the level of sanctions that society imposes for crimes by committing fewer or less serious crimes. The literature on the deterrent effect of the death penalty repeats the earlier debate, but at a more impassioned level. For example, critics of capital punishment have contended that extreme sanctions for murder can have little, if any, deterrent effect because most murders are crimes of passion in which family members or acquaintances are involved. In order to know if there is a deterrent effect of capital punishment, we need to know—as we did with other crimes—how many murders were *not* committed because of the fear of punishment.

[25]T. Sellin, CAPITAL PUNISHMENT (1967) 135–160. *See, also,* T. Sellin, THE PENALTY OF DEATH (1980).

effect of executions. First, he compared the homicide rates for adjacent states that did and did not have the death penalty. By making the comparison across neighboring states, Sellin hoped to minimize cultural, economic, demographic, and any other important differences that might have explained variations in the homicide rate across states. His finding was that there was no discernible difference in homicide rates across these adjacent states, implying that the death penalty had no deterrent effect. Second, he compared homicide rates within the same state before and after the death penalty was either abolished or restored and found no significant difference in the rates depending on the legal status of the death penalty. Third, Sellin looked at homicide rates within cities where executions had taken place and been well publicized. There was no difference in the rates just before and just after executions.[26] Lastly, he examined death rates for police officers in states that did and did not have the death penalty. The rate at which officers were killed was the same, regardless of whether that state executed the murderers of police officers.[27] Sellin's overall conclusion from these four tests was that the death penalty does not deter homicides.

There are three central criticisms that have been made of the Sellin study. First, he did not adequately hold "all other things equal." The issue is that, in order to isolate the effect of the death penalty on homicide rates, all the other factors that might influence homicides must be held constant. For example, we know that murders are, for various reasons, higher in urban areas; thus, differences between states in the degree of urbanization should have been netted out before testing for the relationship between executions and homicides. Additionally, young males commit far more homicides than any other group in society; thus, the age distributions across states should have been standardized in order to net out this effect.[28] The contention is not that Sellin did not try to control for the presence of these other influences on homicide rates, because he did.

---

[26]Other studies have confirmed this finding. Indeed, one investigator discerned an *increase* in the homicide rate in California cities in which executions had taken place: W. E. Graves, "A Doctor Looks at Capital Punishment," in THE DEATH PENALTY IN AMERICA (H. Bedau, ed. 1964).

[27]It is often asserted that the death penalty must be kept on the books in order to have a punishment available for hardened criminals already in prison. In the absence of the death penalty, it is argued, these criminals have nothing to lose from killing guards or other inmates, and, therefore, they will commit more of those murders. Sellin compiled a list of 59 criminals who had committed murder while in state or federal prisons in 1965. Forty-three of those murders took place in states that had the death penalty available; only eleven took place in states without a death statute. (The remaining five were in the federal prisons; there is no federal death penalty.) Sellin and others concluded that this evidence undercut this justification for the death penalty. Evaluate this conclusion after you have read the text's discussion of Sellin's four major tests.

[28]The list of other important factors is a long one. We will return to a discussion of the impact of some of these—e.g., unemployment and the racial composition of the population—shortly.

Recall that his first comparison was between adjacent states with and without the death penalty. His intuition was that adjacent states would be very similar in their cultural, political, economic, and other relevant aspects. Thus, homicide rates in Michigan, which has had no capital punishment since 1847, were compared with those in Ohio and Indiana, which did practice the death penalty. No doubt there are some striking similarities among those states, but there are some remarkable dissimilarities, too. The point is that a better econometric technique for testing for a relationship between homicide rates and the death penalty would have minimized the influence of contaminating variables.[29]

The second major shortcoming of the Sellin work is the ambiguity in his definition of "homicides." The correlation we are eager to learn about is that between those homicides for which execution was an available punishment and the number of executions for those homicides. However, the data that Sellin used—and that most investigators have used, for that matter—did not distinguish between those homicides, like first-degree or premeditated murder, for which capital punishment was a sanction, and other homicides, like second-degree murder or non-negligent manslaughter, for which it was not an available sanction. Thus, the greater the extent to which the proportion of these two broad classes of homicides differed across states or over time within the same state, the less reliable are Sellin's conclusions.

The third criticism is that Sellin did not adequately define "death penalty." His comparisons—save in the case of the city studies—were not between the number of executions and the subsequent number of homicides but rather between homicides and whether the state had a death penalty *statute*. The problem is that many states held out the possibility of capital punishment but, in fact, never used it. For example, Massachusetts had a death penalty statute into the late 1960s, but no one had been executed in that state since 1947. In 1960 there were 56 executions in the entire country, and more than half of those were in the South. In 1965, the year in which Sellin's study appeared, there were only 7 executions, even though almost all states had capital punishment statutes.

The inescapable conclusion is that Sellin's contention that there is no deterrent effect to capital punishment is not tenable. The connection between the death penalty and homicide required further and more careful consideration.[30]

---

[29]Notice that Sellin attempted to minimize the impact of these other influences on homicides in other ways, too. For example, he compared murder rates within the same states over time. But this will not fully nullify the problem because the relevant factors—such as the rate of urbanization—could have changed over time.

[30]In a study similar to Sellin's in methodology, Professor Hans Zeisel sought to determine the effects of the unofficial moratorium on executions that occurred between 1968 and 1976. His prediction was that, if there was a deterrent effect of capital punishment, there should have

The most famous study of the deterrent effect of capital punishment is that done by Isaac Ehrlich, an economist.[31] As we will see, Ehrlich's study met most of the objections that had been raised to the Sellin study but contained some new shortcomings. One of the great strengths of the Ehrlich study is its organization: he begins with a coherent, traditional microeconomic model of the behavior of the murderer, proposes hypotheses about the deterrent effect of a number of the independent variables in the model, and then confronts the model with the relevant data to see which of the hypotheses is tenable.

Ehrlich's model is one in which homicide is a rational utility-maximizing activity that may be undertaken if the increase in utility to the killer from committing the crime exceeds his expected costs. (In essence, his model was the one we explained mathematically in the previous chapter as "the economic decision to commit a crime.") Ehrlich allowed certain economic and social variables to capture part of the benefit of homicide to the killer. For example, because there is a strong correlation between the commission of property crimes and homicide, and because Ehrlich suspected that property crimes are correlated with economic and other social factors, he included data on the unemployment rate, the labor force participation rate, the level of wealth, the age composition of the population, and the racial composition of the population. He justified inclusion of the race variable on the grounds that legitimate employment opportunities for blacks, especially for young male blacks, are very limited. Thus, there is a greater tendency for blacks to commit property crimes and, therefore, because of the correlation between those crimes and homicide, to commit murder.

The specification and justification of the expected *costs* of homicide in the Ehrlich model are also an advancement over those offered in previous attempts to measure the deterrent effect of capital punishment.[32] Ehrlich took the expected costs of homicide to be dependent on

---

been a larger *increase* in homicides in those states that had most recently abolished the death penalty than in those states, like Massachusetts, that had had no executions for a much longer time. He found no perceptible increase and concluded that the death penalty did not deter murder. H. Zeisel, *The Deterrent Effect of Capital Punishment: Facts v. Faith,* 1976 THE SUPREME COURT REVIEW 317. The same criticisms that were made of Sellin's work can be made of Zeisel's study. For example, it is not at all clear that 1968 really represents an important breaking point. As noted above, executions had fallen to a very low level as early as 1960.

[31]I. Ehrlich, *The Deterrent Effect of Capital Punishment: A Question of Life and Death,* 65 AM. ECON. REV. 397 (1975). *See also,* Ehrlich, *Capital Punishment and Deterrence: Some Further Thoughts and Additional Evidence,* 85 J. POL. ECON. 741 (1977).

[32]Previous researchers had used three variables to measure the cost of homicide: the certainty of imprisonment, the length of imprisonment, and the number of executions. We have already seen the difficulties that arose in Sellin's and Zeisel's use of the number of executions as an explanatory variable. The data available on the length of imprisonment show only the length of time served by those currently in jail or those released but do not show the length of sentence. Thus, these data inevitably understate the length of imprisonment.

three variables: the probability of being arrested for the crime (to be measured by the total number of arrests for homicide divided by the total
number of reported homicides); the probability of being convicted for homicide, given arrest (measured by the total number of convictions for homicide
divided by the total number of arrests for homicide); and the probability of
execution if convicted (measured by the total number of executions divided
by the total number of convictions for homicide). His choice-theoretic model
of the decision to maximize utility through homicide led to the prediction of
an inverse relationship between each of these three probabilities and homicide rates. Moreover, Ehrlich's model predicted that the strongest deterrent
effect on homicides would arise from an increase in the probability of arrest;
the next strongest, from an increase in the probability of conviction; and the
next strongest, from an increase in the probability of execution. The regression he ran had homicide rates as a function of all these criminal justice system and socio-economic variables. He used time series data for the entire
United States for the period 1933 to 1969.

The result of the study was that the homicide rate was, as predicted,
negatively and significantly correlated with each of the three deterrence
measures. The relative strength of the components of the deterrent effect was
also as predicted. The most dramatic of the conclusions was that one additional execution per year resulted in seven or eight fewer homicides per
year.[33]

An additional finding of the Ehrlich study, a finding frequently overlooked in the debate on capital punishment, is that the deterrent effect of an
improvement in labor market conditions is stronger than that of any of the
criminal justice system variables.[34] Ehrlich posited that the reason for this
conclusion is the strong relationship between the level of unemployment and
the number of property crimes and between the number of property crimes
and the number of homicides.

The Ehrlich study has been strongly criticized on both statistical and
theoretical grounds. The theoretical criticism is subtle. Ehrlich found that
the number of homicides was an inverse function of the probability of being
convicted for murder, which implies that the greater the conviction rate for
homicide, the lower the number of murders. And yet there are reasons for
doubting whether this particular conclusion logically follows. Suppose that
juries know that if they convict a defendant of homicide, the chances of his
being executed are extremely high. Under these circumstances juries may be

---

[33]The Department of Justice cited this particular result in its argument before the Supreme
Court in *Gregg v. Georgia* in favor of the death penalty. Kenneth Wolpin did a study similar to
Ehrlich's for England and Wales for the period 1929 to 1968 and concluded that an additional
execution would have caused four fewer homicides. Wolpin, *Capital Punishment and Homicide:
The English Experience,* 68 AM. ECON. REV. 422 (1978).

[34]Compare this conclusion of Ehrlich's study with the studies cited in the preceding chapter that found no relationship between property crime and unemployment.

reluctant to convict for first-degree murder. If so, then the following paradoxical behavior may result: greater use of execution as the punishment for
certain homicides might lead to fewer convictions, so that the deterrent
effect of both capital punishment and of convictions on subsequent murderers would be diminished. Indeed, there is evidence that precisely this chain
of events occurred in Great Britain. There, before the abolition of the death
penalty in 1965, judges had less discretion to avoid sentencing defendants
guilty of first-degree homicide to execution than did juries and judges in the
United States. As a result, the percentage of murderers in Great Britain who
were found to be insane and thus ineligible for execution was much larger
than it was in the United States. It is not surprising to learn, then, that the
number of first-degree murderers judged insane in Great Britain declined
dramatically after 1965 when the death penalty was abolished. Surely what
explains this remarkable statistic is not a sudden and dramatic improvement
in the mental health of the English criminal class but rather a reluctance on
the part of British judges before 1965 to sentence convicted murderers to
death. Richard Lempert, using this insight into the connection between conviction and reluctance to execute, re-estimated Ehrlich's model and found
that an increase in the use of the death penalty would decrease the
probability of a murderer's being convicted by 17%.[35]

The second type of criticism of Ehrlich's results focuses on two statistical shortcomings in the study. The first is that the conclusions are much too
sensitive to the functional form of the estimation.[36] Ehrlich had offered no
persuasive reason for the particular functional form in which he estimated
his regression, and that raised the unsettling possibility that an alternative,
and equally plausible, functional form would lead to different results.[37] The
second statistical criticism is that Ehrlich's results are much too sensitive to
the time period over which the estimations were made. Recall that Ehrlich's
original study covered the period 1933 to 1969. We know that in the last
seven years of that period the number of executions dropped precipitously,
from 47 in 1962 to 2 in 1967 to 0 in 1968 and 1969. During those same seven
years, crime rates escalated sharply. This suggests that the period 1962–1969
is unusual and might be dropped from the study on the grounds that only
during the period 1933 to 1962 was the murder rate relatively stable and the

---

[35]Lempert, *Desert and Deterrence: An Assessment of the Moral Bases of the Case for Capital
Punishment,* 79 MICH. L. REV. 1177 (1981). Wolpin's work, mentioned above, also noted that, in
order for his conclusions about the deterrent effect of the death penalty in England to hold, a
change in the probability of execution if convicted must not cause a change in the probability of
conviction for murder.

[36]The "functional form" referred to is whether homicide rates are a *linear* function of the
independent variables or a *multiplicative* function or a *logarithmic* function or still some other
form. In general, one's model should nearly uniquely specify the functional form in which the
data will be estimated.

[37]J. Taylor, "Econometric Models of Criminal Behavior," in ECONOMIC MODELS OF CRIM-
INAL BEHAVIOR (J. M. Heineke, ed. 1978).

probability of execution of murderers realistically high for the purposes of detecting a connection between the two series. John Taylor and Peter Passell ran Ehrlich's data for this truncated period and discovered that the result of excluding the period 1962 to 1969 was that the statistical significance of the deterrent relationship between the number of executions and the number of homicides disappeared.[38] The implication is, of course, the unlikely one that capital punishment became a deterrent to homicide only after 1962. That is all the more unlikely in that, as we have seen, after 1962 the number of executions dropped dramatically at the same time that the number of murders increased.[39]

Let us consider one more aspect of this issue of the deterrent effect of the death penalty: its cost. While we do not have specific estimates of some important elements of this cost, we do have strong reasons for believing that the social costs of capital punishment are very high.[40] First, trying a case in which capital punishment is a possible outcome is extremely expensive. Jury selection is more painstaking: state statutes usually give both the prosecution and the defense more peremptory challenges in capital cases, thus allowing each side to dismiss more prospective jurors without having to offer an explanation for the dismissal; additionally, the prosecution usually has a greater number of challenges for cause because a large percentage of prospective jurors will acknowledge a reluctance to impose the death penalty. Both of these factors increase the costs of a capital case because, first, prospective jurors are more closely questioned than they are in non-capital cases so that the costs of seating a jury are much higher and, second, because a larger number of jurors are likely to be dismissed, either peremptorily or for cause, a larger pool of veniremen (potential jurors) must be retained in capital cases. For example, a recent study of California capital cases revealed that jury selection in those cases averaged thirteen days, while jury selection in non-capital cases averaged three days.

Once the jury is selected, the trial itself is probably much more expensive in a capital case than in non-capital cases. Because the stakes are so much higher, both the prosecution and the defense put on more complicated and thorough cases. Moreover, the capital offense trial is typically bifurcated into two trials, one to determine guilt, the other to assess the penalty. The safeguards that have been put in place in the penalty phase of the trial are so

---

[38]Passell & Taylor, *The Deterrent Effect of Capital Punishment: Another View,* 67 AM. ECON. REV. 445 (1977). *See, also,* Klein, Forst, and Filatov, *The Deterrent Effect of Capital Punishment: An Assessment of the Estimates,* in DETERRENCE AND INCAPACITATION (A. Blumenstein *et al.,* ed. 1978).

[39]In response to these criticisms, Ehrlich did a cross-sectional study of the deterrent effect on homicide for various states between 1940 and 1960. Ehrlich, *Capital Punishment and Deterrence: Some Further Thoughts and Additional Evidence,* 85 J. POL. ECON. 741 (1977). Again Ehrlich found a deterrent effect on homicide from increases in the probability of execution. This later study is not subject to the same criticisms that were made of the earlier work, but other objections have been raised to Ehrlich's use of cross-sectional data.

[40]*See* Kaplan, *The Problem of Capital Punishment,* 1983 U. ILL. L. REV. 555, 571–576.

elaborate that it is not unusual for that phase to be nearly as long as the trial on the determination of guilt.

Even after a sentence of death, the costs are high. It is estimated that imprisonment on death row is twice as expensive as imprisonment among the normal prison population. Death row inmates require more elaborate security and supervision. They cannot be employed in the usual prison enterprises so that they make no contribution to the revenues of the prison, as do all the other prisoners. And because of the extreme stress to which death row subjects the inmates, medical and psychiatric costs are much higher.

Lastly, the post-conviction legal proceedings in death cases have become very elaborate and expensive. For example, most states require automatic review of all capital cases by the state's highest court. Not only is this review directly expensive to the prosecution and the defense, it also partially diverts the scarce judicial resources of the state supreme court from other pressing business.[41]

Notice that these considerations of the cost of capital punishment suggest an additional set of questions that need to be answered in order for us to reach sound conclusions on this important public policy issue. We do not have in the literature on the death penalty any good information on the relative net cost or relative net benefit of the various means of achieving a given level of deterrence of homicides. Recall that, according to Ehrlich, improving labor market conditions has a larger deterrent effect than does an additional execution and that changes in the probabilities of arrest and conviction also have a larger deterrent effect than does capital punishment. But what are the relative prices to society of these alternatives? Considering all the relevant factors, which alternative provides the largest deterrent effect per dollar spent? Moreover, we do not yet know whether the deterrent effect, if any, of capital punishment is greater per dollar spent than that of long-term imprisonment, largely because the data on imprisonment are not amenable to answering such a question. (It is also possible that one of the continuing costs of capital punishment is that it is racially discriminatory. See the box on racial discrimination and the death penalty.)

There is no clear conclusion that flows from these various econometric studies on the deterrent effect of the death penalty. One cannot say with any firmness that executions deter or do not deter homicides.[42] Indeed, we are

---

[41]It is, of course, possible that the threat of capital punishment induces someone accused of first-degree murder for which the prosecution intends to seek the death penalty to plea bargain and thus to save the state the expense of a trial.

[42]It is well worth noting that public opinion polls demonstrate that both opponents and proponents of the death penalty declare that their beliefs are not at all dependent on the presence or absence of a deterrent effect for capital punishment. For example, 90% of those in favor of the death penalty say that they are in favor of that sanction even if it could be shown to them conclusively that there is no deterrent effect. Vidmar & Ellsworth, *Public Opinion and the Death Penalty*, 26 STAN. L. REV. 1245 (1974).

Racial Discrimination and the Death Penalty

The majority of the Supreme Court that found capital punishment to be unconstitutional in 1972 did so on the grounds that it was discriminatorily applied, both racially and in other ways. The evidence available at that time supported the conclusion that the death penalty was racially discrim- inatory, especially in the South. For example, a study by Wolfgang and Amsterdam of 3,000 rape convictions in 11 Southern states between 1945 and 1965 showed that, although the execution of blacks convicted of rape was rare (13% were, in fact, executed), blacks were 7 times more likely to be executed for that crime than were whites convicted of the same crime. A black who had raped a white was 18 times more likely to be executed than was any other combination of race and victim. A similar comparison of black and white executions for the same crimes in the North yielded much less evidence of a systematic race differential, although it did find that the sentences of white criminals were much more likely to be commuted than were the sentences of black criminals.

And yet the matter is more subtle than one might suppose. Murder is primarily an *intra*-racial crime. Inter-racial homicides make up less than 10% of the cases. As a first approximation of the problem, we might con- sider whether the rate at which blacks and whites are sentenced to death is the same as the rate at which they commit murders. For the period 1930 to 1967 the murder of a black person was slightly less likely to result in the execution of a black than the murder of a white person was to result in the execution of a white, although there was considerable variation in those rates from year to year. For the period 1967 to 1978 the issue was clear: blacks were less likely to be sentenced to death for murder than were whites.

However, these figures were for the nation as a whole. It could be that, as has been suggested for other aspects of the criminal law, the regions of the country differ in their attitudes toward punishment. This suggests that the studies on the likelihood of death sentences be disaggregated into regional data. When this is done, it appears to be the case that there are subtle regional variations. From 1930 to 1949, blacks were more likely

left with the unsettling feeling that only more and better statistical work can resolve the debate.[43] Worse still, there is a strong likelihood that the relevant

---

[43]For the important position that econometric studies should not be taken as "scientific" but rather as persuasive rhetoric, *see* Leamer, *Let's Take the Con Out of Econometrics*, 73 AM. ECON. REV. 31 (1983). Professor Leamer uses an econometric study of the deterrent effect of capital punishment to demonstrate the impact of the investigator's prior beliefs on his conclu- sions. *Id.* at 40–43.

than whites to be executed in the South and less likely to be executed in the North. For the period 1950 to 1967 these differences disappeared. It is not yet clear what has happened since the restoration of the death penalty in 1976.

The studies of the discrimnatory effect, if any, of the death penalty since *Gregg v. Georgia* was handed down in 1976 have suffered from some of the same statistical problems that plagued the attempts to discover a deterrent effect of the death penalty. For example, those studies that purported to show a far greater likelihood for blacks than for whites to be executed for the same crime frequently failed to control for the prior record of the criminal. An offender with a more serious prior record is much more likely to be sentenced to death than is one with a less serious prior record. Thus, if, for whatever reason, black offenders are more likely to have a more serious prior record, they would be more likely to be sentenced to death than would a white with no prior record who had committed the same crime.

Moreover, most investigators seeking to discover a racial bias in the more recent use of the death penalty have often failed to take into account the severity of the offense. It matters in judging the blameworthiness of the homicide whether it was, for example, committed in a barroom brawl, whether it was done in a calculated and hideous manner, or whether it was part of a homicidal spree. Studies have found that the death sentence is most likely in execution-style and other hideous homicides, regardless of the race of the victim or the offender. If, for whatever reason, blacks are more likely to engage in those more serious homicides, a failure to recognize this aspect might cause some investigators inadvertently to believe that application of the death penalty was racially discriminatory.

But it may be that the discriminatory impact of death sentences is more subtle than these factors can capture. That, at any rate, is the contention of several recent, comprehensive studies of the issue.

statistical evidence cannot ever be produced. To see why, consider that there is general agreement that if the death penalty is to be invoked, it should be invoked only for cold-blooded murders—for example, those who hire themselves out to kill others, those who knowingly plant bombs to kill innocent people, and those who derive pleasure from terrorizing and ultimately killing other human beings. But it is probably the case that that group of homicides is very small, making the demonstration of a deterrent effect of capital punishment on that small class of potential killers extremely difficult. Moreover, it is likely that the number of other variables besides the probability of execution that influences the decisions of this small class of murderers is immense and swamps any potential deterrent effect of capital punishment.[44]

V. HEROIN AND CRIME[45]

In discussions of public policy toward crime, one of the most troubling issues is the connection between drug abuse and criminal offenses. There is believed to be a strong, positive correlation between the use of habituating drugs, such as heroin, and crime, especially property crime. Drug addicts, it is asserted, are often incapable of maintaining a job because the debilitating effects of their habit make it necessary for them to rely upon illegal activities to generate the income to support the addiction.

This is a relatively recent public policy problem. For various reasons there was a well-publicized heroin epidemic that began in the late 1960s in the United States. As evidence of this epidemic, note that the number of deaths in Los Angeles County attributable to heroin use tripled between 1967 and 1971. During the decade of the 1960s the number of heroin users is estimated to have increased ten-fold in Boston. Clearly these dramatic increases were occurring at the same time that the amount of crime, especially property crime, was dramatically increasing. Further evidence of a connection comes from more recent trends in the opposite direction. The heroin epidemic appears to have run its course in the mid-1970s so that the number of users has declined since late in that decade. Simultaneously with this decline in the number of addicts, there has been a decline in the amount of crime in the early 1980s. Thus, it was natural to suspect a cause-and-effect relationship between addiction and crime.[46]

Current policy is directed at breaking the connection between addiction and crime by attempting to curtail the supply of the drug and by reducing the demand. The theory is that, if the risks of marketing the product are increased through governmental action, then some suppliers will leave the business of supplying drugs in favor of less risky activities at the same time

---

[44]This point is forcefully made in Wilson, *supra* note 4, at 188. *See, also,* Barnett, *The Deterrent of Capital Punishment: A Test of Some Recent Studies,* 29 OPER. RES. 346 (1981), in which the point is made that all of the studies on the deterrent effect have omitted such a large number of important variables that none of their conclusions can be taken seriously. For example, Barnett uses some of the recent studies to retrodict (i.e., to "predict" backwards) the number of homicides in given past years and finds their predictions to be wildly inaccurate.

[45]For further material on heroin, *see* John Kaplan, THE HARDEST DRUG: HEROIN AND PUBLIC POLICY (1983).

[46]At the same time heroin use has been declining in this country, its use has been increasing rapidly in Western Europe. By the mid–1980s, Western European countries consumed more illegal heroin than did the United States.

that the higher market price caused by the restriction in supply will induce some consumers to switch their purchases to alternative goods and services.

Some economists have argued that this policy is incorrect because its factual premises are incorrect. Most importantly, they point out that the addict's demand for heroin is likely to be extremely inelastic: that is, his decision about the quantity of heroin to use is not sensitive to variations in its price. Therefore, a restriction in supply and the resulting increase in the market price of heroin will *not* cause the addict to reduce his use of the drug significantly. Instead, it will cause him to *increase* the amount of crime he engages in to produce the ever greater revenue required to support his habit. Thus, current policy, far from reducing the amount of crime attributable to drug addiction, may in fact increase it. The clear implication of this analysis is that the connection between drug use and crime can be broken only by *reducing* the price of heroin, for example, by the government's providing it to registered addicts at a nominal price.

This standard economic analysis is illustrated in Figure 12.7. The demand curve D_A represents an inelastic demand for heroin by addicts. Suppose that the supply curve for heroin is initially representable by S_1. The equilibrium price and quantity are then P_1 and H_1. The total amount spent on heroin by addicts is then $0P_1$ times $0H_1$ or the area of the rectangle $0H_1E_1P_1$. If we make the simplifying assumption that heroin addicts pay for all their heroin by committing crimes, then initially the total expenditure on heroin by addicts comes from committing crimes in the amount of $0H_1E_1P_1$.

Now suppose that the government announces a policy directed at interrupting the flow of heroin to addicts. The immediate economic result of this policy is to reduce the supply of heroin, say, to the supply curve S_2. The new equilibrium price and quantity established after this change is at the price P_2 and the quantity demanded H_2. Note that because of the inelasticity of demand the reduction in the quantity demanded because of the increase in price is not great.

One of the results of inelasticity of demand is that when the price rises, the total expenditures by consumers increases. In Figure 12.7 that means that when price rises to P_2, the total expenditures of heroin addicts on heroin increases to the amount $0P_2$ times $0H_2$, or the rectangle $0H_2E_2P_2$. Clearly, this amount is greater than that spent before the institution of the policy of supply interruption when the price was P_1. Under our assumption that the only source of funds for heroin addicts is crime, the interruption of supply by the authorities inevitably leads heroin addicts to commit more crimes. This perverse outcome can be avoided, the standard economic argument goes, only by *lowering* the price of heroin. If the price is initially P_1, then crime attributable to heroin addicts can be reduced by the government's subsidizing the supply of heroin so as to lower the price. At the limit, the heroin can be made available for free, thus completely severing the connection between addiction and crime.

As attractive and plausible as this analysis is, things are more complicated than this simple model suggests. For example, the inelastic demand

Figure 12.7 The Economics of Heroin and Crime

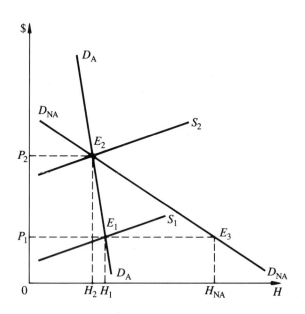

The demand curve D_A represents an inelastic demand for heroin by addicts. Suppose that the supply curve for heroin is initially S_1. The equilibrium price and quantity of heroin are then P_1 and H_1. The total amount spent on heroin by addicts is then OP_1 times OH_1 or the area of the rectangle $OH_1E_1P_1$. If we make the simplifying assumption that heroin addicts pay for all their heroin by committing crimes, then initially the total expenditure on heroin by addicts comes from committing crimes in the amount $OH_1E_1P_1$. Now suppose the government attempts to reduce heroin-related crime by restricting the supply of heroin so that the supply curve becomes S_2. The new equilibrium price and quantity are P_2 and H_2. Because of the inelasticity of demand, the reduction in the quantity of heroin in response to the price increase is not great, and, as a result, the total expenditures by consumers increase. Thus, when the price rises to P_2, the total expenditures of addicts for heroin equal OP_2 times OH_2 or the area $OH_2E_2P_2$, which is clearly greater than the amount spent before the institution of the policy of supply interruption. Under our assumption that the only sources of funds for heroin addicts is crime, the interruption of supply by the authorities inevitably leads heroin addicts to commit more crimes. The standard economic analysis suggests that this perverse result can be avoided only by *lowering* the price of heroin, e.g., by making it freely available to registered addicts.

But suppose that the inelastic demand curve applies only to addicts. Non-addicts may have a much more elastic demand, like that in demand curve D_{NA}. If so, the same price increase from P_1 to P_2 that induces addicts to engage in more crime dissuades non-addicts or casual heroin users from experimenting with the drug. If non-addicts are initially consuming H_{NA} at price P_1, the increase in price to P_2 causes non-addicts to reduce their demand to H_2, a very large drop in demand. It follows that the policy of subsidizing the consumption of heroin by addicts may also lower the price below P_1 to non-addict experimenters and, because of the elasticity of their demand, induce a large amount of experimentation and possible later addiction. Therefore, for the subsidization policy to work, the authorities must somehow maintain a policy of price discrimination in which addicts pay a low price for heroin and all others pay a much higher price.

curve shown in Figure 12.7 may describe the relation between the price and quantity of heroin demanded by *addicts*, but it probably does not describe the demand curve for heroin among *non-addicts*. Those thinking of experimenting with heroin may well have an elastic demand curve for the drug, like that of demand curve D_{NA} in the graph. Thus, the same increase in price that induces addicts to engage in more crime, dissuades non-users or casual heroin users from experimenting with the drug. If non-addicts are initially consuming H_{NA} at price P_1, the increase in price to P_2 causes non-addicts to reduce their demand to H_2, a very large drop in demand. Notice that it follows that the policy of subsidizing the consumption of heroin by addicts may also lower the price below P_1 to non-addict experimenters and, because of the elasticity of their demand, induce a large amount of experimentation and possible later addiction. This suggests that for the subsidization policy to work, the authorities must somehow maintain a policy of price discrimination in which addicts pay a low price and all others pay a higher price. Thus, in the figure a sound public policy would be one that forces addicts to pay a low, or even zero, price while non-addicts pay a high price like P_2. This, in effect, is the solution attempted (until recently) in Great Britain. British addicts may register and obtain heroin from pharmacies at modest prices. Non-addicts (or unregistered addicts) may not purchase heroin from pharmacies, but must, instead, purchase it illegally at a higher price. We will return to the case of Great Britain later.

Our understanding of the pharmacological and social effects of heroin is in its infancy, but we do know enough to question the conventional wisdom about the connection between heroin and crime. For example, it is no longer widely believed that heroin use is necessarily addictive, nor even that it is physically destructive. There are no specific pathologies that result from heroin use, even from heavy heroin use, although there may be adverse, but as yet unknown, long-term consequences of heavy use. The most common ills that arise from heroin use are due to unsterile needles, thrombosed veins, and poisonings from an overdose (frequently from the substance with which the heroin is mixed and not from the heroin itself). There is also some recent evidence of a connection between heroin addiction and acquired immune deficiency syndrome (AIDS), principally because of the sharing of contaminated needles among addicts. Thus, although it is true that the mortality rate among addicts is much higher than that of non-addicts in their age group, it is probably *not* true that their increased mortality is *directly* linked to their use of heroin.

It also appears to be the case that the notion of a pusher who induces otherwise innocent people to experiment with heroin in order to addict them, and thus to create a customer, is a myth. Heroin use spreads in much the same way as does the flu. A "carrier," most frequently a new user, infects his or her peer group by spreading the word about the pleasurable experience he has had. Usually, the group is one that has already experimented with other drugs and with alcohol so that it is receptive to a new experience for which one of its members vouches. Just as the spread of a contagious disease can be halted by quarantine, so the spread of a heroin "epidemic"— as it is usually called—can be halted when there are no more infectable subgroups.

Of these revisions in our knowledge about heroin, perhaps the most surprising is that there is now some doubt about the connection between heroin use and crime. Recall that the conventional wisdom was that heroin use was so debilitating that the habitual user could not meaningfully hold a regular job. His only viable method of raising the money necessary to purchase heroin was crime. Thus, it was widely believed in the late 1970s that something like 50% of all property crime could be attributed to heroin use. That figure is now completely discredited. Although no exact figure is known, more recent and realistic estimates are that addiction accounts for well below 20% of all street crime. At the heart of this doubt is the finding that most addicts, 50–75%, were criminals *before* their heroin addiction developed. Thus, any additional crimes that they commit while addicted may create only a small increase in the crime rate. Moreover, any increase in the amount of crime by a heroin addict is likely to be a short-lived phenomenon, occurring only during a period of particularly heavy use (a "run") in which the addict injects heroin four or five times per day at a total cost of over $100/day. During this period, he may be unable to maintain legitimate work; may have exhausted his, his family's, and his friends' savings; and so must turn to petty crime.

These considerations suggest that one cannot now easily argue for a public policy of curtailing heroin use solely on the grounds that that will reduce the amount of crime. Moreover, they also suggest that the economist's suggestion to subsidize consumption by addicts in order to reduce crime is also incorrect.

The strongest argument for curtailing use may well be that heroin use almost inevitably interferes with the user's ability to enjoy his life fully and to contribute productively to the social good.

These doubts aside, the United States government has made a commitment to the goal of curtailing heroin use (as well as the use of other, more destructive drugs, such as cocaine), and that then raises the important (positive) economic question: what public policy is the most efficient means of achieving this goal? We will discuss the attempts over the past decade or so to curtail heroin use. More recently the drug problem has shifted to a concern with the use of cocaine and its derivative, "crack." The public policy debate on curtailing the use of cocaine and crack has just begun. An understanding of the successes and failures of the war on heroin use of the 1970s and early 1980s is crucial to the formation of good public policy in fighting the use of other drugs.

For the last fifteen years United States government policy has attempted to curtail heroin use principally by restricting the *supply* of heroin and only secondarily by trying to restrict the *demand* for heroin. The supply-restriction policy has taken two forms: attempts to control heroin production in other countries and to make it more difficult to import the substance. Let us use economics to evaluate these policies, first those directed at the supply of heroin and then those directed at the demand for heroin.

Most heroin is produced abroad, and United States consumption for illegal purposes accounts for a tiny fraction of total world output. For example, world production is approximately 1,000 to 2,000 tons per year; total annual U.S. consumption is about 40–50 tons. These figures indicate the very slim likelihood of our government's being able to eradicate world heroin production at a cost that this society would tolerate. Nonetheless, in the early 1970s the government undertook a policy of restricting the supply of heroin to the United States by subsidizing crop substitution programs in those countries that were supplying the bulk of raw material for processing into herion for sale in the United States. It was believed that farmers in those countries grew poppies for processing into heroin because the returns to doing so were significantly larger than those that could be realized from cultivating legal crops, such as rice and wheat. To persuade these foreign farmers to abandon opium as a cash crop, the United States government paid them *not* to grow poppies or subsidized their purchase of inputs—fertilizers, seeds, and so on—for the alternative cash crops. For example, the United States gave Turkey $35 million as part of a crop-substitution policy in 1971. (Turkey was thought at that time to be the source of 80% of the heroin reaching the U.S.) The program lasted until 1974, when the United States government withdrew.

While the program to restrict Turkish supply was operating, Mexico greatly increased its production, even though the cost of growing opium there was much higher than it was in Turkey. By 1974 it was estimated that Mexico provided 80% of the U.S. market. The United States government then entered a crop-substitution agreement with Mexico to restrict poppy production. Unlike the Turkish program, the Mexican program was successful: illegal production there fell by 75% between 1976 and 1980.

The second component of the policy of reducing the supply of heroin in the 1970s was import restriction. The governmment greatly increased the resources it devoted to inspecting personal and commercial imports that were the most likely to contain heroin and other illegal drugs.[47]

By the end of the 1970s the price of heroin in the United States rose, and the purity of the heroin available fell. At about the same time, as we have already seen, the number of heroin addicts is believed to have fallen by about 20%. Although this reduction in the number of addicts followed the heroin-supply-restriction policies, this was more a coincidence than cause-and-effect. Most recent studies of the matter have concluded that the decline in the number of heroin addicts was due to factors other than the government's supply-restriction programs.

---

[47]*See* Peter Reuter, *Eternal Hope: America's Quest for Narcotics Control*, 79 PUB. INTEREST 79 (1985).

Microeconomic theory can explain why the supply-restriction policies had no significant impact on heroin use in this country. Consider first an economic analysis of the crop-substitution programs. First, for most opium farmers there is no easy alternative commercial crop. When they were given fertilizer, irrigation, and other inputs paid for by the United States, the rational response for most of those foreign farmers was to use these inputs to increase their productivity, and consequently their profits, from growing illegal crops. Second, even if it had been extended to other suppliers of heroin, the crop-substitution program could not have had a significant impact on the total world heroin supply because the governments in several important producing areas—notably Afghanistan and the "Golden Triangle" at the junction of Thailand, Burma, and Laos—are fighting insurgency movements in the areas in which poppies are grown and because the governments of some other important producers—such as Iran and Afghanistan—have hostile relations with the United States. Third, and most importantly, entry into the business of growing poppies is very inexpensive so that a reduction in the supply from one country is very likely to be replaced by increased production elsewhere. This is precisely what happened in the 1970s: the crop-substitution program's success in reducing the supply from Turkey led to an increase in the supply from Mexico.

Nor can the policy of reducing the supply of heroin by increasing import restrictions take credit for the decline in the number of addicts from the late 1970s. The reason is that it is not likely that the policy works. First, small amounts of heroin are so valuable that tens of thousands of dollars worth of heroin can be easily concealed and transported by individuals as part of their personal luggage on commercial airlines. Policing the millions of individuals who arrive in this country on commercial airlines cannot be effectively done. Secondly, even if the authorities could make the problem of checking individuals more manageable by focusing on those coming into the United States only from a certain area, it is relatively easy for heroin suppliers to shift among couriers from different countries. A courier is much less likely to be caught if he is part of a large number of people routinely going from the drug-supplying country to the consuming country. For example, most cocaine consumed in the United States comes into the country from Columbia, even though the original product is produced in Peru and Bolivia. The reason for the use of Columbian couriers is that that country is the largest source of legal South American migrants to this country. By contrast, most cocaine is carried to Europe by Brazilians, who are the largest migrating population from South America to Western Europe. Finally, heroin (and cocaine) suppliers can evade import restrictions by avoiding legal immigration points. Examples of this are smuggling by boat into remote harbors or by airplane into private rural airstrips.

An entirely different public policy tack is to try to reduce the *demand* for heroin. In general, demand-affecting policies take one of three forms: the substitution of another, less dangerous, and less debilitating drug for heroin; the free availability of heroin to registered addicts; or a legal proscription on use, which is the current policy.

The first of these programs typically makes the drug methadone freely available to addicts. Methadone is an addictive substance that is usually taken orally under a doctor's supervision. Under those circumstances methadone relieves the heroin addict of the most acute withdrawal symptoms without making it difficult to carry on with an otherwise normal life. But because oral ingestion of methadone does not provide the "high" of injected heroin, a methadone substitution program appeals only to those addicts who have grown tired of the anxieties of being an addict. Thus, the average methadone user is 30–35 years old and has been a heroin user for 10–15 years. This age group accounts for a relatively small fraction of addicts and for an even smaller fraction of the addict population who are responsible for criminal offenses. Methadone maintenance programs are especially unattractive to the younger, most contagious group of heroin users. For those reasons, one should not expect a methadone substitution program to have much impact on the number of heroin addicts or on the amount of crime attributable to heroin addiction. Moreover, as we will shortly see, even if it could reach large numbers of addicts, methadone maintenance programs are extremely expensive.

The policy of making heroin freely available to registered addicts was once a popular alternative but is not now viewed favorably. That program is based on the manner in which the British once dealt with opiate addictions. From the 1920s until 1968 British physicians were allowed to prescribe heroin or morphine to their patients for whom they thought continued use to be the best policy. During that period there were only several hundred addicts in the country, most of whom were members of the middle or upper-middle classes who had become addicted in the course of medical treatment. Between 1961 and 1969 the number of addicts in Britain increased five-fold and the kind of addict changed dramatically: they became much younger, less stable, and part of the youth counter-culture. In response, Parliament changed the system in 1967 to allow only specially licensed physicians located at only a few hospitals and clinics to prescribe opiates. The growth rate in the number of addicts stopped, and in 1968 the price of heroin on the black market in Britain doubled. More recently, the British have begun to move toward oral methadone substitution as their principal policy for dealing with opiate addiction.

One of the benefits of a policy of free availability is the fact that health problems associated with heroin use would probably decline. Recall that the most severe health problems of addiction arise not from the drug itself but rather from the adverse effects of injecting the drug into veins. Injection originally became popular largely because it provided a more efficient method of getting high from a very expensive drug. When heroin's price was low, other, safer methods of use—e.g., oral ingestion—were far more common. Because free availability will, in essence, reduce the price of heroin to registered users, these less risky methods of drug use will increase, and the health problems associated with use will be lowered.

But there are reasons for believing that a program of free availability will impose high social costs and, therefore, will not work in this country.

First, the number of addicts in the United States is orders of magnitude larger than was the British number when it had a policy of free availability. These larger numbers suggest that the total costs of managing a system of free availability in this country would be extraordinarily large. Still, these costs would be less than the costs of a comparably-sized methadone maintenance program. A system of dispensing heroin by prescription to registered addicts at a clinic costs about $2,500 per addict per year, and that figure is about 20% of the cost of a methadone program.

Second, there is the possibility that the free availability program would cause an *increase* in the number of addicts with a consequent increase in the social costs of addiction. Because we do not know what factors cause one to become addicted, it may be the case that free availability would cause a possibly large increase in the number of addicts, as those most susceptible to addiction experiment with the drug. The leakage of legally-prescribed heroin into the black market could be reduced by having registered addicts consume the drug only under supervision at a clinic, but that would increase the cost of this system to approximately $15,000 per addict per year.[48]

Third, the typical addict in the United States shares almost none of the social and demographic characteristics of the British addict of the 1920s to the early 1960s for whom the free availability system was designed. The fact that the British abandoned their system of free availability precisely when the nature of the addict population changed to become more like that of the United States is eloquent testimony against adoption of that system in this country. The free availability system was meant to deal with few, inadvertent, middle-class addicts and is inappropriate when the addict population is large, young, and lower-class.

Fourth, the structure of the medical system in the two countries is entirely different. The British system is highly structured and relatively easily supervised. By contrast, the United States' system is highly competitive, relatively anarchic, and, therefore, difficult to supervise. Given the problems that could arise from the leakage of heroin out of the legal-prescription program, the difficulties of supervising the dispensers argues against adopting the program of free availability in this country.

The current demand-affecting policy is one prohibiting the *possession* and *use* of heroin.[49] The latter part of this policy is very difficult to enforce because it is difficult to observe use. The best *ex post* test of heroin use (urinalysis within 72 hours) is reliable but difficult to compel, and raises other legal problems. Nonetheless, a policy of requiring periodic drug tests

---

[48]One alternative possibility is to use the free-availability-with-clinic-consumption plan to "hook" the addict in the hopes of switching him to methadone within, say, a year. This is the current British practice.

[49]In *Robinson v. California,* 370 U.S. 661 (1962), the United States Supreme Court held a state law making heroin addiction a crime to be unconstitutional. Thus, aside from the inherent problem of defining "addiction," we cannot use criminal sanctions to distinguish between casual, and presumably non-debilitating, use of the drug from debilitating "addiction."

among employees has recently been suggested by a presidential commission as the most effective method of reducing the adverse effects of drugs in the workplace.

Prohibition-of-use does have the benefit of dissuading generally law-abiding citizens from experimenting with the drug. Indeed, after the United States first made the sale, possession, use, and import of heroin and other opiates illegal in the Harrison Act (1914), there was a change in the nature of the addict population much like that that was observed in Britain in the late 1960s; addiction among the middle, upper-middle, and upper classes began to disappear, to be replaced by increasing addiction among the lower classes.[50]

Thus, we see that the connection between heroin use and crime is much more complicated than was once believed and that this fact suggests that, for all its faults, the current policy of prohibiting the use of heroin is probably the most efficient means of dealing with the problems that heroin use imposes on society.

VI. GUN CONTROL

Like many of the other issues in crime and punishment, the issue of the control of guns is one that arouses great passion on both sides. Those who are strongly opposed to further gun control—we will shortly discuss how much control there currently is—are worried that attempts to control the criminal use of guns will inevitably involve the imposition of restrictions on the legitimate use of guns. For example, they perceive attempts to register guns as the inevitable precursor to a policy of more severe restrictions. This camp points to the Second Amendment's guarantee of the right to keep and bear arms as the most important Constitutional buttress for their opposition to gun control. On the other side are those who perceive no legitimate use for certain types of guns, especially handguns, and are willing to impose elaborate restrictions on the use and availability of those guns in an effort to reduce the harm that results from their misuse. For example, the Village of Morton Grove, Illinois, a suburb of Chicago, has banned the keeping of handguns within its jurisdiction.[51]

---

[50]In the early part of the century, opiate addiction was most common among Civil War veterans and among women in rural areas and small towns. Like the early British addicts, these people were far more likely to be members of the middle and upper classes than of the lower classes. One of the most famous examples of opiate addiction among the middle classes is found in Eugene O'Neill's *Long Day's Journey into Night*.

[51]This ordinance has withstood judicial scrutiny, and other jurisdictions are contemplating similar ordinances. Curiously, the citizens of one city, Kenesaw Mountain, Georgia, a town of 5,000, vented their strong feelings about the Morton Grove ban by passing an ordinance that requires the head of every household to own a gun and ammunition.

The issue of gun control is, of course, a terribly complex one. We will see that once we agree on the goal of a control program, designing the optimal policy to implement that goal is not an easy matter.

There is now no doubt that the easy availability of handguns increases the homicide rate.[52] Gun killings increased from 2.5 per 100,000 of population in 1963 to 6.2 per 100,000 in 1973, and since 1966 rates of handgun homicide have increased more than three times as much as homicide by all other means. It does not necessarily follow that restricting the availability of handguns will reduce the homicide rate. It could be that if handguns become more expensive, those bent on committing homicide will substitute other instruments. But most investigators believe that this substitution will be towards less lethal devices, such as knives, and that the homicide rate would indeed fall if the inconvenience and cost of obtaining handguns were increased.

Moreover, the wide and easy availability of handguns probably makes other serious crimes, such as robbery and assault, easier, too. However, in the case of these less serious violent crimes the effects of handgun restrictions may be less desirable. This is because some serious crimes, such as robberies, currently committed with handguns are committed against those—such as youthful men—who are not nearly as vulnerable to attack if the robber does not have a handgun. Additionally, some robberies—such as those against banks or armored cars—may take place only if the criminals have handguns that, they feel, increase their chances of overcoming the presence of armed law enforcement officers. Thus, if handguns become more costly to use, which would be the case, for example, if the punishment for using them in a robbery were greatly increased, some robbers might substitute away from handguns and thus shift their attacks toward more vulnerable groups of the population, such as women and the elderly. While the homicide rate associated with robberies would probably decline, the robbery rate might not change, and the victim population would change.[53] This is a highly speculative response to heightened restrictions on handgun use, but it is sufficiently plausible to make further inquiry desirable.

There are three general ways to regulate guns. First, society might do nothing to restrict access to guns but punish those who use them more severely than those who do not. As the bumper sticker puts it, "Guns don't kill; people do." Second, society can restrict the production and possession of handguns. And third, society can make handguns available only to those who are least likely to use them in a violent way. Let us discuss the economics of these alternatives.

---

[52]Throughout the discussion we will confine our remarks, much as gun control is confined, to handguns. There are three times as many long guns as there are handguns, but handguns account for 75% of all gun murders and 90% of all gun robberies.

[53]See Philip Cook, *The Effect of Gun Availability on Violent Crime Patterns,* in Cook, ed., GUN CONTROL, 63–79 (1981).

Several states have passed legislation that requires more severe and more certain punishment for those who carry a handgun without a permit. For example, Massachusetts passed the Bartley-Fox law in 1974, which amended a long-standing Massachusetts law requiring a license for persons carrying a handgun to add that failure to abide by that provision was to be punished by a mandatory penalty of one year in prison without the possibility of probation, parole, or other diminution of sentence. Several studies have been conducted to measure the impact of Bartley-Fox, and the reported evidence suggests that the result of the law was, first, a reduction in the casual carrying of handguns, and, second, a decline in the proportion of assaults, robberies, and homicides committed with handguns.[54]

These deterrence results of Bartley-Fox have been achieved at a high cost. The law mandates a prison sentence for carrying an unlicensed handgun without exception, and because receiving a permit is difficult unless one has a compelling reason, an ordinary citizen who was unable to get a permit but was carrying a gun solely for the purposes of self-defense would have to be sentenced to a year in prison. This is precisely what happened to a man who had begun to carry a handgun after receiving repeated threats from a coworker. The man was sentenced to a year in prison under Bartley-Fox after he shot the coworker in a subway station when he was knifed. The highest court in Massachusetts affirmed the man's sentence and wrote:

> We are not unaware that some may say that the defendant is to be punished for acting reasonably in face of a serious and real threat. [The defendant did not merely arm himself out of some fear of crime in general.] It was founded on an earlier assault by Michel [the coworker] with a knife and became a real and direct danger when Michel attacked the defendant with a knife at the [subway] station. We are also advised from the record that the defendant is a hardworking family man, without a criminal record, who was respected by his fellow employees (Michel excepted). Michel, on the other hand, appeared to have lacked the same redeeming qualities. He was a convicted felon who had serious charges pending against him at the time of [the defendant's] trial (quite apart from the charge of assaulting the defendant). It is possible that the defendant is alive today only because he carried a gun that day for protection. Before [the legislature mandated the one-year minimum] sentence, [such] special circumstances involving the accused could be reflected reasonably in the sentencing or dispositional aspect of the proceeding. That option is no longer open to the judicial branch of government.[55]

Michigan and other states have tried a different tack: higher mandated imprisonment for those using a handgun to commit a felony. The Michigan Felony Firearms Law provided for a mandatory two-year sentence in prison

---

[54]*See* Wilson, THINKING ABOUT CRIME 135–36 (rev. ed 1983). This reduction in homicides associated with other felonies occurred even though the total number of these offenses was going up in Boston and in other large cities.

[55]As quoted in Kates, *The Battle over Gun Control,* PUBLIC INTEREST (Summer, 1986).

if the offender had a firearm in his possession while committing a felony. The two-year term was to be added to whatever sentence the offender received for commission of the felony. There was no discernible effect of this act on the number of gun-related crimes, apparently because Michigan judges found ways in which to reduce the impact of the Act, for example by reducing the sentence of the felony in order to reduce the impact of the added-on two-year term or by dismissing the gun count. Because the findings on the impact of such laws on handguns and violent crimes are mixed, no strong argument may be made in favor of this alternative until more evidence is available.

The second public policy designed to reduce the connection between handguns and violent crime is to restrict the production and possession of handguns. This alternative has been the one most used by federal, state, and local governments since late in the 19th century when the first laws regulating guns (specifically, concealed weapons) were passed. For example, in 1937 Congress prohibited the use of the U.S. mail for the sale of handguns across state lines, a law that was relatively easily evaded by using private express companies to conduct the mail-order business in guns. The National Firearms Act of 1934 provided for the registration of weapons favored by gangsters (such as machine guns, sawed-off shotguns, and silencers), for the photographing and fingerprinting of registered owners of these weapons, and for a $200 tax to be paid whenever the ownership of these registered weapons was transferred. The Federal Firearms Act of 1938 was an attempt to require mandatory licensing for the manufacturers, importers, and retail dealers in handguns and to provide for penalties if any of those businesses knowingly sold a gun to a convicted criminal. The last act by the federal government to deal with handguns was the Gun Control Act of 1968, a limitation on the importation of inexpensive handguns known as "Saturday Night Specials," which had been involved in assassination attempts on prominent politicians in that year.[56] In 1977 the District of Columbia banned the sale and acquisition of handguns, and, as we have already seen, Morton Grove, Illinois, has banned the possession of handguns.

It is probably fair to say that any further attempts to limit the accessibility to handguns at the federal and state levels is likely to be unsuccessful. First, as the recent episode of the Subway Killer in New York City dramatizes,[57] it is difficult to imagine a legislator urging further restrictions, not because of fear of the political clout of the National Rifle Association (NRA),

---

[56]The impact of this last piece of legislation is discussed in Franklin Zimring, *Firearms and Federal Law: The Gun Control Act of 1968*, 4 J. LEGAL STUD. 133 (1975). See also Gary Keck, *Policy Lessons from Recent Gun Control Research*, 49 LAW & CONTEMPORARY PROBLEMS 1 (1986). In 1986 Congress passed a revision of the 1968 Gun Control Act that weakened several of its key provisions.

[57]In 1985 Bernard Goetz, while riding on the subway in New York City, was confronted by several youths who, in Goetz's estimation, intended to attack and rob him. After they confronted him but before they actually threatened him, Goetz, who was carrying a handgun without a permit, shot and killed one of the youths and injured three others.

but because many people perceive the criminal justice system as having failed to protect them from crime and will, therefore, look unkindly upon a policy of removing their last line of defense (the privately-owned handgun). Second, approximately 20% of American homes already contain a handgun so that it is probably not feasible to have a large impact by restricting future possession or production: the flow may stop, but the stock will still be large. For the same reasons, there is not much likelihood that a governmental policy of buying-back the existing stock of guns will have much impact.

The third policy option—restricting access to guns only to those least likely to use them in a violent way—offers hope for marginal improvement. Federal laws and about one-half of the states currently forbid ownership of handguns by convicted felons, fugitives, minors, current and ex-drug addicts, and those who have been involuntarily committed for mental illness. For this policy to work, there must be better records available to local authorities to determine the criminal and other relevant history of those purchasing handguns. These records are costly to maintain and to check. The sort of changes that would make the system more effective include a lengthened waiting period before a gun may be legally purchased so as to allow a more thorough record check. Also, it might be helpful to require a police report of a stolen or lost handgun. But note that these are marginal improvements. Note, too, that while the policy may be moderately effective at preventing handguns from reaching the proscribed owners by way of licensed dealers, it is not at all likely to be effective in regulating hand-to-hand transactions involving used handguns.

Question 12.4: New handguns are involved in gun crimes at a higher rate than are older handguns. Does it follow that the most efficient gun control policy is one that concentrates on restricting production and possession of *new* handguns, especially by the groups identified in the text, but pays little attention to used handguns? To answer this question is it important to know the degree of substitutability between new and older guns in gun crimes?

CONCLUSION

We have a rare combination of liberties and crime in this society. It could well be that some societies that have less crime than we do may have achieved this by sacrificing some of the liberty of their citizens. Indeed, there is no doubt that the fear of crime has led to a movement in this country to restrict some civil liberties in an effort to reduce crime. For example, there have been proposals to limit an accused person's accessibility to bail, to allow the police to have a good-faith exception to the exclusionary rule (which forbids the use in a criminal prosecution of evidence that was acquired by the police without certain procedural safeguards, such as a search warrant), and to limit the opportunity for unlimited appeals in the judicial system.

It is well to conclude this survey of the economics of crime and punishment by noting how little we really know about crime. Take, for example, the issue of homicide. We do not know why the United States has such a high rate of homicide when compared to the rate in other nations. Nor do we know why Nicaragua, South Africa, and Mexico have rates even higher than ours. Within the United States, there is still much to learn about why the homicide rate varies so greatly among large cities and among the regions of the country. The rate is generally higher in the South, but is this because there is greater poverty in that region or because there is a historical legacy of settling disputes with firearms or for some other reason? There is also a remarkable variation among races and ethnic groups in homicide rates. The homicide rate for black men is ten times higher than for white men; for black women, it is five times higher. In Oakland, California, black males aged 25 to 35 suffer gun homicide at a rate of 120 per 100,000 population, but for all of Alameda County, in which Oakland lies, the rate for black males of that age is only 7.4 per 100,000.[58] For the nation as a whole, the rate for younger black males–those aged 15 to 24–fell throughout the 1970s, but for young white males, it increased from 4.9 per 100,000 in 1965 to 15.5 per 100,000 in 1980.

The state of our knowledge about these matters is extremely elementary. The conclusions of others that we have reported in this survey of the economics of crime and punishment constitute an impressive beginning and a remarkable record of scholarship, but there is much, much more to be learned.

SUGGESTED READINGS

Allen, Francis A., THE DECLINE OF THE REHABILITATIVE IDEAL (1981).

Becker, Gary S., and George Stigler, *Law Enforcement, Malfeasance, and Compensation of Enforcers*, 3 J. LEGAL STUD. 13 (1974).

Friedman, Lee S., *The Use of Multiple Regression Analysis to Test for a Deterrent Effect of Capital Punishment–Prospects and Problems,* CRIMINOLOGY REVIEW YEARBOOK v. 1 (ed. S. Messinger & E. Bittner) (1979).

Heineke, John M., ed., ECONOMIC MODELS OF CRIMINAL BEHAVIOR (1978).

Luksetich, William, and Michael White, CRIME AND PUBLIC POLICY: AN ECONOMIC APPROACH (1982).

Polinsky, A. Mitchell, and Steven Shavell, *The Optimal Tradeoff Between the Probability and Magnitude of Fines*, 69 AM. ECON. REV. 880 (1979).

Polinsky, A. Mitchell, *Private Versus Public Enforcement of Fines*, 9 J. LEGAL STUD. 105 (1980).

Reuter, Peter, DISORGANIZED CRIME: ILLEGAL MARKETS AND THE MAFIA (1983).

Schmidt, Peter, and Ann D. Witte, AN ECONOMIC ANALYSIS OF CRIME AND JUSTICE (1984).

Shavell, Steven, *Criminal Law and the Optimal Use of Nonmonetary Sanctions as a Deterrent*, 85 COL. L. REV. 1232 (1985).

---

[58]By comparison, the homicide rate in Mexico, which has the highest rate in the world, is 17 per 100,000.

Suggested Answers

We believe that answering questions like those sprinkled throughout the text is a very important part of learning law and economics. In the following pages, we have suggested answers to all of the questions posed in the text. We wish to stress the word "suggest." As you may have discovered, some of the questions are immensely complex and require close and lengthy reasoning. Others are relatively straightforward. And still others are so highly speculative that we are not sure what the correct answers might be. We would be highly grateful to those of you who let us know of errors or of different suggestions for answers.

Chapter 2

2.1. Economists generally assume that economic decisionmakers are attempting to maximize something subject to constraints. Thus, consumers are assumed to maximize utility subject to an income constraint, and firms are assumed to maximize profits subject to a production function constraint. Maximization helps to posit the goal or end that the economic decisionmaker seeks. Equilibrium is a state of rest, the condition from which no further endogenous change will occur. The notion of equilibrium helps to specify the point (e.g., the quantity of output produced, the amount of bananas consumed) toward which the maximizing behavior of economic decisionmakers tends.

2.2. Efficiency describes a point of equilibrium with particular characteristics. A *productively efficient* equilibrium describes the condition of a firm or firms in which it is impossible to produce a given level of output at lower cost or, alternatively, to use a given combination of inputs to produce a greater level of output. An *allocatively efficient* equilibrium describes an equilibrium distribution of goods and services among consumers. A particular distribution of goods among consumers is *allocatively efficient* if it is not possible to redistribute the goods so as to make at least one consumer better off without making another consumer worse off.

2.3. In microeconomic theory consumers are assumed to maximize utility subject to an income constraint. The income constraint or budget line is described by the consumer's income and the relative prices of goods and services. The consumer's utility is maximized when she achieves the highest attainable indifference curve. This occurs at the point at which the highest attainable indifference curve is tangent to the budget line, as at point C^* in Figure 2.4. At that point the benefit (i.e., the utility) from spending an additional dollar on any given good is equal for all commodities. That is, at the consumer's constrained maximum the marginal benefit (in terms of the increase in utility) of an additional dollar spent on any good is exactly equal to the marginal cost (i.e., the dollar) of any good.

2.4. a. See Figure A.

   b. The partner who has the children is assumed to have a utility function of $u = cv$, where c equals the weekly child support payment from the other partner and v equals the number of days per week that the children spend with this partner. Initially, $c = 100$ and $v = 4$ days, so that $u = 400$. If the partner paying child support payments wishes to reduce the weekly support payment to $80, then the number of days that the children spend with the other partner must increase to 5 in order for utility to be maintained unchanged at 400.

2.5. Price elasticity of demand measures the responsiveness of consumer's quantity demanded to changes in relative price. Mathematically, price elasticity is defined as the percentage change in the quantity demanded of a commodity divided by the percentage change in the commodity's price. Because quantity demanded and price move in opposite directions (when price declines, quantity demanded increases; when price increases, quantity demanded decreases), the sign of price elasticity will be negative. To avoid having to remember whether -5 is greater or less than -4, economists drop the sign from price elasticity and talk about it as if it were simply a positive number. The ranges of value of price elasticity of demand are inelastic (price elasticity has a value less than 1), unitary elasticity (price elasticity equal to 1), and elastic (price elasticity has a value greater than 1). When price elasticity is greater than 1, the percentage change in quantity demanded is greater than the percentage change in price—e.g., a 10% drop in price gives rise to a 23% increase in quantity demanded.

   There is an interesting relationship between a commodity's price elasticity of demand and total consumer expenditures (price times quantity demanded) on that commodity. When price elasticity of demand is less than one, an increase (decrease) in price will lead to an increase (decrease) in the total amount consumers spend on the commodity. When price elasticity of demand is unitary, consumers will spend the same total amount on the commodity regardless of the price. When price elasticity of demand is greater than one, an increase (decrease) in price will lead to a decrease (increase) in the total amount consumers spend on the commodity.

2.6. Figure B shows the likely supply and demand for heroin in New York City. Notice that the demand curve shown is very steep, which indicates that the price elasticity of demand is less than one. This is assumed to be the demand curve for heroin among heroin addicts, who are not terribly interested in the price of the commodity; whether it is high or low, the quantity they demand is more or less the same. Before the program of suppressing the supply of heroin

Figure A

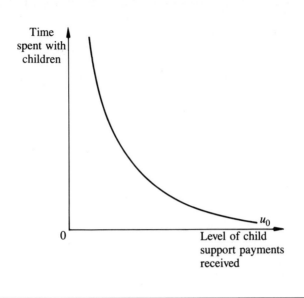

is instituted, the equilibrium price of heroin is P^* and the quantity demanded is H^*. The economic effect of the police commissioner's program is to shift the supply curve up to S'. (That indicates that the cost to heroin suppliers of importing a given amount of heroin has increased.) The new equilibrium price and quantity demanded of heroin are P_1 and H_1. Note that because of the assumed inelasticity of demand, the decline in the quantity demanded, given the increase in price, is small. (That is, because price elasticity is assumed here to be less than 1, the percentage decrease in quantity demanded is smaller— here, *much* smaller—than the percentage increase in price.) Because of the relationship between price elasticity of demand and total consumer expenditures on a commodity, the price increase that follows the police commissioner's crackdown on the suppliers of heroin will cause the total expenditures on heroin by heroin addicts to *increase*. If street crime is the principal or only method by which addicts pay for their habit, then the price increase will cause an *increase* in the amount of street crime, exactly contrary to the result desired or expected by the police commissioner. Notice that if price were reduced from the initial equilibrium of P^* to something like P_2, at the intersection of supply curve S'' and D, the total amount spent by addicts on heroin would fall and so would the amount of street crime.

Our purpose in this question was to suggest a connection between a seemingly arcane microeconomic concept—price elasticity of demand—and an important public policy problem—the connection between heroin addiction and crime. But this is a highly stylized model of the market for heroin. The reality is much more complex. In Chapter 12 we discuss this problem again in much greater depth and with, we think, much more realism.

Figure B

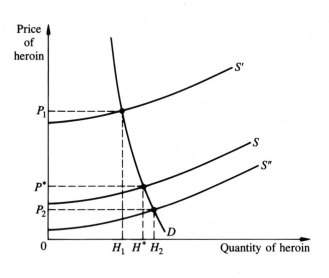

2.7. The expression "There is no such thing as a free lunch" is one of the most famous quotes in all of economics. Its origins are interesting. In order to encourage customers to drink, taverns used to post a sign saying "Free Lunch." The implication was that those who had purchased drink were entitled to eat from the bar's buffet at no extra charge. Clearly the bar expended real resources providing the luncheon buffet, and the explicit and opportunity costs of these resources figure in the bar's determination of the costs of doing business and, therefore, in its calculation of its profits. But what about the bar's customers? Was the lunch really free to them if they purchased a drink? No. The bar must have somehow included a charge for the costs it incurred in putting on the buffet in the prices it charged its customers for drink. The fact that the charge for the buffet is hidden in the price of drink does not make the lunch free.

On many domestic airplane flights, passengers are offered meals at no apparent price. Are these meals "free"?

2.8. Firms are assumed to maximize profits, which are defined as the difference between total costs (including opportunity costs) and total revenues. A firm maximizes profits by choosing that output level for which the marginal cost (the addition to total cost of the last unit of output produced) equals the marginal revenue (the addition to total revenue of the last unit of output produced). (Note that if we call marginal revenue "marginal benefit," then the rule to maximize profits by choosing the output level for which marginal cost equals marginal revenue is exactly equivalent to our general maximization rule of equating marginal cost and marginal benefit.) If the firm finds itself producing an output level for which it is true that marginal revenue exceeds marginal cost, then by producing more output it can add more to total revenue than to total cost and thereby increase its profits. Alternatively, if marginal cost exceeds marginal revenue, the firm should cut back on production: the revenue lost from lower output will be less than the cost savings.

2.9. In a perfectly competitive industry there are a large number of buyers and sellers, so large that no single buyer or seller can influence the market price by his or her individual decisions. Entry and exit of resources into and out of the industry is free. These are the core characteristics of perfect competition about which there is general agreement. There are several other conditions about which there is less widespread agreement, e.g., that all buyers and sellers have perfect and complete information and that products are homogeneous. It is often said that the stock market and the market for agricultural commodities (such as wheat) are examples of perfectly competitive industries.

Monopoly occurs when there is only one seller. (For more on monopoly see the suggested answer to the following question.) By comparison to a perfectly competitive industry, a monopolist produces too little and charges too much. (See Figure 2.9.)

Oligopoly holds where there are only a few sellers, so few that they recognize the interdependence of their decisions. That is, what is optimal for firm A to produce or to charge for its output depends not just on market price, marginal revenue, and the firm's own costs but on what firms B and C produce and charge. This interdependence gives rise to strategic considerations that are best analyzed through the use of game theory and such notions as a Nash equilibrium. The television programming market may be an example of an oligopolistic market.

An imperfectly competitive industry shares some of the aspects of perfectly competitive and monopolized industries. As in perfect competition, there are a large number of sellers, although the number is not as large as in perfect competition. Entry and exit are free. As in monopoly, each seller has some *limited* market control over the consumers of his output. Sellers distinguish their product by brand name, quality, and other characteristics. The market for breakfast cereals is probably imperfectly competitive.

2.10. A monopoly occurs when there is only one seller. There are technological conditions, known as "natural monopoly," that can give rise to monopoly. There are also social welfare conditions that may make a case for the government's granting a monopoly—as with the patent, copyright, and trademark systems (see Chapter 5).

A monopoly can be sustained only if other resources are prevented from flowing into the industry to set up competitive firms. This might happen when a monopolist gains control of the only input that can be used to produce a particular output. Far more common are cases in which the government permits the monopoly to endure by forbidding lawful entry into the industry. Where entry is not so restricted, it will eventually occur, leading to the demise of the monopoly.

A special kind of monopoly is a cartel, which is collusion among otherwise competitive firms that seek to operate as a joint profit-maximizing monopoly. An example is the Organization of Petroleum Exporting Countries (OPEC). OPEC illustrates very well the difficulties that monopolies have in forestalling entry. The more successful the monopoly initially is in raising the price above the competitive level, the greater the incentive to others to enter the industry.

The entry into the petroleum-extracting industry after OPEC's success in raising the price of oil to nearly $33 per barrel was phenomenal, so much so that the OPEC countries now account for less than half of world petroleum output.

2.11. We discussed the adverse effects of a price ceiling with respect to rent control. The price ceiling is set below the equilibrium price so that there is an excess demand for the price-controlled product. Suppliers can make more money supplying unregulated goods and services and so transfer their efforts and resources elsewhere. Those suppliers that remain attempt to keep their profit rates at normal levels by letting the quality of their product (and therefore its costs of production) decline and by insisting on secret payments from consumers over and above the controlled price. Consumers of the controlled product may also alter their behavior in inefficient ways: they may, for example, inefficiently substitute other goods and services for those whose price is controlled.

2.12. General equilibrium is the condition in which all markets are in simultaneous equilibrium. The conditions under which this will happen are that all markets are perfectly competitive and that there are no sources of market failure. (See the answer to the next question.) Given the resources available to the economy, it is not possible for the economy to be productively or allocatively more efficient than it is in general equilibrium. (As we argue in the text, distribution is another matter.)

2.13. Market failure can arise from four sources. The first is non-competitive market structures, such as monopoly (the condition of one seller) and monopsony (the condition of one buyer). We have already examined the reasons why monopoly leads to sub-optimal results. In general, policies of regulation (in the case of natural monopoly) and of antitrust enforcement (in the case of collusion and artificially sustained monopoly) will help to correct for the social costs of monopoly.

The second is external effects, costs and benefits involuntarily imposed on others. In the case of external costs, such as water pollution that results from a firm's discharge of waste chemicals into a nearby stream, the externality-generator does not take into account the costs he has involuntarily imposed on others. As a result, his output costs him less to produce than it should in terms of the social resources his production *really* uses. So, someone who is generating external costs produces too much. To correct for these social costs, he must be induced to "internalize" these external costs, in which case he will reduce his output to the socially optimal level. Policies of taxation and subsidization, of exposure to legal liability, and of prior regulation can help to minimize the social costs of externalities. (We discuss how property law—in Chapters 4 and 5—and tort law—in Chapters 8 and 9—can help in this internalization.)

The third source of market failure is the presence of public goods. These are goods for which the cost of excluding non-paying consumers are so high that no private profit-maximizing firm can earn enough to justify producing the socially optimal amount of the public good. The market fails in respect to public goods in that it produces too little of them. A policy of subsidization of private producers or of public provision of the public good can correct for this failure.

The fourth source of market failure is extreme informational asymmetries. Because of the special characteristics of information, where access to information is highly skewed or where the ability to process information is highly unequal, questions arise about the optimality of otherwise voluntary transactions.

We discuss how contract law—in Chapters 6 and 7—and tort law—in Chapters 8 and 9—can help to correct for problems arising because of informational asymmetries.

2.14. Which of the following will be optimally provided by private profit-maximizing firms and which are public goods?

a. A swimming pool large enough to accommodate hundreds of people. This good does not seem to have either of the characteristics of a public good— non-rivalrous consumption or costliness of excluding non-paying consumers. A fence and charging an entrance fee through a central entrance dispose of the costliness issue. The amount of the pool that one person can consume does depend on the amount that others consume. The swimming pool does not seem to be a public good, and it therefore follows that a private profit-maximizing firm could provide the optimal pool.

b. A fireworks display is clearly a public good. Consumption is non-rivalrous in the sense that one person's enjoyment does not diminish the amount available for another to enjoy. And it is costly to exclude non-paying consumers; they may, after all, simply stand on a hill away from the display and enjoy it without charge. For those reasons it is not surprising that it is municipalities, not private firms, that provide fireworks displays on the 4th of July and that they are generally financed from general tax revenues, not from a user fee.

c. A heart transplant is a private good. Nonetheless, many will shy away from the conclusion that this particular private good should be allocated according to the usual rules prevailing in the market for private goods. For an interesting discussion of this issue, see P. Bobbitt & G. Calabresi, TRAGIC CHOICES.

d. Vaccination against a highly contagious disease is a private good but one that has such strong external benefits that the market will provide sub-optimal amounts of it. Thus, either public provision of vaccination or public subsidization of private provision is called for.

e. A wilderness area could conceivably be a private good. But today wilderness areas and national parks are federally owned and operated, presumably on the theory that these areas should be held in trust for future generations and that private owners would not do that. But there are a few examples of private ownership of natural resources that *do* work. A private organization called the Nature Conservancy attempts to preserve bird sanctuaries, wilderness areas, and other significant natural resources by using the contributions of its members to purchase and hold these areas.

f., g., and h. All three examples of education given here are largely private goods with trace elements of public goods (e.g., in the sense that they contribute to societal well-being by giving those trained a sense of worth and a set of skills). There is general agreement that elementary education has such strong external benefits (in that all citizens are better off when their fellow citizens can read and write and compute) that it should be subsidized or publicly provided.

2.15. *Pareto efficiency* (or *Pareto optimality*) describes a situation of equilibrium from which it is impossible, given the economy's resources, to produce more of one commodity without producing less of another or to make one person better off without making another worse off. Although Pareto efficiency is to be desired, we saw that it does not define a unique distribution of resources among the members of society. The set of Pareto efficient distributions that results from voluntary exchange depends crucially on the initial distribution of resources among the members of the society. Different initial distributions lead to different Pareto optimal outcomes.

A2.1. Let us suggest an answer by reference to an imaginary example. Suppose that drivers of group A are much more likely to be involved in automobile accidents than are members of group B. In general, and assuming that it is relatively inexpensive to distinguish between members of the different groups, insurers would charge a lower premium to members of group B than to members of group A for an insurance policy protecting them against a certain amount of loss from an auto accident. But suppose that the legislature or the courts make it illegal for insurers to charge different premiums to the members of these two groups. What are the consequences?

If the insurer raises the single premium to the level that the risks created by those in group A justifies, then those in group B may substitute self-insurance for market insurance. On the other hand, if the insurer lowers the premium to that justified by the lower-risk group B, the insurance will seem like a bargain to members of the higher-risk group A so that their purchases of insurance will increase significantly. In that case, the insurer's losses from having to pay insurance claims are likely to rise and his profits to fall. Finally, if the insurer attempts to set the premium by splitting the difference between the high premium for the higher-risk group and a low premium for the lower-risk group, the problems of the more extreme solutions are mitigated but not erased. Those with higher risks are more likely to purchase his product, while those with lower risks are more likely to substitute away from market insurance. Things grow more complicated when we allow for the possibility that in addition to altering the single premium, the insurer may attempt to increase the co-payment or deductible provision of his policies on the grounds that members of group B will be more likely to accept that condition than will members of group A.

A2.2. If restrictions on land use become *less* likely, then the potential purchaser's probability estimate on the value of the land moves from point B along TS in Figure A2.4 to a point closer to S. As a result, the expected value of the property increases above I_0. Thus, the maximum amount that the individual is willing to pay for the parcel increases over what it was when his probability estimate on land use restrictions was at B.

A2.3. If the premium on an insurance policy to indemnify the holder against loss in property value is slightly less than ($\$25,000 - I_0$), then the risk-averse person shown in Figure A2.4 would certainly purchase the insurance. His or her certain income after the payment of the premium will give them greater utility than the uncertain prospect of an income of I_0. Thus insured, one would expect the individual to be willing to pay more for the parcel than if the insurance premium were as high as ($\$25,000 - I_1$) or if no insurance were available.

The answer to the final questions depends on the price that the purchaser must pay for the parcel after the insurance is purchased. Clearly, the purchaser will not give up more for the package of insurance and the parcel than when he offered less than I_1. So long as the total amount the purchaser gives up is less than that amount, he or she is better off than when insurance was not available. It follows then that the purchaser cannot be made worse off by the availability of the insurance and may well be made better off.

Chapter 3

3.1. a. Statutes are issued by legislative bodies, usually elected by the citizens of the jurisdiction; a constitution is the work of a constitutional convention, usually a body elected especially for the purpose of drafting the constitution; administrative agency regulations are promulgated by administrative agencies, which are bodies created by the legislature with appointees named by the executive branch, subject to the approval of the legislature; and the holdings of courts we have examined in some depth.

b. Statutes may be legitimately changed by the legislature; sometimes the actions of the legislature are held by the courts to be unconstitutional, i.e., unlawful because they conflict with the constitution of the jurisdiction. In those cases, the legislature must correct the conflict. Constitutions can be amended by the people by a special process outlined in the constitution; usually such fundamental changes in the law require special majorities (typically two-thirds) to be passed. Administrative agency regulations may be changed by subsequent action of the administrative agency and by the legislature; the courts are sometimes asked to adjudicate the interpretation or legitimacy of an administrative agency regulation. As we have seen, the holdings of courts may be changed by higher level appellate courts or by the later holdings of courts.

c. Uniformity and stability for each of the forms of law is the result of fundamental rules laid out in the constitution, in various statutes, and by the political process. We have already examined how the common law system seeks to achieve uniformity and stability through the doctrine of *stare decisis* and the hierarchical relationships among courts. Stability and uniformity in the constitution is aided by the difficulty of legitimately changing it and by the Supreme Court's reluctance to change its interpretation of the Constitution on short notice. Legislatures may alter statutory law almost at will; however, legislatures are reluctant to do that for the sound reason that stability and uniformity are valuable. Presumably the legislature will change the law quickly only when it determines the benefit from doing so to be greater than the cost, which includes, among other things, the heightened uncertainty among the citizenry about the stability and uniformity of the legislature's actions.

d. The complicated system of checks and balances among the legislative, executive, and judicial branches is one of the greatest guarantors of uniformity among the forms of law. As noted above, courts may determine that statutes and administrative agency regulations are in conflict with the fundamental rules laid out in the constitution.

Chapter 4

4.1. Our argument is that the rules of property are a means of giving people liberty over things, not only material things such as land and furniture but also immaterial things such as ideas, as we will see later in this and the following chapter. Religious liberty is the liberty to believe as one likes about spiritual matters, so long as those beliefs do not harm others. Thus, religious liberty is very much like liberty over ideas, a liberty that property law protects, too. Material property may be unequally distributed for a variety of reasons; by contrast, everyone has religious liberty, that is, the freedom to believe as he or she likes. This more equal distribution of religious liberty is due to the fact that every human being has a mind whereas not everyone has material property.

4.2.   After receiving the bid from Clair, Adam values the car at $3,200, which is the opportunity cost of selling it to Blair. (Recall that opportunity cost is defined as the value of the next best use, which is, in this case, selling the car to Clair.) Adam's threat value *vis-a-vis* Blair is now $3,200. The surplus from cooperating with Blair falls to $800. A reasonable solution is for Blair to buy the car for $3,600, leaving Adam with $3,600 and no car and Blair with a car worth $4,000 to her and $1,400 in cash.

4.3.   a.   Arthur's threat value is his expected net gain from trial. Because the value of the kettle is $300, because he has a 50% probability of winning, and because the trial will cost him $50, the expected net value of a trial is $300(0.5) − $50 = $100.

   b.   Betty's threat value is her expected loss from trial. Because the value of the kettle is $300, because she has a 50% probability of losing, and because the trial will cost her $50, the value to her of a trial is −$300(0.5) − $50 = −$150 − $50 = −$200.

   c.   The cost to Arthur and Betty of cooperatively resolving their dispute without trial is $0 because the transaction costs of settling are, by assumption, zero.

   d.   The surplus from cooperating (i.e., from settling the dispute rather than litigating) is $100, which is the sum of the two parties' costs of litigating.

   e.   A reasonable settlement would be for Betty to pay Arthur $150. Thus, Arthur gets his threat value ($100) plus half the surplus ($50). And so does Betty: −$200 (her threat value) + $50 (the saving in litigation costs) = −$150.

   f.:   1.   Assuming that the cost of litigating is still $50, Arthur's net expected gain from litigating is $300(2/3) − $50 = $150.

      2.   Betty believes that the probability of her losing the case and having to pay for the kettle is 1/3. Her probability of winning the case and *not* having to pay for the kettle is 2/3. Thus, Betty's threat value is (−$300)1/3 − $50 = −$150.

      3.   Now the *actual* cooperative surplus from settling rather than litigating is still $100. But because of their optimism, the parties both anticipate doing better from litigating than from cooperating. If the actual cooperative surplus is $100 and each party anticipates a reasonable split of that surplus, then Arthur anticipates receiving $200 from cooperating with Betty in settling the dispute: $150 (his threat value) + $50 (his share of the cooperative surplus) = $200. Betty expects to lose $150 from going to trial; with her share of the cooperative surplus, she would be willing to offer Arthur $100 to settle: −$150 (her threat value) plus $50 (her share of the cooperative surplus) = −$100. What Arthur expects from cooperation ($200) is much greater than what Betty is prepared to offer for cooperating ($100). Thus, neither party prefers cooperating to litigation. The *putative* cooperative surplus is 0.

      4.   Neither party anticipates a surplus from cooperating because each party is optimistic about winning the trial.

4.4.   You will recall at the beginning of our section on suggested answers that we said that there are some questions in the book to which we don't know the answers. This is one of them. There is no correct answer to this question, but a great deal can be learned from discussing and comparing your ideas with those of your colleagues about just distribution and threats *versus* the marginal productivity theory as a method of distributing income and wealth.

4.5. If everyone has free access to a beach, there is a real danger that there will be very little discretion in the use of this resource. The result may be that there are too many people, too many cars, and too many conflicting activities (such as fishing and swimming or free access and the building of beach homes). A rationing device is called for to minimize these and other problems. One such rationing device is assigning private property rights to the beach; another is governmental ownership of the beach but establishing rules of use of the beach and charging a user fee to those who make use of the beach.

4.6. We assume that the invention allows the inventor to accurately predict the weather during the growing season. He determines that the weather will be beautiful and concludes that there will be a bountiful crop at harvest time. He further knows that a large crop means a large supply, that is, that the supply curve of the crop shifts to the right. This will cause the market price of the crop to fall after the harvest. Knowing this, the inventor may enter into contracts to sell quantities of the crop at a price slightly below that expected by others. (His invention is what gives him alone accurate information about the post-harvest price.) When delivery time comes, the inventor will be able to purchase the crop on the spot market at the depressed price and deliver it to his customers for the higher price agreed upon earlier. The difference between what the inventor paid for the crop in the spot market and the price he receives from his promises to sell at the higher price contribute to his profit on the invention.

Chapter 5

5.1. and 5.2. Post, the plaintiff, has sued Pierson, the defendant, for interfering with his property. Post had been chasing a fox, apparently as part of the sport of fox-hunting (or "riding to hounds") when Pierson intervened and killed and carried off the fox. The lower court found for Post, and Pierson appealed. The highest court in New York State reversed that judgment. But its reasons for doing so are not clearly spelled out. The clearest statement we get of the policy issues involved in the decision is in Justice Livingston's minority opinion. So we must infer the majority's position from the statement in the dissent. The issue is how to establish a property right to a wild animal: must the pursuer have actual possession—"manucaption"—of the animal (the majority's view), or is it enough simply to exhibit the intent to catch or kill the animal by chasing it (Justice Livingston's view)? One way to resolve the issue is to ask if some legitimate social goal is more efficiently advanced by one rule rather than another. There are really two closely related legitimate social goals suggested in the opinions here. The first is to minimize the considerable damage done to crops and barnyards by foxes by increasing the incentives of hunters to pursue foxes. The second is to maximize the enjoyment of those who are riding to hounds. (Today, depredations to farms by foxes and the sport of fox hunting are not closely related, but in 1805 they were.)

   Justice Livingston argues that the rule of giving the ownership claim to those originally pursuing a fox will create a heightened incentive for the killing of foxes. He says that under the majority's alternative rule of manucaption, a pursuer of these "wild and noxious beasts" could pursue a fox all day only to see another person rightfully take the fox and that that result could lessen the incentive to hunt foxes. But this distinction between the rules isn't entirely correct. The majority's rule might lessen the fun of riding to hounds, but it does not necessarily lessen the incentive to kill foxes in less sporting ways. In fact, the rules seem equally efficient at contributing to the objective of killing foxes in order to reduce the damage they do to farms. The choice between the rules must be made on other grounds. What may be said in favor of the majority view is that the actual possession rule is clearer, less subject to misinterpretation, and easier to enforce than the intent rule.

5.3.   We argued in the previous chapter that the choice of remedy was in large part a matter of the level of bargaining costs: where those costs are low, an injunction is preferable; when those costs are high, an award of money damages is preferable. As between the owners of copyrighted audiovisual material and the owners of VCRs, those bargaining costs would seem to be high. This argues for an award of money damages. However, determining the appropriate level of damages in this case is difficult. Consider further that it might be most efficient to maintain the appropriate incentive to produce audiovisual material and protect the rights of current copyright holders by imposing a tax on the sale of VCRs or on videotape. (How would you decide whether to tax the machines or the tape?) Establishing the optimal tax level and transferring the proceeds to the copyright holders may well be easier than determining the optimal level of money damages.

The issues raised in this question are very complex. We urge you to consult the articles by Professors Sinclair and Gordon for more complete treatment.

5.4.   One way to approach this question is to ask if the priorities established by statute in the mechanics' lien laws mirror the priorities that would be established in voluntary agreements betweeen a property owner and someone who worked on the property. In essence, the mechanics' lien laws give the worker the property as collateral for the loan to the property owner of the value of the worker's services and materials. If the owner does not pay the debt, the worker may take possession of and sell the property to discharge the debt. Like restrictive covenants discussed later in this chapter, the lien is attached to the property, not to the particular owner who incurred the debt. Thus, if the worker is not paid but does not take possession from the current owner, he may do so from a subsequent owner.

Would a property owner and a worker voluntarily enter into such an agreement? They would if both are thereby made better off. The owner who fully intends to pay may give her home as collateral as a signal of her intention to pay, thus reducing the worker's risk of non-payment. In exchange for this promise of the property as collateral and the consequent lower risk, the worker may offer a lower price for his services.

What about subsequent owners? They may be protected against the burden of the mechanics' lien by investigating the chain of title at the time of purchase. (To be enforceable a mechanic's lien must be recorded.)

5.5.   The rule of distinguishing cardholder liability in the case of loan to another and non-liability above a $50 ceiling in the case of reported theft or loss creates efficient incentives for all parties involved. The co-payment of $50 by the cardholder in the event of theft or loss removes much of the moral hazard problem that cardholders would have if they were not liable: they would have a reduced incentive to take care of their cards or to report their loss. (See the Appendix to Chapter 2 for a definition of moral hazard and an explanation of how co-payment may minimize moral hazard.) The bank and the merchant accepting the card have incentives to check on the identity of the card user because of their liability if the card has been reported lost or stolen. The text argues that non-liability of the bank for expenses incurred when the card is loaned also creates efficient incentives for the card issuer, the cardholder, the merchant, and the card borrower.

When the rules of liability for card charges create efficient incentives, lower costs result. If the market for credit cards is perfectly competitive, the lower costs are passed along entirely to consumers in the form of lower prices (e.g., lower annual fees and lower interest rates). If competition is less than perfect, the lower costs are shared between the card issuer, merchants, and consumers.

5.6.   There are various social goals at issue with regard to property lost or abandoned at sea. The rightful owners have an interest in recovering their property; society has interests in keeping the chain of title unbroken, in keeping shipping lanes clear, and in minimizing debris that floats onto beaches. Salvors are typically awarded their expenses plus a fraction of the value of property they recover. This is true whether the salvor explicitly contracted with the rightful owner or came across it by chance. A rule of granting complete ownership to a salvor without requiring an effort to identify the rightful owner would create the sort of moral hazard problems and title controversies that the text said the law of lost property seeks to avoid. (Notice that these problems may not arise if the rule is that the abandoned property belongs to the state.) The rule of granting the salvor an award of his expenses plus a fraction of the value of the recovered property creates an incentive for chance salvors, as well as professional salvors, to search for lost property at sea and to return it to its rightful owners. (See the discussion of whether and how to enforce a contract between a rescuer and the person rescued in Chapter 7.)

5.7.   This is one of those questions that puts your skills of persuasion to a theoretical test. If you think you've come to grips with the issues of this case, attempt to explain it to someone. (An adage that guides the training of doctors in the complexities of medical procedures is "Watch one, do one, teach one." That seems equally appropriate for the study of law and economics.)

5.8.   Yes. Notice that if damages were temporary, there would be no problem: damages are compensation for a fixed amount of harm over a given time period; the damages rise if the harm is greater in a subsequent time period. But are permanent damages amenable to this adjustment? Certainly. They may be considered as the present discounted value of the amount necessary to compensate the neighbors for a given level of harms for a specified number of future time periods. If the level of harm rises or if the number of future periods during which harm is inflicted rises, the permanent damages previously awarded become under-compensatory. The neighbors should have a new cause of action to have the level of permanent damages increased.

5.9.   We have stressed in this and the previous chapter how the appropriate rules of property rights and remedies can create incentives for the efficient use and protection of property. This question invites you to extend the analysis so as to compare the incentive effects of rules arising from civil litigation with those arising from prior regulation by, say, administrative agency. Consider the matter in relation to *Boomer*. We have explored the ability of this decision to deter the Atlantic Cement Company and other nuisance creators in the future. But suppose that the bothersome emission of noise, smoke, and vibration is regulated by the United States Environmental Protection Agency. The USEPA establishes maximum permissible levels of these emissions and a schedule of penalties for violations. Clearly both the *ex post* and *ex ante* methods can deter. Are they equally effective? Is one less costly to administer? Are these methods of minimizing external effects complements or substitutes?

This is a question about a topic that is at the edge of scholarly interest. No definitive answers are in yet on these questions, but there has been some suggestive speculation. For instance, it is probably true that *ex post* and *ex ante* regulation are perfect substitutes only when all decisionmakers have perfect and complete information. In those circumstances, the externality should be regulated by whichever method is cheaper to administer or more politically palatable. A further implication is that only when there is uncertainty about some important aspect of an externality is one method (or *joint* use of these methods) clearly superior from an efficiency standpoint. For example, suppose that the long-term adverse consequences of exposure to cement dust are thought to be dire but that the scientific evidence is not sufficiently certain to hold someone like the Atlantic Cement Company liable. If the courts cannot act, should the EPA attempt to limit the emission of cement dust until fuller scientific evidence is available? Suppose later that evidence is developed that cement dust is carcinogenic but that the cancer appears, if at all, only 20 years after exposure. The long lapse of time between exposure and harm may mean that evidence suitable for establishing liability may be very difficult to develop. If so, *ex post* regulation may not create sufficiently strong incentives to limit the emission of cement dust. In that case, *ex ante* regulation of the dust emissions by the EPA may be more efficient. (We will discuss some other aspects of uncertainty and the law and of *ex post/ex ante* regulation in the first half of Chapter 9.)

5.10. a. Suppose that someone claims that he has suffered harm because of an externality. It turns out that he knew or should have known that the externality existed. The law may deny recovery on the grounds that the plaintiff "came to the nuisance." In economic terms, one might argue that when one knows or should have known that an externality exists and approaches it, then one has or should have internalized the supposed harm. Someone who moves next door to a stockyard can hardly claim to be unfairly surprised by the existence of the stench and flies. These inconveniences were or should have been taken into account when the person moved in beside the stockyard rather than moving elsewhere.

b. One piece of evidence that there is no externality or, more correctly, that the harm has already been internalized, would be a showing that the land Webb purchased was cheaper precisely because of its proximity to the stockyard. If this is so, then does it not follow that if the land was *not* cheaper then the externality has not been internalized? No. Even if Webb paid too much for the land, the relevant fact is whether there was sufficient information and competition so that the price of the land could have accurately reflected its disamenities. The actual price paid is not conclusive evidence (unless, of course, it indicates that the proximity of the stockyard was a disamenity that caused the price to be lower).

c. The effect of the holding here is really the same whether the defendant is
    excused because the plaintiff came to the nuisance or (as, in fact, the court
    held) the plaintiff wins but must pay for the defendant's relocation costs.
d. Given this rough equivalence of the holdings, it is unlikely that the behav-
    ior of other nuisance creators in Arizona would have been different if the
    defendant had been excused. As a matter of purity of style, excusing the
    defendant would have been a "cleaner" outcome. (In its opinion the
    Supreme Court of Arizona dismisses the coming-to-the-nuisance argument
    on the grounds that the stench and flies from the stockyard constitute a
    public nuisance, that is, a threat to the general health and welfare. While
    this may be true, it seems to be an argument for statutory regulation of
    stockyard location, not a persuasive argument for avoiding the coming-to-
    the-nuisance argument in this civil case.)
e. A cooperative solution between Spur and Webb was likely because the bar-
    gaining costs between them seem to have been low. This point is crucial to
    the contention above that the court's decision and the alternative of excus-
    ing the defendant are roughly equivalent. Recall that the Normative Coase
    Theorem suggests the efficiency of a case is invariant to the assignment of a
    right when bargaining costs are trivial. If the court had excused the defen-
    dant but there was a cooperative surplus between Spur and Webb (in the
    sense that the value to Webb of the nearby land without the stockyards
    exceeded the value to Spur of continuing in business where it was), then the
    two of them may well have bargained to a splitting of that cooperative sur-
    plus. And it is possible that the bargain would have involved Webb's pay-
    ing for Spur to move further out in the country, which is precisely what the
    court ordered and what Spur in fact did.

    The bargaining costs between Spur and the residents would possibly
    have been very high because there would have been so many parties
    involved. This fact changes our indifference about how the court decides
    the case. If the residents are the plaintiffs, then the court should excuse the
    defendant on the grounds that the plaintiffs came to the nuisance for the
    reasons we mentioned above. The residents, if they believe the nuisance not
    to have been internalized, may wish to proceed against Webb for relief.
    Perhaps Webb made fraudulent representations about the amenities of the
    land to the purchasers, many of whom were persons seeking to retire to
    Arizona from distant places. For these purchasers it would have been very
    difficult to examine the premises before buying. Alternatively, the residents
    may wish to make a change through the ballot, e.g., by changing the land
    use ordinances of their locale so as to make Spur unwelcome.
f. Because of the new information, the residents have a cause of action
    against Spur but not against Del Webb. There is nothing that Webb could
    have done to foresee this harm. And because the information is new, there
    was no opportunity for land values to alter to reflect the increased risk of
    cancer because of proximity to the feedlot. The flies and stench have
    become, because of the change in knowledge, an externality. How should
    the externality be internalized? Because bargaining costs between Spur and
    the residents are high, there is small likelihood of a cooperative solution.
    Instead, the court must determine the amount of damage that the defen-
    dant has inflicted and assess a judgment against Spur for that amount. The
    implication is that here as in *Boomer* if Spur remains in its current location,

the residents may bring a new action for a similar amount of money in the future. If it is cheaper for Spur to pay the damages than to incur the costs of relocation, it will remain and the harm will have been internalized. However, it is possible that Spur will make the initial payment and decide to avoid future liability by moving where its activities inflict minimal harm on others. (Spur moved its feedlot to an Indian reservation where the population density was low and its net income would be lightly taxed.)

5.11. The problems that are likely to arise because of interference with the fundamental liberty of the individual are immense. The quasi-utilitarian calculation that society would be better off if the talented pianist made music rather than fixed cars ignores the value to this individual of his personal autonomy and the value to others of seeing individuals being allowed to pursue their own goals. The practical enforcement problems of compelling individuals to do things that they don't want to do are also immense, especially when the compulsion involves such intimate things as personal talent.

A less coercive alternative to defining communal rights to an individual's talents is for society to subsidize the individual in order to induce him or her to pursue the life that gives society greater pleasure. Thus, one might argue on these grounds in favor of subsidizing the income of all musicians: without the subsidy many of the musicians would take up less socially pleasing but more individually rewarding lives.

For a superb discussion of the philosophical issues raised by this question, see the piece by Professor Kronman.

5.12. The question has been phrased so that there is no doubt of the legitimacy of the government's taking: it is truly for a public purpose—the provision of a public good. What is at issue here is the computation of "just compensation." The situation in which a monopolist (one seller) faces a monopsonist (one buyer) is known as a "bilateral monopoly." In the absence of governmental intervention, the price and quantity at which an exchange takes place in a bilateral monopoly are indeterminate. In our example of the governmental purchase of a parcel of land for use as a satellite tracking station, there is no controversy about the quantity of land to be purchased. The dispute is about the price. The monopolist landowner hopes to maximize his profits by charging a price that is consistent with marginal cost being equal to marginal revenue. In Figure C that is the price P_1. The monopsonist (the government) wishes to pay as little for this parcel as possible. That is the price P_2 in the figure. (*MFC* stands for marginal factor cost and is the analog for a monopsonist of the monopolist's marginal revenue curve; the *MFC* curve tells the single buyer of the input by how much his total payments for all units of the input will rise if he purchases one more unit.) (For the sake of reference a roughly competitive price, P_c, is also shown.) If there were bargaining between the government and the parcel owner, the price would be somewhere between P_1 and P_2 depending on the relative bargaining skills of the parties. If there were no constraint on the government, then it is likely that the price paid for the parcel would be close to P_2. But the existence of the just compensation requirement for compulsory sales to the government should compel the government to take the parcel at a price closer to P_c than to P_2.

5.13. a. Recall that a public good is a commodity or service that has two closely-related characteristics: consumption of the good by one person does not diminish the amount available for consumption by others, and the high

Figure C

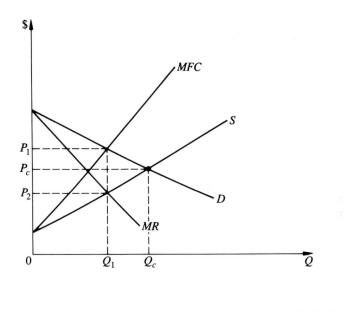

cost to private providers of excluding non-paying beneficiaries of the good or service. The jobs to be provided by the expansion of the General Motors plant do not fit either of these criteria. Employment is a private good. Worse still, this isn't even a very skillful bargain by the government: as the dissent notes, General Motors has given no assurances to the state that it will preserve a certain number of jobs.

b. Presumably the residents of this area derive a large subjective value from being part of this ethnic neighborhood. It is unlikely that this value is so widely held that a determination of the market value of the homes in this area would reflect this subjective value. As a result, just compensation at fair market value will almost certainly undercompensate the people in Poletown.

c. Instead of taking private property to induce GM to remain in Detroit, the City of Detroit (and State of Michigan) might have given GM a tax holiday (the right not to pay corporation and other taxes for a specific period of time); or it might have directly subsidized GM's acquisition of private property from general tax revenues. Neither of these alternatives is open to the sort of objections that can be raised against the taking of land in Poletown.

5.14. a. The rule proposed by Holmes to distinguish a non-compensable from a compensable regulation is roughly that if a regulation diminishes the value of private property by a small amount, it does not amount to a taking but that if the regulation diminishes the value of the property by a large amount, then the regulation amounts to a taking. In his words, "The general rule at least is, that while property may be regulated to a certain extent, if regulation goes too far it will be recognized as a taking ... As we already said, this is a question of degree—and therefore cannot be disposed of by general propositions." There is no hard and fast rule for determining by what percentage the property value must decline in order for the regulation to become a taking. And as the question suggests, there probably can be no solution to this ambiguity. Not knowing the threshold, governments are likely to push the effect of regulations further and further while risk-averse individuals are likely to be extraordinarily cautious about investments whose value might decline precipitously because of governmental regulation without hope of compensation. On the other hand, the mere act of specifying a threshold might induce a different set of inefficiencies by government and individuals. Both of these problems would be minimized if the option plan proposed in the previous section were adopted.

b. The crucial concept in determining the reduction in value is "opportunity cost." That is, the difference between the property's current value and its value in its next best use is the appropriate measure of diminution in value because of governmental regulation. The power company would like to exaggerate the diminution in value because of the regulation forbidding nuclear power plant construction near an earthquake fault; thus, it might contend that the regulation diminishes the value of the parcel from its value as a nuclear power plant to zero. But the regulation does not forbid alternative uses of the property. If the land could safely be used, for example, as a housing site, then the diminution in value is the value to the power company of the land as a nuclear power plant site minus its value as the site for a housing development.

c. Clearly, yes. Suppose that instead of regulating the property and thereby diminishing its value (with uncertainty as to whether the diminution is large enough to constitute a taking) the government purchases the right to restrict the use of the owner's property for a specified number of years. The maximum price that the government would have to pay is, of course, the difference between the property's value in unrestricted uses and its value when restricted. But because this is an option, the price that the government would have to pay the private property owner would reflect the parties' estimates of the probability of regulation, of the diminution in value, and other factors. This scheme should be appealing to government if it is cheaper than the demoralization and litigation costs of uncompensated regulatory takings; it would be appealing to individual property owners if it reduces the risk of uncompensated takings.

Chapter 6

6.1. a. Consideration served as an outward signal that deliberation had taken place by both parties. The common law courts did not usually concern themselves with whether the deliberation had been done skillfully or stupidly (unless, of course, there was fraud or coercion). Because the classical theory perceived contract as a *subjective* meeting of the minds, there was no attempt to determine the *objective* worth of the consideration.

b. She might have agreed for any number of plausible reasons. For example, she might have been willing to pay the extraordinary premium for U.S. dollars in the implicit understanding that the transaction was to be kept secret.

c. If she could have easily learned the true 1942 exchange rate between dollars and drachmae but did not, then the contract should be enforced. If it was impossible for her to have had that knowledge or if Batsakis lied to her about the true value, then the enforceability of the contract is open to question.

d. If Batsakis was a monopolist, this would explain (at least in part) the extraordinarily high price Demotsis paid. The court might consider enforcing the contract but at a lower, more nearly competitive price. (We will discuss this possible remedy in Chapter 7 when we explain the modern doctrine of unconscionability.)

 It is not likely that Batsakis was a monopolist. Entry into the business of lending is easy. Nonetheless, it is possible that Batsakis *was* a monopolist. Perhaps, for example, the government had banned most foreign exchange transactions, and Batsakis was the only licensed currency exchanger or the only unlicensed exchanger willing to assume the risk of illegally lending dollars to individuals.

e. The borrower's expectations or ability to repay are not relevant to the rule-creation aspect of his or her decision. One could go farther and say that if the court were to consider these matters, and depending on what the court said, it could have a deleterious effect on the behavior of future contracting parties. For example, if the court were to excuse Demotsis because she is unable to repay Batsakis, this might induce future borrowers to enter into contracts they knowingly could not repay.

f. As in the last question, a decision to enforce the contract but at a price of $750 could have an injurious effect on future contractual exchanges in Texas. If lenders and borrowers could have their mutual promises re-written in this fashion, then terms to which they agreed would be less secure. In short, for lenders there would be more risk, and they would probably begin to charge higher rates to borrowers. (Of course, it is possible that the court could justify its revision of the contract terms on the grounds of Batsakis' monopoly, fraud, coercion, or the like. If so, then enforcing the contract but at $750 could *increase* the efficiency of future contractual exchanges.)

g. If future contracting parties are aware that a court will *not* evaluate the objective value of consideration but only its existence, they each will be more certain that the consideration and the terms of the contract are adequate according to their own subjective evaluation.

6.2. a. Consideration is one of the most important elements in differentiating serious from frivolous promises: a promise supported by consideration is generally assumed to have been made seriously. But there are other conceivable indicators of seriousness and deliberation, e.g., making a promise in public (as in *Hamer*) or in writing.

b. The standard argument is that relations within the family ought to be outside the common law of contracts and torts. One reason is that the continuing and intimate nature of the relationship within the family makes informal solutions to contract-like and tortious problems better than the formal letter of the common law. Thus, a promise by a father to purchase a sports car for his daughter if she gets straight A's is not generally enforceable. Also, in tort law spouses are protected by the doctrine of interspousal tort immunity from a tort action for harm suffered at the hands of their partner. (In some states battered wives or husbands are now allowed to bring tort actions against their spouses.)

c. The reliance must be detrimental to the promisee and reasonable. If there was no reasonableness constraint and if evidence of detrimental reliance was sufficient to get a contract enforced, promisees might lock promisors into performing a contract by instantaneously incurring any sort of debt as evidence of reliance on the performance.

d. It is sometimes said that the uncle did not benefit from his nephew's abstinence but that only the nephew benefited. (Moreover, because the nephew benefited from his abstinence, that act cannot count as consideration. Consideration is something that is of detriment to the promisor and of benefit to the promisee.) But this is probably not a correct description of what happened. The uncle's utility was probably increased by his nephew's abstinence. The problem lies in finding some tangible and believable evidence of this increase in utility.

Actually the court here did not hold that the uncle had to benefit from the nephew's abstinence for the contract to be enforceable. The court says that "[i]t is sufficient that [the nephew] restricted his lawful freedom of action ... upon the faith of his uncle's agreement, and now, having fully performed the conditions imposed, it is of no moment whether such performance actually proved a benefit to the promisor." But the court further says that if it had attempted to determine whether the uncle benefited from the nephew's abstinence, "we see nothing in this record that would permit a determination that the uncle was not benefited in a legal sense."

e. One objection to the court's enforcing such a promise is that the promise would be "merely a gift" and that the nephew loses nothing if the gift is not made. Unlike the actual case, there are no conditions to be fulfilled and no consideration. Thus, this promise of a gift was not part of an exchange and would not have been enforceable under the classical bargain theory of contract. Nonetheless, gifts should be enforced when the promisee reasonably relies to his detriment on the completion of the gift.

6.3. The bargain theory would interpret the computer company's May 10 letter of a firm offer as an *unenforceable* promise because nothing was given by the client in exchange for the offer. Accordingly, there was no contract to breach, and the client is not entitled to relief.

However, it is almost certainly true that on May 10 the computer company *wanted* to be bound by its firm offer to deliver a computer at a given price. The anticipated benefit of being so bound is that it increases the likelihood of the client's doing business with this computer company and not another. The client, of course, expects and wants the firm offer to be binding. On the grounds that these and future parties benefit by making firm offers enforceable, the computer company should be held to have breached a contract and the client should be given relief.

6.4. Let's compare the effect of the different remedies. If there is no remedy, then future promisors of gifts may be more extravagant and less cautious in making donative promises. Those to whom such promises are made will become more skeptical and reduce their reliance on donative promises. If the remedy is compensation for reasonable detrimental reliance, then promisors will tend to make more cautious gifts, and promisees will tend to incur only reasonable reliance expenses. Also, reliance damages may be relatively easy to measure. If the remedy is expectation damages, promisors will be even more cautious about making gift promises; promisees may be less cautious in determining the believability of the promise.

Different remedies may be in order if the crucial issues are different. With donative promises reasonable reliance is the crucial issue; with bargain promises expectations are relatively more important.

6.5. Businesses can make commitments to consumers to repair and service their products. Businesses can give access to technology and other business secrets or can commit to certain product or machine design specifications as hostages to other business customers. Less tangible to other consumers and other businesses but equally important, a business's reputation is a hostage to a happy long-term relationship.

Chapter 7

7.1. This is a fundamental question that has different but mutually reinforcing answers. With regard to the explicit question in the text, A's threat to harm B unless she engages in a transaction destroys B's security in her person. This destruction can be faulted on both moral and efficiency grounds. For example, one might argue that everyone is entitled by reason of morality to liberty over his or her person. That freedom may be surrendered only voluntarily. (And only, perhaps, temporarily; an argument may be made that no one should be allowed even voluntarily to become a slave for the rest of his or her life.) Threatening someone's freedom over her person is, therefore, immoral.

Not allowing a destructive threat to B's person also promotes efficiency. If such threats were allowed, people would incur costs to avoid being so threatened; they might carry weapons, avoid being alone, or surround themselves with hired toughs. These costs of avoiding being coerced would be reduced (but not eliminated) by adopting a legal rule of not enforcing promises elicited by coercive, destructive threats.

7.2. Sea captains have a legal duty to rescue ships and cargo in distress. The captains in this case threatened not to do their legal duty, which would have resulted in the destruction of valuable cargo. Thus, their threat involved destruction of value, not merely the refusal to participate in its creation. And as we have seen, promises extracted under threats to destroy existing values should not be enforced on both moral and efficiency grounds.

7.3. The crucial point in this hypothetical situation is that the person duped was a young girl. Her age is such that we may doubt her ability to have a good idea of the *objective* value of the contract. We should presume competency to engage in a (truly) mutually beneficial exchange only where that objective valuation can be made and then compared with an individual's subjective valuation.

7.4. One might sensibly argue that once someone is drunk or high, the burden falls on the sober contractual partner to refrain from entering into a promise until the other party is also sober. This position would hold whether the inebriated person was a casual indulger or an addict. The point is that the probability of competence (and the probability of avoiding a dispute about whether the promise was void because of incompetence) would be much higher when both parties are sober.

Notice, by the way, that tort law adopts a similar position when dealing with the possibility of avoiding an accident as between a sober and an inebriated person. According to so-called "dram shop laws," a bartender (and in some cases a social host or hostess) who continues to sell or give an inebriated person alcohol or drugs becomes responsible for harms that the inebriate may subsequently commit.

7.5.   The circumstances in this famous case are highly unusual. Nonetheless, sufficiently similar circumstances are likely to arise in the future so that a clear rule in this case could have influenced the behavior of future contracting parties. The opinion that this contract is void because there was "no true meeting of the minds" is not particularly helpful. An economic analysis can provide clearer guidelines.

The problem that has arisen to frustrate the performance of the contract is the unforeseen contingency that there were two ships named *Peerless*. If this contingency could have been foreseen by one of the contractual parties at a reasonable cost, then responsibility for non-performance in the event of the contingency could have been and should have been assigned in the contract. Presumably, the parties would have assigned responsibility for nonperformance in the event of that contingency to the party who could have more cheaply taken steps to prevent or insure against this contingency. For example, if either of the parties had had extensive business dealings in the England-India cotton trade, he could or should have known that there were two ships named *Peerless*.

Notice, however, that if neither party could have foreseen this contingency, then the issue is no longer so much one of creating a rule to induce efficient risk allocation as it is one of apportioning unavoidable losses between two innocent parties. If there is a content to the expression "no true meeting of the minds," it is precisely to cover those circumstances in which a contingency that was not foreseeable at reasonable cost has arisen to frustrate contract performance. In those circumstances the task of the court becomes one of equitably dividing the unavoidable loss.

7.6.   a.   If the information is productive, it will change the economic incentives facing the owner and may, therefore, cause him to change his behavior. (If the information is merely redistributive, then it is not likely to change incentives and thereby behavior; redistributive information merely changes the identity of the economic agent, the person who receives the economic reward.) Here, if the owner knows the cow is fertile, he will breed her rather than butcher her.

b.   The contractual price can help to make this determination. Suppose that a fertile cow would sell for $800 (the majority opinion says a fertile cow was worth between $750 and $1000) and a barren beef cow would sell for $80. And further suppose that the contract price between Sherwood and Walker was $440. What does that price tell us? One way to interpret the price is as an explicit discounting of the probability that the cow is barren. Imagine that the buyer Sherwood supposed the probability that this allegedly barren cow was in fact fertile to be 0.5. If so, then the expected value of the cow to him might be 0.5($800) + 0.5($80) = $440. In short, if the price was higher than the value of the cow as meat, that higher price must reflect a premium for the possibility that Rose is fertile. (This does not preclude a sale price of $80 or of $800 from being interpreted as an explicit assignment of risk.)

c. Sherwood would have no incentive to invest time and effort in discovering such facts if the payoff from such information goes to Walker.

d. Professionals assume the risk of mistaking the fertility of a cow as part of their job.

7.7. a. In the absence of bargaining or transaction costs, the party who places the highest value on the crane (Beta) will end up with it, regardless of how the contract is enforced.

b. Omega relied on Alpha's offer to the extent that it turned down Beta's higher offer and thereby made less on the sale than it otherwise would have. Eventually the crane will end up with Beta. Whether Omega or Alpha realizes the surplus from selling to Beta is a matter for further discussion.

c. Here, because of the assumption of low bargaining costs, the crane will end up in Beta's hands regardless of how the contract is enforced. However, future contracting parties might be induced to be more careful about transmitting bids and in verifying them by either voiding the contract between Omega and Alpha or enforcing it according to its terms.

7.8. The costs of foreseeing all contingencies are clearly too high. On efficiency grounds it is desirable that contractual parties internalize the risks of ever more contingencies up to the point where the marginal cost of including the allocation of risk of one more contingency is equal to the marginal benefit of that allocation. This general condition may be difficult to apply in practice. Consider its application to the *Batchelor's Peas* case. Was the offense to the Armistice Day viewers foreseeable at reasonable cost? Has the ad agency had a lot or only a little experience with contracts for flying signs? Could either party have foreseen this harm more cheaply than the other? We need more facts to answer these questions.

7.9. No. The buyer *should* be suspicious of a conditional statement and should push the seller farther. Notice that there is a difference between the circumstance here and an *intentional* falsehood.

7.10. The informational asymmetry in this case concerns productive facts, not destructive facts, so the economic analysis suggests that the contract should be enforced. Enforcing the contract will reward people like Schmidt for the cost of discovering minerals. If the buyer had acquired the information casually and fortuitously, as did Organ in *Organ v. Laidlaw,* rather than by an investment, the economic case for compensating him is weakened.

7.11. This is a destructive fact by the buyer, an affirmative and intentional misrepresentation that may have caused the seller to sell to him when, if she had known the truth, she would have sold to someone else. The court should rescind the contract.

7.12. Here are some hints: In *Scissor-Tail,* there is monopoly power, whereas banking is remarkably unconcentrated. In *A & M* there was a one-shot transaction, whereas in *Perdue* there is a continuing relationship between banker and client. (Think about the "end-game" problem of bargaining theory, described in a box in the preceding chapter, to see why market failures are unlikely in small, repeated transactions.) Furthermore, in *A & M* the contract clause in dispute concerns loss allocation, whereas in *Perdue* it concerns a charge. (In general, are buyers better informed about charges or losses in contracts?) Finally, notice that *Scissor-Tail* and *A & M* both involve a large loss suffered by one party, whereas *Perdue* involves a small loss suffered by a whole class of people.

7.13. a.   *Williams* might possibly be considered a case of transactional incapacity; if the terms and conditions of sale are such that the buyer was likely to be incapable of understanding them and if the seller knew that or should have known that, then the contract should be void on the grounds of the buyer's transactional incapacity. One might also contend that price ignorance is relevant to an unconscionability claim in *Williams*. *Scissor-Tail* probably does not qualify as an instance of unconscionability under any of Eisenberg's criteria. The contract was between professionals who had participated in these concerts many times before. When he signed the contract, Graham recognized who the arbitrators would be in the event of a dispute. *A & M* is also an example of a contract between professionals engaged in a routine business transaction. There would seem to be no unconscionability on Eisenberg's criteria. In *Perdue* the only criterion that might be relevant to a claim of unconscionability is price ignorance, but the claim does not seem to be strong.

b.   One might void a contract induced by an advertisement as unconscionable on Eisenberg's criteria if the heart of the issue was misrepresentation but the misrepresentation stopped short of being a fraud. For example, the contract for the sale of the grasshopper killer cited at the beginning of Chapter 6 might be considered unconscionable on those grounds. On the other hand (economists always come equipped with two hands so that they may say of any thorny issue, "On the one hand, . . ." and "On the other hand, . . ."; it is said that there is actually a one-handed economist somewhere who is capable of reaching a definite conclusion, but we doubt that story because, on the one hand, . . .), to void a contract induced by an ad that was misrepresentational but not fraudulent would impose a chill on advertising and reduce the benefits of ads.

The criterion of price ignorance is difficult to pin down. We are inclined to think that it would be very rare to void a contract induced by an advertised price—even where the ad wrongly said that there was no lower price to be had.

c.   Disputes about value are best resolved by bargaining in a competitive market. Where that is impossible (see the second half of Chapter 4), correction of market failures by collective action *may* be warranted.

The costs of requiring manufacturers to justify their prices will be partly passed on to consumers in the form of higher prices, partly to shareholders of the corporation in the form of lower profits, and partly to employees of the firm in the form of lower wages or employment.

7.14. It could be that the terms are efficient in the sense that there are lots of music publishing companies with whom the young songwriter might have signed and that the terms efficiently allocate the risk that this songwriter, like most young songwriters, will not be successful. Why do you think the plaintiff brought this action? The most likely reason is that he has, contrary to the odds, been successful and finds the constraints imposed on him when he originally signed with the publisher to be confining. The House of Lords voided the contract as being unconscionable. Assume that it is, in fact, not unconscionable, but rather, an efficient allocation of risk. What effect might the decision have on the fortunes of other young songwriters who do not yet have contracts and on those who do have the standard form here held void? Music publishers and untried songwriters must find some alternative method of allocating between them the risks that are inherent in the business. If the terms that were here held to be unconscionable were the most efficient method of doing that, then this decision will impose unnecessary costs on future contracting parties.

See Trebilcock, *The Doctrine of Inequality of Bargaining Power: Post-Benthamite Economics in the House of Lords,* 26 U. TORONTO L. J. 359 (1976).

7.15. One of the most important factors leading to the ability to prevent risk or to insure against loss is access to information. One aspect of that is the length of time in the business. Another is information about preventive technology. Another important factor besides information is the availability of self-insurance possibilities. In general, it would seem to be the case that those firms that have cheaper access to prevention also have cheaper access to insurance.

7.16. The relevant question is whether Taylor (the performer) or Caldwell (the concert hall owner) could have prevented or insured against the unavailability of the hall due to this contingency at lower cost. The fact that it is physically impossible to perform in the hall is really beside the point. Caldwell probably has better information about the fireworthiness of the hall and its risks of being destroyed by fire. Moreover, being a professional impressario, he was better able to arrange an alternative venue for the concert than was the performer. In short, Caldwell breached the contract and should be responsible to Taylor for damages. Such a holding, made on those grounds, is likely to induce more efficient risk allocation among future contracting parties.

7.17. There are very complicated antitrust issues involved here. Nonetheless, let's simplify. If the formation of a secret uranium price cartel was foreseeable at reasonable cost, then Westinghouse was the better bearer of the risk of that contingency's arising to frustrate performance of the contract. If the risk was not foreseeable at reasonable cost, then no efficiency goal would be served by laying the losses entirely on either party—Westinghouse or the utilities.

7.18. Imagine that you are the builder and that you realize that you are going to be a week late in completing the contract. The construction contract imposes a penalty of $10,000 per week on you for late completion, even though the true loss to the other party is only $5,000 per week. Should you inefficiently spend an extra $9,000 per week to complete the contract and avoid paying the $10,000 penalty? If the conditions of the Positive Coase Theorem hold (viz., low bargaining costs), you will not. Assuming that you discover early enough that you will be late, you can always "threaten" to incur the extra costs (added shifts, overtime, etc.) to complete on time. If these additional costs of hurrying completion are high enough, it may pay you to offer the other party, say, $6,000 in exchange for his not pressing his claim for the $10,000 liquidated damages. He would be willing to take this money because it covers his losses and gives him something extra. You would be willing to make such a payment because it is less than the liquidation damages. As a credible threat, you can induce the other party to take less than $10,000 because you can always hurry your performance (at a cost) and thereby deprive him of the excess over $5,000 that you offer.

7.19. The presence of monopoly or of severe informational asymmetries are factors determining whether the contract with the Anxious Alumnus should be enforced. It is difficult to imagine circumstances in which the Anxious Alumnus has that special information (either through monopoly or a severe informational asymmetry) and is not justified on our earlier distinction between productive and destructive facts in having it and using it.

7.20. Despite our argument that liquidated damages clauses can be efficiency enhancing, it would be a mistake to require every enforceable contract to contain a liquidation clause. The general principle for determining whether to add another contractual clause is that the clause is to be added if the (expected) marginal cost of inclusion is less than the (expected) marginal benefits. The danger in requiring liquidation clauses is that this may induce some parties to include clauses for which the marginal costs are greater than the marginal benefits. Consider the impact on contracts for fungible goods of a requirement of a liquidation clause. It is unlikely that either party places a large subjective valuation on performance of a contract for a fungible good. Thus, a requirement to insert a liquidation clause can be easily accommodated by inserting routine language about alternative performance in the event of breach. But for contracts covering goods or services that are *not* fungible (or are fungible but for which one party places a high subjective valuation, as is the case with the Anxious Alumnus) the costs of requiring a liquidation clause could be very high. Simply consider what information is conveyed to the seller of a seemingly fungible good when the buyer says he wants ten times the market value of a good as liquidated damages. This is a clear indication to the seller that the buyer places a large subjective valuation on performance (or is crazy), and this revelation invites the seller to bargain for a large share of the buyer's surplus. There is no efficiency or equity reason to encourage this sort of bargaining, and, therefore, there is no good reason to require a liquidation clause in these circumstances. In general, as we will see, designing the appropriate remedy for breach can more efficiently and equitably protect the buyer's subjective valuation.

Contracting parties are likely to include a liquidation clause when there is a surplus from doing so (i.e., when the marginal costs of doing so are less than the marginal benefits).

7.21. If the photographer (or any other contractual party who stands to suffer an extraordinary loss from breach) notifies the film company of his special conditions, the two parties can then bargain about assignment of the risk of this loss at the time the contract is formed. Without this notification the parties do not have an opportunity to assign risk efficiently. (It is possible that no agreeable price can be reached. This might explain, e.g., why it is that film companies typically include a blanket waiver of liability with every roll of film.) If so, the photographer may choose to self-insure by taking extra rolls of film, by mailing them separately, by developing them himself, or the like.

7.22. a. $2,000.
  b. $1,000 = $11,000 − $10,000
  c. $400 = $11,000 − $10,500 − $100.
  d. $100.
  e. $9,500 = $10,000 − $500.

7.23. When bargaining costs are nil, there is no need for a mitigation requirement. There are two reasons. First, responsibility for mitigation in the event of breach may well have been assigned as part of the contract, e.g., in a liquidation clause. Second, the costs of dealing with mitigation can be costlessly renegotiated between parties after a breach has occurred. If Xavier fails to complete his contractual obligation on time and if he is responsible for *all* of Yvonne's losses, she has a reduced incentive to sell her supplemental food and may, in fact, choose to let it spoil. But this spoilage and waste is unlikely. Suppose that Yvonne has $400 worth of supplemental food. Xavier can pay her $500 for the food, re-sell it for $300, and lose only $200 rather than $400.

Could you justify the requirement to mitigate damages on the grounds of the Normative Hobbes Theorem of Chapter 4 (legal rules should be structured so as to minimize the harm from private disagreements)?

7.24. It is difficult to imagine a more wrong-headed and outrageous opinion than the majority opinion in *Peevyhouse*. Clearly, the outcome is unfair, but it is also wildly inefficient. What is particularly galling is the majority's inaccurate and pretentious invocation of economics to justify their outrageous result.

a. Breach could be efficient here if the parties had faced efficient incentives to perform or breach. But because the court has made such a hash of things, we can say without fear of error that the breach was inefficient. Indeed, the rule enunciated by the majority seems to *encourage* inefficient breach. After the case was handed down, there was no compelling legal reason for a coal company not to promise to restore land (regardless of cost) after strip-mining even though the company had no intention whatsoever of doing it.

b. The coal company could have taken precaution against nonperformance by such actions as retaining the services of a landscape architect, purchasing large amounts of topsoil, seedlings, plants, etc.—all of which would have been evidence of an intention *not* to breach. The promisees' reliance could have taken such forms as planning to plant commercial crops or ornamental trees on their land after restoration and purchasing equipment and supplies relevant to that action, planning to give a lawn party, and foregoing other offers to landscape after the mining.

The court's decision will cause precautionary expenditures to fall (because breach will be excused more easily in the future) and reliance expenditures also to fall (because of heightened uncertainty that the contractual promises will be fulfilled).

c. (If you agree, you're in deep trouble in this class.) Both the diminished-value and cost-of-performance measures use *objective* measures of harm from breach. The most likely reason that the court favors the diminished-value measure is that the courts assume (wrongly) that there are no subjective values attached by the Peevyhouses to performance of the contract. If that were true, then the fall in the *objective* value of the farm would be an appropriate measure. But if that assumption is false, then the cost-of-performance measure is the better measure because it protects any subjective value on performance much more effectively.

d. As noted in the previous paragraph, the court's measure of the benefits of restoration is purely objective in that it uses only market values. In court one could have asked the Peevyhouses for their subjective valuation, but unfortunately the answer would not be believable: they have a strong incentive at that point to exaggerate this subjective value. We would strongly prefer to have prior evidence on this subjective value as, for example, might have been contained in a liquidation clause *but only if* there are no actual constraints on the amount of damages that may be specified in a liquidation clause. Such evidence would have been monetary. However, we may not have direct evidence on the *extent* of subjective value but merely that the breachee has some indeterminate subjective valuation on performance. That would seem to be true here because, as the majority opinion says, "In addition to the usual covenants found in a coal mining lease, defendant specifically agreed to perform certain restorative and remedial work at the end of the lease period." The plaintiffs would not have insisted on this clause if they had not placed a high value on restoration.

e. After the decision, one would expect coal companies readily to agree to restoration work whether they intended to perform or not. There is no reason to discount the lease price as deeply because there is a lowered intention to perform.

The landowner's options for protection of their subjective valuation are greatly restricted by this case. Before *Peevyhouse* the option of including seemingly punitive liquidated damages clauses was not available. After *Peevyhouse* the enforceability of a simple clause agreeing to restore strip-mined property is in doubt. The landowner can minimize uncompensated loss by leasing only property with a low subjective value and withholding leases for parcels with a higher subjective value.

7.25. The court in *Jacob & Youngs v. Kent* determined that the appropriate measure of damages was diminution in value and that because there was no perceptible difference between Cohoes and Reading pipe, there was no reduction in the *objective* value of the house because the wrong brand of pipe was used. The cost-of-performance measure of damages would have involved the contractor's incurring expenses of $200,000 (several times the value of the home) to replace the pipe.

Even if Kent placed a very high subjective valuation on the pipe installed, it is very hard to believe that that subjective value was greater than the objective value of the home. Should that fact cause the court to act as if there was no subjective value? Clearly not. As outrageous as the $200,000 figure is, there is a plausible argument to be made for making that the basis of Kent's award. Despite the fact that that figure may overstate the value that the home owner places on having the correct kind of pipe installed in his home, it may well be that the contractor never incurs $200,000 in repairs. If it is true, as the court says, that the home is not worth that much, the contractor can always offer to rebuild the home with the correct pipe for much less than $200,000. Alternatively, Kent and the contractor may settle their dispute for a payment far less than that required to rebuild the home or effect the repairs.

There is another good reason that the court should choose the cost-of-performance figure over the diminution-in-value measure of damages. That is that there does not appear to be any excuse for the contactor's not having used the appropriate pipe. Simply put, contractual parties are entitled to have terms of the contract enforced. If the court made that point forcefully in this case by adopting the cost-of-performance measure, that would serve as a strong signal to other contracting parties that the terms of the contract, however idiosyncratic they may seem, are entitled to enforcement.

7.26. The court should have awarded the Peevyhouses specific performance of the contract to have their land restored. That would have efficiently protected the Peevyhouses' subjective valuation on their property by allowing them to bargain with the Garland Coal Company to establish the value to them of restoration, rather than relying on the court's outrageous measure of that value.

7.27. In *Jacob & Youngs* an award of specific performance would have been roughly equivalent to the award of cost-of-performance money damages: Kent's subjective valuation on the particular pipe used in his home would have been efficiently protected.

7.28. A complete answer to this question is probably worthy of publication. Here are the elements of that answer. Specific performance as the routine remedy efficiently induces the parties to allocate risk of non-performance at the time the contract is formed and most efficiently induces them to settle a dispute about responsibility for losses arising from breach. To the extent that it accomplishes these things, specific performance creates better incentives for the promisee to rely on the other party's promise and for the promisor to take the efficient amount of precaution against non-performance.

7.29. It is possible that R paid a lower than market rental rate for L's property precisely because L insisted on the limitations that it not be sub-let and that it be used only as a saloon. Suppose that without those restrictions the monthly rent would have been $600, but that with them it was $500. Under a specific performance L is entitled to a stream of income of $500/month for another three years. Wouldn't this cause L inefficiently *not* to mitigate his losses from R's breach? No. As was the case in our discussion in question 7.18 of the possibility of bargaining out of a seemingly punitive liquidation clause, R can make an offer to L to waive the clauses not allowing sub-letting or use of the property for any purpose other than a saloon. Suppose, for example, that H would be willing to pay $400 per month to use the property as a clothing store. R could offer L $600 per month for the remainder of his lease in exchange for L's waiving the two clauses. R could collect $400/month from H and pay an additional $200 of his own money. He would be better off under this arrangement than if he had to pay $500/month to L. H is presumably better off than if he had to pay the full $600/month (assuming that is the going rate for the lease of comparable property). And L may be better off than if he simply accepted $500/month from R for the remainder of the lease. The only difference between this scenario and the one in which L would bear responsibility for mitigating damages is who bears the costs of renegotiating the lease (e.g., the costs of locating and bargaining with H): under specific performance, R bears those costs; under a mitigation requirement, L may bear them.

7.30. Suppose that the breachee who has been awarded specific perfomance presses the breacher for compensation for consequential and unforeseeable damages in return for not enforcing the specific performance decree. If the asking price of the breachee exceeds the cost to the breacher of performance, the breacher can always insert liquidation clauses limiting damages to direct and reasonably foreseeable amounts.

Chapter 8

8.1. A contract suit enabled the plaintiff in *Hawkins* to ask for expectation damages, the amount of money that would place him on the indifference curve he expected to reach had the promise been fully performed. With a tort suit the most he could have obtained is the equivalent of reliance damages in contracts. Reliance damages are compensatory in the sense that they return the victim to the indifference curve he or she would have been on had the injury never occurred. Expectation damages are always at least as large as reliance damages

Figure D

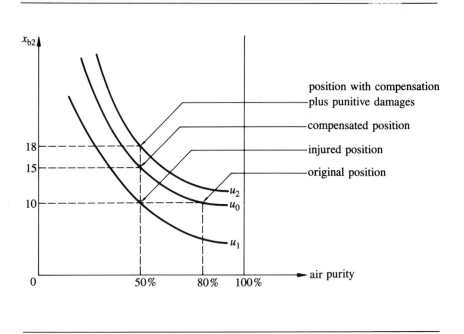

and are frequently larger in that they seek to put the victim on the indifference curve he or she expected to reach if a contractual promise had been fulfilled. (See Figure D accompanying the next answer.)

8.2. When the victim is allowed to recover compensatory damages *and* punitive damages, he is placed on a higher indifference curve than his pre-accident curve. Figure D above repeats the example in the text to show this point. Giving the victim compensatory damages sufficient to purchase an additional 5 units of x_{b2} returned him to his original indifference curve, U_0. If punitive damages are given that allow the victim to purchase an additional 3 units of x_{b2}, the victim is placed on indifference curve U_2, which is higher than the original curve, U_0.

8.3. In most states courts do not allow a defendant-injurer to invoke the so-called "seat-belt defense" to escape or mitigate liability. (However, in a recent case in Michigan a defendant charged with negligent homicide has contended that he is innocent of homicide because the people in the other car would not have been killed if they had been wearing their seat belts, as they were required to do by Michigan law.) This reluctance may at first blush strike one as inefficient because it relieves the plaintiff-victim of the responsibility of taking a relatively costless action (putting on a seat belt) that would greatly reduce the extent of personal injury in the event of an accident. The argument is that the appropriate form of the negligence rule is negligence with a defense of contributory negligence or a form of comparative negligence because both evaluate the plaintiff's actions with respect to a legal standard of care. If there is no legal standard of care facing the plaintiff, the argument is that the plaintiff will have only a weak incentive to take precaution. But this line of argument is not correct. As the answer to the next question makes clear in more detail, simple negligence—here, placing the plaintiff under no obligation to comply with a duty of care such as wearing a seat belt—places residual responsibility on the potential plaintiff: if the potential defendant complies with the legal standard of care, then the victim will bear responsibility for all his losses. The rationally self-interested potential victim should presume that potential injurers are taking sufficient precaution to escape liability. If so, the wisest thing for the potential victim to do is to take expected cost-minimizing precaution, such as wearing a seat belt. (Be certain you read the answer to the next question.)

8.4.   There is really no mystery about how negligence with contributory negligence induces efficient precaution by both parties. What is unusual here is the contention that simple negligence will also induce efficient precaution by both parties. We know that potential injurers will be led by rational self-interest to take efficient precaution under either form of the negligence rule. But how will the potential victim be induced to take efficient precaution under simple negligence? If potential victims know that potential injurers will take efficient precaution under simple negligence, then injurers will not be held liable for any losses to victims of accidents. This means that under simple negligence victims will bear *residual responsibility* for their accident losses. This exposure to residual responsibility should induce potential victims to take an expected cost-minimizing amount of precaution. As we noted in the previous answer, this suggests that the seat-belt defense of the previous question is not necessary to induce potential victims to use seat belts. (As we will see in the next chapter, the equivalent efficiency of the various forms of the negligence rule is due to our assumption of certainty. When we introduce uncertainties [e.g., in how accurately a jury will evaluate a party's precaution with respect to the legal standard of care], we can draw efficiency distinctions among the forms of negligence.)

8.5.   a.   The Hand Rule proposes taking total costs rather than *marginal* calculations of cost and benefit. Recall that our formulation determines x^*, the social-cost minimizing level of precaution, as the level for which the marginal cost of precaution, w, equals the marginal benefits of precaution, $p'(x)A$. When there are no fixed costs associated with an accident, the total and marginal cost methods of calculating x^* lead to the same level of precaution.

In practice, the marginal values may not be as readily available as the total values so that the cruder and easier calculation of the total cost Hand Rule (set x^* at the level of precaution for which $p(x)A = wx$) must be used.

   b.   To determine whether to incur the $25 expense of keeping the bargee present, we must compare the marginal cost of precaution ($25) with the marginal benefit (the reduction in the expected accident costs from taking the precaution). The rule for determining x^* is $w = p'(x)A$. If $w > p'(x)A$, then $x < x^*$ and the injurer is negligent. If $w < p'(x)A$, then $x > x^*$ and the injurer is not liable. Here $w = 25, $A = $100,000$, and $p'(x) = 0.001 - 0.0005 = 0.0005$. Thus, $p'(x)A = 0.0005($100,000) = 50. Because $w < p'(x)A$, the barge owner would be negligent if he did not pay the bargee to be present.

   c.   We implicitly answered this question when we argued that in negligence the crucial variable for the court to determine is the social-cost minimizing level of care—that is, the legal duty of care. If the court sets x^* correctly,

Figure E

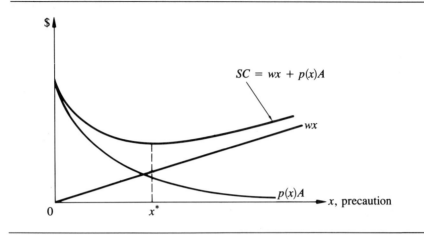

then the potential injurer will find it in his interests to comply with that legal standard of care, regardless of what accident losses he anticipates. The behavior of a potential injurer facing a form of the negligence standard is not sensitive to the size of A, except in the unusual case where he makes such a serious underestimate of the accident losses that he minimizes his private costs by taking a level of precaution that is below the legal standard. (*See* Figure 8.4.)

What about the barge owner (the potential victim) who has an extraordinarily valuable cargo? Such a barge owner (like contractual parties who anticipate exceptional losses) will probably take special steps to protect himself against these extraordinary losses, e.g., by purchasing special insurance coverage.

d. The Hand Rule formulation (both that in *U.S. v. Carroll Towing* and our marginal formulation) implies risk-neutrality or, more accurately, no risk at all. We have assumed that everything is known. In the following chapter we discuss the effect of uncertainty and of attitudes toward risk on behavior under different liability rules.

8.6 and 8.7. These questions point up a very important difference between negligence and strict liability. The crucial variable inducing efficient incentives under negligence is the legal standard of care. If that legal duty is set correctly at the social cost-minimizing level of precaution, x^*, then the level of damages that is assessed against a wrongdoer becomes unimportant. We argued that when faced with a negligence standard, the rational decisionmaker will take enough precaution to satisfy the legal standard of care, wherever that is set.

Under strict liability there is no legal standard of care, compliance with which will relieve the injurer of liability. What is optimal for the rationally self-interested potential injurer to do under strict liability depends on the level of expected accident costs. We can show this most easily in a graph. Suppose in Figure E that $p(x)A$ represents the expected accident costs and $SC = wx + $

Figure F

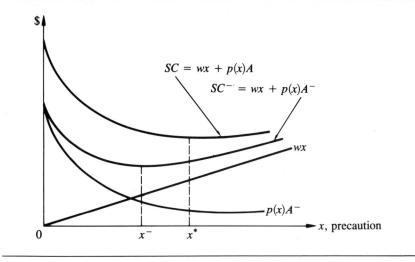

$p(x)A$ represents the expected social costs when damages are set equal to perfectly compensatory damages. x^* then gives the level of precaution that minimizes the potential injurer's expected costs. It is also the *socially* optimal level of precaution.

But now suppose that damages are set too low, at A^-, which is less than perfectly compensatory damages, A. $p(x)A^-$ represents expected accident costs and $SC^- = wx + p(x)A^-$, social costs when damages are less than perfectly compensatory. (These curves are shown in Figure F. For the sake of reference the expected social costs, SC, and the efficient level of precaution, x^*, when damages are perfectly compensatory are shown.) Note that when expected damages are less than perfectly compensatory the potential injurer minimizes his costs by choosing $x^- < x^*$.

Finally, when damages are expected to be above the level of perfect compensation under strict liability, potential injurers minimize their expected costs at a level of precaution above the social optimum. Figure G, with A^+ indicating the super-compensatory damages and x^+ the cost-minimizing level of care, shows this. We leave its exposition to you.

Notice that these questions add something to our criteria for choosing between negligence and strict liability. Errors are possible under either standard: by mis-specifying the legal standard of care under negligence and by mis-specifying the level of damages under strict liability. For a given type of accident, if it is easier to get the legal standard correct than to set damages correctly at perfect compensation, then all other things equal, negligence should be preferred to strict liability. If it is easier to set damages correctly than to determine the legal standard correctly, strict liability should be preferred to negligence. (Recall, however, that there are other criteria that are relevant to choosing between these two liability standards, viz., whether precaution is unilateral or bilateral and whether the activity level influences the probability or severity of harm.)

Figure G

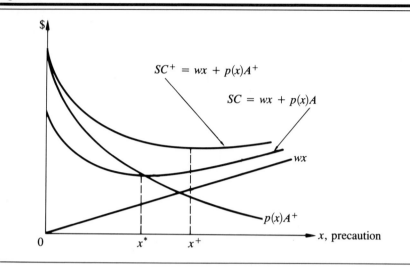

8.8. a. Strict liability. Precaution here is unilateral: the construction company is the only party that has a realistic opportunity of reducing the probability or severity of injury. Before blasting they could determine if anyone in the area is likely to be sensitive, and if so, they could take steps to minimize the probability or severity of harm, e.g., pay to transport the potential victims elsewhere while blasting takes place. In addition to unilateral precaution, there is no reason that damages should be difficult to measure and thus *not* be perfectly compensatory.

  b. Strict liability on the manufacturer (and possibly the retailer). Again, precaution is unilateral in that only the injurer can realistically take steps to reduce the probability or severity of injury. For example, the manufacturer could have made a tamper-proof package and warned consumers not to take its cold remedy if the seal was broken.

  c. A form of the negligence rule because precaution is bilateral. The driver was speeding; the pedestrian was crossing the street against a red light. (1.) However, if the predestrian is a blind woman with a cane, then the driver should be strictly liable because precaution has become unilateral. (2.) It might be argued that in these circumstances the opportunity cost of precaution, w, is very high so that the cost-minimizing duty of care on the driver is low. But the law is reluctant to craft special standards of care. It generally does so only when the injurer is clearly in a special category, such as children. It is unlikely that the heart surgeon qualifies as such a category. Notice, too, that the problem would have been avoided if the surgeon had ridden to the hospital in a police car whose siren was blaring. (3.) If the pedestrian is a child, then a case can be made for holding the driver strictly liable. In part this depends on the age of the child: a 4-year-old crossing against the light is one thing; a 12-year-old doing so is another. (4.) What is a minor child doing driving a car? This makes the situation very complicated. Perhaps the car is stolen. Perhaps the minor's mother is sitting beside the driver giving instructions.

Chapter 9

9.1.   a.   When there is a great deal of competition, there is a presumption that the prevailing prices, quantities, and quality of output are efficient. (Only for an externality would this general statement not hold true. That is, despite its other efficiencies, a competitive industry might engage in too much of an external-cost generating activity or not enough of an external-benefit generating activity. That issue does not arise in this case.) The implication is that if all the firms in a competitive industry do not have a radio-receiving set, then it must not be cost-effective to have such a set; if it were, everyone would have one or there would be a trend toward everyone's having such a set. If such a set is cost-effective, in the sense that the marginal cost of installing such a set is less than the marginal benefit, the first company to install such a set would be able to offer its services at a lower price than does its competitors. That firm's profits would increase and other firms would then follow its lead.

   b.   A monopolistic or cartelized industry is inefficient. It is possible—but not certain—that one of the inefficiencies is not to have radio receiving sets on coastwise tugs, even though a competitive industry would have adopted them. If the industry is monopolistically or imperfectly competitive or oligopolistic so that some firms have receiving sets and others do not, then matters become more complex. Some firms, for example, may have chosen to increase the quality of their service by having a set; others, by some other amenity. In such a circumstance the court would have to determine fault (as the opinion suggests) by determining what the social-cost minimizing level of precaution is with regard to receiving sets and then determining whether a particular firm complied with or violated that standard of care.

   c.   Information on insurance rates would be helpful. If it revealed, all other things equal, a lower rate for those firms with receiving sets, then that is evidence that having a set is cost-justified. If there was no difference between rates for firms with and without sets, that would reveal that the alternative precaution of remaining close enough to shore to observe storm warnings was deemed just as good at minimizing loss from foundering.

   d.   As noted in parts b and c, the comparison should be between the cost of a receiving set and the expected benefit from having it. That expected benefit would be the reduced probability of loss from having a set times the accident losses in the event of an accident. (If there were further benefits—for example, a faster transit time because a receiving set allows a tug to stay further away from the shore, those should be computed as well.)

   e.   This is an extraordinarily broad question that touches on all the material raised in this book. We have argued that, in general, the forces in a competitive market maximize allocative and productive efficiency. Thus, a competitive market would induce optimal precaution. However, we have also seen that there are well-known circumstances in which the competitive market does not work very well—e.g., when there are severe informational asymmetries and when there are uncompensated external effects. In this and the previous chapter we have examined the ability of tort liability standards to induce potential wrongdoers and potential injurers to take precaution that they would not take in a competitive market. An alternative or a complementary social policy to tort liability is administrative agency regulations that explicitly govern behavior before an injury occurs (or an external cost is imposed). You might try to view the tort liability standards and regulation and the competitive market as alternative (or complementary) methods of achieving the desirable social goal of efficiency.

9.2. a. The Hand Rule holds that if a party's cost of precaution is less than the expected benefit (in the form of a reduction in the expected probability and severity of an accident) then that party is at fault. Here the cost is $5 and the expected benefit is $(1/25,000) \times \$678,000 = \$27.12$. The defendant was negligent in not giving the exam.

b. As the previous question indicated, if ophthalmology was a competitive industry (and it probably was), then the widespread custom of offering tonometry to people like Ms. Helling argues that the test was cost-effective.

c. (1.) The exposure to tort liability transmits a signal to potential injurers only when someone in a similar situation is held liable for a victim's losses. If those under 40 who have contracted glaucoma have not sued for negligent omission of tonometry, then the tort system has not indicated to ophthalmologists that they should change their testing procedures. (There are, of course, other methods of signaling the need to change—e.g., competitive pressures and *ex ante* governmental regulation.) (2.) To the extent that this code of silence prevailed among doctors, it would be difficult to develop evidence of the faultiness of not administering a particular test.

Under either of these (and some other) circumstances, some but not all ophthalmologists would administer tonometry to those under the age of 40.

9.3. It does seem strange that, in general, recoveries are larger for unintentionally inflicting a crippling injury than for unintentionally killing someone. But there may be a simple economic explanation for this. When someone is unintentionally crippled, they should be compensated for their lost opportunities for the remainder of their lives in a lump-sum payment. The present discounted value of these lost opportunities can be extremely large, especially so the younger the victim and the greater the value of the lost opportunities. However, when the victim dies, so do those lost opportunities and, therefore, the ability to recover for them; the only recovery that can be had is by the decedent's family and dependents and only for well-defined losses attributable to the decedent's absence. Tragic though the loss may be, these losses to the survivors tend to be less than the decedent's lost opportunities.

The potential inefficiency of this anomalous situation is that it might induce injurers who have unintentionally inflicted harm to minimize their losses by killing the victim. For example, if a driver has struck a pedestrian and severely injured her, he might reduce his liability by backing up and running over the victim again until she is dead. Most people are prevented from behaving in this hideous manner by moral constraints. But if those constraints are not enough, the act of returning to kill is not an unintentional harm, as was the initial injury. Instead, it is an intentional harm, for which there are severe criminal sanctions.

9.4. a. $\$6,000 = (0.8 \times \$10,000) + (0.2 \times (-\$10,000))$.
$= \$8,000 - \$2,000.$

b. Let P be the value of punitive damages that makes the expected payoff from breaking the fiduciary duty 0. Thus,
$$0 = 0.8 \times \$10,000 + (0.2 \times (-\$10,000 - P))$$
$$0 = \$8,000 - \$2,000 - 0.2P$$

$$0.2P = \$6,000$$
$$P = \$30,000.$$

  c. The punitive multiple equals

$$(\$10,000 + \$30,000) \; / \; \$10,000 = 4.$$

9.5.   a. The court may certainly do so and call this amount "punitive damages," but it is confusing to call an excluded element of compensatory damages "punitive damages."

  b. One possible reason is that punitive damages might have deterred Joe whereas the threat of compensatory damages apparently did not.

  c. If compensatory damages refers to the indifference value—the value at which the victim is indifferent as to whether he suffers no harm or he suffers harm with damages—then he will be an eager victim.

9.6.   In the figures given, the cost of redesigning the gas tank location so as to reduce the probability and severity of accidents is approximately \$10. The benefit to doing so is a savings of \$200,000 per burn death, \$67,000 per burn injury, and \$700 per burned car. For the sake of simplicity, let us ignore the losses arising from burn injuries and burned cars and concentrate on death, the worst outcome. Then, for the purposes of determining Ford's liability for failure to redesign, we may calculate the probability, P, of such an accident by using the Hand Rule:

$$\$10 = P \times \$200,000,$$
$$P = 10/200,000 = 0.00005.$$

9.7.   There is no dispute about the cost figures. Some contemporaries argued that in calculating the benefits of redesign, Ford was callous in putting a dollar figure on death and injury. But as Professor Epstein has argued in an exceptionally clear piece cited in the text of this section, Ford cannot be faulted for having performed the calculation. After all, if the tort liability system is to encourage optimal precaution, calculations like those reproduced in the text *must* be undertaken. (One may, of course, find fault with the figures actually used; for example, one could contend that the cost attributed to burn deaths was far too low.) We cannot, on the one hand, try to induce safety by exposing potential injurers to liability for failure to consider the external costs of their actions and then simultaneously criticize and punish them for making those calculations.

9.8.   The case for imposing punitive damages on Ford is very weak. None of the factors we have discussed in the text suggests that compensation would be inadequate. (Moreover, as we have seen, it is not even clear that Ford is at fault.) In circumstances like those of this case, punitives might be called for if Ford was not only negligent but grossly so. Consider an example based on the figures developed in Question 9.6. Suppose that the figure that Ford used to calculate the probability of a rear-end fire resulting in death was 0.00005. (This is the figure we calculated above.) But suppose that the true probability was twice that: 0.0001. If so, the expected benefit of redesign would become 0.0001 $\times$ \$200,000 = \$20, and Ford would clearly be at fault for failing to redesign the gas tank location. So far, there seems to be no need to impose punitives. But suppose that the true figure for the probability of death from rear-end collision given Ford's location of the tank was not 0.00005 but rather 0.005, one hundred times as large as Ford had thought. The true benefit of redesign would then become 0.005 $\times$ \$200,000 = \$1,000. This expected benefit is so large by comparison to the \$10 cost of redesign that it makes Ford's failure to redesign something more than mere negligence. This negligence is so extreme that it borders on the intentional and should be punished; an error in precaution this large requires more than compensation. (We will return to this sort of situation in Chapter 11, when we discuss the economic rationale for criminal sanctions.)

9.9. Under a comparative fault standard, the apportionment of fault in this case depends crucially on the actual probability of rear-end collisions that might rupture the gas tank. Clearly, the actions of the driver and passengers in leaving the gas tank cap off was faulty so that there is at least a *prima facie* case to be made for holding them partially at fault for their harm.

It is likely that the uncertainty about the interpretation of the appropriate level of care would induce Ford and other car makers to make their cars safer.

9.10. If the injured person is a fellow employee, the analysis of this section still applies (the employer should be vicariously liable) but with a major caveat: the contractual allocation of the risk of harm on the job as between the employer and the injured employee may govern. It is not likely but nonetheless possible that in his employment contract the injured employee agreed to waive a tort action against fellow employees or the employer. (An old common law doctrine known as the "fellow servant rule" excused employers from liability for employee harms due to the fault of a fellow employee.) If he did not, then it still seems most efficient to make the employer liable.

9.11. The justification for the distinction was apparently that although parents could not at reasonable cost control their children's actions, husbands could at reasonable cost control their adult wives.

9.12. We saw in Chapter 7 that contract law treats a person who is drunk as incapacitated so that a promise that a drunk makes is unenforceable. Similarly, tort law recognizes that a drunk is no longer capable of making reasonable decisions about precaution although his condition creates a high probability of causing harm. One way to reduce this probability or to make accidents involving drunks less severe is to make sober people responsible for the drunk's actions. As between the drunk and the bartender or social host, there is now a situation of what we have called unilateral precaution: only the sober bartender can guide the drunk into taking adequate precaution.

It is worth thinking about whether the bartender or social host should bear complete or only partial liability for the drunk's action. Are social hosts more likely to help if liability is shared with the drunk? Will helpers avoid drunks if they realize they become fully responsible for the drunks' actions? If so, can this effect be reduced by applying comparative fault principles to the helper?

9.13. There is a balance to be struck here: we would like rescuers to come to the aid of others (see the example of distress in the section on unconscionability in Chapter 7) but to do so in a reasonable manner. This argues for holding *B* liable for negligent rescue. But suppose that there is uncertainty in the determination of the appropriate standard of legal care (what we will call "evidentiary uncertainty" later in the chapter). Rescuers might become so fearful of being held liable that they might avoid giving aid. This is clearly an undesirable consequence of imposing liability for negligent rescue. It may well be that the only way to avoid this consequence is to allow an action against rescuers only where there is willful, wanton, or gross negligence.

9.14. The assumption of the risk defense seems to be controlling.

9.15. In both exceptions the rescuer is a professional whose professional skills are required to effect the rescue. In contract law the fiction is that the professional has an "implicit" contract with the person rescued or with the owner of the rescued property. The suggestion is that if the person benefited had been conscious or present, he would have agreed to pay the usual and customary fee of the professional. (Contrast this analysis of the compensation of the professional rescuer with the analysis of the fortuitous rescuer in the discussion of distress as an unconscionability defense in Chapter 7. Recall that we discussed the case of a symphony musician rescued in the desert by an amateur geologist. The rescuer had insisted on $100,000 or one-third of the musician's wealth, whichever was greater. The musician agreed, was saved, but later refused to honor the terms of the contract on the grounds that they were unconscionable. We argued, following Professor Eisenberg, that the geologist was entitled to his opportunity costs plus a bonus. In the case of a professional rescuer we argued only for the usual and customary fee with no bonus. What is the distinction?)

9.16. The analogy to the case of the Indian surgeon seems appropriate. As detestable as Dr. Eddingfield's actions are, they are not reachable by a tort action. The most compelling reason for this conclusion is that there is no overwhelming case for forcing an exchange in circumstances where there are relatively low transaction or bargaining costs. Once the law begins such compulsion, there is no clear stopping point.

9.17. Recall our discussion in Chapter 4 of the distinction between a private bad—an external cost imposed only on one person or a very few people—and a public bad—an external cost imposed on many parties. We argued there that the appropriate remedy for a private bad was an injunction because that remedy clearly delineates rights and induces the parties to solve their disagreement through negotiation. For a public bad the costs of achieving a bargaining solution are too high so that the court must undertake a hypothetical market transaction and determine, through the levying of compensatory damages, the appropriate price to impose on the wrongdoer.

The same factors apply to the issue of settling disputes when litigation is costly. If only a few parties are involved, bargaining costs are low and a settlement is likely. If many parties are involved, bargaining costs are high. It is possible that if the bargaining costs exceed litigation costs, a trial will result.

We will return to the important issue of litigation *versus* settlement in the next chapter.

9.18. There are at least three hypotheses to explain the surprisingly limited use of seat belts.

First, it could be that the decision not to wear belts is a utility-maximizing decision made by rationally self-interested economic actors. These people may have accurately estimated the expected benefits of wearing seat belts with due regard to the probability of being involved in an accident, the probability of being injured in the event that one was not wearing a belt, and the severity of injuries from not wearing a belt in various kinds of accidents. They also may have accurately compared these expected benefits with the perceived costs of wearing belts—e.g., the discomfort and inconvenience—and have concluded that the costs exceed the benefits.

A second hypothesis is that only a small fraction of people wear their seat belts because they have made an inaccurate estimate of the benefits. Principally because of a lack of information about such matters as the true probability of harm in the event of an accident, many people may have erroneously concluded that the expected benefits of seat belts are less than the costs.

A third hypothesis holds that people mis-estimate the benefits from wearing seat belts because of an inability to make the relevant calculation, not because of a lack of information. Most people simply do not use the expected utility method of making decisions under uncertainty. They use alternative methods, such as the availability heuristic, that make far fewer demands on their information-processing abilities. If the best available evidence is that one has not had an automobile accident, nor has anyone he knows, the available information suggests (erroneously) that the probability of being involved in an accident is zero. Therefore, there is no need to wear a seat belt.

Notice that the public policy recommendations of the three hypotheses are quite different. If the first hypothesis is correct, then there is no basis for a policy to encourage seat belt use: people are already acting on accurate information and maximizing their welfare by rationally comparing costs and benefits of seat belt use. If the second hypothesis is correct, then the costs of accidents can be reduced and welfare increased by a policy of encouraging the dissemination of accurate information about the relevant probabilities and magnitudes of harm. Once decisionmakers have that accurate information they will reassess the costs and benefits of seat belt use and a larger fraction of the population will routinely use them. In addition to information-dissemination, this hypothesis might argue for the imposition of fines for failure to wear a seat belt. If the third hypothesis is correct, a more aggressive policy of intervention is called for —e.g., the mandatory inclusion of passive restraints, such as air bags, in all automobiles.

See R. J. Arnould & H. Grabowski, *Auto Safety Regulation: An Analysis of Market Failure*, 12 BELL J. ECON. 27 (1981).

9.19. The modern tort action is for *intentional* infliction of emotional distress. The reported actions for recovery on the grounds of the unintentional or negligent infliction of emotional distress are very few. The law was understandably reluctant to allow recovery even for this intentional harm because, among other things, it is so difficult to measure the damages. The action proposed here against the drug companies would be for the negligent infliction of emotional distress. Whether to allow such an action depends on the answers to questions we have been investigating in this and the previous chapter. Can one compute perfectly compensatory damages for this harm? Is this an instance of unilateral or bilateral precaution? Can a social-cost-minimizing level of care be defined for this harm? Our intuition is that the tort liability system is not an appropriate public policy instrument for creating efficient incentives to minimize the social costs of this harm. Defining the efficient legal standard of care for negligent infliction of emotional distress would seem to be extremely difficult, if not impossible. That makes negligence suspect. But just as certainly, strict liability is inappropriate because determining the level of perfectly compensatory damages for emotional distress is impossible.

9.20. It is possible that the horseman can recover from the manufacturer on a negligence theory: the manufacturer may not have adequately observed his duty of care to strangers who were injured through a defect in the wheel. (There is no contractual relation between the horseman and the wheel manufacturer.) It is not likely that the horseman can recover from the wagon owner unless there was some specific act of negligence on his part—e.g., in not maintaining his wagon in a safe fashion or in not driving carefully.

What about a passenger in the wagon? Can he recover from the manufacturer? From the wagon owner?

9.21. Applying the comparative advantage theory, we might argue that the exclusion of liability for consequential damages and the exclusion of liability for all persons except the original purchaser efficiently allocate risk as between all concerned parties. For example, the exclusion of liability for consequential damages places responsibility for insuring against those losses on the party who is best placed to estimate the extent of insurance required—the person who might be harmed. The tire manufacturer is not well enough informed about the consequential damages that might be suffered by the average customer to underwrite insurance in this area as efficiently as can commercial insurers. The original purchaser is induced by this warranty term to purchase his own disability, medical, liability, and life insurance. If the exclusion of consequential damages is not allowed, the manufacturer (and possibly the retailer) must become partial insurers of their customers' losses; as a result, their costs of providing the product rise and so the retail price rises. Notice that the price rises for all customers, even those who can find insurance elsewhere at a lower price.

The comparative advantage theory suggests a similar defense of the exclusion from warranty coverage of all but the original purchaser. This exclusion allows the manufacturer (through his agent, the retailer) in theory to assess the original purchaser's likelihood of using the warranty. The manufacturer has no control at all over the other users of the product and would probably not willingly assume liability for their injuries. The inclusion of others in the warranty coverage creates moral hazard and adverse selection problems for the manufacturer: the original purchaser's incentive to screen those to whom he loans his product is removed completely, thus increasing the probability of the insurable event's occurring.

9.22. Recall from the previous chapter that negligence is the more efficient tort liability standard when there is bilateral precaution and when it is relatively easier to determine the social-cost-minimizing level of care than to determine perfectly compensatory damages. Strict liability is more efficient when there is unilateral precaution and when it is relatively easier to determine perfectly compensatory damages than to determine the social-cost-minimizing level of care. It is probably the case with regard to product-related injuries that there is unilateral precaution (the manufacturer is the party who has an overwhelming advantage in reducing the probability or severity of an accident) and that perfectly compensatory damages are relatively easy to determine. Nonetheless, with the traditional defenses in product-related torts (voluntary assumption of risk and product misuse) strict liability looks very much like a negligence standard. That is, the difference between strict products liability with the traditional defenses and a form of the negligence standard is probably minimal. Given that, a switch to a negligence standard is not likely to sacrifice much, if any, efficiency in the provision of safe products. Note also that the imposition of a recovery cap under a negligence standard does not diminish the incentive to take efficient precaution so long as the legal standard of care is set at the social-cost-minimizing level.

9.23. Plaintiffs' incentive to ask for punitives would be greatly diminished by the proposed scheme. If the plaintiff can recover none of the punitives, then he has no incentive to ask for them. Thus, punitives may not be asked for or awarded in circumstances in which they are, in fact, warranted. This is the opposite extreme from the current case in which plaintiffs have a strong (and probably inefficient) incentive to ask for punitives in a wide range of torts, even where punitive damages are unwarranted. Neither extreme is efficient. Some compromise is necessary: perhaps the appropriate public policy is to allow successful plaintiffs to receive a fraction of the punitive award with the bulk going to the State or to an umbrella charitable organization.

9.24. Let's concede for the moment that no-fault does involve higher premiums. The quotation suggests that the no-fault system is a bad bargain in that the insured pays higher premium for lowered coverage. This is not a fair description of the system. The reason that drivers may be willing to pay higher premiums under no-fault is that the certainty of recovery is greater. That is, the expected payment (the probability of recovery times the amount recovered) is thought to be greater under no-fault. This would be true if the percentage increase in the probability of recovery was greater than the percentage decrease in the amount recovered.

9.25. The no-fault system appears to do nothing to induce efficient precaution. It is commonly argued by non-economists that drivers do not think about their exposure to liability in deciding on the safety of their driving so that there is no efficiency impact on automobile safety of *any* tort liability standard. The principal inducement to drive safely is a regard for one's own health. Therefore, a move to no-fault will not, it is argued, reduce incentives to drive safely. This argument is premised on a factual assertion for which there is not conclusive evidence. In fact, the better evidence is that potential injurers *are* sensitive to liability considerations. *See* R. Grayson, *Deterrence in Automobile Liability Insurance* (unpublished Ph.D. diss., U. Chi. Grad. Sch. of Bus., 1971) and E. Landes, *Insurance, Liability, and Accidents: A Theoretical and Empirical Investigation of No-Fault Accidents*, 25 J. LAW & ECON. 49 (1982). But also see J. O'Connell & S. Levmore, *A Reply to Landes: A Faulty Study of No-Fault's Effect on Fault?*, 48 MO. L. REV. 649 (1983).

9.26. The alleged tort done to Mrs. Melvin is invasion of privacy. If recovery is allowed for this tort, then those with an interesting or sordid past that they would rather keep secret are allowed to do so unless they explicitly waive their right to privacy. This would be true for prospective employees as well as those like Mrs. Melvin who are private citizens not seeking employment. But for public figures a different approach is justified. Public figures implicitly contract away their right to privacy about their lives. While this might discourage some worthy candidates from seeking public office (Governor Cuomo of New York gave as a partial reason for not seeking the Democratic candidacy for President in 1988 his concern for his family's privacy), it also brings to the fore those who have relatively spotless lives or who have a thick hide for public criticism, both desirable qualities in high public officials.

Chapter 10

10.1. a. In order to determine how much the frequency of trials will increase in equilibrium when the values of hard and soft strategies change, we must solve the following equations:

for plaintiffs: $0(p) + 0.8(1 - p) = 0.2p + 0.5(1 - p)$,

where p indicates the proportion of plaintiffs adopting a hard strategy and $(1 - p)$ is therefore the proportion of plaintiffs adopting a soft strategy and the equality indicates equilibrium in the sense that the expected values of a hard and a soft strategy are the same; and

for defendants: $0.2q + 0.5(1 - q) = 0(q) + 0.8(1 - q)$,

where q indicates the proportion of defendants adopting a hard strategy and $(1 - q)$ is therefore the proportion of defendants adopting a soft strategy.

Solving these equations yields

$$p = q = 0.6.$$

A trial occurs when both parties adopt hard strategies. Thus, the frequency of trial is

$$p \times q = 0.36, \text{ or } 36\%.$$

Notice that this is a much higher frequency of trial than that calculated in the text when the relative value of playing a hard strategy was lower.

b. Recall that we have previously assumed that the expected return from litigation under a hard strategy by both parties is $500 and that the cost of litigation is also $500. (Thus, the entries in the northwest cell of the matrix are 0.) You would fully expect that if the cost of litigation fell from $500 to $400, all other things being equal, the frequency of litigation would increase. Let's demonstrate that result.

The new entries in the cells of the matrix indicate the change in expected returns under lower litigation costs. For plaintiffs, the equilibrium condition is now

$$0.1p + 0.6(1 - p) = 0.4p + 0.5(1 - p),$$

where p is the proportion of plaintiffs who adopt a hard strategy. And for defendants the equilibrium condition is

$$0.1q + 0.6(1 - q) = 0.4q + 0.5(1 - q),$$

where q is the proportion of defendants who adopt a hard strategy.

Solving both equations yields

$$p = q = 0.25.$$

A trial will occur when both parties adopt a hard strategy, so that the frequency is given by $p \times q = .0625$ or about 6%. Notice that this is higher than the frequency calculated when litigation was more expensive but much lower than the frequency when the relative value of a hard strategy increased.

c. This question deals with the same issues as parts a and b but in a more general way.

Assuming that p is still the proportion of plaintiffs who adopt a hard strategy, the equilibrium condition for plaintiffs is

$$(0.5s - t)p + .6s(1 - p) = 0.4sp + 0.5s(1 - p).$$

Solving for p gives

$$p = 0.1s/t.$$

The value for q (the proportion of defendants adopting a hard strategy) is obtainable by substituting q for p in the preceding expressions, so that $q = 0.1s/t$.

In general terms, the frequency of trials is determined by the percentage of plaintiffs and defendants who simultaneously adopt a hard strategy. Thus, the frequency of trials (f) is

$$f = p \times q = [0.1s/t]^2 = .01s^2t^2.$$

Figure H

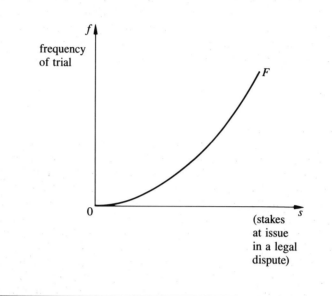

For those of you who know calculus, the sensitivity of trial frequency to changes in the stakes at issue and the level of litigation costs can be calculated by taking the partial derivative of f with respect to s and t. The first partial of this product with respect to s is

$$0.02s/t^2.$$

Because this is a positive number, the frequency of trials increases as s, the stakes at issue, increase. The second partial of f with respect to s is

$$0.02/t^2.$$

Because this is also a positive number, the frequency of trials increases with s at an increasing rate. Graphically, the relationship between f and s looks like the line labelled F in Figure H.

The first partial of f with respect to t is

$$-0.02s^2/t^3.$$

Because this is a negative number, the frequency of trials decreases as the cost of litigation increases. The second partial of f with respect to t is

$$0.06s^2/t^4.$$

Because this is a positive number, the frequency of trials decreases with t but at an increasing rate. This is somewhat confusing (in the "Yes, we have no bananas" vein), so perhaps a picture will help. Graphically, the relationship between f and t looks like the line labelled L in Figure I.

These relationships are generally true only to the extent that our figures in the matrices are accurate.

10.2. (Recall that we dealt with this matter of optimism on both sides in a legal dispute in Question 4.1. We saw there that when each side expected to win a trial the putative cooperative surplus from settling rather than litigating was 0. Thus, we showed that optimism on both sides increased the frequency of trials. See the suggested answer to that question.) An optimist will prefer the British

Figure I

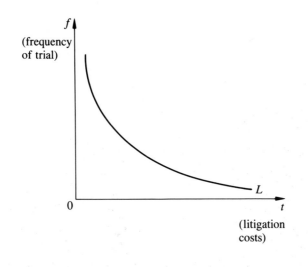

rule because his expected net gain from litigation will be higher under that rule than under the American rule. Additionally, optimism on both sides induces more trials. It follows that more trials should occur under the British rule.

10.3. The British rule will cause fewer nuisance suits because the threat position of an undeserving plaintiff is weakened by facing the prospect of paying the defendant's trial costs.

10.4. The strategic theory developed in the text would have to be elaborated to answer this question fully. However, we *can* say that if disputants are risk averse and if all other things are equal, the British rule will discourage suits.

10.5. The benefits of a more efficient legal rule accrue in part to a particular plaintiff and in part to the rest of society. There is no easy way for plaintiffs to secure payment from those future parties who enjoy some of the benefits of a more efficient rule. This suggests that voluntary market exchange cannot internalize all of the benefits of a more efficient rule. As a result, in the absence of appropriate societal intervention, a socially sub-optimal amount of litigation may be brought by plaintiffs if they must bear the full cost of litigation. Apparently society recognizes this external benefit of more efficient rules because some of the costs of litigation are borne by society from the public fisc. Plaintiffs and defendants pay only a portion of the costs of operating the court system. (Can you make sense of the exceptions to this general statement—that is, can you explain particular instances, e.g., the rent-a-judge system or arbitration, in which private parties bear *all* the costs of dispute resolution?)

However, we have also recognized in this chapter that there are circumstances in which plaintiffs litigate inefficiently. For example, when both parties are optimistic, there will be too many trials. Thus, there are contrasting forces pushing litigants in opposite directions: the market induces them to litigate too little; other factors induce them to litigate too much. In the absence of further analysis, it is very difficult to judge whether the net effect of these contrasting forces is to produce just the right amount of litigation, too little, or too much.

The rules for summarily dismissing complaints and for imposing court costs on those who bring frivolous or malicious suits would seem to indicate that the law has identified some of the circumstances in which the social costs of litigation are greater than the social benefits and has adopted rules to minimize these net social costs.

10.6. Judges only have before them the facts presented by the parties that are relevant to the instant case. They are not particularly well positioned to consider the impact of their rule-making on alternative circumstances and decisionmakers in the future. Thus, judges guard against the dangers of overinclusion, of deciding broad matters of social policy rather than resolving a particular fact situation. Legislators, in contrast, have access to expert testimony and debate about the impact of rules on wide varieties of people, place, and circumstance and can thus better anticipate the effects and avoid the dangers of overinclusion. Thus, legislators frame general laws and leave their interpretation to judges.

Chapter 11

11.1. We have suggested that the term "victimless crime" implies that society or the social fabric, rather than a single individual, is the victim. Counterfeiting is a crime in two senses: it imposes extraordinary costs on individuals and on society. For example, counterfeiting causes losses to the individuals who accept the counterfeit currency. But by threatening the value and acceptability of the currency, it also raises the cost to everyone of engaging in mutually beneficial exchange.

Other aspects of counterfeiting that are important in explaining why it is a crime are that it is an *intentional* wrong and that it is frequently difficult to apprehend and convict counterfeiters. Why these are elements of a crime will become evident shortly.

11.2. One might argue that speeding or running a stop light or stop sign when no one was around or no one was injured are examples of inchoate crimes. But why can one not alternatively argue that they are examples of "negligence in the air," faulty actions that result in no harm? The reason for punishing speeding and running a stop sign as inchoate crimes is twofold. First, the probability of harm from those actions is very high; society does not want its members to be subjected to such large risks. Second, there may be a large detrimental spillover effect from the failure to punish inchoate crimes. Those who get away with such actions as speeding or running a stop sign may deduce that it is acceptable to scoff at other laws as well, thus imposing even more risks on other members of society.

11.3. The theory we have proposed draws a sharp distinction between the basis of a civil complaint and a criminal complaint. The two complaints are not, as the compromise statute seems to indicate, substitutes; they are complements. If the widow and her children received compensation sufficient to satisfy their civil complaint, that should discharge the civil but not the criminal complaint. The State's reason for proceeding against Garoutte (that he grossly violated a duty of care and thereby caused a death) is still intact. The criminal complaint should continue.

11.4. She should not be excused from either the civil or criminal complaints. With regard to the civil complaint, Frankie clearly violated the legal duty of care she owed to Jonny. With regard to the criminal complaint, she may have violated statutes against reckless driving or reckless endangerment or the like. There were safer alternatives available to her; for example, she could have asked for a police escort. The sirens are specifically intended to allow an officer to violate speed laws in the event of an emergency; the siren sound gives a clear warning to other citizens to get out of the way.

11.5. The obvious difference between Frankie's pleasure in causing harm and Ford's decision about the location of the gas tank is intent. In the text example Frankie intended to cause harm. Ford did not intend to cause harm; indeed, it is possible (depending on the figures, as discussed in a suggested answer in Chapter 9) that Ford genuinely thought that little or no harm would result from its design of the gas tank location.

The distinction bears stressing again. The optimal amount of intentional harm may well be zero because society does not and should not count as a benefit the pleasure the perpetrator of the harm enjoyed. But the optimal amount of unintentional harm is not zero because there are legitimate benefits (such as Ford's profits) that a potential injurer may balance against the costs that a shortfall in precaution may involuntarily inflict on others.

11.6. a. In our discussion in Chapter 9 of the reasons for punitive damages and in this chapter of the reasons for criminal liability, there is little difference between punitives in civil litigation and sanctions in criminal complaints. (Historically this was true. It was only within the last two or three hundred years that criminal law became distinct from the area of intentional torts. The two areas still bear a strong resemblance to one another.)

b. Bankruptcy may present problems if the value of the firm's assets is less than the amount of compensation plus punishment. In a few rare instances the law allows a "piercing of the corporate veil," that is, reaching out to the corporation's owners and going after their personal assets to satisfy a claim against the corporation. This could happen if the corporation committed an intentional tort for which its assets were inadequate, and it could therefore be appropriate if the corporation is guilty of a crime.

c. Traditionally the doctrine of *respondeat superior* did not extend to an employee's intentional torts and by implication to the employee's crimes. However, the recent trend has been toward holding the employer at least partially responsible for the intentional torts of his employees. It is not unlikely that the doctrine will be further extended to make employers partially responsible for employee crimes. But there is no obvious economic reason for either of these extensions. They are almost certainly due to the trend toward increasing the likelihood that victims can recover, a trend we observed most clearly in the case of products liability. Employers generally have more money than do their employees; thus, a victim of an employee's intentional tort or crime will be more likely to recover if he or she is allowed to proceed against the employer.

11.7. The intersection at a positive value along the vertical axis indicates that even when there is no crime, there may be a punishment. This may be taken to mean several things—that inchoate crimes are punished, or that errors are made in criminal prosecutions in which innocent people are punished.

Chapter 12

12.1. a. 0.5 (0.5 × 3 + 0.5 × 1)

 0.5 (1.5 + 0.5) = 0.5 (2) = 1 year.

 b. 6 months is the minimum sentence that the prosecutor would accept in exchange for a plea of guilty; 18 months is the maximum sentence that the defendant would accept in plea bargaining.

 c. 1 year = 6 months + 6 months.

 d. 1 year.

 e. (1.) 18 months.

 (2.) 6 months.

 f. 9 months = 0.5 × 18 months.

 g. 12 months.

 h. (1.) acquittal.

 (2.) 3 years.

12.2. Good time laws are used in every prison system in the country. Apparently even hardened criminals respond to the implicit prices created by variations in punitive sanctions.

12.3. Let's take the easier question first. The analysis of this and the previous chapter suggests that fines should replace imprisonment wherever that is feasible. Allowing criminals to work to discharge their "debt [literally] to society" in the form of a fine is clearly superior to the present system of nearly automatic incarceration.

 Victim compensation funds are another matter. The most likely explanation for their recent popularity is that they are a second-best solution to a profound problem: the judgment-proof criminal. To see this problem, we must return to the basic notion of why there are both crimes and civil wrongs. We have repeatedly stressed that for nearly every crime there is an associated civil wrong. In theory there should be a concurrent civil trial with every criminal trial, and in the civil trial the victim should receive perfect compensation. But many criminals are judgment proof; they do not have the resources to pay either their victims nor a fine as a criminal sanction. Longstanding practice has been to deal with this sort of criminal by incarcerating him and forgetting about compensation for the victim. The recent rise of the victim compensation fund is an attempt to correct the neglect of victims of judgment-proof criminals. But that innovation does not go far enough. A better idea is to replace automatic incarceration of even judgment-proof criminals with the imposition of a fine that would both compensate the victim and pay the criminal fine by requiring the criminal to work to discharge this debt, a sort of "workfare" for criminals. Wage garnishment and other forms of involuntary servitude would keep a flow of funds coming from the judgment-proof criminal. Victim compensation funds could still play a role: the victim could be compensated immediately out of general state revenues and the criminal could then pay the State back for this loan of the funds to compensate the victim as well as working to discharge his criminal fine. This scheme no doubt has large practical problems, but its benefits could be considerable.

12.4. Criminals will substitute a relatively cheaper for a relatively more expensive commodity. Thus, if gun control focuses only on new handguns and raises their price relative to the alternatives by making the acquisition of these new guns extremely costly, especially for criminals, then they will switch to cheaper alternatives, such as older handguns and other weapons (e.g., long guns and knives).

CASE INDEX

NAME INDEX

SUBJECT INDEX